Personalized Learning

In MyOBLab you are treated as an individual with specific learning needs.

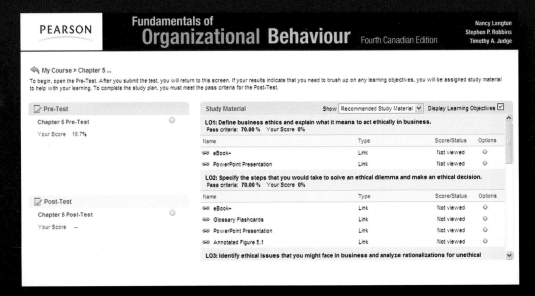

The study and assessment resources that come with your textbook allow you to review content and develop what you need to know, on your own time, and at your own pace.

MyOBLab provides

- Auto-graded quizzes and assignments
- A personalized study plan that tells you what to study based on your quiz results
- Annotated exhibits and tables from the text
- Self-Assessment Library with 51 behavioural questionnaires
- Student PowerPoint slides
- Videos: Acadia/Pearson Video Portal featuring interviews with over 70 executives from a variety of companies, plus CBC video cases from your textbook

Save Time. Improve Results. www.pearsoned.ca/myoblab

Fundamentals of
Organizational
Behaviour

Fourth Canadian Edition

Nancy Langton
University of British Columbia

Stephen P. Robbins
San Diego State University

Timothy A. Judge
University of Florida

Pearson Canada
Toronto

Library and Archives Canada Cataloguing in Publication

Langton, Nancy
Fundamentals of organizational behaviour / Nancy Langton, Stephen P. Robbins, Timothy A. Judge.—
4th Canadian ed.

Includes index.
ISBN 978-0-13-712851-8

1. Organizational behavior—Textbooks. I. Robbins, Stephen P., 1943– II. Judge, Tim III. Title.

HD58.7.L34 2011   658.3   C2010-900566-X

ISBN 978-0-13-712851-8

Vice-President, Editorial Director: Gary Bennett
Editor-in-Chief: Nicole Lukach
Acquisitions Editor: Karen Elliott
Executive Marketing Manager: Cas Shields
Developmental Editor: Su Mei Ku
Production Editor: Imee Salumbides
Copy Editor: Martin Tooke
Proofreader: Leanne Rancourt
Production Coordinator: Andrea Falkenberg
Compositor: MPS Limited, A Macmillan Company
Photo and Literary Permissions Researcher: Pre-Press PMG
Art Director: Julia Hall
Cover and Interior Designer: Anthony Leung
Cover Image: Veer Inc.

Brief Contents

Contents

PART 3
INTERACTING EFFECTIVELY 192

CHAPTER 6 Communication, Conflict, and Negotiation 192

Preface

Welcome to the fourth Canadian edition of *Fundamentals of Organizational Behaviour* by Nancy Langton, Stephen P. Robbins, and Timothy A. Judge. This edition takes a fresh approach to organizational behaviour coverage through more relevant examples, updated theory coverage, and a continued emphasis on pedagogically sound design. Based on earlier reviews we have found that potential users want chapters that have the right balance of theory and application material and are relevant to student learning.

General Content and Approach

- *Relevance.* The text reminds both teacher and student alike that we have entered the twenty-first century and must contend with a new paradigm of work that may be considerably different from the past. The new paradigm is more globally focused and competitive, relies more heavily on part-time and contract jobs, and places a higher premium on entrepreneurial acumen, either within the traditional workplace structure, as an individual seeking out an alternative job, or as the creator of your own new business.

    When the first Canadian edition of our textbook *Organizational Behaviour: Concepts, Controversies, Applications* appeared, it emphasized that OB is for everyone, from the bottom-rung employee to the CEO, as well as anyone who has to interact with others to accomplish a task. We continue to emphasize this theme in *Fundamentals of Organizational Behaviour*. We remind readers of the material's relevance beyond a "9-to-5" job through each chapter's feature, **OB for You**, which outlines how OB can be used by individuals in their daily lives. We also include the feature **OB in the Street**, which further emphasizes how OB applies outside the workplace.

- *Writing style.* We continue to make clarity and readability the hallmarks of this text. Our reviewers describe the text as "conversational," "interesting," "student-friendly," and "very clear and understandable." Students say they really like the informal style and personal examples.

- *Examples, examples, examples.* From our teaching experience, we know that students may not remember a concept, but they will remember an example. Moreover, a good example goes a long way in helping students to better understand a concept. You will find this book to be packed full of recent real-world examples drawn from a variety of organizations: business and not-for-profit, large and small, and local and international. We have also used photos to provide additional examples and information by expanding the captions.

- *Comprehensive literature coverage.* This book follows in the path of Langton/Robbins/Judge, *Organizational Behaviour: Concepts, Controversies, and Applications*, Fifth Canadian Edition, in its comprehensive and up-to-date coverage of OB from both academic journals and business periodicals.

- *Skill-building emphasis.* Each chapter's **OB at Work** is full of exercises to help students make the connections between theories and real-world applications. Exercises at the end of each chapter reinforce critical thinking, behavioural analysis, and team building.

Highlights of the Fourth Canadian Edition

In this edition, we have

- Added more exhibits to help clarify material and revised exhibits to make them clearer

- Introduced **OB Around the Globe** vignettes to emphasize the global nature of today's workplace

- Updated the research base significantly, and continued to include more references to research in the text

- Highlighted additional self-assessment exercises that students could do on MyOBLab at **www.pearsoned.ca/myoblab**.

Chapter-by-Chapter Highlights: What's New

Here is a summary of the key changes that we made to this edition.

Chapter 1: What Is Organizational Behaviour?

- Added a new section "The Importance of Interpersonal Skills"

- Completely revised the discussion "OB Looks Beyond Common Sense"

- Added the following new discussions under the topic "Challenges at the Organizational Level"

  - "Helping Employees with Work–Life Balance"

  - "Creating a Positive Work Environment"

- Created a new exhibit that summarizes the essential points of OB (Exhibit 1-4)

Chapter 2: Perception, Personality, and Emotions

- Revised the section "Factors Influencing Perception"

- Rewrote the discussion of stereotyping

- Considerably reworked the discussion of personality, including:

  - A new "Measuring Personality" section

  - Expanded coverage of heredity

  - Significantly revised section "Myers-Briggs Type Indicator"

  - Rewritten section "The Big Five Personality Model," with a new exhibit (Exhibit 2-5)

  - New discussions of core self-evaluation and narcissism

- Significantly rewrote the discussion of emotional labour and emotional intelligence

Chapter 3: Values, Attitudes, and Their Effects in the Workplace

- Added "Hofstede's Framework for Assessing Cultures" with an exhibit (Exhibit 3-3)

- Revised the sections "Generation X" and "The Ne(x)t Generation"

- Significantly revised the section "Attitudes," including:

  - Fully rewritten coverage of job satisfaction and productivity

  - All-new sections called "What Causes Job Satisfaction?" and "Employee Engagement"

Chapter 4: Motivating Self and Others

- Related the discussion "Goal-Setting Theory" to "stretch goals" and "management by objectives (MBO)"

- Expanded the discussion on "self-efficacy," including a new exhibit on the joint effects of goals and self-efficacy on performance (Exhibit 4-8)

- Added a discussion on "organizational justice" under the section "Fair Process and Treatment" with an exhibit to illustrate three models of justice (Exhibit 4-10)

- Included a section "Provide Performance Feedback" with a new *OB in Action: Giving More Effective Feedback*

Chapter 5: Working in Teams

- Created a new exhibit on teamwork skills (Exhibit 5-5)

- Revised the section "Personality" in relations to team composition

- Introduced the term "reflexivity" in the discussion of common purpose under "Team Process"

Chapter 6: Communication, Conflict, and Negotiation

- Rewrote and updated the discussion of e-mail

- Significantly revised the discussion of instant messaging with the inclusion of text messaging

- Extended discussion of distributive bargaining and integrative bargaining

Chapter 7: Power and Politics

- Expanded the section "Influence Tactics"

- Extended and updated the discussion of workplace bullying and sexual harassment

- Fully revised the research findings on impression management techniques

Chapter 8: Leadership

- Significantly reorganized the chapter

- Rewrote the section "Trait Theory: Are Leaders Different from Others?"

- Added a new section called "Full Range of Leadership Model" including a new exhibit (Exhibit 8-6)

- Revised the content on self-leadership (or self-management), including a new **OB in Action** called "Engaging in Self Leadership"

- Included a discussion of authentic leadership

Chapter 9: Decision Making, Creativity, and Ethics

- Completely rewrote discussions of intuition and intuitive decision making

- Revised "Judgment Shortcuts" section with new topics, including confirmation bias, randomness error, winner's curse, and hindsight bias

- Added a new "Effectiveness and Efficiency" section

- Completely revised "Creativity in Organizational Decision Making" with new discussions of creative potential and the three-component model of creativity (which includes a new exhibit—Exhibit 12-5).

Chapter 10: Organizational Culture and Change

- Created a new exhibit on the discussion of appreciative inquiry (Exhibit 10-8)

- Significantly revised the section "Individual Resistance" with a completely reworked exhibit (Exhibit 10-9)

- Extensively rewrote the discussion "Overcoming Resistance to Change"

Pedagogical Features

The pedagogical features of *Fundamentals of Organizational Behaviour*, Fourth Canadian Edition, are designed to complement and reinforce the textual material. This book offers the most complete assortment of pedagogy available in any OB book on the market.

- The text is developed in a "story-line" format that emphasizes how the topics fit together. Each chapter opens with a concept map of key questions related to a main example that threads through the chapter. The opening vignette is shorter, and it is carried throughout the chapter to help students apply a story to the concepts they are learning. The questions from the concept map appear in the margin of the text to indicate where they are addressed. The chapter ends with each of the opening questions repeated and answered to summarize the contents of the chapter.

- Keyed examples, **OB in the Street**, **OB in the Workplace**, (NEW!) **OB Around the Globe**, **Focus on Ethics**, and **Focus on Diversity** help students see the links between theoretical material and applications.

IN THE STREET

What It's Like to Play Next to Tiger Woods

Are people less motivated if they expect to lose? A recent study by Berkeley professor Jennifer Brown considered whether playing in a tournament with Tiger Woods increased other golfers' performances or decreased them.[30] On the one hand, individuals might be more motivated to try hard in the presence of a great player. Alternatively, individuals might feel that they were less likely to win, and thus not try as hard.

Brown noted that between 1999 and 2006, players who had to qualify for PGA Tour events averaged 1 to 4 strokes under par. Players who automatically qualified averaged 3 to 6 strokes under par. Woods, by contrast, averaged 10 to 14 strokes under par. In games where Woods played, however, players averaged about a stroke more per tournament.

If money motivated unconditionally, then there should not be any effect on other players if Woods is playing in the tournament. However, if players believe they are less likely to win the top prize, they may be less motivated by the money.

Brown found that the better players tended to play worse than their average when Woods was playing. She also found that when Woods was in his slump period (2003 and 2004), the top competitors' scores were not affected when he played.

Brown's findings suggest that when players are less likely to expect to win, they do not play as well.

- **OB in Action** features provide tips for using the concepts of OB in everyday life. For instance, OB in Action features includes *Practices of Successful Organizations*, *The Magnificent Seven Principles*, and *Managing Virtual Teams*.

> **OB in ACTION**
>
> **The Magnificent Seven Principles**
>
> → *Dignity of human life.* The lives of **people are to be respected**.
> → *Autonomy.* All **persons are intrinsically valuable** and **have the right to self-determination**.
> → *Honesty.* **The truth should be told** to those who have a right to know it.
> → *Loyalty.* **Promises, contracts, and commitments** should be **honoured**.
> → *Fairness.* **People should be treated justly**.
> → *Humaneness.* Our **actions ought to accomplish good**, and we should **avoid doing evil**.
> → *The common good.* Actions should accomplish **the greatest good for the greatest number** of people.[10]

- To help instructors and students readily spot significant discussions of research findings, we have included a research icon in the margin where these discussions appear. This helps emphasize the strong research foundation that underlies OB.

RESEARCH FINDINGS: TEAM DIVERSITY

Managing diversity on teams is a balancing act (see Exhibit 5-7 on page 173).[44] On the one hand, a number of researchers have suggested that diversity brings a greater number of ideas, perspectives, knowledge, and skills to the group, which can be used to perform at a higher level.[45] On the other hand, researchers have suggested that diversity can lead people to recall stereotypes and therefore bring bias into their evaluations of people who are different from them.[46] Diversity can thus make it more difficult to unify the team and reach agreements.[47] We consider some of the evidence to help us resolve these opposing views.

- Margin definitions have been differentiated to help students separate concepts from theories. Definitions of terms and concepts appear in blue and definitions of theories appear in magenta, making them stand out for easier studying.

> **McClelland's theory of needs** Achievement, power, and affiliation are three important needs that help explain motivation.
>
> **need for achievement** The drive to excel, to achieve in relation to a set of standards, to strive to succeed.

- Integrated questions (in the form of yellow notes) throughout the chapters encourage students to think about how OB applies to their everyday lives and engage students in their reading of the material. These questions first appear in the chapter opener, under the heading **OB Is For Everyone**, and then appear throughout.

OB Is for Everyone

- Ever wonder what causes flurries of activity in groups?
- Should individuals be paid for their "teamwork" or their individual performance?
- Why do some teams seem to get along better than others?
- Is building a team just from people who are friends a good idea?
- Why don't some team members pull their weight?

Should individuals be paid for their "teamwork" or their individual performance?

- Summary and Implications provides responses to the outcomes-based questions at the beginning of each chapter, while the **Snapshot Summary** provides a study tool that helps students see the overall connection among concepts studied within each chapter.

- Each chapter concludes with **OB at Work**, a set of resources designed to help students apply the lessons of the chapter. Included in OB at Work are the following continuing and new features:

  - **For Review** and **For Critical Thinking** provide thought-provoking questions to review the chapter and consider ways to apply the material presented.

  - **OB for You** outlines how OB can be used by individuals in their daily lives.

  - **Point/Counterpoint** features promote debate on contentious OB issues.

  - **Learning About Yourself Exercises** with (NEW!) **More Learning About Yourself Exercises**, **Breakout Group Exercise**, **Working with Others Exercises**, and **Ethical Dilemma Exercises** are all now featured in every chapter. We have found great value in using application exercises in the classroom. The many new exercises included here are ones that we have found particularly stimulating in our own classrooms. Our students say that they both like these exercises and learn from them.

  - **Case Incident** features deal with real-world scenarios and require students to exercise their decision-making skills. Each case will enable an instructor to quickly generate class discussion on a key theme within each chapter.

  - **CBC Video Case Incidents** present CBC cases tied to the material in each chapter. The segments were carefully selected by Frederick A. Starke of the University of Manitoba. The video cases provide instructors with audiovisual material to engage students' attention.

  - **From Concepts to Skills** provides a wide range of applications for the *Fundamentals* user. The section begins with a practical set of tips on topics such as "Reading Emotions," "Setting Goals," and "Solving Problems Creatively," which demonstrate real-world applications of OB theories. This is followed by the features *Practising Skills* and *Reinforcing Skills*. *Practising Skills* presents an additional case or group activity to apply the chapter's learning objectives. *Reinforcing Skills* asks students to talk about the material they have learned with others, or to apply it to their own personal experiences.

Supplements

We have created an outstanding supplements package for *Fundamentals of Organizational Behaviour*, Fourth Canadian Edition. In particular, we have introduced MyOBLab, an online study tool for students and an online homework and assessment tool for faculty. An access code to MyOBLab at **www.pearsoned.ca/myoblab** is included with this textbook and students can also purchase access online. MyOBLab provides students with an assortment of tools to help enrich and expedite learning. It lets students assess their understanding through auto-graded tests and assignments, develop a personalized study plan to address areas of weaknesses, and practise a variety of learning tools to master organizational behaviour principles. Some of these tools are described below.

- *Auto-Graded Tests and Assignments.* MyOBLab comes with two sample tests per chapter. These were prepared by Angela Kelleher (University of British Columbia). Students can work through these diagnostic tests to identify areas they have not fully understood. These sample tests generate a personalized study plan. Instructors can also assign these sample tests or create assignments, quizzes, or tests using a mix of publisher-supplied content and their own custom exercises.

- *Personalized Study Plan.* In MyOBLab, students are treated as individuals with specific learning needs. Students have limited study time so it is important for them to study as effectively as possible. A personalized study plan is generated from each student's results on sample tests. Students can clearly see the topics they have mastered—and, more importantly, the concepts they need to work on.

- *PowerPoint Slides.* This tool provides students with highlights and visuals of key concepts. These were prepared by David Parker (George Brown College).

- *Glossary Flashcards.* This study aid is useful for students' review of key concepts.

- *Pearson eText.* Students can study without leaving the online environment. They can access the eText online, including annotated text figures prepared by Cathy Heyland (Selkirk College).

- *Self-Assessment Library.* The Self-Assessment Library helps students create a skills portfolio. It is an interactive library containing behavioural questionnaires that help students discover things about themselves, their attitudes, and their personal strengths and weaknesses. Learning more about themselves gives students interesting insights into how they might behave in an organizational setting and motivates them to learn more about OB theories and practices that they can apply today and in the future.

- *HR Implications.* This feature spotlights those facets of each chapter topic that are relevant to human resource management.

- *MySearchLab.* MySearchLab helps students quickly and efficiently make the most of their research time by providing four exclusive databases of reliable source content including the EBSCO Academic Journal and Abstract Database, New York Times Search by Subject Archive, "Best of the Web" Link Library, and Financial Times Article Archive and Company Financials.

The following materials are available for instructors:

Instructor's Resource CD-ROM (ISBN 978-0-13-213421-7). This resource provides all of the following supplements in one convenient package:

- *Instructor's Resource Manual with Video Guide* (ISBN 978-0-13-213420-0). Prepared by Angela Kelleher, the Instructor's Resource Manual includes learning objectives, chapter outlines and synopses, annotated lecture outlines, teaching guides for in-text exercises, a summary and analysis of the **Point/Counterpoint** features, and answers to questions found under **For Review**, **For Critical Thinking**, **Case Incidents**, and **Video Case Incidents**. There are additional cases, exercises, and teaching materials as well.

- *Electronic Transparencies in PowerPoint®* (ISBN 978-0-13-213418-7). Prepared by David Parker (George Brown College), this package includes over 400 slides of content and exhibits from the text, prepared for electronic presentation.

- *Pearson TestGen* (ISBN 978-0-13-213419-4). Prepared by Richard Michalski (McMaster University), this test-generating and grading software allows instructors to assemble their own customized tests from the questions included in the TestGen. The TestGen contains over 1500 items, including multiple-choice, true/false, and discussion questions that relate not only to the body of the text but to **From Concepts to Skills**, **Point/Counterpoint**, and case materials. For each question, we have provided the correct answer, a page reference to the text, a difficulty rating (easy, moderate, or challenging), and a classification (recall or applied). TestGen enables instructors to administer tests on a local area network, have the tests graded electronically and have the results prepared in electronic or printed reports. TestGen is compatible with Windows and Macintosh operating systems, and can be downloaded from the TestGen website located at www.pearsoned.ca/testgen. Contact your local sales representative for details and access.

- *CBC/Pearson Canada DVD Video Library* (ISBN 978-0-13-213458-3). Pearson Canada has developed an exciting video package consisting of 10 segments from CBC programs and from Prentice Hall's *Organizational Behavior,* 13th edition Video Library. These segments show students issues of organizational behaviour as they affect real Canadian individuals and companies. Teaching notes are provided in the *Instructor's Resource Manual with Video Guide*. These cases were prepared by Frederick A. Starke of the University of Manitoba.

- *Image Library* (ISBN 978-0-13-213416-3). This package provides instructors with images to enhance their teaching.

Innovative Solutions Team. Pearson's Innovative Solutions Team works with faculty and campus course designers to ensure that Pearson technology products, assessment tools, and online course materials are tailored to meet your specific needs. This highly qualified team is dedicated to helping schools take full advantage of a wide range of educational technology, by assisting in the integration of a variety of instructional materials and media formats.

Acknowledgments

A number of people worked hard to give this fourth Canadian edition of *Fundamentals of Organizational Behaviour* a new look. Su Mei Ku, who has been the developmental editor on almost all of my projects, again outdid her always excellent performance. Her wit, good humour, helpfulness, support, and organizational skills made working on this textbook immensely easier. Su Mei served as a much-valued sounding board throughout the editorial process and also helped me significantly during manuscript preparation and the review of pages.

   I received incredible support for this project from a variety of people at Pearson Canada. Karen Elliott, acquisitions editor, is a wonderful cheerleader for the project. Anthony Leung produced yet another beautiful interior and cover design. Imee Salumbides served as the Production Editor for this project, managing a variety of tasks. Steve O'Hearn, President of Higher Education, and Gary Bennett, Vice-President, Editorial Director of Higher Education, are extremely supportive on the management side of Pearson Canada. This kind of support makes it much easier for an author to get work done and meet dreams and goals. Pre-Press PMG was very helpful in doing the photo and literary permission research. There are a variety of other people at Pearson who also had their hand in making sure that the manuscript would be transformed into this book and then delivered to your hands. To all of them I extend my thanks for jobs well done. The Pearson sales team is an exceptional group, and I know they will do everything possible to make this book successful. I continue to appreciate and value their support and interaction, particularly that of Cas Shields, executive marketing manager.

   Martin Tooke was copyeditor for the project and made sure everything was in place and written clearly. Leanne Rancourt, as the proofreader, was diligent about checking for consistency throughout the text. Their keen eyes helped to make these pages look good.

My family and friends are often ignored during the busier parts of writing a text book. They accept this graciously and provide food, support, and encouragement, as necessary. I am grateful for their support. Particular thanks goes to the members of the Carnavaron Quilt Guild who provided Monday night breaks from gruelling writing sessions and always asked how things were going and encouraged me along the way.

Finally, I want to acknowledge the many reviewers of this textbook for their detailed helpful comments. I appreciate the time and care that they put into their reviewing: Ian Anderson (Algonquin College), Fran Clarke (Durham College), Ike Hall (British Columbia Institute of Technology), Judith Hunter (Sheridan College), Lorna L. Kaufman (Vancouver Island University), Mohamed Khan (Centennial College), Kandey Larden (Langara College), Rorri McBlane (Capilano University), Graham Rodwell (Douglas College), Lynne Siemens (University of Victoria), Zina Suissa (Dawson College), James Voulakos (George Brown College), and Yanelia Yabar (Red Deer College).

I dedicate this book to my father, Peter X. Langton. He was a man of many talents, and his understanding of organizational behaviour may have been greater than my own.

Nancy Langton
January 2010

Nancy Langton received her Ph.D. from Stanford University. Since completing her graduate studies, Dr. Langton has taught at the University of Oklahoma and the University of British Columbia. Currently a member of the Organizational Behaviour and Human Resources division in the Sauder School of Business, UBC, she teaches at the undergraduate, MBA and Ph.D. level and conducts executive programs on attracting and retaining employees, time management, family business issues, as well as women and management issues. Dr. Langton has received several major three-year research grants from the Social Sciences and Humanities Research Council of Canada, and her research interests have focused on human resource issues in the workplace, including pay equity, gender equity, and leadership and communication styles. She is currently conducting longitudinal research with entrepreneurs in the Greater Vancouver Region, trying to understand the relationship between their human resource practices and the success of their businesses. Her articles on these and other topics have appeared in such journals as *Administrative Science Quarterly*, *American Sociological Review*, *Sociological Quarterly*, *Journal of Management Education*, and *Gender, Work and Organizations*. She has won Best Paper commendations from both the Academy of Management and the Administrative Sciences Association of Canada.

Dr. Langton routinely wins high marks from her students for teaching. She has been nominated many times for the Commerce Undergraduate Society Awards, and has won several honourable mention plaques. She has also won the Sauder School of Business's most prestigious award for teaching innovation, The Talking Stick. The award was given for Dr. Langton's redesign of the undergraduate organizational behaviour course as well as the many activities that were a spin-off of these efforts. She was also part of the UBC MBA Core design team that won the Alan Blizzard award, a national award that recognizes innovation in teaching.

Dr. Langton's passion for teaching has taken a new direction in recent years through the Sauder School of Business's Africa Initiative. Specifically, she is the faculty advisor for Social Entrepreneurship 101 (SE101), a three-week program where UBC and Kenyan university students teach young people living in Nairobi how to write business plans. She took her fourth student team to Nairobi in summer 2009. You can read more about the project at www.africa.sauder.ubc.ca.

In Dr. Langton's "other life," she is fascinated with the artistry of quiltmaking, and one day hopes to win first prize at *Visions*, the juried show for quilts as works of art. When she is not designing quilts, she is either reading novels (often suggested by a favourite correspondent), or studying cookbooks for new ideas. All of her friends would say that she makes from scratch the best pizza in all of Vancouver.

Stephen P. Robbins received his Ph.D. from the University of Arizona and has taught at the University of Nebraska at Omaha, Concordia University in Montreal, the University of Baltimore, Southern Illinois University at Edwardsville, and San Diego State University. Dr. Robbins' research interests have focused on conflict, power, and politics in organizations, as well as on the development of effective interpersonal skills. His articles on these and other topics have appeared in journals such as *Business Horizons, California Management Review, Business and Economic Perspectives, International Management, Management Review, Canadian Personnel and Industrial Relations,* and *The Journal of Management Education.*

Dr. Robbins is the world's bestselling textbook author in the areas of management and organizational behaviour. His most recent textbooks include *Organizational Behavior,* 13th ed. (Prentice Hall, 2009), *Essentials of Organizational Behavior,* 9th ed. (Prentice Hall, 2008), *Fundamentals of Management,* 6th ed., with David DeCenzo (Prentice Hall, 2008), and *Supervision Today!,* 5th ed., with David DeCenzo (Prentice Hall, 2007). In addition, Dr. Robbins is the author of the global best-sellers *The Truth About Managing People,* 2nd ed. (Financial Times Press, 2008) and *Decide & Conquer* (Financial Times Press, 2004).

An avid participant in masters' track-and-field competition, Dr. Robbins has set numerous indoor and outdoor age-group world sprint records since turning 50 in 1993. He has won more than a dozen indoor and outdoor US national titles at 60, 100, 200, and 400 meters, and has won seven gold medals at the World Masters Championships.

Timothy A. Judge received his Ph.D. from the University of Illinois at Urbana-Champaign and has taught at the University of Florida in Gainesville, Cornell University in Ithaca, Charles University in the Czech Republic, and Comenius University in Slovakia. Dr. Judge's research interests have focused on personality, moods, and emotions; job attitudes; leadership and influence behaviours; and careers (person–organization fit, career success). His articles on these and other topics have appeared in journals such as *Journal of Organizational Behavior, Personnel Psychology, Academy of Management Journal, Journal of Applied Psychology, European Journal of Personality,* and *European Journal of Work and Organizational Psychology.* He has also co-authored a book with H.G. Heneman III, *Staffing Organizations,* 5th ed. (Mendota House/Irwin, 2006).

In 1995, Dr. Judge received the Earnest J. McCormick Award for Distinguished Early Career Contributions from the Society for Industrial and Organizational Psychology, and in 2001, he received the Larry L. Cummings Award for mid-career contributions from the Organizational Behavior Division of the Academy of Management. In 2007, he received the Professional Practice Award from the Institute of Industrial and Labor Relations, University of Illinois.

Dr. Judge enjoys golf, cooking and baking, literature (he's a particular fan of Thomas Hardy and is a member of the Thomas Hardy Society), and keeping up with his three children.

Chapter *1*

What Is Organizational Behaviour?

An organization decides it will hire people with few skills and job experience. What challenges might its managers face?

1 What is organizational behaviour?

2 Isn't organizational behaviour common sense? Or just like psychology?

3 How does knowing about organizational behaviour make work and life more understandable?

4 What challenges do managers and employees face in the workplace of the twenty-first century?

*C*harles Chang started Port Coquitlam, BC-based Sequel Naturals, which makes premium natural health supplements, in April 2001.[1] The nutritional supplement industry was growing rapidly at the time, and six years later his annual revenue was $5.4 million and he had gone from 2 employees to 40.

Despite his strong sales record, by early 2007 the young entrepreneur realized that he had to resolve the people issues facing his company. He had recently hired a controller with "disorganized accounting practices" who caused $400 000 in inventory to be written off. The personality conflicts among his staff made it difficult to get work done. He was having trouble expanding into the United States, and renovations on a new location were behind schedule. All of these problems led to Sequel posting a loss of $300 000 at the end of 2006, after a profit of $1.4 million the previous year.

Chang says that one of his problems in running his business was that he was not an "HR guy"—that is, he did not pay much attention to people issues. Instead, he paid far more attention to sales and development issues because that is what he knew. But no one else was paying attention to the people issues either, so there was no real leadership for the employees, which is why the personality conflicts were taking over.

The challenges that managers such as Charles Chang face illustrate several concepts you will find as you study the field of organizational behaviour. Let's take a look, then, at what organizational behaviour is.

OB *Is for Everyone*

- Why do some people do well in organizational settings while others have difficulty?
- Do you know what a "typical" organization looks like?
- Does job satisfaction really make a difference?
- Are you ready to assume more responsibility at work?
- What people-related challenges have you noticed in the workplace?
- Why should you care about understanding other people?

1 What is organizational
behaviour?

organizational behaviour A field
of study that investigates the
impact of individuals, groups, and
structure on behaviour within
organizations; its purpose is to apply
such knowledge toward improving
organizational effectiveness.

Defining Organizational Behaviour

Organizational behaviour (often abbreviated as OB) is a field of study that looks at the impact that individuals, groups, and structure have on behaviour within organizations. Behaviour refers to what people do in an organization and how they perform. Because the organizations studied are often business organizations, OB is frequently applied to topics such as jobs, absenteeism, turnover, productivity, motivation, working in groups, and job satisfaction. Managers apply the knowledge gained from OB research to help them manage their organizations more effectively.

OB Is for Everyone

Why do some people do well in organizational settings while others have difficulty?

It may seem natural to think that the study of OB is for leaders and managers of organizations. After all, they often set the agenda for everyone else. However, OB is for everyone. For instance, many employees have informal leadership roles. They are often expected to move beyond simply providing labour to playing a more proactive role in achieving organizational success. As well, managers are increasingly asking employees to share in their decision-making processes rather than simply follow orders. For instance, employees in some retail stores can make decisions about when to accept returned items on their own, without involving the manager. Thus, in many organizations, the roles of managers and employees have become blurred.[2]

OB is not just for managers and employees. Entrepreneurs and self-employed individuals may not act as managers, but they certainly interact with other individuals and organizations as part of their work. In fact, much of OB is relevant beyond the workplace.

Microsoft understands how organizational behaviour affects an organization's performance. The company maintains good employee relationships by providing a great work environment, generous benefits, and challenging jobs. The two-storey wall painting shown here is one of 4500 pieces of contemporary art displayed at Microsoft's corporate campus for employees' enjoyment. Other benefits, such as valet parking, dry-cleaning and laundry services, free grocery delivery, and take-home meals, help employees focus on their work. At Microsoft, employee loyalty and productivity are high, contributing to the company's growth to over $60 billion in annual revenue since its founding in 1975.

OB applies equally well to all situations in which you interact with others. In fact, OB is relevant anywhere that people come together and share experiences, work on goals, or meet to solve problems. The study of OB can shed light on the interactions among family members, the voluntary group that comes together to do something about reviving the downtown area, students working as a team on a class project, the parents who sit on the board of their child's daycare centre, or even the members of a lunchtime pickup basketball team. Throughout this textbook, a feature called *OB in the Street* will help you understand these broader connections.

The Importance of Interpersonal Skills

Although practising managers have long understood the importance of interpersonal (people) skills to organizational effectiveness, business schools have been slower to get the message. Until the late 1980s, business school curricula emphasized the technical aspects of management, specifically focusing on economics, accounting, finance, and quantitative techniques. Course work in human behaviour and people skills received minimal attention relative to the technical aspects of management. Over the past two decades, however, business faculty have come to realize the importance that an understanding of human behaviour plays in determining organizational effectiveness, and required courses on people skills have been added to many curricula. As the director of leadership at MIT's Sloan School of Management recently put it, "M.B.A. students may get by on their technical and quantitative skills the first couple of years out of school. But soon, leadership and communication skills come to the fore in distinguishing those whose careers really take off."[3]

Recognition of the importance of developing interpersonal skills is closely tied to the need for organizations to attract and retain high-performing employees. Regardless of labour market conditions, outstanding employees are always in short supply.[4] Companies with reputations as good places to work—such as Toronto-based Environics Communications, Regina-based SaskCentral, Vancouver-based Karo Group, Markham, Ontario-based Ceridian Canada, and Toronto-based TD Bank Financial Group—have a big advantage. A recent study found that wages and benefits are not the main reasons people like their jobs or stay with an employer. Far more important is the quality of the employee's job and the supportiveness of the work environment.[5] In addition, creating a pleasant workplace appears to make good economic sense. For instance, companies with reputations as good places to work have been found to generate superior financial performance.[6]

We have come to understand that technical skills are necessary, but they are not enough to succeed in the workplace. In today's increasingly competitive and demanding workplace, individuals need to have good people skills. This textbook has been written to help managers and employees develop those people skills. To learn more about the kinds of skills needed in the workplace, look at the *Working With Others Exercise* on page 26.

What Do We Mean by Organization?

Do you know what a "typical" organization looks like?

An **organization** is a consciously coordinated social unit, made up of a group of people who work together on common goals on a relatively continuous basis. Manufacturing and service firms are organizations, and so are schools, hospitals, churches, military units, retail stores, police departments, volunteer organizations, start-ups, and local, provincial, and federal government agencies. Thus, when we say "organization" throughout this textbook, we are

organization A consciously coordinated social unit, made up of a group of people who work together on common goals on a relatively continuous basis.

referring not only to large manufacturing firms but also to small mom-and-pop stores, as well as to the variety of other forms of organization that exist. Businesses that employ no more than 10 people make up 75 percent of the Canadian marketplace. In Canada, small and mid-sized businesses now make up 45 percent of the gross national product, up from 25 percent 20 years ago.[7]

The examples in this textbook present various organizations so that you gain a better understanding of the many types that exist. Though you might not have considered this before, the college or university you attend is every bit as much a "real" organization as is Hudson's Bay Company or Air Canada or the Toronto Raptors. A small, for-profit organization that hires people with limited skills to renovate and build in the inner city of Winnipeg is as much a real organization as is London, Ontario-based EllisDon, one of North America's largest construction companies. Therefore, the theories we cover should be considered in light of the variety of organizations you may encounter. We try to point out instances where the theory may be less applicable (or especially applicable) to a particular type of organization. For the most part, however, you should expect that the discussions in this textbook apply across the broad spectrum of organizations. Throughout, we highlight applications to a variety of organizations in our feature *OB in the Workplace*.

OB: Making Sense of Behaviour in Organizations

> As Charles Chang took more responsibility for managing people at Sequel Naturals, he considered what he could do to make sure his employees felt motivated.[8] He started with a profit-sharing plan and performance bonuses. He worked toward creating a better organizational culture. He used weekly staff meetings to give recognition rewards, and he regularly holds all-staff retreats. What can Chang learn from organizational behaviour to do an even better job of managing his employees?

2 Isn't organizational behaviour common sense? Or just like psychology?

We have thus far considered why OB can be applied in a variety of settings. In this next section, we consider the other fields of study that have contributed to OB and discuss the fact that OB is a scientific discipline, with careful research that is conducted to test and evaluate theories.

The Building Blocks of OB

OB is an applied behavioural science that is built upon contributions from a number of behavioural disciplines. The main areas are psychology, sociology, social psychology, anthropology, and political science.[9] As we will learn, psychology's contributions have been mainly at the individual or micro level of analysis. The other four disciplines have contributed to our understanding of macro concepts, such as group processes and organization. Exhibit 1-1 presents an overview of the major contributions to the study of OB.

The Rigour of OB

Whether you want to respond to the challenges of the Canadian workplace, which we discuss later in this chapter, manage well, guarantee satisfying and rewarding employment for yourself, or know how to work better in groups and teams, it pays to understand organizational behaviour. OB provides a systematic approach to the study of behaviour in organizations, as well as groups and teams. Underlying this systematic approach is the belief that behaviour is not random. Thus, research studies are conducted and are the basis for all of the claims made in this textbook. OB is even being adopted by other disciplines, as *OB in the Street* shows.

EXHIBIT 1-1 Toward an OB Discipline

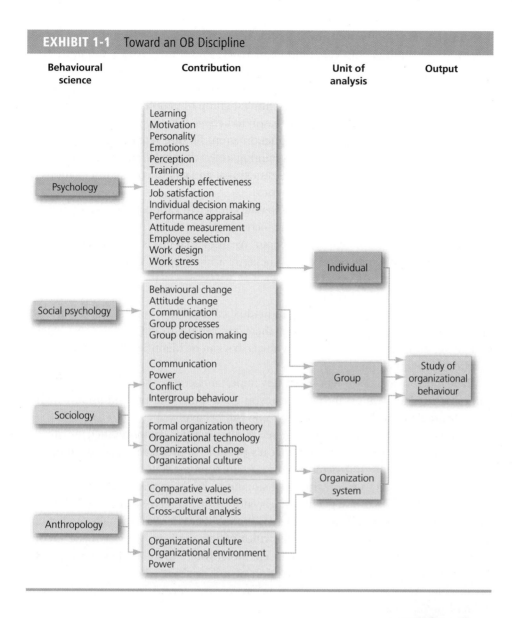

Is OB Just for the Workplace?

Can finance learn anything from OB? It may surprise you to learn that, increasingly, other business disciplines are employing OB concepts.[10] Marketing has the closest overlap with OB. Trying to predict consumer behaviour is not that different from trying to predict employee behaviour. Both require an understanding of the dynamics and underlying causes of human behaviour, and there is a lot of correspondence between the disciplines.

What is perhaps more surprising is the degree to which the so-called hard disciplines are making use of soft OB concepts. Behavioural finance, behavioural accounting, and behavioural economics (also called *economic psychology*) all have grown in importance and interest in the past several years.

On reflection, the use of OB by these disciplines should not be so surprising. Your common sense will tell you that humans are not perfectly rational creatures, and in many cases, our actions do not conform to a rational model of behaviour.

Although some elements of irrationality are incorporated into economic thought, finance, accounting, and economics researchers find it increasingly useful to draw from OB concepts.

For example, investors have a tendency to place more weight on private information (information that only they, or a limited group of people, know) than on public information, even when there is reason to believe that the public information is more accurate. To understand this phenomenon, finance researchers use OB concepts. In addition, behavioural accounting research might study how feedback influences auditors' behaviour, or the functional and dysfunctional implications of earnings warnings on investor behaviour.

The point is that while you take separate courses in various business disciplines, the lines between them are becoming increasingly blurred as researchers draw from common disciplines to explain behaviour. We think that this is a good thing because it more accurately matches the way managers actually work, think, and behave.

OB Looks at Consistencies

Certainly there are differences among individuals. Placed in similar situations, people do not all act exactly alike. However, there are certain fundamental consistencies underlying the behaviour of most individuals that can be identified and then modified to reflect individual differences.

These fundamental consistencies are very important because they allow predictability. For instance, when you get into your car, you make some definite and usually highly accurate predictions about how other people will behave.

What may be less obvious is that there are rules (written and unwritten) in almost every setting. Thus, it can be argued that it's possible to predict behaviour (undoubtedly, not always with 100 percent accuracy) in supermarkets, classrooms, doctors' offices, elevators, and in most structured situations. For instance, do you turn around and face the doors when you get into an elevator? Almost everyone does. Is there a sign inside the elevator that tells you to do this? Probably not! Just as we make predictions about drivers, where there are definite rules of the road, so we can make predictions about the behaviour of people in elevators, where there are few written rules. This example supports a major foundation of this textbook: Behaviour is generally predictable, and the *systematic study* of behaviour is a means to making reasonably accurate predictions.

OB Looks Beyond Common Sense

Each of us watches the actions of others and attempts to interpret what we see. Unfortunately, a casual or commonsensical approach to reading others can often lead to erroneous predictions. However, you can improve your predictive ability by supplementing your intuitive opinions with a more systematic approach.

Underlying the systematic approach used in this textbook is the belief that behaviour is not random. Behaviour is generally predictable in that even seemingly random behaviour is guided by an underlying probability of whether that behaviour will occur. When we use the phrase **systematic study**, we mean looking at relationships, attempting to attribute causes and effects, and basing our conclusions on scientific evidence—that is, on data gathered under controlled conditions and measured and interpreted in a reasonably rigorous manner. Exhibit 1-2 illustrates the common methods researchers use to study topics in OB.

An approach that complements systematic study is **evidence-based management (EBM)**. EBM involves basing managerial decisions on the best available scientific evidence. We would want doctors to make decisions about patient care based on the latest available evidence, and EBM argues that we want managers to do the same. That means managers must become more scientific in how they think about management

systematic study Looking at relationships, attempting to attribute causes and effects, and drawing conclusions based on scientific evidence.

evidence-based management (EBM) Basing managerial decisions on the best available scientific evidence.

EXHIBIT 1-2   Research Methods in OB

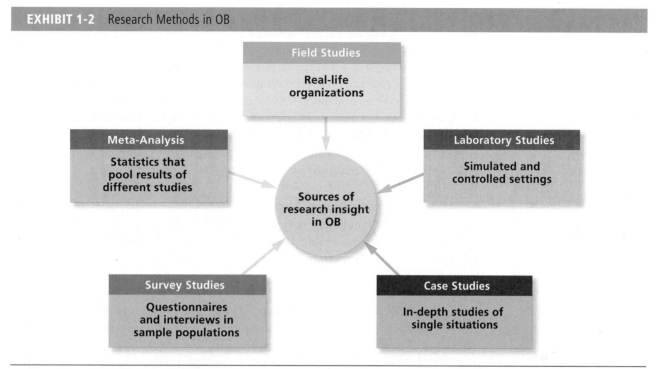

Source: J. R. Schermerhorn, J. G. Hunt, and R. N. Osborn, *Organizational Behavior*, 9th ed., 2005, p. 4. Copyright © 2005 John Wiley & Sons, Inc. Reprinted with permission of John Wiley & Sons, Inc.

problems. For example, a manager might consider a managerial question, search for the best available evidence based on research conducted that applies to that question, and apply the research results to the question or case at hand. You might think it's difficult to argue against this (what manager would argue that decisions should not be based on evidence?), but the vast majority of management decisions are still made "on the fly," with little or no systematic study of available evidence.[11]

Systematic study and EBM add to **intuition**, or those "gut feelings" about "why I do what I do" and "what makes others tick." If we make all decisions with intuition or gut instinct, we are likely making decisions with incomplete information—sort of like making an investment decision with only half the data. The limits of relying on intuition are made worse by the fact that we tend to overestimate the accuracy of what we think we know. A recent survey revealed that 86 percent of managers thought their organization was treating their employees well. However, only 55 percent of employees thought they were well treated.[12]

Some of the conclusions we make in this textbook, based on reasonably substantive research findings, will support what you always knew was true. But you will also be exposed to research evidence that runs counter to what you may have thought was common sense. One of the objectives of this textbook is to encourage you to enhance your intuitive views of behaviour with a systematic analysis, in the belief that such analysis will improve your accuracy in explaining and predicting behaviour.

If understanding behaviour were simply common sense, we would not observe many of the problems that occur in the workplace, because managers and employees would know how to behave. Unfortunately, as you will see from examples throughout the textbook, many individuals and managers exhibit less than desirable behaviour in the workplace. With a stronger grounding in OB, you might be able to avoid some of these mistakes. This chapter's *Point/Counterpoint* on page 24 looks at how systematic OB is.

intuition A gut feeling not necessarily supported by research.

OB Has Few Absolutes

There are few, if any, simple and universal principles that explain OB. In contrast, the physical sciences—chemistry, astronomy, and physics, for example—have laws that are consistent and apply in a wide range of situations. Such laws allow scientists to generalize about the pull of gravity or to confidently send astronauts into space to repair satellites. However, as one noted behavioural researcher concluded, "God gave all the easy problems to the physicists." Human beings are complex. Because we are not alike, our ability to make simple, accurate, and sweeping generalizations is limited. Two people often act differently in the same situation, and the same person's behaviour changes in different situations.

OB Takes a Contingency Approach

contingency approach An approach taken by OB that considers behaviour within the context in which it occurs.

Just because people can behave differently at different times does not mean, of course, that we cannot offer reasonably accurate explanations of human behaviour or make valid predictions. It does mean, however, that OB must consider behaviour within the context in which it occurs—known as a **contingency approach**. In other words, OB's answers "depend upon the situation." For example, OB scholars would avoid stating that everyone likes complex and challenging work (the general concept). Why? Because not everyone wants a challenging job. Some people prefer the routine over the varied or the simple over the complex. In other words, a job that is appealing to one person may not be to another, so the appeal of the job is contingent on the person who holds it.

Consistent with the contingency approach, the *Point/Counterpoint* feature included in each chapter presents debates on some of the more controversial issues in OB. These debates highlight the fact that within OB there is disagreement on many issues. The *Point/Counterpoint* format gives you the opportunity to explore different points of view on an issue, discover how diverse perspectives complement and oppose each other, and gain insight into some of the current debates in the OB field.

How Will Knowing OB Make a Difference?

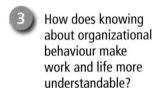

3 How does knowing about organizational behaviour make work and life more understandable?

When we talk about the impact of OB in each chapter, we consider the impact on both the workplace and the individual (see our features *OB in the Workplace* and *OB in the Street*). So let's begin our discussion of OB's impact by looking broadly at how knowing about OB makes a difference in the workplace, before we look at how OB affects us individually.

In the Workplace

From a management point of view, understanding OB can help you manage well. The evidence indicates that managing people well makes for better corporations overall.

Each year, *Report on Business* (*ROB*) magazine publishes a list of the "50 Best Employers in Canada." The magazine's 2009 list noted that each of the top companies "believes in praise, believes in people, and feels their employees' goals should be one with the overall corporate plan." Managing well also makes a difference to the bottom line. Despite a challenging economic period, companies that were ranked in the Best Employers' list exceeded the industry average annual total shareholder return by more than 14 percent.[13]

While the survey shows that managing well adds to the bottom line, it also shows that managing well provides managers with day-to-day returns. *ROB*'s 50 best employers have low turnover, and employees want to stay with their firms—even when they are offered higher-paying jobs by other companies. Employees with the 50 best employers who participated in the *ROB* survey did not mention money. Instead, they noted that the company recognizes their performance in little ways that make a difference.

The simple message is this: Managing people well pays off. Doing so may also lead to greater **organizational commitment**. We use this term to describe the degree to which an employee identifies with the organization and wishes to maintain membership in the organization.[14] This type of commitment is often called **affective commitment**, which describes the strength of an individual's emotional attachment to, identification with, and involvement in the organization. Employees who are highly committed go beyond expected behaviours to provide extra service, extra insight, or whatever else is needed to get the job done. There is some concern that extreme organizational commitment can have negative effects, in that employees with strong organizational commitment may behave unethically to protect the organization. However, this concern should not be a reason to avoid encouraging commitment. One benefit of having committed employees is that they are less resistant to change when organizations need to carry out changes.

Finally, managing well may improve organizational citizenship behaviour, a topic we discuss later in this chapter.

organizational commitment The degree to which an employee identifies with the organization and wishes to remain with the organization.

affective commitment The strength of an individual's emotional attachment to, identification with, and involvement in the organization.

For You as an Individual

You may be wondering exactly how OB applies to you if you are still in school and not yet working. Or you may want to know how OB applies to you if you are planning to run your own business or work for a small nonprofit organization, rather than a large organization. Or you may be asking yourself how OB applies to you if you are not planning on being a manager. We look at each of these scenarios below to help you see that OB is relevant in a variety of situations.

"What if I Am 'Just' a Student?"

You may think that OB is only useful once you reach the workplace. However, many of the concepts that apply to organizations also apply to teamwork, something many students have to do. As a team member, it's important to know how personality differences affect the ability of people to work together. You may need to motivate members of your team. Or you may want to know how to create a more effective team or solve conflict in a team. Individually or as part of a team, you also have decisions to make and need to know how to communicate with others. All of these topics are covered by OB.

"What if I Am Not Going to Work in a Large Organization?"

You may think that when we say "organization" we are referring to large financial firms in office towers, to the exclusion of the variety of other forms of organization that exist. You may be thinking that you want to work in a small business, or in your family's business, so OB has no relevance for you. But this would be short-sighted. Throughout your life you will work with a variety of organizations, and OB will help you better understand how those organizations work.

"What if I Do Not Want to Be a Manager?"

Many of us carry around a simplistic view of work organizations, with the participants divided into set categories: owners, leaders and/or managers, and employees. These distinct roles are found most often in large, publicly held organizations. Distinct organizational roles become more blurred when we discuss smaller, privately owned firms.

When we talk about leadership in organizations, we typically mean the person or persons responsible for setting the overall vision of the organization, although leadership can come from informal sources as well. While managers and leaders have seen their roles expand as a result of factors such as globalization and e-commerce, employees are also being asked to "move beyond their traditional role as inputs to the process of achieving organizational goals."[15] More and more employees are taking on this new role and responsibility. In particular, The Conference Board of Canada says that in high-performance organizations, "Employees are willing to be accountable for their own and the organization's success."[16] To be accountable means that employees "take charge of their own careers, decide what skills they need to acquire and determine where they wish to employ these skills."[17]

You may be thinking that you are not planning to work in an organization at all because you would prefer to be self-employed. While self-employed individuals often do not act as managers, they certainly interact with other individuals and organizations as part of their work. Thus, the study of OB is just as important for the sole proprietor or entrepreneur as for those who work in large organizations. It gives all of us more insight into how to work with others, and how to prepare to become employees in the twenty-first-century workplace.

Today's Challenges in the Canadian Workplace

Six years after starting Sequel Naturals, Charles Chang was reflecting on the fact that his employees were having daily squabbles because of personality conflicts.[18] His general manager was no better than he was at managing people. He decided he needed to move out of his home office and spend more time working side by side with his employees at headquarters. He then tackled the people issues.

Chang built a management team to handle operations, sales, marketing, and finances. He took over the HR (human resources) role, hired 20 new employees, and fired "five problematic employees." He started holding Monday morning staff meetings in which he made everyone aware of the company's performance goals. "I want everyone to know those numbers inside and out," he says. Once his changes were in place, he said, "We went from being unmanaged to extremely managed, and staying on top of our numbers is how we'll stay that way."

Chang is committed to being a good employer, surrounded by a good team. Will keeping them focused on the numbers be enough? What factors affect good teamwork? How can Chang motivate his employees to perform well in their jobs?

4 What challenges do managers and employees face in the workplace of the twenty-first century?

OB considers that organizations are made up of levels, moving up from the individual, to the group, to the entire organizational structure. Each level contributes to the variety of activities that occur in today's workplace. Exhibit 1-3 presents the three levels of analysis we consider in this textbook and shows that as we move from the individual level to the organization systems level, we deepen our understanding of behaviour in organizations. The three basic levels are like building blocks: Each level is constructed upon the previous level. Group concepts grow out of the foundation we lay out in the section on individual behaviour. We then overlay structural constraints on the individual and group in order to arrive at OB.

When we look at the different levels in the organization, we recognize that each has challenges that can affect how the levels above and/or below might operate. We consider the challenges at the individual, group, and organizational levels.

Challenges at the Individual Level

At the individual level, managers and employees need to learn how to work with people who may be different from themselves in a variety of dimensions, including personality, perception, values, and attitudes.

Individuals also have different levels of job satisfaction and motivation, and these affect how managers manage employees.

More organizations expect employees to be empowered and to take on more responsibility than ever before. This expectation puts demands on both managers and employees.

EXHIBIT 1-3   Basic OB Model

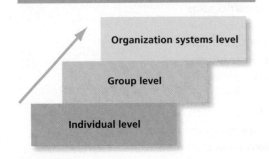

Organization systems level

Group level

Individual level

Perhaps the greatest challenge facing individuals (and organizations) is how to behave ethically, as the findings from the Gomery Commission, looking into the $250-million sponsorship scandal of the Liberal party, show. At his sentencing hearing, Jean Brault, found guilty of defrauding the government of $1.23 million on contracts that his company, Montreal-based Groupaction Marketing, obtained, claimed the external pressures he faced led to his actions: "I'm not trying to excuse what I did, but essentially it's the political demands, the demands on me, that led me to take that first step."[19]

Individual Differences

People enter groups and organizations with certain characteristics that influence their behaviour, the more obvious of these being personality characteristics, perception, values, and attitudes. These characteristics are essentially intact when an individual joins an organization, and for the most part, there is little that those in the organization can do to alter them. Yet they have a very real impact on behaviour. In this light, we look at perception, personality, values, and attitudes, and their impact on individual behaviour in Chapters 2 and 3.

Job Satisfaction

Does job satisfaction really make a difference?

Employees are increasingly demanding satisfying jobs. As we discuss in Chapter 3, less than half of Canadian employees are very satisfied with their jobs. The belief that satisfied employees are more productive than dissatisfied employees has been a basic assumption among managers for years. Although there is evidence that questions that causal relationship,[20] it can be argued that society should be concerned not only with the quantity of life—that is, with concerns such as higher productivity and material acquisitions—but also with its quality. Researchers with strong humanistic values argue that satisfaction is a legitimate objective of an organization. They believe that organizations should be responsible for providing employees with jobs that are challenging and intrinsically rewarding. This chapter's *Ethical Dilemma Exercise*, on pages 26–27, questions the extent to which organizations should be responsible for helping individuals achieve balance in their lives.

Employers can pay the price when employees are not satisfied with working conditions. Bank tellers at Toronto-Dominion Bank and Canadian Imperial Bank of Commerce in Sudbury, Ontario, voted to join the United Steelworkers of America in 2005. Employees at a Sears Canada department store in Sudbury also pursued the possibility of joining the Steelworkers in 2005. Brian Whalen, a maintenance worker for the store, said that "job satisfaction levels . . . have declined dramatically over the past two years." He noted that employees were upset about low hourly wages, a benefits package that was not affordable, and job security.[21] While unionization does not necessarily increase job satisfaction, it does provide a mechanism for employees to have some bargaining power with their employers.

Toronto-based RBC Financial Group, Canada's largest financial institution in terms of assets, commands the respect of many business leaders. In a 2005 KPMG/ Ipsos Reid poll of 250 Canadian CEOs, the company ranked first in five out of the eight categories, including "Best Long-Term Investment Value," "Human Resources Management," "Financial Performance," "Corporate Social Responsibility," and "Corporate Governance."

Motivation

A 2009 survey found that 22 percent of Canadian employees were expressing decreased loyalty to their companies over the previous year, and this increased to 36 percent for employees working in organizations that had laid off employees following the downturn in the economy.[22] Employers are thus facing a demotivated workforce. To address this concern, Chapter 4 discusses the importance of rewards in motivating employees. You may find the discussion of motivation and rewards particularly interesting in *Case Incident—How a UPS Manager Cut Turnover*, on pages 27–28, where a manager faces the challenges of motivating different types of employees in order to reduce turnover.

Empowerment

Are you ready to assume more responsibility at work?

At the same time that managers are being held responsible for employee satisfaction and happiness, they are also being asked to share more of their power. If you read any popular business magazine nowadays, you will find that managers are referred to as "coaches," "advisers," "sponsors," or "facilitators," rather than "bosses."[23]

In many organizations, employees have become *associates* or *teammates*.[24] The roles of managers and employees have blurred as the responsibilities of employees have grown. Decision making is being pushed down to the operating level, where employees are being given the freedom to make choices about schedules, procedures, and solving work-related problems.

empowerment Giving employees responsibility for what they do.

What is happening is that managers are empowering employees. **Empowerment** means managers are putting employees in charge of what they do. In the process, managers are learning how to give up control, and employees are learning how to take responsibility for their work and make appropriate decisions. The roles for both managers and employees are changing, often without much guidance on how to perform these new roles.

How widespread are these changes in the workplace? While we have no specific Canadian data, a survey by the American Management Association of 1040 executives found that 46 percent of their companies were still using a hierarchical structure, but 31 percent defined their companies as empowered.[25] *OB in the Workplace* looks at how WestJet Airlines empowers its employees.

OB IN THE WORKPLACE

WestJet Airlines' Employees Work Together

What do empowered employees do? Calgary-based WestJet Airlines employees are given lots of freedom to manage themselves.[26] When the company was started in 1996, Clive Beddoe, the company's founder and chair of the board, was determined to create a company "where people wanted to manage themselves."

At WestJet, employees are asked to be responsible for their tasks, rather than rely on supervisors to tell them what to do. Instead of being given directions, employees are given guidelines for behaviour. For instance, flight attendants are directed to serve customers in a caring, positive, and cheerful manner. How do they carry that out? It's up to them. Employees also share tasks. When a plane lands, all employees on the flight, even those who are flying off-duty, are expected to prepare the plane for its next takeoff. Beddoe does not excuse himself from helping out when he is on a flight. It's not unusual, he says, for him to "schmooze with the passengers and help our flight attendants pick up garbage."

Sean Durfy, WestJet's president, explains why empowerment is a good business model: "If you empower people to do the right things, then they will. If you align the interests of the people with the interests of the company, it's very powerful. That's what we do." WestJet's empowerment culture is admired by others as well. In 2008, the company placed first on Waterstone Human Capital's "Canada's 10 Most Admired Corporate Cultures" for the third time in a row.

Throughout this textbook you will find references to empowerment. We discuss it in terms of power in Chapter 7, and we discuss how leaders contribute to empowerment in Chapter 8.

Behaving Ethically

In an organizational world characterized by cutbacks, expectations of increasing worker productivity, and tough competition in the marketplace, it's not altogether surprising that many employees feel pressured to cut corners, break rules, and engage in other forms of questionable practices. For example, should they "blow the whistle" if they uncover illegal activities taking place in their company? Should they follow orders with which they do not personally agree? Do they give an inflated performance evaluation to an employee whom they like, knowing that such an evaluation could save that employee's job? Do they allow themselves to "play politics" in the organization if it will help their career advancement?

Ethics starts at the individual level. While the word refers to moral conduct, **ethics** is also the study of moral values or principles that guide our behaviour and inform us whether actions are right or wrong. Ethics helps us "do the right thing," such as not padding expense reports, or not phoning in sick to attend the opening of *The Dark Knight*.

Individuals as well as organizations can face ethical dilemmas. As we show in Chapter 9, the study of ethics does not come with black and white answers. Rather, many factors need to be considered in determining the ethical thing to do. Those individuals who strive hard to create their own set of ethical values and those organizations that encourage an ethical climate in the face of financial and other pressures will be more likely to do the right thing.

Throughout this textbook you will find references to ethical and unethical behaviour. The *Focus on Ethics* vignettes provide thought-provoking illustrations of how various organizations deal with ethics.

ethics The study of moral values or principles that guide our behaviour and inform us whether actions are right or wrong.

Challenges at the Group Level

What people-related challenges have you noticed in the workplace?

The behaviour of people in groups is more than the sum total of all the individuals acting in their own way. People's behaviour when they are in a group differs from their behaviour when they are alone. Therefore, the next step in developing an understanding of OB is the study of group behaviour.

Chapter 5 lays the foundation for an understanding of the dynamics of group and team behaviour. That chapter discusses how individuals are influenced by the patterns of behaviour they are expected to exhibit, what the team considers to be acceptable standards of behaviour, and how to make teams more effective.

Chapters 6 and 7 examine some of the more complex issues of interaction: communication, conflict, and negotiation; and power and politics. These two chapters give you an opportunity to think about how communication processes sometimes become complicated because of office politicking and interpersonal and group conflict.

Few people work entirely alone, and some organizations make widespread use of teams. Therefore, most individuals interact with others during the workday. This can lead to a need for greater interpersonal skills. The workplace is also made up of people from a variety of backgrounds. Thus, learning how to work with people from different cultures has become more important. We review some of the challenges that occur at the group level below.

Working with Others

Much of an individual's success in any job involves developing good interpersonal, or "people," skills. In fact, The Conference Board of Canada identified the skills that form the foundation for a high-quality workforce in today's workplace as communication, thinking, learning, and working with others. Positive attitudes and behaviours and an ability to take responsibility for one's actions are also key skills, according to the Conference Board.[27] Because many people will work in small and medium-sized firms in the future, Human Resources and Skills Development Canada has noted that additional important skills are team building and priority management.[28]

In Canada's increasingly competitive and demanding workplace, neither managers nor employees can succeed on their technical skills alone. They must also have good people skills. Management professor Jin Nam Choi of McGill University reports that research shows that 40 percent of managers either leave or stop performing within 18 months of starting at an organization "because they have failed to develop relationships with bosses, colleagues or subordinates."[29] Choi's comment underscores the importance of developing interpersonal skills. This book has been written to help you develop those people skills, whether as an employee, manager, or potential manager.

To learn more about the interpersonal skills needed in today's workplace, read *From Concepts to Skills* on pages 29–31.

Workforce Diversity

Why should you care about understanding other people?

workforce diversity The mix of people in organizations in terms of gender, race, ethnicity, disability, sexual orientation, and age, and demographic characteristics such as education and socio-economic status.

Organizations are becoming more diverse, employing a greater variety of people in terms of gender, race, ethnicity, sexual orientation, and age. A diverse workforce includes, for instance, women, Aboriginal peoples, Asian Canadians, African Canadians, Indo-Canadians, people with disabilities, gays and lesbians, and senior citizens. It also includes people with different demographic characteristics, such as education and socio-economic status. The ability to adapt to many different people is one of the most important and broad-based challenges facing organizations. We discuss **workforce diversity** issues in Chapter 3.

One of the challenges in Canadian workplaces is the mix of generations working side by side: the Elders (those over 60), Baby Boomers (born between the mid-1940s and mid-1960s), Generation Xers (born between the mid-1960s and early 1980s), and the Net Generation (born between 1977 and 1997). Due to their very different life experiences, they bring different values and different expectations to the workplace.

We used to assume that people in organizations who differed from the stereotypical employee would somehow simply fit in. We now know that employees do not set aside their cultural values and lifestyle preferences when they come to work. Organizations therefore try to accommodate diverse groups of people by addressing their different lifestyles, family needs, and work styles.[30] We need to keep in mind that what motivates one person may not motivate another. One person may like a straightforward and open style of communication that another finds uncomfortable and threatening. To work effectively with different people, we need to understand how culture shapes them and learn to adapt our interaction style.

The *Focus on Diversity* feature found throughout the textbook helps create awareness of the diversity issues that arise in organizations. Our first example looks at ways that Regina-based SGI focuses on the diversity of its employees.

FOCUS ON **DIVERSITY**

SGI: Top Diversity Employer

How does an organization accommodate its diverse employees? Regina-based Saskatchewan Government Insurance (SGI) must have some clue.[31] The company was named one of Canada's top diversity employers in 2008. Its workforce demonstrates SGI's commitment to diversity: 10 percent of employees are Aboriginal, 4.4 percent are visible minorities, and 7.5 percent have a disability.

SGI has developed a number of programs to support its workforce. The Aboriginal Network provides an opportunity for First Nations employees to talk about their own issues and also get career counselling. "It works at removing barriers for people," says Jon Schubert, the company's president. "We want to be an employer of choice for Aboriginal Canadians."

The company also hosts a diversity celebration each year with "performances from different cultural groups—from Greek traditional dancing to First Nation dancing." This helps employees learn about each other's heritages.

For its 2009 brokers' calendar, SGI encouraged Canadian artists to submit works of art that reflect the different cultural perspectives found in Canada. Such works might reflect, for example, "an ethnic glimpse of Oktoberfest in Kitchener, a powwow in Saskatoon."

SGI strives to have a workforce that is as diverse as its customers—a goal, Schubert says, that "just makes good business sense."

Workforce diversity has important implications for management practice. Managers need to shift their philosophy from treating everyone alike to recognizing differences. They need to respond to those differences in ways that will ensure employee retention and greater productivity, while at the same time not discriminating against certain groups. This shift includes, for instance, providing diversity training and revising benefit programs to be more "family-friendly."

Diversity, if positively managed, can increase creativity and innovation in organizations, as well as improve decision making by providing different perspectives on problems.[32] When diversity is not managed properly, there is potential for higher turnover, miscommunication, and more interpersonal conflicts.

Challenges at the Organizational Level

OB becomes more complex when we move to the organizational level of analysis. Just as groups are not the sum total of individuals, so organizations are not the sum total of individuals and groups. There are many more interacting factors that place constraints on individual and group behaviour. In Chapter 8 we consider how leadership and management affect employee behaviour. In Chapter 9 we discuss decision making and creativity, and then look at the issues of ethics and corporate social responsibility. In Chapter 10 we look at organizational culture, which is generally considered the glue that holds organizations together. We also discuss organizational change in Chapter 10. As we have noted already, and as will become clear throughout the textbook, change has become a key issue for organizations.

Canadian businesses face many challenges in the twenty-first century. Their ability to be as productive as US businesses is constantly tested.[33] The need to develop effective employees and to manage human resource issues such as absenteeism and turnover is critical. Meanwhile, Canadian businesses face greater competition because of the global economy. Many companies have expanded their operations overseas, which means they have to learn how to manage people from different cultures.

Improving Quality and Productivity

Increased competition is forcing managers to reduce costs and, at the same time, improve both productivity and the quality of the products and services their organization offers.

An organization or group is productive if it achieves its goals and does so by transferring inputs (labour and raw materials) to outputs (finished goods or services) at the lowest cost.

productivity A performance measure including effectiveness and efficiency.

effectiveness The achievement of goals.

efficiency The ratio of effective work output to the input required to produce the work.

Productivity implies a concern for both **effectiveness** (achieving goals) and **efficiency** (watching costs). The late management expert Peter Drucker stated that *effectiveness* is "doing the right thing," while *efficiency* is "doing things right."[34] For example, a hospital is *effective* when it successfully meets the needs of its patients. It is *efficient* when it can do so at a low cost. If a hospital manages to achieve higher output from its present staff—say, by reducing the average number of days a patient is confined to a bed, or by increasing the number of staff–patient contacts per day— we say that the hospital has gained productive *efficiency*. Similarly, a student team is effective when it puts together a group project that gets a high mark. It is efficient when all the members manage their time appropriately and are not at each other's throats.

As you study OB, you will begin to understand those factors that influence the effectiveness and efficiency of individuals, groups, and the overall organization.

Developing Effective Employees

One of the major challenges facing organizations in the twenty-first century is how to engage employees effectively so that they are committed to the organization. We use the term **organizational citizenship behaviour (OCB)** to describe discretionary behaviour that is not part of an employee's formal job requirements, but that nevertheless promotes the effective functioning of the organization.[35] Recent research has also looked at expanding the work on OCB to include team behaviour.[36]

organizational citizenship behaviour (OCB) Discretionary behaviour that is not part of an employee's formal job requirements, but that nevertheless promotes the effective functioning of the organization.

Successful organizations need employees who will go beyond their usual job duties, providing performance that is beyond expectations. In today's dynamic workplace, where tasks are increasingly done in teams and where flexibility is critical, organizations need employees who will engage in "good citizenship" behaviours, such as making constructive statements about their work group and the organization, helping others on their team, volunteering for extra job activities, avoiding unnecessary conflicts, showing care for organizational property, respecting the spirit as well as the letter of rules and regulations, and gracefully tolerating the occasional work-related impositions and nuisances.

Toronto-based BBDO Canada encourages an entrepreneurial spirit as a way of inspiring OCB. The ad agency's president and CEO Gerry Frascione notes that a team leader on the Campbell Soup account overheard a Campbell's representative musing about a program that would launch Campbell's Soup ads when the temperature dipped. "Instead of waiting to get approvals, she acted very entrepreneurially and took it upon herself and made the whole thing happen in one week," says Frascione. "She went back to the client, analyzed the situation, fleshed out the opportunity, came up with an integrated communication plan, came up with a budget, and it was all done within five days."[37]

Organizations want and need employees who will do those things that are not in any job description. The evidence indicates that organizations that have such employees outperform those that do not.[38] As a result, OB is concerned with organizational citizenship behaviour.

Helping Employees with Work–Life Balance

Employees are increasingly complaining that the line between work and nonwork time has become blurred, creating personal conflicts and stress.[39] At the same time, however, today's workplace presents opportunities for workers to create and structure their work roles.

A number of forces have contributed to blurring the lines between employees' work life and personal life. First, the creation of global organizations means their world never sleeps. At any time and on any day, for instance, thousands of General Electric employees are working somewhere. The need to consult with colleagues or customers 8 or 10 time zones away means that many employees of global firms are "on call" 24 hours a day. Second, communication technology allows employees to do their work at home, in their cars, or on the ski slopes at Whistler. This lets many people in technical and professional jobs do their work at any time and from any place. Third, organizations are asking employees to put in longer hours.

Employees are increasingly recognizing that work is affecting their personal lives, and they are not happy about it. Recent studies suggest that employees want jobs that give them flexibility in their work schedules so they can better manage work–life conflicts.[40] In fact, evidence indicates that balancing work and life demands now surpasses job security as an employee priority.[41] In addition, the next generation of employees is likely to show similar concerns.[42] A majority of college and university students say that attaining a balance between personal life and work is a primary career goal. They want "a life" as well as a job. Organizations that do not help their people achieve work–life balance will find it increasingly difficult to attract and retain the most capable and motivated employees.

Creating a Positive Work Environment

Although competitive pressures on most organizations are stronger than ever, we have noticed an interesting turn in both OB research and management practice, at least in some organizations. Instead of responding to competitive pressures by "turning up the heat," some organizations are trying to realize a competitive advantage by encouraging a positive work environment. For example, Jeff Immelt and Jim McNerney, both disciples of Jack Welch (former CEO of GE), have tried to maintain high performance expectations (a characteristic of GE's culture) while also encouraging a positive work environment in their organizations (GE and Boeing, respectively). "In this time of turmoil and cynicism about business, you need to be passionate, positive leaders," Immelt recently told his top managers.

At the same time, a real growth area in OB research has been **positive organizational scholarship** (also called *positive organizational behaviour*), which concerns how organizations develop human strengths, foster vitality and resilience, and unlock potential. Researchers in this area argue that too much of OB research and management practice has been targeted toward identifying what is wrong with organizations and their employees. In response, these researchers try to study what is *good* about organizations.[43]

positive organizational scholarship An area of OB research that concerns how organizations develop human strengths, foster vitality and resilience, and unlock potential.

For example, positive organizational scholars have studied a concept called "reflected best-self"—asking employees to think about situations in which they were at their "personal best" to understand how to exploit their strengths. These researchers argue that we all have things at which we are unusually good, yet too often we focus on addressing our limitations and too rarely think about how to exploit our strengths.[44]

Although positive organizational scholarship does not deny the presence (or even the value) of the negative (such as critical feedback), it does challenge researchers to look at OB through a new lens. It also challenges organizations to think about how to exploit their employees' strengths rather than dwell on their limitations. For instance, WestJet makes use of employees' cheerful, outgoing personalities to provide better customer service.

Global Competition

In recent years, Canadian businesses have faced tough competition from the United States, Europe, Japan, and even China, as well as from other companies within our borders. To survive, they have had to reduce costs, increase productivity, and improve quality. A number of Canadian companies have found it necessary to merge in order to survive. For instance, Rona, the Boucherville, Quebec-based home improvement store, bought out Lansing, Revy, and Revelstoke in recent years in order to defend its turf against the Atlanta, Georgia-based Home Depot. That may not be enough to keep it from being swallowed up by the Mooresville, North Carolina-based Lowe's home improvement company, however.

Some employers are starting to outsource jobs to other countries, where labour costs are lower. For instance, Toronto-based Dell Canada's technical service lines are handled by technicians working in India. Toronto-based Wall & Associates, a full-service chartered accounting and management consulting firm, outsources document management to Uganda. Employees in Uganda are willing to work for $1 an hour to sort and record receipts. While these wages might seem low, on average, Ugandans make only $1 a day.

These changes in the workplace, and the loss of jobs to international outsourcing, mean that the actual jobs that employees perform, and even those of managers to whom they report, are in a permanent state of change. To stay employable under these conditions, employees need to continually update their knowledge and skills to meet new job requirements.[45] Today's managers and employees have to learn to live with flexibility, spontaneity, uncertainty, and unpredictability.

Managing and Working in a Multicultural World

Twenty or thirty years ago, national borders protected most firms from foreign competitive pressures. This is no longer the case. Trading blocks such as the North American

Dallas, Texas-based Pizza Hut is responding to globalization by expanding its restaurants and delivery services worldwide. Pizza Hut introduced pizza to Chinese consumers in 1990. Today, Pizza Hut management targets mainland China as the number one market for new restaurant development because of the country's enormous growth potential. In this photo, a Pizza Hut employee passes out free samples in Nanjing to promote its delivery service. Managers expect delivery to become increasingly important as economic activity continues to expand, placing increased time demands on Chinese families.

EXHIBIT 1-4 The Fundamentals of OB

OB considers the multiple levels in an organization: individual, group, and organizational.

OB is built from the wisdom and research of multiple disciplines, including psychology, sociology, social psychology, and anthropology.

OB takes a systematic approach to the study of organizational phenomena. It is research-based.

OB takes a contingency approach to the consideration of organizational phenomena. Recommendations depend on the situation.

Free Trade Agreement (NAFTA) and the European Union (EU) have greatly reduced tariffs and barriers to trade, and North America and Europe are no longer the only continents with highly skilled labour. The Internet also helps companies become more globally connected by opening up international sales and by increasing opportunities to carry on business. Even small firms can bid on projects in different countries and compete with larger firms through the Internet. An implication of all these changes is that you could find yourself managing or working in a multicultural environment.

OB in Summary

We have discussed the meaning of OB throughout this chapter, and revealed different aspects of what OB covers. The essential points of OB that you should keep in mind as you study this topic are illustrated in Exhibit 1-4

Summary and Implications

1 What is organizational behaviour? Organizational behaviour (OB) is a field of study that investigates the impact that individuals, groups, and structure have on behaviour within an organization. It uses that knowledge to make organizations work more effectively. Specifically, OB focuses on how to improve productivity, reduce both absenteeism and turnover, and increase employee job satisfaction. OB also helps us understand how people can work together more effectively in the workplace.

OB recognizes differences, helps us see the value of workforce diversity, and calls attention to practices that may need to be changed when managing and working in different countries. It can help improve quality and employee productivity by showing managers how to empower their people, as well as how to design and implement change programs. It offers specific insights to improve people skills.

2 Isn't organizational behaviour common sense? Or just like psychology? OB is built on contributions from a number of behavioural disciplines, including psychology, sociology, social psychology, anthropology, and political science.

We all hold generalizations about the behaviour of people. Some of our generalizations may provide valid insights into human behaviour, but many are wrong. If understanding behaviour were simply common sense, we would see fewer problems in the workplace, because managers and employees would know how to behave. OB provides a systematic approach to improving predictions of behaviour that would be made from common sense alone.

3 How does knowing about organizational behaviour make work and life more understandable? From a management point of view, knowing OB can help you manage well. Managing people well pays off. It may also lead employees to have greater organizational commitment. From an individual point of view, knowing OB can help you understand why the workplace functions in the way it does. OB can also help you understand how to deal with others if you decide to start your own business.

4 **What challenges do managers and employees face in the workplace of the twenty-first century?** OB considers three levels of analysis—the individual, the group, and the organization—which, combined, help us understand behaviour in organizations. Each level has different challenges. At the individual level, we encounter employees who have different characteristics, and thus we consider how to better understand and make the most of these differences. Because employees have become more cynical about their employers, job satisfaction and motivation have become important issues in today's organizations. Employees are also confronted with the trend toward an empowered workplace. Perhaps the greatest challenge individuals (and organizations) face is how to behave ethically.

At the group level, individuals are increasingly expected to work in teams, which means that they need to do so effectively. Employees are expected to have good interpersonal skills. The workplace is now made up of people from many different backgrounds, requiring a greater ability to understand those different from ourselves.

At the organizational level, Canadian businesses face many challenges in the twenty-first century. They face ongoing competition at home and from US businesses, as well as growing competition from the global marketplace. Productivity is critical. It has become essential to develop effective employees who are committed to the organization. By putting people first, organizations can generate a committed workforce, but taking this approach becomes a challenge for businesses that focus solely on the bottom line. Organizations also have to learn how to be more sensitive to cultural differences, not only because Canada is a multicultural country, but also because competitive companies often develop global alliances or set up plants in foreign countries, where being aware of other cultures becomes a key to success.

OB at Work

For Review

1. Define *organizational behaviour.*

2. What is an organization? Is the family unit an organization? Explain.

3. "Behaviour is generally predictable, so there is no need to formally study OB." Do you agree or disagree with this statement? Why?

4. What does it mean to say OB takes a contingency approach in its analysis of behaviour?

5. What are the three levels of analysis in our OB model? Are they related? If so, how?

6. What are some of the challenges and opportunities that managers face as we move into the twenty-first century?

7. Why is job satisfaction an important consideration for OB?

8. What are effectiveness and efficiency, and how are they related to OB?

For Critical Thinking

1. "OB is for everyone." Build an argument to support this statement.

2. Why do you think the subject of OB might be criticized as being "only common sense," when we would rarely hear such a comment about a course in physics or statistics? Do you think this criticism of OB is fair?

3. On a scale of 1 to 10, measuring the sophistication of a scientific discipline in predicting phenomena, mathematical physics would probably be a 10. Where do you think OB would fall on the scale? Why?

4. Can empowerment lead to greater job satisfaction?

OB for You

- As you journey through this course in OB, bear in mind that the processes we describe are as relevant to you as an individual as they are to organizations, managers, and employees.

- When you work together with student teams, join a student organization, or volunteer time to a community group, know that your ability to get along with others has an effect on your interactions with the other people in the group and the achievement of the group's goals.

- If you are aware of how your perceptions and personality affect your interactions with others, you can be more careful in forming your initial impression of others.

- By knowing how to motivate others who are working with you, how to communicate effectively, and when to negotiate and compromise, you can get along in a variety of situations that are not necessarily work-related.

OB *At Work*

Point

Looking for the Quick Fix to OB Issues

Walk into your nearest major bookstore. You will undoubtedly find a large section of books devoted to management and managing human behaviour. A close look at the titles will find there is certainly no shortage of popular books on topics related to OB. To illustrate the point, consider the following popular book titles that are currently available on the topic of leadership:

- *Outliers: The Stories of Success* (Little, Brown, and Company, 2008)

- *The Leadership Teachings of Geronimo* (Sterling House, 2002)

- *Catch! A Fishmonger's Guide to Greatness* (Berrett-Koehler, 2003)

- *Strengths Based Leadership: Great Leaders, Teams, and Why People Follow* (Gallup, 2008)

- *Leadership Wisdom from the Monk Who Sold His Ferrari* (Hay House, 2003)

- *Sway: The Irresistible Pull of Irrational Behavior* (Doubleday, 2008)

- *Beyond Basketball: Coach K's Keywords for Success* (Warner Business Books, 2006)

- *Bhagavad Gita on Effective Leadership* (iUniverse, 2006)

- *If Harry Potter Ran General Electric: Leadership Wisdom from the World of the Wizards* (Currency/Doubleday, 2006)

Organizations are always looking for leaders; and managers and manager-wannabes are continually looking for ways to improve their leadership skills. Publishers respond to this demand by offering hundreds of titles that claim to provide insights into the complex subject of leadership. People hope that there are "shortcuts" to leadership success and that books like these can provide them with the secrets to leadership that others know and that they can quickly learn.

Counterpoint

Beware of the Quick Fix!

We all want to find quick and simple solutions to our complex problems. But here is the bad news: On problems related to OB, the quick and simple solutions are often wrong because they fail to consider the diversity among organizations, situations, and individuals. As Einstein said, "Everything should be made as simple as possible, but not simpler."

When it comes to trying to understand people at work, there is no shortage of simplistic ideas that books and consultants promote. And these books are not just on leadership. Consider three recent bestsellers. *Who Moved My Cheese?* is a metaphor about two mice that is meant to convey the benefits of accepting change. *Fish!* tells how a fish market in Seattle made its jobs motivating. And *Whale Done!* proposes that managers can learn a lot about motivating people from techniques used by whale trainers at Sea World in San Diego. Are the "insights" from these books generalizable to people working in hundreds of different countries, in a thousand different organizations, and doing a million different jobs? It's very unlikely.

Popular books on OB often have cute titles and are fun to read. But they can be dangerous. They make the job of managing people seem much simpler than it really is. They are also often based on the authors' opinions rather than substantive research.

OB is a complex subject. There are few, if any, simple statements about human behaviour that are generalizable to all people in all situations. Should you really try to apply leadership insights you got from a book on Shakespeare or Attila the Hun to managing software engineers in the twenty-first century?

The capitalist system ensures that when a need exists, opportunistic individuals will surface to fill that need. When it comes to managing people at work, there is clearly a need for valid and reliable insights to guide managers and those aspiring to managerial positions. However, most of the offerings available at your local bookstore tend to be simplistic solutions. To the degree that people buy these books and enthusiastically expect them to provide them with the secrets to effective management, they do a disservice to themselves and those they are trying to manage.

OB *At Work*

The Competing Values Framework: Identifying Your Interpersonal Skills

From the list below, identify what you believe to be your strongest skills, and then identify those in which you think your performance is weak. You should identify about 4 strong skills and 4 weak skills.[46]

1. Taking initiative
2. Goal setting
3. Delegating effectively
4. Personal productivity and motivation
5. Motivating others
6. Time and stress management
7. Planning
8. Organizing
9. Controlling

10. Receiving and organizing information
11. Evaluating routine information
12. Responding to routine information
13. Understanding yourself and others
14. Interpersonal communication
15. Developing subordinates
16. Team building

17. Participative decision making
18. Conflict management
19. Living with change
20. Creative thinking
21. Managing change
22. Building and maintaining a power base
23. Negotiating agreement and commitment
24. Negotiating and selling ideas

Scoring Key

These skills are based on the Competing Values Framework (pages 29–31), and they appear in detail in Exhibit 1-5 on page 29. Below, you will see how the individual skills relate to various managerial roles. Using the skills you identified as strongest, identify which roles you feel especially prepared for right now. Then, using the skills you identified as weakest, identify areas in which you might want to gain more skill. You should also use this information to determine whether you are currently more internally or externally focused, or oriented more toward flexibility or control.

Director: 1, 2, 3	Mentor: 13, 14, 15
Producer: 4, 5, 6	Facilitator: 16, 17, 18
Coordinator: 7, 8, 9	Innovator: 19, 20, 21
Monitor: 10, 11, 12	Broker: 22, 23, 24

After reviewing how your strengths and weaknesses relate to the skills that today's managers and leaders need, as illustrated in Exhibit 1-6 (page 30), you should consider whether you need to develop a broader range of skills.

More Learning About Yourself Exercises

An additional self-assessment relevant to this chapter appears on MyOBLab (**www.pearsoned.ca/myoblab**).

IV.G.1 How Much Do I Know About OB?

When you complete the additional assessment, consider the following:

1. Am I surprised about my score?
2. Would my friends evaluate me similarly?

OB *At Work*

BREAKOUT **GROUP** EXERCISES

Form small groups to discuss the following topics, as assigned by your instructor:

1. Consider a group situation in which you have worked. To what extent did the group rely on the technical skills of the group members vs. their interpersonal skills? Which skills seemed most important in helping the group function well?

2. Identify some examples of "worst jobs." What conditions of these jobs made them unpleasant? To what extent were these conditions related to behaviours of individuals?

3. Develop a list of "organizational puzzles," that is, behaviour you have observed in organizations that seemed to make little sense. As the term progresses, see if you can begin to explain these puzzles, using your knowledge of OB.

WORKING WITH **OTHERS** EXERCISE

Interpersonal Skills in the Workplace

This exercise asks you to consider the skills outlined in the Competing Values Framework on page 25 to develop an understanding of managerial expertise. Steps 1–4 can be completed in 15–20 minutes.

1. Using the skills listed in the *Learning About Yourself Exercise,* identify the 4 skills that you think all managers should have.

2. Identify the 4 skills that you think are least important for managers to have.

3. In groups of 5–7, reach a consensus on the most-needed and least-needed skills identified in steps 1 and 2.

4. Using Exhibit 1-6 on page 30, determine whether your "ideal" managers would have trouble managing in some dimensions of organizational demands.

5. Your instructor will lead a general discussion of your results.

ETHICAL **DILEMMA** EXERCISE

What Is the Right Balance Between Work and Personal Life?

When you think of work–life conflicts, you may tend to think of people in lower levels of organizations who might not have as much flexibility in determining their workday.[47] However, a recent survey of 179 CEOs revealed that many of them struggle with this issue. For instance, 31 percent said they have a high level of stress in their lives; 47 percent admitted that they would sacrifice some compensation for more personal time; and 16 percent considered changing jobs in the past six months to reduce stress or sacrifices made in their personal lives.

Most of these surveyed executives conceded that they had given up, and continue to give up, a lot to get to the top in their organizations. They are often tired from the extensive and exhausting travel their jobs demand, not to mention an average 60-hour workweek. Yet most feel the climb to the CEO position was worth whatever sacrifices they have had to make.

Jean Stone, while not representative of the group, indicates the price that some of these executives have had to pay. As senior VP and chief operating officer of Dukane Corporation, an Illinois-based manufacturer of electronic communications equipment, Stone describes herself as highly achievement-oriented. She has an intense focus on her job and admits to having lost sight of her personal life. Recently divorced after a 10-year marriage, she acknowledges that "career and work pressures were a factor in that."

How much emphasis on work is *too much*? What is the right balance between work and personal life? How much would you be willing to give up to be CEO of a major company? And if you were a CEO, what ethical responsibilities, if any, do you think you have to help your employees balance their work–family obligations?

CASE INCIDENT

How a UPS Manager Cut Turnover

Katriona Roeder is district manager for UPS's operation in Buffalo, New York.[48] She is responsible for $225 million in revenue, 2300 employees, and the processing of some 45 000 packages an hour. When she took over in Buffalo, she faced a serious problem: Turnover was out of control. Part-time employees—who load, unload, and sort packages, and who account for half of Buffalo's workforce—were leaving at the rate of 50 percent a year. Cutting this turnover rate became her highest priority.

The entire UPS organization relies heavily on part-time employees. In fact, it has historically been the primary inroad to becoming a full-time employee. Most of UPS's current executives, for instance, began as part-timers while attending college or university, then moved into full-time positions. In addition, UPS has always treated its part-timers well. They are given high pay, flexible work hours, full benefits, and substantial financial aid to go back to school. Yet these pluses did not seem to be enough to keep employees at UPS in Buffalo.

Roeder developed a comprehensive plan to reduce turnover. It focused on improving hiring, communication, the workplace, and supervisory training.

Roeder began by modifying the hiring process to screen out people who essentially wanted full-time jobs. She reasoned that unfulfilled expectations were frustrating the hires whose preferences were for full-time work. Given that it typically took new part-timers six years to work up to a full-time job, it made sense to try to identify people who actually preferred part-time work.

Next, Roeder analyzed the large database of information that UPS had on her district's employees. The data led her to the conclusion that she had five distinct groups working for her—differentiated by ages and stages in their careers. In addition, these groups had different needs and interests. In response, Roeder modified the communication style and motivation techniques she used with each employee to reflect the group to which

he or she belonged. For instance, Roeder found that college students are most interested in building skills that they can apply later in their careers. As long as these employees saw that they were learning new skills, they were content to keep working at UPS. So Roeder began offering them Saturday classes for computer-skill development and career-planning discussions.

Many new UPS employees in Buffalo were intimidated by the huge warehouse in which they had to work. To lessen that intimidation, Roeder improved lighting throughout the building and upgraded break rooms to make them more user-friendly. To further help new employees adjust, she turned some of her best shift supervisors into trainers who provided specific guidance during new hires' first week. She also installed more personal computers on the floor, which gave new employees easier access to training materials and human resource information on UPS's internal network.

Finally, Roeder expanded training so supervisors had the skills to handle increased empowerment. Recognizing that her supervisors—most of whom were part-timers themselves—were the ones best equipped to understand the needs of part-time employees, she made sure they learned how to assess difficult management situations, how to communicate in different ways, and how to identify the needs of different people. Supervisors learned to demonstrate interest in their employees as individuals. For instance, they were taught to inquire about employees' hobbies, where they went to school, and the like.

Four years after implementation, Roeder's program was showing impressive results. Her district's attrition rate had dropped from 50 percent to 6 percent. During the first quarter of that year, not one part-timer left a night shift. Annual savings attributed to reduced turnover, based largely on lower hiring costs, are estimated to be around $1 million. Additional benefits that the Buffalo district has gained from a more stable workforce include a 20 percent reduction in lost workdays due to work-related injuries and a drop from 4 percent to

1 percent in packages delivered on the wrong day or at the wrong time.

Questions

1. In dollars-and-cents' terms, why did Katriona Roeder want to reduce turnover?

2. What are the implications from this case for motivating part-time employees?

3. What are the implications from this case for managing in future years when there may be a severe labour shortage?

4. Is it unethical to teach supervisors "to demonstrate interest in their employees as individuals"? Explain.

5. What facts in this case support the argument that OB should be approached from a contingency perspective?

VIDEO CASE INCIDENT

CASE 1   Control at TerraCycle

Tom Szaky is a young Canadian who was admitted to prestigious Princeton University in the United States a few years ago.[49] One day he discovered a friend's worm composter. When he learned that worms eat garbage, he got an idea for a business. So he quit Princeton and, together with Jon Beyer, started TerraCycle, a company that makes plant fertilizer from worm droppings. Now he is trying to make a fortune off worms. Each year the size of the company has tripled. It now has 45 full-time employees and annual sales of about $5 million.

Szaky says that things at TerraCycle are never fully under control, and he does not want them to be. He says that when you are frantically doing everything you can to make your business a success, it is almost inevitable that things will be slightly out of control. The company's rapid growth is part of the control problem.

Betsy Cotton, chief financial officer (CFO) of the company, says (with some humour) that she is the most disliked person in the company. She does a wide variety of tasks—cutting cheques, depositing cheques at the bank, running the candy machine, reporting to investors and to the board of directors, providing feedback on how well a product is selling, and providing decision support for things like the advisability of leasing certain office space.

Cotton feels that the company is too reactive and does not have a good planning process. She agrees that it's good when people are excited about new ideas and about the future, but people think about those things in ways that are too abstract, so they do not develop detailed execution plans. She notes that by the time she gets information about an issue, all that can be done is to react to it. She would rather see more proactive planning. Cotton also senses a certain resistance to structure in the

company. When people are excited about their work, imposing order seems like it goes against what the company is all about.

Szaky notes that older people and people in the production area want more defined work processes, but developing those is time-consuming. Younger people and people in innovation want less-defined work processes, but that can lead to bad decisions. He realizes that you cannot launch a product without a control process, but you have to walk a fine line between too little and too much process. You also have to dream big and take calculated risks. For example, the least-risky thing would be to package a chemical product in a new bottle, but Szaky says you should not always do the least-risky thing. TerraCycle has a vision to package organic fertilizer in reused bottles, and there are risks associated with that vision.

Questions

1. What is organizational behaviour? How is the concept relevant to a company like TerraCycle?

2. The textbook notes that there are workplace "challenges" at the individual, group, and organizational levels. Explain the extent to which these challenges are evident at TerraCycle. How might TerraCycle address these challenges?

3. What does it mean to take a contingency perspective to organizational behaviour? How does the contingency idea apply to TerraCycle?

4. What is organizational citizenship behaviour? Explain why it might be particularly important at a company like TerraCycle.

OB At Work

From Concepts to Skills

Developing Interpersonal Skills

We note in the chapter that having a broad range of interpersonal skills to draw on makes us more effective organizational participants. So what kinds of interpersonal skills does an individual need in today's workplace? Robert Quinn, Kim Cameron, and their colleagues have developed a model known as the "Competing Values Framework" that can help us identify some of the most useful skills.[50] They note that the range of issues organizations face can be divided along two dimensions: an internal-external and a flexibility-control focus. This is illustrated in Exhibit 1-5. The internal-external dimension refers to the extent that organizations focus on one of two directions: either inwardly, toward employee needs and concerns and/or production processes and internal systems; or outwardly, toward such factors as the marketplace, government regulations, and the changing social, environmental, and technological

conditions of the future. The flexibility-control dimension refers to the competing demands of organizations to stay focused on doing what has been done in the past vs. being more flexible in orientation and outlook.

Because organizations face the competing demands shown in Exhibit 1-5, it becomes obvious that managers and employees need a variety of skills to help them function within the various quadrants at different points. For instance, the skills needed to operate an efficient assembly-line process are not the same as those needed to scan the environment or to create opportunities in anticipation of changes in the environment. Quinn and his colleagues use the term *master manager* to indicate that successful managers learn and apply skills that will help them manage across the range of organizational demands; at some times moving toward flexibility, at others moving toward control, sometimes being more internally focused, sometimes being more externally driven.[51]

As organizations increasingly cut their layers, reducing the number of managers while also relying more on the use of teams in the workplace, the skills of the master manager apply as well to the employee. In other words, considering the Competing Values Framework, we can see that both managers and individual employees need to learn new skills and new ways of interpreting their organizational contexts. Continuing to use traditional skills and practices that worked in the past is not an option. The growth in self-employment also indicates a need to develop more interpersonal skills, particularly for anyone who goes on to build a business that involves hiring and managing employees.

Exhibit 1-6 outlines the many skills required of today's manager. It gives you an indication of the complex roles that managers and employees fill in the changing workplace. The skills are organized in terms of four major roles: maintaining flexibility, maintaining control, maintaining an external focus, and maintaining an internal focus. The *Learning About Yourself Exercise* on page 25 helps you identify your own strengths and weaknesses in these skill areas so that you can have a better sense of how close you are to becoming a successful manager. For instance, on the flexibility side, organizations want to inspire their

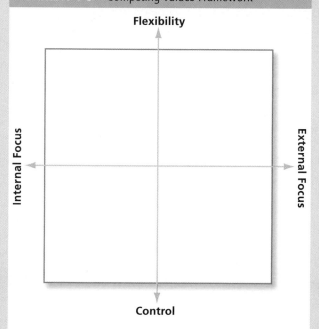

EXHIBIT 1-5 Competing Values Framework

Flexibility

Internal Focus

External Focus

Control

Source: Adapted from K. Cameron and R. E. Quinn, *Diagnosing and Changing Organizational Culture: Based on the Competing Values Framework* (Reading, MA: Addison Wesley Longman, 1999).

OB *At Work*

employees toward high-performance behaviour. Such behaviour includes looking ahead to the future and imagining possible new directions for the organization. To do these things, employees need to think and act like mentors and facilitators. It is also important to have the skills of innovators and brokers. On the control side, organizations need to set clear goals about productivity expectations, and they have to develop and implement systems to carry out the production process. To be effective on the production side, employees need to have the skills of monitors, coordinators, directors, and producers. The *Working With Others Exercise* on page 26 will help you better understand how closely your views on the ideal skills of managers and leaders match the skills needed to be successful in the broad range of activities that managers and leaders encounter.

At this point, you may wonder whether it is possible for people to learn all of the skills necessary to become a master manager. More important, you may wonder whether we can change our individual style, say from more controlling to more flexible. Here is what Peggy Kent, chair, president, and CEO of Century Mining Corporation (a mid-tier Canadian gold producer), said about how her managerial style changed from controlling to more flexible over time: "I started out being very dictatorial. Everybody in head office reported to me. I had to learn to trust other executives so we could work out problems together."[52] So, while it is probably true that each of us has a preferred style of operating, it is also the case that we can enhance the skills we have or develop new ones if that is something we choose to do. Learning to work well with others, listening to others, and building trust are skills that are certainly worth trying to master.

Practising Skills

As the father of two young children, Marshall Rogers thought that serving on the board of Marysville Daycare would be a good way to stay in touch with those who cared for his children during the day.[53] But he never

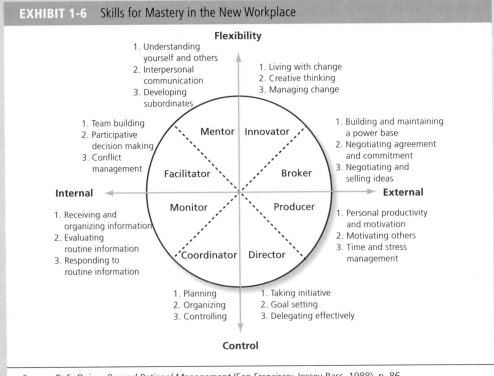

EXHIBIT 1-6	Skills for Mastery in the New Workplace

Flexibility

1. Understanding yourself and others
2. Interpersonal communication
3. Developing subordinates

1. Living with change
2. Creative thinking
3. Managing change

1. Team building
2. Participative decision making
3. Conflict management

Mentor   Innovator

1. Building and maintaining a power base
2. Negotiating agreement and commitment
3. Negotiating and selling ideas

Facilitator   Broker

Internal   **External**

Monitor   Producer

1. Receiving and organizing information
2. Evaluating routine information
3. Responding to routine information

Coordinator   Director

1. Personal productivity and motivation
2. Motivating others
3. Time and stress management

1. Planning
2. Organizing
3. Controlling

1. Taking initiative
2. Goal setting
3. Delegating effectively

Control

Source: R. E. Quinn, *Beyond Rational Management* (San Francisco: Jossey-Bass, 1988), p. 86.

dreamed that he would become involved in union-management negotiations with daycare-centre workers.

Late one Sunday evening, in his ninth month as president of the daycare centre, Rogers received a phone call from Grace Ng, a union representative of the Provincial Government Employees' Union (PGEU). Ng informed Rogers that the daycare workers would be unionized the following week. Rogers was stunned to hear this news. Early the next morning, he had to present his new marketing plan to senior management at Techtronix Industries, where he was vice-president of marketing. Somehow he made it through the meeting, wondering why he had not been aware of the employees' unhappiness, and how this action would affect his children.

Following his presentation, Rogers received documentation from the Labour Relations Board indicating that the daycare employees had been working to unionize themselves for more than a year. Rogers immediately contacted Xavier Breslin, the board's vice-president, and together they determined that no one on the board had been aware that the daycare workers were unhappy, let alone prepared to join a union.

Hoping that there was some sort of misunderstanding, Rogers called Emma Reynaud, the Marysville supervisor. Reynaud attended most board meetings, but had never mentioned the union-organizing drive. Yet Reynaud now told Rogers that she had actively encouraged the other daycare workers to consider joining the PGEU because the board had not been interested in the employees' concerns, had not increased their wages sufficiently over the past two years, and had not maintained communication channels between the board and the employees.

All of the board members had full-time jobs elsewhere, and many were upper- and middle-level managers in their own companies. They were used to dealing with unhappy employees in their own workplaces, although none had experienced a union-organizing drive. Like Rogers, they had chosen to serve on the board of Marysville to stay informed about the day-to-day events of the centre. They had not really thought of themselves as the centre's employer, although, as board members, they represented all the parents of children enrolled at Marysville. Their main tasks on the daycare-centre board had been setting fees for the children and wages for the daycare employees. The board members usually saw the staff members several times a week, when they picked up their children, yet the unhappiness represented by the union-organizing drive was surprising to all of them. When they met at an emergency board meeting that evening, they tried to evaluate what had gone wrong at Marysville.

Questions

1. If you were either a board member or a parent, how would you know that the employees taking care of your children were unhappy with their jobs?

2. What might you do if you learned about their unhappiness?

3. What might Rogers have done differently as president of the board?

4. In what ways does this case illustrate that knowledge of OB can be applied beyond your own workplace?

Reinforcing Skills

1. Talk to several managers you know and ask them what skills they think are most important in today's workplace. Ask them to specifically consider the use of teams in their workplaces, and what skills their team members most need to have but are least likely to have. How might you use this information to develop greater interpersonal skills?

2. Talk to several managers you know and ask them what skills they have found to be most important in doing their jobs. Why did they find these skills most important? What advice would they give a would-be manager about skills worth developing?

Chapter **2** *Perception, Personality, and Emotions*

Can a company win best employer in Canada awards *and* be regarded as the worst employer in Canada?

1   What is perception?

2   What causes people to have different perceptions of the same situation?

3   Can people be mistaken in their perceptions?

4   Does perception really affect outcomes?

5   What is personality and how does it affect behaviour?

6   Can emotions help or get in the way when we are dealing with others?

W almart Canada.[1] Just the thought of the retailer being in Canada upsets some people. There was strong resistance when Walmart first announced it was coming to Canada in 1994, and a belief that the retailer would somehow destroy the fabric of Canadian society. Fourteen years after its arrival, Mississauga, Ontario-based Walmart Canada employs more than 77 000 Canadians in 309 stores across Canada.

The company has been ranked as one of Canada's best employers on the Hewitt Associates survey of Canada's Best Employers five times between 2001 and 2007. It has also appeared on KPMG's list of Canada's 25 Most Admired Corporate Cultures. The Retail Council of Canada (RCC) presented former president and CEO Mario Pilozzi with the 2007 Distinguished Canadian Retailer of the Year award, noting that Walmart Canada has "one of the lowest staff turnover rates in the Canadian retail industry." In presenting the award, RCC also noted that "more than 100 Canadian communities have lobbied or petitioned to have a Walmart built in their towns" in recent years. With all of these positive statements about Walmart Canada, how can the perception of the company be so negative for some individuals?

All of our behaviour is somewhat shaped by our perceptions, personalities, emotions, and experiences. In this chapter, we consider the role that perception plays in affecting the way we see the world and the people around us. We also consider how personality characteristics affect our attitudes toward people and situations. We then consider how emotions shape many of our work-related behaviours.

OB *Is for Everyone*

- Who do you tend to blame when someone makes a mistake? Ever wonder why?
- Have you ever misjudged a person? Do you know why?
- Are people born with their personalities?
- Do you think it is better to be a Type A or a Type B personality?
- Ever wonder why the grocery clerk is always smiling?

Perception Defined

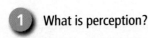

What is perception?

perception The process by which individuals select, organize, and interpret their sensory impressions in order to give meaning to their environment.

Perception is the process by which individuals select, organize, and interpret their sensory impressions in order to give meaning to their environment. However, what we perceive can be substantially different from objective reality. We often disagree about what is real.

Why is perception important in the study of organizational behaviour (OB)? Simply because people's behaviour is based on their perception of what reality is, not on reality itself. *The world as it is perceived is the world that is behaviourally important.* Paul Godfrey, CEO of the Toronto Blue Jays, notes that "a lot of things in life are perception." He claims that as chair of Metropolitan Toronto for 11 years, he had little real power, but people believed he could get things done, and so he did.[2]

Factors Influencing Perception

In summer 2005, Walmart Canada faced a vote by the Vancouver City Council on whether the retailer would be allowed to open a store in the southern part of the city.[3] Walmart Canada had bought the property that it was planning to develop in 2001 for $20 million, on advice from the city's planning department. The company proposed an environmentally friendly design, trying to appease the council's "green" views. Nonetheless, the council voted against the proposal, claiming that having a Walmart in the city would lead to more cars, and also harm neighbourhood shops.

Andrew Pelletier, director of corporate affairs for Walmart Canada, expressed dismay at city council's decision. He noted that Walmart Canada had polled more than 4000 Vancouver residents, and "81 per cent were in support of the development." "That's four to one in favour," he said. "There is no question people want this store. I've been talking to seniors and people on fixed incomes who don't have a car and they were looking for discount shopping. I feel very sorry for them." The city council and Vancouver residents appear to have had different perceptions of the same situation. What factors might have influenced these different perceptions?

What causes people to have different perceptions of the same situation?

How do we explain that individuals may look at the same thing, yet perceive it differently, and both be right? A number of factors affect perception. These factors can be found in the *perceiver*, in the object or *target* being perceived, or in the context of the *situation* in which the perception is made. Exhibit 2-1 summarizes the factors influencing perception. This chapter's *Working With Others Exercise* on page 69 will help you understand how your perceptions affect your evaluation of others.

The Perceiver

When an individual ("the perceiver") looks at a target and attempts to interpret what he or she sees, that interpretation is heavily influenced by the perceiver's personal characteristics. Personal characteristics that affect perception include a person's attitudes, personality, motives, interests, past experiences, and expectations. For instance, if you expect police officers to be authoritative, young people to be lazy, or individuals holding public office to be unscrupulous, you may perceive them as such, regardless of their actual traits. Our attitudes, motives, interests, and past experiences all shape the way we perceive an event.

The Target

A target's characteristics can affect what is perceived. Loud people are more likely to be noticed in a group than are quiet ones. So, too, are extremely attractive or unattractive individuals. Novelty, motion, sound, size, and other attributes of a target shape the way we see it.

EXHIBIT 2-1 Factors That Influence Perception

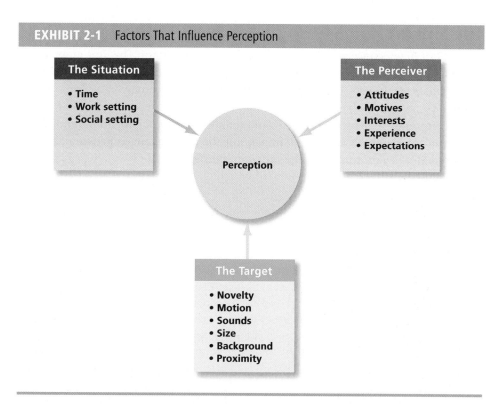

The Situation
- Time
- Work setting
- Social setting

The Perceiver
- Attitudes
- Motives
- Interests
- Experience
- Expectations

Perception

The Target
- Novelty
- Motion
- Sounds
- Size
- Background
- Proximity

Because targets are not looked at in isolation, the relationship of a target to its background influences perception. For instance, people who are female, black, or members of any other clearly distinguishable group will tend to be perceived as similar not only in physical terms but in other unrelated characteristics as well.

People's expectations about what employees working for a full-service web development agency should look like often leave them startled when they meet Jason Billingsley (left) and Justin Tilson (foreground), two of the founders of Vancouver-based Elastic Path Software (formerly Ekkon Technologies). Both men are in wheelchairs after a skiing accident for Billingsley and a mountain bike accident for Tilson. "It's an eye-opener sometimes," says Billingsley. "You've been talking on the phone for two or three weeks before you meet someone and they have no clue, and they kind of walk in and you see a little 'oh.'"

The Situation

The context in which we see objects or events is also important. The time at which we see an object or event can influence attention, as can location, light, heat, or any number of situational factors. For example, at a nightclub on Saturday night, you may not notice a young guest "dressed to the nines." Yet that same person so attired for your Monday morning management class would certainly catch your attention (and that of the rest of the class). Neither the perceiver nor the target changed between Saturday night and Monday morning, but the situation is different.

Perceptual Errors

In their review of whether to allow Walmart Canada to develop a site in south Vancouver, city council decided that having a Walmart in Vancouver was not in the best interests of the city's residents. They noted the increase in the amount of traffic and the potential harm to local businesses as some of the reasons to reject Walmart Canada's application for development. Meanwhile, Walmart Canada felt city residents supported the application, citing their own polling data. These differences in responses might suggest that city council, Vancouver residents, or Walmart Canada were engaged in making perceptual errors, perhaps sticking to their own views rather than honestly listening to the views of those who disagreed with them. What might have caused this to happen?

3 Can people be mistaken in their perceptions?

It can be difficult to perceive and interpret what others do. As a result, we develop shortcuts to make this task more manageable. These shortcuts are often very helpful—they allow us to make accurate perceptions quickly and provide valid information for making predictions. However, they are not foolproof. They can and do get us into trouble. For instance, when we make a bad first impression on someone, that perception may lead them to treat us poorly or dismiss us as a prospective employee or teammate. Some of the errors that distort the perception process include attribution theory, selective perception, the halo effect, contrast effects, projection, and stereotyping.

Attribution Theory

attribution theory The theory that when we observe what seems to be atypical behaviour by an individual, we attempt to determine whether it is internally or externally caused.

Who do you tend to blame when someone makes a mistake? Ever wonder why?

Attribution theory explains how we judge people differently, depending on the cause we attribute to a given behaviour.[4] Basically, the theory suggests that when we observe an individual's behaviour, we try to determine whether the individual is responsible for the behaviour (the cause is internal), or whether something outside the individual caused the behaviour (the cause is external). Whether we realize it or not, we use attribution theory whenever we try to come up with explanations for why people behaved the way they did.

In trying to understand another person's behaviour, then, we consider whether the behaviour was internally or externally caused. *Internally* caused behaviour is believed to be under the personal control of the individual; that is, the person *chooses* to engage in the behaviour. *Externally* caused behaviour is believed to result from outside causes; that is, the person does not have control over his or her actions and is *forced* into the behaviour by the situation. For example, while waiting for one of your team members who is late for a meeting, you could imagine either an internal or an external reason for the lateness. An internal reason might be that the team member must have partied into the wee hours of the morning and then overslept. An external attribution might be that there was a major automobile accident that tied up traffic.

EXHIBIT 2-2 Attribution Theory

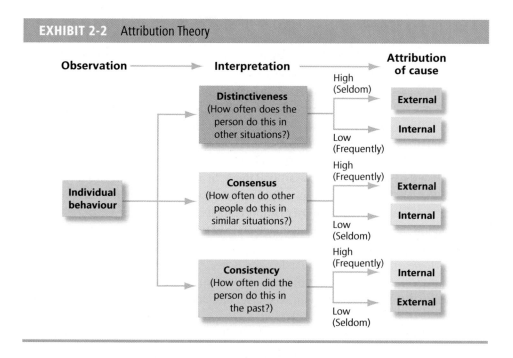

Rules for Determining Attribution

In trying to determine whether behaviour is internally or externally caused, we rely on three rules about the behaviour: (1) distinctiveness, (2) consensus, and (3) consistency. Exhibit 2-2 summarizes the main elements in attribution theory.

Distinctiveness **Distinctiveness** refers to whether an individual acts similarly across a variety of situations. Is the student always underperforming (being late for class, goofing off in team meetings, not answering urgent emails) or is the student's behaviour in one situation unusual from what he shows in other situations? If the behaviour is unusual, the observer is likely to make an external attribution. If this action is not unusual, the observer will probably judge it as internally caused.

Consensus **Consensus** considers how an individual's behaviour compares with others in the same situation. If everyone who is faced with a similar situation responds in the same way, we can say the behaviour shows consensus. When consensus is high, an external attribution is given to an individual's behaviour. But if an individual's behaviour is different from everyone else's, you would conclude the cause for that individual's behaviour was internal.

Consistency Finally, an observer looks for **consistency** in an action that is repeated over time. If a student is usually on time for class (she has not been late all term), being 10 minutes late will be perceived differently from the way it is when the student is routinely late (almost every class). If a student is almost always late, the observer is likely to attribute lateness to internal causes. If the student is almost never late, then lateness will be attributed to external causes.

How Attributions Get Distorted

One of the more interesting findings from attribution theory is that there are errors or biases that distort attributions. For instance, there is substantial evidence that when we judge the behaviour of other people, we tend to put more emphasis on internal or personal factors and less emphasis on external factors.[5] This is called the **fundamental attribution error** and can explain why a sales manager is prone to attribute the poor

distinctiveness A behavioural rule that asks whether an individual acts similarly across a variety of situations.

consensus A behavioural rule that asks if everyone faced with a similar situation responds in the same way.

consistency A behavioural rule that asks whether the individual has been acting in the same way over time.

fundamental attribution error The tendency to underestimate the influence of external factors and overestimate the influence of internal factors when making judgments about the behaviour of others.

performance of his or her sales agents to laziness rather than to the innovative product line introduced by a competitor. Recent research suggests that journalists often engage in the fundamental attribution error when they over-attribute firm performance to the CEO's characteristics. This attribution error results in the creation of "celebrity CEOs."[6]

self-serving bias The tendency for individuals to attribute their own successes to internal factors while putting the blame for failures on external factors.

Research suggests that individuals tend to overestimate their own good behaviour and underestimate the good behaviour of others.[7] We use **self-serving bias** when we judge ourselves. This means that when we are successful, we are more likely to believe it was because of internal factors, such as ability or effort. When we fail, however, we blame external factors, such as luck. In general, people tend to believe that their own behaviour is more positive than the behaviour of those around them. In a recent study, managers suggested that even though they were not responsible for the past poor performance of employees, they felt that they could help employees improve their behaviour in the future.[8]

Attribution theory was developed largely in the United States on the basis of experiments with Americans, but there is no particular reason to believe it would not apply in Canada. However, evidence from Japan[9] and Korea[10] suggests we should be careful in making attribution theory predictions in non-Western countries or in those with strong collectivist traditions, such as Spain, Portugal, and some Eastern European countries.

Selective Perception

selective perception People's selective interpretation of what they see based on their interests, background, experience, and attitudes.

Have you ever misjudged a person? Do you know why?

Because it is impossible for us to absorb everything we see, we engage in **selective perception**. Any characteristic that makes a person, object, or event stand out will increase the probability that we see that characteristic, rather than the whole package of characteristics. This tendency explains why, for example, you are more likely to notice cars like your own.

How does selectivity work as a shortcut in judging other people? Since we cannot absorb all that we see, we take in bits and pieces. Those bits and pieces are not chosen randomly, but are selectively chosen according to our interests, background, experience, and attitudes. For instance, you are listening to your instructor while surfing the net. The next thing you know, the instructor is calling on you, asking a question, but you have no idea what to answer because you got involved in an online auction on eBay and lost track of the classroom discussion. While you were surfing, the eBay auction became more important than what your instructor was saying, and you tuned her out. However, had she said "tomorrow's test will cover the following topics," you might have snapped to attention again, knowing that you needed that information to study effectively.

Selective perception also allows us to "speed-read" others, but we may draw inaccurate pictures as a result. Because we see what we want to see, we can make unwarranted conclusions about an ambiguous situation. Selective perception can also make us draw wrong conclusions about co-workers who have suffered serious illnesses, as *Focus on Diversity* shows.

FOCUS ON **DIVERSITY**

Underestimating Employees Who Have Been Seriously Ill

Does having had a serious illness mean that you cannot do your job? Lynda Davidson learned the hard way that suffering a mental illness and then getting treatment for it does not necessarily give one a clean bill of health at work.[11] When she returned to work after treatment, though she made her targets and earned her bonuses, her contract was not renewed. She later took a job as program manager at the Canadian Mental Health Association in Toronto.

Another Toronto woman suffered a similar fate when she was diagnosed with acute leukemia. After treatment, she returned to work at a large financial services organization only to find that she could not get any promotions. "I had the sense that people no longer took me seriously. I think people looked at me and thought, 'She's going to die,'" the woman said. It took moving to a different department where no one knew her to get ahead in her job.

It is not uncommon for employees with critical, chronic illnesses to feel that their jobs have been harmed by their illnesses. Employers and co-workers apparently perceive that those employees cannot function at the same level that they had prior to the illnesses. Describing a recent study done in the United States by the National Coalition for Cancer Survivorship, Dr. Ross Gray, a research psychologist at the Toronto-Sunnybrook Regional Cancer Centre, noted: "The study found that employers and co-workers overestimate the impact of cancer on people's lives. Decisions get made about advancement or capability that are out of line with the realities."

Halo Effect

When we draw a general impression about an individual on the basis of a single characteristic, such as intelligence, likeability, or appearance, a **halo effect** is operating. This often happens when students evaluate their instructor. Students may give more weight to a single trait, such as enthusiasm, and allow their entire evaluation to be affected by how they judge the instructor on that one trait. Thus, an instructor may be quiet, assured, knowledgeable, and highly qualified, but if his or her presentation style lacks enthusiasm, those students would probably give the instructor a low rating.

halo effect Drawing a general impression of an individual on the basis of a single characteristic.

The reality of the halo effect was confirmed in a classic study. Subjects were given a list of traits and asked to evaluate the person to whom those traits applied.[12] When traits such as intelligent, skillful, practical, industrious, determined, and warm were used, the person was judged to be wise, humorous, popular, and imaginative. When cold was substituted for warm, a completely different set of perceptions was obtained, though otherwise the list was identical. Clearly, the subjects were allowing a single trait to influence their overall impression of the person being judged.

Contrast Effects

There is an old saying among entertainers who perform in variety shows: Never follow an act that has children or animals in it.

This example demonstrates how **contrast effects** can distort perceptions.[13] We do not evaluate a person in isolation. Our reaction to one person is often influenced by other people we have recently encountered.

contrast effects The concept that our reaction to one person is often influenced by other people we have recently encountered.

Consider what happens when a manager interviews job candidates from a pool of applicants. The evaluation of a candidate can be affected by his or her place in the interview schedule. The candidate is likely to receive a better evaluation if interviewed after a mediocre applicant, and a worse evaluation if interviewed after a strong applicant.

Projection

It is easy to judge others if we assume that they are similar to us. For instance, if you want challenge and responsibility in your job, you assume that others want the same. Or you are honest and trustworthy, so you take it for granted that other people are

projection Attributing one's own characteristics to other people.

equally honest and trustworthy. This tendency for people to attribute their own characteristics to other people—which is called **projection**—can distort perceptions.

People who engage in projection tend to perceive others according to what they themselves are like rather than perceiving others as they really are. Because they always judge people as similar to themselves, when they observe someone who is actually like them their perceptions are naturally correct. But when they observe others who are not like them, their perceptions are not so accurate.

Stereotyping

stereotyping Judging someone on the basis of one's perception of the group to which that person belongs.

heuristics Judgment shortcuts in decision making.

When we judge someone on the basis of our perception of the group to which he or she belongs, we are using the shortcut called **stereotyping**.

We rely on generalizations every day because they help us make decisions quickly. They are a means of simplifying a complex world. It's less difficult to deal with an unmanageable number of stimuli if we use **heuristics** (judgment shortcuts in decision making) or stereotypes. The problem occurs, of course, when we generalize inaccurately or too much. In organizations, we frequently hear comments that represent stereotypes based on gender, age, race, religion, ethnicity, and even weight:[14] "Women will not relocate for a promotion," "men are not interested in child care," "older workers cannot learn new skills," "Asian immigrants are hard-working and conscientious," "overweight people lack discipline." Stereotypes can be so deeply ingrained and powerful that they influence life-and-death decisions. One study showed that, controlling for a wide array of factors (such as aggravating or mitigating circumstances), the degree to which black defendants in US murder trails looked stereotypically black essentially doubled their odds of receiving a death sentence if convicted.[15]

Obviously, one of the problems of stereotypes is that they are widespread, despite the fact that they may not contain a shred of truth or that they may be irrelevant. Perhaps they are widespread only because many people are making the same inaccurate

Muslim women in Canada often experience discrimination in being hired, or how their co-workers treat them, when they were a hijab. Co-workers of nurse Sharon Hoosein, shown here, were surprised when she announced she would be returning from her maternity leave. They assumed that because of her religion she would be expected to stay at home to raise children rather than work.

perception based on a false premise about a group. Stanford Graduate School of Business professor John Jost has uncovered another problem with stereotypes: They can be used to support the status quo.[16] He notes that when people buy into stereotypes about disadvantaged groups, they are less likely to challenge the consequences of the stereotype. For instance, subjects exposed to stereotypes such as "poor but happy" were less likely to respond negatively to ideas of social inequality. One implication of Jost's research is that we need to be aware of the effects of stereotypes on how we evaluate the world around us. Stereotypes can lead to strong negative reactions, such as prejudice, which we describe below.

Prejudice

Prejudice is an unfounded dislike of a person or group based on their belonging to a particular stereotyped group. For instance, an individual may dislike people of a particular religion, or state that she does not want to work with someone of a particular ethnicity. Prejudice can lead to negative consequences in the workplace and, in particular, to discrimination.[17] For instance, an individual of a particular ethnic group might be passed over for a management position because of the belief that employees might not see that person as a good manager. In another instance, an individual in his fifties who is looking for work but cannot find a job may be discriminated against because of the belief that younger workers are more appealing than older workers. Prejudice generally starts with stereotypes and then has negative emotional content added.

prejudice An unfounded dislike of a person or group based on their belonging to a particular stereotyped group.

Why Do Perception and Judgment Matter?

Walmart Canada receives mixed reviews from Canadians, who seem to either love the company or hate it.[18] Supporters cite such things as low prices and the increase in jobs that the company has brought. Critics complain about low wages and the loss of local businesses once the company arrives. At least some studies suggest that Walmart benefits communities where it opens stores. For instance, when Walmart arrived in Stettler, Alberta (near Calgary), in 2004, there was a great deal of apprehension. Subsequently, Boston Pizza and Tim Hortons have come to the town. "It's been very positive, and it's created many more shoppers coming to our community," said Alan Willis of the Stettler and Region Marketing Corporation.

Walmart's management is aware that the company is not universally liked by Canadians. For instance, when Walmart Canada announced in August 2008 that all new stores would be designed to be more energy efficient, and existing stores would be made more environmentally friendly, one might have expected this announcement to be greeted with enthusiasm. But the company anticipated that there would be some who would be cynical about the company's motives. "Some might say we're just another company trying to endear itself to the Canadian public by hopping on the green movement. That perspective misses the point," CEO David Cheesewright said. Can negative perceptions of Walmart by individuals make it impossible to recognize any good that the company does?

People in organizations are always judging each other. For instance, people typically go through an employment interview before being hired. Interviewers make perceptual judgments during the interview, which then affect whether the individual is hired. Studies show that if negative information is exposed early in the interview, it tends to be more heavily weighted than if that same information comes out later.[19] When multiple interviewers are present, agreement among interviewers is often poor; that is, different interviewers see different things in the same candidate and thus arrive at different conclusions about the applicant. If the employment interview is an important input into the hiring decision—and it usually is—you should recognize that perceptual factors influence who is hired and, eventually, the quality of an organization's labour force.

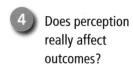 **4** Does perception really affect outcomes?

This chapter's *Ethical Dilemma Exercise—Hiring Based on Body Art* on pages 69–70 illustrates how the perception of tattoos affects hiring practices.

An employee's performance appraisal is another process that depends very much on perceptual factors.[20] An employee's future is closely tied to his or her appraisal—promotions, pay raises, and continuation of employment are among the most obvious outcomes. Although the appraisal can be objective (e.g., a salesperson is appraised on how many dollars of sales he or she generates in a given territory), many jobs are evaluated in subjective terms. Subjective measures are easier to implement, they provide managers with more freedom to do as they like, and many jobs do not readily lend themselves to objective measures. Subjective measures are, by definition, judgmental. The evaluator forms a general impression of an employee's work. To the degree that managers use subjective measures in appraising employees or choosing whom to promote, what the evaluator perceives to be good or bad employee characteristics or behaviours will significantly influence the outcome of the appraisal. One recent study found that managers in both Hong Kong and the United States were more likely to promote individuals who were more similar to themselves.[21] One's behaviour may also be affected by perceptions. Below we discuss how the self-fulfilling prophecy can lead to people's engaging in behaviour that is expected of them.

Managers are not the only people making judgments at work. When a new person joins a work team, he or she is immediately "sized up" by the other team members. McMaster University professor Kathleen Martin found that even small things can make a difference in how a team member is viewed. In her study, students read descriptions of individuals and were then asked to evaluate 12 personality characteristics of "Tom" or "Mary."[22] Some of these descriptions included information about whether "Tom" or "Mary" exercised. Students evaluated nonexercisers more negatively on every personality and physical characteristic than those described as exercisers. In fact, those described as nonexercisers were rated more negatively than those for whom no information about exercise was provided. Martin noted, "When Mary and Tom were described as exercisers, they were considered to be harder workers, more confident, braver, smarter, neater, happier, and more sociable than the non-exerciser."

Self-Fulfilling Prophecy

There is an impressive amount of evidence that demonstrates that people will attempt to validate their perceptions of reality, even when those perceptions are faulty.[23] This characteristic is particularly relevant when we consider performance expectations on the job.

self-fulfilling prophecy A concept that proposes a person will behave in ways consistent with how he or she is perceived by others.

The terms **self-fulfilling prophecy** and *Pygmalion effect* have evolved to characterize the fact that people's expectations determine their behaviour. In other words, if a manager expects big things from his people, they are not likely to let him down. Similarly, if a manager expects people to perform minimally, they will tend to behave so as to meet those low expectations. The result then is that the expectations become reality.

An interesting illustration of the self-fulfilling prophecy is a study undertaken with 105 soldiers in the Israeli Defense Forces who were taking a 15-week combat command course.[24] The four course instructors were told that one-third of the specific incoming trainees had high potential, one-third had normal potential, and the potential of the rest was unknown. In reality, the trainees were randomly placed into those categories by the researchers. The results confirmed the existence of a self-fulfilling prophecy. The trainees whom instructors were told had high potential scored significantly higher on objective achievement tests, exhibited more positive attitudes, and held their leaders in higher regard than did the other two groups. The instructors of the supposedly high-potential trainees got better results from them because the instructors expected better performance. Expectations may not be the only factor leading to the self-fulfilling prophecy, however. In some cases, it is the treatment that individuals receive from instructors and others that accounts for higher performance. For instance, instructors might put more time and effort into those individuals who are expected to perform better.

As you can see, perception plays a large role in how people are evaluated. Personality, which we review below, is another major factor affecting how people relate in the workplace.

Personality

Why are some people quiet and passive, while others are loud and aggressive? Are certain personality types better adapted for certain job types? What do we know from theories of personality that can help us explain and predict the behaviour of leaders such as Stephen Harper, Michael Ignatieff, or Barack Obama? How do we explain the risk-taking nature of Donald Trump, who still sees himself as the greatest businessman in America even though Trump Entertainment Resorts went into bankruptcy protection for part of 2004 and 2005 and filed for bankruptcy in February 2009, after Trump resigned from the board? In this section, we will attempt to answer such questions.

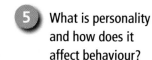

5 What is personality and how does it affect behaviour?

What Is Personality?

When we talk of personality we do not mean that a person has charm, a positive attitude toward life, a smiling face, or is a finalist for "Miss Congeniality." When psychologists talk of personality, they mean a dynamic concept describing the growth and development of a person's whole psychological system. Rather than looking at parts of the person, personality looks at the whole person. Gordon Allport produced the most frequently used definition of personality more than 70 years ago. He said personality is "the dynamic organization within the individual of those psychophysical systems that determine his unique adjustments to his environment."[25] For our purposes, you should think of **personality** as the stable patterns of behaviour and consistent internal states that determine how an individual reacts to and interacts with others. It is most often described in terms of measurable traits that a person exhibits.

personality The stable patterns of behaviour and consistent internal states that determine how an individual reacts to and interacts with others.

Measuring Personality

The most important reason managers need to know how to measure personality is that research has shown that personality tests are useful in hiring decisions. Scores on personality tests help managers forecast who is the best fit for a job.[26] And some managers want to know how people score on personality tests to better understand and more effectively manage the people who work for them. Far and away the most common means of measuring personality is through self-report surveys, with which individuals evaluate themselves by rating themselves on a series of factors, such as "I worry a lot about the future." Though self-report measures work well when well constructed, one weakness of these measures is that the respondent might lie or practise impression management—that is, the person could "fake it" on the test to create a good impression. This is especially a concern when the survey is the basis for employment. Another problem is accuracy. In other words, a perfectly good candidate could have just been in a bad mood when the survey was taken.

Observer ratings provide an independent assessment of personality. Instead of a person self-reporting, a co-worker or another observer does the rating (sometimes with the subject's knowledge and sometimes without). Even though the results of self-reports and observer ratings are strongly correlated, research suggests that observer ratings are a better predictor of success on the job.[27] However, each can tell us something unique about an individual's behaviour in the workplace.

Personality Determinants

An early argument in personality research centred on whether an individual's personality was predetermined at birth, or the result of the individual's interaction with his or her environment. Clearly, there is no simple answer. Personality appears to be a result of both influences. In addition, today we recognize a third factor—the situation. Thus, an adult's personality is now generally considered to be made up of both hereditary and environmental factors, moderated by situational conditions.

Heredity

Are people born with their personalities?

Heredity refers to those factors that were determined at conception. Physical stature, facial attractiveness, gender, temperament, muscle composition and reflexes, energy level, and biological rhythms are characteristics that are generally considered to be either completely or largely influenced by your parents' bio-logical, physiological, and inherent psychological makeup. The heredity approach argues that the ultimate explanation of an individual's personality is genetic.

If personality characteristics were *completely* dictated by heredity, they would be fixed at birth and no amount of experience could alter them. If genetics resulted in your being tense and irritable as a child, for example, it would not be possible for you to change those characteristics as you grew into an adult. But personality characteristics are not completely dictated by heredity.

Researchers have found that genetics can explain about 50 percent of the personality differences and more than 30 percent of the variation in occupational and leisure interests found in individuals. In other words, blood-related siblings are likely to have more similar personalities, occupations, and leisure interests than unrelated people.

Does personality change over one's lifetime? Most research in this area suggests that while some aspects of our personalities do change over time, the rank orderings do not change very much. For example, people's scores on measures of conscientiousness tend to increase as they get older. However, there are still strong individual differences in conscientiousness, and despite the fact that most of us become more responsible over time, people tend to change by about the same amount, so that the rank order stays roughly the same.[28] For instance, if you are more conscientious than your sibling now, that is likely to be true in 20 years, even though you both should become more conscientiousness over time.

Personality Traits

The early work in the structure of personality revolved around attempts to identify and label enduring characteristics that describe an individual's behaviour. Popular characteristics include shy, aggressive, submissive, lazy, ambitious, loyal, and timid. Those characteristics, when they are exhibited in a large number of situations, are called **personality traits**.[29] The more consistent the characteristic and the more often it occurs in different situations, the more important that trait is in describing the individual. The "Myers-Briggs Type Indicator" and the "Big Five Personality Model," which we discuss below, are two methods that have been used to determine personality traits. A recent study suggests that personality traits are common across a variety of cultures.[30]

Our personality traits, by the way, are evaluated differently by different people. This is partly a function of perception, which we discussed earlier in the chapter. In Exhibit 2-3, you will note that Lucy tells Linus a few things about his personality.

personality traits Enduring characteristics that describe an individual's behaviour.

EXHIBIT 2-3

Source: *Peanuts* reprinted with permission of United Features Syndicate, Inc.

A number of early research efforts tried to identify the *primary* traits that govern behaviour.[31] However, for the most part, they resulted in long lists of traits that were difficult to generalize from and provided little practical guidance to organizational decision makers. Two exceptions are the Myers-Briggs Type Indicator and the Big Five Personality Model. Over the past 20 years, these two approaches have become the dominant frameworks for identifying and classifying traits.

The Myers-Briggs Type Indicator

The **Myers-Briggs Type Indicator (MBTI)** is the most widely used personality-assessment instrument in the world.[32] It's a 100-question personality test that asks people how they usually feel or act in particular situations. On the basis of their answers, individuals are classified as extraverted or introverted (E or I), sensing or intuitive (S or N), thinking or feeling (T or F), and judging or perceiving (J or P). These terms are defined as follows:

> **Myers-Briggs Type Indicator (MBTI)** A personality test that taps four characteristics and classifies people into 1 of 16 personality types.

- *Extraverted/introverted.* Extraverted individuals are outgoing, sociable, and assertive. Introverts are quiet and shy. E/I measures where we direct our energy when dealing with people and things.

- *Sensing/intuitive.* Sensing types are practical and prefer routine and order. They focus on details. Intuitives rely on unconscious processes and look at the "big picture." This dimension looks at how we process information.

- *Thinking/feeling.* Thinking types use reason and logic to handle problems. Feeling types rely on their personal values and emotions.

- *Judging/perceiving.* Judging types want control and prefer their world to be ordered and structured. Perceiving types are flexible and spontaneous.

These classifications together describe 16 personality types. To illustrate, let's look at three examples:

- *INTJs are visionaries.* They usually have original minds and great drive for their own ideas and purposes. They are skeptical, critical, independent, determined, and often stubborn.

- *ESTJs are organizers.* They are realistic, logical, analytical, decisive, and have a natural head for business or mechanics. They like to organize and run activities.

- *ENTPs are conceptualizers.* They are innovative, individualistic, versatile, and attracted to entrepreneurial ideas. They tend to be resourceful in solving challenging problems, but may neglect routine assignments.

A book profiling 13 contemporary businesspeople who created super-successful firms including Apple Computer, FedEx, Honda Motors, Microsoft, and Sony found that all are intuitive thinkers (NTs).[33] This result is particularly interesting because intuitive thinkers represent only about 5 percent of the population.

The MBTI is widely used by organizations including Apple Computer, AT&T, Citigroup, GE, 3M, many hospitals and educational institutions, and even the US Armed Forces. In spite of its popularity, the evidence is mixed as to whether the MBTI is a valid measure of personality—with most of the evidence suggesting that it is not.[34] One problem is that it forces a person into either one type or another (that is, you are either introverted or extraverted). There is no in-between, though people can be both extraverted and introverted to some degree. The best we can say is that the MBTI can be a valuable tool for increasing self-awareness and providing career guidance. But because results tend to be unrelated to job performance, managers probably should not use it as a selection test for job candidates.

The Big Five Personality Model

The most widely accepted model of personality is the five-factor model of personality—more typically called the "Big Five."[35] An impressive body of research supports the notion that five basic personality dimensions underlie all others and include most of the significant variations in human personality.[36] The Big Five personality factors are as follows:

- **Extraversion**. This dimension captures a person's comfort level with relationships. Extraverted individuals are sociable, talkative, and assertive.

- **Agreeableness**. This dimension refers to how readily a person will go along with others. Highly agreeable people are good-natured, cooperative, warm, and trusting.

- **Conscientiousness**. This dimension is a measure of a person's reliability. People who score high on conscientiousness are responsible, dependable, persistent, and achievement-oriented.

- **Emotional stability**. This dimension taps a person's ability to withstand stress. People high on emotional stability are calm, self-confident, and secure.

- **Openness to experience**. The final dimension addresses a person's range of interests and fascination with novelty. People high on openness to experience are imaginative, artistically sensitive, and intellectual.

Exhibit 2-4 shows the characteristics for the high and low dimensions of each Big Five personality factor.

Research on the Big Five has found a relationship between the personality dimensions and job performance.[37] As the authors of the most-cited review put it, "The preponderance of evidence shows that individuals who are dependable, reliable, careful, thorough, able to plan, organized, hardworking, persistent, and achievement-oriented tend to have higher job performance in most if not all occupations."[38] In addition, employees who score higher in conscientiousness develop higher levels of job knowledge, probably because highly conscientious people exert greater levels of effort on their jobs. The higher levels of job knowledge then contribute to higher levels of job performance.[39]

Although conscientiousness is the Big Five trait most consistently related to job performance, the other traits are related to aspects of performance in some situations. All five traits also have other implications for work and for life, as summarized in Exhibit 2-5.

extraversion A personality factor that describes the degree to which someone is sociable, talkative, and assertive.

agreeableness A personality factor that describes the degree to which someone is good-natured, cooperative, warm, and trusting.

conscientiousness A personality factor that describes the degree to which someone is responsible, dependable, persistent, and achievement-oriented.

emotional stability A personality factor that describes the degree to which someone is calm, self-confident, and secure.

openness to experience A personality factor that describes the degree to which someone is imaginative, artistically sensitive, and intellectual.

Indra Nooyi, CEO and chair of PepsiCo, scores high on all personality dimensions of the Big Five Model. She is described as sociable, agreeable, conscientious, emotionally stable, and open to experiences. These personality traits have contributed to Nooyi's high job performance and career success at PepsiCo; she joined the company in 1994 as senior vice-president of strategy and development, and she was promoted to president and chief financial officer before moving into the firm's top position.

EXHIBIT 2-4   Big Five Personality Factors

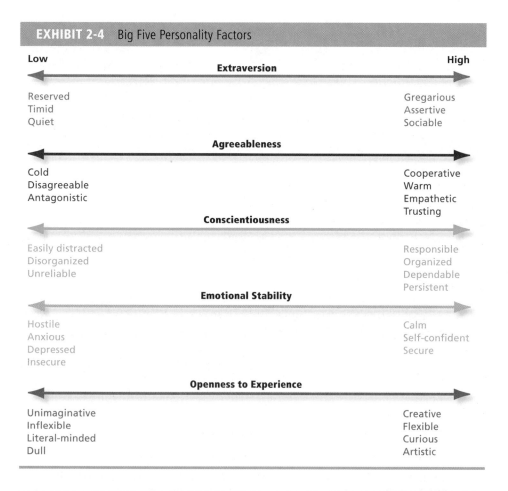

Low	**Extraversion**	High
Reserved		Gregarious
Timid		Assertive
Quiet		Sociable

Agreeableness

Cold	Cooperative
Disagreeable	Warm
Antagonistic	Empathetic
	Trusting

Conscientiousness

Easily distracted	Responsible
Disorganized	Organized
Unreliable	Dependable
	Persistent

Emotional Stability

Hostile	Calm
Anxious	Self-confident
Depressed	Secure
Insecure	

Openness to Experience

Unimaginative	Creative
Inflexible	Flexible
Literal-minded	Curious
Dull	Artistic

EXHIBIT 2-5   How the Big Five Traits Influence OB

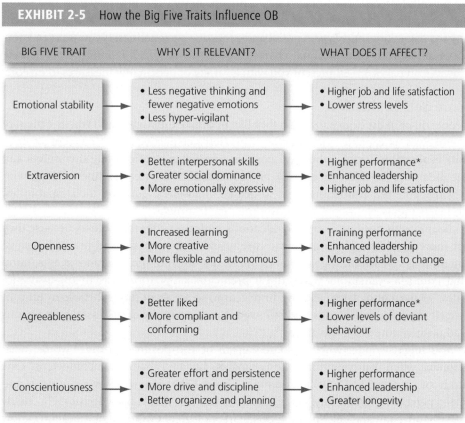

BIG FIVE TRAIT	WHY IS IT RELEVANT?	WHAT DOES IT AFFECT?
Emotional stability	• Less negative thinking and fewer negative emotions • Less hyper-vigilant	• Higher job and life satisfaction • Lower stress levels
Extraversion	• Better interpersonal skills • Greater social dominance • More emotionally expressive	• Higher performance* • Enhanced leadership • Higher job and life satisfaction
Openness	• Increased learning • More creative • More flexible and autonomous	• Training performance • Enhanced leadership • More adaptable to change
Agreeableness	• Better liked • More compliant and conforming	• Higher performance* • Lower levels of deviant behaviour
Conscientiousness	• Greater effort and persistence • More drive and discipline • Better organized and planning	• Higher performance • Enhanced leadership • Greater longevity

*In jobs requiring significant teamwork or frequent interpersonal interactions.

It is not always easy for friends to share top management roles, but Anton Rabie (left), president and COO, and Ronnen Harary (right), CEO, of Toronto-based Spin Master, like the arrangement. Rabie is an extravert, while Harary is an introvert. The childhood friends feel their personalities complement each other, making an ideal management team.

Major Personality Attributes Influencing OB

In this section, we will evaluate specific personality attributes that have been found to be powerful predictors of behaviour in organizations. The first relates to one's core self-evaluation. The others are Machiavellianism, narcissism, self-monitoring, propensity for risk-taking, and Type A and B and proactive personalities. If you want to know more about your own personal characteristics, this chapter's *Learning About Yourself Exercises* on pages 63–68 present you with a variety of personality measures to explore.

Core Self-Evaluation

core self-evaluation The degree to which an individual likes or dislikes himself or herself, whether the person sees himself or herself as capable and effective, and whether the person feels in control of his or her environment or powerless over the environment.

People differ in the degree to which they like or dislike themselves and whether they see themselves as capable and effective. This self-perspective is the concept of **core self-evaluation**. People who have positive core self-evaluations like themselves and see themselves as effective, capable, and in control of their environment. Those with negative core self-evaluations tend to dislike themselves, question their capabilities, and view themselves as powerless over their environment.[40]

People with positive core self-evaluations perform better than others because they set more ambitious goals, are more committed to their goals, and persist longer at attempting to reach these goals. For example, one study of life-insurance agents found that core self-evaluations were critical predictors of performance. In life-insurance sales, 90 percent of sales calls end in rejection, so an agent has to believe in him- or herself to persist. In fact, this study showed that the majority of successful salespersons had positive core self-evaluations.[41]

You might wonder whether someone can be too positive. In other words, what happens when someone thinks he is capable, but he is actually incompetent? One study of *Fortune* 500 CEOs, for example, showed that many are overconfident, and their perceived infallibility often causes them to make bad decisions.[42] Teddy Forstmann, chair and CEO of the sports marketing giant IMG, said of himself, "I know God gave me an unusual brain. I can't deny that. I have a God-given talent for seeing potential."[43] One might say that people like Forstmann are overconfident, but very often we humans sell ourselves short and are less happy and effective than we could be because of it. If we decide we cannot do something, for example, we won't try, and not doing it only reinforces our self-doubts.

Machiavellianism

The personality characteristic of **machiavellianism** (Mach) is named after Niccolò Machiavelli, who wrote in the sixteenth century on how to gain and use power. An individual high in machiavellianism is highly practical, maintains emotional distance, and believes that ends can justify means. "If it works, use it" is consistent with a high-Mach perspective.

A considerable amount of research has been directed toward relating high- and low-Mach personalities to certain behavioural outcomes.[44] High Machs manipulate more, win more, are persuaded less, and persuade others more than do low Machs.[45] Think of Donald Trump interacting with the characters on *The Apprentice*. Yet these high-Mach outcomes are moderated by situational factors. It has been found that high Machs flourish (1) when they interact face to face with others rather than indirectly; (2) when the situation has a minimum number of rules and regulations, thus allowing latitude for improvisation; and (3) when low Machs get distracted by emotional involvement with details irrelevant to winning.[46]

Should we conclude that high Machs make good employees? That answer depends on the type of job and whether you consider ethical implications in evaluating performance. In jobs that require bargaining skills (such as labour negotiation) or that offer substantial rewards for winning (as in commissioned sales), high Machs will be productive. But if the ends cannot justify the means, if there are absolute standards of behaviour, or if the three situational factors noted in the preceding paragraph are not in evidence, our ability to predict a high Mach's performance will be severely curtailed. If you are interested in determining your level of machiavellianism, you might want to complete *Learning About Yourself Exercise #1* on page 63.

machiavellianism The degree to which an individual is pragmatic, maintains emotional distance, and believes that ends can justify means.

Narcissism

Hans likes to be the centre of attention. He likes to look at himself in the mirror a lot. He has extravagant dreams and seems to consider himself a person of many talents. Hans is a narcissist. The term is from the Greek myth of Narcissus, the story of a man so vain and proud that he fell in love with his own image. In psychology, **narcissism** describes a person who has a grandiose sense of self-importance, requires excessive admiration, has a sense of entitlement, and is arrogant.[47] Some research suggests that narcissism can be seen as a combination of the Big Five traits of extraversion and agreeableness; narcissists tend to be disagreeable extraverts.[48]

A study found that while narcissists thought they were *better* leaders than their colleagues, their supervisors actually rated them as *worse* leaders. For example, an Oracle executive described that company's CEO, Larry Ellison, as follows: "The difference between God and Larry is that God does not believe he is Larry."[49] Because narcissists often want to gain the admiration of others and receive affirmation of their superiority, they tend to "talk down" to those who threaten them, treating others as if they were inferior. Narcissists also tend to be selfish and exploitive, and they often carry the attitude that others exist for their benefit.[50] Studies indicate that narcissists are rated by their bosses as less effective at their jobs than others, particularly when it comes to helping other people.[51]

narcissism The tendency to be arrogant, have a grandiose sense of self-importance, require excessive admiration, and have a sense of entitlement.

Self-Monitoring

Some people are better able to pay attention to the external environment and respond accordingly, a characteristic known as **self-monitoring**.[52] Individuals high in

self-monitoring A personality trait that measures an individual's ability to adjust behaviour to external, situational factors.

self-monitoring show considerable ability to adjust and adapt their behaviour to the situations they are in. They are highly sensitive to external cues and can behave differently in different situations. High self-monitors are capable of presenting striking contradictions between their public personae and their private selves.

Low self-monitors cannot disguise themselves in the same way. They tend to display their true dispositions and attitudes in every situation; hence, there is high behavioural consistency between who they are and what they do.

Research suggests that high self-monitors tend to pay closer attention to the behaviour of others and are more capable of conforming than are low self-monitors.[53] In addition, high self-monitoring managers tend to be more mobile in their careers and receive more promotions (both internal and cross-organizational).[54] Recent research found that self-monitoring is also related to job performance and emerging leaders.[55] Specifically, high self-monitors are more likely to be high performers and more likely to become leaders. To determine whether you are a high or low self-monitor, you might want to complete *Learning About Yourself Exercise #2* on page 64.

Risk-Taking

risk-taking A person's willingness to take chances or risks.

People differ in their willingness to take chances. Matthew Barrett, the former CEO and chair of Bank of Montreal, and Frank Stronach, chair of Magna International, are good examples of high risk-takers. The tendency to assume or avoid risk has been shown to have an impact on how long it takes managers to make a decision and how much information they require before making their choice. For instance, 79 managers worked on simulated exercises that required them to make hiring decisions.[56] High **risk-taking** managers made more rapid decisions and used less information in making their choices than did the low risk-taking managers. Interestingly, the decision accuracy was the same for both groups.

Although previous studies have shown managers in large organizations to be more risk averse than are growth-oriented entrepreneurs who actively manage small businesses,

Richard Branson's tendency to take risks aligns with his job demands as an entrepreneur. Branson, founder and chairman of London-based Virgin Group, starts risky ventures that compete against industry giants. His Virgin Atlantic airline, for example, has taken market share from British Airways and has earned a reputation as one of the financially healthiest airlines in the world. Branson's risk-taking personality extends to his leisure activities of speedboat racing, skydiving, and ballooning.

recent findings suggest that managers in large organizations may actually be more willing to take risks than entrepreneurs.[57] For the work population as a whole, there are also differences in risk propensity.[58] As a result, it makes sense to recognize these differences and even to consider aligning risk-taking propensity with specific job demands. For instance, a high risk-taking propensity may lead to more effective performance for a stock trader in a brokerage firm because that type of job demands rapid decision making. On the other hand, a willingness to take risks might prove a major obstacle to an accountant who performs auditing activities. The latter job might be better filled by someone with a low risk-taking propensity. If you are interested in determining where you stand on risk-taking, you might want to complete *Learning About Yourself Exercise #3* on pages 65–66.

Type A and Type B Personalities

Do you think it is better to be a Type A or a Type B personality?

Do you know any people who are excessively competitive and always seem to be pushed for time? If you do, it's a good bet that those people have a **Type A personality**. An individual with a Type A personality is "aggressively involved in a chronic, incessant struggle to achieve more and more in less and less time, and, if required to do so, against the opposing efforts of other things or other persons."[59] In North American culture, such characteristics tend to be highly prized and positively associated with ambition and the successful acquisition of material goods.

Type A personality A personality with aggressive involvement in a chronic, incessant struggle to achieve more and more in less and less time and, if necessary, against the opposing efforts of other things or other people.

Type As

- Are always moving, walking, and eating rapidly

- Feel impatient with the rate at which most events take place

- Strive to think or do two or more things at once

- Cannot cope with leisure time

- Are obsessed with numbers, measuring their success in terms of how many or how much of everything they acquire

In contrast to the Type A personality is the Type B, who is exactly the opposite. Type Bs are "rarely harried by the desire to obtain a wildly increasing number of things or participate in an endless growing series of events in an ever-decreasing amount of time."[60]

Type Bs

- Never suffer from a sense of time urgency with its accompanying impatience

- Feel no need to display or discuss either their achievements or accomplishments unless such exposure is demanded by the situation

- Play for fun and relaxation, rather than to exhibit their superiority at any cost

- Can relax without guilt

Type As are often impatient, hurried, competitive, and hostile, but these traits tend to emerge most often when a Type A individual experiences stress or challenge.[61] Type As are fast workers because they emphasize quantity over quality. In managerial positions, Type As demonstrate their competitiveness by working long hours and, not infrequently, making poor decisions because they make them too fast. Stressed Type As are also rarely creative. Because of their concern with quantity and speed, they rely on past experiences when faced with problems. They will not allocate the time that is necessary to develop unique solutions to new problems. They seldom vary in their responses to specific challenges in their environment, and so their behaviour is easier to predict than that of Type Bs.

Are Type As or Type Bs more successful in organizations? Despite the hard work of Type As, Type Bs are the ones who appear to make it to the top. Great salespeople are usually Type As; senior executives are usually Type Bs. Why? The answer lies in the tendency of Type As to trade off quality of effort for quantity. Promotions in corporate and professional organizations "usually go to those who are wise rather than to those who are merely hasty, to those who are tactful rather than to those who are hostile, and to those who are creative rather than to those who are merely agile in competitive strife."[62]

Recent research has looked at the effect of job complexity on the cardiovascular health of both Type A and Type B individuals to see whether Type As always suffered negative health consequences.[63] Type B individuals did not suffer negative health consequences from jobs with psychological complexity. Type A workers who faced high job complexity had higher death rates from heart-related disorders than Type As who faced lower job complexity. These findings suggest that, health-wise, Type B workers suffer less when handling more complex jobs than do Type As. It also suggests that Type As who face lower job complexity do not encounter the same health risks as Type As who face higher job complexity.

If you are interested in determining whether you have a Type A or Type B personality, you might want to complete *Learning About Yourself Exercise #4* on page 67.

Proactive Personality

Did you ever notice that some people actively take the initiative to improve their current circumstances or create new ones while others sit by, passively reacting to situations? The former individuals have been described as having proactive personalities.[64]

People with a **proactive personality** identify opportunities, show initiative, take action, and persevere until meaningful change occurs. They create positive change in their environment, regardless or even in spite of constraints or obstacles.[65]

proactive personality A person who identifies opportunities, shows initiative, takes action, and perseveres until meaningful change occurs.

Not surprisingly, proactives have many desirable behaviours that organizations look for. For instance, the evidence indicates that proactives are more likely to be seen as leaders and are more likely to act as change agents within the organization.[66] Other actions of proactives can be positive or negative, depending on the organization and the situation. For example, proactives are more likely to challenge the status quo or voice their displeasure when situations are not to their liking.[67] If an organization requires people with entrepreneurial initiative, proactives make good candidates; however, these are people who are also more likely to leave an organization to start their own business.[68] As individuals, proactives are more likely to achieve career success.[69] This is because they select, create, and influence work situations in their favour. Proactives are more likely to seek out job and organizational information, develop contacts in high places, engage in career planning, and demonstrate persistence in the face of career obstacles. For an interesting look at how personality can contribute to business success, you might want to read this chapter's *Case Incident—A Diamond Personality* on pages 70–71.

Personality and National Culture

There are certainly no common personality types for a given country. You can, for instance, find high and low risk-takers in almost any culture. Yet a country's culture should influence the dominant personality characteristics of its population. Let's build this case by looking at one personality attribute—core self-evaluation.

There is evidence that cultures differ in terms of people's relationship to their environment.[70] In some cultures, such as those in North America, people believe that they can dominate their environment. People in other societies, such as Middle Eastern countries, believe that life is essentially preordained. Notice the close parallel to positive and negative core self-evaluation. We should expect a larger proportion of employees with positive core self-evaluations in the Canadian and American workforces than in the Saudi Arabian or Iranian workforces.

One caveat regarding personality tests is that they may be subject to cultural bias when used on samples of people other than those for whom the tests were designed. For instance, on common American personality tests, British people are characterized as "less dominant, achievement-orientated or flexible than Americans, but more self-controlled."[71] An example of a bias that can appear in such tests is that only 10 percent of British men answer "true" to the statement "I very much like hunting," while 70 percent of American men agree.[72] When these tests are used to select managers, they may result in the selection of individuals who are not as suitable in the British workplace as they would be in the American workplace.

Emotions

Former Vancouver city councillor Anne Roberts was a vocal opponent of Walmart Canada opening a store in the city.[73] She was so concerned that a new city council would overturn the views of the previous council, which had denied a permit to Walmart, that she wondered if the retailer was interfering with city elections. "It would be of great concern if a big American corporation was influencing our local election. If they are contributing to the NPA [one of the city's political parties], Walmart is interfering with our political process," said Roberts.

Sam Sullivan, who was running for mayor at the time, was willing to entertain another vote by city council on whether Walmart could open its doors in Vancouver if he was elected. Still, he denied that Walmart was contributing to his campaign. "I usually don't get involved in fundraising, but after I heard her accusations I had to ask. And in fact Walmart has not contributed any money to the NPA. There is no conspiracy theory here," said Sullivan. Could emotions have affected how each individual viewed Walmart's impact on the city?

Each of us has a range of personality characteristics, but we also bring with us a range of emotions. Given the obvious role that emotions play in our everyday lives, it might surprise you to learn that, until very recently, the topic of emotions was given little or no attention in the field of OB. When emotions were considered, the discussion focused on strong negative emotions—especially anger—that interfered with an employee's ability to do his or her job effectively. Emotions were rarely viewed as constructive or able to stimulate performance-enhancing behaviours.

Certainly some emotions, particularly when exhibited at the wrong time, can reduce employee performance. But this does not change the reality that employees bring an emotional component with them to work every day, and that no study of OB could be comprehensive without considering the role of emotions in workplace behaviour.

6 Can emotions help or get in the way when we are dealing with others?

What Are Emotions?

Emotions are intense feelings that are directed at someone or something.[74] Emotions are *reactions* to an object; they are not lasting personality traits. You show your emotions when you are "happy about something, angry at someone, afraid of something."[75]

emotions Intense feelings that are directed at someone or something.

How many emotions are there? In what ways do they vary? There are dozens of emotions, including anger, contempt, enthusiasm, envy, fear, frustration, disappointment, embarrassment, disgust, happiness, hate, hope, jealousy, joy, love, pride, surprise, and sadness. There have been numerous research efforts to limit and define the dozens of emotions into a fundamental or basic set of emotions.[76] But some researchers argue that it makes no sense to think of basic emotions because even emotions we rarely experience, such as shock, can have a powerful effect on us.[77]

In contemporary research, psychologists have tried to identify basic emotions by studying facial expressions (see the facial expressions in *From Concepts to Skills* on pages 72–73).[78] One problem with this approach is that some emotions are too complex to be easily represented on our faces. Take love, for example. Many think of love as the most universal of all emotions,[79] yet it's not easy to express a loving emotion with one's face only. Also, cultures have norms that govern emotional expression, so how we *experience* an emotion is not always the same as how we *show* it. And many companies today offer anger management programs to teach people to contain or even hide their inner feelings.[80]

It's unlikely that psychologists or philosophers will ever completely agree on a set of basic emotions, or even whether it makes sense to think of basic emotions. Still, researchers generally agree on six essentially universal emotions—anger, fear, sadness, happiness, disgust, and surprise—with most other emotions subsumed under one of these six categories.[81] Some researchers even plot these six emotions along a continuum: happiness—surprise—fear—sadness—anger—disgust.[82] The closer any two emotions are to each other on this continuum, the more likely it is that people will confuse them. For instance, we sometimes mistake happiness for surprise, but rarely do we confuse happiness and disgust.

Choosing Emotions: Emotional Labour

Ever wonder why the grocery clerk is always smiling?

If you have ever had a job working in retail sales or waiting on tables in a restaurant, you know the importance of "being nice." Even though there were days when you did not feel cheerful, you knew management expected you to be upbeat when dealing with customers. So you faked it, and in so doing, you expressed *emotional labour*.

Every employee expends physical and mental labour when they put their bodies and cognitive capabilities, respectively, into their job. But jobs also require **emotional labour**. Emotional labour is an employee's expression of organizationally desired emotions while at work.[83] For instance, crying may or may not be acceptable in the workplace, as *OB in the Workplace* shows.

emotional labour When an employee expresses organizationally desired emotions during interpersonal interactions.

OB IN THE WORKPLACE

Shed Those Tears

Can crying hurt you at work? Kathryn Brady, 34, is a finance manager for a large corporation.[84] Occasionally she has had bosses who have driven her to tears. Brady argues that when she has cried, it has been out of frustration, not weakness. "The misinterpretation that I'm whiny or weak is just not fair," she says.

Although that "old school" wisdom still holds true in many places, it is changing in others. George Merkle, CEO of a San Antonio credit company, does not mind if his employees cry. If someone cries, he says, "No apology needed. I know it's upsetting, and we can work our way through it." When Hillary Clinton was running to be the nominee for US president in 2008, it was said that showing tears had actually made her more likeable.

Surveys indicate that women are more likely to cry at work than men, but that may be changing, too. When 6'3" 253-pound football tight end Vernon Davis cried after being selected in the first round of the NFL draft, nobody accused him of being a wimp.

To many, however, these emotional displays are signs of weakness. On the reality TV show *The Apprentice: Martha Stewart*, Stewart warned one of the contestants not to cry. "Cry, and you're out of here," she said. "Women in business don't cry, my dear."

The concept of emotional labour emerged from studies of service jobs. Airlines expect their flight attendants, for instance, to be cheerful; we expect funeral directors to be sad; and we expect doctors to be emotionally neutral. But really, emotional labour is relevant to almost every job. Your managers expect you, for example, to be courteous, not hostile, in interactions with co-workers. The true challenge arises when employees have to project one emotion while simultaneously feeling another.[85] This difference is **emotional dissonance**, and it can take a heavy toll on employees. Bottled-up feelings of frustration, anger, and resentment can eventually lead to emotional exhaustion and burnout.[86] It is because of emotional labour's increasing importance in effective job performance that an understanding of emotion has gained heightened relevance within the field of OB.

emotional dissonance Inconsistencies between the emotions people feel and the emotions they show.

Emotional labour creates dilemmas for employees. There are people with whom you have to work that you just do not like. Maybe you consider their personality abrasive. Maybe you know they have said negative things about you behind your back. Regardless, your job requires you to interact with these people on a regular basis. So you are forced to pretend to be friendly.

It can help you, on the job especially, if you separate emotions into *felt* or *displayed emotions*.[87] **Felt emotions** are an individual's actual emotions. In contrast, **displayed emotions** are those that the organization requires employees to show and considers appropriate in a given job. They are not natural; they are learned. "The ritual look of delight on the face of the first runner-up as the [winner] is announced is a product of the display rule that losers should mask their sadness with an expression of joy for the winner."[88] Similarly, most of us know that we are expected to act sad at funerals, regardless of whether we consider the person's death to be a loss, and to pretend to be happy at weddings, even if we do not feel like celebrating.[89]

felt emotions An individual's actual emotions.

displayed emotions Emotions that are organizationally required and considered appropriate in a given job.

Effective managers have learned to be serious when giving an employee a negative performance evaluation and to hide their anger when they have been passed over for promotion. A salesperson who has not learned to smile and appear friendly, regardless of his true feelings at the moment, is not typically going to last long in most sales jobs. How we *experience* an emotion is not always the same as how we *show* it.[90]

Yet another point is that displaying fake emotions requires us to suppress the emotions we really feel (not showing anger toward a customer, for example). In other words, the individual has to "act" to keep her job. **Surface acting** is hiding one's inner feelings and hiding emotional expressions in response to display rules. For example, when an employee smiles at a customer even when he does not feel like it, he is surface acting. **Deep acting** is trying to modify one's true inner feelings based on display rules. A health care provider trying to genuinely feel more empathy for her patients is deep acting.[91] Surface acting deals with one's *displayed* emotions, and deep acting deals with one's *felt* emotions. Research shows that surface acting is more stressful to employees than deep acting because it entails faking one's true emotions.[92] For further discussion on the costs and benefits of emotional display rules in organizations, read this chapter's *Point/Counterpoint* on page 62.

surface acting Hiding one's inner feelings to display what is expected.

deep acting Trying to modify one's true inner feelings to match what is expected.

Why Should We Care About Emotions in the Workplace?

There are a number of reasons to be concerned about understanding emotions in the workplace.[93] People who know their own emotions and are good at reading others' emotions may be more effective in their jobs. That, in essence, is the theme underlying recent research on emotional intelligence.[94] The entire workplace can be affected by positive or negative workplace emotions, another issue we consider below. One recent study found that when leaders were in a positive mood, individual group members experienced better moods, and groups had a more positive tone. Groups whose leaders had a positive mood also found it easier to coordinate tasks and expended less effort when doing their work.[95]

Emotional Intelligence

Diane Marshall is an office manager. Her awareness of her own and others' emotions is almost zero. She is moody and unable to generate much enthusiasm or interest in her employees. She does not understand why employees get upset with her. She often overreacts to problems and chooses the most ineffectual responses to emotional situations.[96] Diane Marshall has low emotional intelligence. **Emotional intelligence (EI)** is a person's ability to (1) be self-aware (to recognize one's own emotions when one experiences them), (2) detect emotions in others, and (3) manage emotional cues and information. People who know their own emotions and are good at reading emotional cues—for instance, knowing why they are angry and how to express themselves without violating norms—are most likely to be effective.[97]

Several studies suggest that EI plays an important role in job performance. One study looked at the characteristics of engineers at Lucent Technologies (now Alcatel-Lucent) who were rated as stars by their peers. The researchers concluded that stars were better at relating to others. That is, it was EI, not IQ, that characterized high performers. Another illuminating study looked at the successes and failures of 11 American presidents—from Franklin Roosevelt to Bill Clinton. They were evaluated on six qualities—communication, organization, political skill, vision, cognitive style, and emotional intelligence. It was found that the key quality that differentiated the successful (such as Roosevelt, Kennedy, and Reagan) from the unsuccessful (such as Johnson, Carter, and Nixon) was emotional intelligence.[98] Some researchers argue that emotional intelligence is particularly important for leaders.[99]

A recent poll of human resource managers asked the question, How important is it for your workers to demonstrate EI to move up the corporate ladder?[100] Forty percent replied "Very Important." Another 16 percent said "Moderately Important." Irene Taylor, a consultant with Toronto-based Praxis Canada, says her company "has conducted EQ assessments on about 300 Canadian lawyers over the past five years." She also says that demand to get into the company's EI coaching program is high.

EI has been a controversial concept in OB; it has supporters and detractors. In the following sections, we review the arguments for and against the effectiveness of EI in OB. If you are interested in determining your EI, you might want to complete *Learning About Yourself Exercise #5* on pages 67–68. This chapter's *From Concepts to Skills* on pages 72–73 gives you some insight into reading the emotions of others.

The Case for EI

The arguments in favour of EI include its intuitive appeal, the fact that EI predicts criteria that matter, and the idea that EI is biologically based.

Intuitive Appeal There is a lot of intuitive appeal to the EI concept. Almost everyone would agree that it is good to possess street smarts and social intelligence. People who can detect emotions in others, control their own emotions, and handle social interactions well will have a powerful leg up in the business world, so the thinking goes.[101] As just one example, partners in a multinational consulting firm who scored above the median on an EI measure delivered $1.2 million more in business than did the other partners.[102]

EI Predicts Criteria That Matter More and more evidence is suggesting that a high level of EI means a person will perform well on the job. One study found that EI predicted the performance of employees in a cigarette factory in China.[103] Another study

emotional intelligence (EI) An assortment of noncognitive skills, capabilities, and competencies that influence a person's ability to succeed in coping with environmental demands and pressures.

found that being able to recognize emotions in others' facial expressions and to emotionally "eavesdrop" (that is, pick up subtle signals about peoples' emotions) predicted peer ratings of how valuable those people were to their organization.[104] Finally, a review of 59 studies indicated that, overall, EI correlated moderately with job performance.[105]

EI Is Biologically Based One study has shown that people with damage to the part of the brain that governs emotional processing (lesions in an area of the prefrontal cortex) score significantly lower than others on EI tests. Even though these brain-damaged people scored no lower on standard measures of intelligence than people without the same brain damage, they were still impaired in normal decision making. Specifically, when people were playing a card game in which there is a reward (money) for picking certain types of cards and a punishment (a loss of money) for picking other types of cards, the participants with no brain damage learned to succeed in the game, while the performance of the brain-damaged group worsened over time. This study suggests that EI is neurologically based in a way that is unrelated to standard measures of intelligence, and that people who suffer neurological damage score lower on EI and make poorer decisions than people who are healthier in this regard.[106]

The Case Against EI

For all its supporters, EI has just as many critics. Its critics say that EI is vague and impossible to measure, and they question its validity.

EI Is Too Vague a Concept To many researchers, it's not clear what EI is. Is it a form of intelligence? Most of us would not think that being self-aware or self-motivated or having empathy is a matter of intellect. Moreover, different researchers often focus on different skills, making it difficult to get a definition of EI. One researcher may study

Meg Whitman, former CEO and director of eBay, is a leader with high emotional intelligence. She is described as self-confident yet humble, trustworthy, culturally sensitive, and expert at building teams and leading change. Shown here, Whitman welcomes Gloria Arroyo, president of the Philippine Islands, to eBay headquarters.

self-discipline. Another may study empathy. Another may look at self-awareness. As one reviewer noted, "The concept of EI has now become so broad and the components so variegated that . . . it is no longer even an intelligible concept."[107]

EI Cannot Be Measured Many critics have raised questions about measuring EI. Because EI is a form of intelligence, for instance, there must be right and wrong answers about it on tests, they argue. Some tests do have right and wrong answers, although the validity of some of the questions on these measures is questionable. For example, one measure asks you to associate particular feelings with specific colours, as if purple always makes us feel cool and not warm. Other measures are self-reported, meaning that there is no right or wrong answer. For example, an EI test question might ask you to respond to the statement "I'm good at 'reading' other people." In general, the measures of EI are diverse, and researchers have not subjected them to as much rigorous study as they have measures of personality and general intelligence.[108]

The Validity of EI Is Suspect Some critics argue that because EI is so closely related to intelligence and personality, once you control for these factors, EI has nothing unique to offer. There is some foundation to this argument. EI appears to be highly correlated with measures of personality, especially emotional stability.[109] But there has not been enough research on whether EI adds insight beyond measures of personality and general intelligence in predicting job performance. Still, among consulting firms and in the popular press, EI is wildly popular. For example, one company's promotional materials for an EI measure claimed, "EI accounts for more than 85 percent of star performance in top leaders."[110] To say the least, it's difficult to validate this statement with the research literature.

Weighing the arguments for and against EI, it's still too early to tell whether the concept is useful. It *is* clear, though, that the concept is here to stay.

Negative Workplace Emotions

Negative emotions can lead to a number of deviant workplace behaviours. Anyone who has spent much time in an organization realizes that people often engage in voluntary actions that violate established norms and threaten the organization, its members, or both. These actions are called **employee deviance**.[111] They fall into categories such as production (leaving early, intentionally working slowly); property (stealing, sabotage); political (gossiping, blaming co-workers); and personal aggression (sexual harassment, verbal abuse).[112]

Many of these deviant behaviours can be traced to negative emotions. For instance, envy is an emotion that occurs when you resent someone for having something that you do not have but strongly desire—such as a better work assignment, larger office, or higher salary.[113] It can lead to malicious deviant behaviours. Envy, for example, has been found to be associated with hostility, "backstabbing," and other forms of political behaviour, as well as with negatively distorting others' successes and positively distorting one's own accomplishments.[114] Evidence suggests that people who feel negative emotions, particularly those who feel angry or hostile, are more likely than people who do not feel negative emotions to engage in deviant behaviour at work.[115]

employee deviance Voluntary actions that violate established norms and threaten the organization, its members, or both.

Summary and Implications

1 **What is perception?** *Perception* is the process by which individuals organize and interpret their impressions in order to give meaning to their environment. Individuals behave in a given manner based not on the way their environment actually is but, rather, on what they see or believe it to be. An organization may spend millions of dollars to create a pleasant work environment for its employees. However, despite these expenditures, an employee who believes that his or her job is lousy will behave accordingly.

2 **What causes people to have different perceptions of the same situation?** A number of factors operate to shape and sometimes distort perception. These factors can be present in the *perceiver,* in the object or *target* being perceived, or in the context of the *situation* in which the perception is made. The perceiver's attitudes, motives, interests, and past experiences all shape the way he or she sees an event. The target's characteristics also affect what is perceived. Novelty, motion, sounds, size, and other characteristics of a target shape the way it is seen. Objects or events that are unrelated are often perceived together because they are close physically or in timing. Persons, objects, or events that are similar to each other also tend to be viewed as a group. The setting in which we see objects or events also affects how they are perceived.

3 **Can people be mistaken in their perceptions?** Perceiving and interpreting what others do is difficult and takes time. As a result, we develop shortcuts to make this task more manageable. These shortcuts, described by attribution theory, selective perception, the halo effect, contrast effect, projection, and stereotyping, are often valuable—they can sometimes allow us to make accurate perceptions quickly and provide valid data for making predictions. However, they are not foolproof. They can and do get us into trouble.

4 **Does perception really affect outcomes?** The evidence suggests that what individuals perceive about their work situations influences their productivity more than the situations do. Whether a job is actually interesting or challenging is irrelevant. Whether a manager actually helps employees to structure their work more efficiently and effectively is far less important than how employees perceive the manager's efforts. Similarly, issues such as fair pay, the validity of performance appraisals, and the adequacy of working conditions are not judged "objectively." Rather, individuals interpret conditions surrounding their jobs based on how they *perceive* their jobs.

5 **What is personality and how does it affect behaviour?** *Personality* is the stable patterns of behaviour and consistent internal states that determine how an individual reacts to and interacts with others. A review of the personality literature offers general guidelines that can lead to effective job performance. As such, it can improve hiring, transfer, and promotion decisions. Personality attributes give us a framework for predicting behaviour. Personality affects how people react to others and the types of jobs that they may desire. For example, individuals who are shy, introverted, and uncomfortable in social situations would probably make poor salespeople. Individuals who are submissive and conforming might not be effective as advertising "idea" people. Be aware, though, that measuring personality is not an exact science, and as you no doubt learned from the discussion of attribution theory, it is easy to attribute personality characteristics in error.

SNAPSHOT SUMMARY

1 **Perception Defined**

2 **Factors Influencing Perception**
The Perceiver
The Target
The Situation

3 **Perceptual Errors**
Attribution Theory
Selective Perception
Halo Effect
Contrast Effects
Projection
Stereotyping

4 **Why Do Perception and Judgment Matter?**
Self-Fulfilling Prophecy

5 **Personality**
What Is Personality?
Measuring Personality
Personality Determinants
Personality Traits
Major Personality Attributes Influencing OB
Personality and National Culture

6 **Emotions**
What Are Emotions?
Choosing Emotions: Emotional Labour
Why Should We Care About Emotions in the Workplace?

6 **Can emotions help or get in the way when we are dealing with others?**
Emotions are intense feelings that are directed at someone or something. Positive emotions can be motivating for everyone in the workplace. Negative emotions may make it difficult to get along with others. Can managers control the emotions of their colleagues and employees? No. Emotions are a natural part of an individual's makeup. At the same time, managers err if they ignore the emotional elements in OB and assess individual behaviour as if it were completely rational. Managers who understand the role of emotions will significantly improve their ability to explain and predict individual behaviour.

Do emotions affect job performance? Yes. Emotions, especially negative ones, can hinder performance. That is probably why organizations, for the most part, try to remove emotions from the workplace. But emotions can also enhance performance. How? Two ways.[116] First, emotions can increase arousal levels, thus acting as motivators to higher performance. Second, emotional labour recognizes that feelings can be part of a job's required behaviour. So, for instance, the ability to effectively manage emotions in leadership and sales positions may be critical to success in those positions. Research also indicates the importance of emotional intelligence—the assortment of noncognitive skills, capabilities, and competencies that influence a person's ability to succeed in coping with environmental demands and pressures.

OB at Work

For Review

1. Define *perception*.

2. What is attribution theory? What are its implications for explaining behaviour in organizations?

3. What is stereotyping? Give an example of how stereotyping can create perceptual distortion.

4. Give some positive results of using shortcuts when judging others.

5. Describe the factors in the Big Five model. Evaluate which factor shows the greatest value in predicting behaviour.

6. What behavioural predictions might you make if you knew that an employee had (a) an external locus of control? (b) a low-Mach score? (c) low self-esteem? (d) a Type A personality?

7. To what extent do people's personalities affect how they are perceived?

8. What is emotional labour and why is it important to understanding OB?

9. What is emotional intelligence and why is it important?

For Critical Thinking

1. How might the differences in experience of students and instructors affect each of their perceptions of classroom behaviour (e.g., students' written work and class comments)?

2. An employee does an unsatisfactory job on an assigned project. Explain the attribution process that this person's manager will use to form judgments about this employee's job performance.

3. One day your boss comes in and he is nervous, edgy, and argumentative. The next day he is calm and relaxed. Does this behaviour suggest that personality traits are not consistent from day to day?

4. What, if anything, can managers do to manage emotions? Are there ethical implications in any of these actions? If so, what are they?

5. Give some examples of situations where expressing emotions openly might improve job performance.

OB for You

- The discussion of perception might get you thinking about how you view the world. When we perceive someone as a troublemaker, for instance, this may be only a perception and not a real characteristic of the other person. It is always good to question your perceptions, just to be sure that you are not reading something into a situation that is not there.

- One important thing to consider when looking for a job is whether your personality will fit the organization to which you are applying. For instance, it may be a highly structured organization. If you, by nature, are much less formal, this may not be a good fit for you.

- Sometimes personalities get in the way when working in groups. You may want to see if you can figure out ways to get personality differences working in favour of group goals.

- Emotions need not always be suppressed when working with others. While emotions can sometimes hinder performance, positive emotions can motivate you and those around you.

OB *At Work*

Point

Display Rules Make Good Business Sense

Organizations today realize that good customer service means good business. After all, who wants to end a shopping trip at the grocery store with a surly cashier? Research clearly shows that organizations that provide good customer service have higher profits than those with poor customer service.[117] An integral part of customer-service training is to set forth display rules to teach employees to interact with customers in a friendly, helpful, professional way—and evidence indicates that such rules work: Having display rules increases the odds that employees will display the emotions expected of them.[118]

As one Starbucks manager says, "What makes Starbucks different is our passion for what we do. We're trying to provide a great experience for people, with a great product. That's what we all care about."[119] Starbucks may have good coffee, but a big part of the company's growth has been the customer experience. For instance, the cashiers are friendly and will get to know you by name if you are a repeat customer.

Asking employees to act friendly is good for them, too. Research shows that employees of organizations that require them to display positive emotions actually feel better as a result.[120] And if someone feels that being asked to smile is bad for him, that person does not belong in the service industry in the first place.

Counterpoint

Display Rules Do Not Make Sense

Organizations have no business trying to regulate the emotions of their employees. Companies should not be "the thought police" and force employees to feel and act in ways that serve only organizational needs. Service employees should be professional and courteous, yes, but many companies expect them to take abuse and refrain from defending themselves. That's wrong. As philosopher Jean Paul Sartre wrote, we have a responsibility to be authentic—true to ourselves—and within reasonable limits, organizations have no right to ask us to be otherwise.

Service industries have no business teaching their employees to be smiling punching bags. Most customers might even prefer that employees be themselves. Employees should not be openly nasty or hostile, of course, but who appreciates a fake smile? Think about trying on an outfit in a store and the clerk automatically says it looks "absolutely wonderful" when you know it does not and you sense that the clerk is lying. Most customers would rather talk with a "real" person than someone enslaved to an organization's display rules. Furthermore, if an employee does not feel like slapping on an artificial smile, then it's only going to create friction between her and her employer.[121]

Finally, research shows that forcing display rules on employees takes a heavy emotional toll.[122] It's unnatural to expect someone to smile all the time or to passively take abuse from customers, clients, or fellow employees. Organizations can improve their employees' psychological health by encouraging them to be themselves, within reasonable limits.

How Machiavellian Are You?

For each statement, circle the number that most closely resembles your attitude.[123]

Statement	Disagree			Agree	
	A Lot	A Little	Neutral	A Little	A Lot
1. The best way to handle people is to tell them what they want to hear.	1	2	3	④	5
2. When you ask someone to do something for you, it is best to give the real reason for wanting it rather than giving reasons that might carry more weight.	1	2	3	4	⑤
3. Anyone who completely trusts anyone else is asking for trouble.	1	2	3	④	5
4. It is hard to get ahead without cutting corners here and there.	1	②	3	4	5
5. It is safest to assume that all people have a vicious streak, and it will come out when given a chance.	①	2	3	4	5
6. One should take action only when it is morally right.	①	2	3	4	5
7. Most people are basically good and kind.	1	2	3	④	5
8. There is no excuse for lying to someone else.	1	2	③	4	5
9. Most people more easily forget the death of their fathers than the loss of their property.	1	2	③	4	5
10. Generally speaking, people will not work hard unless they are forced to do so.	1	②	3	4	5

Scoring Key

To obtain your Mach score, add the number you have checked on questions 1, 3, 4, 5, 9, and 10. For the other 4 questions, reverse the numbers you have checked: 5 becomes 1, 4 is 2, 2 is 4, and 1 is 5. Total your 10 numbers to find your score. The higher your score, the more machiavellian you are. Among a random sample of American adults, the national average was 25.

27

OB *At Work*

Are You a High Self-Monitor?

Indicate the degree to which you think the following statements are true or false by circling the appropriate number. For example, if a statement is always true, circle the 5 next to that statement.[124]

0	**=**	**Certainly, always false**
1	**=**	**Generally false**
2	**=**	**Somewhat false, but with exceptions**
3	**=**	**Somewhat true, but with exceptions**
4	**=**	**Generally true**
5	**=**	**Certainly, always true**

1. In social situations, I have the ability to alter my behaviour if I feel that something else is called for.   0   1   2   ③   4   5

2. I am often able to read people's true emotions correctly through their eyes.   0   1   2   ③   4   5

3. I have the ability to control the way I come across to people, depending on the impression I wish to give them.   0   1   ②   3   4   5

4. In conversations, I am sensitive to even the slightest change in the facial expression of the person I'm conversing with.   0   1   2   3   ④   5

5. My powers of intuition are quite good when it comes to understanding others' emotions and motives.   0   1   2   3   ④   5

6. I can usually tell when others consider a joke in bad taste, even though they may laugh convincingly.   0   1   2   3   ④   5

7. When I feel that the image I am portraying isn't working, I can readily change it to something that does.   0   1   2   ③   4   5

8. I can usually tell when I've said something inappropriate by reading the listener's eyes.   0   1   2   3   4   ⑤

9. I have trouble changing my behaviour to suit different people and different situations.   0   ①   2   3   4   5

10. I have found that I can adjust my behaviour to meet the requirements of any situation I find myself in.   0   1   2   3   ④   5

11. If someone is lying to me, I usually know it at once from that person's manner of expression.   0   1   2   ③   4   5

12. Even when it might be to my advantage, I have difficulty putting up a good front.   0   1   2   ③   4   5

13. Once I know what the situation calls for, it's easy for me to regulate my actions accordingly.   0   1   2   3   ④   5

47

Scoring Key

To obtain your score, add up the numbers circled, except reverse scores for questions 9 and 12. On those, a circled 5 becomes a 0, 4 becomes 1, and so forth. High self-monitors are defined as those with scores of 53 or higher.

OB *At Work*

Are You a Risk-Taker?

For each of the following situations, indicate the minimum odds of success you would demand before recommending that one alternative be chosen over another.[125] Try to place yourself in the position of the adviser to the central person in each of the situations.

1. Mr. B, a 45-year-old accountant, has recently been informed by his physician that he has developed a severe heart ailment. The disease will be sufficiently serious to force Mr. B to change many of his strongest life habits—reducing his workload, drastically changing his diet, giving up favourite leisure-time pursuits. The physician suggests that a delicate medical operation could be attempted. If successful, the operation would completely relieve the heart condition. But its success cannot be assured, and in fact the operation might prove fatal.

   Imagine that you are advising Mr. B. Listed below are several probabilities or odds that the operation will prove successful. Check the *lowest probability* that you would consider acceptable for the operation to be performed.

   _____ Place a check mark here if you think that Mr. B should not have the operation, no matter what the probabilities.

   _____ The chances are 9 in 10 that the operation will be a success.

   _____ The chances are 7 in 10 that the operation will be a success.

   __✓___ The chances are 5 in 10 that the operation will be a success.

   _____ The chances are 3 in 10 that the operation will be a success.

   _____ The chances are 1 in 10 that the operation will be a success.

2. Mr. D is the captain of University X's varsity football team. University X is playing its traditional rival, University Y, in the final game of the season. The game is in its final seconds, and Mr. D's team, University X, is behind in the score. University X has time to make one more play. Mr. D, the captain, must decide on a strategy. Would it be best to try a play that would be almost certain to work and try to settle for a tie score? Or, on the other hand, should he try a more complicated and risky play that would bring victory if it succeeded or defeat if it failed?

   Imagine that you are advising Mr. D. Listed below are several probabilities or odds that the risky play will work. Check the *lowest probability* that you would consider acceptable for the risky play to be attempted.

   _____ Place a check mark here if you think that Mr. D should not attempt the risky play, no matter what the probabilities.

   _____ The chances are 9 in 10 that the risky play will work.

   __✓___ The chances are 7 in 10 that the risky play will work.

   _____ The chances are 5 in 10 that the risky play will work.

   _____ The chances are 3 in 10 that the risky play will work.

   _____ The chances are 1 in 10 that the risky play will work.

3. Ms. K is a successful businesswoman who has taken part in a number of civic activities of considerable value to the community. Ms. K has been approached by the leaders of her political party as a possible candidate in the next provincial election. Ms. K's party is a minority party in the constituency, though the party has won occasional elections in the past. Ms. K would like to hold political office, but to do so would involve a serious financial sacrifice, since the party does not have enough campaign funds. She would also have to endure the attacks of her political opponents in a heated campaign.

(Continued)

OB *At Work*

LEARNING ABOUT **YOURSELF** EXERCISE #3 (Continued)

Imagine that you are advising Ms. K. Listed below are several probabilities or odds of Ms. K's winning the election in her constituency. Check the *lowest probability* that you would consider acceptable to make it worthwhile for Ms. K to run for political office.

_____ Place a check mark here if you think that Ms. K should not run for political office, no matter what the probabilities.

✓ The chances are 9 in 10 that Ms. K will win the election.

_____ The chances are 7 in 10 that Ms. K will win the election.

_____ The chances are 5 in 10 that Ms. K will win the election.

_____ The chances are 3 in 10 that Ms. K will win the election.

_____ The chances are 1 in 10 that Ms. K will win the election.

4. Ms. L, a 30-year-old research physicist, has been given a 5-year appointment by a major university laboratory. As she considers the next 5 years, she realizes that she might work on a difficult long-term problem. If a solution to the problem could be found, it would resolve basic scientific issues in the field and bring high scientific honours. If no solution were found, however, Ms. L would have little to show for her 5 years in the laboratory, and it would be hard for her to get a good job afterward. On the other hand, she could, as most of her professional associates are doing, work on a series of short-term problems for which solutions would be easier to find. Those solutions would be of lesser scientific importance.

Imagine that you are advising Ms. L. Listed below are several probabilities or odds that a solution will be found to the difficult long-term problem that Ms. L has in mind. Check the *lowest probability* that you would consider acceptable to make it worthwhile for Ms. L to work on the more difficult long-term problem.

_____ Place a check mark here if you think Ms. L should not choose the long-term, difficult problem, no matter what the probabilities.

_____ The chances are 9 in 10 that Ms. L will solve the long-term problem.

✓ The chances are 7 in 10 that Ms. L will solve the long-term problem.

_____ The chances are 5 in 10 that Ms. L will solve the long-term problem.

_____ The chances are 3 in 10 that Ms. L will solve the long-term problem.

_____ The chances are 1 in 10 that Ms. L will solve the long-term problem.

Scoring Key

These situations were based on a longer questionnaire. Your results are an indication of your general orientation toward risk rather than a precise measure. To calculate your risk-taking score, add up the chances you were willing to take and divide by 4. (For any of the situations in which you would not take the risk, regardless of the probabilities, give yourself a 10.) The lower your number, the more risk-taking you are.

7

OB At Work

LEARNING ABOUT **YOURSELF** EXERCISE #4

Are You a Type A?

Circle the number on the scale below that best characterizes your behaviour for each trait.[126]

1. Casual about appointments	1	2	3	4	5	6	7	⑧	Never late
2. Not competitive	1	2	3	4	5	⑥	7	8	Very competitive
3. Never feel rushed	1	2	3	4	5	⑥	7	8	Always feel rushed
4. Take things one at a time	1	2	3	4	5	6	⑦	8	Try to do many things at once
5. Slow doing things	1	2	3	4	⑤	6	7	8	Fast (eating, walking, etc.)
6. Express feelings	①	2	3	4	5	6	7	8	"Sit on" feelings
7. Many interests	①	2	3	4	5	6	7	8	Few interests outside work

Scoring Key

Total your score on the 7 questions. Now multiply the total by 3. A total of 120 or more indicates that you are a hard-core Type A. Scores below 90 indicate that you are a hard-core Type B. The following gives you more specifics:

Points	Personality Type
120 or more	A1
106–119	A
100–105	A2
90–99	B1
Less than 90	B

102.

LEARNING ABOUT **YOURSELF** EXERCISE #5

What's Your EI at Work?

Evaluating the following 25 statements will allow you to rate your social skills and self-awareness, the components of emotional intelligence (EI).[127]

EI, the social equivalent of IQ, is complex, in no small part because it depends on some pretty slippery variables—including your innate compatibility, or lack thereof, with the people who happen to be your co-workers. But if you want to get a rough idea of how your EI stacks up, this quiz will help.

As honestly as you can, estimate how you rate in the eyes of peers, bosses, and subordinates on each of the following traits, on a scale of 1 to 4, with 4 representing strong agreement, and 1 representing strong disagreement.

___4___ I usually stay composed, positive, and unflappable even in trying moments.

___4___ I can think clearly and stay focused on the task at hand under pressure.

___3___ I am able to admit my own mistakes.

___4___ I usually or always meet commitments and keep promises.

___3___ I hold myself accountable for meeting my goals.

___4___ I'm organized and careful in my work.

(Continued)

LEARNING ABOUT **YOURSELF** EXERCISE #5 (Continued)

2	I regularly seek out fresh ideas from a wide variety of sources.
3	I'm good at generating new ideas.
4	I can smoothly handle multiple demands and changing priorities.
3	I'm result-oriented, with a strong drive to meet my objectives.
3	I like to set challenging goals and take calculated risks to reach them.
4	I'm always trying to learn how to improve my performance, including asking advice from people younger than I am.
4	I readily make sacrifices to meet an important organizational goal.
4	The company's mission is something I understand and can identify with.
4	The values of my team—or of our division or department, or the company—influence my decisions and clarify the choices I make.
4	I actively seek out opportunities to further the overall goals of the organization and enlist others to help me.
3	I pursue goals beyond what is required or expected of me in my current job.
4	Obstacles and setbacks may delay me a little, but they don't stop me.
4	Cutting through red tape and bending outdated rules are sometimes necessary.
4	I seek fresh perspectives, even if that means trying something totally new.
4	My impulses or distressing emotions don't often get the best of me at work.
3	I can change tactics quickly when circumstances change.
2	Pursuing new information is my best bet for cutting down on uncertainty and finding ways to do things better.
3	I usually don't attribute setbacks to a personal flaw (mine or someone else's).
4	I operate from an expectation of success rather than a fear of failure.

Scoring Key

Total your score. A score below 70 indicates very low EI. EI can be improved. Says Daniel Goleman, author of *Working with Emotional Intelligence,* "Emotional intelligence can be learned, and in fact we are each building it, in varying degrees, throughout life. It's sometimes called maturity. EQ is nothing more or less than a collection of tools that we can sharpen to help ensure our own survival." 88

More Learning About Yourself Exercises

Additional self-assessments relevant to this chapter appear on MyOBLab (**www.pearsoned.ca/myoblab**).

IV.C.2 What Are My Gender Role Perceptions?
IV.A.I Am I a Narcissist?
IV.D.1 How Are You Feeling Right Now?
I.E.1 What's My Emotional Intelligence Score?

When you complete the additional assessments, consider the following:

1. Am I surprised about my score?
2. Would my friends evaluate me similarly?

OB *At Work*

BREAKOUT **GROUP** EXERCISES

Form small groups to discuss the following topics, as assigned by your instructor:

1. Think back to your perception of this course and your instructor on the first day of class. What factors might have affected your perceptions of what the rest of the term would be like?

2. Describe a situation in which your perception turned out to be wrong. What perceptual errors did you make that might have caused this to happen?

3. Compare your scores on the *Learning About Yourself Exercises* at the end of the chapter. What conclusions could you draw about your group based on these scores?

WORKING WITH **OTHERS** EXERCISE

Evaluating Your Stereotypes

1. Your instructor will choose 4 volunteers willing to reveal an interesting true-life background fact about themselves. Examples of such background facts are as follows:

   • I can perform various dances, such as polka, rumba, bossa nova, and salsa.

   • I am the youngest of four children, and I attended a Catholic high school.

   • Neither of my parents attended school beyond grade 8.

   • My mother is a homemaker and my father is an author.

2. The instructor will put the 4 facts on the board without revealing to which person each belongs, and the 4 students will remain in the front of the room for the first part of the group discussion below.

3. Students in the class should silently decide which fact belongs to which person.

4. Students should break into groups of about 5 or 6 and try to reach consensus about which fact belongs to which person. Meanwhile, the 4 students can serve as observers to group discussions, listening in on rationales for how students decide to link the facts with the individuals.

5. After 15 minutes of group discussion, several groups will be asked to present their consensus to the class, with justifications.

6. The classroom discussion will focus on perceptions, assumptions, and stereotyping that led to the decisions made.

7. At the end of the discussion, the instructor will reveal which fact belongs to each student.

ETHICAL **DILEMMA** EXERCISE

Hiring Based on Body Art

When Christine Giacomoni applied for a job at the Sherwood Park (Alberta) location of the Real Canadian Superstore, she was wearing a nose stud.[128] She got the job. Six months later, however, she was told that she could no longer wear her small nose stud at work. The company had just recently decided to apply their policy for front-line workers about no nose studs to employees like Giacomoni, who worked in the deli.

The United Food and Commercial Workers (UFCW), Giacomoni's union, grieved this action for her. The complaint ended up in front of a labour arbitrator. The union argued that this company was out of touch with reality. The company argued that nose studs offended customers. They hired Ipsos Reid to survey shoppers, and the results of the poll indicated that "a significant portion" of shoppers would stop shopping at a store that allowed employee facial piercings.

(Continued)

OB *At Work*

Ultimately, a judge ruled against Real Canadian Superstore's policy. Meanwhile, Giacomoni left to take a job at TELUS, in part because of the store's policy against her piercing. TELUS does not mind that she has a nose stud.

Many employees are aware that tattoos and body piercings can hurt one's chances of being hired. Consider Russell Parrish, 29, who lives near Orlando, Florida, and has dozens of tattoos on his arms, hands, torso, and neck. In searching for a job, Parrish walked into 100 businesses, and in 60 cases, he was refused an application. "I want a career," Parrish says, "I want the same shot as everybody else."

Employers are mixed in their reactions to employees with tattoos or piercings. At Vancouver-based Whitespot, employees cannot have visible tattoos (or pink or blue hair). They are allowed a small, simple nose stud. BC's Starbucks shops don't allow any pierced tongues or visible tattoos. Staff may not wear more than two reasonably sized earrings per ear. At Victoria-based Arq Salon, nearly everyone has a tattoo, "We work in an artistic field," manager Yasmin Morris explains, then adds that staff cannot wear jeans. "We don't want people to look too casual."

A survey of employers revealed that 58 percent indicated that they would be less likely to hire someone with visible tattoos or body piercings. The career centre at the University of Calgary's Haskayne School of Business advises students to "start out understated" when it comes to piercing. "We coach our students to be conservative, and if they do have any facial piercings, we suggest they remove them for the first interview until they find out what the culture's like in the organization," centre director Voula Cocolakis said. "We don't want them to be taken out of the 'yes' pile because of a facial piercing. We want them to interview and compete in the job market based on their qualifications."

In-house policies toward tattoos vary because, legally, employers can do as they wish. As long as the rule is applied equally to everyone (it would not be permissible to allow tattoos on men but not on women, for example), policies against tattoos are perfectly legal. Though not hiring people with tattoos is discrimination, it is not a form of discrimination that is covered by the Canadian Human Rights Act.

Thirty-six percent of those aged 18 to 25 and 40 percent of those aged 26 to 40 have at least one tattoo, whereas only 15 percent of those over 40 do, according to a fall 2006 survey by the Pew Research Center. One study in *American Demographics* suggested that 57 percent of senior citizens viewed visible tattoos as "freakish."

How does the matter of perception explain why some employers ban tattoos while others don't mind them? Is it fair for employers to reject applicants who have tattoos? Is it fair to require employees, if hired, to conceal their tattoos? Should it be illegal to allow tattoos to be a factor at all in the hiring process?

CASE INCIDENT

A Diamond Personality

Oscar Rodriguez, a 38-year-old entrepreneur, owns an Internet business that sells loose diamonds to various buyers.[129] Business is booming. In 2004, Rodriguez had sales of $2.06 million—a 140 percent increase from 2003. Rodriguez's database of almost 60 000 available diamonds is one of the largest in the industry and is valued, according to him, at over $350 million. Needless to say, he is optimistic about his business venture.

The future was not always so bright. In 1985, Rodriguez moved from his native Puerto Rico to Gainesville, Florida, with little ability to speak English. There, he attended community college and worked at a local mall to support himself. After graduation, his roommate's girlfriend suggested that he work at a local jeweller. "I thought she was crazy. I didn't know anything about jewellery," says Rodriguez, but he took her advice. Though he worked hard and received his Diamonds and Diamonds Grading certification from the Gemological Institute of America, he was not satisfied with his progress. "I quickly realized that working there, I was just going to get a salary with a raise here and there. I would never become anything. That drove me to explore other business ventures. I also came to really know diamonds—their pricing and their quality."

In 1997, tired of working for someone else, Rodriguez decided to open his own jewellery store. However, business did not boom. "Some of my customers were telling me they could find diamonds for less on the Internet. It blew my mind." Rodriguez recognized an opportunity and began contacting well-known diamond dealers to see whether they would be interested in selling their gems online. Rodriguez recalls one conversation with a prominent dealer who told him, "You cannot sell diamonds on the Internet. You will not survive." Discouraged, Rodriguez says he then made a mistake. "I stopped working on it. If you have a dream, you have to keep working harder at it."

A year later, Rodriguez did work harder at his dream and found a dealer who agreed to provide him with some diamonds. Says Rodriguez, "Once I had one, I could approach others. Business started to build. The first three months I sold $200 000 worth of diamonds right off the bat. And that was just me. I started to add employees and eventually closed the jewellery store and got out of retail." Although Rodriquez does have some diamonds in inventory, he primarily acts as a connection point between buyers and suppliers, giving his customers an extraordinary selection from which to choose.

Rodriguez is now a savvy entrepreneur, and his company, Abazias.com, went public in October 2003.

Why is Rodriguez successful? Just ask two people who have known him over the years. Gary Schneider, a realtor who helped build Rodriguez's building, says, "Oscar is a very ambitious young man. I am not surprised at all how successful he is. He is an entrepreneur in the truest sense of the word." One of Rodriguez's former real estate instructors, Howard Freeman, concurs. "I am not surprised at all at his success," says Freeman. "Oscar has

always been an extremely motivated individual with a lot of resources. He has a wonderful personality and pays close attention to detail. He also has an ability to stick to things. You could tell from the beginning that he was going to persevere, and I am proud of him."

Rodriguez is keeping his success in perspective, but he also realizes his business's potential: "I take a very small salary, and our overhead is $250 000 a year. I am not in debt, and the business is breaking even. I care about the company. I want to keep everything even until we take off, and then it may be another ball game."

Questions

1. What factors do you think have contributed to Rodriguez's success? Was he merely "in the right place at the right time," or are there characteristics about him that contribute to his success?

2. How do you believe Rodriguez would score on the Big Five dimensions of personality (extraversion, agreeableness, conscientiousness, emotional stability, openness to experience)? Which ones would he score high on? Which ones might he score low on?

3. Do you believe that Rodriguez is high or low on core self-evaluation? On what information did you base your decision?

4. What information about Rodriguez suggests that he has a proactive personality?

VIDEO CASE INCIDENT

| CASE 2 | How Bad Is Your Boss? | CBC |

Everybody has a boss, and it seems that everybody has a "bad boss" story.[130] Here are seven questions that will help you determine if your boss is one of the bad ones. Answer each question with a "yes" or "no."

1. Has your boss ever embarrassed you in front of co-workers?

2. Does your boss have a tough time making decisions or sticking to them once they are made?

3. Does your boss take you for granted?

4. Does your boss hog the limelight when things go well and blame others when things go wrong?

5. Does your boss argue about everything?

6. Is your boss clear about what he or she expects of you?

7. Does your boss pile on the work without any thought as to what you are already doing?

If you answered "yes" to just one or two questions, your boss is probably fine (let's face it, a boss can occasionally slip up). If you answered "yes" to 3–6 questions, you have a boss that is likely to make you feel pretty bad on various occasions. But be careful when confronting your boss. If you are going to complain, you should cite

(Continued)

very specific instances of your boss's bad behaviour. You must also realize that if you are not happy with your boss, chances are that your boss is also unhappy with you. If you answered "yes" to all 7 questions, you have a big problem. You probably cannot run fast enough to keep up.

What should you do if you have a bad boss? If you want to better the situation, you might try discussing your concerns with your boss. Be sure to document your experiences and be very specific about the kinds of things that concern you. Jack Welch, the legendary former CEO of General Electric, says that bosses must realize that they are only as good as the people who work for them. If a boss does not develop good people, the boss's unit will underperform and the boss's own career plans will be affected. If the boss behaves badly, Welch thinks employees should not whine and be a victim. Instead, they should just quit.

The practical implications of the seven questions listed above can be profound for employees. For example, for question #3, Shaun Belding, a management consultant, says that the most common complaint from employees is that they are not given any recognition for the work they do. For question #4, this type of boss behaviour sucks the creativity out of an organization because people have no incentive to come up with new ideas if they are not going to get credit for those ideas. For question #7, the fact is that bad bosses are simply not aware of the workloads of their employees. They just expect that all their requests will be met.

Some bosses are taking action to improve their performance. Robert Lemieux, the director of sales at the Delta Chelsea Hotel, is a young executive moving up the corporate ladder. He would like to be a top manager some day. He currently supervises a staff of 50, and he knows he has to be a great boss if he wants to get to the top. So, he goes to a "boss boot camp" run by Lindsay Sukornyk, a consultant who whips bosses into shape. She first interviews Lemieux's employees to find out what they really think of him. She discovers that his employees think he is professional and intuitive, and that he cares about them. So far so good. But she also hears that he is standoffish, and that he over-promises and under-delivers. He is also seen by employees as too hands-on. Lemieux has to learn to let go and to let employees take ownership of ideas.

At boot camp, Lemieux is owning up to his weaknesses in front of his employees and learning to trust them to do their jobs on their own. From now on, he will be doing less talking and more listening. The employees seem to like the idea, because they want him to coach them, not get involved in all the details and always be the "fixer." As they review his performance, they point out a few areas where he still needs to improve, but Lemieux is on the road to being a better boss.

Questions

1. Think of a boss you have had and answer the seven questions listed above. Was your boss good or bad? Give brief examples of incidents that led you to answer "yes" to any question.

2. Think of a boss you have had and evaluate your boss on the Big Five personality factors. What impact did the Big Five have on your boss being a good or bad manager? Give examples to illustrate your reasoning.

3. Think of a boss you have had and give several examples of how the various factors in Exhibit 2-1 influenced your perception of your boss.

4. Think of a specific "bad" behaviour your boss exhibited. Use the model in Exhibit 2-2 to analyze the behaviour and determine whether it had an internal or external cause. Does your conclusion match the attribution you made at the time of the behaviour?

From Concepts to Skills

Reading Emotions

Understanding another person's felt emotions is very difficult. But we can learn to read others' displayed emotions.[131] We do this by focusing on verbal, nonverbal, and paralanguage cues.

The easiest way to find out what someone is feeling is to ask. Saying something as simple as "Are you OK? What's the problem?" can often provide you with the information to assess an individual's emotional state. But relying on a verbal response has two drawbacks. First, almost all of us conceal our emotions to some extent for privacy and to reflect social expectations. So we might be unwilling to share our true feelings. Second, even if we want to verbally convey our feelings, we may be unable to do so. As we noted earlier, some people have difficulty understanding their own emotions and, hence, are unable to express them verbally. So, at best, verbal responses provide only partial information.

You are talking with a co-worker. Does the fact that his back is rigid, his teeth are clenched, and his facial muscles tight tell you something about his emotional state? It probably should. Facial expressions, gestures, body movements, and physical distance are nonverbal cues that can provide additional insights into what a person is feeling. The facial expressions shown in Exhibit 2-6, for instance, are a window into a person's feelings. Notice the difference in facial features: the height of the cheeks, the raising or lowering of the brow, the turn of the mouth, the positioning of the lips, and the configuration of muscles around the eyes. Even something as subtle as the distance someone chooses to put between him- or herself and you can convey how much intimacy, aggressiveness, repugnance, or withdrawal that person feels.

When you speak with someone, you may notice a sharp change in the tone of her voice and the speed at which she speaks. You are tapping into the third source of information on a person's emotions—paralanguage. This is communication that goes beyond the specific spoken words. It includes pitch, amplitude, rate, and voice quality of speech. Paralanguage reminds us that people convey their feelings not only in what they say, but also in how they say it.

Practising Skills

Part A. Form groups of two. Each person is to spend a couple of minutes thinking of a time in the past when she or he was emotional about something. Examples might include being upset with a parent, sibling, or friend; being excited or disappointed about an academic or athletic achievement; being angry with someone over an insult or slight; being disgusted by something someone has said or done; or being happy because of something good that happened. Do not share this event with the other person in your group.

Part B. Now you will conduct two role plays. Each will be an interview. In the first, one person will play the interviewer and the other will play the job applicant. The job is for a summer management internship with a large retail chain. Each role play will last no longer than 10 minutes. The interviewer is to conduct a normal job interview, except you are to continually rethink the emotional episode you envisioned in Part A. Try hard to convey this emotion while, at the same time, being professional in interviewing the job applicant.

Part C. Now reverse positions for the second role play. The interviewer becomes the job applicant and vice versa. The new interviewer will conduct a normal job interview, except that he or she will continually rethink the emotional episode chosen in Part A.

Part D. Spend 10 minutes analyzing the interview, with specific attention focused on these questions: What emotion(s) do you think the other person was conveying? What cues did you pick up? How accurate were you in reading those cues?

EXHIBIT 2-6 Facial Expressions and Emotions

Each picture portrays a different emotion. Try to identify them before looking at the answers.

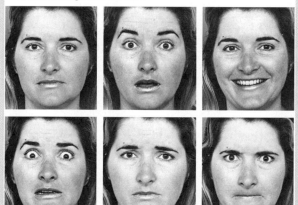

Top, left to right: neutral, surprise, happiness. Bottom: fear, sadness, anger.

Source: S. E. Taylor, L. A. Peplan, and D. O. Sears, *Social Psychology*, 9th ed. (Upper Saddle River, NJ: Prentice Hall, 1997), p. 98; photographs by Paul Ekman, Ph.D. Used with permission.

Reinforcing Skills

1. Rent a DVD of an emotionally laden film such as *Death of a Salesman* or *12 Angry Men.* Carefully watch the actors for clues to the emotions they are exhibiting. Try to determine the various emotions projected and explain how you arrived at your conclusion.

2. Spend a day specifically looking for emotional cues in the people with whom you interact. Did this improve communication?

Chapter 3

Values, Attitudes, and Their Effects in the Workplace

At KPMG Canada, diversity is valued and respected. How does this affect the company's workplace?

1 What are values?

2 How can we understand values across cultures?

3 Are there unique Canadian values?

4 What are attitudes and why are they important?

ichael Bach is the first director of diversity for Toronto-based KPMG Canada, a position he was promoted to in 2006.[1] Bach is a signal that KPMG is committed to an inclusive workplace.

"I'm here to remove barriers. At the core, we want everyone to be able to bring their whole self to work and we want everyone to feel they have the ability to succeed regardless of anything other than their ability to do their job," says Bach.

Generally, we expect that an organization's values, like those of an individual, will be reflected in corresponding behaviour and attitudes. If a company stated that it valued workforce diversity, and yet no behaviour followed from that statement, we would question whether that value was really so important to the company. However, in KPMG's case, the company backs up its value statements with concrete policies and actions to show support for its values. Does having strong values make for a better workplace?

In this chapter, we look more carefully at how values influence behaviour and consider the relationship between values and attitudes. We then consider two specific issues that arise from our discussion of values and attitudes: job satisfaction and organizational commitment.

OB *Is for Everyone*

- How do countries differ in their values?
- What can you learn about OB from Aboriginal culture?
- What would you need to know to set up a business in Asia?
- Are Gen-Xers really different from their elders?

Values

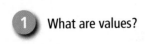

What are values?

Is capital punishment right or wrong? How about employment equity guidelines in hiring? If a person likes power, is that good or bad? The answers to these questions are value-laden. Some might argue, for example, that capital punishment is right because it is a suitable punishment for crimes such as murder. However, others might argue just as strongly that no government has the right to take anyone's life.

values Basic convictions that a specific mode of conduct or end-state of existence is personally or socially preferable to an opposite or converse mode of conduct or end-state of existence.

Values represent basic convictions that "a specific mode of conduct or end-state of existence is personally or socially preferable to an opposite or converse mode of conduct or end-state of existence."[2] They contain a judgmental element in that they carry an individual's ideas as to what is right, good, or desirable. Values generally influence attitudes and behaviour.[3]

Values tend to be relatively stable and enduring.[4] Most of our values are formed in our early years—with input from parents, teachers, friends, and others. As children, we are told that certain behaviours or outcomes are always desirable or always undesirable. There are few grey areas. It is this absolute or "black-or-white" learning of values that more or less ensures their stability and endurance.

We examine two frameworks for understanding values: Milton Rokeach's terminal and instrumental values and Kent Hodgson's general moral principles.

Rokeach Value Survey

terminal values Goals that individuals would like to achieve during their lifetimes.

instrumental values Preferable ways of behaving.

Milton Rokeach classified the values that people hold into two sets, with each set containing 18 individual value items.[5] One set, called **terminal values**, refers to desirable end-states of existence. These are the goals that individuals would like to achieve during their lifetimes, such as a comfortable life or happiness. The other set, called **instrumental values**, refers to preferable ways of behaving, such as being courageous or helpful. Exhibit 3-1 gives common examples for each of these sets.

EXHIBIT 3-1 Terminal and Instrumental Values in Rokeach's Value Survey	
Terminal Values	**Instrumental Values**
A comfortable life (a prosperous life)	Ambitious (hard-working, aspiring)
An exciting life (a stimulating, active life)	Broad-minded (open-minded)
A sense of accomplishment (lasting contribution)	Capable (competent, effective)
A world at peace (free of war and conflict)	Cheerful (lighthearted, joyful)
A world of beauty (beauty of nature and the arts)	Clean (neat, tidy)
Equality (brotherhood, equal opportunity for all)	Courageous (standing up for your beliefs)
Family security (taking care of loved ones)	Forgiving (willing to pardon others)
Freedom (independence, free choice)	Helpful (working for the welfare of others)
Happiness (contentedness)	Honest (sincere, truthful)
Inner harmony (freedom from inner conflict)	Imaginative (daring, creative)
Mature love (sexual and spiritual intimacy)	Independent (self-reliant, self-sufficient)
National security (protection from attack)	Intellectual (intelligent, reflective)
Pleasure (an enjoyable, leisurely life)	Logical (consistent, rational)
Salvation (saved, eternal life)	Loving (affectionate, tender)
Self-respect (self-esteem)	Obedient (dutiful, respectful)
Social recognition (respect, admiration)	Polite (courteous, well-mannered)
True friendship (close companionship)	Responsible (dependable, reliable)
Wisdom (a mature understanding of life)	Self-controlled (restrained, self-disciplined)

Source: M. Rokeach, *The Nature of Human Values* (New York: Free Press, 1973), p. 56.

| EXHIBIT 3-2 | Value Ranking of Executives, Union Members, and Activists (Top Five Only) | | | | | |

EXECUTIVES		UNION MEMBERS		ACTIVISTS	
Terminal	Instrumental	Terminal	Instrumental	Terminal	Instrumental
1. Self-respect	1. Honest	1. Family security	1. Responsible	1. Equality	1. Honest
2. Family security	2. Responsible	2. Freedom	2. Honest	2. A world of peace	2. Helpful
3. Freedom	3. Capable	3. Happiness	3. Courageous	3. Family security	3. Courageous
4. A sense of accomplishment	4. Ambitious	4. Self-respect	4. Independent	4. Self-respect	4. Responsible
5. Happiness	5. Independent	5. Mature love	5. Capable	5. Freedom	5. Capable

Source: Based on W. C. Frederick and J. Weber, "The Values of Corporate Managers and Their Critics: An Empirical Description and Normative Implications," in *Business Ethics: Research Issues and Empirical Studies,* ed. W. C. Frederick and L. E. Preston (Greenwich, CT: JAI Press, 1990), pp. 123–144.

Several studies confirm that these sets of values vary among groups.[6] People in the same occupations or categories (e.g., corporate managers, union members, parents, students) tend to hold similar values. For instance, one study compared corporate executives, members of the steelworkers' union, and members of a community activist group. Although a good deal of overlap was found among the three groups,[7] there were also some very significant differences (see Exhibit 3-2). The activists had value preferences that were quite different from those of the other two groups. They ranked "equality" as their most important terminal value; executives and union members ranked this value 12 and 13, respectively. Activists ranked "helpful" as their second-highest instrumental value. The other two groups both ranked it 14. These differences are important, because executives, union members, and activists all have a vested interest in what corporations do. These differences make it difficult when these groups have to negotiate with each other and can create serious conflicts when they contend with each other over the organization's economic and social policies.[8]

ethics The study of moral values or principles that guide our behaviour and inform us whether actions are right or wrong.

Hodgson's General Moral Principles

Ethics is the study of moral values or principles that guide our behaviour and inform us whether actions are right or wrong. Thus, ethical values are related to moral judgments about right and wrong.

In recent years, there has been concern that individuals are not grounded in moral values. It is believed that this lack of moral roots has resulted in a number of business scandals, such as those at WorldCom, Enron, Hollinger International, and in the sponsorship scandal of the Canadian government.

Management consultant Kent Hodgson has identified seven general moral principles that individuals should follow when making decisions about behaviour. He calls these "the Magnificent Seven" and suggests that they are universal values that managers should use to make *principled, appropriate,* and *defensible* decisions.[9] They are presented in *OB in Action—The Magnificent Seven Principles.* We discuss the issue of ethics further in Chapter 9.

OB in ACTION

The Magnificent Seven Principles

→ *Dignity of human life.* The lives of **people are to be respected.**

→ *Autonomy.* All **persons are intrinsically valuable** and **have the right to self-determination.**

→ *Honesty.* **The truth should be told** to those who have a right to know it.

→ *Loyalty.* **Promises, contracts,** and **commitments** should be **honoured.**

→ *Fairness.* **People should be treated justly.**

→ *Humaneness.* Our **actions ought to accomplish good,** and we should **avoid doing evil.**

→ *The common good.* Actions should accomplish **the greatest good for the greatest number** of people.[10]

Assessing Cultural Values

> KPMG Canada's decision to value diversity in its workplace reflects a dominant value of Canada as a multicultural country.[11] The approach to diversity is very different in the United States, which considers itself a melting pot with respect to different cultures. KPMG Canada has other values that guide employees. These include integrity, respect, open and honest communication, and commitment to community. What do we know about the values of other countries? What values make Canada unique?

2 How can we understand values across cultures?

In Chapter 1, we noted that managers have to become capable of working with people from different cultures. Thus it is important to understand how values differ across cultures.

Hofstede's Framework for Assessing Cultures

How do countries differ in their values?

One of the most widely referenced approaches for analyzing variations among cultures was done in the late 1970s by Geert Hofstede.[12] He surveyed more than 116 000 IBM employees in 40 countries about their work-related values and found that managers and employees vary on five value dimensions of national culture:

power distance A national culture attribute that describes the extent to which a society accepts that power in institutions and organizations is distributed unequally.

- *Power distance.* **Power distance** describes the degree to which people in a country accept that power in institutions and organizations is distributed unequally. A high rating on power distance means that large inequalities of power and wealth exist and are tolerated in the culture, as in a class or caste system that discourages upward mobility of its citizens. A low power distance rating characterizes societies that stress equality and opportunity.

individualism A national culture attribute that describes the degree to which people prefer to act as individuals rather than as members of groups.

- *Individualism vs. collectivism.* **Individualism** is the degree to which people prefer to act as individuals rather than as members of groups and believe in individual rights above all else. Collectivism emphasizes a tight social framework in which people expect others in groups of which they are a part to look after them and protect them.

masculinity A national culture attribute that describes the extent to which the culture favours traditional masculine work roles of achievement, power, and control.

femininity A national culture attribute that sees little differentiation between male and female roles; women are treated as the equals of men in all respects.

- *Masculinity vs. femininity.* Hofstede's construct of **masculinity** is the degree to which the culture favours traditional masculine roles, such as achievement, power, and control, as opposed to viewing men and women as equals. A high masculinity rating indicates the culture has separate roles for men and women, with men dominating the society. A high **femininity** rating means the culture sees little differentiation between male and female roles and treats women as the equals of men in all respects.

uncertainty avoidance A national culture attribute that describes the extent to which a society feels threatened by uncertain and ambiguous situations and tries to avoid them.

- *Uncertainty avoidance.* The degree to which people in a country prefer structured over unstructured situations defines their **uncertainty avoidance**. In cultures that score high on uncertainty avoidance, people have an increased level of anxiety about uncertainty and ambiguity, and use laws and controls to reduce uncertainty. Cultures low on uncertainty avoidance are more accepting of ambiguity and are less rule-oriented, take more risks, and more readily accept change.

long-term orientation A national culture attribute that emphasizes the future, thrift, and persistence.

short-term orientation A national culture attribute that emphasizes the past and present, respect for tradition, and fulfillment of social obligations.

- *Long-term vs. short-term orientation.* This is the newest addition to Hofstede's typology. It focuses on the degree of a society's long-term devotion to traditional values. People in a culture with **long-term orientation** value virtues such as thrift and persistence that are oriented to future rewards. In a culture with **short-term orientation**, people value virtues related to the past and present, such as saving "face" and honouring social obligations.

How do different countries score on Hofstede's dimensions? Exhibit 3-3 shows the ratings for the countries for which data are available. For example, power distance is

EXHIBIT 3-3 Hofstede's Cultural Values by Nation

Country	Power Distance		Individualism vs. Collectivism		Masculinity vs. Femininity		Uncertainty Avoidance		Long- vs. Short-Term Orientation	
	Index	Rank	Index	Rank	Index	Rank	Index	Rank	Index	Rank
Argentina	49	35–36	46	22–23	56	20–21	86	10–15		
Australia	36	41	90	2	61	16	51	37	31	22–24
Austria	11	53	55	18	79	2	70	24–25	31	22–24
Belgium	65	20	75	8	54	22	94	5–6	38	18
Brazil	69	14	38	26–27	49	27	76	21–22	65	6
Canada	39	39	80	4–5	52	24	48	41–42	23	30
Chile	63	24–25	23	38	28	46	86	10–15		
Colombia	67	17	13	49	64	11–12	80	20		
Costa Rica	35	42–44	15	46	21	48–49	86	10–15		
Denmark	18	51	74	9	16	50	23	51	46	10
Ecuador	78	8–9	8	52	63	13–14	67	28		
El Salvador	66	18–19	19	42	40	40	94	5–6		
Finland	33	46	63	17	26	47	59	31–32	41	14
France	68	15–16	71	10–11	43	35–36	86	10–15	39	17
Germany	35	42–44	67	15	66	9–10	65	29	31	22–24
Great Britain	35	42–44	89	3	66	9–10	35	47–48	25	28–29
Greece	60	27–28	35	30	57	18–19	112	1		
Guatemala	95	2–3	6	53	37	43	101	3		
Hong Kong	68	15–16	25	37	57	18–19	29	49–50	96	2
India	77	10–11	48	21	56	20–21	40	45	61	7
Indonesia	78	8–9	14	47–48	46	30–31	48	41–42		
Iran	58	29–30	41	24	43	35–36	59	31–32		
Ireland	28	49	70	12	68	7–8	35	47–48	43	13
Israel	13	52	54	19	47	29	81	19		
Italy	50	34	76	7	70	4–5	75	23	34	19
Jamaica	45	37	39	25	68	7–8	13	52		
Japan	54	33	46	22–23	95	1	92	7	80	4
Korea (South)	60	27–28	18	43	39	41	85	16–17	75	5
Malaysia	104	1	26	36	50	25–26	36	46		
Mexico	81	5–6	30	32	69	6	82	18		
The Netherlands	38	40	80	4–5	14	51	53	35	44	11–12
New Zealand	22	50	79	6	58	17	49	39–40	30	25–26
Norway	31	47–48	69	13	8	52	50	38	44	11–12
Pakistan	55	32	14	47–48	50	25–26	70	24–25	0	34
Panama	95	2–3	11	51	44	34	86	10–15		
Peru	64	21–23	16	45	42	37–38	87	9		
Philippines	94	4	32	31	64	11–12	44	44	19	31–32
Portugal	63	24–25	27	33–35	31	45	104	2	30	25–26
Singapore	74	13	20	39–41	48	28	8	53	48	9
South Africa	49	35–36	65	16	63	13–14	49	39–40		
Spain	57	31	51	20	42	37–38	86	10–15	19	31–32
Sweden	31	47–48	71	10–11	5	53	29	49–50	33	20
Switzerland	34	45	68	14	70	4–5	58	33	40	15–16
Taiwan	58	29–30	17	44	45	32–33	69	26	87	3
Thailand	64	21–23	20	39–41	34	44	64	30	56	8
Turkey	66	18–19	37	28	45	32–33	85	16–17		
United States	40	38	91	1	62	15	46	43	29	27
Uruguay	61	26	36	29	38	42	100	4		
Venezuela	81	5–6	12	50	73	3	76	21–22		
Yugoslavia	76	12	27	33–35	21	48–49	88	8		
Regions:										
Arab countries	80	7	38	26–27	53	23	68	27		
East Africa	64	21–23	27	33–35	41	39	52	36	25	28–29
West Africa	77	10–11	20	39–41	46	30–31	54	34	16	33

Scores range from 0 = extremely low on dimension to 100 = extremely high.

Note: 1 = highest rank. LTO ranks: 1 = China; 15-16 = Bangladesh; 21 = Poland; 34 = lowest.

Source: Copyright Geert Hofstede BV, hofstede@bovt.nl. Reprinted with permission.

higher in Malaysia than in any other country. Canada is tied with the Netherlands as one of the top five individualistic countries in the world, falling just behind the United States, Australia, and Great Britain. Canada also tends to be short-term in orientation and is low in power distance (people in Canada tend not to accept built-in class differences between people). Canada is also relatively low on uncertainty avoidance, meaning that most adults are relatively tolerant of uncertainty and ambiguity. Canada scores relatively high on masculinity, meaning that most people emphasize traditional gender roles (at least relative to countries such as Denmark, Finland, Norway, and Sweden).

You will also notice regional differences. Western and Northern nations such as Canada and the Netherlands tend to be more individualistic. Compared with other countries, poorer countries such as Mexico and the Philippines tend to be higher on power distance. South American nations tend to be higher than other countries on uncertainty avoidance, and Asian countries tend to have a long-term orientation.

Hofstede's cultural dimensions have been enormously influential on OB researchers and managers. Nevertheless, his research has been criticized. First, although Hofstede's work was updated and reaffirmed by a Canadian researcher at the Chinese University of Hong Kong (Michael Bond), who conducted research on values in 22 countries on 5 continents,[13] the original work is more than 30 years old and was based on a single company (IBM). A lot has happened on the world scene since then. Some of the most obvious changes include the fall of the Soviet Union, the transformation of Central and Eastern Europe, the end of apartheid in South Africa, the spread of Islam throughout the world today, and the rise of China as a global power. Second, few researchers have read the details of Hofstede's methodology closely and are therefore unaware of the many decisions and judgment calls he had to make (for example, reducing the number of cultural values to just five). Some results are unexpected. For example, Japan, which is often considered a highly collectivist nation, is considered only average on collectivism under Hofstede's dimensions.[14] Despite these concerns, many of which Hofstede refutes,[15] he has been one of the most widely cited social scientists ever, and his framework has left a lasting mark on OB.

The GLOBE Framework for Assessing Cultures

Begun in 1993, the Global Leadership and Organizational Behavior Effectiveness (GLOBE) research program is an ongoing cross-cultural investigation of leadership and national culture. Using data from 825 organizations in 62 countries, the GLOBE team identified nine dimensions on which national cultures differ.[16]

The GLOBE dimensions are defined as follows:

- *Assertiveness.* The extent to which a society encourages people to be tough, confrontational, assertive, and competitive vs. modest and tender. This is essentially equivalent to Hofstede's quantity-of-life dimension.

- *Future orientation.* The extent to which a society encourages and rewards future-oriented behaviours such as planning, investing in the future, and delaying gratification. This is essentially equivalent to Hofstede's long-term/short-term orientation.

- *Gender differentiation.* The extent to which a society maximizes gender role differences.

- *Uncertainty avoidance.* As did Hofstede, the GLOBE team defined this term as a society's reliance on social norms and procedures to alleviate the unpredictability of future events.

- *Power distance.* Like Hofstede, the GLOBE team defined this as the extent to which members of a society expect power to be unequally shared.

- *Individualism/collectivism.* Again, this term was defined, as was Hofstede's, as the extent to which individuals are encouraged by societal institutions to be integrated into groups within organizations and society.

- *In-group collectivism.* In contrast to focusing on societal institutions, this dimension encompasses the extent to which members of a society take pride in membership in small groups, such as their family and circle of close friends, and the organizations in which they are employed.

- *Performance orientation.* The extent to which a society encourages and rewards group members for performance improvement and excellence.

- *Humane orientation.* The extent to which a society encourages and rewards individuals for being fair, altruistic, generous, caring, and kind to others. This closely approximates Hofstede's quality-of-life dimension.

The GLOBE study confirms that Hofstede's dimensions are still valid. The main difference between Hofstede's dimensions and the GLOBE framework is that the latter added dimensions, such as humane orientation and performance orientation.

Which framework is better? That is hard to say, and each has its adherents. We give more emphasis to Hofstede's dimensions here because they have stood the test of time and the GLOBE study confirmed them. However, researchers continue to debate the differences between these frameworks, and future studies may, in time, favour the more nuanced perspective of the GLOBE study.[17]

In this chapter's *Working With Others Exercise* on page 100, you have the opportunity to compare the cultural values of two countries and determine how differences might affect group behaviour. The *Ethical Dilemma Exercise* on page 101 asks you to consider when something is a gift and when it is a bribe. Different cultures take different approaches to this question.

Values in the Canadian Workplace

Studies have shown that when individual values align with organizational values, the results are positive. Individuals who have an accurate understanding of the job requirements and the organization's values adjust better to their jobs and have greater levels of satisfaction and organizational commitment.[18] In addition, shared values between the employee and the organization lead to more positive work attitudes,[19] lower turnover,[20] and greater productivity.[21]

 Are there unique Canadian values?

Individual and organizational values do not always align. Moreover, within organizations, individuals can have very different values. Two major factors lead to a potential clash of values in the workplace: cultural differences and generational differences. Let's look at the implications of both factors in the Canadian workplace.

Cultural Differences

Canada is a multicultural country. One in five Canadians is an immigrant, according to the 2006 Census.[22] In 2006, 46 percent of Metropolitan Toronto's population, 40 percent of Vancouver's population, and 21 percent of Montreal's population were made up of immigrants.[23] The 2006 Census found that 20.1 percent of Canada's population spoke neither of the country's two official languages as their first language. In Vancouver and Toronto, this rate was 41 percent and 44 percent, respectively, so considerably more than one-third of the population of those two cities does not speak either English or French as a first language.[24] Of those who speak other languages, 16 percent speak Chinese (mainly Mandarin or Cantonese). The other dominant languages in Canada are Italian (in fourth place), followed by German, Punjabi, and Spanish.[25] These figures indicate the very different cultures that are part of the Canadian fabric of life.

Though we live in a multicultural society, there are some tensions among people from different races and ethnic groups. For instance, a Statistics Canada survey on ethnic diversity found that while most Canadians (93 percent) say they have never or rarely experienced unfair treatment because of their ethnicity or culture, 20 percent of visible minorities reported having been unfairly treated sometimes or often.[26]

Canadians often define themselves as "not Americans" and point out differences in the values of the two countries. The Pew Global Attitudes Project identified a number of differences between Canadian and American values.[27] Exhibit 3-4 shows some of the highlights of that study.

In his book *Fire and Ice*, pollster Michael Adams finds that there is a growing dissimilarity between Canadian and American values. The two groups differ in 41 of the 56 values that Adams examined. For 24 values the gap has actually widened between 1992 and 2000, indicating that Canadians' social values are growing more distinct from those of Americans.[28] Adams suggests that the September 11, 2001, attacks have affected the personality of Americans. He finds Americans are more accepting of patriarchy and hierarchy these days, and he concludes that it is "the supposedly bold, individualistic Americans who are the nodding conformists, and the supposedly shy, deferential and law-abiding Canadians who are most likely to assert their personal autonomy and political agency."[29]

In what follows, we identify a number of cultural values that influence workplace behaviour in Canada. Be aware that these are generalizations, and it would be a mistake

EXHIBIT 3-4 Canadian and American Value Differences		
	Percentage Who Completely Agree with Statement	
Statement	**Canadians**	**Americans**
The impact of globalization on their country can be described as very good.	36	21
People are better off in a free market, despite inequality.	19	28
It is more important that government ensure that nobody is in need than that government stay out of the way.	52	34
It is the responsibility of government to tend to the very poor who cannot take care of themselves.	43	29
Immigrants have a very good influence on how well things are going.	19	8
Religion should be a matter of private faith, kept separate from government policy.	71	55
Homosexuality is a way of life that should be accepted by society.	69	51

Source: The Pew Research Center for the People and the Press, *Views of a Changing World 2003* (Washington, DC: The Pew Research Center for the People and the Press, June 2003).

to assume that everyone coming from the same cultural background acts similarly. Rather, these overviews are meant to encourage you to think about cultural differences and similarities so that you can better understand people's behaviour.

Francophone and Anglophone Values

One of the larger cultural issues that confronts Canada is the question of Quebec separatism and anglophone-francophone differences. Thus, it may be of interest to managers and employees in Canadian firms to be aware of some of the potential cultural differences when managing in francophone environments compared with anglophone environments. A number of studies have shown that English-speaking Canadians and French-speaking Canadians have distinctive values. Francophones have been found to be more collectivist, or group-oriented, with a greater need for achievement, while anglophones have been found to be more individualist, or I-centred.[30] Francophones have also been shown to be more concerned about the interpersonal aspects of the workplace than task competence.[31] They have also been found to be more committed to their work organizations.[32] Anglophones have been shown to take more risks.[33] By contrast, a recent study examining work values in French- and English-speaking Canada found that French-speaking Canadians were not risk-takers and had the highest values for "reducing or avoiding ambiguity and uncertainty at work."[34]

The many faces that represent Canada's multiculturalism are illustrated by this crowd of commuters making their way to Union Station in downtown Toronto.

Some studies have looked at the difference between francophone and anglophone personality characteristics. One study found that on the Meyers-Briggs personality test, francophones were more likely to be introverted, sensing, thinking, and judging. Anglophones were more likely to be intuitive, feeling, and perceiving.[35] A 2008 study, however, suggests that anglophones and francophones are not very different personality-wise.[36]

Other studies have found that anglophone managers tended to value autonomy and intrinsic job values, such as achievement, and thus were more achievement-oriented, while francophone managers tended to value affiliation and extrinsic job values, such as technical supervision.[37] A study conducted at the University of Ottawa and Laval University suggests that some of the differences reported in previous research may be decreasing.[38] Another study indicates that French Canadians have become more like English Canadians in valuing autonomy and self-fulfillment.[39] These studies are consistent with the recent study that suggests there are few differences between francophones and anglophones.[40]

However, there is evidence of some continuing differences in lifestyle values. A recent Canadian Institute for Health Information report noted that Quebecers experience more stress than other Canadians.[41] The study also found that Quebecers smoke more, have the highest workplace absenteeism rate, and are less physically active than the rest of the country. Another study found that French-speaking Canadians and English-speaking Canadians have different values regarding cultural activities. For example, francophones are more likely to attend symphonic, classical, or choral music performances than anglophones. Anglophones are more likely to read newspapers, magazines, and books than francophones.[42]

Even though they have some cultural and lifestyle value differences, francophone and anglophone managers today have been exposed to similar types of organizational theories during their post-secondary school training, which might also influence their outlooks as managers. Thus we would not expect to find large differences in the way that firms in francophone Canada are managed compared with those in the rest of Canada. Throughout the textbook, you will see a number of examples of Quebec-based businesses that support this conclusion.

Aboriginal Values

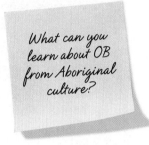

What can you learn about OB from Aboriginal culture?

Entrepreneurial activity among Canada's Aboriginal peoples has been growing, as has the number of partnerships and alliances between Aboriginal and non-Aboriginal businesses. There are now more than 27 000 Aboriginal-owned businesses in Canada. Fourteen percent of Aboriginal business owners live on reserves, while 86 percent live off reserves. Between 1996 and 2001, the growth rate of Aboriginal businesses was huge: They increased by nearly 31 percent, a rate nine times higher than Canadian businesses overall.[43]

With this strong increase in both the number of Aboriginal businesses and the number of partnerships and alliances between Aboriginal and non-Aboriginal businesses, it is important to examine whether and how each culture manages differently.[44] "Aboriginal values are usually perceived (by non-Aboriginals) as an impediment to economic development and organizational effectiveness."[45] Such values include reluctance to compete, a time orientation different from the Western one, and an emphasis on consensus decision making.[46] Aboriginal peoples do not necessarily agree that these values are business impediments, however. Saskatoon-based First Nations Bank of Canada, for example, posted its fifth straight year of profitability in 2005.

Although Canadian businesses and government have historically assumed that "non-Native people must teach Native people how to run their own organizations," the First Nations of Canada are not convinced.[47] They believe that traditional culture, values, and languages can help build a self-sustaining economy. Moreover, they believe that their cultural values may actually be a positive force in conducting business.[48]

In recent years, Canadian businesses facing Native land claims have met some difficulties in trying to accommodate demands for appropriate land use. In some cases, *accommodation* can mean less logging or mining by businesses until land claims are worked out. In order to achieve better communication between businesses and Native leaders, Cliff Hickey and David Natcher, two anthropologists from the University of Alberta, collaborated with the Little Red River Cree Nation in northern Alberta to develop a new model for forestry operations on First Nations land.[49] The anthropologists sought to balance the Native community's traditional lifestyle with the economic concerns of forestry operations. *OB in Action—Ground Rules for Developing Business Partnerships with Aboriginal Peoples* outlines several of Hickey and

OB in ACTION

Ground Rules for Developing Business Partnerships with Aboriginal Peoples

→ Modify management operations to **reduce negative impact on wildlife species**.

→ Modify operations to **ensure community access** to lands and resources.

→ **Protect** all those **areas identified by community members** as having biological, cultural, and historical significance.

→ **Recognize and protect Aboriginal and treaty rights** to hunting, fishing, trapping, and gathering activities.

→ **Increase** forest-based **economic opportunities** for community members.

→ **Increase** the **involvement of community members** in decision making.[50]

Natcher's recommended ground rules, which they say could be used in oil and gas developments as well. Johnson Sewepagaham, chief of the Little Red River Cree, said his community will use these recommendations to resolve difficulties on treaty lands for which Vernon, BC-based Tolko Industries and High Level, Alberta-based Footner Forest Products jointly hold forest tenure. The two companies presented their General Development Plan to the Cree in fall 2008.[51]

Lindsay Redpath of Athabasca University has noted that Aboriginal cultures are more collectivist in orientation than are non-Aboriginal cultures in Canada and the United States.[52] Aboriginal organizations are much more likely to reflect and advance the goals of the community. There is also a greater sense of family within the workplace, with greater affiliation and loyalty. Power distance in Aboriginal cultures is smaller than in non-Aboriginal cultures of Canada and the United States, and there is an emphasis on consensual decision making. Aboriginal cultures are lower on uncertainty avoidance than non-Aboriginal cultures in Canada and the United States. Aboriginal organizations and cultures tend to have fewer rules and regulations. Each of these differences suggests that businesses created by Aboriginal peoples will differ from non-Aboriginal businesses, and both research and anecdotal evidence support this view.[53] For instance, Richard Prokopanko, director of corporate affairs for Montreal-based Alcan, says that a move from handling issues in a generally legalistic, contract-oriented manner to valuing more dialogue and collaboration has helped ease some of the tension that had built up over 48 years between Alcan and First Nations people.[54]

Asian Values

What would you need to know to set up a business in Asia?

The largest visible minority group in Canada are the Chinese. Over 1 million people of this group live in Canada and represent 26 percent of the country's visible minority population.[55] The Chinese in this country are a diverse group; they come from different countries (e.g., China, Hong Kong, Malaysia), speak different languages, and practise different religions. The Chinese are only one part of the entire influence of East and Southeast Asian values that affect Canadian society. It is predicted that by 2017, almost one-half of all visible minorities in Canada will come from two groups, South Asian and Chinese, and that these groups will be represented in almost equal numbers.[56] As well, many Canadian organizations, particularly those in British Columbia, conduct significant business with Asian firms. Asian cultures differ from Canadian culture on many of the GLOBE dimensions discussed earlier. For instance, Asian cultures tend to exhibit greater power distance and greater collectivism. These differences in values can affect individual interactions.

Professor Rosalie Tung of Simon Fraser University and her student Irene Yeung examined the importance of *guanxi* (personal connections with the appropriate authorities or individuals) for a sample of North American, European, and Hong Kong firms doing business with companies in mainland China.[57] They suggest that their findings will also be relevant in understanding how to develop relationships with firms from Japan, South Korea, and Hong Kong.

"*Guanxi* refers to the establishment of a connection between two independent individuals to enable a bilateral flow of personal or social transactions. Both parties must derive benefits from the transaction to ensure the continuation of such a relationship."[58] *Guanxi* relations are based on reciprocation, unlike Western networked relationships, which may be characterized more by self-interest. *Guanxi* relationships are meant to be long-term and enduring, in contrast with the immediate gains sometimes expected in Western relationships. *Guanxi* also relies less on institutional law, and more on personal power and authority, than do Western relationships. Finally, *guanxi* relations are governed more by the notion of shame (i.e., external pressures on performance), while Western relations often rely on guilt (i.e., internal pressures on performance) to maintain agreements. *Guanxi* is seen as extremely important for business success in China—more than such factors as right location, price, or strategy, or product differentiation and quality. For Western firms wanting to do business with Asian firms, an understanding of *guanxi* and an effort to build relationships are important strategic advantages.

Our discussion about differences in cross-cultural values should suggest to you that understanding other cultures matters. When Canadian firms develop operations across Canada, south of the border, or overseas, employees need to understand other cultures in order to work more effectively and get along with others.

Generational Differences

In his book *Sex in the Snow,* pollster Michael Adams attempted to identify the social values of today's Canadians.[59] He found that within three broad age groups of adult Canadians—the Elders (those over 60), Baby Boomers (born between the mid-1940s and the mid-1960s), and Generation Xers (born between the mid-1960s and the early 1980s)—there are at least 12 quite distinct "value tribes." We present the age groups and discuss some of their values in what follows. For further information on these different value tribes and an opportunity to see where you might be classified in terms of your social values, visit the Environics Research Group website.

In the discussion of values that follows, bear in mind that we present broad generalizations, and you should certainly avoid stereotyping individuals on the basis of these generalizations. There are individual differences in values. For instance, not every Baby Boomer thinks alike, and neither does every member of Generation X. Thus, the important point about the values discussion is that you should try to understand how others might view things differently from you, even when they are exposed to the same situation.

The Elders

These individuals are characterized as "playing by the rules," and their core values are belief in order, authority, discipline, the Judeo-Christian moral code, and the Golden Rule (do unto others as you would have others do unto you). About 80 percent of the Elders resemble this description of traditional values, although there are variations within that 80 percent in the strength of fit.

Baby Boomers

This cohort was influenced heavily by the civil rights movement, the women's movement, the Beatles, the Vietnam War, and baby-boom competition. The view of Baby Boomers as a somewhat spoiled, hedonistic, rebellious group belies the four categories of Boomers: autonomous rebels (25 percent), anxious communitarians (20 percent), connected enthusiasts (14 percent), and disengaged Darwinists (41 percent). So, unlike the Elders, the Boomers are a bit more fragmented in their views. Yet all but the disengaged Darwinists reflect, to some extent, the stereotypes of this generation: rejection of authority, skepticism regarding the motives of big business and government, a strong concern for the environment, and a strong desire for equality in the workplace and society. Of course, the disengaged Darwinists, the largest single group, do not fit this description well. The Darwinists are characterized as angry, intimidated by change, and anxious about their professional and financial futures.

Generation X

Are Gen-Xers really different from their elders?

The lives of *Xers* (*Generation Xers*) have been shaped by global- ization, two-career parents, MTV, AIDS, and computers. They value flexibility, life options, and the achievement of job satisfaction. Xers are skeptical, particularly of authority. They also enjoy team-oriented work. In search of balance in their lives, Xers are less willing to make personal sacrifices for the sake of their employer than previous generations were. On the Rokeach value survey, they rate high on true friendship, happiness, and pleasure.

Despite these common values, Generation Xers can be divided into five tribes. Thrill-seeking materialists (25 percent) desire money and material possessions, as well as recognition, respect, and admiration. Aimless dependants (27 percent) seek financial independence, security, and stability. Social hedonists (15 percent) are experience-seeking, committed to their own pleasure, and seek immediate gratification. New Aquarians (13 percent) are experience-seeking, and also egalitarian and ecologically minded. Finally, autonomous post-materialists (20 percent) seek personal autonomy and self-fulfillment, and are concerned about human rights.

The Ne(x)t Generation

Since Adams' book appeared, another generation has been identified. The most recent entrants to the workforce were born between 1977 and 1997. The Nexters (also called Netters, Millennials, Generation Yers, and Generation Nexters) grew up during prosperous times. They have high expectations and seek meaning in their work. Nexters have life goals more oriented toward becoming rich (81 percent) and famous (51 percent) than do Generation Xers (62 percent and 29 percent, respectively). Nexters are at ease with diversity and are the first generation to take technology for granted. They have lived much of their lives with ATMs, DVDs, cellphones, laptops, and the Internet. More than other generations, they tend to be questioning, socially conscious, and entrepreneurial. At the same time, some have described Nexters as needy. One employer said, "This is the most high-maintenance workforce in the history of the world. The good news is they're also going to be the most high-performing."[60]

In this chapter's *Learning About Yourself Exercise* on page 99, you have the opportunity to examine some of the things that you value.

The Generations Meet in the Workplace

An understanding that individuals' values differ but tend to reflect the societal values of the period in which they grew up can be a valuable aid in explaining and predicting behaviour. Baby Boomers currently dominate the workplace, but their years of being in charge are limited. In 2013, half of them will be at least 55 and 18 percent will be over 60.[61] As Boomers move into head offices, the "play-by-the-rules," "boss-knows-best" Elders are being replaced by somewhat more egalitarian Boomers. They dislike the command-and-control rules that were part of their parents' lives, although the Boomers have also been described as workaholics. Meanwhile, the Generation Xers in the workplace are comfortable in adapting, but also want more experiences. They are not in awe of authority. Most important, they are not interested in copying the workaholic behaviour of their parents. Managing the expectations of each of these very different groups is not an easy task. It requires managers to be flexible, observant, and willing to adjust more to the individual needs of these different employees. Members of the Net Generation will certainly change the face of the workplace in significant ways. They have mastered a communication and information system that many of their parents have yet to understand.

Attitudes

Managers at KPMG Canada consider diversity a competitive advantage.[62] Mario Paron, chief officer of human resources, explains the company's views: "KPMG believes all our initiatives are fundamental business goals about attracting the brightest and best people. This is a real business strategy for us."

To create an attitude of inclusivity among employees, KPMG conducts diversity training for all employees, including a mandatory web-based program that encourages "dialogue about diversity, ethnic and cultural issues." Michael Bach also makes sure that potential hires are representative of the community. "It's about getting everyone to think about diversity in everyday life in everything they do," he says. Thus, KPMG Canada understands the link between organizational values and employee attitudes. The training is meant to help employees have greater awareness of cultural and style differences. So how do attitudes get formed, and can they really be changed?

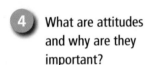

4 What are attitudes and why are they important?

attitudes Positive or negative feelings about objects, people, or events.

Attitudes are evaluative statements—either positive or negative—about objects, people, or events. When I say "I like my job," I am expressing my attitude to work. Attitudes are thus judgment responses to situations.

Attitudes are not the same as values because values are convictions about what is important, but the two are interrelated. In organizations, attitudes are important because they affect job behaviour. Employees may believe, for example, that supervisors, auditors, managers, and time-and-motion engineers are all conspiring to make employees work harder for the same or less money. This may then lead to a negative attitude toward management when an employee is asked to stay late and help on a special project. *Case Incident—Gourmet Foods Works on Employee Attitudes* on pages 101–102 highlights how changes in attitudes can help a company's bottom line.

Employees may be negatively affected by the attitudes of their co-workers or clients. In *From Concepts to Skills* on page 103, we discuss whether it is possible to change someone's attitude, and how that might happen in the workplace.

Ben Barry (left), president of Ben Barry Agency, is trying to change the attitudes toward waif-like models through his modelling agency. Sixty percent of his models are atypical: bigger, shorter, older, or different from what the public usually expects. He has received a number of awards, including "One of the 25 Leaders of Tomorrow" from *Maclean's* magazine.

OB Around the Globe looks at how attitudes about appropriate behaviour in the workplace differ for Londoners and Americans.

OB AROUND THE GLOBE

California Moves to London

Can California "comfortable" take over London "fashion"? Silicon Valley, California, has established an outpost in London.[63] You do not need to know much about Silicon Valley or London to see a culture clash in the making here. London is famous (or notorious, depending on your point of view) for its formality—business suits, formal lunches, conservative offices, and polite, proper communication. California is renowned for just the opposite culture. So which culture wins?

So far, it seems, California. At Google's London offices, the California touches include foosball tables, bean bag chairs, giant games, and catered sandwiches (rather than a three-course meal). The dress code is business casual, even though most of the employees at Google's London headquarters are British. "You can be serious without a suit," says one Google Londoner who has grown accustomed to the California style.

When another Londoner, Nigel Thornton, was hired by Amgen, he was surprised by the number of emails soliciting his opinion and by the different customs. "The funny thing about Americans in our office is that they are always eating or drinking something," said Thornton. "Brits are still used to just breakfast, lunch, and dinner."

When British visit the offices of DVS Shoe Company (based in Torrance, California), they are often surprised by the informal dress and low-key atmosphere. "They'll see us dressed casual," says Erik Ecklund, a DVS manager, "and say, 'Man, you guys should have told us.'"

A person can have thousands of attitudes, but organizational behaviour focuses our attention on a limited number of job-related attitudes. These job-related attitudes tap positive or negative evaluations that employees hold about aspects of their work environment. In the following, we consider three important attitudes that affect organizational performance: job satisfaction, organizational commitment, and employee engagement.

Job Satisfaction

The term **job satisfaction** refers to an individual's general attitude toward his or her job. A person with a high level of job satisfaction holds positive attitudes toward the job, while a person who is dissatisfied with his or her job holds negative attitudes toward the job. When people speak of employee attitudes, more often than not they mean job satisfaction. In fact, the terms are frequently used interchangeably.

A recent Canadian Policy Research Networks survey on job satisfaction found that only 40 percent of Canadian employees are very satisfied with their jobs. By comparison, 47 percent of American employees are happy with their work and 54 percent of Danish employees are highly satisfied.[64] On the other hand, almost 40 percent of

job satisfaction An individual's general attitude toward his or her job.

Canadian employees would not recommend their companies as good places to work. Forty percent also believe that they never see any of the benefits from their companies' making money. Almost 40 percent report that red tape and bureaucracy are among the biggest barriers to job satisfaction. A majority of the workforce (55 percent) says that they feel the "pressure of having too much to do."

What Causes Job Satisfaction?

Think about the best job you have ever had. What made it so? Chances are you probably liked the work you did. In fact, of the major job-satisfaction factors (work itself, pay, advancement opportunities, supervision, co-workers), enjoying the work is almost always the one most strongly linked to high levels of overall job satisfaction. Interesting jobs that provide training, variety, independence, and control satisfy most employees.[65] In other words, most people prefer work that is challenging and stimulating over work that is predictable and routine.

There is an interesting relationship between salary and job satisfaction. For people who are poor (for example, living below the poverty line) or who live in poor countries, pay does correlate with job satisfaction. But once an individual reaches a level of comfortable living (in Canada, that occurs at about $40 000 a year, depending on the region and family size), the relationship virtually disappears. In other words, people who earn $80 000 are, on average, no happier with their jobs than those who earn close to $40 000.[66] When we discuss motivation in Chapter 4, this might suggest that money may be less likely to motivate, once people reach a comfortable level of living. This idea would also be consistent with Maslow's hierarchy of needs, also discussed in Chapter 4.

Job satisfaction is not just about job conditions. Personality also plays a role. People who are less positive about themselves are less likely to like their jobs. Research has shown that people who have positive **core self-evaluations**—who believe in their inner worth and basic competence—are more satisfied with their jobs than those with negative core self-evaluations. Not only do they see their work as more fulfilling and challenging, but they are more likely to gravitate toward challenging jobs in the first place. Those with negative core self-evaluations set less ambitious goals and are more likely to give up when confronting difficulties. Thus, they are more likely to be stuck in boring, repetitive jobs than those with positive core self-evaluations.[67]

So what are the consequences of job satisfaction? We examine this question below.

core self-evaluation The degree to which an individual likes or dislikes himself or herself, whether the person sees himself or herself as capable and effective, and whether the person feels in control of his or her environment or powerless over the environment.

Job Satisfaction and Productivity

The idea that "happy workers are productive workers" developed in the 1930s and 1940s, largely as a result of findings by researchers conducting the Hawthorne studies at Western Electric. Based on those conclusions, managers worked to make their employees happier by focusing on working conditions and the work environment. Then, in the 1980s, an influential review of the research suggested that the relationship between job satisfaction and job performance was not particularly high. The authors of that review even went so far as to label the relationship as "illusory."[68]

More recently, a review of more than 300 studies corrected some errors in that earlier review. It estimated that the correlation between job satisfaction and job performance is moderately strong. This conclusion also appears to be generalizable across international contexts. The correlation is higher for complex jobs that provide employees with more discretion to act on their attitudes.[69]

We cannot be entirely sure, however, whether satisfaction causes productivity or productivity causes satisfaction.[70] In other words, if you do a good job, you intrinsically feel good about it. In addition, your higher productivity should increase your recognition, your pay level, and your likelihood of promotion. Cumulatively, these rewards, in turn, increase your level of satisfaction with the job. Most likely, satisfaction can lead to high levels of performance for some people, while for others, high performance is satisfying. *Point/Counterpoint* on page 98 further explores the debate on whether job satisfaction is created by the situation or by an individual's characteristics.

As we move from the individual level to that of the organization, we also find support for the satisfaction-performance relationship.[71] When satisfaction and productivity data are gathered for the organization as a whole, we find that organizations with more satisfied employees tend to be more effective than organizations with less satisfied employees.

Job Satisfaction and Organizational Citizenship Behaviour

In Chapter 1, we defined **organizational citizenship behaviour (OCB)** as discretionary behaviour that is not part of an employee's formal job requirements and is not usually rewarded, but that nevertheless promotes the effective functioning of the organization.[72] Individuals who are high in OCB will go beyond their usual job duties, providing performance

When it comes to keeping its employees happy, Google seems to spare no expense. The company provides its workers with a multitude of benefits, including chef-prepared food, a gym with state-of-the-art equipment, a masseuse, on-site car washes, oil changes, haircuts, dry cleaning, free on-site doctor and dentist, child care next door, and free high-tech shuttle buses. According to a recent survey, employees believe that benefits are the most important factor that might increase job satisfaction.

that is beyond expectations. Examples of such behaviour include helping colleagues with their workloads, taking only limited breaks, and alerting others to work-related problems.[73] More recently OCB has been associated with the following workplace behaviours: "altruism, conscientiousness, loyalty, civic virtue, voice, functional participation, sportsmanship, courtesy, and advocacy participation."[74] Organizational citizenship is important, as it can help the organization function more efficiently and more effectively.[75] Recent work by York University professors Sabrina Salamon and Yuval Deutsch suggest that OCB may be a way for individuals to signal to managers and co-workers abilities that might not be immediately observable.[76]

It seems logical to assume that job satisfaction should be a major determinant of an employee's OCB.[77] Satisfied employees would seem more likely to talk positively about an organization, help others, and go beyond the normal expectations in their jobs.[78] Moreover, satisfied employees might be more prone to go beyond the call of duty because they want to reciprocate their positive experiences. Consistent with this thinking, early discussions of OCB assumed that it was closely linked with satisfaction.[79] Some evidence, however, suggests that satisfaction does influence OCB, but through perceptions of fairness.[80]

There is, then, a modest overall relationship between job satisfaction and OCB.[81] But job satisfaction is unrelated to OCB when fairness is considered.[82] What does this mean? Basically, job satisfaction comes down to a belief that there are fair outcomes, treatment, and procedures in the workplace.[83] If you do not feel that your manager, the organization's procedures, or its pay policies are fair, your job satisfaction is likely to suffer significantly. However, when you perceive organizational processes and outcomes to be fair, trust is developed. When you trust your employer, your job

organizational citizenship behaviour (OCB) Discretionary behaviour that is not part of an employee's formal job requirements, but that nevertheless promotes the effective functioning of the organization.

satisfaction increases, and you are more willing to voluntarily go beyond your formal job requirements. Recent research suggests that OCB can be applied cross-culturally, although the exact form of OCB might be different in non–North American countries.[84]

Job Satisfaction and Customer Satisfaction

Employees in service jobs often interact with customers. Since the management of service organizations should be concerned with pleasing those customers, it is reasonable to ask: Is employee satisfaction related to positive customer outcomes? For front-line employees who have regular contact with customers, the answer is yes.

The evidence indicates that satisfied employees increase customer satisfaction and loyalty.[85] Why? In service organizations, customer retention and defection are highly dependent on how front-line employees deal with customers. Satisfied employees are more likely to be friendly, upbeat, and responsive—which customers appreciate. Because satisfied employees are less prone to turnover, customers are more likely to encounter familiar faces and receive experienced service. These qualities build customer satisfaction and loyalty. In addition, the relationship seems to apply in reverse: Dissatisfied customers can increase an employee's job dissatisfaction. Employees who have regular contact with customers report that rude, thoughtless, or unreasonably demanding customers adversely affect the employees' job satisfaction.[86]

How Employees Can Express Dissatisfaction

Dissatisfied employees are more likely to miss work, but the correlation is moderate—usually less than –0.40.[87] Dissatisfied employees are also more likely to quit their

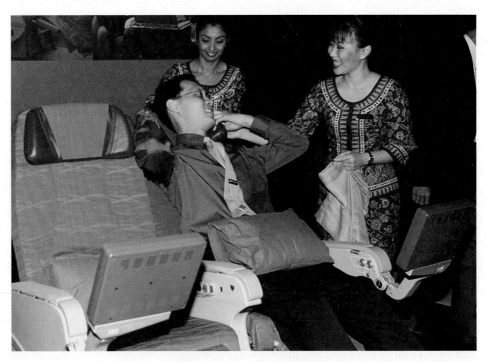

Service organizations know that whether customers are satisfied and loyal depends on how front-line employees deal with customers. Singapore Airlines has earned a reputation among world travellers for outstanding customer service. The airline's "putting people first" philosophy applies to both its employees and customers. In recruiting flight attendants, the airline selects people who are warm, hospitable, and happy to serve others. Through extensive training, Singapore Airlines moulds recruits into attendants focused on complete customer satisfaction.

jobs, and the correlation is stronger than what we found for absenteeism.[88] However, a person's general disposition toward life moderates the job satisfaction-turnover relationship.[89] Some individuals gripe more than others and such individuals, when dissatisfied with their jobs, are less likely to quit than those who are more positively disposed toward life. So if two employees are equally dissatisfied, the one most likely to quit is the one with the highest predisposition to be happy or satisfied with life in general. Likely these individuals do not feel trapped and are willing to exert more control over the situation and look for another job.

The evidence suggests that employees express dissatisfaction in a number of ways.[90] For example, rather than quit, employees can complain, be insubordinate, steal organizational property, or avoid some of their work responsibilities. Researchers argue that these behaviours are indicators of a broader syndrome that we would term *deviant behaviour in the workplace* (or *employee withdrawal*).[91] The key is that if employees do not like their work environment, they will respond somehow. Exhibit 3-5 illustrates a model that can be used to examine individual responses to dissatisfaction along two dimensions: whether they are constructive or destructive and whether they are active or passive. Four types of behaviour result:[92]

- **Exit**. Actively attempting to leave the organization, including looking for a new position as well as resigning. This is a destructive action from the point of view of the organization.

- **Voice**. Actively and constructively trying to improve conditions, including suggesting improvements, discussing problems with superiors, and some forms of union activity.

- **Loyalty**. Passively but optimistically waiting for conditions to improve, including speaking up for the organization in the face of external criticism and trusting the organization and its management to do the right thing.

- **Neglect**. Passively allowing conditions to worsen, including chronic absenteeism or lateness, reduced effort, and increased error rate.

exit Dissatisfaction expressed by actively attempting to leave the organization.

voice Dissatisfaction expressed by actively and constructively attempting to improve conditions.

loyalty Dissatisfaction expressed by passively waiting for conditions to improve.

neglect Dissatisfaction expressed by passively allowing conditions to worsen.

EXHIBIT 3-5 Responses to Job Dissatisfaction

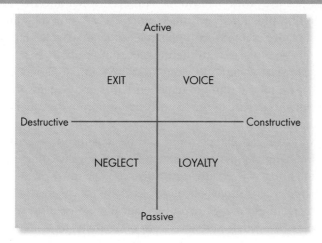

Exit and neglect behaviours encompass our performance variables—productivity, absenteeism, and turnover. But this list expands employee response to include voice and loyalty—constructive behaviours that allow individuals to tolerate unpleasant situations or to revive satisfactory working conditions. It helps us to understand situations, such as those sometimes found among unionized employees, where low job satisfaction is coupled with low turnover.[93] Union members often express dissatisfaction through the grievance procedure or through formal contract negotiations. These voice mechanisms allow the union members to continue in their jobs while convincing themselves that they are acting to improve the situation.

Organizational Commitment

Organizational commitment A state in which an employee identifies with a particular organization and its goals, and wishes to maintain membership in the organization.

affective commitment An individual's emotional attachment to, identification with, and involvement in the organization.

normative commitment The obligation an individual feels to staying with the organization.

continuance commitment An individual's calculation to stay with the organization based on the perceived costs of leaving the organization.

Organizational commitment is defined as a state in which an employee identifies with a particular organization and its goals, and wishes to maintain membership in the organization.[94]

Professor John Meyer at the University of Western Ontario and his colleagues have identified and developed measures for three types of commitment:[95]

- **Affective commitment**. An individual's relationship to the organization: his or her emotional attachment to, identification with, and involvement in the organization.

- **Normative commitment**. The obligation an individual feels to staying with the organization.

- **Continuance commitment**. An individual's calculation that it is in his or her best interest to stay with the organization based on the perceived costs of leaving the organization.

A positive relationship appears to exist between organizational commitment and job productivity, but it is a modest one.[96] A review of 27 studies suggested that the relationship between commitment and performance is strongest for new employees, and it is considerably weaker for more experienced employees.[97] And, as with job involvement, the research evidence demonstrates negative relationships between organizational commitment and both absenteeism and turnover.[98]

Affective commitment is strongly associated with positive work behaviours such as performance, attendance, and citizenship. Normative commitment is less strongly associated with positive work behaviours. However, when affective and normative commitment decline, individuals are much more likely to quit their jobs.[99]

Because continuance commitment reflects an individual's calculation that it is in his or her best interest to stay with the organization (perhaps because it would be difficult to find a job elsewhere), it is often associated with negative work behaviours. People in highly paid jobs and union members with good benefits may exhibit continuance commitment because of the rewards received from the job, rather than their preference for the job itself.[100]

The notion of organizational commitment has changed in recent years. Twenty years ago, employees and employers had an unwritten loyalty contract, with employees typically remaining with a single organization for most of their careers. This notion has become increasingly obsolete. As such, "measures of employee-firm attachment, such as commitment, are problematic for new employment relations."[101] Canadian business consultant Barbara Moses notes that "40-somethings still value loyalty: they think people should be prepared to make sacrifices, to earn their way. The 20-somethings are saying, 'No, I want to be paid for my work; I have no belief in the goodness of organizations, so I'm going to be here as long as my work is meaningful.'"[102]

How can companies increase organizational commitment? Research on a number of companies known for employees with high organizational commitment identified five reasons why employees commit themselves:[103]

- They are proud of [the company's] aspirations, accomplishments, and legacy; they share its values.

- They know what each person is expected to do, how performance is measured, and why it matters.

- They are in control of their own destinies; they savour the high-risk, high-reward work environment.

- They are recognized mostly for the quality of their individual performance.

- They have fun and enjoy the supportive and highly interactive environment.

These findings suggest a variety of ways for organizations to increase the commitment of employees. Additionally, a recent study conducted in five countries suggests that an individual's organizational commitment is strongly associated with whether the employee finds the work interesting.[104] Earlier in the chapter we discussed the role of satisfaction on organizational citizenship behaviour (OCB). We should also note that when individuals have high organizational commitment, they are likely to engage in more OCB.

Employee Engagement

A new concept is **employee engagement**, an individual's involvement with, satisfaction with, and enthusiasm for the work he or she does. For example, we might ask employees about the availability of resources and the opportunities to learn new skills, whether they feel their work is important and meaningful, and whether their interactions with co-workers and supervisors are rewarding.[105] Highly engaged employees have a passion for their work and feel a deep connection to their company; disengaged employees have essentially "checked out"—putting time but not energy or attention into their work.

employee engagement An individual's involvement with, satisfaction with, and enthusiasm for the work he or she does.

A recent study of nearly 8000 business units in 36 companies found that, compared with other companies, those whose employees had high average levels of engagement had higher levels of customer satisfaction, were more productive, had higher profits, and had lower levels of turnover and accidents.[106] Toronto-based Molson Coors found that engaged employees were five times less likely to have safety incidents, and when one did occur, it was much less serious and less costly for the engaged employee than for a disengaged one ($63 per incident vs. $392). Engagement becomes a real concern for most organizations because surveys indicate that few employees—between 17 percent and 29 percent—are highly engaged by their work.

Because of some of these promising findings, employee engagement has attracted quite a following in many business organizations and management consulting firms. However, the concept is relatively new, so we have a lot to learn about how engagement relates to other concepts, such as job satisfaction, organizational commitment, or intrinsic motivation to do one's job well. Engagement may be broad enough that it captures the intersection of these variables. In other words, it may be what these attitudes have in common.

Summary and Implications

1 **What are values?** Values guide how we make decisions about and evaluations of behaviours and events. They represent basic convictions about what is important, right, and good to the individual. Although they do not have a direct impact on behaviour, values strongly influence a person's attitudes. So knowledge of an individual's values can provide insight into his or her attitudes.

2 **How can we understand values across cultures?** Geert Hofstede found that managers and employees vary on five value dimensions of national culture. These include power distance, individualism vs. collectivism, masculinity vs. femininity, uncertainty avoidance, and long-term vs. short-term orientation. His insights were expanded by the GLOBE project, an ongoing cross-cultural investigation of leadership and national culture.

3 **Are there unique Canadian values?** In his recent books, pollster Michael Adams identifies the social values of today's Canadians. He finds that within three broad age groups of adult Canadians—the Elders (those over 60), Baby Boomers (born between the mid-1940s and mid-1960s), and Generation Xers (born between the mid-1960s and the early 1980s)—there are at least 12 quite distinct "value tribes." More recently, discussion has turned to the Net Generation, now in their early 20s, who are the newest entrants to the workplace. Canada is a multicultural country, and there are a number of groups that contribute to its diverse values, such as Aboriginal peoples, French Canadians, and various immigrant groups. Canadian values differ from American values and those of its other trading partners in a variety of ways.

4 **What are attitudes and why are they important?** Attitudes are positive or negative feelings about objects, people, or events. Attitudes affect the way people respond to situations. When I say "I like my job," I am expressing my attitude to work and I am likely to be more committed in my behaviour than if my attitude was one of not liking my job. A person can have thousands of attitudes, but OB focuses our attention on a limited number of job-related attitudes. These job-related attitudes tap positive or negative evaluations that employees hold about aspects of their work environment. Most of the research in OB has been concerned with three attitudes: job satisfaction, organizational commitment, and employee engagement.

OB at Work

For Review

1. Describe the five value dimensions of national culture proposed by Geert Hofstede.

2. Compare Aboriginal and non-Aboriginal values.

3. How might differences in generational values affect the workplace?

4. What might explain low levels of employee job satisfaction in recent years?

5. Are satisfied employees productive employees? Explain your answer.

6. What is the relationship between job satisfaction and absenteeism? Job satisfaction and turnover? Which is the stronger relationship?

7. Contrast exit, voice, loyalty, and neglect as employee responses to job satisfaction.

For Critical Thinking

1. "Thirty-five years ago, young employees we hired were ambitious, conscientious, hard-working, and honest. Today's young employees don't have the same values." Do you agree or disagree with this manager's comments? Support your position.

2. Do you think there might be any positive and significant relationship between the possession of certain personal values and successful career progression in organizations such as Merrill Lynch, the Canadian Union of Postal Workers (CUPW), and the City of Regina's police department? Discuss.

3. "Managers should do everything they can to enhance the job satisfaction of their employees." Do you agree or disagree? Support your position.

4. When employees are asked whether they would again choose the same work or whether they would want their children to follow in their footsteps, fewer than half typically answer "yes." What, if anything, do you think this implies about employee job satisfaction?

OB for You

■ You will encounter many people who have values different from yours in the classroom, in various kinds of activities in which you participate, as well as in the workplace. You should try to understand value differences and to figure out ways to work positively with people who are different from you.

■ Though we often try to generalize about people's values based on either their generation or their culture, not all people in a group hold the same values. Be prepared to look beyond the group characteristics to understand the person.

■ The variety of possible responses to dissatisfaction (exit, voice, loyalty, neglect) gives you alternatives to consider when you are feeling dissatisfied with a situation. Neglect may be an easy way to respond, but consider whether voice might be more effective.

OB *At Work*

Point

Managers Create Job Satisfaction

A review of the evidence has identified four factors conducive to high levels of employee job satisfaction: mentally challenging work, equitable rewards, supportive working conditions, and supportive colleagues.[107] Importantly, each of these factors is controllable by management.

Mentally challenging work. People prefer jobs that give them opportunities to use their skills and abilities and offer a variety of tasks, freedom, and feedback on how well they are doing. These characteristics make work mentally challenging.

Equitable rewards. Employees want pay systems and promotion policies that they perceive as just, unambiguous, and in line with their expectations. When pay is seen as fair based on job demands, individual skill level, and community pay standards, satisfaction is likely to result. Similarly, employees seek fair promotion policies and practices. Promotions provide opportunities for personal growth, more responsibilities, and increased social status. Individuals who perceive that promotion decisions are made in a fair and just manner, therefore, are likely to experience satisfaction from their jobs.

Supportive working conditions. Employees want work environments that support personal comfort and good job performance. Studies demonstrate that employees prefer physical surroundings that are not dangerous or uncomfortable. Most employees also prefer working relatively close to home, in clean and relatively modern facilities, and with adequate tools and equipment.

Supportive colleagues. People get more out of work than merely money or tangible achievements. For most employees, work also fills the need for social interaction. Not surprisingly, therefore, having friendly and supportive co-workers leads to increased job satisfaction. The behaviour of an employee's manager is also a major determinant of satisfaction. Studies generally find that employee satisfaction increases when the immediate supervisor is understanding and friendly, offers praise for good performance, listens to employees' opinions, and shows a personal interest in them.

Counterpoint

Satisfaction Is Individually Determined

The notion that managers and organizations can control the level of employee job satisfaction is inherently attractive. It fits nicely with the view that managers directly influence organizational processes and outcomes. Unfortunately there is a growing body of evidence challenging the notion that managers control the factors that influence employee job satisfaction. Contemporary research indicates that employee job satisfaction is largely genetically determined.[108]

Whether people are happy or not is essentially determined by their gene structure. You either have happy genes or you don't. Approximately 80 percent of people's differences in happiness, or subjective well-being, has been found to be attributable to their different genes.

Analysis of satisfaction data for a selected sample of individuals over a 50-year period found that individual results were consistently stable over time, even when these people changed employers and occupations. This and other research suggests that an individual's disposition toward life—positive or negative—is established by his or her genetic makeup, holds over time, and carries over into his or her disposition toward work.

Given these findings, there is probably little that most managers can do to influence employee satisfaction. In spite of the fact that managers and organizations go to extensive lengths to try to improve employee job satisfaction through manipulating job characteristics, working conditions, and rewards, these actions are likely to have little effect. The only place where managers will have significant influence is through their control of the selection process. If managers want satisfied employees, they need to make sure their selection process screens out the negative, maladjusted, troublemaking fault-finders who derive little satisfaction in anything job-related. This is probably best achieved through personality testing, in-depth interviewing, and careful checking of applicants' previous work records.

OB At Work

What Do You Value?

There are 16 items in the list below. Rate how important each one is to you on a scale of 0 (not important) to 100 (very important). Write a number between 0 and 100 on the line to the left of each item.[109]

Not Important					**Somewhat Important**					**Very Important**
0	10	20	30	40	50	60	70	80	90	100

_____ **1.** An enjoyable, satisfying job.

_____ **2.** A high-paying job.

_____ **3.** A good marriage.

_____ **4.** Meeting new people; social events.

_____ **5.** Involvement in community activities.

_____ **6.** My religion.

_____ **7.** Exercising, playing sports.

_____ **8.** Intellectual development.

_____ **9.** A career with challenging opportunities.

_____ **10.** Nice cars, clothes, home, and so on.

_____ **11.** Spending time with family.

_____ **12.** Having several close friends.

_____ **13.** Volunteer work for nonprofit organizations, such as the Canadian Cancer Society.

_____ **14.** Meditation, quiet time to think, pray, and so on.

_____ **15.** A healthy, balanced diet.

_____ **16.** Educational reading, television, self-improvement programs, and so on.

Scoring Key

Transfer the numbers for each of the 16 items to the appropriate column; then add up the 2 numbers in each column.

	Professional	**Financial**	**Family**	**Social**
	1. _____	2. _____	3. _____	4. _____
	9. _____	10. _____	11. _____	12. _____
Totals	_____	_____	_____	_____

	Community	**Spiritual**	**Physical**	**Intellectual**
	5. _____	6. _____	7. _____	8. _____
	13. _____	14. _____	15. _____	16. _____
Totals	_____	_____	_____	_____

The higher the total in any value dimension, the higher the importance you place on that value set. The closer the numbers are in all 8 dimensions, the more well rounded you are.

OB *At Work*

More Learning About Yourself Exercises

Additional self-assessments relevant to this chapter appear on MyOBLab (**www.pearsoned.ca/myoblab**).

IV.C.1 What's My Attitude toward Older People?

I.B.3 How Satisfied Am I with My Job?

IV.B.1 Am I Engaged?

I.E.1 What's My Emotional Score?

When you complete the additional assessments, consider the following:

1. Am I surprised about my score?

2. Would my friends evaluate me similarly?

BREAKOUT **GROUP** EXERCISES

Form small groups to discuss the following topics, as assigned by your instructor. Each person in the group should first identify 3 to 5 key personal values.

1. Identify the extent to which values overlap in your group.

2. Try to uncover with your group members the source of some of your key values (e.g., parents, peer group, teachers, church).

3. What kind of workplace would be most suitable for the values that you hold most closely?

WORKING WITH **OTHERS** EXERCISE

Understanding Cultural Values

Objective To compare the cultural values of two countries, and determine how differences might affect group behaviour.

Time Approximately 30 minutes.

Procedure

1. Break into groups of 5 or 6.

2. Pretend that you are a group of students working on a project. Half of you are from Canada and hold typically "Canadian" cultural values; the other half are from the country assigned and hold that country's cultural values.

3. Consider the values of power distance, individualism/collectivism, and uncertainty avoidance, and discuss the differences between Canadian cultural values and the values of the country assigned to you. (Refer to Exhibit 3-3 on page 79 to identify the values of your assigned country.)

4. Answer the following questions:
What challenges might you expect in working together?
What steps could be taken to work together more effectively?

ETHICAL **DILEMMA** EXERCISE

Is It a Bribe or a Gift?

The Corruption of Foreign Public Officials Act prohibits Canadian firms from making payments to foreign government officials with the aim of gaining or maintaining business.[110] But payments are acceptable if they don't violate local laws. For instance, payments to officers working for foreign corporations are legal. Many countries don't have such legal guidelines.

Bribery is a common way of doing business in many underdeveloped countries. Government jobs there often don't pay very well, so it's tempting for officials to supplement their income with bribes. In addition, in many countries, the penalties for demanding and receiving bribes are few or nonexistent.

You are a Canadian who works for a large European multinational computer manufacturer. You are currently working to sell a $5 million system to a government agency in Nigeria. The Nigerian official who heads up the team that will decide who gets this contract has asked you for a payment of $20 000. He says this payment will not guarantee you get the order, but without it he cannot be very encouraging. Your company's policy is very flexible on the issue of "gifts" to facilitate sales. Your boss says that it's OK to pay the $20 000, but only if you can be relatively assured of the order.

You are not sure what you should do. The Nigerian official has told you specifically that any payment to him is not to be mentioned to anyone else on the Nigerian team. You know for certain that three other companies are also negotiating, but it's unconfirmed whether two of those companies have turned down the payment request.

What would you do?

CASE INCIDENT

Gourmet Foods Works on Employee Attitudes

Gourmet Foods is a huge grocery and drug company. It has more than 2400 supermarkets, and its Premier and Polar brands make it the fifth-largest drugstore company in North America.[111] In a typical year, shoppers will make 1.4 billion trips through its stores.

Gourmet Foods competes against tough businesses. Walmart, in particular, has been eating away at its market share. In 2001, with revenues flat and profits falling, the company hired Larry Johnston to turn the business around.

Johnston came to Gourmet Foods from General Living Medical Systems. It was while he was at General Living that Johnston met a training specialist named Roger Nelson. Nelson endeared himself to Johnston when the latter hired Nelson to help him with a serious problem. At the time, Johnston had been sent to Paris to fix General Living's European division. The division made CT scanners. Over the previous decade, four executives had been brought in to turn the division around and try to make it profitable. All had failed. Johnston responded to the challenge by initiating some important changes—he made a number of acquisitions, he closed down inefficient plants, and he moved factories to Eastern European countries to take advantage of lower labour costs. Then he brought in

Nelson to charge up the troops. "After we got Roger in," says Johnston, "people began to live their lives differently. They came to work with a spring in their step." In three years, the division was bringing in annual profits of $100 million. Johnston gives a large part of the credit for this turnaround to Nelson.

What is Nelson's secret? He provides motivation and attitude training. Here is an example of Nelson's primary program—called the Successful Life Course. It lasts three days and begins each morning at 6 a.m. The first day begins with a chapter from an inspirational handout, followed by 12 minutes of yoga-like stretching. Then participants march up a hill, chanting, "I know I can, I know I can." This is followed by breakfast and then a variety of lectures on attitude, diet, and exercise. But the primary focus of the program is on attitude. Says Nelson, "It's your attitude, not your aptitude, that determines your altitude." Other parts of the program include group hugs, team activities, and mind-control relaxation exercises.

Johnston believes strongly in Nelson's program. "Positive attitude is the single biggest thing that can change a business," says Johnston. He sees Nelson's program as a

(Continued)

OB *At Work*

critical bridge linking employees with customers: "We're in the business of maintenance and acquisition of customers." With so many shoppers going through his stores, Johnston says there are "a lot of opportunities for customer service. We've got to energize the associates." To prove he is willing to put his money where his mouth is, Johnston has committed $10 million to this training. By the end of 2006, 10 000 managers will have taken the course. They, in turn, will train all 190 000 Gourmet Foods "associates," with the help of tapes and books.

Nelson claims his program works. He cites success at companies such as Allstate, Milliken & Co., and Abbott Labs. "The goal is to improve mental, physical, and emotional well-being," he says. "We as individuals determine the success of our lives. Positive thoughts create positive actions."

Questions

1. Explain the logic as to how Nelson's three-day course could positively influence Gourmet Foods' profitability.

2. Johnston says, "Positive attitude is the single biggest thing that can change a business." How valid and generalizable do you think this statement is?

3. If you were Johnston, what could you do to evaluate the effectiveness of your $10 million investment in Nelson's training program?

4. If you were a Gourmet Foods employee, how would you feel about going through Nelson's course? Explain your position.

VIDEO CASE INCIDENT

| CASE 3 | Flair Bartending | CBC |

Remember *Cocktail*, the movie in which Tom Cruise was a flashy bartender?[112] That style of bartending actually has a name. It's called *flair bartending*. Gavin MacMillan is the top-ranked Canadian flair bartender, and second-ranked in the world. He is also an author and the owner of a bartender-for-hire business called *Movers and Shakers*. Now he is developing a brand-new idea for a bartender school called *Bartender 1*. Eventually, he wants to franchise the idea across Canada, the United States, and the world. He wants to earn enough money to buy a yacht with a helicopter pad on it.

Potential franchisees will like his idea to use an actual bar to teach students flair bartending. MacMillan does not rent space; rather, he borrows a bar for an evening to hold his classes. On one Monday evening, he is at a Toronto bar that is closed, but he has talked the owner into letting him run his class there for free. In return, the bar gets first pick of the graduates of MacMillan's bartending school.

In his first class of 12 students, MacMillan's expenses are $11 000, against $6000 in revenues. He hopes to reduce the cost of running future classes by re-using demonstration equipment. He needs to prove his concept works before he franchises it.

MacMillan discovers there is no problem finding students who want to be bartenders, but there is a problem finding people who can be instructors. There are only about 10 flair bartenders in Toronto and 40 in all of Canada. Finding teachers is not MacMillan's only problem. He is a perfectionist who is always fussing over the little things. Sometimes he focuses so much on the details that he does not see the big picture. He also lacks time to do all the things he wants to do.

MacMillan designed, built, and financed a portable bar to sell to golf courses and hotels. He brings his idea to a business group that runs entrepreneurial self-help sessions. He tells the group that he wants to make 10 of the portable bars in order to be more cost-effective, and he wants the group to help him with ideas to market the bar. But one of the group members questions whether MacMillan should even pursue the idea, noting he already has too many balls in the air. He needs to prioritize.

Two months later, MacMillan is conducting a two-day bartending course at the University of Guelph. His school is now making money, and everything is going well because he listened to the advice about focusing on just a few projects. He has stopped putting energy into his portable bar for the moment, and he has begun delegating duties to others.

Questions

1. What is the difference between terminal and instrumental values? Which of the terminal and instrumental values shown in Exhibit 3-1 apply to Gavin MacMillan?

2. Consider the following statement: *"Individuals who place a great deal of emphasis on the pursuit of money and material possessions are quite narrow in their perspective and are missing out on the really important nonmaterial things in life like friends, family, and helping others. They are also showing a lack of concern for the environment because their desire to acquire things like a yacht leads to environmental damage."* Do you agree or disagree with the statement? Explain, and be sure to consider the importance of values in your discussion.

3. Explain the difference between "values," "attitudes," and "job satisfaction." How do these ideas apply in practice to Gavin MacMillan? Give examples.

From *Concepts* to *Skills*

Changing Attitudes

Can you change unfavourable employee attitudes? Sometimes! It depends on who you are, the strength of the employee's attitude, the magnitude of the change, and the technique you choose to try to change the attitude.

People are most likely to respond to changes suggested by someone who is liked, credible, and convincing. If people like you, they are more apt to identify and adopt your message. Credibility implies trust, expertise, and objectivity. So you are more likely to change someone's attitude if that person views you as believable, knowledgeable about what you're saying, and unbiased in your presentation. Finally, successful attitude change is enhanced when you present your arguments clearly and persuasively.

It's easier to change a person's attitude if he or she is not strongly committed to it. Conversely, the stronger the belief in the attitude, the harder it is to change it. Also, attitudes that have been expressed publicly are more difficult to change because doing so requires admitting having made a mistake.

It's also easier to change attitudes when the change required is not very significant. To get a person to accept a new attitude that varies greatly from his or her current position requires more effort. It may also threaten other deeply held attitudes.

All attitude-change techniques are not equally effective across situations. Oral persuasion techniques are most effective when you use a positive, tactful tone; present strong evidence to support your position; tailor your argument to the listener; use logic; and support your evidence by appealing to the person's fears, frustrations, and other emotions. But people are more likely to embrace change when they can experience it. The use of training sessions in which employees share and personalize experiences, and practise new behaviours, can be powerful stimulants for change. Consistent with self-perception theory, changes in behaviour can lead to changes in attitudes.

Practising Skills

Form groups of 2. Person A is to choose any topic that he or she feels strongly about and state his or her position on the topic in 30 words or less. Person B's task will be to try to change Person A's attitude on this topic. Person B will have 10 minutes to make his or her case. When the time is up, the roles are reversed. Person B picks the topic and Person A has 10 minutes to try to change Person B's attitude.

Potential topics (you can choose *either* side of a topic) include the following: politics; the economy; world events; social practices; or specific management issues, such as that organizations should require all employees to undergo regular drug testing, there is no such thing as organizational loyalty any more, the customer is always right, and layoffs are an indication of management failures.

Questions

1. Were you successful in changing the other person's attitude? Why or why not?

2. Was the other person successful in changing your attitude? Why or why not?

3. What conclusions can you draw about changing the attitudes of yourself and others?

Reinforcing Skills

1. Try to convince a friend or relative to go with you to see a movie or play that you know he or she does not want to see.

2. Try to convince a friend or relative to try a different brand of toothpaste.

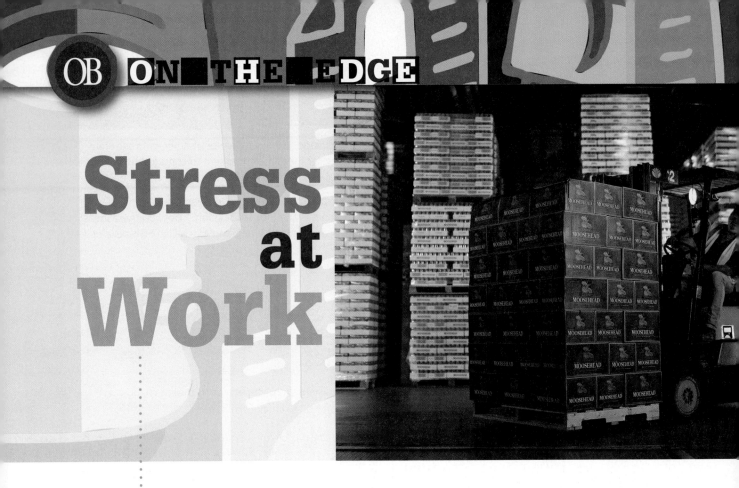

Stress at Work

Saint John, New Brunswick-based Moosehead Breweries switched to running its beer production plant 24 hours a day, up from 16 hours, in 2007.[1] The increase in hours had an immediate effect. "Running 24 hours a day has caused significant stresses," said Michael Lee, Moosehead's vice-president of human resources.

The plant's managers are working with employees to deal with the stress. "Our Employment Assistance Program has always been vibrant. But now we are doing more presentations on shift work to help our employees deal with the changes," says Lee.

Moosehead's employees have a good, well-grounded role model in the company's president, Andrew Oland. He regularly attends 6 a.m. spin classes at a local fitness centre. His wife, Leslie, notes that "Andrew is a very involved parent who tries very hard to set aside time for his family."

Being sensitive to workplace stress is putting increased responsibilities on managers. When Janie Toivanen was diagnosed with severe depression in September 2002, she approached her employer, Vancouver-based Electronic Arts Canada, to request indefinite stress leave.[2] Instead, just days later, she was fired. After working there for six years, she "felt like she had been thrown away." Toivanen thought EA cared about its employees, and could not believe it would not do anything to help her as she struggled to overcome her illness. She subsequently filed a complaint with the BC Human Rights Tribunal and in 2006 was awarded, among other things, $20 000 for injury to her dignity, feelings, and self-respect and $19 744 in severance pay.

Are We Overstressed?

Stress appears to be a major factor in the lives of many Canadians. A recent survey conducted by Statistics Canada found that Canadians experience a great deal of stress, with those from Quebec topping the list.[3] The survey also found that women were more stressed than men. The inset *Stress Across the Country, 2005,* reports the findings.

The impact of stress on the Canadian economy is huge, costing an estimated $33 billion each year in lost productivity, and considerably more than that in medical costs. To address these costs, Prime Minister Stephen Harper announced the creation of the Mental Health Commission of Canada in 2007. At the launch of the commission, Harper noted that mental health disorders are "now the fastest-growing category of disability insurance claims in Canada."[5]

Shannon Wagner, a clinical psychologist and a specialist in workplace stress research at the University of Northern British Columbia, notes that changes in the nature of jobs may be increasing the levels of stress in the workplace. While many jobs are not as physically demanding, they are often more mentally demanding. "A lot of people now are identifying techno-stress and the 24/7 workday, which we didn't have even 10 or 15 years ago, this feeling of being constantly plugged in, of checking email 500 times a day."[6]

An additional problem is that employees are increasingly asked to donate labour to their employers, according to professor Linda Duxbury of Carleton University's Sprott School of Business and professor Chris Higgins of the Richard Ivey School of Business at the University of Western Ontario. Their survey of 31 571 Canadians found that in the previous month half of them had worked an extra 2.5 days of unpaid overtime, and more than half had donated 3.5 days of working at home to catch up.[7] Canadians are frequently reporting that they want more balance in their work and family lives.[8]

Jobs and Stress Levels

How do jobs rate in terms of stress? The inset *The Most and Least Stressful Jobs* on page 106 shows how selected occupations ranked in an evaluation of 250 jobs. Among the criteria used in the rankings were overtime, quotas, deadlines, competitiveness, physical demands, environmental conditions, hazards encountered, initiative required, stamina required, win-lose situations, and working in the public eye.

Stress is not something that can be ignored in the workplace. A 2005 poll by Ipsos Reid found that 66 percent of the CEOs surveyed said that "stress, burnout or other physical and mental health issues" have a negative effect on productivity.[9] A 2001 study conducted in 15 developed countries found that individuals who report that they are stressed in their jobs are 25 percent more likely to quit and 25 percent more likely to miss days of work.[10] Canadian, French, and Swedish employees reported the highest stress levels. In Canada, 41 percent of employees noted that they "often" or "always" experience stress at work, while only 31 percent of employees in Denmark and Switzerland reported stress levels this high. "In the wake of years of fiscal downsizing, workers across all sectors are working harder and longer than ever while trying to balance family responsibilities," said Scott Morris, former head of the Vancouver-based consulting firm Priority Management Systems.[11] Daniel Ondrack, a professor at the Joseph L. Rotman School of Management at the University of Toronto, notes that "one of the major reasons for absenteeism is the logistical problems workers face in just getting to work, including transporting children to school and finding daycare. Single parents, especially female, have to juggle all the daycare and family responsibilities, and that makes it extremely difficult for people to keep up with work demands."[12]

What Is Stress?

Stress is a dynamic condition in which an individual is confronted with an opportunity, demand, or resource related to what the individual desires and for which the outcome is perceived to be both uncertain and important.[13] This is a complicated definition. Let's look at its components more closely.

Stress Across the Country, 2005[4]

Region	% with no life stresses	% with quite a lot of stress
Alberta	9.8	22.4
Atlantic Canada	13.1	18.4
British Columbia	13.2	22.7
Ontario	10.6	23.1
The Prairies	9.9	20.5
Quebec	14.4	26.0

The Most and Least Stressful Jobs

How do jobs rate in terms of stress? According to *Health* magazine, the top 10 most and least stressful jobs are as follows.[14]

Ten Most Stressful Jobs	Ten Least Stressful Jobs
1. Inner-city high school teacher	1. Forester
2. Police officer	2. Bookbinder
3. Miner	3. Telephone line worker
4. Air traffic controller	4. Toolmaker
5. Medical intern	5. Millwright
6. Stockbroker	6. Repairperson
7. Journalist	7. Civil engineer
8. Customer-service/complaint worker	8. Therapist
9. Secretary	9. Natural scientist
10. Waiter	10. Sales representative

Stress is not necessarily bad in and of itself. Although stress is typically discussed in a negative context, it also has a positive value.[15] It's an opportunity when it offers potential gain. Consider, for example, the superior performance that an athlete or stage performer gives in "clutch" situations. Such individuals often use stress positively to rise to the occasion and perform at or near their maximum. Similarly, many professionals see the pressures of heavy workloads and deadlines as positive challenges that enhance the quality of their work and the satisfaction they get from their job. In short, some stress can be good, and some can be bad.

Recently, researchers have argued that challenge stressors—or stressors associated with workload, pressure to complete tasks, and time urgency—operate quite differently from hindrance stressors—or stressors that keep you from reaching your goals (red tape, office politics, confusion over job responsibilities). Although research on challenge and hindrance stress is just starting to accumulate, early evidence suggests that challenge stressors are less harmful (produce less strain) than hindrance stressors.[16]

More typically, stress is associated with demands and resources. Demands are responsibilities, pressures, obligations, and even uncertainties that individuals face in the workplace. Resources are things within an individual's control that can be used to resolve the demands. For example, when you take a test at school, you feel stress because you confront opportunities and performance pressures. To the extent that you can apply resources to the demands—such as being prepared for the exam—you will feel less stress.

Under the demands and resources perspective on stress, having resources to cope with stress is just as important in offsetting stress as demands are in increasing it.[17] This model has received increasing support in the literature.[18]

Causes of Stress

A variety of changes in the workplace have resulted in additional causes of stress. We identify some of these key changes below:[19]

- *Environmental factors.* Evidence indicates that uncertainty is the biggest reason people have trouble coping with organizational changes.[20] Two types of environmental uncertainty are economic and technological. Changes in the business cycle create *economic uncertainties*. When the economy is contracting, for example, people become increasingly anxious about their job security. *Technological change* is another environmental factor that can cause stress. Because new innovations can make an employee's skills and experience obsolete in a very short time, computers, robotics, automation, and similar forms of technological innovation are a threat to many people and cause them stress.

- *Organizational factors.* There is no shortage of factors within an organization that can cause stress. Pressures to avoid errors or complete tasks in a limited time, work overload, a demanding and insensitive boss, and unpleasant co-workers are a few examples. We have categorized these factors around task, role, and interpersonal demands.[21]

- *Task demands* are factors related to a person's job. They include the design of the individual's job (autonomy, task variety, degree of automation), working conditions, and the physical work layout. Assembly lines, for instance, can put pressure on people when the line's speed is perceived as excessive. Similarly, working in an overcrowded room or in a visible location where noise and interruptions are constant can increase anxiety and stress.[22] Increasingly, as customer service becomes ever more important, emotional labour is a source of stress.[23] Do you think you could put on a happy face when you are having a bad day?

- *Role demands* relate to pressures placed on a person as a function of the particular role he or she plays in the organization.

- *Interpersonal demands* are pressures created by other employees. Lack of social support from colleagues and poor interpersonal relationships can cause stress, especially among employees with a high social need.

- *Personal factors.* The typical individual works about 40 to 50 hours a week. But the experiences and problems that people encounter in the other 120-plus nonwork hours each week can spill over to the job. Our final category, then, encompasses factors in the employee's personal life. Primarily, these factors are family issues, personal economic problems, and inherent personality characteristics.

- National surveys consistently show that people hold *family* and personal relationships dear. Marital difficulties, the breaking off of a relationship, and discipline troubles with children are examples of relationship problems that create stress for employees that are not left at the front door when they arrive at work.[24]

- Furthermore, about one in eight workers was responsible for providing some form of care for aging parents in 1997, and one survey found that one in three was doing so in 2002.[25] Being a caregiver is an additional stress

both at home and at work. Studies indicate that those who have difficulties finding effective child care or elder care have lower work performance and increased absenteeism, decreased satisfaction, and lower physical and psychological well-being.[26]

- *Economic* problems created by individuals overextending their financial resources is another set of personal troubles that can create stress for employees and distract their attention from their work. Regardless of income level—people who make $80 000 per year seem to have as much trouble handling their finances as those who earn $18 000—some people are poor money managers or have wants that always seem to exceed their earning capacity.

- Studies in three diverse organizations found that stress symptoms reported prior to beginning a job accounted for most of the variance in stress symptoms reported nine months later.[27] This led the researchers to conclude that some people may have an inherent tendency to accentuate negative aspects of the world in general. If this is true, then a significant individual factor that influences stress is a person's basic disposition. That is, stress symptoms expressed on the job may actually originate in the person's *personality*.

Consequences of Stress

Stress manifests itself in a number of ways. For instance, an individual who is experiencing a high level of stress may develop high blood pressure, ulcers, irritability, difficulty in making routine decisions,

FactBox

- Mental illness accounts for 40% of disability claims and sick leaves in Canada.

- Every day, 500 000 Canadians are absent from work due to mental health problems.

- About 8% of Canadians take medication for depression and other mental health conditions.

- Almost 21% of employees will suffer from mental illness at some point in their work life.

- One-third of Canadians don't take all of their vacation days, saving their employers $8 billion a year.

- When Canadians do go on holiday, 36% of them take work and check their office voice mail and email.[28]

A fact that tends to be overlooked when stressors are reviewed individually is that stress is an additive phenomenon.[29] Stress builds up. Each new and persistent stressor adds to an individual's stress level. A single stressor may seem relatively unimportant in and of itself, but if it is added to an already high level of stress, it can be "the straw that breaks the camel's back."

loss of appetite, accident proneness, and the like. These symptoms can be placed under three general categories: physiological, psychological, and behavioural symptoms.[30]

- *Physiological symptoms.* Most of the research on stress suggests that it can create changes in metabolism, increase heart and breathing rates, increase blood pressure, cause headaches, and induce heart attacks. An interesting aspect of illness in today's workplace is the considerable change in how stress shows up. In the past, older workers were the ones claiming sick leave, workers' compensation, and short- and long-term disability—most often in cases of catastrophic illness such as heart attacks, cancer, and major back surgeries. These days, however, it is not unusual for long-term disability programs to be filled with employees in their 20s, 30s, and 40s. Employees are claiming illnesses that are either psychiatric (such as depression) or more difficult to diagnose (such as chronic fatigue syndrome or fibromyalgia, a musculoskeletal discomfort). The increase in disability claims may be the result of downsizing taking its toll on the psyches of those in the workforce.[31]

- *Psychological symptoms.* Job dissatisfaction is "the simplest and most obvious psychological effect" of stress.[32] However, stress also shows itself in other psychological states—for instance, tension, anxiety, irritability, boredom, and procrastination.

- The evidence indicates that when people are placed in jobs that make multiple and conflicting demands or in which there is a lack of clarity as to the person's duties, authority, and responsibilities, both stress and dissatisfaction increase.[33]

    Similarly, the less control that people have over the pace of their work, the greater the stress and dissatisfaction. More research is needed to clarify the relationship, but the evidence suggests that jobs providing a low level of variety, significance, autonomy, feedback, and identity create stress and reduce satisfaction and involvement in the job.[34]

- *Behavioural symptoms.* Behaviourally related stress symptoms include changes in productivity, absence, and turnover, as well as changes in eating habits, increased smoking or consumption of alcohol, rapid speech, fidgeting, and sleep disorders. More recently, stress has been linked to aggression and violence in the workplace.

Why Do Individuals Differ in Their Experience of Stress?

Some people thrive on stressful situations, while others are overwhelmed by them. What is it that differentiates people in terms of their ability to handle stress? What individual difference variables moderate the relationship between potential stressors and experienced stress? At least four variables—perception, job experience, social support, and personality—have been found to be relevant moderators.

- *Perception.* Individuals react in response to their *perception* of reality rather than to reality itself. Perception, therefore, moderates the relationship between a potential stress condition and an employee's reaction to it. For example, one person might fear losing his job because the company is laying off staff, while another might perceive the situation as an opportunity to receive a large severance allowance and start a small business. Similarly, what one employee perceives as a challenging job may be viewed as threatening and demanding by others.[35] So the stress potential in environmental, organizational, and individual factors does not lie in objective conditions. Rather, it lies in an employee's interpretation of those factors.

- *Job experience.* Experience on the job tends to be negatively related to work stress. Two explanations have been offered.[36] First, people who experience more stress on the job when they are first hired may be more likely to quit. Therefore, people who remain with the organization longer are those with more stress-resistant traits or those who are more resistant to the stress characteristics of their organization. Second, people eventually develop coping mechanisms to deal with stress. Because this takes time, senior members of the organization are more likely to be fully adapted and should experience less stress.

- *Social support.* There is increasing evidence that social support— that is, collegial relationships with co-workers or supervisors— can buffer the impact of stress.[37] The logic underlying this moderating variable is that social support helps ease the negative effects of even high-strain jobs.

    For individuals whose work associates are unhelpful or even actively hostile, social support may be found outside the job. Involvement with family, friends, and community can provide the

support—especially for those with a high social need—that is missing at work, and this can make job stressors more tolerable.

- *Personality.* Personality not only affects the degree to which people experience stress but also how they cope with it. Perhaps the most widely studied personality trait in stress is Type A personality, which we discussed in Chapter 2. Type A—particularly that aspect of Type A that manifests itself in hostility and anger—is associated with increased levels of stress and risk for heart disease.[38] More specifically, people who are quick to anger, maintain a persistently hostile outlook, and project a cynical mistrust of others are at increased risk of experiencing stress in situations.

How Do We Manage Stress?

Both the individual and the organization can take steps to help the individual manage stress. Below we discuss ways that individuals can manage stress, and then we examine programs that organizations use to help employees manage stress.

Individual Approaches

An employee can take personal responsibility for reducing his or her stress level. Individual strategies that have proven effective include time management techniques, physical exercise, relaxation techniques, and a close social support network.

- *Time management.* Many people manage their time poorly. The things we have to accomplish in any given day or week are not necessarily beyond completion if we manage our time properly. The well-organized employee, like the well-organized student, can often accomplish twice as much as the person who is poorly organized. So understanding and using basic time management principles can help individuals cope better with tensions created by job demands.[39] A few of the more well-known time management principles are: (1) making daily lists of activities to be accomplished; (2) prioritizing activities by importance and urgency; (3) scheduling activities according to the priorities set; and (4) knowing your daily cycle and handling the most demanding parts of your job during the high part of your cycle, when you are most alert and productive.[40]

- *Physical activity.* Noncompetitive physical exercise, such as aerobics, walking, jogging, swimming, and riding a bicycle, has long been recommended by physicians as a way to deal with excessive stress levels. These forms of physical exercise increase heart capacity, lower at-rest heart rate, provide a mental diversion from work pressures, and offer a means to "let off steam."[41]

- *Relaxation techniques.* Individuals can teach themselves to reduce tension through relaxation techniques such as meditation, hypnosis, and biofeedback. The objective is to reach a state of deep relaxation, where you feel physically relaxed, somewhat detached from the immediate environment, and detached from body sensations.[42] Fifteen or twenty minutes a day of deep relaxation releases tension and provides a person with a pronounced sense of peacefulness. Importantly, significant changes in heart rate, blood pressure, and other physiological factors result from achieving the deep relaxation condition.

- *Building social supports.* Having friends, family, or colleagues to talk to provides an outlet when stress levels become excessive. Expanding your social support network, therefore, can be a means for tension reduction. It provides you with someone to listen to your problems and to offer a more objective perspective on the situation.

The inset *Tips for Reducing Stress* offers additional ideas for managing stress.

Tips for Reducing Stress

- At least two or three times a week, spend time with supportive friends or family.

- Ask for support when you are under pressure. This is a sign of health, not weakness.

- If you have spiritual or religious beliefs, increase or maintain your involvement.

- Use a variety of methods to reduce stress. Consider exercise, nutrition, hobbies, positive thinking, and relaxation techniques such as meditation or yoga.[43]

Organizational Approaches

Employees who work at Montreal-based Ericsson Canada, a global telecommunications supplier, have access to a comprehensive wellness program. They can engage in activities that address their intellectual, emotional, social, physical, and spiritual well-being. "The program has really evolved over the years," says Louise Leonhardt, manager of human resources. "We've found it helps people balance their life, just like the on-site daycare does."

Employees who work at Toronto-based BCS Communications, a publishing, advertising, and public relations agency, receive biweekly shiatsu massages, paid for by the company. The company spends about $700 a month for the massages, equivalent to the amount it used to spend providing coffee to the employees. "It's in my company's best interest to have my employees be healthy," says Caroline Tapp-McDougall, the BCS group publisher.[44]

Most firms that have introduced wellness programs have found significant benefits. Health Canada reports that businesses get back $3.39 for each corporate dollar they invest in wellness initiatives. For individuals with three to five risk factors (such as high cholesterol, being overweight, or smoking) the return was $2.04 for each dollar spent.[45] The savings come about because there is less turnover, greater productivity, and reduced medical claims.[46] About 64 percent of Canadian companies surveyed by Health Canada offered some sort of wellness initiative, including stop-smoking programs, stress courses, and back-pain management programs; 17.5 percent of companies offered on-site wellness programs.[47]

So what can organizations do to reduce employee stress? In general, strategies to reduce stress include improved processes for choosing employees, placement of employees in appropriate jobs, realistic goal setting, designing jobs with employee needs and skills in mind, increased employee involvement, improved organizational communication, offering employee sabbaticals, and, as mentioned, establishment of corporate wellness programs.

Certain jobs are more stressful than others, but individuals also differ in their response to stress situations. We know, for example, that individuals with little experience or a negative core self-evaluation tend to be more prone to stress. Selection and placement decisions should take these facts into consideration. Although management should not restrict hiring to only experienced individuals with a positive core self-evaluation, such individuals may adapt better to high-stress jobs and perform those jobs more effectively.

Research shows that individuals perform better when they have specific and challenging goals and receive feedback on how well they are progressing toward them.[48] The use of goals can reduce stress as well as provide motivation. Specific goals that are perceived as attainable clarify performance expectations. Additionally, goal feedback reduces uncertainties as to actual job performance. The result is less employee frustration, role ambiguity, and stress.

Creating jobs that give employees more responsibility, more meaningful work, more autonomy, and increased feedback can reduce stress because these factors give the employee greater control over work activities and lessen dependence on others. Of course, not all employees want jobs with increased responsibility. The right job for employees with a low need for growth might be less responsibility and increased specialization. If individuals prefer structure and routine, more structured jobs should also reduce uncertainties and stress levels.

Increasing formal organizational communication with employees reduces uncertainty by lessening role ambiguity and role conflict. Given the importance that perceptions play in moderating the stress-response relationship, management can also use effective communications as a means to shape employee perceptions. Remember that what

Reducing Stress in the Workplace

- Avoid electronic monitoring of staff. Personal supervision generates considerably less stress.

- Allow employees time to recharge after periods of intense or demanding work.

- Deliver important information that significantly affects employees face to face.

- Encourage positive social interactions between staff to promote problem-solving around work issues and increase emotional support.

- Keep in mind that staff need to balance privacy and social interaction at work. Extremes can generate stress.[49]

employees categorize as demands, threats, or opportunities are merely interpretations, and those interpretations can be affected by the symbols and actions communicated by management.

What some employees need is an occasional escape from the frenetic pace of their work. In recent years, companies such as Charles Schwab, DuPont, L.L.Bean, Nike, and 3Com have begun to provide extended voluntary leaves.[50] These *sabbaticals*— ranging in length from a few weeks to several months—allow employees to travel, relax, or pursue personal projects that consume time beyond normal vacation weeks. Proponents argue that these sabbaticals can revive and rejuvenate workers who might be headed for burnout.

Our final suggestion is to offer organizationally supported wellness programs. These programs focus on the employee's total physical and mental condition.[51] For example, they typically include workshops to help people quit smoking, control alcohol use, lose weight, eat better, and develop a regular exercise program. The assumption underlying most wellness programs is that employees need to take personal responsibility for their physical and mental health. The organization is merely a vehicle to make this happen. The inset *Reducing Stress in the Workplace* offers additional ideas.

Research Exercises

1. Look for data on stress levels in other countries. How do these data compare with the Canadian data presented above? Are the sources of stress the same in different countries? What might you conclude about how stress affects people in different cultures?

2. Find out what three Canadian organizations in three different industries have done to help employees manage stress. Are there common themes in these programs? Did you find any unusual programs? To what extent are these programs tailored to the needs of the employees in those industries?

Your Perspective

1. Think of all of the technological changes that have happened in the workplace in recent years, including email, BlackBerrys, and intranets. What are the positive benefits of this change? What are the downsides? As an employee facing the demand to "stay connected" to your workplace, how would you try to maintain a balance in your life?

2. How much responsibility should individuals take for managing their own stress? To what extent should organizations become involved in the personal lives of their employees when trying to help them manage stress? What are the pros and cons for whether employees or organizations take responsibility for managing stress?

Want to Know More?

If you are wondering how stressed you are, go to **www.heartandstroke.ca** and click on "Risk assessment." The site also offers tips on reducing stress.

FACE**OFF**

When organizations provide on-site daycare facilities, they are filling a needed role in parents' lives and making it easier for parents to attend to their job demands rather than worry about child-care arrangements.

When employees expect organizations to provide child care, they are shifting their responsibilities to their employers, rather than keeping their family needs and concerns private. Moreover, it is unfair to give child-care benefits when not all employees have children.

Chapter 4 Motivating Self and Others

The BC Lions football team ended the 2007 season with a team record of 14 wins. How does motivation affect how the team performs?

1. What is motivation?

2. How do needs motivate people?

3. Are there other ways to motivate people?

4. Do equity and fairness matter?

5. How can rewards and job design motivate employees?

6. What kinds of mistakes are made in reward systems?

*B*y most accounts, Vancouver-based BC Lions head coach Wally Buono is not a particularly warm person.[1] Buono is a hard taskmaster with his BC Lions players and coaches, and he is not afraid to make tough decisions.

Buono wants to coach winners, not losers. As a coach, Buono has the winningest record in the Canadian Football League (CFL), achieving that milestone in September 2009. His teams have been to seven Grey Cups, and the BC Lions have finished first in the West four times, gone to the Grey Cup twice, and won the 2006 CFL championship under his leadership. In 2007, the BC Lions finished the season with 14 wins (3 losses and 1 tie), setting a franchise record. In 2008, however, their record was not as good, winning 11 and losing 7 games.

Buono seems to motivate by being tough. He's not afraid to criticize his players publicly and will give them a long list of their faults during contract negotiations. He claims that he gives only two performance reviews to players: "Once when I warn you and once when I cut you."

Buono's players may not like him personally, but they spend hours in training each day because "guys wanna get better," explained slotback Geroy Simon.

This chapter examines the subject of motivation and rewards in some detail. It looks at what motivation is, key motivation theories, and how motivation theories and reward systems can be used effectively in the workplace.

OB *Is for Everyone*

- Are managers manipulating employees when they link rewards to productivity? Is this ethical?
- Why do some managers do a better job of motivating people than others?
- How important is fairness to you?
- What can you do if you think your salary is unfair?
- When might job redesign be an appropriate motivational tool?
- Ever wonder why employees do some strange things?

Defining Motivation

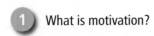
What is motivation?

motivation The internal and external forces that lead an individual to work toward a goal.

Following the lead of professors Gary Latham of the Joseph L. Rotman School of Management at the University of Toronto and Craig Pinder of the Faculty of Business at the University of Victoria, we define **motivation** as the internal and external factors that lead an individual to engage in goal-related behaviour. Motivation can affect the intensity, direction, and persistence a person shows in working toward a goal.[2] *Intensity* is concerned with how hard a person tries. This is what most of us focus on when we talk about motivation. However, high intensity is unlikely to positively affect job performance unless the effort is channelled in a *direction* that is useful. Finally, the effort requires *persistence.* This is a measure of how long a person can maintain his or her effort. Motivated individuals stay with a task long enough to achieve their goal.

Many people incorrectly view motivation as a personal trait—that is, some have it and others do not. Along these lines, Douglas McGregor has proposed two distinct views of human beings. **Theory X**, which is basically negative, suggests that employees dislike work, will try to avoid it, and must be coerced, controlled, or threatened with punishment to achieve goals. **Theory Y**, which is basically positive, suggests that employees like work, are creative, seek responsibility, and will use self-direction and self-control if they are committed to the goals.[3]

Theory X The assumption that employees dislike work, will attempt to avoid it, and must be coerced, controlled, or threatened with punishment to achieve goals.

Theory Y The assumption that employees like work, are creative, seek responsibility, and will exercise self-direction and self-control if they are committed to the goals.

Our knowledge of motivation tells us that neither of these theories fully accounts for employee behaviour. What we know is that motivation is the result of the interaction of the individual and the situation. Certainly, individuals differ in their basic motivational drives. But the same employee who is quickly bored when pulling the lever on a drill press may enthusiastically pull a slot machine lever in Casino Windsor for hours. You may read a thriller at one sitting, yet find it difficult to concentrate on a textbook for more than 20 minutes. It's not necessarily you—it's the situation. So as we analyze the concept of motivation, keep in mind that the level of motivation varies both between individuals and within individuals at different times. What motivates people will also vary for both the individual and the situation.

intrinsic motivators A person's internal desire to do something due to such things as interest, challenge, and personal satisfaction.

extrinsic motivators Motivation that comes from outside the person and includes such things as pay, bonuses, and other tangible rewards.

Motivation theorists talk about **intrinsic motivators** and **extrinsic motivators**. Extrinsic motivators come from outside the person and include such things as pay, bonuses, and other tangible rewards. Intrinsic motivators come from a person's internal desire to do something, motivated by such things as interest, challenge, and personal satisfaction. Individuals are intrinsically motivated when they genuinely care about their work, look for better ways to do it, and are energized and fulfilled by doing it well.[4] The rewards the individual gets from intrinsic motivation come from the work itself, rather than from external factors such as increases in pay or compliments from the boss.

Are individuals mainly intrinsically or extrinsically motivated? Theory X suggests that people are almost exclusively driven by extrinsic motivators. However, Theory Y suggests that people are more intrinsically motivated. Intrinsic and extrinsic motivation may reflect the situation, however, rather than individual personalities.

For example, suppose your mother has asked you to take her to a meeting an hour away and then drop off your twin brother somewhere else. You may be willing to drive her, without any thought of compensation, because it will make you feel nice to do something for her. That is intrinsic motivation. But if you have a love-hate relationship with your brother, you may insist that he buy you lunch for helping out. Lunch would then be an extrinsic motivator—something that came from outside yourself and motivated you to do the task.

Recent research suggests that perceptions of managers regarding whether employees are intrinsically or extrinsically motivated vary by culture.[5] North American managers perceive employees as more extrinsically than intrinsically motivated and tend to give better performance appraisals to employees whom they perceive to be intrinsically motivated. Asian managers perceive employees as equally motivated by intrinsic and extrinsic factors. Latin American managers perceive employees as more intrinsically than extrinsically motivated and give higher performance evaluations to those they believe are more intrinsically motivated. Though managers from the three cultures have different perceptions of their employees, employees in all three cultures said that they were motivated more by intrinsic than extrinsic rewards.

Needs Theories of Motivation

Theories of motivation generally fall into two categories: needs theories and process theories. *Needs theories* describe the types of needs that must be met in order to motivate individuals. *Process theories* help us understand the actual ways in which we and others can be motivated. There are a variety of needs theories, including Maslow's hierarchy of needs, Alderfer's ERG theory,[6] McClelland's theory of needs,[7] and Herzberg's motivation-hygiene theory (sometimes called the *two-factor theory*). We briefly review these to illustrate the basic properties of needs theories.

2 How do needs motivate people?

Maslow's Hierarchy of Needs Theory

It is probably safe to say that the best-known theory of motivation is Abraham Maslow's hierarchy of needs.[8] He hypothesized that every human being has a hierarchy of five needs:

- *Physiological.* Includes hunger, thirst, shelter, sex, and other bodily needs.

- *Safety.* Includes security and protection from physical and emotional harm.

- *Social.* Includes affection, belongingness, acceptance, and friendship.

- *Esteem.* Includes internal esteem factors such as self-respect, autonomy, and achievement; and external esteem factors such as status, recognition, and attention.

- *Self-actualization.* Includes growth, achieving one's potential, and self-fulfillment. This is the drive to become what one is capable of becoming.

As each of these needs becomes substantially satisfied, the next need becomes more important to fulfill. In terms of Exhibit 4-1, the individual moves up the steps of the needs hierarchy. From the perspective of motivation, the theory would say that while no need is ever fully satisfied, a substantially satisfied need no longer motivates. So if you want to motivate someone, according to Maslow, you need to understand what level of the hierarchy that person is currently on and focus on satisfying the needs at or above that level.

Maslow's needs theory continues to be widely recognized some 60 years after he proposed it, particularly among practising managers. The practical significance of Maslow's theory is widely accepted.[9] The theory is intuitive and easy to understand. Unfortunately, research does not generally validate the theory, although research does suggest that people have basic needs that are important to them and motivate them to get along with others.[10] Maslow himself provided no empirical evidence for his theory. Several studies that examined the theory found little support for the prediction that needs form the hierarchy proposed by Maslow, that unsatisfied needs motivate, or that a satisfied need moves a person to seek satisfaction at a new need level.[11]

EXHIBIT 4-1   Maslow's Hierarchy of Needs

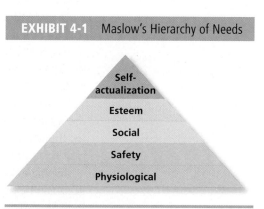

ERG Theory

Clayton Alderfer has reworked Maslow's hierarchy of needs to align it more closely with the empirical research. His revised need hierarchy is called **ERG theory**.[12]

Alderfer argues that there are three groups of core needs—existence, relatedness, and growth—hence the name: ERG theory. The *existence* group is concerned with our basic material existence requirements. They include the items that Maslow considered to be physiological and safety needs. The *relatedness* group is concerned with our desire for maintaining important interpersonal relationships. These social and status desires require interaction with others if they are to be satisfied, and they align with Maslow's social need and the external component of Maslow's esteem need. Finally, the *growth* group is concerned with our intrinsic desire for personal development. This group includes the intrinsic component of Maslow's esteem need and the characteristics included under self-actualization.

Aside from substituting three needs for five, how does Alderfer's ERG theory differ from Maslow's? In contrast to the hierarchy of needs theory, the ERG theory demonstrates that (1) more than one need may be working at the same time, and (2) if the gratification of a higher-level need is stifled, the desire to satisfy a lower-level need increases. ERG theory is more consistent with our knowledge of individual differences among people. Variables such as education, family background, and cultural environment can alter the importance or driving force that a group of needs holds for a particular person.

Several studies have supported ERG theory,[13] but there is also evidence that it does not work in some organizations.[14] Overall, however, ERG theory represents a more valid version of the need hierarchy.

McClelland's Theory of Needs

McClelland's theory of needs was developed by David McClelland and his associates to help explain motivation.[15] The theory focuses on three needs: achievement, power, and affiliation. They are defined as follows:

- *Need for achievement*. The drive to excel, to achieve in relation to a set of standards, to strive to succeed.

- *Need for power*. The need to make others behave in a way that they would not have behaved otherwise.

- *Need for affiliation*. The desire for friendly and close interpersonal relationships.

Some people have a compelling drive to succeed. They are striving for personal achievement rather than the rewards of success per se. They have a desire to do something better or more efficiently than it has been done before. This drive is the achievement need (*nAch*). From research into the achievement need, McClelland found that high achievers differentiate themselves from others by their desire to do things better.[16]

The need for power (*nPow*) is the desire to have impact, to be influential, and to control others. Individuals high in nPow enjoy being "in charge," strive for influence over others, prefer to be placed in competitive and status-oriented situations, and tend to be more concerned with prestige and gaining influence over others than with effective performance.

The third need isolated by McClelland is affiliation (*nAff*). This need has received the least attention from researchers. Individuals with a high affiliation motive strive for friendship, prefer cooperative situations rather than competitive ones, and desire relationships that involve a high degree of mutual understanding.

Relying on an extensive amount of research, some reasonably well-supported predictions can be made based on the relationship of these needs to job performance. First, individuals with a high need to achieve prefer and will be motivated by job situations with personal responsibility, feedback, and an intermediate degree of risk. Second, people with a high achievement need are interested in how well they do personally and not in influencing others to do well. Thus, they may not make good managers.[17] Third, the best managers are high in their need for power and low in their need for affiliation.[18]

Motivation-Hygiene Theory

The motivation-hygiene theory was proposed by psychologist Frederick Herzberg.[19] Herzberg investigated the question "What do people want from their jobs?" in an effort to determine what might lead to a person's success or failure at work.

He found that intrinsic factors—such as achievement, recognition, the work itself, responsibility, advancement, and growth—seem to be related to job satisfaction. Herzberg also found that there were characteristics that led to job dissatisfaction. The factors that caused dissatisfaction were extrinsic—such as company policy and administration, supervision, interpersonal relations, and working conditions.

Herzberg's research led him to conclude that the opposite of satisfaction is not dissatisfaction, as was traditionally believed. Removing dissatisfying characteristics from a job does not necessarily make the job satisfying. As illustrated in Exhibit 4-2, Herzberg proposes a dual continuum: the opposite of "Satisfaction" is "No Satisfaction," and the opposite of "Dissatisfaction" is "No Dissatisfaction."

Herzberg explained that the factors leading to job satisfaction were *motivators* that are separate and distinct from the *hygiene factors* that lead to job dissatisfaction. Thus managers who try to get rid of factors that create job dissatisfaction can create more pleasant workplaces, but not necessarily more motivated ones. Hygiene factors include company policy and administration, supervision, interpersonal relations, working conditions, and salary. When these factors are adequate, people will not be dissatisfied; however, neither will they be satisfied. Motivating factors include achievement, recognition, the work itself, responsibility, and growth. These are the characteristics that people find intrinsically rewarding or motivating.

Herzberg's theory has received some criticism.[20] However, it has been widely read and few managers are unfamiliar with his recommendations. Over the past 40 years the popularity of jobs that allow employees greater responsibility in planning and controlling their work can probably be attributed largely to Herzberg's findings and recommendations.

Summarizing Needs Theories

All needs theories of motivation, including Maslow's hierarchy of needs, Alderfer's ERG theory, McClelland's theory of needs, and Herzberg's motivation-hygiene theory (or the two-factor theory), propose a similar idea: Individuals have needs that, when unsatisfied, will result in motivation. For instance, if you have a need to be praised, you may work harder at your task in order to receive recognition from your manager or other co-workers. Similarly, if you need money and you are asked to do something, within reason, that offers money as a reward, you will be motivated to complete the task in order to earn the money. Where needs theories differ is in the types of needs they consider, and whether they propose a hierarchy of needs

Anne Sweeney is a high achiever. Since joining the Walt Disney Company in 1996, Sweeney has led the transition of the struggling Disney Channel from a premium cable service to a basic network, quintupling the channel's subscriber base. As co-chair of Disney's Media Networks, Sweeney is trying to achieve a turnaround for Disney's ABC Family channel. In addition, when Sweeney became president of ABC Television in 2004, she accepted the challenging goal of lifting the network from its last-place position.

EXHIBIT 4-2   Contrasting Views of Satisfaction and Dissatisfaction

Traditional view

Dissatisfaction   Satisfaction

Herzberg's view

Hygiene Factors

Dissatisfaction   No Dissatisfaction

Motivators

No Satisfaction   Satisfaction

EXHIBIT 4-3   Relationship of Various Needs Theories

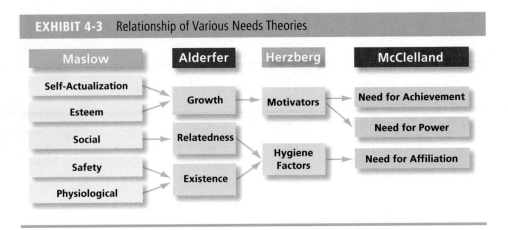

(where some needs have to be satisfied before others) or simply a list of needs. Exhibit 4-3 illustrates the relationship of the four needs theories to each other. While the theories use different names for the needs, and also have different numbers of needs, we can see that they are somewhat consistent in the types of needs addressed. Exhibit 4-4 indicates the contribution of and empirical support for each theory.

EXHIBIT 4-4   Summarizing the Various Needs Theories

Theory	Maslow	Alderfer	Herzberg	McClelland
Is there a hierarchy of needs?	The theory argues that lower-order needs must be satisfied before one progresses to higher-order needs.	More than one need can be important at the same time. If a higher-order need is not being met, the desire to satisfy a lower-level need increases.	Hygiene factors must be met if a person is not to be dissatisfied. They will not lead to satisfaction, however. Motivators lead to satisfaction.	People vary in the types of needs they have. Their motivation and how well they perform in a work situation are related to whether they have a need for achievement, power, or affiliation.
What is the theory's impact/ contribution?	The theory enjoys wide recognition among practising managers. Most managers are familiar with it.	The theory is seen as a more valid version of the need hierarchy. It tells us that achievers will be motivated by jobs that offer personal responsibility, feedback, and moderate risks.	The popularity of giving workers greater responsibility for planning and controlling their work can be attributed to his findings (see, for instance, the job characteristics model). It shows that more than one need may operate at the same time.	The theory tells us that high-need achievers do not necessarily make good managers, since high achievers are more interested in how they do personally.
What empirical support/ criticisms exist?	Research does not generally validate the theory. In particular, there is little support for the hierarchical nature of needs. The theory is criticized for how data were collected and interpreted.	It ignores situational variables.	It is not really a *theory* of motivation: It assumes a link between satisfaction and productivity that was not measured or demonstrated.	It has mixed empirical support, but the theory is consistent with our knowledge of individual differences among people. Good empirical support exists on needs achievement in particular.

Needs Theories in the Workplace

What can we conclude from the needs theories? We can safely say that individuals have needs and that they can be highly motivated to achieve those needs. The types of needs, and their importance, vary by individual, and probably vary over time for the same individual as well. When rewarding individuals, one should consider their specific needs. Some employees may be struggling to make ends meet, while others are looking for more opportunities to reach self-actualization. Individual needs also change over time, depending on one's stage in life. Obviously, in a workplace it would be difficult to design a reward structure that could completely take into account the specific needs of each employee. At Burnaby, BC-based TELUS, employees earn points through a variety of job-related activities. They then choose gifts from a catalogue that lists rewards and their point values. To get an idea of the factors that might motivate you in the workplace, turn to this chapter's *Learning About Yourself Exercise* on pages 148–149.

Process Theories of Motivation

What does the life of a Canadian Football League assistant coach look like? It's definitely not glamorous.[21] The coaches work long hours, they can be fired without notice if the team's owner or the head coach thinks they are responsible for the poor play of the team, and they work long hours without pensions or benefits.

Dan Dorazio, an offensive line coach with the BC Lions, faced a choice after his team beat the Calgary Stampeders: stay in Calgary overnight, or drive home to Abbotsford, BC, and arrive just before midnight. Tired after a long day of coaching, he still was not able to rest. He was expected to have the Calgary game tape analyzed before sunrise, so that the coaches could plan the post-game practice with the players later in the afternoon. Dorazio chose to drive home, and, after a brief nap, go into his office at 4 a.m.

What would make an assistant coach show up for work, day after day, under these conditions?

While needs theories identify the different needs that could be used to motivate individuals, process theories focus on the broader picture of *how* someone can set about motivating another individual. Process theories include *expectancy theory* and *goal-setting theory*. Focusing greater attention on these process theories might help you understand how to motivate yourself or someone else.

3 Are there other ways to motivate people?

Expectancy Theory

Currently, one of the most widely accepted explanations of motivation is Victor Vroom's **expectancy theory**.[22]

From a practical perspective, expectancy theory says that an employee will be motivated to exert a high level of effort when he or she believes the following:

- That the effort will lead to good performance

- That good performance will lead to organizational rewards, such as a bonus, a salary increase, or a promotion

- That the rewards will satisfy his or her personal goals

The theory, therefore, focuses on the three relationships (expectancy, instrumentality, and valence) illustrated in Exhibit 4-5 on page 120 and described below. This exhibit also provides an example of how you might apply the theory.

expectancy theory The theory that individuals are motivated based upon their evaluation of whether their effort will lead to good performance, whether good performance will be followed by a given outcome, and whether that outcome is attractive to them.

Effort-Performance Relationship

The effort-performance relationship is commonly called **expectancy**. It refers to the individual's perception of how probable it is that exerting a given amount of effort will

expectancy The belief that effort is related to performance.

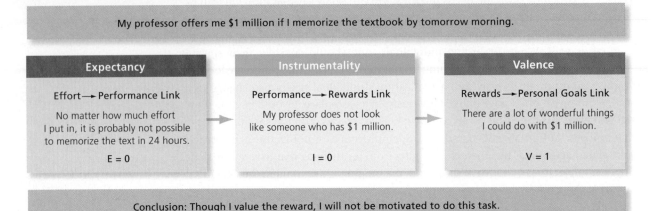

EXHIBIT 4-5   How Does Expectancy Theory Work?

My professor offers me $1 million if I memorize the textbook by tomorrow morning.

Expectancy	Instrumentality	Valence
Effort → Performance Link	Performance → Rewards Link	Rewards → Personal Goals Link
No matter how much effort I put in, it is probably not possible to memorize the text in 24 hours.	My professor does not look like someone who has $1 million.	There are a lot of wonderful things I could do with $1 million.
E = 0	I = 0	V = 1

Conclusion: Though I value the reward, I will not be motivated to do this task.

lead to good performance. For example, employees are sometimes asked to perform tasks for which they do not have suitable skills or training. When that is the case, they will be less motivated to try hard, because they already believe that they will not be able to accomplish what they are being asked to do. Expectancy can be expressed as a probability, and ranges from 0 to 1.

In the opening vignette, we saw that the BC Lions players were willing to work hard for a demanding coach. These players likely felt that their efforts, such as spending extra time training, would lead to good performance.

In general, an employee's expectancy is influenced by the following:

- Self-esteem

- Previous success

- Help from supervisors and subordinates

- Information

- Proper materials and equipment[23]

Coach Wally Buono's observation on motivation highlights the importance of the expectancy link in motivating individuals. According to Buono, motivation "is really the function of the person that you hire . . . . You need to be able to give [staff and players] the proper setting . . . atmosphere . . . tools so they're not hindered from doing what they have to do."[24]

The *Point/Counterpoint* discussion on page 148 further examines whether failure motivates or demotivates.

Performance-Rewards Relationship

Are managers manipulating employees when they link rewards to productivity? Is this ethical?

instrumentality The belief that performance is related to rewards.

The performance-rewards relationship is commonly called **instrumentality**. It refers to the individual's perception of whether performing at a particular level will lead to the attainment of a desired outcome. In particular, will the performance be acknowledged by those who have the power to allocate rewards? Instrumentality ranges from −1 to +1. A negative instrumentality indicates that high performance reduces the chances of getting the desired outcome. An instrumentality of 0 indicates that there is no relationship between performance and receiving the desired outcome.

In a study by the Angus Reid Group, only 44 percent of employees said the workplace recognizes employees who excel at their job.[25] Thus, one possible source of low motivation is the employee's belief that no matter how hard he or she works, the performance will not be recognized. BC Lions offensive line coach Dan Dorazio works long hours at his job because he does feel that his efforts are recognized by the head coach and by the players on the team.

Rewards–Personal Goals Relationship

Why do some managers do a better job of motivating people than others?

The rewards–personal goals relationship is commonly called **valence**. It refers to the degree to which organizational rewards satisfy an individual's personal goals or needs and the attractiveness of those potential rewards for the individual. Unfortunately, many managers are limited in the rewards they can distribute, which makes it difficult to personalize rewards. Moreover, some managers incorrectly assume that all employees want the same thing. They overlook the motivational effects of differentiating rewards. In either case, employee motivation may be lower because the specific need the employee has is not being met through the reward structure. Valence ranges from –1 (very undesirable reward) to +1 (very desirable reward).

valence The value or importance an individual places on a reward.

Vancouver-based Radical Entertainment, creator of such digital entertainment as *Crash® Mind Over Mutant* and *Scarface: The World Is Yours,* makes sure it meets the needs of its employees because it does not want to lose them to the United States.[26] The company employs a "Radical fun guru" whose job is to make the workplace so much fun that no one wants to leave. The company provides free food all day, including catered lunches a few times a week, and there is a log cabin on-site, fitted with big screens, DVDs, and gaming equipment, where employees can take time out to recharge during their long workdays. Radical Entertainment offers these benefits to meet the needs of its young employees, who find greater motivation from being part of a cool workplace than having a bigger pension plan.

Expectancy Theory in the Workplace

Does expectancy theory work? Although it has its critics,[27] most of the research evidence supports the theory.[28] Research in cross-cultural settings has also indicated support for expectancy theory.[29]

Exhibit 4-6 shows how managers can increase the motivation of employees, using insights from expectancy theory. Managers can take

Golfers such as Ontario's Alena Sharp illustrate the effectiveness of the expectancy theory of motivation, where rewards are tied to effort and outcome. Players on the LPGA tour are paid strictly according to their performance, unlike members of professional sports teams. Sharp's first LPGA Tour victory came in 2004. As Sharp put more effort into her play, she increased her earnings. In 2007, she earned $223 258, which greatly exceeded her earnings of $97 422 for 2006.

EXHIBIT 4-6   Steps to Increasing Motivation, Using Expectancy Theory

Improving Expectancy	Improving Instrumentality	Improving Valence
Improve the ability of the individual to perform.	Increase the individual's belief that performance will lead to reward.	Make sure that the reward is meaningful to the individual.
• Make sure employees have skills for the task. • Provide training. • Assign reasonable tasks and goals.	• Observe and recognize performance. • Deliver rewards as promised. • Indicate to employees how previous good performance led to greater rewards.	• Ask employees what rewards they value. • Give rewards that are valued.

steps to improve expectancy, instrumentality, and valence. *OB in the Street* demonstrates how expectancy theory works on the golf course.

OB IN THE STREET

What It's Like to Play Next to Tiger Woods

Are people less motivated if they expect to lose? A recent study by Berkeley professor Jennifer Brown considered whether playing in a tournament with Tiger Woods increased other golfers' performances or decreased them.[30] On the one hand, individuals might be more motivated to try hard when in the presence of a great player. Alternatively, individuals might feel that they were less likely to win, and thus not try as hard.

Brown noted that between 1999 and 2006, players who had to qualify for PGA Tour events averaged 1 to 4 strokes under par. Players who automatically qualified averaged 3 to 6 strokes under par. Woods, by contrast, averaged 10 to 14 strokes under par. In games where Woods played, however, players averaged about a stroke more per tournament.

If money motivated unconditionally, then there should not be any effect on other players if Woods is playing in the tournament. However, if players believe they are less likely to win the top prize, they may be less motivated by the money.

Brown found that the better players tended to play worse than their average when Woods was playing. She also found that when Woods was in his slump period (2003 and 2004), the top competitors' scores were not affected when he played.

Brown's findings suggest that when players are less likely to expect to win, they do not play as well.

Goal-Setting Theory

You have heard the phrase a number of times: "Just do your best. That's all anyone can ask." But what does "do your best" mean? Do we ever know if we have achieved that vague goal? Might you have done better in your high school English class if your parents had said, "You should strive for 75 percent or higher on all your work in English" instead of "do your best"?

goal What an individual is trying to accomplish.

The research on goal setting by Edwin Locke and his colleague Professor Gary Latham at the University of Toronto shows that intentions to work toward a goal are a major source of work motivation.[31] A **goal** is "what an individual is trying to accomplish; it is the object or aim of an action."[32] Goals tell an employee what needs to be done and how much effort will need to be expended.[33]

Goal-setting theory has an impressive base of research support. But as a manager, how do you put the theory into action? That is often left up to the individual manager or leader. Some managers explicitly set aggressive performance targets—what General Electric called "stretch goals." For example, some CEOs, such as Procter & Gamble's A. G. Laffey and SAP's Hasso Plattner, are known for the demanding performance goals they set. The problem with leaving it up to the individual manager is that, in many cases, managers do not set goals. A recent survey revealed that when asked whether their job had clearly defined goals, only a minority of employees agreed.[34]

management by objectives (MBO) An approach to goal setting in which specific measurable goals are jointly set by managers and employees; progress on goals is periodically reviewed, and rewards are allocated on the basis of this progress.

A more systematic way to implement goal setting is through a **management by objectives (MBO)** program.[35] In MBO, managers and employees jointly set performance

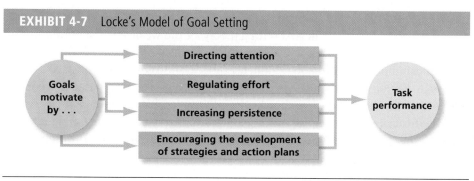

EXHIBIT 4-7   Locke's Model of Goal Setting

Source: Adapted from E. A. Locke and G. P. Latham, *A Theory of Goal Setting and Task Performance* (Englewood Cliffs, NJ: Prentice Hall, 1980). Reprinted with permission of Edwin A. Locke.

goals that are tangible, verifiable, and measurable; progress on goals is periodically reviewed, and rewards are allocated on the basis of this progress.

How Does Goal Setting Motivate?

According to Locke, goal setting motivates in four ways (see Exhibit 4-7):[36]

- *Goals direct attention.* Goals indicate where individuals should direct their efforts when they are choosing among things to do. For instance, recognizing that an important assignment is due in a few days, goal setting may encourage you to say no when friends invite you to a movie this evening.

- *Goals regulate effort.* Goals suggest how much effort an individual should put into a given task. For instance, if earning a high mark in accounting is more important to you than earning a high mark in organizational behaviour (OB), you will likely put more effort into studying accounting.

- *Goals increase persistence.* Persistence represents the effort spent on a task over time. When people keep goals in mind, they will work hard on them, even in the face of obstacles.

- *Goals encourage the development of strategies and action plans.* Once goals are set, individuals can develop plans for achieving those goals. For instance, a goal to become more fit may include plans to join a gym, work out with friends, and change eating habits.

In order for goals to be effective, they should be "SMART." SMART stands for

- Specific: Individuals know exactly what is to be achieved.

- Measurable: The goals proposed can be tracked and reviewed.

- Attainable: The goals, even if difficult, are reasonable and achievable.

- Results-oriented: The goals should support the vision of the organization.

- Time-bound: The goals are to be achieved within a stated time.

From Concepts to Skills on page 155 gives further ideas on how to effectively engage in goal setting.

Goal-setting theory is consistent with expectancy theory. The goals can be considered the effort-performance link—in other words, the goals determine what must be done. Feedback can be considered the performance-rewards relationship, where the individual's efforts are recognized. Finally, the implication of goal setting is that the achievement of the goals will result in intrinsic satisfaction (and may of course be linked to external rewards).

Contingency Factors in Goal Setting

Are there any contingencies in goal-setting theory, or can we take it as a universal truth that difficult and specific goals will always lead to higher performance? Feedback is one of the most important factors that influences the relationship between goals and performance. Recent research suggests that when individuals receive negative feedback, they lower their goals, and when they receive positive feedback, they raise their goals.[37]

self-efficacy An individual's belief that he or she is capable of performing a task.

Self-efficacy (also known as *social cognitive theory* or *social learning theory*) refers to an individual's belief that he or she is capable of performing a task.[38] The higher your self-efficacy, the more confidence you have in your ability to succeed in a task. So, in difficult situations, people with low self-efficacy are more likely to lessen their effort or give up altogether, while those with high self-efficacy will try harder to master the challenge.[39] In addition, individuals high in self-efficacy seem to respond to negative feedback with increased effort and motivation, while those low in self-efficacy are likely to lessen their effort when given negative feedback.[40]

Managers can help their employees achieve high levels of self-efficacy by bringing together insights from goal-setting theory and self-efficacy theory. As Exhibit 4-8 shows, when a manager sets difficult goals for employees, this leads employees to have a higher level of self-efficacy, and also leads them to set higher goals for their own performance. Why is this the case? Research has shown that setting difficult goals for people communicates confidence. For example, imagine that your boss sets a high goal for you, and you learn it is higher than the goals she has set for your co-workers. How would you interpret this? As long as you did not feel you were being picked on, you would probably think, "Well, I guess my boss thinks I'm capable of performing better than others." This then sets into motion a psychological process in which you are more confident in yourself (higher self-efficacy) and you set higher personal goals, causing you to perform better both in the workplace and outside it.

In addition to feedback and self-efficacy, three other factors have been found to influence the goals-performance relationship. These are goal commitment, task characteristics, and national culture. Goal-setting theory presupposes that an individual is committed to the goal; that is, he or she is determined not to lower or abandon the

EXHIBIT 4-8   Joint Effects of Goals and Self-Efficacy on Performance

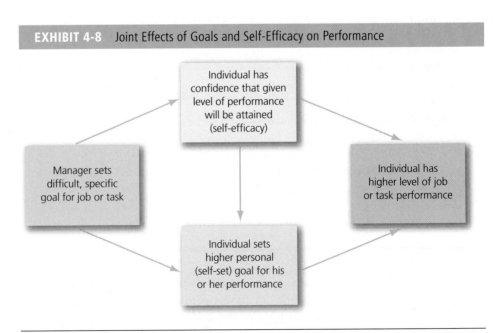

Source: Based on E. A. Locke and G. P. Latham, "Building a Practically Useful Theory of Goal Setting and Task Motivation: A 35-Year Odyssey," *American Psychologist*, September 2002, pp. 705–717.

goal. This is most likely to occur when goals are made public, when the individual has an internal locus of control, and when the goals are self-set rather than assigned.[41]

Research indicates that individual goal setting does not work equally well on all tasks. The evidence suggests that goals seem to have a greater effect on performance when tasks are simple rather than complex; well-learned rather than new; and independent rather than interdependent.[42] On interdependent tasks, group goals are preferable. Finally, goal-setting theory is culture-bound. It's well adapted to countries such as Canada and the United States because its key components align reasonably well with North American cultures. Following the GLOBE measures from Chapter 3, it assumes that employees will be reasonably independent (not too high a score on power distance), that managers and employees will seek challenging goals (low in uncertainty avoidance), and that performance is considered important by both (high in performance orientation). So do not expect goal setting to necessarily lead to higher employee performance in countries such as Portugal or Chile, where the opposite conditions exist.

Our overall conclusion is that intentions—as articulated in terms of hard and specific goals—are a potent motivating force. Under the proper conditions, they can lead to higher performance.

Responses to the Reward System

Geroy Simon, a receiver for the BC Lions football team, felt he was in a pretty good position when he negotiated for a contract extension in May 2006.[43] He had the most receptions and most yards of all BC Lions receivers in 2005 and ranked sixth in team history for receptions and touchdowns. But he was not content with just considering how he stood on his team. He also looked to the salary of receivers on other teams, focusing in particular on Edmonton Eskimos receiver Jason Tucker, the CFL's 2005 receiving yards leader.

"I know what I'm worth," said Simon, who knew that Tucker had already signed a contract for close to $200 000 earlier in the year. "I think it'll be a short negotiation once we really get going." Ultimately, Simon signed a four-year extension to his contract with pay similar to Tucker's. He led the league in receiving in 2007 and finished as the second best receiver in 2008. Did the higher salary motivate Simon to be a better player? Did he make the right salary comparison?

To a large extent, motivation theories are about rewards. The theories suggest that individuals have needs and will exert effort to have those needs met. The needs theories specifically identify those needs. Goal-setting and expectancy theories portray processes by which individuals act and then receive desirable rewards (intrinsic or extrinsic) for their behaviour.

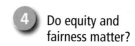 **4** Do equity and fairness matter?

Three additional process theories ask us to consider how individuals respond to rewards. *Equity theory* suggests that individuals evaluate and interpret rewards. *Fair process* goes one step further, suggesting that employees are sensitive to a variety of fairness issues in the workplace that extend beyond the reward system but also affect employee motivation. *Cognitive evaluation theory* examines how individuals respond to the introduction of extrinsic rewards for intrinsically satisfying activities.

Equity Theory

How important is fairness to you?

Equity theory suggests that employees compare their job inputs (i.e., effort, experience, education, competence, creativity) and outcomes (i.e., salary levels, raises, recognition, challenging assignments, working conditions) with those of others. We perceive what we get from a job situation (the outcomes mentioned above) in relation to what we put into it (the inputs mentioned

equity theory Individuals compare their job inputs and outcomes with those of others and then respond so as to eliminate any inequities.

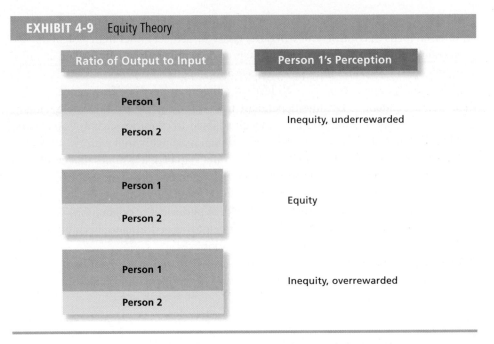

EXHIBIT 4-9   Equity Theory

above), and then we compare our outcome-input ratio with the outcome-input ratio of relevant others. (This idea is illustrated in Exhibit 4-9.) If we perceive our ratio to be equal to that of the relevant others with whom we compare ourselves, a state of equity is said to exist. We perceive our situation as fair—that justice prevails. When we see the ratio as unequal, we experience this as inequity.

Imagine that you wrote a case analysis for your marketing professor and spent 18 hours researching and writing it. Your classmate spent 6 hours doing her analysis. Each of you received a mark of 75 percent. It is likely that you would perceive this as unfair, as you worked considerably harder (i.e., exerted more effort) than your classmate. J. Stacy Adams has proposed that those experiencing inequity are motivated to do something to correct it.[44] Thus, you might be inclined to spend considerably less time on your next assignment for your marketing professor.

What Happens When We Feel Treated Inequitably?

What can you do if you think your salary is unfair?

When individuals feel that they have been treated inequitably, they generally act to reduce that inequity. Based on equity theory, they can be predicted to make one of six choices, with some of them being more negative to the organization than others.[45] We can illustrate these by considering possible responses that BC Lions receiver Geroy Simon can make if he thinks his salary is unfair compared with that of the other receivers in his reference group.

- *Change their inputs* (for example, Simon can decide to exert less effort).

- *Change their outcomes* (for example, Simon can work harder than ever to show that he really does deserve higher pay—as he did in the 2006 season, when he won Most Valuable Player).

- *Adjust perceptions of self* (for example, Simon could think to himself, "Maybe I don't really have the same experience as some of the other guys playing receiver").

- *Adjust perceptions of others* (for example, Simon could think, "Jason Tucker of the Eskimos has worked at his job a lot longer, and may deserve greater pay").

- *Choose a different referent* (for example, Simon could consider what other receivers with his same statistics receive).

- *Leave the field* (for example, Simon could start looking at other teams, hoping that he can be picked up by one of them at the end of the season).

Bear in mind that being treated equitably is not the same as being treated equally. Equity theory tells us that people who perform better should observe that they are rewarded better than those who do not perform as well. Thus poor performers should also observe that they receive lesser rewards than those who perform at a higher level. Paying equally would mean that everyone is paid the same, regardless of performance.

RESEARCH FINDINGS: EQUITY THEORY

Equity theory has generally been supported, with a few minor qualifications.[46] First, inequities created by overpayment do not seem to have a significant impact on behaviour in most work situations. Apparently, people have a great deal more tolerance of overpayment inequities than of underpayment inequities, or are better able to rationalize them. Second, not all people are equity sensitive.[47] For example, some employees simply do not worry about how their rewards compare with those of others. Predictions from equity theory are unlikely to be very accurate with these individuals.

After the 2005 season ended for the BC Lions, Geroy Simon's contract was up for renewal. He wanted a similar salary to Edmonton Eskimo's receiver Jason Tucker, based on his performance during the year. Simon's salary was increased and he led the league in receiving in 2007 and finished as the second best receiver in 2008.

Equity Theory in the Workplace

It is important to note that while most research on equity theory has focused on pay, employees seem to look for equity in the distribution of other organizational rewards. For instance, it has been shown that the use of high-status job titles, as well as large and lavishly furnished offices, may function as desirable outcomes for some employees in their equity equations.[48]

Equity theory demonstrates that, for most employees, motivation is influenced significantly by relative rewards, as well as by absolute rewards. However, some key issues are still unclear.[49] For instance, how do employees handle conflicting equity signals, such as when unions point to other employee groups who are substantially *better off*, while management argues how much things have *improved*? How do employees define inputs and outcomes? How do they combine and weigh their inputs and outcomes to arrive at totals? Despite these problems, equity theory continues to offer some important insights into employee motivation.

Fair Process and Treatment

Recent research has been directed at redefining what is meant by equity, or fairness.[50] Historically, equity theory focused on **distributive justice**, or the perceived fairness of the *amount* and *allocation* of rewards among individuals. But increasingly, equity is thought of from the standpoint of **organizational justice**, which we define as an overall perception of what is fair in the workplace. In other words, under organizational justice, fairness or equity can be subjective, and it resides in the perception of

distributive justice The perceived fairness of the amount and allocation of rewards among individuals.

organizational justice An overall perception of what is fair in the workplace.

procedural justice The perceived fairness of the process used to determine the distribution of rewards.

interactional justice The quality of the interpersonal treatment received from a manager.

the person. Thus, organizational justice notes that people also care about **procedural justice**—the perceived fairness of the *process* used to determine the distribution of rewards. (This includes having a voice in a decision and feeling that the outcome is adequately explained.) And they care, too, about **interactional justice**—the quality of the *interpersonal treatment* received from a manager.[51] (Being treated with dignity, concern, and respect are examples.) Exhibit 4-10 shows a model of organizational justice.

Why does the manner in which an employee is treated matter? When people are treated in an unjust manner (at least in their own eyes), they respond by retaliating (for example, by badmouthing a supervisor).[52] Because interactional justice or injustice is intimately tied to the person who communicates the information (usually one's supervisor), whereas procedural injustice often results from impersonal policies, we would expect perceptions of injustice to be towards one's supervisor. Generally, that is what the evidence suggests.[53]

Of these three forms of justice, distributive justice is most strongly related to satisfaction with outcomes (for example, satisfaction with pay) and organizational commitment. Procedural justice relates most strongly to job satisfaction, employee trust, withdrawal from the organization, job performance, and organizational citizenship behaviour. There is less evidence on how interactional justice affects employee behaviour.[54]

Managers can take several steps to foster employees' perceptions of fairness. First, they should realize that employees are especially sensitive to unfairness in procedures when bad news has to be communicated (that is, when distributive justice is low). Thus, when managers have bad news to communicate, it's especially important to openly share information about how allocation decisions are made, follow consistent and unbiased procedures, and engage in similar practices to increase the perception of

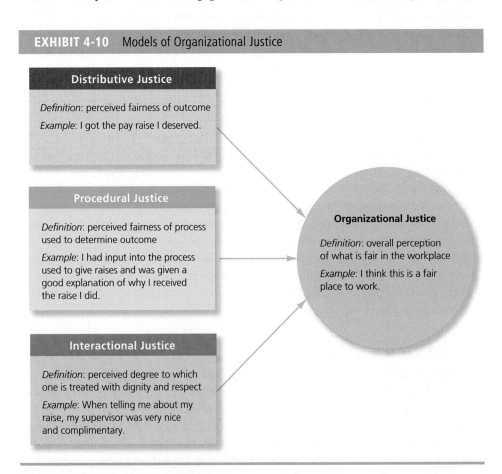

EXHIBIT 4-10   Models of Organizational Justice

Distributive Justice

Definition: perceived fairness of outcome

Example: I got the pay raise I deserved.

Procedural Justice

Definition: perceived fairness of process used to determine outcome

Example: I had input into the process used to give raises and was given a good explanation of why I received the raise I did.

Interactional Justice

Definition: perceived degree to which one is treated with dignity and respect

Example: When telling me about my raise, my supervisor was very nice and complimentary.

Organizational Justice

Definition: overall perception of what is fair in the workplace

Example: I think this is a fair place to work.

procedural justice. Second, when addressing perceived injustices, managers need to focus their actions on the source of the problem. Professor Daniel Skarlicki at the Sauder School of Business at the University of British Columbia has found that it is when unfavourable outcomes are combined with unfair procedures or poor interpersonal treatment that resentment and retaliation (e.g., theft, badmouthing, sabotage) are most likely.[55]

Case Incident—Bullying Bosses on page 153 describes what could happen to the motivation and behaviour of employees who have bullies for bosses.

Cognitive Evaluation Theory

Several researchers suggest that the introduction of extrinsic rewards, such as pay, for work effort that was *previously rewarding intrinsically* (i.e., that was personally satisfying) will tend to decrease the overall level of a person's motivation.[56] This proposal—which has come to be called **cognitive evaluation theory**—has been extensively researched, and a large number of studies have been supportive.[57] Additionally, Alfie Kohn, often cited for his work on rewards, argues that people are actually punished by rewards and do inferior work when they are enticed by money, grades, or other incentives. His extensive review of incentive studies concluded that "rewards usually improve performance only at extremely simple—indeed, mindless—tasks, and even then they improve only quantitative performance."[58]

cognitive evaluation theory Offering extrinsic rewards (e.g., pay) for work effort that was previously rewarding intrinsically will tend to decrease the overall level of a person's motivation.

Extrinsic vs. Intrinsic Rewards

Historically, motivation theorists have generally assumed that intrinsic motivators are independent of extrinsic motivators. That is, the stimulation of one would not affect the other. But cognitive evaluation theory suggests otherwise. It argues that when extrinsic rewards are used by organizations as payoffs for superior performance, the intrinsic rewards, which are derived from individuals doing what they like to do, are reduced.

In other words, when extrinsic rewards are given to someone for performing an interesting task, it causes intrinsic interest in the task itself to decline. For instance, although a taxi driver expects to be paid for taking your best friend to the airport, you do not expect your friend to pay you if you volunteer to drive her to the airport. In fact, the offer of pay might diminish your pleasure in doing a favour for your friend.

Why would such an outcome occur? The popular explanation is that the individual experiences a loss of control over his or her own behaviour when it is being rewarded by external sources. This causes the previous intrinsic motivation to diminish. Extrinsic rewards can produce a shift—from an internal to an external explanation—in an individual's perception of why he or she works on a task. If you are reading a novel a week because your contemporary literature instructor requires you to, you can attribute your reading behaviour to an external source. If you stop reading novels the moment the course ends, this is more evidence that your behaviour was due to an external source. However, if you find yourself continuing to read a novel a week when the course ends, your natural inclination is to say, "I must enjoy reading novels because I'm still reading one a week!"

 RESEARCH FINDINGS: EXTRINSIC AND INTRINSIC REWARDS

Although further research is needed to clarify some of the current ambiguity, the evidence does lead us to conclude that the interdependence of extrinsic and intrinsic rewards is a real phenomenon.[59] A large body of research shows that large external rewards can undermine the positive performance of employees.[60] When employees work for a large reward, they will explain their behaviour through that reward—"I did it for the money." However, in the absence of large rewards, employees are more likely to reflect on the interesting nature of the work or the benefits of being an organizational member to explain their behaviour. When an organization provides employees with intrinsically interesting work, they will often work longer and harder than one might predict from the actual external rewards.

In studies dating back to the 1940s, employees have always ranked other items, such as being shown appreciation for work done, feeling "in" on things, and having interesting work, as being more important to them than their salaries.[61] Employees at both Southwest Airlines and AES, an independent producer of electrical power with offices in the United States, Argentina, China, Hungary, and other countries, indicated that they appreciated the positive working climates of these organizations more than the financial rewards they received.[62]

Increasing Intrinsic Motivation

Our discussion of motivation theories and our discussion of how to apply motivation theories in the workplace focuses mainly on improving extrinsic motivation. Professor Kenneth Thomas of the Naval Postgraduate School in Monterey, California, has developed a model of intrinsic motivation that draws from the job characteristics model and cognitive evaluation theory.[63] He identifies four key rewards that increase an individual's intrinsic motivation:

- *Sense of choice.* The opportunity to select what one will do and perform the way one thinks best. Individuals can use their own judgment to carry out the task.

- *Sense of competence.* The feeling of accomplishment for doing a good job. People are more likely to feel a sense of accomplishment when they carry out challenging tasks.

- *Sense of meaningfulness.* The opportunity to pursue worthwhile tasks. Individuals feel good about what they are doing and believe that what they are doing matters.

- *Sense of progress.* The feeling of accomplishment that one is making progress on a task, and that it is moving forward. Individuals feel that they are spending their time wisely in doing their jobs.

Thomas also identified four sets of behaviours managers can use to create intrinsic rewards for their employees:

- *Leading for choice.* Empowering employees and delegating tasks

- *Leading for competence.* Supporting and coaching employees

- *Leading for meaningfulness.* Inspiring employees and modelling desired behaviours

- *Leading for progress.* Monitoring and rewarding employees

Exhibit 4-11 presents the building blocks that increase the likelihood that intrinsic rewards are motivational.

Creating a Motivating Workplace: Rewards and Job Redesign

How can rewards and job design motivate employees?

Organizations use specific incentives to motivate individuals, teams, and the entire organization to achieve organizational goals such as productivity, reduced turnover, and leadership effectiveness. They can also redesign jobs to create more motivating workplaces.

EXHIBIT 4-11   Building Blocks for Intrinsic Rewards

Leading for Choice	Leading for Competence
• Delegated authority • Trust in workers • Security (no punishment) for honest mistakes • A clear purpose • Information	• Knowledge • Positive feedback • Skill recognition • Challenge • High, noncomparative standards
Leading for Meaningfulness	**Leading for Progress**
• A noncynical climate • Clearly identified passions • An exciting vision • Relevant task purposes • Whole tasks	• A collaborative climate • Milestones • Celebrations • Access to customers • Measurement of improvement

Source: Reprinted with permission of the publisher. From *Intrinsic Motivation at Work: Building Energy and Commitment.* Copyright © K. Thomas. Berrett-Koehler Publishers Inc., San Francisco, CA. All rights reserved. www.bkconnection.com.

Employee Recognition: Showing People That They Matter

Expectancy theory tells us that a key component of motivation is the link between performance and reward (that is, having your behaviour recognized). Employee recognition programs cover a wide spectrum of activities. They range from a spontaneous and private "thank you" on up to widely publicized formal programs in which specific types of behaviour are encouraged and the procedures for attaining recognition are clearly identified.[64] Recognition may not be enough for some jobs, however, as Exhibit 4-12 suggests.

Sometimes, however, the link between reward and performance is unclear, as the *Ethical Dilemma Exercise* on page 152 shows.

A survey of Canadian firms in 2004 by Hewitt Associates found that 34 percent of companies recognized individual or group achievements with cash or merchandise.[65] At the same time, recognizing employees can cost little or no money. Toronto-based KPMG is one company that has created a "thank-you culture" to recognize good work and deeds. Recognition is a way of "reinforcing our corporate values," says Val Duffey, KPMG's Toronto-based human resource director. "We acknowledge that recognition is critical to motivating, satisfying and retaining the best employees."[66] Not all employees feel they get recognition, however. In a recent *Globe and Mail* web poll, 27 percent of respondents said that they had never received a compliment from their bosses, and 10 percent said that they had received the last compliment from their bosses over a year ago.[67]

Organizations can recognize employees in numerous ways. The *Globe and Mail* awards the Stephen Godfrey Prize for Newsroom Citizenship. Vancouver-based Purdy's Chocolates recognizes employees on their birthdays and

EXHIBIT 4-12

Source: From the *Wall Street Journal,* October 21, 1997. Reprinted by permission of Cartoon Features Syndicate.

Purdy's Chocolates shows its employees that they matter. The company pays its employees about 20 percent higher than the industry average and provides them with medical and dental benefits. It also has a variety of recognition programs, which signal to employees that they are valued as important contributors to the company's success. As a result, turnover at the company is low—the average employee has been with the company for nine years. The company was voted by its 800 employees as one of the "50 Best Employers in Canada" in 2002, 2004, 2008, and 2009.

variable-pay programs Reward programs in which a portion of an employee's pay is based on some individual and/or organizational measure of performance.

when they move, get married, or have children. As well, Purdy's recognizes employees who reach their five-year anniversary with the company at an annual luncheon, with out-of-town employees flown in for the event.[68] Other ways of recognizing performance include sending personal notes or emails for good performance, putting employees on prestigious committees, sending them for training, and giving someone an assistant for a day to help clear backlogs.

Employee recognition may reduce turnover in organizations, particularly that of good employees. When executives were asked the reasons why employees left for jobs with other companies, 34 percent said it was due to lack of recognition and praise, compared with 29 percent who mentioned low compensation, 13 percent who mentioned limited authority, and 8 percent who cited personality problems.[69]

Variable-Pay Programs: Improving Productivity

A large body of research suggests that pay is far more motivational than some motivation theorists such as Maslow and Herzberg suggest.[70] Consistent with this research, managers generally look at ways to manipulate pay to improve performance by considering a variety of incentive schemes. Some of these are individually based, some are team-based, and some reward all members of the organization for working together toward productivity goals. The rewards used are all forms of **variable-pay programs**. What differentiates these forms of compensation from more traditional programs is that they do not pay a person only for time on the job or seniority. Instead, a portion of an employee's pay is based on some individual and/or organizational measure of performance. Unlike more traditional base-pay programs, with variable pay there is no guarantee that just because you made $60 000 last year, you will make the same amount this year. Instead, earnings fluctuate annually based on performance.[71]

The number of employees who have variable-pay programs has been rising in Canada. A 2007 nationwide survey of Canadian firms by Hewitt Associates found that 80 percent of them have variable-pay programs in place, compared with 43 percent in 1994.[72] Today, more than 70 percent of US companies have some form of variable-pay plan, up from only about 5 percent in 1970.[73] Unfortunately, recent survey data indicate that most employees still do not see a strong connection between pay and performance. Only 29 percent say that when they do a good job their performance is rewarded.[74] Variable-pay programs are more common among non-unionized companies; only about 8 percent of unionized employees were subject to variable-pay plans in 2004.[75]

Variable-pay programs can be applied at individual, team, and company-wide levels, making it possible to link rewards to the appropriate level of performance. Below, we briefly describe some examples of incentives at these different levels of the organization.

Individual-Based Incentives

Piece-Rate Wages Piece-rate wages are one of the earliest forms of individual performance pay. They have long been popular as a means for compensating production employees. In a **piece-rate pay plan**, employees are paid a fixed sum for each unit of production completed. When an employee gets no base salary and is paid only for what he or she produces, this is a pure piece-rate plan. People who work at baseball parks selling peanuts and soft drinks frequently are paid this way. They might get to keep 25 cents for every bag of peanuts they sell. If they sell 200 bags during a game, they make $50. If they sell only 40 bags, their take is a mere $10. Sales associates who are paid commissions based on sales also have a form of piece-rate pay plan.

Many organizations use a modified piece-rate pay plan, where employees earn a base hourly wage plus a piece-rate differential. For example, a legal typist might be paid an hourly wage plus a certain rate per typed page. Or a sales associate might be paid a base salary plus commissions on sales. Such modified plans provide a basic security net while still offering a productivity incentive.

Bonuses Bonuses are becoming an increasingly popular form of individual incentive in Canada.[76] They are used by such companies as Molson Coors Brewing Company, Ontario Hydro Energy, and the Bank of Montreal. Bonuses can be used for reasons other than improving performance. A recent study showed that 39 percent of small and medium-sized companies used bonuses as a retention strategy, so that employees would not look for jobs elsewhere.[77] In spring 2006, in the hopes of having no labour unrest during the 2010 Olympics, the BC provincial government offered bonuses of about $3000 to every public sector employee whose union signed a four-year (or longer) collective agreement. As a result of the bonus offer, all affected unions settled their contracts before the March 31 deadline set by the provincial government.

> **piece-rate pay plan** An individual-based incentive plan in which employees are paid a fixed sum for each unit of production completed.

Using employee performance software, convenience store retailer 7-Eleven measures the efforts of 2400 store managers and 30 000 employees at company-owned stores in Canada and the United States. The company ties employee compensation to performance outcomes based on 7-Eleven's five fundamental strategic initiatives—product assortment, value, quality, service, and cleanliness—as well as for meeting goals set for new products. The system identifies top performers and rewards them with incentive bonuses.

Bonuses are not free from organizational politics (which we discuss in Chapter 7), and they can sometimes result in negative behaviour. When using bonuses, managers should be mindful of potential unexpected behaviours that may arise when employees try to ensure that they will receive bonuses.

Group-Based Incentives

Gainsharing

gainsharing A group-based incentive plan in which improvements in group productivity determine the total amount of money to be shared.

The variable-pay program that has received the most attention in recent years is undoubtedly **gainsharing**.[78] This is a formula-based group incentive plan. Improvements in group productivity—from one period to another—determine the total amount of money that is to be allocated. The productivity savings can be divided between the company and employees in any number of ways, but 50-50 is fairly typical.

Gainsharing differs from profit-sharing, discussed below. Gainsharing focuses on productivity gains rather than profits, and so it rewards specific behaviours that are less influenced by external factors. Employees in a gainsharing plan can receive incentive awards even when the organization is not profitable.

Gainsharing was initially popular only in large unionized manufacturing companies,[79] such as Montreal-based Molson Coors Brewing Company and Montreal-based Hydro-Québec. This has changed in recent years, with smaller companies, such as Delta, BC-based Avcorp Industries, and governments, such as Ontario's Kingston Township and Town of Ajax, also introducing gainsharing. Gainsharing has been found to improve productivity in a majority of cases and often has a positive impact on employee attitudes.[80]

Organizational-Based Incentives

There are two major forms of organizational-based pay-for-performance programs: profit-sharing and stock option plans, including employee stock ownership plans.

Profit-Sharing Plans

profit-sharing plan An organization-wide plan in which the employer shares profits with employees based on a predetermined formula.

A **profit-sharing plan** is an organization-wide plan in which the employer shares profits with employees based on a predetermined formula. The plan can distribute direct cash outlays or stock options. Though senior executives are most likely to be rewarded through profit-sharing plans, employees at any level can be recipients. For instance, IKEA divided every penny rung up in its 152 stores on October 8, 1999, among its 44 000 staffers in 28 countries. This amounted to $2500 for each employee.[81]

Be aware that profit-sharing plans focus on past financial results. They do not necessarily focus employees on the future, because employees and managers look for ways to cut costs today without considering longer-term organizational needs. They also tend to ignore factors such as customer service and employee development, which may not be seen as directly linked to profits. In addition, employees who work in companies in cyclical industries would see inconsistent rewards in such a plan. For example, a financial services company would offer few or no rewards during slumping economic periods and substantial rewards during times of economic growth. Fluctuating rewards may not work for all employees. Employees at St. John's, Newfoundland-based Fishery Products International were quite upset when the $750 profit-sharing cheques they received in 2000 were reduced to just 10 percent of that for 2001 because of lower profits. Allan Moulton, a union representative of the employees, said, "It's extremely hard for [employees] . . . to see that [the company] realized profits, and they expected to see some benefits from the profits they generated."[82]

Stock Options and Employee Stock Ownership Plans

Some companies try to encourage employees to adopt the values of top management by making them owners of their firms. The idea is that employees will be more likely to think about the consequences of their behaviour on the bottom line if they own part of the company. Employees can become owners of the company either through being granted stock options or through an **employee stock ownership plan (ESOP)**.[83] Stock options give employees the right to buy stocks in the company at a later date for a guaranteed price. ESOPs are company-established benefit plans in which employees acquire stock as part of their benefits.

Canadian companies lag far behind the United States in the use of ESOPs because Canada's tax environment is less conducive to such plans. More recently, both the dot-com meltdown and the high-tech meltdown have made employees more reluctant to accept stock options instead of cash. Lisa Slipp, head of executive compensation at Toronto-based consulting firm Mercer Human Resource Consulting, notes that "people are recognizing the reality of stock options, that they are attractive in an up market and less so in a down market."[84] Nevertheless, Edmonton-based PCL Constructors has been owned by its employees since 1977, with 80 percent of employees owning shares. Ross Grieve, the company's president and CEO, says that ownership "elevates [the employees'] commitment to the organization."[85]

 RESEARCH FINDINGS: ESOPs

The research on ESOPs indicates that they increase employee satisfaction.[86] But their impact on performance is less clear. For instance, one study compared 45 companies with ESOPs against 238 companies without ESOPs.[87] Companies with ESOPs outperformed those without, both in terms of employment and sales growth. Other studies on companies with ESOPs have shown disappointing results.[88] More important, ESOPs can sometimes focus employees on trying to increase short-term stock prices while not worrying about the impact of their behaviour on the long-term effectiveness of the organization.

ESOPs have the potential to increase employee job satisfaction and work motivation. For this potential to be realized, employees need to experience ownership psychologically.[89] Some employees may not be fully aware of how their performance affects company performance, or they may not feel that they have any control over company performance. So, in addition to having a financial stake in the company, employees need to be kept regularly informed on the status of the business and also have the opportunity to exercise influence over the business.

Linking Productivity-Related Incentives to Motivation Theories

Variable-pay programs are probably most compatible with expectancy theory predictions. Specifically, under these plans, individuals should perceive a strong relationship between their performance and the rewards they receive and thus be more motivated. They should also be more productive.

However, the evidence is mixed, at best.[90] One study that followed the careers of 1000 top economists found that they put in more effort early in their careers, at a time when productivity-related incentives had a larger impact.[91] A recent study of Finnish white-collar employees found that higher levels of pay and more frequent payments positively affected productivity, while lower levels of pay did not improve productivity.[92] Other studies generally support the idea that organizations with profit-sharing plans or gainsharing plans have higher levels of profitability and productivity than those without.[93] But there are studies that question the effectiveness of pay-for-performance approaches, suggesting they can lead to less group cohesiveness.[94] Although some researchers note that much of the evidence supporting pay for

employee stock ownership plan (ESOP) A company-established benefit plan in which employees acquire stock as part of their benefits.

performance "is based on anecdotal testimonials and one-time company cases, rather than on methodologically more rigorous empirical studies,"[95] a number of researchers have shown that the connection between pay and performance is linked to productivity improvement.[96] This is supported by a recent study in Canada that looked at both unionized and non-unionized workplaces, and found that variable-pay plans result in "increased productivity, a safer work environment a better understanding of the business by employees, and little risk of employees losing base pay," according to Prem Benimadhu, a former analyst with The Conference Board of Canada.[97]

Using pay for performance can be difficult for some managers. They worry about what should constitute performance and how it should be measured. There is also some belief by managers and employees alike that wages should keep pace with inflation, independent of performance issues. Other barriers include salary scales keyed to what the competition is paying; traditional compensation systems that rely heavily on specific pay grades and relatively narrow pay ranges; and performance appraisal practices that produce inflated evaluations and expectations of full rewards.

Of course, from the employees' perspective, the major concern about pay-for-performance programs is a potential drop in earnings. *Pay for performance* means employees must share in the risks as well as the rewards of their employers' businesses. They are not guaranteed the same salary each year under this system. A recent Conference Board of Canada study may ease some fears about this particular concern. There was no evidence that pay for performance led to a reduction in salary in unionized settings. Instead, it "is used as an 'add-on' to the employees' base salary."[98] Pay for performance may also be more successful when organizations are more transparent about financial conditions. Ottawa-based Lee Valley Tools, which has a pay-for-performance program, uses quarterly newsletters to let employees know how much profit is forecast. Being informed helps employees understand how their efforts will pay off for them. Robin Lee, the company's president, says "sharing information and profits promotes an atmosphere in which hard work, innovation and efficiency pay off for everybody."[99]

What About Teamwork?

Incentive pay, especially when it is awarded to individuals, can have a negative effect on group cohesiveness and productivity, and in some cases may not offer significant benefits to a company.[100] For example, Montreal-based National Bank of Canada offered a $5 employee bonus for every time employees referred clients for loans, mutual funds, or other bank products. But the bonus so upset employees that the plan was abandoned after just three months.[101] Tellers complained that the bonus caused colleagues to compete against one another. Meanwhile, the bank could not determine whether the referrals actually generated new business.

Organized labour is, in general, cool to the idea of pay for performance. Andrew Jackson, director of the Social and Economic Policy Department at the Canadian Labour Congress, explains that "it hurts co-operation in the workplace. It can lead to competition between workers, speeding up the pace of work. It's a bad thing if it creates a stressful work environment where older workers can't keep up."[102] Pay for performance can also be problematic if work is speeded up to such unfair levels that employees can injure themselves. Still, not all unions oppose pay for performance, and the benefits and drawbacks of such incentive plans must be carefully considered before they are introduced.

If an organization wants a group of individuals to function as a "team" (which we define in Chapter 5), emphasis needs to be placed on team-based rewards rather than individual rewards. We will discuss the nature of team-based rewards in Chapter 5.

Motivating Beyond Productivity

In recent years, organizations have been paying for performance on bases other than strict productivity. Compensation experts Patricia Zingheim and Jay Schuster note the following activities that merit additional compensation:[103]

- *Commissions beyond sales.* Commissions might be determined by customer satisfaction and/or sales team outcomes, such as meeting revenue or profit targets.

- *Leadership effectiveness.* Rewards can be determined by employee satisfaction or measures of how the manager handles his or her employees.

- *New goals.* Rewards go to all employees who contribute to specific organizational goals, such as customer satisfaction, cycle time, or quality measures.

- *Knowledge workers in teams.* Rewards are linked to the performance of knowledge workers and/or professional employees who work on teams.

- *Competency and/or skills.* Rewards are based on employees' abstract knowledge or competencies—for example, knowledge of technology, the international business context, customer service, or social skills.

Exhibit 4-13 compares the strengths and weaknesses of variable-pay programs, team-based rewards, and skill-based pay programs. **Skill-based pay** is based on how many skills an employee has or how many jobs he or she can do.

skill-based pay Pay based on how many skills an employee has or how many jobs he or she can do.

While rewarding individuals for something other than performance may make sense in some instances, not everyone agrees that these rewards are fair. *OB in the Street* questions whether athletic scholarships should be given for athletic skills only, with little concern for academic merit or financial need.

EXHIBIT 4-13	Comparing Various Pay Programs	
Approach	**Strengths**	**Weaknesses**
Variable pay	• Motivates for performance. • Cost-effective. • Clearly links organizational goals and individual rewards.	• Individuals do not always have control over factors that affect productivity. • Earnings vary from year to year. • Can cause unhealthy competition among employees.
Team-based rewards	• Encourages individuals to work together effectively. • Promotes goal of team-based work.	• Difficult to evaluate team performance sometimes. • Equity problems could arise if all members paid equally.
Skill-based pay	• Increases the skill levels of employees. • Increases the flexibility of the workforce. • Can reduce the number of employees needed.	• Employers may end up paying for unneeded skills. • Employees may not be able to learn some skills, and thus feel demotivated.

OB IN THE STREET

Scholarships for Jocks: Skills or Smarts?

Should university athletes be awarded money just for their athletic abilities? Jack Drover, athletic director at Mount Allison University in Sackville, New Brunswick, thinks not.[104] He objects to student-athlete awards that are often offered because of what coaches and teams need rather than what the individual student needs.

Many university presidents react negatively to schools using financial rewards to recruit athletes. Some high school athletes can get full-tuition scholarships to university, even though they have not achieved high marks in school. While not every university finds this problematic, others feel awarding scholarships that do not recognize academic achievement or financial need is "an affront to the values of higher education."

Schools across the country interpret the rules for scholarships differently, which may affect the quality of school sports teams. Universities in Ontario (which rarely give athletic scholarships to first-year students) have had particular difficulty competing with schools across the country. For example, since 1995 only two football teams in Ontario have won the Vanier Cup: the Ottawa Gee Gees (2000) and the Wilfrid Laurier Golden Hawks (2005); the University of Ottawa is one of the few schools in the province that gives many athletic scholarships. In contrast, the Saint Mary's Huskies of Halifax, Nova Scotia, have been in the Vanier Cup final four times since 1999, winning twice. Rivals claim that a reason for the team's successes is its "plentiful" athletic scholarships.[105] Some members of Canadian Interuniversity Sport (CIS) suggest that a level playing field, with no scholarships granted to first-year athletes except in cases of financial need and academic merit, would be fairer to all teams. CIS chief executive officer Marg MacGregor, however, argues that "We're asking a lot of our students when we say compete every weekend and practise all the time without any support."

Designing Motivating Jobs

When might job redesign be an appropriate motivational tool?

Either as an alternative or a supplement to various reward programs, managers can consider redesigning jobs to make them more motivating. OB researchers Richard Hackman from Harvard University and Greg Oldham from the University of Illinois explored the nature of good jobs through their **job characteristics model (JCM)**.[106] The JCM identifies five core job dimensions and their relationship to personal and work outcomes.

Building on Herzberg's motivation-hygiene theory, the JCM focuses on the content of jobs rather than the context of jobs and can be considered as a way of motivating employees and increasing job satisfaction.

Job enrichment, an application of the JCM, refers to the vertical expansion of jobs. It increases the degree to which employees control the planning, execution, and evaluation of their work. An enriched job organizes tasks so that an employee does a complete activity. It expands employees' freedom and independence, increases responsibility, and provides feedback, so individuals will be able to assess and correct their own performance.[107]

Core Job Dimensions

According to the JCM, any job can be described in terms of five core job dimensions:

- *Skill variety.* The degree to which the job requires a variety of different activities so the employee can use a number of different skills and talents.

---

job characteristics model (JCM) A model that identifies five core job dimensions and their relationship to personal and work outcomes.

job enrichment The vertical expansion of jobs; increases the degree to which employees control the planning, execution, and evaluation of their work.

skill variety The degree to which the job requires a variety of different activities.

- *Task identity*. The degree to which the job requires completion of a whole and identifiable piece of work.

- *Task significance*. The degree to which the job has a substantial impact on the lives or work of other people.

- *Autonomy*. The degree to which the job provides substantial freedom, independence, and discretion to the individual in scheduling the work and determining the procedures to be used in carrying it out.

- *Feedback*. The degree to which carrying out the work activities required by the job results in the individual's obtaining direct and clear information about the effectiveness of his or her performance.

Jobs can be rated as high or low on these dimensions. Examples of jobs with high and low ratings appear in Exhibit 4-14.

Critical Psychological States

The JCM, presented in Exhibit 4-15 on page 140, links the five core job dimensions to three critical psychological states:[108]

- *Experienced meaningfulness*. The model predicts that if an employee's task is meaningful, the employee will view the job as important, valuable, and

task identity The degree to which the job requires completion of a whole and identifiable piece of work.

task significance The degree to which the job has a substantial impact on the lives or work of other people.

autonomy The degree to which the job provides substantial freedom, independence, and discretion to the individual in scheduling the work and determining the procedures to be used in carrying it out.

feedback The degree to which individuals obtain direct and clear information about the effectiveness of their performance.

EXHIBIT 4-14	Examples of High and Low Job Characteristics
Skill Variety	
High variety	The owner-operator of a garage who does electrical repair, rebuilds engines, does body work, and interacts with customers
Low variety	A body shop worker who sprays paint eight hours a day
Task Identity	
High identity	A cabinet maker who designs a piece of furniture, selects the wood, builds the object, and finishes it to perfection
Low identity	A worker in a furniture factory who operates a lathe solely to make table legs
Task Significance	
High significance	Nursing the sick in a hospital intensive care unit
Low significance	Sweeping hospital floors
Autonomy	
High autonomy	A telephone installer who schedules his or her own work for the day, makes visits without supervision, and decides on the most effective techniques for a particular installation
Low autonomy	A telephone operator who must handle calls as they come according to a routine, highly specified procedure
Feedback	
High feedback	An electronics factory worker who assembles a radio and then tests it to determine if it operates properly
Low feedback	An electronics factory worker who assembles a radio and then routes it to a quality control inspector who tests it for proper operation and makes needed adjustments

Source: G. Johns, *Organizational Behavior: Understanding and Managing Life at Work*, 4th ed. Copyright © 1997. Adapted by permission of Pearson Education, Inc., Upper Saddle River, NJ.

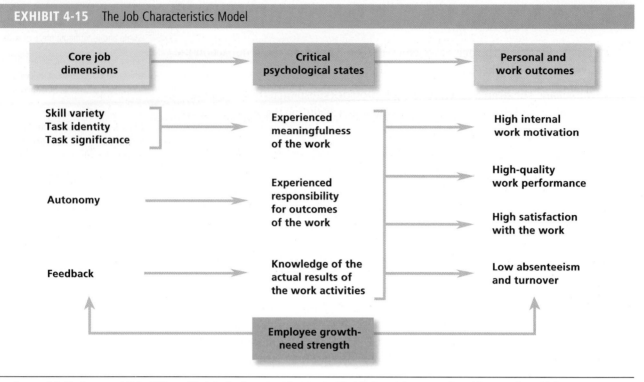

EXHIBIT 4-15   The Job Characteristics Model

Source: J. R. Hackman and G. R. Oldham, *Work Design* (excerpted from pages 78–80). Copyright © 1980 by Addison-Wesley Publishing Co. Reprinted by permission of Addison-Wesley Longman.

worthwhile. (Notice how in Exhibit 4-15 skill variety, task identity, and task significance combine to create meaningful work.)

- *Experienced responsibility for outcomes.* Employees feel a sense of personal responsibility for results when their jobs give them greater autonomy.

- *Knowledge of the actual results.* Feedback helps employees know whether they are performing effectively. The feedback can come from managers, clients, co-workers, or the nature of the task itself.

The model suggests that the more employees experience meaningfulness, responsibility, and knowledge of the actual results, the greater their motivation, performance, and satisfaction, and the lower their absenteeism and likelihood of leaving the organization.[109] As Exhibit 4-15 shows, the links between the job dimensions and the outcomes are moderated or adjusted by the strength of the individual's growth need—in other words, the employee's desire for self-esteem and self-actualization. This means, for example, that not every employee will respond favourably to a job with skill variety, task identity, task significance, autonomy, or feedback. Those with high self-esteem and self-actualization needs will respond more favourably than others with different needs.

Caveat Emptor: Apply Motivation Theories Wisely

6 What kinds of mistakes are made in reward systems?

Applying motivation theories without giving performance feedback makes little sense. Second, when managers are not careful, they can send the wrong signals by how they use rewards. Third, rewards may not always be necessary. Finally, while motivation theories generally work well in Canada and the United States, they do not always work successfully in other cultures. We examine these issues below. When applying motivation theories in the workplace, managers should be aware of the kinds of signals rewards send, how rewards are viewed in different cultures, and whether rewards are essential.

Beware the Signals That Rewards Send

Ever wonder why employees do some strange things?

Perhaps more often than we would like, organizations engage in what has been called "the folly of rewarding A, while hoping for B."[110] Organizations do this when they hope that employees will engage in one type of behaviour yet they reward another type. Managers of Vancouver's bus drivers had hoped that by increasing the number of days a driver had to be out sick to get paid, bus drivers would take fewer days off. Instead, the bus drivers simply stayed out sick for more days, so that they could collect their sick pay. To prevent this problem, managers might have considered giving bonuses for perfect attendance. Hoping for a behaviour you are not rewarding is unlikely to make that behaviour occur to any great extent. In fact, as expectancy theory suggests, individuals will generally perform in ways to raise the probability of receiving the rewards offered.

Exhibit 4-16 provides further examples of common management reward follies. Research suggests that there are three major obstacles to ending these follies:[111]

- *Individuals are unable to break out of old ways of thinking about reward and recognition practices.* This approach is demonstrated when management emphasizes quantifiable behaviours to the exclusion of nonquantifiable behaviours; when management is reluctant to change the existing performance system; and when employees have an entitlement mentality (i.e., they do not support changing the reward system because they are comfortable with the current behaviours that are rewarded).

EXHIBIT 4-16 Management Reward Follies

We hope for . . .	But we reward . . .
Teamwork and collaboration	The best team members
Innovative thinking and risk-taking	Proven methods and not making mistakes
Development of people skills	Technical achievements and accomplishments
Employee involvement and empowerment	Tight control over operations and resources
High achievement	Another year's effort
Long-term growth; environmental responsibility	Quarterly earnings
Commitment to total quality	Shipping on schedule, even with defects
Candour; surfacing bad news early	Reporting good news, whether it's true or not; agreeing with the manager, whether or not (s)he's right

Sources: Constructed from S. Kerr, "On the Folly of Rewarding A, While Hoping for B," *Academy of Management Executive* 9, no. 1 (1995), pp. 7–14; and "More on the Folly," *Academy of Management Executive* 9, no. 1 (1995), pp. 15–16.

- *Organizations often do not look at the big picture of their performance system.* Thus, rewards are allocated at subunit levels, with the result that units often compete against each other.

- *Both management and shareholders often focus on short-term results.* They do not reward employees for longer-range planning.

Organizations would do well to ensure that they do not send the wrong message when offering rewards. When organizations outline an organizational objective of "team performance," for example, but reward each employee according to individual productivity, does this send a message that teams are valued? Or when a retailer tells commissioned employees that they are responsible for monitoring and replacing stock as necessary, are employees more likely to concentrate on making sales or stocking the floor? Employees motivated by the promise of rewards will do those things that earn them the rewards they value.

Provide Performance Feedback

For employees to understand the relationship between rewards and performance, as well as considering whether rewards are equitable, they need to be given performance feedback. For many managers, however, few activities are more unpleasant than providing performance feedback to employees.[112] In fact, unless pressured by organizational policies and controls, managers are likely to ignore this responsibility.[113] Why the reluctance to give performance feedback? There seem to be at least three reasons.

First, managers are often uncomfortable discussing performance weaknesses directly with employees. Even though almost every employee could stand to improve in some areas, managers fear a confrontation when presenting negative feedback.

Second, many employees tend to become defensive when their weaknesses are pointed out. Instead of accepting the feedback as constructive and a basis for improving performance, some employees challenge the evaluation by criticizing the manager or redirecting blame to someone else. A survey of 151 area managers in Philadelphia, for instance, found that 98 percent encountered some type of aggression after giving employees negative appraisals.[114]

Finally, employees tend to have an inflated assessment of their own performance. Statistically speaking, half of all employees must be below-average performers. But the evidence indicates that the average employee's estimate of his or her own performance level generally falls around the 75th percentile.[115] So even when managers are providing good news, employees are likely to perceive it as not good enough.

The solution to the performance feedback problem is not to ignore it, but to train managers to conduct constructive feedback sessions. An effective review—one in which the employee perceives the appraisal as fair, the manager as sincere, and the climate as constructive—can result in the employee's leaving the interview in an upbeat mood, informed about the performance areas needing improvement, and determined to correct the deficiencies.[116] In addition, the performance review should be designed more as a counselling activity than a judgment process. This can best be accomplished by allowing the review to evolve out of the employee's own self-evaluation. For more tips on performance feedback, see *OB in Action—Giving More Effective Feedback.*

Can We Just Eliminate Rewards?

Alfie Kohn, in his book *Punished by Rewards,* argues that "the desire to do something, much less to do it well, simply cannot be imposed; in this sense, it is a mistake to talk about motivating other people. All we can do is set up certain conditions that will maximize the probability of their developing an interest in what they are doing and remove the conditions that function as constraints."[117]

Creating a Motivating Work Environment

Based on his research and consulting experience, Kohn proposes actions that organizations can take to create a motivating work environment.[119]

Abolish Incentive Pay Paying people generously and fairly makes sure they do not feel exploited and takes pay off their minds. As a result, employees will be more able to focus on the goals of the organization rather than have their paycheques as their main goal.

Re-evaluate Evaluation Instead of making performance appraisals look and feel like a punitive effort—who gets raises, who gets promoted, who is told he or she is performing poorly— the performance evaluation system might be structured more like a two-way conversation to trade ideas and questions, done continuously, not as a competition. The discussion of performance should not be tied to compensation. "Providing feedback that employees can use to do a better job ought never to be confused or combined with controlling them by offering (or withholding) rewards."[120]

Create the Conditions for Authentic Motivation A noted economist recently summarized the evidence about pay for productivity as follows: "Changing the way workers are *treated* may boost productivity more than changing the way they are *paid*."[121] There is some consensus about what the conditions for creating authentic motivation might be: helping employees rather than putting them under surveillance; listening to employee concerns and thinking about problems from their viewpoint; and providing plenty of feedback so they know what they have done right and what they need to improve.[122]

Support Collaboration People are more likely to perform better in well-functioning groups where they can get feedback and learn from each other.[123] Therefore, it is important to provide the necessary supports to create well-functioning teams.

Pay Attention to Content People are generally the most motivated when their jobs give them an opportunity to learn new skills, provide variety in the tasks that are performed, and enable them to demonstrate competence. Some of this can be fostered by carefully matching people to their jobs and by giving them the opportunity to try new jobs. It is also possible to increase the meaningfulness of many jobs.

But what about jobs that do not seem inherently interesting? One psychologist suggests that in cases where the jobs are fundamentally unappealing, the manager might acknowledge frankly that the task is not fun, give a meaningful rationale for why it must be done, and then give people as much choice as possible in how the task is completed.[124] One sociologist studying a group of garbage collectors in San Francisco discovered that they were quite satisfied with their work.[125] Their satisfaction came from the way the work and the company were organized: Relationships among the crew were important, the tasks and routes were varied to provided interest, and the company was set up as a cooperative, so that each employee owned a share of the company and thus felt "pride of ownership."

Provide Choice "We are most likely to become enthusiastic about what we are doing— and all else being equal, to do it well—when we are free to make decisions about the way we carry out a task."[126] Extrinsic rewards (and punishments too) actually remove choice, because they focus us on rewards, rather than on tasks or goals. Research suggests that burnout, dissatisfaction, absenteeism, stress, and coronary heart disease are related

---

OB in ACTION

Giving More Effective Feedback

Managers can use the following tips to give more effective feedback:

→ Relate feedback to existing performance goals and clear expectations.

→ Give specific feedback tied to observable behaviour or measurable results.

→ Channel feedback toward key result areas.

→ Give feedback as soon as possible.

→ Give positive feedback for improvement, not just final results.

→ Focus feedback on performance, not personalities.

→ Base feedback on accurate and credible information.[118]

to situations where individuals did not have enough control over their work.[127] By *choice* we do not mean lack of management, but rather involving people in the decisions that are to be made. A number of case studies indicate that participative management, when it includes full participation by everyone, is successful.[128]

These actions represent an alternative to simply providing more and different kinds of incentives to try to induce people to work more effectively. They suggest that providing the proper environment may be more important than the reward structure.

Motivation Theories Are Culture-Bound

Reward strategies that have been used successfully in Canada and the United States do not always work successfully in other cultures. Take, for instance, a study comparing sales representatives at a large electronics company in the United States with one in Japan. The study found that while Rolex watches, expensive dinners, and fancy vacations were valued rewards for star performers in the United States, taking the whole sales team bowling was more appreciated in Japan. The study's authors found that "being a member of a successful team with shared goals and values, rather than financial rewards, is what drives Japanese sales representatives to succeed."[129]

Why do our motivation theories perform less well when we look at their use in countries beyond Canada and the United States? Most current motivation theories were developed in the United States and so take US cultural norms for granted.[130] That may account for why Canada and the United States, which have more individualistic cultures, rely more heavily on extrinsic motivating factors than some other countries.[131] Japanese and German firms rarely make use of individual work incentives because their cultures are more collectivist.[132]

Many of the social-psychological theories of motivation rely heavily on the idea of motivating the individual through individual rewards. Thus they emphasize, particularly in an organizational context, the meaning of "pay" and give little attention to the informal rewards that come from group norms and prestige from peers.[133] Exhibit 4-17 presents a quick summary of the cultural differences in motivation observed by a number of studies.

Motivation theories also assume that needs are similar across societies. For instance, Maslow's needs hierarchy argues that people start at the physiological level and then move progressively up the hierarchy in this order: physiological, safety, social, esteem,

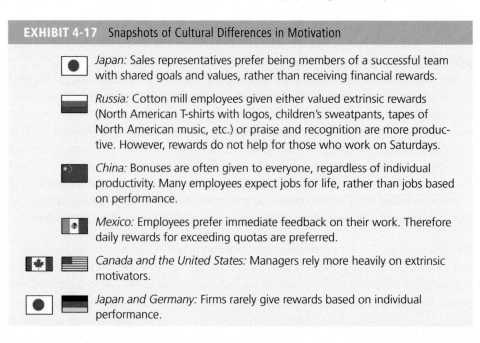

EXHIBIT 4-17   Snapshots of Cultural Differences in Motivation

Japan: Sales representatives prefer being members of a successful team with shared goals and values, rather than receiving financial rewards.

Russia: Cotton mill employees given either valued extrinsic rewards (North American T-shirts with logos, children's sweatpants, tapes of North American music, etc.) or praise and recognition are more productive. However, rewards do not help for those who work on Saturdays.

China: Bonuses are often given to everyone, regardless of individual productivity. Many employees expect jobs for life, rather than jobs based on performance.

Mexico: Employees prefer immediate feedback on their work. Therefore daily rewards for exceeding quotas are preferred.

Canada and the United States: Managers rely more heavily on extrinsic motivators.

Japan and Germany: Firms rarely give rewards based on individual performance.

and self-actualization. This hierarchy, if it applies at all, aligns well with American culture and reasonably well with Canadian culture. However, in countries such as Austria, Denmark, and Germany, where uncertainty avoidance characteristics are strong, security needs would be at the top of the needs hierarchy. Countries that score high on humane orientation characteristics—Indonesia, Egypt, and Malaysia—would have social needs on top.[134] We would predict, for instance, that group work will motivate employees more when the country's culture scores high on the humane orientation criterion.

Equity theory has gained a relatively strong following in Canada and United States. That is no surprise, since North American reward systems assume that employees are highly sensitive to equity in the granting of rewards and expect pay to be tied closely to performance. However, recent evidence suggests that in collectivist cultures, especially in the former socialist countries of Central and Eastern Europe, employees expect rewards to reflect their individual needs as well as their performance.[135] Moreover, consistent with a legacy of Communism and centrally planned economies, employees show an entitlement attitude—they expect outcomes to be *greater* than their inputs.[136] These findings suggest that Canadian- and US-style pay practices may need modification, especially in Russia and former Communist countries, in order to be perceived as fair by employees.

These international findings indicate that it is important to consider the internal norms of a country when developing an incentive plan rather than simply import a plan that works well in Canada and the United States.

Putting It All Together

While it is always dangerous to synthesize a large number of complex ideas into a few simple guidelines, the following suggestions summarize the essence of what we know about motivating employees in organizations:

- *Recognize individual differences.* Employees have different needs and should not be treated alike. Managers should spend the time necessary to understand what is important to each employee and then align goals, level of involvement, and rewards with individual needs. This chapter's *Working With Others Exercise* on pages 150–151 gives you an opportunity to understand the different needs of a diverse workforce.

- *Use goals and feedback.* Employees should have hard, specific goals, as well as feedback on how well they are faring in pursuit of those goals.

- *Allow employees to participate in decisions that affect them.* Employees can contribute to a number of decisions that affect them: setting work goals, choosing their own benefits packages, solving productivity and quality problems, and the like. This can increase employee productivity, commitment to work goals, motivation, and job satisfaction.

- *When giving rewards, be sure that they are clearly related to the performance desired.* It is important that employees perceive a clear link between rewards and the type of performance expected. How closely rewards are *actually* correlated to performance criteria is less important than the *perception* of this relationship. If individuals perceive that there is little relation between the performance desired and the rewards they receive, the results will be low performance, a decrease in job satisfaction, and an increase in turnover and absenteeism.

- *Check the system for equity.* Employees should be able to perceive rewards as matching the inputs they bring to the job. At a simplistic level, this means that experience, skills, abilities, effort, and other obvious inputs should explain differences in performance and, hence, pay, job assignments, and other obvious rewards.

Summary and Implications

1 **What is motivation?** Motivation is the process that accounts for an individual's intensity, direction, and persistence of effort toward reaching a goal. *Intensity* is concerned with how hard a person tries. This is the element most of us focus on when we talk about motivation. However, high intensity is unlikely to lead to good job performance unless the effort is channelled in a useful *direction*. Finally, the effort requires *persistence*.

2 **How do needs motivate people?** All needs theories of motivation, including Maslow's hierarchy of needs, Alderfer's ERG theory, McClelland's theory of needs, and Herzberg's motivation-hygiene theory (sometimes called the *two-factor theory*) propose a similar idea: Individuals have needs that will result in motivation. Needs theories suggest that motivation will be high to the degree that the rewards individuals receive for high performance satisfy their dominant needs.

3 **Are there other ways to motivate people?** Process theories focus on the broader picture of how someone can set about motivating another individual. Process theories include expectancy theory and goal-setting theory. Expectancy theory says that an employee will be motivated to exert a high level of effort when he or she believes (1) that the effort will lead to good performance; (2) that good performance will lead to organizational rewards, such as a bonus, a salary increase, or a promotion; and (3) that the rewards will satisfy his or her personal goals.

Goal-setting theory suggests that intentions to work toward a goal are a major source of work motivation. That is, goals tell an employee what needs to be done and how much effort will need to be expended. Specific goals increase performance; difficult goals, when accepted, result in higher performance than do easy goals; and feedback leads to higher performance than does nonfeedback.

4 **Do equity and fairness matter?** Individuals look for fairness in the reward system. Rewards should be perceived by employees as related to the inputs they bring to the job. At a simplistic level, this means that experience, skills, abilities, effort, and other obvious inputs should explain differences in performance and, hence, pay, job assignments, and other obvious rewards.

5 **How can rewards and job design motivate employees?** When organizations want to reward individuals for specific high performance, they often turn to employee recognition programs. Recognizing an employee's superior performance often costs little or no money.

When organizations want to improve productivity, they often use variable-pay programs. With these programs, a portion of an employee's pay is based on some individual and/or organizational measure of performance.

Managers can enrich jobs following the job characteristics model. The model tells us that jobs that offer skill variety, task identity, task significance, autonomy, and feedback tend to be more motivating for employees.

6 **What kinds of mistakes are made in reward systems?** Individuals are responsive to the signals sent out by organizations, and if they determine that some activities are not valued, they may not engage in them, even when the firm expects employees to do so. Rewards should be linked to the type of performance expected. Rewards are also culture-bound. Individuals respond to rewards in general and specific rewards differently, depending upon what culture they come from. Finally rewards are not always necessary. In the right context, individuals often motivate themselves intrinsically and can achieve quite high levels of performance doing so. We also know that giving rewards for things that were previously done for intrinsic motivation will decrease motivation.

OB at Work

For Review

1. What are the implications of Theories X and Y for motivation practices?

2. Identify the variables in expectancy theory.

3. Describe the four ways in which goal setting motivates.

4. Explain cognitive evaluation theory. How applicable is it to management practice?

5. What are the pluses and minuses of variable-pay programs from an employee's viewpoint? From management's viewpoint?

6. What is an ESOP? How might it positively influence employee motivation?

7. Define the five core dimensions in the JCM.

8. Describe three jobs that score high on the JCM. Describe three jobs that score low.

9. What can firms do to create more motivating environments for their employees?

For Critical Thinking

1. Identify three activities you really enjoy (for example, playing tennis, reading a novel, going shopping). Next, identify three activities you really dislike (for example, visiting the dentist, cleaning the house, following a low-fat diet). Using expectancy theory, analyze each of your answers to assess why some activities stimulate your effort while others do not.

2. Identify five different bases by which organizations can compensate employees. Based on your knowledge and experience, is performance the basis most used in practice? Discuss.

3. "Employee recognition may be motivational for the moment, but it doesn't have any staying power. Why? Because employees can't take recognition to Roots or The Bay!" Do you agree or disagree? Discuss.

4. "Performance can't be measured, so any effort to link pay with performance is a fantasy. Differences in performance are often caused by the system, which means the organization ends up rewarding the circumstances. It's the same thing as rewarding the weather forecaster for a pleasant day." Do you agree or disagree with this statement? Support your position.

5. Your textbook argues for recognizing individual differences. It also suggests paying attention to members of diverse groups. Does this view contradict the principles of equity theory? Discuss.

OB for You

- To motivate yourself to finish a particularly long and dry chapter in a textbook, plan a snack break. Or buy yourself a new CD once that major accounting assignment is finished.

- The people you interact with appreciate recognition. Consider including a brief note on a nice card to show thanks for a job well done. Or you might send a basket of flowers. Sometimes just sending a pleasant, thankful email is enough to make a person feel valued. All of these things are easy enough to do and appreciated greatly by the recipient.

- Be aware of the kinds of things that motivate you, so you can choose jobs and activities that suit you better.

OB *At Work*

Point

Failure Motivates

It's sad but true that many of the best lessons we learn in life are from our failures. Often when we are riding on the wings of success, we coast—until we crash to earth. Take the example of Dan Doctoroff. Doctoroff is a successful New York investment banker who spent five years obsessed with bringing the 2012 Olympics to New York. In his efforts, he used $4 million of his own money, travelled half a million miles, worked 100-hour weeks, and staked his reputation on achieving a goal many thought was foolhardy.

What happened? New York was not selected, and all Doctoroff's efforts were in vain. His immediate reaction? He felt "emotionally paralyzed." But Doctoroff is not sorry he made the effort. He said he learned a lot about himself in trying to woo Olympic decision makers in 78 countries. Colleagues had once described him as brash and arrogant. As a result of his efforts, Doctoroff said, he learned to listen more and talk less. He also said that losing made him realize how supportive his wife and three teenage children could be.

Not only does failure bring perspective to people such as Doctoroff, it often provides important feedback on how to improve. The important thing is to learn from the failure and to persist. As Doctoroff says, "The only way to ensure you'll lose is not to try." One of the reasons successful people fail so often is that they set their own bars so high. Harvard's Rosabeth Moss Kanter, who has spent her career studying executives, says, "Many successful people set the bar so high that they don't achieve the distant goal. But they do achieve things that wouldn't have been possible without that bigger goal."[137]

Counterpoint

Failure Demotivates

Do people learn from failure? We have seen people who persist in a failed venture just because they think persistence is a virtue or because their ego is involved, even when logic suggests they should move on. One research study found that managers often illogically persist in launching new products, even when the evidence becomes clear that the product is going nowhere. As the authors note, "It sometimes takes more courage to kill a product that's going nowhere than to sustain it." So the thought of learning from failure is a nice ideal, but most people are too defensive to do that.

Moreover, there is ample evidence that when people fail they often rationalize their failures to preserve their self-esteem, and thus don't learn at all. Although the example of Dan Doctoroff is interesting, it's not clear he has done anything but rationalize his failure. It's human nature. Research shows that when we fail, we often engage in external attributions—blaming the failure on bad luck or powerful others—or we devalue what we failed to get ("It wasn't that important to me anyway," we may tell ourselves). These rationalizations may not be correct, but that is not the point. We engage in them not to be right but to preserve our often fragile self-esteem. We need to believe in ourselves to motivate ourselves, and because failing undermines that self-belief, we have to do what we can to recover our self-confidence.[138]

In sum, although it is a nice story that failure is actually good, as one songwriter wrote, "The world is not a song." Failure hurts, and to either protect ourselves or recover from the pain, we often do not learn from failure—we rationalize it away.

LEARNING ABOUT **YOURSELF** EXERCISE

What Motivates You?

Circle the number that most closely agrees with how you feel. Consider your answers in the context of your current job or a past work experience.[139]

	Strongly Disagree			Strongly Agree	
1. I try very hard to improve on my past performance at work.	1	2	3	4	5
2. I enjoy competition and winning.	1	2	3	4	5

OB At Work

3. I often find myself talking to those around me about nonwork matters.	1	2	3	4	5
4. I enjoy a difficult challenge.	1	2	3	4	5
5. I enjoy being in charge.	1	2	3	4	5
6. I want to be liked by others.	1	2	3	4	5
7. I want to know how I am progressing as I complete tasks.	1	2	3	4	5
8. I confront people who do things I disagree with.	1	2	3	4	5
9. I tend to build close relationships with co-workers.	1	2	3	4	5
10. I enjoy setting and achieving realistic goals.	1	2	3	4	5
11. I enjoy influencing other people to get my way.	1	2	3	4	5
12. I enjoy belonging to groups and organizations.	1	2	3	4	5
13. I enjoy the satisfaction of completing a difficult task.	1	2	3	4	5
14. I often work to gain more control over the events around me.	1	2	3	4	5
15. I enjoy working with others more than working alone.	1	2	3	4	5

Scoring Key

To determine your dominant needs—and what motivates you—place the number 1 through 5 that represents your score for each statement next to the number for that statement.

Achievement	**Power**	**Affiliation**
1. _____	2. _____	3. _____
4. _____	5. _____	6. _____
7. _____	8. _____	9. _____
10. _____	11. _____	12. _____
13. _____	14. _____	15. _____
Totals: _____	_____	_____

Add up the total of each column. The sum of the numbers in each column will be between 5 and 25 points. The column with the highest score tells you your dominant need.

More Learning About Yourself Exercises

Additional self-assessments relevant to this chapter appear on my MyOBLab (**www.pearsoned.ca/myoblab**).

I.C.5   What Are My Course Performance Goals?

I.C.8   What's My Job's Motivating Potential?

IV.A.3 How Confident Am I in My Abilities to Succeed?

II.B.5 How Good Am I at Disciplining Others?

When you complete the additional assessments, consider the following:

1. Am I surprised about my score?

2. Would my friends evaluate me similarly?

OB At Work

BREAKOUT **GROUP** EXERCISES

Form small groups to discuss the following topics, as assigned by your instructor:

1. One of the members of your team continually arrives late for meetings and does not turn drafts of assignments in on time. Choose one of the available theories and indicate how the theory explains the member's current behaviour and how the theory could be used to motivate the group member to perform more responsibly.

2. You are unhappy with the performance of one of your instructors and would like to encourage the instructor to present livelier classes. Choose one of the available theories and indicate how the theory explains the instructor's current behaviour. How could you as a student use the theory to motivate the instructor to present livelier classes?

3. Harvard University recently changed its grading policy to recommend to instructors that the average course mark should be a B. This was the result of a study showing that more than 50 percent of students were receiving an A or A– for coursework. Harvard students are often referred to as "the best and the brightest," and they pay $27 000 (US) for their education, so they expect high grades. Discuss the impact of this change in policy on the motivation of Harvard students to study harder.

WORKING WITH **OTHERS** EXERCISE

Rewards for a Diverse Workforce

Purpose   To learn about the different needs of a diverse workforce.[140]

Time   Approximately 40 minutes.

Directions   Divide the class into groups of approximately 6 students. Each group is assigned 1 of the following people and is to determine the best benefits package for that person.

- Lise is 28 years old. She is a divorced mother of 3 children, aged 3, 5, and 7. She is the department head. She earns $37 000 a year in her job and receives another $3600 a year in child support from her ex-husband.

- Ethel is a 72-year-old widow. She works 25 hours a week to supplement her $8000 annual pension. Including her hourly wage of $7.75, she earns $18 075 a year.

- John is a 34-year-old black male born in Trinidad who is now a Canadian resident. He is married and the father of two small children. John attends college at night and is within a year of earning his bachelor's degree. His salary is $24 000 a year. His wife is an attorney and earns approximately $54 000 a year.

- Sanjay is a 26-year-old physically impaired Indo-Canadian male. He is single and has a master's degree in education. Sanjay is paralyzed and confined to a wheelchair as a result of a car accident. He earns $29 000 a year.

- Wei Mei is a single 22-year-old immigrant. Born and raised in China, she came to Canada only three months ago. Wei Mei's English needs considerable improvement. She earns $18 000 a year.

- Mike is a 16-year-old white male in his 2nd year of high school. He works 15 hours a week after school and during vacations. He earns $7.75 an hour, or approximately $6045 a year.

Background

Our 6 participants work for a company that has recently installed a flexible benefits program. Instead of the traditional "one benefits package fits all," the company is allocating an additional 25 percent of each employee's annual pay to be used for discretionary benefits. Those benefits and their annual costs are listed on the next page.

Benefit Yearly Cost

Extended medical care (for services such as private hospital room, eyeglasses, and dental care that are not provided by the province's health insurance plan) for employee:

Plan A (No deductible and pays 90%)	$3000
Plan B ($200 deductible and pays 80%)	$2000
Plan C ($1000 deductible and pays 70%)	$ 500

Extended medical care for dependants (same deductibles and percentages as above):

Plan A	$2000
Plan B	$1500
Plan C	$ 500
Supplementary dental plan	$ 500

Life insurance:

Plan A ($25 000 coverage)	$ 500
Plan B ($50 000 coverage)	$1000
Plan C ($100 000 coverage)	$2000
Plan D ($250 000 coverage)	$3000
Mental health plan	$ 500
Prepaid legal assistance	$ 300
Vacation	2% of annual pay for each week, up to 6 weeks a year
Pension at retirement equal to approximately 50% of final annual earnings	$1500
Four-day workweek during the three summer months	4% of annual pay (available only to full-time employees)
Daycare services (after company contribution) for all of an employee's children, regardless of number	$2000
Company-provided transportation to and from work	$ 750
University tuition reimbursement	$1000
Language class tuition reimbursement	$ 500

The Task

1. Each group has 15 minutes to develop a flexible benefits package that consumes 25 percent (and no more!) of its character's pay.

2. After completing Step 1, each group appoints a spokesperson who describes to the entire class the benefits package the group has arrived at for its character.

3. The entire class then discusses the results. How did the needs, concerns, and problems of each participant influence the group's decision? What do the results suggest for trying to motivate a diverse workforce?

OB *At Work*

ETHICAL **DILEMMA** EXERCISE

Are CEOs Paid Too Much?

Critics have described the astronomical pay packages given to Canadian and American CEOs as "rampant greed."[141] In 2006, the average compensation of Canada's 100 best-paid CEOs was $8 528 304. This was more than 218 times what the average full-time Canadian employee made.[142]

How do you explain such large pay packages for CEOs? Some say this represents a classic economic response to a situation in which the demand is great for high-quality top-executive talent and the supply is low. Other arguments in favour of paying executives millions a year are the need to compensate people for the tremendous responsibilities and stress that go with such jobs; the motivating potential that seven- and eight-figure annual incomes provide to senior executives and those who might aspire to be; and the influence of senior executives on the company's bottom line.

Critics of executive pay practices in Canada and the United States argue that CEOs choose board members whom they can count on to support ever-increasing pay for top management. If board members fail to "play along," they risk losing their positions, their fees, and the prestige and power inherent in board membership.

In addition, it is not clear that executive compensation is tied to firm performance. For instance, KPMG found in one survey that for 40 percent of the respondents there was no correlation between the size of the bonus and how poorly or well the company fared. Consider the data in Exhibit 4-18, which illustrates the disconnect that can sometimes happen between CEO compensation and firm performance. *National Post Business* writers calculated that the CEOs noted in the exhibit were overpaid, based on their company's performance in 2007.

Is high compensation of CEOs a problem? If so, does the blame for the problem lie with CEOs or with the shareholders and boards that knowingly allow the practice? Are Canadian and American CEOs greedy? Are these CEOs acting unethically? Should their pay reflect more closely some multiple of their employees' wages? What do you think?

EXHIBIT 4-18   2007 Compensation of Canada's "Most Overpaid" CEOs*

CEO(s)	Was Paid (3-Yr Avg.)	Should Have Been Paid	Amount Overpaid
1. James Balsillie and Michael Lazarides Research In Motion Waterloo, Ontario	$76 871 000	$ 1 537 000	$75 334 000
2. Jeffrey Orr and Robert Gratton Power Financial Montreal, Quebec	$59 555 000	$11 911 000	$47 644 000
3. Kevin MacArthur, Ian Telfer, and Robert McEwan Goldcorp Vancouver, British Columbia	$ 8 238 000	$ 1 730 000	$ 6 508 000
4. Donald Walker, Siegfried Wolf, and Frank Stronach Magna International Aurora, Ontario	$33 054 000	$ 7 272 000	$25 782 000
5. Robert Gannicott Harry Winston Diamond Corp. Toronto, Ontario	$ 2 706 000	$ 649 000	$ 2 057 000

National Post Business calculated a "Bang for the Buck" formula, taking into account CEO performance variables.

Source: D. Dias, "Bang for the Buck," *National Post Business*, November 2007, p. 20. Material reprinted with the express permission of National Post Company, a CanWest Partnership.

OB *At Work*

Bullying Bosses

"It got to where I was twitching, literally, on the way into work," states Carrie Clark, a 52-year-old retired teacher and administrator.[143] After enduring 10 months of repeated insults and mistreatment from her supervisor, she finally quit her job. "I had to take care of my health."

Although many individuals recall bullies from their elementary school days, some are realizing that bullies can exist in the workplace as well. And these bullies do not just pick on the weakest in the group; rather, any subordinate in their path may fall prey to their torment, according to Dr. Gary Namie, director of the Workplace Bullying and Trauma Institute. Dr. Namie further says workplace bullies are not limited to men—women are at least as likely to be bullies. However, gender discrepancies are found in victims of bullying, as women are more likely to be targets.

What motivates a boss to be a bully? Dr. Harvey Hornstein, a retired professor from Teachers College at Columbia University, suggests that supervisors may use bullying as a means to subdue a subordinate who poses a threat to the supervisor's status. In addition, supervisors may bully individuals to vent frustrations. Many times, however, the sheer desire to wield power may be the primary reason for bullying.

What is the impact of bullying on employee motivation and behaviour? Surprisingly, even though victims of workplace bullies may feel less motivated to go to work every day, it does not appear that they discontinue performing their required job duties. However, it does appear that victims of bullies are less motivated to perform extra-role or citizenship behaviours. Helping others, speaking positively about the organization, and going beyond the call of duty are behaviours that are reduced as a result of bullying. According to Dr. Bennett Tepper of the University of North Carolina, fear may be the reason that many employees continue to perform their job duties. And not all individuals reduce their citizenship behaviours. Some continue to engage in extra-role behaviours to make themselves look better than their colleagues.

What should you do if your boss is bullying you? Don't necessarily expect help from co-workers. As Emelise Aleandri, an actress and producer from New York who left her job after being bullied, stated, "Some people were afraid to do anything. But others didn't mind what was happening at all, because they wanted my job." Moreover, according to Dr. Michelle Duffy of the University of Kentucky, co-workers often blame victims of bullying in order to resolve their guilt. "They do this by wondering whether maybe the person deserved the treatment, that he or she has been annoying or lazy, they did something to earn it," states Dr. Duffy. One example of an employee who observed this phenomenon first-hand is Sherry Hamby, who was frequently verbally abused by her boss and then eventually fired. She stated, "This was a man who insulted me, who insulted my family, who would lay into me while everyone else in the office just sat there and let it happen. The people in my office eventually started blaming me."

What can a bullied employee do? Dr. Hornstein suggests that employees try to ignore the insults and respond only to the substance of the bully's gripe. "Stick with the substance, not the process, and often it won't escalate," he states. Of course, that is easier said than done.

Questions

1. What aspects of motivation might workplace bullying reduce? For example, are there likely to be effects on an employee's self-efficacy? If so, what might those effects be?

2. If you were a victim of workplace bullying, what steps would you take to try to reduce its occurrence? What strategies would be most effective? What strategies might be ineffective? What would you do if one of your colleagues were a victim of an abusive supervisor?

3. What factors do you believe contribute to workplace bullying? Are bullies a product of the situation, or do they have flawed personalities? What situations and what personality factors might contribute to the presence of bullies?

OB At Work

CASE 4   ## Human Resources at KPMG

Bruce Pfau, vice-president of human resources at KPMG, says that the company is dealing with a shortage of qualified people who can take on the many new tasks created by new accounting regulations.[144] The accounting scandals at firms such as Enron and WorldCom and the failure of accounting firm Arthur Andersen have led to a lot of litigation in the industry, which has created a challenging work environment for many accounting firms. In addition to this industry-wide problem, the top management at KPMG determined that "employee engagement" scores were lower than what the company wanted, and only 50 percent of employees felt that KPMG was a great place to work.

Pfau recognizes that KPMG is in a war for talent with other accounting firms. The company needs to attract the best people, and to do that, it needs to have what he calls a "superior employment proposition." Undergraduates are telling KPMG what they want from an ideal employer—great career development, good economic rewards, good benefits, a great work–life balance, and global experience.

To create the desired "superior employment proposition," KPMG makes sure that it is sharing the firm's economic success with its employees. Over 85 percent of employees receive bonuses at the end of the year, and many more employees receive on-the-spot bonuses (called "encore awards" at KPMG) of $100, $200, or $500 for a job well done. The company has also changed the mix of retirement plans, tripled contributions to pension plans, makes sure people have adequate time off, and has a good vacation policy. The number one priority is career development. People are trained not just in the area of technical skills, but also in leadership and project management skills.

The company has also launched the Employee Career Architecture (ECA) program. As a result of information generated in focus groups, KPMG found that what employees wanted most in their career was to have a close relationship with their performance manager or mentor so they could have in-depth conversations about their career. The company provides resources and tools that help make employee conversations with their performance manager valuable to the employee. For example, Suzanne Barnum, the performance manager for Meredith Ferguson, has regular discussions with Meredith about the behaviours that will make Meredith more successful. Meredith says that people can go on the ECA and determine if there is a domestic or foreign rotation position that is available.

Pfau says that rotations are a win-win proposition because employees learn a lot and come back with more skills that will help the company. Turnover at KPMG is now very low, and the company is hiring people who have high grade point averages from very good schools. There has also been an improvement in engagement scores. These things combined save the company millions of dollars each year.

Questions

1. What is the difference between extrinsic and intrinsic motivation? To what extent do the human resource practices and managerial behaviour at KPMG encourage intrinsic motivation? Explain.

2. Briefly summarize the main points in the debate about the effect of monetary rewards on employee motivation. Do you think that KPMG should continue to give bonuses to employees?

3. KPMG is a multinational firm. What sort of advice would you offer to KPMG management about motivating people across different cultures?

4. To what extent are KPMG's current motivation practices consistent with the recommendations made by Alfie Kohn? Give examples.

5. KPMG spends a significant amount of time getting input from both current and potential employees regarding what they want in a job. Why is this so important to the organization?

From *Concepts* to *Skills*

Setting Goals

You can be more effective at setting goals if you use the following eight suggestions.[145]

1. *Identify the key tasks you want to accomplish*. Goal setting begins by defining what it is that you want to accomplish.

2. *Establish specific and challenging goals for each key task*. Identify the level of performance you want to accomplish for each task. Specify the targets toward which you are working.

3. *Specify the deadlines for each goal*. Putting deadlines on each goal reduces ambiguity. Deadlines, however, should not be set arbitrarily. Rather, they need to be realistic given the tasks to be completed.

4. *Allow the employee to participate actively*. When employees participate in goal setting, they are more likely to accept the goals. However, it must be sincere participation. That is, employees must perceive that you are truly seeking their input, not just going through the motions.

5. *Prioritize goals*. When you have more than one goal, it's important to rank the goals in order of importance. The purpose of prioritizing is to encourage you to take action and expend effort on each goal in proportion to its importance.

6. *Rate goals for difficulty and importance*. Goal setting should not encourage people to choose easy goals. Instead, goals should be rated for their difficulty and importance. When goals are rated, individuals can be given credit for trying to reach difficult goals, even if they don't fully achieve them.

7. *Build in feedback mechanisms to assess goal progress*. Feedback lets you know whether your level of effort is sufficient to attain the goal. Set deadlines for when you will evaluate how you are performing. You should review your progress frequently.

8. *Link rewards to goal attainment*. It's natural for you to get discouraged when working toward your goals. Link rewards to the achievement of goals to help encourage you more.

Practising Skills

Tammie Arnold worked her way through college while holding down a part-time job bagging groceries at the Food Town supermarket chain. She liked working in the food industry, and when she graduated she accepted a position with Food Town as a management trainee. Over the next three years, Arnold gained experience in the grocery store industry and in operating a large supermarket. About a year ago, Arnold received a promotion to store manager at one of the chain's locations. One of the things she has liked about Food Town is that it gives store managers a great deal of autonomy in running their stores. The company provides very general guidelines to its managers. Top management is concerned with the bottom line; for the most part, how the store manager gets there is up to him or her. Now that Arnold is finally a store manager, she wants to use goal setting to motivate her employees. She likes the idea that everyone should have clear goals to work toward and then be evaluated against those goals.

The store employs 70 people, although except for the managers most work only 20 to 30 hours per week. There are six people reporting to Arnold: an assistant manager; a weekend manager; and grocery, produce, meat, and bakery managers. The only highly skilled jobs belong to the butchers, who have strict training and regulatory guidelines. Other less skilled jobs include cashier, shelf stocker, maintenance employee, and grocery bagger.

Arnold has come to you for advice on how to design a goal-setting program for her store. Specifically describe how she should go about setting goals in her new position. Include examples of goals for the jobs of butcher, cashier, and bakery manager.

Reinforcing Skills

1. Set personal and academic goals you want to achieve by the end of this term. Prioritize and rate them for difficulty.

2. Where do you want to be in five years? Do you have specific five-year goals? Establish three goals you want to achieve in five years. Make sure these goals are specific, challenging, and measurable.

5 *Working in Teams*

How can a team go from being at the top of the league to near the bottom in just a few short months?

1. What are teams and groups?

2. Does everyone use teams?

3. Do groups and teams go through stages while they work?

4. How do we create effective teams?

5. How do virtual teams work?

6. Are teams always the answer?

When the Ottawa Senators started the 2007–08 hockey season, they were the runner-up for the 2007 Stanley Cup.[1] They had lost to the Anaheim Ducks, who beat them in five games. While disappointed in the outcome, the team had something to be proud of: It was the first time the team had made it to the Cup finals since the Senators became an NHL expansion team in 1992–93. They were 12–3 in playoff games before making it to the final.

They started the new season confidently, with thoughts of avenging themselves in the 2008 Stanley Cup playoffs. The team got off to a record 15–2 start, only to become one of the worst teams in the NHL in the second half of the season. The Senators lost to the Pittsburgh Penguins in the first round of the playoffs.

How could the team essentially self-destruct in such a short period of time? There was a lot of finger pointing to go around, but the main answer was that "the team" stopped acting like a team. One of the team's goalies, notable for off-the-field antics, refused to take any responsibility for the team losing in the playoffs. "It was a really bad year for me—the worst year I've had, on and off the ice. It just wasn't enjoyable at all," said Ray Emery.

For teams to excel, a number of conditions need to be met. Effective teams need wise leadership, a variety of resources, and a way to solve problems. Team members need to be dedicated, and they need to build trust. In this chapter, we examine why teams have become so popular in the workplace, how groups and teams develop, how to create effective teams, how virtual teams work, and when a team is your best option to get work done.

OB Is for Everyone

- Ever wonder what causes flurries of activity in groups?
- Should individuals be paid for their "teamwork" or their individual performance?
- Why do some teams seem to get along better than others?
- Is building a team just from people who are friends a good idea?
- Why don't some team members pull their weight?

Teams vs. Groups: What's the Difference?

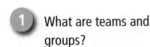
What are teams and groups?

group Two or more people with a common relationship.

team A small number of people who work closely together toward a common objective and are accountable to one another.

There is some debate about whether groups and teams are really separate concepts, or whether the terms can be used interchangeably. We think that there is a subtle difference between the terms. A **group** is two or more people with a common relationship. Thus a group could be co-workers or people meeting for lunch or standing at the bus stop. Unlike teams, groups do not necessarily engage in collective work that requires interdependent effort.

A **team** is "a small number of people with complementary skills who are committed to a common purpose, performance goals, and approach for which they hold themselves mutually accountable."[2] Groups become teams when they meet the following conditions:[3]

- Team members share *leadership*.
- Both individuals and the team as a whole share *accountability* for the work of the team.
- The team develops its own *purpose* or *mission*.
- The team works on *problem solving* continuously, rather than just at scheduled meeting times.
- The team's measure of *effectiveness* is the team's outcomes and goals, not individual outcomes and goals.

Thus while not all groups are teams, all teams can be considered groups. Much of what we discuss in this chapter applies equally well to both. We will offer some suggestions on creating effective teams later in the chapter. This chapter's *Point/Counterpoint* on page 185 discusses whether sports teams are good models for helping us understand how teams function in the workplace.

At the Louis Vuitton factory in Ducey, France, all employees work in problem-solving teams, with each team focusing on one product at a time. Team members are encouraged to suggest improvements in manufacturing work methods and processes as well as product quality. When a team was asked to make a test run on a prototype of a new handbag, team members discovered that decorative studs were causing the bag's zipper to bunch up. The team alerted managers, who had technicians move the studs away from the zipper, which solved the problem.

Why Have Teams Become So Popular?

Pick up almost any business newspaper or magazine today and you will read how teams have become an essential part of the way business is done in companies such as Zellers, Xerox, Sears Canada, General Electric, AT&T, Hewlett-Packard, Motorola, Apple Computer, DaimlerChrysler AG, 3M, Australian Airlines, Johnson & Johnson, and London Life Insurance Company. How do we explain the current popularity of teams? As organizations have restructured themselves to compete more effectively and efficiently, they have turned to teams as a better way to use employee talents. Management has found that teams are more flexible and responsive to changing events than are traditional departments or other forms of permanent groupings. Teams have the capability to quickly assemble, deploy, refocus, and disband. The extensive use of teams creates the *potential* for an organization to generate greater outputs with no increase in inputs. Notice, however, we said "potential." Creating a team does not lead magically to positive results. As well, merely calling a group a *team* will not automatically increase its level of performance.

Do teams work? The evidence suggests that teams typically outperform individuals when the tasks being done require multiple skills, judgment, and experience.[4] As organizations have restructured to compete more effectively and efficiently, they have turned to teams as a way to better use employee talents. Management has found that teams are more flexible and responsive to changing events than traditional departments or other forms of permanent groupings. Teams can quickly assemble, deploy, refocus, and disband. Teams also can be more motivational. Recall from the job characteristics model in Chapter 4 that having greater task identity is one way of increasing motivation. Teams allow for greater task identity, with team members working on tasks together.

As we show later in this chapter, successful, or high-performing, teams have certain common characteristics. If management hopes to gain increases in organizational performance through the use of teams, it must ensure that its teams possess these characteristics.

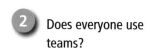 **2** Does everyone use teams?

Stages of Group and Team Development

> As the Ottawa Senators headed into training camp in July 2008, following their disappointing 2007–08 season, they faced a number of questions.[5] Would they ever qualify for the playoffs again? What was their new coach, Craig Hartsburg, going to be like? Who would fill some of the key positions, such as defenceman and winger? Could they all work well together again? To rebuild a successful team that makes it to the Stanley Cup finals, the Senators will have to go through several stages. So what stages do teams go through as they develop?

3 Do groups and teams go through stages while they work?

While we make a distinction between groups and teams, some of the stages of development they go through are similar. In this section, we discuss two models of group development. The five-stage model describes the standardized sequence of stages groups pass through. The recently discovered punctuated-equilibrium model describes the pattern of development specific to temporary groups with deadlines. These models apply as readily to teams.

The Five-Stage Model

From the mid-1960s, it was believed that groups passed through a standard sequence of five stages.[6] As shown in Exhibit 5-1 on page 160, these five stages have been labelled *forming, storming, norming, performing,* and *adjourning.* Although we now know that not all groups pass through these stages in a linear fashion, the five-stage model of group development can still help in addressing your anxieties about working in

EXHIBIT 5-1   Stages of Group Development and Accompanying Issues

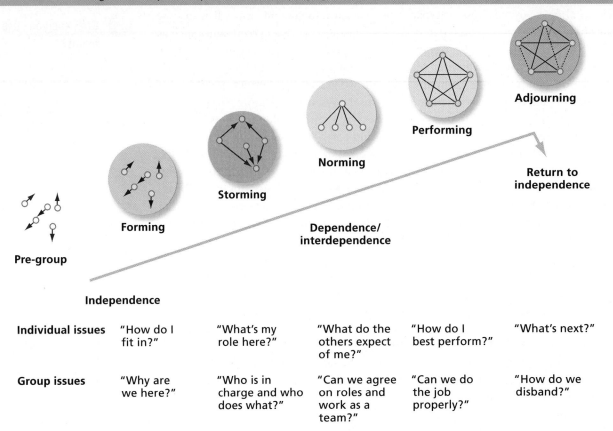

Individual issues	"How do I fit in?"	"What's my role here?"	"What do the others expect of me?"	"How do I best perform?"	"What's next?"
Group issues	"Why are we here?"	"Who is in charge and who does what?"	"Can we agree on roles and work as a team?"	"Can we do the job properly?"	"How do we disband?"

groups and teams. The model shows how individuals move from being independent to working interdependently with group members.

- *Stage I: Forming.* Think about the first time you met with a new group that had been put together to accomplish a task. Do you remember how some people seemed silent and others felt confused about the task you were to accomplish? Those feelings arise during the first stage of group development, know as forming. **Forming** is characterized by a great deal of uncertainty about the group's purpose, structure, and leadership. Members are "testing the waters" to determine what types of behaviour are acceptable. This stage is complete when members have begun to think of themselves as part of a group.

- *Stage II: Storming.* Do you remember how some people in your group just did not seem to get along, and sometimes power struggles even emerged? These reactions are typical of the **storming** stage, which is one of intragroup conflict. Members accept the existence of the group, but resist the constraints that the group imposes on individuality. Furthermore, there is conflict over who will control the group. When this stage is complete, a relatively clear hierarchy of leadership will emerge within the group.

  Some groups never really emerge from the storming stage, or they move back and forth through storming and the other stages. A group that remains forever planted in the storming stage may have less ability to complete the task because of all the interpersonal problems.

- *Stage III: Norming.* Many groups resolve the interpersonal conflict and reach the third stage, in which close relationships develop and the group demonstrates

forming The first stage in group development, characterized by much uncertainty.

storming The second stage in group development, characterized by intragroup conflict.

cohesiveness. There is now a strong sense of group identity and camaraderie. The group develops **norms**, acceptable standards of behaviour that are shared by the group's members. All groups have established norms that tell members what they ought and ought not to do under certain circumstances. When agreed to and accepted by the group, norms act as a means of influencing the behaviour of group members with a minimum of external controls. This **norming** stage is complete when the group structure solidifies and the group has assimilated a common set of expectations about what defines correct member behaviour.

norms Acceptable standards of behaviour within a group that are shared by the group's members.

- *Stage IV: Performing.* Next, and you may have noticed this in some of your own group interactions, some groups just seem to come together well and start to do their work. This fourth stage, when significant task progress is being made, is called **performing**. The structure at this point is fully functional and accepted. Group energy has moved from getting to know and understand each other to performing the task at hand.

norming The third stage in group development, characterized by close relationships and cohesiveness.

performing The fourth stage in group development, when the group is fully functional.

- *Stage V: Adjourning.* For permanent work groups, performing is the last stage in their development. However, for temporary committees, teams, task forces, and similar groups that have a limited task to perform, there is an **adjourning** stage. In this stage, the group prepares to split up. High task performance is no longer the group's top priority. Instead, attention is directed toward wrapping up activities. Group members' responses vary at this stage. Some members are upbeat, basking in the group's accomplishments. Others may be depressed over the loss of camaraderie and friendships gained during the work group's life.

adjourning The final stage in group development for temporary groups, where attention is directed toward wrapping up activities rather than task performance.

Putting the Five-Stage Model into Perspective

Many interpreters of the five-stage model have assumed that a group becomes more effective as it progresses through the first four stages. While that is usually true, what makes a group effective is more complex than this model acknowledges. Under some

Having passed through the forming, storming, and norming phases of group development, this group of women at Delphi Delco Electronics factory in Mexico now functions as a permanent work group in the performing stage. Their structure is functional and accepted, and each day they begin their work with a small shift meeting before performing their tasks.

conditions, high levels of conflict lead to high group performance, as long as the conflict is directed toward the task and not toward group members. So we might expect to find situations in which groups in Stage II outperform those in Stage III or Stage IV. Similarly, groups do not always proceed clearly from one stage to the next. Sometimes, in fact, several stages go on simultaneously, as when groups are storming and performing at the same time. Groups even occasionally move backwards to previous stages. Therefore, you should not assume that all groups follow the five-stage process precisely or that Stage IV is always the most preferable.

The five-stage model ignores organizational context.[7] For instance, a study of a cockpit crew in an airliner found that, within 10 minutes, three strangers assigned to fly together for the first time had become a high-performing group. How could a group come together so quickly? The answer lies in the strong organizational context surrounding the tasks of the cockpit crew. This context provided the rules, task definitions, information, and resources needed for the group to perform. They did not need to develop plans, assign roles, determine and allocate resources, resolve conflicts, and set norms the way the five-stage model predicts.

Within the workplace, some group behaviour takes place within a strong organizational context, and the five-stage development model might have limited applicability for those groups. However, there are a variety of situations in the workplace in which groups are assigned to tasks and the individuals do not know each other. They must therefore work out interpersonal differences at the same time as they work through the assigned tasks.

The Punctuated-Equilibrium Model

Ever wonder what causes flurries of activity in groups?

Temporary groups with deadlines do not seem to follow the previous model. Studies indicate that temporary groups with deadlines have their own unique sequence of action (or inaction):[8]

- The first meeting sets the group's direction.

- The first phase of group activity is one of inertia.

- A transition takes place at the end of the first phase, which occurs exactly when the group has used up half its allotted time.

- The transition initiates major changes.

- A second phase of inertia follows the transition.

- The group's last meeting is characterized by high levels of productive activity.

This pattern is called the *punctuated-equilibrium model*, developed by Professor Connie Gersick, a Visiting Scholar at the Yale University School of Management, and is shown in Exhibit 5-2.[9] It is important for you to understand these shifts in group behaviour. If you are ever in a group that is not working well, knowing about the shifts could help you think of ways to make the group move to a more productive phase.

Phase 1

As a group member and possibly a group leader, you need to recognize that the first meeting sets the group's direction. A framework of behavioural patterns and assumptions through which the group will approach its project emerges in this first meeting. These lasting patterns can appear as early as the first few seconds of the group's life.

EXHIBIT 5-2   The Punctuated-Equilibrium Model

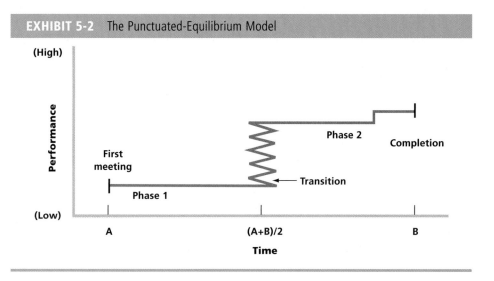

Once set, the group's direction becomes accepted and is unlikely to be re-examined throughout the first half of the group's life. This is a period of inertia—that is, the group tends to stand still or become locked into a fixed course of action. Even if it gains new insights that challenge initial patterns and assumptions, the group does not act on these new insights in Phase 1. You may recognize that in some groups, during the early period of trying to get things accomplished, no one really did his or her assigned tasks. You may also recognize this phase as one in which everyone carries out the tasks, but not in a very coordinated fashion. Thus, the group is performing at a relatively low level. This does not necessarily mean that it is doing nothing at all, however.

Phase 2

At some point, the group moves out of the inertia stage and recognizes that work needs to get completed. One of the more interesting discoveries made in these studies was that each group experienced its transition at the same point in its calendar—precisely halfway between its first meeting and its official deadline. The similarity occurred despite the fact that some groups spent as little as an hour on their projects while others spent six months. It was as if the groups universally experienced a mid-life crisis at this point. The midpoint appears to work like an alarm clock, heightening members' awareness that their time is limited and that they need to "get moving." When you work on your next group project, you might want to examine when your group starts to "get moving."

This transition ends Phase 1 and is characterized by a concentrated burst of changes, dropping of old patterns, and adoption of new perspectives. The transition sets a revised direction for Phase 2, which is a new equilibrium or period of inertia. In this phase, the group executes plans created during the transition period. The group's last meeting is characterized by a final burst of activity to finish its work. There have been a number of studies that support the basic premise of punctuated equilibrium, though not all of them found that the transition in the group occurred exactly at the midpoint.[10]

Applying the Punctuated-Equilibrium Model

Let's use this model to describe some of your experiences with student teams created for doing group term projects. At the first meeting, a basic timetable is established. Members size up one another. They agree they have nine weeks to complete their projects.

The instructor's requirements are discussed and debated. From that point, the group meets regularly to carry out its activities. About four or five weeks into the project, however, problems are confronted. Criticism begins to be taken seriously. Discussion becomes more open. The group reassesses where it has been and aggressively moves to make necessary changes. If the right changes are made, the next four or five weeks find the group developing a first-rate project. The group's last meeting, which will probably occur just before the project is due, lasts longer than the others. In it, all final issues are discussed and details resolved.

In summary, the punctuated-equilibrium model characterizes deadline-oriented groups and teams as exhibiting long periods of inertia interspersed with brief revolutionary changes triggered primarily by members' awareness of time and deadlines. To use the terminology of the five-stage model, the group begins by combining the *forming* and *norming* stages, then goes through a period of *low performing*, followed by *storming*, then a period of *high performing*, and, finally, *adjourning*.

Several researchers have suggested that the five-stage and punctuated-equilibrium models are at odds with each other.[11] However, it makes more sense to view the models as complementary: The five-stage model considers the interpersonal process of the group, while the punctuated-equilibrium model considers the time challenges that the group faces.[12] Group members and managers may want to use the implications of the punctuated-equilibrium model to either shorten the deadlines for tasks (so that less time is wasted getting to the midpoint of the time period) or to build in more goals and rewards for the first half of the time period (to help overcome the inertia that occurs during that phase).

Creating Effective Teams

When Craig Hartsburg took over as coach for the Ottawa Senators, he was facing a team that did not have a good reputation.[13] They had finished near the bottom of the league, and the team had a reputation as a "party squad." There were concerns that the team lacked discipline, and one reporter asked him if he was considering 10 p.m. curfews and giving out alarm clocks. While he laughed at that suggestion, he said, "We have some really good players, star players, and I think we also have a great group of role players here, so the thing is, we've got to get them buying in, all in, to the program." Hartsburg also noted that the team had to work on trust: trust in the team as a whole, in the coaches, and in the individual players. What other factors might contribute to the effectiveness of the Ottawa Senators?

4 How do we create effective teams?

When we consider team effectiveness, we refer to such objective measures as the team's productivity, managers' ratings of the team's performance, and aggregate measures of member satisfaction. Some of the considerations necessary to create effective teams are outlined next. However, we are also interested in team process. Exhibit 5-3 provides a checklist of the characteristics of an effective team.

There is no shortage of efforts that try to identify the factors that lead to team effectiveness.[14] However, studies have taken what was once a "veritable laundry list of characteristics"[15] and organized them into a relatively focused model with four general categories (summarized in Exhibit 5-4):[16]

- Resources and other contextual influences that make teams effective

- Team composition

- Work design

- Team process (those things that go on in the team that influence how effective the team is)

EXHIBIT 5-3   Characteristics of an Effective Team

1. **Clear purpose**	The vision, mission, goal, or task of the team has been defined and is now accepted by everyone. There is an action plan.
2. **Informality**	The climate tends to be informal, comfortable, and relaxed. There are no obvious tensions or signs of boredom.
3. **Participation**	There is much discussion, and everyone is encouraged to participate.
4. **Listening**	The members use effective listening techniques such as questioning, paraphrasing, and summarizing to get out ideas.
5. **Civilized disagreement**	There is disagreement, but the team is comfortable with this and shows no signs of avoiding, smoothing over, or suppressing conflict.
6. **Consensus decisions**	For important decisions, the goal is substantial but not necessarily unanimous agreement through open discussion of everyone's ideas, avoidance of formal voting, or easy compromises.
7. **Open communication**	Team members feel free to express their feelings on the tasks as well as on the group's operation. There are few hidden agendas. Communication takes place outside of meetings.
8. **Clear rules and work assignments**	There are clear expectations about the roles played by each team member. When action is taken, clear assignments are made, accepted, and carried out. Work is distributed among team members.
9. **Shared leadership**	While the team has a formal leader, leadership functions shift from time to time depending on the circumstances, the needs of the group, and the skills of the members. The formal leader models the appropriate behaviour and helps establish positive norms.
10. **External relations**	The team spends time developing key outside relationships, mobilizing resources, and building credibility with important players in other parts of the organization.
11. **Style diversity**	The team has a broad spectrum of team-player types including members who emphasize attention to task, goal setting, focus on process, and questions about how the team is functioning.
12. **Self-assessment**	Periodically, the team stops to examine how well it is functioning and what may be interfering with its effectiveness.

Source: G. M. Parker, *Team Players and Teamwork: The New Competitive Business Strategy* (San Francisco: Jossey-Bass, 1990), Table 2, p. 33.
Copyright © 1990 by Jossey-Bass Inc., Publishers. Reprinted by permission of John Wiley & Sons, Inc.

EXHIBIT 5-4   A Model of Team Effectiveness

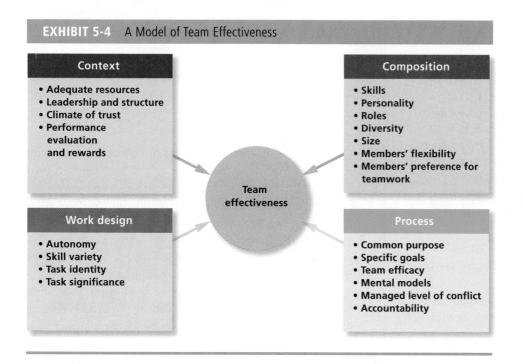

Becoming a team player is not easy, as *OB in the Street* demonstrates.

Top Skeleton Racer Finds Teamwork a Real Challenge

Is being a team player all that tough? Jeff Pain spent much of the 2000s trying his best not to be a team player, even though he was part of the Canadian men's skeleton team (a skeleton sled is a one-person racing toboggan).[17] Much of Pain's negativity toward teamwork was directed at team member Duff Gibson, his rival for over five years. "When Duff started skeleton [in 1999], I had a difficult time with my team dynamics because I felt that I knew a lot more than the people I was sliding with," says Pain. "I didn't want to share information with them and I carried that mistaken belief right up to [2004]. That was probably my and Duff's worst year."[18]

In summer 2004, Pain, Gibson, and fellow team member Paul Boehm decided to work together to share information about the tracks they were competing on, and then tried to help each other out.

Pain and Gibson improved their times and reached the highest level in international standings. Pain admits that learning how to be more of a team player has helped him improve in a sport that he was thinking of quitting because of his unhappiness with other team members. "I really insulated myself, and that didn't create a good environment for me or the team," Pain says.[19] At the 2006 Olympics, the two teammates wound up taking the top spots in skeleton racing: Gibson won gold, and Pain won silver.

Harming Your Team

→ **Refuse to share** issues and concerns. Team members refuse to share information and engage in silence, avoidance, and meetings behind closed doors where not all members are included.

→ **Depend** too much **on the leader**. Members rely too much on the leader and do not carry out their responsibilities.

→ **Fail to follow through** on decisions. Teams do not take action after decision making, showing that the needs of the team have low priority, or members are not committed to the decisions that were made.

→ **Hide conflict.** Team members do not reveal that they have a difference of opinion and this causes tension.

→ **Fail at conflict resolution**. Infighting, put-downs, and attempts to hurt other members damage the team.

→ **Form subgroups.** The team breaks up into smaller groups that put their needs ahead of the team as a whole.[21]

Keep in mind two caveats as you review the issues that lead to effective teams:

- First, teams differ in form and structure. Since the model we present attempts to generalize across all varieties of teams, you need to be careful not to rigidly apply the model's predictions to all teams.[20] The model should be used as a guide, not as an inflexible prescription.

- Second, the model assumes that it's already been determined that teamwork is preferable over individual work. Creating "effective" teams in situations in which individuals can do the job better is equivalent to solving the wrong problem perfectly.

OB in Action—Harming Your Team presents actions that can make a team ineffective. You might want to evaluate your own team experiences against this checklist to give you some idea of how well your team is functioning or to understand what might be causing problems for your team. Then consider the factors that lead to more effective teams below. *Case Incident—Team-Building Retreats* on pages 188–189 examines whether corporate retreats build effective teams and increase productivity among employees. For an applied look at the process of building an effective team, see the *Working With Others Exercise* on pages 187–188, which asks you to build a paper tower with teammates and then analyze how the team performed.

Team Context

Teams can require a great deal of maintenance to function properly. They need management support as well as an organizational structure that supports teamwork. The four contextual factors that appear to be most significantly related to team performance are adequate resources, effective leadership, a climate of trust, and a performance evaluation and reward system that reflects team contributions.

Adequate Resources

All work teams rely on resources outside the team to sustain them. A scarcity of resources directly reduces the ability of a team to perform its job effectively. As one set of researchers concluded after looking at 13 factors potentially related to team performance, "perhaps one of the most important characteristics of an effective work group is the support the group receives from the organization."[22] This includes technology, adequate staffing, administrative assistance, encouragement, and timely information. Teams must receive the necessary support from management and the larger organization if they are going to succeed in achieving their goals.

Kerri Molinaro, president of Burlington, Ontario-based IKEA Canada, believes that teams are the best way to bring employees together. IKEA's leadership style is informal, and the company values people who are humble and trustworthy. This also makes them good team members.

Leadership and Structure

Leadership plays a crucial role in the development and success of teams. As the Ottawa Senators started losing more and more games in early 2008, John Paddock, the team's coach, was fired for not doing enough to keep the team together.

Professor Richard Hackman of Harvard University, who is a leading expert on teams, suggests that the role of team leader involves the following:[23]

- Creating a real team rather than a team in name only

- Setting a clear and meaningful direction for the team's work

- Making sure that the team structure will support its working effectively

- Ensuring that the team operates within a supportive organizational context

- Providing expert coaching

There are some practical problems that must be resolved when a team first starts working together. Team members must agree on who is to do what and ensure that all members contribute equally in sharing the workload. The team also needs to determine how schedules will be set, what skills need to be developed, how the team will resolve conflicts, and how the team will make and modify decisions. Agreeing on the specifics of work and how they fit together to integrate individual skills requires team leadership and structure. This, incidentally, can be provided directly by management or by the team members themselves. Although you might think there is no role for leaders in self-managed teams, that could not be further from the truth. It is true that, in self-managed teams, team members absorb many of the duties typically assumed by managers. However, a manager's job becomes managing outside (rather than inside) the team.

Leadership is especially important in multi-team systems—where different teams need to coordinate their efforts to produce a desired outcome. In such systems, leaders need to empower teams by delegating responsibility to them, and they need to play the role of facilitator, making sure the teams are coordinating their efforts so that they work together rather than against one another.[24] The *Learning About Yourself Exercise* on pages 186–187 will help you evaluate how suited you are to building and leading a team.

Recent research suggests that women may make better team leaders than men. "The more women participating equally in a project, the better the outcome," suggests Professor Jennifer Berdahl of the Joseph L. Rotman School of Management at the University of Toronto.[25] Berdahl's research, which looked at 169 students enrolled in her organizational behaviour courses, found that in predominantly female teams, women shared leadership roles and were more egalitarian in how they worked. Male-led teams, whether they were predominantly male groups or mixed-gender groups, received poorer grades on their projects than teams where women shared leadership roles.[26]

Sometimes teams need coaches more than they need leaders. Though workplace teams often report that they receive little coaching compared with leadership,[27] productivity-related coaching may help teams perform more effectively. In particular, coaching may be best at three particular stages in the team's history: "at the beginning for effort-related (motivational) interventions, near the midpoint for strategy-related (consultative) interventions, and at the end of a task cycle for (educational) interventions that address knowledge and skill."[28]

Teams do not always need a leader. For instance, the evidence indicates that self-managed work teams often perform better than teams with formally appointed leaders.[29] Leaders can also obstruct high performance when they interfere with self-managed teams.[30] On self-managed teams, team members absorb many of the duties typically assumed by managers.

Climate of Trust

Members of effective teams trust each other. For team members to do this, they must feel that the team is capable of getting the task done and they must believe that "the team will not harm the individual or his or her interests."[31] Interpersonal trust among team members facilitates cooperation, reduces the need to monitor one another's behaviour, and bonds members around the belief that others on the team will not take advantage of them. Team members are more likely to take risks and expose vulnerabilities when they believe they can trust others on their team. *OB in Action—Building Trust* shows the dimensions that underlie the concept of trust.

Team members must also trust their leaders.[32] Trust in leadership is important in that it allows the team to be willing to accept and commit to their leader's goals and decisions. Management at Mississauga, Ontario-based Flynn Canada invests in their employees to make sure that they become good team players. The company helps employees learn to trust each other, so that they can work effectively. Employees are encouraged to take pride in their work and the outcomes of their work. They are encouraged to be open with one another. "Personally, what attracted me to Flynn is that it's got scale and horsepower but it has a heart and soul; it's not just another corporate entity. We are authentic in our interactions with each other. What you see is what you get," says Gerard Montocchio, vice-president of human resources.

OB in ACTION

Building Trust

The following actions, in order of importance, help build one's trustworthiness.

→ **Integrity**—built through **honesty** and **truthfulness**.

→ **Competence**—demonstrated by technical and interpersonal **knowledge** and **skills**.

→ **Consistency**—shown by **reliability**, **predictability**, and **good judgment** in handling situations.

→ **Loyalty**—one's willingness to **protect** and **stand up** for another person.

→ **Openness**—one's willingness to **share ideas** and **information** freely.[33]

Performance Evaluation and Rewards

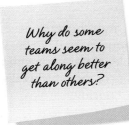

Should individuals be paid for their "teamwork" or their individual performance?

How do you get team members to be both individually and jointly accountable? The traditional individually oriented evaluation must be modified to reflect team performance.[34]

Individual performance evaluations, fixed hourly wages, individual incentives, and the like are not consistent with the development of high-performance teams. So in addition to evaluating and rewarding employees for their individual contributions, management should consider group-based appraisals, profit sharing, gainsharing, small-group incentives, and other system modifications that will reinforce team effort and commitment. Ignoring these factors may affect the level of trust that develops in the team.[35]

One additional consideration when deciding whether and how to reward team members is the effect of pay dispersion on team performance. Research by Nancy Langton, your Vancouver-based author, shows that when there is a large discrepancy in wages among group members, collaboration is lowered.[36] A study of baseball players' salaries also found that teams in which players were paid more similarly often outperformed teams with highly paid "stars" and lowly paid "scrubs."[37]

Team Composition

Why do some teams seem to get along better than others?

This category includes variables that relate to how teams should be staffed. In this section, we address the skills, personality, and roles of team members, the diversity and size of the team, member flexibility, and members' preference for teamwork.

Skills

To perform effectively, a team requires three different types of skills:

1. It needs people with *technical expertise.*

2. It needs people with the *problem-solving* and *decision-making* skills to be able to identify problems, generate alternatives, evaluate those alternatives, and make competent choices.

3. It needs people with good listening, feedback, conflict resolution, and other *interpersonal skills.*[38]

No team can achieve its performance potential without developing all three types of skills. The right mix is crucial. Too much of one at the expense of others will result in lower team performance. But teams do not need to have all the complementary skills in place at the beginning. It's not uncommon for one or more members to take responsibility to learn the skills in which the group is deficient, thereby allowing the team to reach its full potential. Exhibit 5-5 on page 170 identifies some important teamwork skills that help teams function well.

Personality

Teams have different needs, and people should be selected for the team on the basis of their personalities and preferences, as well as the team's needs for diversity and specific roles. We demonstrated in Chapter 2 that personality has a significant influence on individual employee behaviour. Personality also influences team behaviour.

Many of the dimensions identified in the Big Five personality model have been shown to be relevant to team effectiveness. A recent review of the literature suggested

EXHIBIT 5-5 Teamwork Skills	
Orients Team to Problem-Solving Situation	Assists the team in arriving at a common understanding of the situation or problem. Determines the important elements of a problem situation. Seeks out relevant data related to the situation or problem.
Organizes and Manages Team Performance	Helps team establish specific, challenging, and accepted team goals. Monitors, evaluates, and provides feedback on team performance. Identifies alternative strategies or reallocates resources to address feedback on team performance.
Promotes a Positive Team Environment	Assists in creating and reinforcing norms of tolerance, respect, and excellence. Recognizes and praises other team members' efforts. Helps and supports other team members. Models desirable team member behaviour.
Facilitates and Manages Task Conflict	Encourages desirable and discourages undesirable team conflict. Recognizes the type and source of conflict confronting the team and implements an appropriate resolution strategy. Employs "win-win" negotiation strategies to resolve team conflicts.
Appropriately Promotes Perspective	Defends stated preferences, argues for a particular point of view, and withstands pressure to change position for another that is not supported by logical or knowledge-based arguments. Changes or modifies position if a defensible argument is made by another team member. Projects courtesy and friendliness to others while arguing position.

Source: G. Chen, L. M. Donahue, and R. J. Klimoski, "Training Undergraduates to Work in Organizational Teams," *Academy of Management Learning & Education* 3, no. 1 (March 2004), p. 40.

that three of the Big Five traits were especially important for team performance.[39] Specifically, teams that rate higher on mean levels of conscientiousness and openness to experience tend to perform better. Moreover, the minimum level of team member agreeableness also matters: Teams did worse when they had one or more highly disagreeable members. Perhaps one bad apple *can* spoil the whole bunch!

Senior product scientists Syed Abbas and Albert Post and technology team manager Laurie Coyle functioned as a high-ability team in developing Unilever's new Dove Nutrium bar soap. In solving the complex problems involved in product innovation, the intelligent members of Unilever's research and development teams have advanced science degrees, the ability to think creatively, and the interpersonal skills needed to perform effectively with other team members.

Research has also provided us with a good idea about why these personality traits are important to teams. Conscientious people are valuable in teams because they are good at backing up other team members, and they are also good at sensing when that support is truly needed. Open team members communicate better with one another and throw out more ideas, which leads teams composed of open people to be more creative and innovative.[40]

Roles

In groups, each individual fills a particular **role**. By this term, we mean a set of expected behaviour patterns of a person in a given position in a social unit. Within almost any group, two sets of role relationships need to be considered: task-oriented roles and maintenance roles. **Task-oriented roles** are performed by group members to ensure that the tasks of the group are accomplished. These roles include initiators, information seekers, information providers, elaborators, summarizers, and consensus makers. **Maintenance roles** are carried out to ensure that group members maintain good relations. These roles include harmonizers, compromisers, gatekeepers, and encouragers.

Effective teams maintain some balance between task orientation and maintenance of relations. Exhibit 5-6 on page 172 identifies a number of task-oriented and maintenance behaviours in the key roles that you might find in a team.

On many teams, there are individuals who will be flexible enough to play multiple roles and/or complete each other's tasks. This is an obvious plus to a team because it greatly improves its adaptability and makes it less reliant on any single member.[41] Selecting members who themselves value flexibility, and then cross-training them to be able to do one another's jobs, should lead to a higher level of team performance over time.

Occasionally within teams, you will see people take on **individual roles** that are not productive for keeping the team on task. When this happens, the individual is demonstrating more concern for himself or herself than the team as a whole.

Most roles, whether in the workplace or in our personal lives, are governed by **role expectations**, that is, how others believe a person should act in a given situation. **Role conflict** exists when an individual finds that complying with one role requirement may make it more difficult to comply with another.[42] At the extreme, it can include situations in which two or more role expectations are mutually contradictory!

Diversity

Group diversity refers to the presence of a heterogeneous mix of individuals within a group.[43] Individuals can be different not only in functional characteristics (jobs, positions, expertise, or work experiences) but also in demographic or cultural characteristics (age, race, sex, and citizenship).

RESEARCH FINDINGS: TEAM DIVERSITY

Managing diversity on teams is a balancing act (see Exhibit 5-7 on page 173).[44] On the one hand, a number of researchers have suggested that diversity brings a greater number of ideas, perspectives, knowledge, and skills to the group, which can be used to perform at a higher level.[45] On the other hand, researchers have suggested that diversity can lead people to recall stereotypes and therefore bring bias into their evaluations of people who are different from them.[46] Diversity can thus make it more difficult to unify the team and reach agreements.[47] We consider some of the evidence to help us resolve these opposing views.

role A set of expected behaviours of a person in a given position in a social unit.

task-oriented roles Roles performed by group members to ensure that the tasks of the group are carried out.

maintenance roles Roles performed by group members to maintain good relations within the group.

individual roles Roles performed by group members that are not productive for keeping the team on task.

role expectations How others believe a person should act in a given situation.

role conflict A situation in which an individual finds that complying with one role requirement may make it more difficult to comply with another.

group diversity The heterogeneous mix of individuals within a group.

EXHIBIT 5-6	Roles Required for Effective Team Functioning		
	Function	**Description**	**Example**
Roles that build task accomplishment	*Initiating*	Stating the goal or problem, making proposals about how to work on it, setting time limits.	"Let's set up an agenda for discussing each of the problems we have to consider."
	Seeking information and opinions	Asking group members for specific factual information related to the task or problem, or for their opinions about it.	"What do you think would be the best approach to this, Jack?"
	Providing information and opinions	Sharing information or opinions related to the task or problems.	"I worked on a similar problem last year and found . . ."
	Clarifying	Helping one another understand ideas and suggestions that come up in the group.	"What you mean, Sue, is that we could . . ."
	Elaborating	Building on one another's ideas and suggestions.	"Building on Don's idea, I think we could . . ."
	Summarizing	Reviewing the points covered by the group and the different ideas stated so that decisions can be based on full information.	Appointing a recorder to take notes on a blackboard.
	Consensus testing	Providing periodic testing on whether the group is nearing a decision or needs to continue discussion.	"Is the group ready to decide about this?"
Roles that build and maintain a team	*Harmonizing*	Mediating conflict among other members, reconciling disagreements, relieving tensions.	"Don, I don't think you and Sue really see the question that differently."
	Compromising	Admitting error at times of group conflict.	"Well, I'd be willing to change if you provided some help on . . ."
	Gatekeeping	Making sure all members have a chance to express their ideas and feelings and preventing members from being interrupted.	"Sue, we haven't heard from you on this issue."
	Encouraging	Helping a group member make his or her point. Establishing a climate of acceptance in the group.	"I think what you started to say is important, Jack. Please continue."

Source: "Team Processes," in *Managing for the Future*, ed. D. Ancona, T. Kochan, M. Scully, J. Van Maanen, and D. E. Westney (Cincinnati, OH: South-Western College Publishing, 1996), p. 9.

In a study examining the effectiveness of teams of strangers and teams of friends on bargaining, researchers found that teams of strangers gained greater profit than teams of friends when teams reported to a supervisor.[48] However, teams of friends were more cohesive than teams of strangers. Another study of 60 teams found that in effective teams, about 50 percent of the individuals considered themselves friends, which underscores the importance of teams' developing friendships.[49] However, the researchers

EXHIBIT 5-7	Advantages and Disadvantages of Diversity
Advantages	**Disadvantages**
Multiple perspectives	Ambiguity
Greater openness to new ideas	Complexity
Multiple interpretations	Confusion
Increased creativity	Miscommunication
Increased flexibility	Difficulty in reaching a single agreement
Increased problem-solving skills	Difficulty in agreeing on specific actions

Source: Adapted from N. J. Adler, *International Dimensions of Organizational Behavior*, 4th ed., p. 109. © 2002 South-Western, a part of Cengage Learning, Inc. Reproduced by permission www.cengage.com/permissions.

Is building a team just from people who are friends a good idea?

also found that in teams that reported almost 100 percent friendship, performance was much lower. These groups tended to isolate themselves from others and not seek outside influences. The research on friendships in teams suggests that teams of friends may be less concerned with productivity and more concerned with maintaining their relationship than are teams of strangers.

Recent studies have examined the effect of heterogeneous values on performance and suggest that value differences may have a greater influence than functional, demographic, or cultural differences.[50] Professor Margaret Neale of Stanford University's Graduate School of Business examined the impact of three types of diversity on group performance: informational, demographic, and value-goal diversity.[51] She found that these different forms of diversity generate different types of conflict. Informational diversity is associated with constructive conflict, with team members debating about the best course of action. Neale considers this positive conflict. Demographic diversity can result in interpersonal conflict, which, if left unresolved, can destroy the group. Groups that have value-goal diversity may face the most damage from the diversity. When team members do not agree on values and goals, it is hard for them to function. However, if a team works through differences to reach consensus on values and goals, team members then know one another's intentions.

Overall, studies suggest that the strongest case for diversity on work teams can be made when these teams are engaged in problem-solving and decision-making tasks.[52] Heterogeneous teams may have qualities that lead to creative or unique solutions.[53] The lack of a common perspective also means diverse teams usually spend more time discussing issues, which decreases the possibility that a weak alternative will be chosen. Although diverse groups have more difficulty working together and solving problems, this goes away with time as the members come to know one another. A recent study supports this idea; teams with high expertise diversity were found to perform better when team members were committed to the team than when team members showed low commitment.[54]

Recent research suggests that when team members share a common belief that diversity will affect their performance positively, they set the foundation for the team to manage the diversity in a positive way. Specifically, if team members set out early to try to learn about one another in order to understand and make the most of their differences, this will have a positive effect on the team.[55] Laurie Milton, at the Haskayne School of Business at the University of Calgary, along with several co-authors, found that even 10 minutes spent sharing personal information when group members first started working together lowered group conflict and improved creative performance.[56] When group members did not share personal information at the beginning of their work, they were less likely to do so later.

The research findings, taken as a whole, suggest that diversity can bring added benefits to the team, but to do so, team members must have some common values, and they need to be willing to share information about themselves early on. Thus we can expect that diversity begins to provide extra value to the team once team members get to know one another and the team becomes more cohesive. *Focus on Diversity* examines the impact of diversity on learning to work together in teams.

FOCUS ON **DIVERSITY**

Questioning the Impact of Diversity

Do diverse teams really have more difficulty learning how to work together? A study of groups of Caucasian and Chinese men living in Canada examined whether being a token ethnic member in a group (the only Chinese or the only Caucasian) would affect participation and influence levels in groups.[57] Some groups worked face to face, others by computer only.

The study found that in the face-to-face groups, Caucasian males, whether tokens or dominants in their groups, had higher participation levels on average than Chinese males. However, in face-to-face groups dominated by Chinese males, the Chinese males also had relatively high participation rates. Only the token Chinese males scored low in participation or influence on their groups.

In the computer-only groups, the ethnicity of group members could be determined in some groups, while for others it could not. In those groups where the ethnicity of team members was unknown there were no differences in the participation rates of Chinese and Caucasian men.

This research suggests that participation and influence may be less a cultural issue and more related to how individuals respond to visible differences when interacting with diverse team members.

Size

Generally speaking, the most effective teams have fewer than 10 members. And experts suggest using the smallest number of people who can do the task. Unfortunately, there is a tendency for managers to make teams too large. While a minimum of four or five members may be necessary to develop a diversity of views and skills, managers seem to seriously underestimate how coordination problems can dramatically increase as team members are added. When teams have excess members, cohesiveness and mutual accountability decline, social loafing increases, and more and more people do less talking compared to others. So in designing effective teams, managers should try to keep the number of members at less than 10. If a work unit is larger and you want a team effort, consider breaking the unit into subteams. Uneven numbers in teams may help build in a mechanism to break ties and resolve conflicts, while an even number of team members may foster the need to create more consensus.

Size and Social Loafing One of the most important findings related to the size of a team has been labelled **social loafing**. Social loafing is the tendency of individuals to expend less effort when working collectively than when working individually.[58] It directly challenges the logic that the productivity of the team as a whole should at least equal the sum of the productivity of each individual in that team.

social loafing The tendency of individuals to expend less effort when working collectively than when working individually.

Studies indicate that these employees in Miles, China, collecting harvest grapes for the production of red wine will perform better in a group than when working alone. In collectivist societies such as China, employees show less propensity to engage in social loafing. Unlike individualistic cultures such as the United States, where people are dominated by self-interest, the Chinese are motivated by in-group goals.

Why don't some team members pull their weight?

What causes this social loafing effect? It may be due to a belief that others in the team are not carrying their fair share. If you view others as lazy or inept, you can re-establish equity by reducing your effort. Another explanation is the dispersion of responsibility. Because the results of the team cannot be attributed to any single person, the relationship between an individual's input and the team's output is clouded. In such situations, individuals may be tempted to become "free riders" and coast on the team's efforts. In other words, there will be a reduction in efficiency when individuals believe that their contribution cannot be measured. To reduce social loafing, teams should not be larger than necessary and individuals should be held accountable for their actions. You might also consider the ideas presented on dealing with shirkers in this chapter's *Ethical Dilemma Exercise* on page 188.

Member Flexibility

Teams made up of flexible individuals have members who can complete each other's tasks. This is an obvious plus to a team because it greatly improves its adaptability and makes it less reliant on any single member.[59] Selecting members who themselves value flexibility, then cross-training them to be able to do each other's jobs, should lead to a higher level of team performance over time.

Members' Preference for Teamwork

Not every employee is a team player. Given the option, many employees will "select themselves out" of team participation. When people who would prefer to work alone are required to team up, there is a direct threat to the team's morale.[60] This suggests that, when selecting team members, individual preferences should be considered, as well as abilities, personalities, and skills. High-performing teams are likely to be composed of people who prefer working as part of a team.

Work Design

Effective teams need to work together and take collective responsibility to complete significant tasks. They must be more than a "team-in-name-only."[61] The work design category includes variables such as freedom and autonomy, the opportunity to use a variety of skills and talents, the ability to complete a whole and identifiable task or product, and the participation in a task or project that has a substantial impact on others. The evidence indicates that these characteristics enhance member motivation and increase team effectiveness.[62] These work design characteristics motivate teams because they increase members' sense of responsibility for and ownership of the work, and because they make the work more interesting to perform.[63] These recommendations are consistent with the job characteristics model we presented in Chapter 4.

Team Process

Process variables make up the final component of team effectiveness. The process category includes member commitment to a common purpose; establishment of specific goals; team efficacy; a managed level of conflict; and a system of accountability.

Common Purpose

reflexivity A characteristic of effective teams, allowing them to reflect on and adjust their master plan when necessary.

Effective teams have a common and meaningful purpose that provides direction, momentum, and commitment for members.[64] This purpose is a vision. It's broader than specific goals.

A recent study of 23 National Basketball Association teams found that "shared experience"—tenure on the team and time on court—tended to reduce turnover and boost win-loss performance significantly. Why do you think teams that stay together longer tend to play better?

Members of successful teams put a tremendous amount of time and effort into discussing, shaping, and agreeing on a purpose that belongs to them both collectively and individually. This common purpose, when accepted by the team, becomes the equivalent of what celestial navigation is to a ship's captain—it provides direction and guidance under any and all conditions. Like the proverbial ship following the wrong course, teams that do not have good planning skills are doomed; perfectly executing the wrong plan is a lost cause.[65] Effective teams also show **reflexivity**, meaning that they reflect on and adjust their master plan when necessary. A team has to have a good plan, but it also has to be willing and able to adapt when conditions call for it.[66]

Specific Goals

Successful teams translate their common purpose into specific, measurable, and realistic performance goals. Just as we demonstrated in Chapter 4 how goals lead individuals to higher performance, so goals also energize teams. These specific goals facilitate clear communication. They also help teams maintain their focus on achieving results.

Consistent with the research on individual goals, team goals should be challenging. Difficult goals have been found to raise team performance on those criteria for which they are set. So, for instance, goals for quantity tend to raise quantity, goals for speed tend to raise speed, goals for accuracy tend to raise accuracy, and so on.[67]

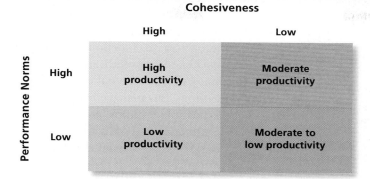

EXHIBIT 5-8 Relationship among Team Cohesiveness, Performance Norms, and Productivity

Teams should also be encouraged to develop milestones—tangible steps toward completion of the project. This allows teams to focus on their goals and evaluate progress toward the goals. The milestones should be sufficiently important and readily accomplished so that teams can celebrate some of their accomplishments along the way.

Team Efficacy

Effective teams have confidence in themselves. They believe they can succeed. We call this *team efficacy*.[68]

Success breeds success. Teams that have been successful raise their beliefs about future success which, in turn, motivates them to work harder. One of the factors that helps teams build their efficacy is **cohesiveness**—the degree to which members are attracted to one another and are motivated to stay on the team.[69] Though teams differ in their cohesiveness, it is important because it has been found to be related to the team's productivity.[70]

Studies consistently show that the relation between cohesiveness and productivity depends on the performance-related norms established by the group.[71] If performance-related norms are high (for example, high output, quality work, cooperation with individuals outside the group), a cohesive group will be more productive than a less cohesive group. If cohesiveness is high and performance norms are low, productivity will be low. If cohesiveness is low and performance norms are high, productivity increases—but less than in the high cohesiveness–high norms situation. Where cohesiveness and performance-related norms are both low, productivity will tend to fall into the low-to-moderate range. These conclusions are summarized in Exhibit 5-8. *OB in Action—Creating a Team Charter* provides a way for teams to develop productivity norms when the team first forms.

Most studies of cohesiveness focus on *socio-emotional cohesiveness*, the "sense of togetherness that develops when individuals derive emotional satisfaction from group

cohesiveness The degree to which team members are attracted to one another and are motivated to stay on the team.

OB in ACTION
Creating a Team Charter

When you form a new team, you may want to develop a team charter, so that everyone agrees on the basic norms for group performance. Consider including answers to the following in your charter:

→ What are team members' **names and contact information** (phone, email)?

→ How will **communication** among team members take place (phone, email)?

→ What will the **team ground rules** be (where and when to meet, attendance expectations, workload expectations)?

→ How will **decisions** be made (consensus, majority vote, leader rules)?

→ What **potential conflicts** may arise within the team? Among team members?

→ How will **conflicts be resolved** by the group?[72]

OB in ACTION

Increasing Group Cohesiveness

Increasing socio-emotional cohesiveness

→ Keep the group relatively **small**.

→ Strive for a **favourable public image** to increase the status and prestige of belonging.

→ Encourage **interaction** and **cooperation**.

→ Emphasize members' **common characteristics** and interests.

→ **Point out environmental threats** (e.g., competitors' achievements) to rally the group.

Increasing instrumental cohesiveness

→ Regularly update and **clarify the group's goal(s)**.

→ Give every group member a **vital "piece of the action."**

→ Channel each group member's special talents toward the **common goal(s)**.

→ **Recognize** and equitably reinforce **every member's contributions**.

→ Frequently remind group members they **need one another** to get the job done.[74]

participation."[73] There is also *instrumental cohesiveness:* the "sense of togetherness that develops when group members are mutually dependent on one another because they believe they could not achieve the group's goal by acting separately." Teams need to achieve a balance of these two types of cohesiveness to function well. *OB in Action—Increasing Group Cohesiveness* indicates how to increase both socio-emotional and instrumental cohesiveness.

What, if anything, can management do to increase team efficacy? Two possible options are helping the team to achieve small successes and skill training. Small successes build team confidence. As a team develops an increasingly stronger performance record, it also increases the collective belief that future efforts will lead to success. In addition, managers should consider providing training to improve members' technical and interpersonal skills. The greater the abilities of team members, the greater the likelihood that the team will develop confidence and the capability to deliver on that confidence.

Managed Level of Conflict

Conflict on a team is not necessarily bad. Though relationship conflicts—those based on interpersonal incompatibilities, tension, and animosity toward others—are almost always dysfunctional, teams that are completely void of conflict are likely to be less effective, with the members becoming withdrawn and only superficially harmonious. Often, if there were no conflict, the alternative was not agreement, but apathy and disengagement. Teams that avoid conflict also tend to have lower performance levels, forget to consider key issues, or remain unaware of important aspects of their situation.[75] Effective teams are characterized by an appropriate level of conflict.[76]

Kathleen Eisenhardt of the Stanford Graduate School of Business and her colleagues studied top management teams in technology-based companies to understand how they manage conflict.[77] Their research identified six tactics that helped the teams successfully manage the interpersonal conflict that can accompany group interactions. These are presented in *OB in Action—Reducing Team Conflict*. By handling the interpersonal conflict well, the teams were able to achieve their goals without letting conflict get in the way.

OB in ACTION

Reducing Team Conflict

→ Work with **more, rather than less, information**, and debate on the basis of **facts**.

→ Develop **multiple alternatives** to enrich the level of debate.

→ Develop commonly agreed-upon **goals**.

→ Use **humour** when making tough decisions.

→ Maintain a **balanced power** structure.

→ Resolve issues **without forcing consensus**.[78]

Groups need mechanisms by which they can manage the conflict, however. From the research reported above, we could conclude that sharing information and goals and striving to be open and get along are helpful strategies for negotiating our way through the maze of conflict. A sense of humour and a willingness to understand the points of others without insisting that everyone agree on all points are also important. Group members should try to focus on the issues rather than on personalities and strive to achieve fairness and equity in the group process.

Accountability

Successful teams make members individually and jointly accountable for the team's purpose, goals, and approach.[79]

They clearly define what they are individually responsible for and what they are jointly responsible for. *From Concepts to Skills* on pages 190–191 discusses how to conduct effective team meetings.

Twenty-First Century Teamwork: Virtual Teams

When we think of teams, we often picture face-to-face interactions. **Virtual teams**, however, seldom interact face-to-face and they use computer technology to tie together physically separated members in order to achieve a common goal.[80] They enable people to collaborate online—using communication links such as wide-area networks, videoconferencing, and email—whether team members are only a room away or continents apart. Virtual teams are so pervasive, and technology has advanced so far, that it's probably a bit of a misnomer to call these teams "virtual." Nearly all teams today do at least some of their work remotely.

Providing that team members are comfortable with using technology, virtual teams can do all the things that other teams do—share information, make decisions, complete tasks. They can include members from the same organization or link an organization's members with employees from other organizations (suppliers and joint partners). They can convene for a few days to solve a problem, a few months to complete a project, or exist permanently.[81] Often they can be more efficient at tasks as well, because of the ease of sharing information through email and voice mail. Virtual teams also make it possible for people who are in different geographical and time zones to work together.

Virtual teams can suffer from the limited social contact of team members. This can lead to bonding problems, which the research on teams suggests is important for team performance. One recent meta-analysis of 27 studies of virtual teams questioned whether members of virtual teams ever bonded in the traditional sense.[82] Lack of bonding can lead to slower and less accurate performance than is the case for face-to-face teams.

Virtual teams can also suffer from the absence of *paraverbal* and *nonverbal* cues in their communications. In face-to-face conversation, people use paraverbal (tone of voice, inflection, voice volume) and nonverbal (eye movement, facial expression, hand gestures, and other body language) cues to provide increased meaning. In virtual communications, team members are not able to duplicate the normal give-and-take of face-to-face discussion. As a result, virtual team members often have less social rapport and are more at risk of misunderstanding one another.

Virtual Teams and Trust

There has been some concern that, because virtual teams lack face-to-face interaction, it may be more difficult to build trust among individuals. However, two recent studies examining how virtual teams work on projects indicate that virtual teams can develop close interaction and trust; these qualities simply evolve differently than in face-to-face groups.[83] In face-to-face groups, trust comes from direct interaction, over time. In virtual teams, trust is either established at the outset or it generally does not develop. The researchers found that initial electronic messages set the tone for how interactions occurred throughout the entire project. In one team, for instance, when the appointed leader sent an introductory message that had a distrustful tone, the team suffered low morale and poor performance throughout the duration of the project. The researchers suggest that virtual teams should start with an electronic "courtship," where members provide some personal information. Then the teams should assign clear roles to members, helping members to identify with each other. Finally, the researchers noted that teams whose members had a positive attitude (eagerness, enthusiasm, and intense

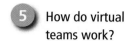

5 How do virtual teams work?

virtual teams Teams that seldom interact face-to-face and use computer technology to tie together physically dispersed members in order to achieve a common goal.

action orientation in messages) did considerably better than teams that had one or more pessimists. The article by S. L. Jarvenpaa, K. Knoll, and D. E. Leidner cited in endnote 83 of this chapter provides more detail on this subject; you might find the team experience reported there interesting.

Creating Virtual Workspaces

It is obvious that virtual teams must rely on technology to communicate. But what is the best way to do this? Team members can be overwhelmed with email, drowning in messages to the point of failing to read them. To better understand the problem, a recent study looked at 54 teams from 26 companies operating in a wide variety of industries.[84] The researchers found that 83 percent of the teams they studied used virtual workspaces (also known as virtual meeting rooms) to communicate. The virtual workspace is a team website on a company's intranet designed to help remind team members of their "decisions, rationales, and commitments." The virtual workspace can have "walls" or links to information about each person, and discussion forums with topic threads that cover important issues and problems. The discussion forums can also serve as places to post work-in-progress to get feedback. Exhibit 5-9 shows an example of a virtual workspace for a project at Shell.

Tips for managers who want to improve the way virtual teams function include the following: ensure that the team addresses feelings of isolation that members might

---

EXHIBIT 5-9   An Illustration of a Virtual Workspace

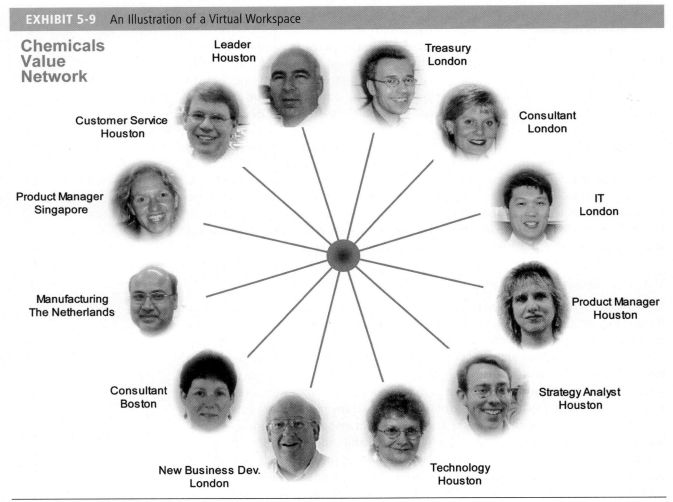

Source: Reprinted by permission of Shell Chemical LP.

have; ensure that team members have a mix of interpersonal and technical skills; and pay careful attention to evaluating performance and providing recognition and feedback.[85] By engaging in spontaneous communication with virtual team members, managers can also reduce the likelihood and impact of conflict.[86] For more tips on improving the way virtual teams function, see *OB in Action—Managing Virtual Teams*.

Beware! Teams Are Not Always the Answer

Despite considerable success in the use of teams, they are not necessarily appropriate in all situations, as Exhibit 5-10 on page 182 suggests. Teamwork takes more time and often more resources than individual work. Teams, for instance, have greater communication demands, conflicts to be managed, and meetings to be run. In their enthusiasm to enjoy the benefits of teams, some managers have introduced them into situations where the work is better done by individuals. A 2003 study done by Statistics Canada found that the introduction of teamwork lowered turnover in the service industries, for both high- and low-skilled employees. However, manufacturing companies experienced higher turnover if they introduced teamwork and formal teamwork training, compared with not doing so (15.8 percent vs. 10.7 percent).[88]

How do you know if the work of your group would be better done in teams? It has been suggested that three tests be applied to see if a team fits the situation:[89]

- *Can the work be done better by more than one person?* Simple tasks that do not require diverse input are probably better left to individuals.

- *Does the work create a common purpose or set of goals for the people in the group that is more than the sum of individual goals?* For instance, the service departments of many new-car dealers have introduced teams that link customer service personnel, mechanics, parts specialists, and sales representatives. Such teams can better manage collective responsibility for ensuring that customers' needs are properly met.

- *Are the members of the group interdependent?* Teams make sense where there is interdependence between tasks—where the success of the whole depends on the success of each one *and* the success of each one depends on the success of the others. Soccer, for instance, is an obvious *team* sport because of the interdependence of the players. Swim teams, by contrast, are not really teams, but groups of individuals whose total performance is merely the sum of the individual performances. Others have outlined the conditions under which organizations would find teams more useful: "when work processes cut across functional lines; when speed is important (and complex relationships are involved); when the organization mirrors a complex, differentiated, and rapidly changing market environment; when innovation and learning have priority; and when the tasks that have to be done require online integration of highly interdependent performers."[90]

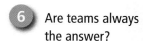

6 Are teams always the answer?

OB in ACTION

Managing Virtual Teams

Establishing trust and commitment, encouraging communication, and assessing team members pose tremendous challenges for virtual team managers. Here are a few tips to make the process easier:

- → Establish **regular times** for group interaction.
- → Set up **firm rules** for communication.
- → Use **visual forms of communication** where possible.
- → **Copy** the good points of **on-site teams**. For example, allow time for informal chit-chat and socializing, and celebrate achievements.
- → **Give and receive feedback** and offer assistance on a regular basis. Be persistent with people who are not communicating with you or each other.
- → Agree on **standard technology** so all team members can work together easily.
- → Consider using **360-degree feedback** to better understand and evaluate team members. This type of feedback comes from the full circle of daily contacts that an employee might have, including supervisors, peers, subordinates, and clients.
- → Provide a **virtual workspace** via an intranet, website, or bulletin board.
- → Note which employees **effectively use email** to build team rapport.
- → **Smooth the way for the next assignment** if membership on the team, or the team itself, is not permanent.
- → **Be available** to employees, but do not wait for them to seek you out.
- → Encourage **informal, off-line conversation** between team members.[87]

EXHIBIT 5-10

Source: S. Adams, *Build a Better Life by Stealing Office Supplies* (Kansas City, MO: Andrews and McMeal, 1991), p. 31. Dilbert reprinted with permission of United Features Syndicate.

Summary and Implications

1 **What are teams and groups?** Groups and teams differ. The output of a group is simply the sum of individual efforts. A team, because of the close collaboration among members, produces output that is greater than the sum of individual efforts.

2 **Does everyone use teams?** Teams have become an essential part of the way business is being done these days. In fact, it is more surprising to find an organization that does not use teams. As organizations focus on effectiveness and efficiency, they find that teams are a good way to manage talent. Teams are more flexible and responsive to changing events than are traditional departments or other forms of permanent groupings. Teams have the capability to quickly assemble, deploy, refocus, and disband.

3 **Do groups and teams go through stages while they work?** Two different models illustrate how teams and groups develop. The first, the five-stage model, describes the standard sequence of stages groups pass through: forming, storming, norming, performing, and adjourning. Through these stages, group members learn how to settle conflicts and develop norms, which enable them to perform. The second, the punctuated-equilibrium model, describes the pattern of development specific to temporary groups with deadlines. In this model, the group shows two great periods of activity. The first peak in activity takes place after the midpoint of the project, a time in which the team performs at a higher level than it did previously. The second peak takes place right before the project comes due.

4 How do we create effective teams? For teams to be effective, careful consideration must be given to resources, the team's composition, work design, and process variables. The four contextual factors that appear to be most significantly related to team performance are the presence of adequate resources, effective leadership, a climate of trust, and a performance evaluation and reward system that reflects team contributions. Effective teams are neither too large nor too small—typically they range in size from 5 to 12 people. They have members who fill role demands, are flexible, and who prefer to be part of a group. Teams will be more effective if members have freedom and autonomy to do their tasks and believe that the task will have a substantial impact on others. Finally, effective teams have members committed to a common purpose and specific team goals.

5 How do virtual teams work? Virtual teams can do many of the same things face-to-face teams can, but they have more challenges, especially when it comes to team-member bonding and building trust. To help build understanding among teammates, members should provide some personal information early on, and they should also be clear on one another's roles from the outset. Researchers have found that virtual teams with members who have positive attitudes do better than teams with pessimistic members. Often, virtual teams communicate, discuss ideas, post work-in-progress, and exchange feedback through a virtual workspace via an intranet, website, or bulletin board.

6 Are teams always the answer? Teams are not necessarily appropriate in every situation. How do you know if the work of your group would be better done in teams? It's been suggested that three tests be applied to see if a team fits the situation: (1) Can the work be done better by more than one person? (2) Does the work create a common purpose or set of goals for the people in the group that is more than the sum of individual goals? and (3) Are the members of the group interdependent? This third test asks whether the success of the whole depends on the success of each one *and* the success of each one depends on the success of the others.

OB at Work

For Review

1. How can teams increase employee motivation?

2. Describe the five-stage model of group development.

3. Describe the punctuated-equilibrium model of group development.

4. What are the characteristics of an effective team?

5. How can team members harm their team?

6. What is the difference between task-oriented roles and maintenance roles?

7. What are the effects of team size on performance?

8. How can a team minimize social loafing?

9. Contrast virtual and face-to-face teams.

10. What conditions favour creating a team, rather than letting an individual perform a given task?

For Critical Thinking

1. How could you use the punctuated-equilibrium model to understand group behaviour better?

2. Have you experienced social loafing as a team member? What did you do to prevent this problem?

3. Would you prefer to work alone or as part of a team? Why? How do you think your answer compares with that of others in your class?

4. What effect, if any, do you expect that workforce diversity has on a team's performance and satisfaction?

OB for You

- Know that you will be asked to work on teams and groups both during your post-secondary years and later in life, so understanding how teams work is an important skill to have.

- Think about the roles that you play on teams. Teams need task-oriented people to get the job done, but they also need maintenance-oriented people who help keep people working together and feeling committed to the team.

- Help your team set specific, measurable, realistic goals, as this leads to more successful outcomes.

Point

Sports Teams Are Good Models for Workplace Teams

Studies from hockey, football, soccer, basketball, and baseball have found a number of elements in successful sports teams that can be applied to successful work teams.[91]

Successful teams integrate cooperation and competition. Effective team coaches get athletes to help one another but also push one another to perform at their best. Sports teams with the best win-loss records had coaches who promoted a strong spirit of cooperation and a high level of healthy competition among their players.

Successful teams score early wins. Early successes build teammates' faith in themselves and their capacity as a team. For instance, research on hockey teams of relatively equal ability found that 72 percent of the time the team that was ahead at the end of the first period went on to win the game. So managers should provide teams with early tasks that are simple and provide "easy wins."

Successful teams avoid losing streaks. Losing can become a self-fulfilling prophecy. A couple of failures can lead to a downward spiral if a team becomes demoralized and believes it is helpless to end its losing streak. Managers need to instill the confidence in team members that they can turn things around when they encounter setbacks.

Practice makes perfect. Successful sports teams execute on game day but learn from their mistakes in practice. A wise manager carves out time and space in which work teams can experiment and learn.

Successful teams use halftime breaks. The best coaches in basketball and football use halftime during a game to reassess what is working and what is not. Managers of work teams should build in similar assessments at about the halfway point in a team project to evaluate how the team can improve.

Winning teams have a stable membership. Studies of professional basketball teams have found that the more stable a team's membership, the more likely the team is to win. The more time teammates have together, the more able they are to anticipate one another's moves and the clearer they are about one another's roles.

Successful teams debrief after failures and successes. The best sports teams study the game video. Similarly, work teams need to take time to routinely reflect on both their successes and failures and to learn from them.

Counterpoint

Sports Teams Are Not the Model for All Teams

There are flaws in using sports as a model for developing effective work teams. Here are just four caveats.[92]

All sports teams are not alike. In baseball, for instance, there is little interaction among teammates. Rarely are more than two or three players directly involved in a play. The performance of the team is largely the sum of the performance of its individual players. In contrast, basketball has much more interdependence among players. Usually all players are involved in every play, team members have to be able to switch from offence to defence at a moment's notice, and there is continuous movement by all, not just the player with the ball. The performance of the team is more than the sum of its individual players. So when using sports teams as a model for work teams, you have to make sure you are making the correct comparison.

Work teams are more varied and complex. In an athletic league, teams vary little in their context, the design of the team, and the design of the task. But from one work team to the next, these factors can vary tremendously. As a result, coaching plays a much more significant part in a sports team's performance than in the workplace. Performance of work teams is more a function of getting the team's structural and design variables right. So, in contrast to sports, managers of work teams should focus less on coaching and more on getting the team set up for success.

A lot of employees cannot relate to sports metaphors. Not everyone on work teams is conversant in sports. Team members from different cultures also may not know the sports metaphors you are using. Most Canadians, for instance, are unfamiliar with the rules and terminology of Australian football.

Work team outcomes are not easily defined in terms of wins and losses. Sports teams usually measure success in terms of wins and losses. Such measures of success are rarely as clear for work teams. Managers who try to define success in wins and losses imply that the workplace is ethically no more complex than the playing field, which is rarely true.

OB *At Work*

How Good Am I at Building and Leading a Team?

Use the following rating scale to respond to the 18 questions on building and leading an effective team:[93]

Strongly Disagree	Disagree	Slightly Disagree	Slightly Agree	Agree	Strongly Agree
1	2	3	4	5	6

1.	I am knowledgeable about the different stages of development that teams can go through in their life cycles.	1 2 3 4 5 6
2.	When a team forms, I make certain that all team members are introduced to one another at the outset.	1 2 3 4 5 6
3.	When the team first comes together, I provide directions, answer team members' questions, and clarify goals, expectations, and procedures.	1 2 3 4 5 6
4.	I help team members establish a foundation of trust among themselves and between themselves and me.	1 2 3 4 5 6
5.	I ensure that standards of excellence, not mediocrity or mere acceptability, characterize the team's work.	1 2 3 4 5 6
6.	I provide a great deal of feedback to team members regarding their performance.	1 2 3 4 5 6
7.	I encourage team members to balance individual autonomy with interdependence among other team members.	1 2 3 4 5 6
8.	I help team members become at least as committed to the success of the team as to their own personal success.	1 2 3 4 5 6
9.	I help team members learn to play roles that assist the team in accomplishing its tasks, as well as building strong interpersonal relationships.	1 2 3 4 5 6
10.	I articulate a clear, exciting, passionate vision of what the team can achieve.	1 2 3 4 5 6
11.	I help team members become committed to the team vision.	1 2 3 4 5 6
12.	I encourage a win-win philosophy in the team; that is, when one member wins, every member wins.	1 2 3 4 5 6
13.	I help the team avoid making the group's survival more important than accomplishing its goal.	1 2 3 4 5 6
14.	I use formal process-management procedures to help the group become faster, more efficient, and more productive, and to prevent errors.	1 2 3 4 5 6
15.	I encourage team members to represent the team's vision, goals, and accomplishments to outsiders.	1 2 3 4 5 6
16.	I diagnose and capitalize on the team's core competence.	1 2 3 4 5 6
17.	I encourage the team to achieve dramatic breakthrough innovations, as well as small continuous improvements.	1 2 3 4 5 6
18.	I help the team work toward preventing mistakes, not just correcting them after the fact.	1 2 3 4 5 6

Scoring Key

The authors of this instrument propose that it assesses team development behaviours in five areas: diagnosing team development (items 1, 16); managing the forming stage (items 2–4); managing the storming stage (items 10–12, 14, 15); managing the norming stage (items 6–9, 13); and managing the performing stage (items 5, 17, 18). Add up your score. Your total score will range between 18 and 108.

LEARNING ABOUT **YOURSELF** EXERCISE (Continued)

Based on a norm group of 500 business students, the following can help estimate where you are relative to others:

95 or above = You are in the top quartile of being able to build and lead a team

72–94 = You are in the second quartile

60–71 = You are in the third quartile

Below 60 = You are in the bottom quartile

More Learning About Yourself Exercises

An additional self-assessment relevant to this chapter appears on MyOBLab (**www.pearsoned.ca/myoblab**).

IV.E.2 Do Others See Me as Trustworthy?

When you complete the additional assessment, consider the following:

1. Am I surprised about my score?

2. Would my friends evaluate me similarly?

BREAKOUT **GROUP** EXERCISES

Form small groups to discuss the following topics, as assigned by your instructor:

1. One of the members of your team continually arrives late for meetings and does not turn drafts of assignments in on time. In general this group member is engaging in social loafing. What can the members of your group do to reduce social loafing?

2. Consider a team with which you have worked. Using the information in Exhibit 5-6 on page 172, consider whether there were more task-oriented or maintenance-oriented roles in the group. What impact did this have on the group's performance?

3. Identify 4 or 5 norms that a team could put into place near the beginning of its life to help it function better over time.

WORKING WITH **OTHERS** EXERCISE

The Paper Tower Exercise

Step 1 Each group will receive 20 index cards, 12 paper clips, and 2 marking pens.[94] Groups have 10 minutes to plan a paper tower that will be judged on the basis of 3 criteria: height, stability, and beauty. No physical work (building) is allowed during this planning period.

Step 2 Each group has 15 minutes for the actual construction of the paper tower.

Step 3 Each tower will be identified by a number assigned by your instructor. Each student is to individually examine all the paper towers. Your group is then to come to a consensus as to which tower is the winner (5 minutes). A spokesperson from your group should report its decision and the criteria the group used in reaching it.

(Continued)

OB *At Work*

WORKING WITH OTHERS EXERCISE (Continued)

Step 4   In your small groups, discuss the following questions (your instructor may choose to have you discuss only a subset of these questions):

a.   What percentage of the plan did each member of your group contribute, on average?

b.   Did your group have a leader? Why or why not?

c.   How did the group generally respond to the ideas that were expressed during the planning period?

d.   To what extent did your group follow the five-stage model of group development?

e.   List specific behaviours exhibited during the planning and building sessions that you felt were helpful to the group. Explain why you found them helpful.

f.   List specific behaviours exhibited during the planning and building sessions that you felt were dysfunctional to the group. Explain why you found them dysfunctional.

ETHICAL DILEMMA EXERCISE

Dealing with Shirkers

We have noted that one of the most common problems in groups is social loafing, which means group members contribute less than if they were working on their own. We might call such individuals "shirkers"—those who are contributing far less than other group members.

Most of us have experienced social loafing, or shirking, in groups. And we may even admit to times when we shirked ourselves. We discussed earlier in the chapter some ways of discouraging social loafing, such as limiting group size, holding individuals responsible for their contributions, and setting group goals. While these tactics may be effective, in our experience, many students simply work around shirkers. "We just did it ourselves—it was easier that way," says one group member.

Consider the following questions for dealing with shirking in groups:

1.   If group members end up "working around" shirkers, do you think this information should be communicated to the instructor so that this individual's contribution to the project is judged more fairly? If so, does the group have an ethical responsibility to communicate this to the shirking group member? If not, isn't the shirking group member unfairly reaping the rewards of a "free ride"?

2.   Do you think confronting the shirking group member is justified? Does this depend on the skills of the shirker (whether he or she is capable of doing good-quality work)?

3.   Social loafing has been found to be higher in Western, more individualist nations than in other countries. Do you think this means we should tolerate shirking on the part of North American workers to a greater degree than if it occurred with someone from Asia?

CASE INCIDENT

Team-Building Retreats

Team-building retreats are big business. Companies believe such retreats, where team members participate in activities ranging from mountain climbing, to trust-building exercises (in which, for example, team mem-bers let themselves fall backwards into their colleagues' arms), to Iron Chef–inspired cooking contests (used by UBS, Hewlett-Packard, and Verizon) can foster effective teamwork.[95]

But why do organizations have teammates participate in activities that seem irrelevant to the organization's primary activities? Pat Finelli, vice-president of marketing for Toronto-based Pizza Pizza, believes that corporate retreats aid team building, which in turn improves company performance. Finelli took his staff members to Hockley Valley Resort (which features spa treatments) in Orangeville, Ontario, so that his employees could have time for both meetings and relaxation. He explains that the trip "was part thank-you for the previous year's success, but included a lot of brainstorming to come up with ways to surpass the company's goals for next year." He believes that spa treatments motivate employees. "When they're relaxed and feeling good, they give back to you and they're more open to thinking."

Given the level of expense for such retreats, not all companies are keen on providing team-building activities outside the organization. According to Susan Harper, a business psychologist, "team-building has definitely gone down. People are reluctant to spend money on what they think is not an absolute necessity." Howard Atkins, chief financial officer at Wells Fargo, believes otherwise: "I know intuitively the payback here is huge. It's a very small investment to make for the payback we are going to get."

Hard-drive maker Seagate takes it even further. Every year, Seagate flies roughly 200 managers to New Zealand to participate in "Eco Seagate," its annual team-building exercise. The tab? $9800 per manager. Chief financial officer Charles Pope says it's one of the last things he would cut from Seagate's budget.

It is clear that companies that invest in team-building retreats think they are worth the investment. Sometimes, though, they have unintended consequences. In 2001, a dozen Burger King employees burned themselves while participating in a "fire walk"—a team-building exercise that requires teammates to walk barefoot across an 8-foot pit of burning-hot coals. The results were injured employees and some very negative publicity for Burger King. In 2006, an employee of security systems company Alarm One was award $1.7 million in damages in a lawsuit in which she claimed she had been spanked on the job as part of a camaraderie-building exercise. One observer of these retreats said, "Most of the time, people asking for these activities are not interested in real teamwork building. What they really want is entertainment."

Some companies are taking team-building exercises in a different direction, having their employees engage in hands-on volunteer work. When the breweries Molson and Coors merged, they wanted to use a team-building exercise to acquaint the executive teams, but they did not want to go the route of the typical golf outings or a ropes course. So, they helped Habitat for Humanity build a home. UPS has new managers participate in various community projects, such as distributing second-hand medical equipment in developing countries.

It is questionable whether team-building exercises such as mountain climbing, cooking contests, and fire walks result in improved company financial performance, and it may be better to think of such activities as morale boosters. According to Merianne Liteman, a professional corporate retreat organizer, "Where good retreats have a quantifiable effect is on retention, on morale, on productivity." Daryl Jesperson, CEO of RE/MAX International, says, "There is a productivity boost anytime you have one of these. People feel better about themselves, they feel better about the company, and as a result will do a better job."

Questions

1. Do you believe that team-building activities increase productivity? Why or why not? What other factors might be responsible for increases in profitability following a corporate retreat?

2. What are some other ways (besides those described above) to build effective teams and increase teamwork among company employees? How might these alternatives be better or worse than corporate retreats?

3. What should companies do about employees who lack athletic talent but are still pressured to participate in physical activities with their colleagues? How might poor performance by those with low athletic ability affect their status within the organization?

4. How might you increase teamwork when team members are not often in direct contact with one another? Can you think of any "electronic" team-building exercises?

OB At Work

CASE 5

Teams at Kluster

Kluster is a web-based company that invites individuals and companies to send in ideas for new products so they can get feedback from others.[96] Within the company, teams have been formed to pursue various projects. Peter Wadsworth is an engineer on "the Illuminator project" team, which focuses on the web-based, community-driven product development platform that is designed to facilitate good decision making about new product ideas. The team is where all kinds of people and organizations meet to pitch ideas, work on projects, and design products and events. In short, it focuses on anything that requires decision making and deliverables. The team's reward system facilitates teamwork and provides both financial and status rewards to high performers. It does not provide incentives to naysayers or those who simply want to bash ideas. People are allowed to do that, but they won't get very far with that kind of behaviour.

Wadsworth says that Ben Kaufman, Kluster's CEO, comes up with many ideas, but every day the team meets to talk about the website and other important issues. People on the Illuminator team have to be disciplined, stay on task, be honest, and exercise self-leadership because Ben does not get involved in everyone's work. But he does want status reports on how things are going. Employees are based in various locations and are also on the road a lot. Each person has milestones that must be reached week by week, and they all have "to-do" lists to guide their work. They all know that they have a good thing going and enjoy being around talented people.

The website enables the team to accomplish goals and to come up with solutions. Tom Pasley, the project manager, says that everyone has to work together using different skill sets. It is fun to get things done as a group, and it is more rewarding than individual work.

Kaufman believes that everyone wants to receive feedback about their work. They may not act on the feedback, but they do want to hear reactions. He also realizes that sometimes people need a break from the team. He says that as long as tasks are being completed on time and employees are communicating well, he does not demand that they come in to the office.

Hitch, a graphic designer, says that all different kinds of people work at Kluster—some are very blunt, some are the calm voice of reason, and some are very creative. But whatever they are like, they focus on bouncing ideas back and forth. No one assumes that they are any better than anyone else.

Questions

1. What are the various types of teams that are found in organizations? Which type of team is the Illuminator team? Explain your reasoning.

2. What are the benefits of a team-based approach? What are the challenges? How have members of the Illuminator project overcome these challenges?

3. This chapter lists 12 characteristics of effective teams. Make a tentative assessment of how the Illuminator team scores on each of the 12 characteristics.

4. What three questions should be asked before the decision is made to form a team? What are the answers to these questions in terms of the Illuminator project? Is a team the best way to proceed?

5. Ben Kaufman says that it is important to make sure that people occasionally get a break from the team. Why do you think he said this?

From Concepts to Skills

Conducting a Team Meeting

Team meetings have a reputation for inefficiency. For instance, noted Canadian-born economist John Kenneth Galbraith once said, "Meetings are indispensable when you don't want to do anything."

When you are responsible for conducting a meeting, what can you do to make it more efficient and effective? Follow these 12 steps:[97]

1. *Prepare a meeting agenda*. An agenda defines what you hope to accomplish at the meeting. It should state the meeting's purpose; who will be in attendance; what, if any, preparation is required of each participant; a detailed list of items to be covered; the specific time and location of the meeting; and a specific finishing time.

2. *Distribute the agenda in advance*. Participants should have the agenda far enough in advance that they can adequately prepare for the meeting.

3. *Consult with participants before the meeting*. An unprepared participant cannot contribute to his or her full potential. It is your responsibility to ensure that members are prepared, so check with them ahead of time.

4. *Get participants to go over the agenda*. The first thing to do at the meeting is to have participants review the agenda, make any changes, and then approve the final agenda.

5. *Establish specific time limits*. Meetings should begin on time and have a specific time for completion. It is your responsibility to specify these times and to hold to them.

6. *Maintain focused discussion*. It is your responsibility to give direction to the discussion; to keep it focused on the issues; and to minimize interruptions, disruptions, and irrelevant comments.

7. *Encourage and support participation of all members*. To maximize the effectiveness of problem-oriented meetings, each participant must be encouraged to contribute. Quiet or reserved personalities need to be drawn out so their ideas can be heard.

8. *Maintain a balanced style*. The effective group leader pushes when necessary and is passive when need be.

9. *Encourage the clash of ideas*. You need to encourage different points of view, critical thinking, and constructive disagreement.

10. *Discourage the clash of personalities*. An effective meeting is characterized by the critical assessment of ideas, not attacks on people. When running a meeting, you must quickly intercede to stop personal attacks or other forms of verbal insult.

11. *Be an effective listener*. You need to listen with intensity, empathy, and objectivity, and do whatever is necessary to get the full intended meaning from each participant's comments.

12. *Bring proper closure*. You should close a meeting by summarizing the group's accomplishments; clarifying what actions, if any, need to follow the meeting; and allocating follow-up assignments. If any decisions are made, you also need to determine who will be responsible for communicating and implementing them.

Practising Skills

Jameel Saumur is the leader of a five-member project team that has been assigned the task of moving his engineering firm into the booming area of high-speed intercity rail construction. Saumur and his team members have been researching the field, identifying specific business opportunities, negotiating alliances with equipment vendors, and evaluating high-speed rail experts and consultants from around the world. Throughout the process, Tonya Eckler, a highly qualified and respected engineer, has challenged a number of things Saumur has said during team meetings and in the workplace. For example, at a meeting two weeks ago, Saumur presented the team with a list of 10 possible high-speed rail projects and started evaluating the company's ability to compete for them. Eckler contradicted virtually all of Saumur's comments, questioned his statistics, and was quite pessimistic about the possibility of getting contracts on these projects. After this latest display of displeasure, two other group members, Bryan Worth and Maggie Ames, are complaining that Eckler's actions are damaging the team's effectiveness. Eckler was originally assigned to the team for her unique expertise and insight. If you had to advise this team, what suggestions would you make to get the team on the right track to achieve its fullest potential?

Reinforcing Skills

1. Interview three managers at different organizations. Ask them about their experiences in managing teams. Have each describe teams that they thought were effective and why they succeeded. Have each also describe teams that they thought were ineffective and the reasons that might have caused this.

2. Contrast a team you have been in in which members trusted one another with another team you have been in in which members lacked trust in one another. How did the conditions in each team develop? What were the consequences in terms of interaction patterns and performance?

6 Communication, Conflict, and Negotiation

An employer faces employees who feel disconnected from the company they helped make a success. Will communication help reduce tensions?

1 How does communication work?

2 What are the barriers to communication?

3 What are other issues in communication?

4 What is conflict?

5 How can conflict be resolved?

6 How does one negotiate effectively?

It is not every day that an oil company reaches a major milestone, so when Fort McMurray, Alberta-based Suncor Energy's oil sands operation did so in 2006 by producing its billionth barrel of oil, it was a time for reflection.[1] The company's workforce had changed significantly in recent years. Only 17 percent of the oil sands employees had worked at the company for more than 10 years. Almost half had been there less than 2 years. Senior executives felt that it was time to bring the workforce together to build a more cohesive culture.

Suncor grew tremendously during the previous 10 years, but employees felt that this was done at their expense. Many were feeling burned out from long hours and lack of recognition. Senior management decided to address these problems through a coordinated communications program that would bring all the employees together and help them understand where the company was going next and how employees' concerns would be addressed.

In this chapter we explore the foundations of communication and then consider the effects of communication on conflict and negotiation.

OB *Is for Everyone*

- What information should be sent by which communication channel?
- How can you communicate better when you're stressed out?
- Ever notice that communicating via email can lead to misunderstandings?
- Does body language really make a difference?
- What factors hinder cross-cultural communication?
- Is conflict always bad?
- Should you try to win at any cost when you bargain?

The Communication Process

1 How does communication work?

Research indicates that poor communication is probably the most frequently cited source of interpersonal conflict.[2] Individuals spend nearly 70 percent of their waking hours communicating—writing, reading, speaking, listening—which means that they have many opportunities in which to engage in poor communication. A WorkCanada survey of 2039 Canadians in six industrial and service categories explored the state of communication in Canadian businesses.[3] The survey found that 61 percent of senior executives believed they did a good job of communicating with employees. However, those who worked below the senior executives did not share this feeling—only 33 percent of the managers and department heads believed that senior executives were effective communicators. Lower-level employees reported that communication was even worse: Only 22 percent of hourly workers, 27 percent of clerical employees, and 22 percent of professional staff reported that senior executives did a good job of communicating with them. Good communication skills are very important to your career success. A 2007 study of recruiters found that they rated communication skills as *the* most important characteristic of an ideal job candidate.[4]

communication The transfer and understanding of a message between two or more people.

Despite these communication problems, no group can exist without **communication**, which is the transfer and understanding of a message between two or more people. Communication can be thought of as a process, or flow, as shown in Exhibit 6-1. The model indicates that communication is both an interactive and iterative process. The sender has to keep in mind the receiver (or audience) and in finalizing the communication, may decide to revisit decisions about the message, the encoding, and/or the feedback. For instance, a manager may want to convey a message face to face, and then may not be able to do so for some reason. The message sent by email or voice mail may need to be framed differently than the message that would have been delivered face to face. Similarly, you may decide on a message, and then realize the medium that you have chosen will make the message too complicated. Writing 10 emails to set up a simple lunch appointment may convince you midway through the process to pick up the telephone to finalize the details.

We discussed perception in Chapter 2. The communication process is significantly affected by the sender's perception of the receiver and the receiver's perception of the sender. For instance, if the receiver does not trust the sender, he or she may interpret intended positive statements in a negative manner.

Encoding and Decoding

encoding Converting a message to symbolic form.

decoding Interpreting a sender's message.

Messages are **encoded** (converting a message to symbolic form) by a sender and **decoded** (interpreting a sender's message) by a receiver. Four factors have been described that affect message encoding and decoding: skill, attitudes, knowledge, and the socio-cultural system. For example, our success in communicating to you depends on our writing skills and your reading skills. Communication success also includes speaking, listening, and reasoning

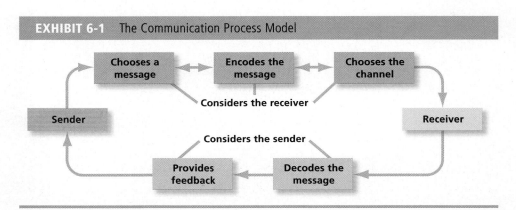

EXHIBIT 6-1   The Communication Process Model

skills. As we discussed in Chapter 3, our interactions with others are affected by our attitudes, values, and beliefs. Thus, the attitudes of the sender and receiver toward each other will affect how the message is transmitted. Clearly, the amount of knowledge the source and receiver hold about a subject will affect the clarity of the message that is transferred. Finally, our position in the socio-cultural system affects our ability to successfully engage in communication. Messages sent and received by people of equal rank are sometimes interpreted differently than messages sent and received by people in very different positions.

The Message

The **message** is the actual physical product from the source encoding. "When we speak, the speech is the message. When we write, the writing is the message. When we paint, the picture is the message. When we gesture, the movements of our arms, the expressions on our face are the message."[5] Our message is affected by the code, or group of symbols, that we use to transfer meaning; the content of the message itself; and the decisions that we make in selecting and arranging both codes and content. A poor choice of symbols, and confusion in the content of the message, can cause problems.

message What is communicated.

Messages can also get "lost in translation" when two parties formalize their understanding through contracts. Contracts are meant to be written in legal terms, for lawyers, but these may not always capture the underlying meaning of the parties' understandings. Collective agreements written between management and unions sometimes suffer from this problem as well. When either management or union leaders point to the collective agreement for every interaction in the workplace, they are relying on the encoding of their negotiations, but this may not permit some of the flexibility that was intended in some cases.

The Channel

What information should be sent by which communication channel?

The **channel** is the medium through which a message travels. It is selected by the source, who must determine which channel is formal and which one is informal. Formal channels are established by organizations to transmit messages about the job-related activities of members. Traditionally, they follow the authority network within the organization. Other forms of messages, such as personal or social messages, follow the informal channels in the organization. Examples of channels include formal memos, voice mail, email, and meetings. Choosing a poor channel, or one with a high noise level, can distort communication. Suncor chose to communicate its message of change through formal meetings that all employees attended.

channel The medium through which a message travels.

Why do people choose one channel of communication over another—for instance, a phone call instead of a face-to-face talk? One answer might be anxiety! An estimated 5 to 20 percent of the population suffers from debilitating **communication apprehension**, or anxiety, which is undue tension and anxiety about oral communication, written communication, or both.[6] We all know people who dread speaking in front of a group, but some people may find it extremely difficult to talk with others face to face or become extremely anxious when they have to use the telephone. As a result, they may rely on memos, letters, or email to convey messages when a phone call would not only be faster but also more appropriate.

communication apprehension Undue tension and anxiety about oral communication, written communication, or both.

But what about the 80 to 95 percent of the population who do not suffer from this problem? Is there any general insight we might be able to provide regarding choice of communication channel? The answer is a qualified "yes." A model of media richness has been developed to explain channel selection among managers.[7]

Research has found that channels differ in their capacity to convey information. Some are rich in that they have the ability to (1) handle multiple cues at the same

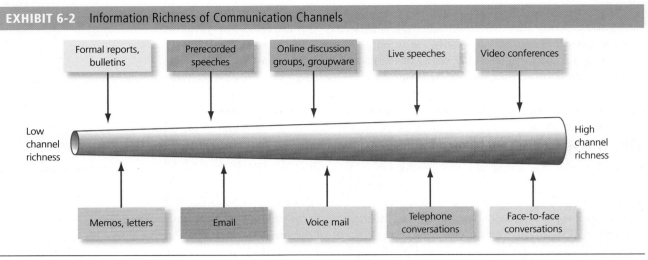

EXHIBIT 6-2   Information Richness of Communication Channels

Formal reports, bulletins — Prerecorded speeches — Online discussion groups, groupware — Live speeches — Video conferences

Low channel richness ... High channel richness

Memos, letters — Email — Voice mail — Telephone conversations — Face-to-face conversations

Sources: Based on R. H. Lengel and R. L. Daft, "The Selection of Communication Media as an Executive Skill," *Academy of Management Executive,* August 1988, pp. 225–232; and R. L. Daft and R. H. Lengel, "Organizational Information Requirements, Media Richness, and Structural Design," *Managerial Science,* May 1996, pp. 554–572. Reproduced from R. L. Daft and R. A. Noe, *Organizational Behavior* (Fort Worth, TX: Harcourt, 2001), p. 311.

channel richness The amount of information that can be transmitted during a communication episode.

time, (2) allow rapid feedback, and (3) be very personal. Others are lean in that they score low on these three factors. As Exhibit 6-2 on page 196 illustrates, face-to-face conversation scores highest in terms of **channel richness** because it provides for the maximum amount of information to be transmitted during a communication episode. That is, it offers multiple information cues (words, postures, facial expressions, gestures, intonations), immediate feedback (both verbal and nonverbal), and the personal touch of "being there." Impersonal written media such as formal reports and bulletins rate lowest in richness. Two students were suspended from class for choosing YouTube, a very rich channel, to distribute their message. Their actions also raised concerns about privacy in the classroom, as *Focus on Ethics* reveals.

FOCUS ON **ETHICS**

YouTube's Darker Side

Is it okay for students to post a teacher's outburst on YouTube? Two grade 9 students from École Secondaire Mont-Bleu in Gatineau, Quebec, were suspended from school after teachers discovered a video the students had posted on YouTube.[8] One of the students provoked the teacher during class time while the other secretly taped the scene for about 50 minutes with a compact digital camera.

The students, who have academic problems, were in a special-education class. The teacher had 33 years of experience and specialized in teaching students with learning disabilities. After the incident, the teacher went on sick leave, and his union said, "He is so embarrassed that he may never return to class."

There was no apparent explanation for why the students decided to provoke and then film the teacher. Other students have said that "the teacher was good at helping them improve their grades."

"I think students are just trying to embarrass the teachers they don't like," school board president Jocelyn Blondin said. "In the future, students will have to keep their cellphones in their pockets and use them outside of class," she predicted shortly after the incident.

Teachers and school boards are trying to determine strategies for handling these kinds of events in classrooms. The Gatineau school no longer allows personal electronic devices in the classroom. In Ontario, changes to the Safe Schools Act made in 2007 state that students who engage in online bullying are to be suspended from classes.

The choice of one channel over another depends on whether the message is routine or nonroutine. Routine messages tend to be straightforward and have a minimum of ambiguity. Nonroutine messages are likely to be complicated and have the potential for misunderstanding. Individuals can communicate routine messages efficiently through channels that are lower in richness. However, they can communicate nonroutine messages more effectively by selecting rich channels. Evidence indicates that high-performing managers tend to be more media-sensitive than low-performing managers.[9] In other words, they are better able to match appropriate media richness with the ambiguity involved in the communication.

One study found that managers found it easier to deliver bad news (layoffs, promotion denials, and negative feedback) via email, and that the messages were delivered more accurately this way. This does not mean that sending negative information through email is always recommended. One of the co-authors of the study noted that "offering negative comments face-to-face is often taken as a sign that the news is important and the deliverer cares about the recipient."[10]

The media richness model is consistent with organizational trends and practices of the past decade. It is not just coincidence that more and more senior managers, like those at Suncor, have been using meetings to facilitate communication and regularly leaving the isolated sanctuary of their executive offices to manage by walking around. These executives are relying on richer channels of communication to transmit the more ambiguous messages they need to convey. The past decade has been characterized by organizations closing facilities, imposing large layoffs, restructuring, merging, consolidating, and introducing new products and services at an accelerated pace—all nonroutine messages high in ambiguity and requiring the use of channels that can convey a large amount of information. It is not surprising, therefore, to see the most effective managers expanding their use of rich channels.

feedback loop The final link in the communication process; it puts the message back into the system as a check against misunderstandings.

The Feedback Loop

The final link in the communication process is the **feedback loop**. Feedback lets us know whether understanding has been achieved. If the feedback loop is to succeed in preventing miscommunication, the receiver needs to give feedback and the sender needs to check for it. Many receivers forget that there is a responsibility involved in communication: to give feedback. For instance, if you sit in a boring lecture, but never discuss with the instructor ways that the delivery could be improved, you have not engaged in communication with your instructor.

When either the sender or the receiver fails to engage in the feedback process, the communication is effectively one-way communication. Two-way communication involves both talking and listening. Many managers communicate poorly because they fail to use two-way communication.[11]

One of the greatest difficulties managers have is providing performance feedback. Suncor deliberately built a feedback

Companies use the technique of 360-degree feedback to ensure that individuals get feedback from co-workers and subordinates. As a senior vice-president with Scotiabank, Claude Norfolk found that sometimes feedback hurts. "I was really surprised, for example, to find out that I needed to work on my listening skills, because I thought I was a pretty good listener." Turns out his wife agreed with Norfolk's colleagues. Still, he found value in the exercise. Feedback almost always brings with it valuable insights, which we can use for greater understanding.

mechanism into its communication with employees. After each session, employees were asked to fill out surveys in which they were asked to evaluate their reactions to the company's new message of change. In *From Concepts to Skills*, on page 227, we discuss strategies for providing performance feedback. We also provide some practice exercises for doing so.

The Context

All communication takes place within a context, and violations of that context may create additional problems in sending and receiving messages. For instance, the context of a workplace presents different expectations about how to interact with people than does the context of a bus stop. The workplace may demand more formal interaction, while communication at a bus stop is generally expected to be informal. In some situations, informal communication can look unprofessional, and thus be viewed negatively. In other situations, formal communication can make others feel awkward if the formality is out of place. Thus, it is important to consider context in both encoding the message and choosing the channel.

Barriers to Effective Communication

When Suncor Energy decided to approach its employees to discuss plans for the future and their impact, the company faced a significant organizational challenge.[12] Employees had never been asked to attend off-site meetings outside working hours. There were 3000 employees to address, and putting them all in one room at the same time was both logistically impossible and would have prevented the message from being heard. Suncor's communication team decided to work with groups of 500 employees at a time, holding six 90-minute meetings during a two-week period.

With logistics resolved, the communication team still had to consider the best way to deliver the message of change. Hearing from senior management was important, but might not engage the audience very much, causing them to tune out. So the team included humour and interactivity in the meeting agenda. Are there other things the communication team might have considered to make sure everyone was listening at the meetings?

2 **What are the barriers to communication?**

A number of factors have been identified as barriers to communication. The more prominent ones are filtering, selective perception, defensiveness, information overload, and language.

Filtering

filtering A sender's manipulation of information so that it will be seen more favourably by the receiver.

Filtering occurs when a sender manipulates information so that the receiver will view it more favourably. For example, when a manager tells a senior executive what the manager thinks the executive wants to hear, the manager is filtering information. Does this happen much in organizations? Sure! As information is passed up to senior executives, employees must condense and summarize it so that those on top do not become overloaded with information. The personal interests and perceptions of what is important by those doing the summarizing will result in filtering.

The major determinant of filtering is the number of levels in an organization's structure. The more levels in an organization's hierarchy, the more opportunities there are for filtering information.

Selective Perception

Receivers in the communication process selectively see and hear based on their needs, motivations, experience, background, and other personal characteristics. Receivers also project their interests and expectations into communications as they decode them. For example, the employment interviewer who believes that young people are more interested in spending time on leisure and social activities than working extra hours to further their careers is likely to be influenced by that stereotype when interviewing young job applicants. As we discussed in Chapter 2, we do not see reality; rather, we interpret what we see and call it "reality."

Defensiveness

When people feel that they are being threatened, they tend to react in ways that reduce their ability to achieve mutual understanding. That is, they become defensive—engaging in behaviours such as verbally attacking others, making sarcastic remarks, being overly judgmental, and questioning others' motives. So when individuals interpret another's message as threatening, they often respond in ways that hinder effective communication.

Information Overload

Individuals have a finite capacity for processing data. When the information we have to work with exceeds our ability to process it, the result is **information overload**. With emails, phone calls, faxes, meetings, and the need to keep current in one's field, more and more employees are suffering from too much information. The information can be distracting as well. A recent study of employees who have tracking software on their computers found that they clicked on their email program more than 50 times in the course of a day, and used instant messaging 77 times. The study also found that on average, employees visited 40 websites during the workday.[13]

information overload The state of having more information than one can process.

What happens when individuals have more information than they can sort out and use? They tend to select out, ignore, pass over, or forget information. Or they may put off further processing until the overload situation is over. Regardless, the result is lost information and less effective communication.

Language

Words mean different things to different people. "The meanings of words are not in the words; they are in us."[14] Age, education, and cultural background are three of the more obvious variables that influence the language a person uses and the definitions he or she gives to words. For instance, when Alanis Morissette sang "Isn't It Ironic?" middle-aged English professors complained that she completely misunderstood the meaning of "irony"—but the millions who bought her CD understood what she meant.

Even with a common language, such as English, our usage of that language is far from uniform. For example, in many organizations, employees come from diverse backgrounds and, therefore, have different patterns of speech. Additionally, the grouping of employees into departments creates specialists who develop their own jargon or technical language. In large organizations, members are also often widely dispersed geographically—even operating in different countries—and individuals in each location will use terms and phrases that are unique to their area. In hierarchical organizations, sometimes the language of senior executives can be confusing to operative employees who are unfamiliar with management jargon.

Senders tend to assume that the words and terms they use mean the same to the receiver as they do to themselves. This, of course, is often incorrect and can create communication difficulties. The multicultural environment of many of today's workplaces makes communication issues even more complex. In many workplaces, there are people whose first language is something other than English. This means that even more opportunities arise for confusion about meaning. It is therefore important to be aware that your understanding of the particular meaning of a word or phrase may not be shared by all. Exhibit 6-3 on page 200 shows individuals who have very different views on what words to use.

THE FAR SIDE® BY GARY LARSON

© 1994 FarWorks, Inc. All Rights Reserved/Dist. by Creators Syndicate   Larson

The Far Side® by Gary Larson © 1994 FarWorks, Inc. All Rights Reserved. Used with permission.

"Well, actually, Doreen, I rather resent being called a 'swamp thing.' ... I prefer the term 'wetlands-challenged-mutant.'"

Source: The Far Side by Gary Larson, Copyright © 1994 for Works, Inc. All rights reserved. Used with permission.

Communicating Under Stress

How can you communicate better when you're stressed out?

One of the most difficult times to communicate properly is when one is under stress. While stress can arise from any number of situations, it can be particularly stressful to have to communicate in something other than one's first language. One consultant has identified several tips for communicating under stress. These tips are also appropriate for less stressful communication.[15]

- *Speak clearly.* Be direct about what you want to say, and avoid hiding behind words. For instance, as difficult as it might be to say "You did not receive the position," the listener is better able to process the information when it is spoken that directly.

- *Be aware of the nonverbal part of communicating.* Tone, facial expression, and body language send signals that may or may not be consistent with your message. In a stressful situation, it is best to speak in a neutral manner.

- *Think carefully about how you state things.* In many situations, it is better to be restrained so that you do not offend your listener. For instance, when you threaten someone if they do not do exactly what you want ("I insist on speaking to your manager this minute"), you simply escalate the situation. It is better to state what you want calmly, so that you can be heard accurately.

Current Issues in Communication

How organizations communicate with their employees plays an important role in whether the employees actually hear the message.[16] Prior to the meetings with the oil sands employees, Suncor Energy had a negative image in the minds of some of its employees. Surveys showed that employees felt disconnected from senior managers and did not think that management "had their best interests in mind." Less than a third of the employees felt they received enough recognition for their work.

The company developed a multi-pronged approach to getting out its message of change to employees. The company already had a weekly employee newsletter called *Update*. Management used the newsletter to build interest in the upcoming meetings. The meetings were conducted using a variety of forms of communication, including speeches by the management team and video documentaries of the company's history. Other videos showed employees discussing the challenges they faced in their work environment and talking positively about the future. There were question-and-answer sessions to encourage employee involvement. There were also "fun videos," such as a fake newscast from the future and a *Star Trek* parody.

Because there were six meetings scheduled, the Suncor communication team was able to adjust subsequent presentations based on feedback from earlier sessions. After the first meeting, the management team learned that employees thought the answers to their questions were "too long and hard to understand." Answers were shortened and simplified for the later sessions.

The result of all of this attention to how best to communicate? The employees felt more positive about the future of Suncor, and they changed their views about their leaders. More than 50 percent said they felt their contributions were recognized, compared with 32 percent prior to the meetings. So what can managers do to make communication more effective?

How are electronics changing the way people communicate with each other in organizations? How important is nonverbal communication? What does silence have to do with communicating? Why do men and women often have difficulty communicating with each other? How can individuals improve their cross-cultural communication? We address each of these issues below.

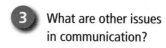

3 What are other issues in communication?

Electronic Communications

Since the early 1980s, we have been subjected to an onslaught of new electronic ways to communicate. Electronic communications (including email, text messaging, networking software, Internet or web logs (blogs), and video conferencing) make it possible for you to work even if you are away from your workstation. These technologies are largely reshaping the way we communicate in organizations.[17] You can be reached when you are in a meeting; having a lunch break; visiting a customer's office across town; watching a movie in a crowded theatre; or playing golf on a Saturday morning. The line between an employee's work and nonwork life is no longer distinct, meaning all employees theoretically can be "on call" 24 hours a day.

Organizational boundaries become less relevant as a result of electronic communications. Why? Because networked computers allow employees to jump vertical levels within the organization, work full-time at home or someplace other than "the office," and have ongoing communications with people in other organizations.

David Breda, co-owner of Leader Plumbing and Heating, a mechanical contractor in Woodbridge, Ontario, finds online collaboration a major boon to his business. His employees, mostly plumbers, are able to exchange real-time information, and thus be more efficient in their work.

Email

Ever notice that communicating via email can lead to misunderstandings?

Email's growth has been spectacular, and its use is now so pervasive that it's hard to imagine life without it. As a communication tool, email has a long list of benefits. Email messages can be quickly written, edited, and stored. They can be distributed to one person or thousands with a click of a mouse. They can be read, in their entirety, at the convenience of the recipient. And the cost of sending formal email messages to employees is a fraction of the cost of printing, duplicating, and distributing a comparable letter or brochure.

Email, of course, is not without drawbacks. Email has added considerably to the number of hours worked per week, according to a study by Christina Cavanagh, former professor of management communications at the Richard Ivey School of Business, University of Western Ontario.[18] One researcher suggests that knowledge workers devote about 28 percent of their day to email.[19] While the increase in the volume of email seems to have slowed, up just 9 percent between 2006 and 2007 (compared with 26 percent between 2005 and 2006), the volume of junk mail shows no let-up.[20] Canadians divert 42 percent of their email directly to "junk mail" folders, according to a 2007 Ipsos Reid study. Over one-third of the survey respondents said they had trouble handling all of their email, and only 43 percent thought that email increased efficiency at work, down from 52 percent in 2006.

The following are some of the most significant limitations of email and what organizations should do to reduce or eliminate these problems:

- *Misinterpreting the message.* It's true that we often misinterpret verbal messages, but the potential for misinterpretation with email is even greater. One research team found that we can accurately decode an email's intent and tone only

50 percent of the time, yet most of us vastly overestimate our ability to send and interpret clear messages. If you are sending an important message, make sure you reread it for clarity. And if you are upset about the presumed tone of someone else's message, keep in mind that you may be misinterpreting it.[21]

- *Communicating negative messages.* When companies have negative information to communicate, managers need to think carefully. Email may not be the best way to communicate the message. When RadioShack decided to lay off 400 employees, it was widely criticized for doing it via email. Employees need to be careful communicating negative messages via email, too. Justen Deal, 22, wrote an email critical of some strategic decisions made by his employer, pharmaceutical giant Kaiser Permanente. In the email, he criticized the "misleadership" of Kaiser CEO George Halvorson and questioned the financing of several information technology projects. Within hours, Deal's computer was seized; he was later fired.[22]

- *Overuse of email.* An estimated 6 trillion emails are sent every year, and someone has to answer all those messages! As people become established in their careers and their responsibilities expand, so do their inboxes. Some people, such as venture capitalist Fred Wilson, have become so overwhelmed by email that they have declared "email bankruptcy." Recording artist Moby sent an email to all those in his address book announcing that he was taking a break from email for the rest of the year. Although you probably do not want to declare email bankruptcy, or could not get away with it even if you did, you should use email wisely, especially when you are contacting people inside the organization who may already be wading through lots of email messages every day.[23]

- *Email emotions.* We tend to think of email as a sort of sterile, faceless form of communication. But that does not mean it's unemotional. As you no doubt know, emails are often highly emotional. One CEO said, "I've seen people not talk to each other, turf wars break out and people quit their jobs as a result of emails." Email tends to make senders feel free to write things they would never be comfortable saying in person. Facial expressions tend to temper our emotional expressions, but in email, there is no other face to look at, and so many of us fire away. An increasingly common way of communicating emotions in email is with emoticons (see Exhibit 6-4). For example, Yahoo!'s email software allows users to pick from over 60 graphical emoticons. Although emoticons used to be considered for personal use only, adults are increasingly using them in business emails. Still, some see them as too informal for business use.

  When others send flaming messages, remain calm and try not to respond in kind. Also, when writing new emails, try to temper your own tendencies to quickly fire off messages.[24]

- *Privacy concerns.* There are two privacy issues with email. First, you need to be aware that your emails may be, and often are, monitored. Also, you cannot always trust that the recipient of your email will keep it confidential. For these reasons, you should not write anything you would not want made public. One survey found that nearly 40 percent of companies have employees whose only job is to read other employees' email. You are being watched—so be careful what you email![25]

Focus on Ethics illustrates that employees cannot assume that their email is private.

EXHIBIT 6-4   Showing Emotions in Email

Email need not be emotion-free. Over the years, email users have developed a way of displaying text, as well as a set of symbols (*emoticons*) for expressing emotions. For instance, the use of all caps (as in THIS PROJECT NEEDS YOUR IMMEDIATE ATTENTION!) is the email equivalent of shouting. The following highlights some emoticons:

:)	Smile	:-e	Disappointed
<g>	Grin	:-@	Scream
:(	Frown	:-0	Yell
;)	Wink	:-D	Shock or surprise
:-[	Really sad face	:'(	Crying

FOCUS ON **ETHICS**

Your Email Can Get You Fired

Should your email be safe from your manager's eyes? A 2008 poll conducted by Environics found that 35 percent of Canadians say they have sent emails from their work-based email address that they worry could come back to hurt them.[26] Even so, about the same percentage of employees believe their employers probably check on email accounts, and 52 percent think their employer has the right to do so. Moreover, 30 percent of Canadians know someone who has been disciplined because of an email sent at work.

While a City of Toronto employee was merely disciplined after sending "inappropriate" pictures using a city computer, Fred Jones (not his real name) was fired from a Canadian company for forwarding dirty jokes to his clients.[27] Until this incident, Jones had been a high-performing employee who sold network computers for his company. Jones thought that he was only sending the jokes to clients who liked them, and assumed the clients would tell him if they did not want to receive the jokes. Instead, a client complained to the company about receiving the dirty jokes. After an investigation, the company fired Jones. Jones is still puzzled about being fired. He views his email as private; to him, sending jokes is the same as telling them at the water cooler.

Jones was not aware that under current law, employee information, including email, is not necessarily private. Most federal employees, provincial public sector employees, and employees working for federally regulated industries are covered by the federal Privacy Act and Access to Information Act, in place since 1985. Many private sector employees are not covered by privacy legislation, however.

Ann Cavoukian, Information and Privacy Commissioner of Ontario, notes that "employees deserve to be treated like adults and companies should limit surveillance to rare instances, such as when there is suspicion of criminal activity or harassment."[28] She suggests that employers use respect and courtesy when dealing with employees' email, and she likens email to office phone calls, which generally are not monitored by the employer. It is clearly important, in any event, that employees be aware of their companies' policies on email. *OB in the Street* considers employers' responses to blogging, yet another way to keep in touch with friends, family, and co-workers.

OB IN THE STREET

When a Personal Blog Becomes a Workplace Issue

Should blog entries about work be a concern for employers? Andrew McDonald landed an internship with the television channel Comedy Central, and on his first day at work he started a blog.[29] His supervisors asked him to change various things about the blog, essentially removing all specific references to Comedy Central. Kelly Kreth was fired from her job as a marketing director for blogging about her co-workers. So was Jessa Werner, who later said, "I came to the realization that I probably shouldn't have been blogging about work."

Although some companies have policies in place governing the content of blogs, many do not. Many bloggers think their personal blogs are outside their employer's purview, and 39 percent of individual bloggers say they have posted comments that could be construed as harmful to their company's reputation.

If someone else in a company happens to read a blog entry, there is nothing to keep him or her from sharing that information with others, and the employee could be dismissed as a result. Some companies may not fire an employee over any blog entry short of one that broke the law. But most organizations are unlikely to be so forgiving of any blog entry that might cast a negative light on them. In short, if you are going to have a personal blog, maintain a strict work-personal "firewall."

Instant Messaging and Text Messaging

Instant messaging (IM) and text messaging (TM), which have been popular among teens for more than a decade, are now rapidly moving into business.[30]

The growth of IM and TM has been spectacular. In 2002, Canadians sent 174 million text messages, in 2003 they sent 352 million text messages, in 2004 they sent more than 710 million text messages, and in 2006 they sent 4.3 billion text messages, tripling the number sent in 2005.[31] More people use IM than email as their primary communication tool at work.[32]

IM and TM represent fast and inexpensive means for managers to stay in touch with employees and for employees to stay in touch with each other. In an increasing number of cases, this is not just a luxury, it is a business imperative.

Despite their advantages, IM and TM are not going to replace email. Email is still probably a better device for conveying long messages that need to be saved. IM is preferable for one- or two-line messages that would just clutter up an email inbox. On the downside, some IM/TM users find the technology intrusive and

Facebook founder and CEO Mark Zuckerberg continues to transform communication. He announced a new platform strategy that allows third parties to develop services on the Facebook site, which allows communication opportunities for business entrepreneurs. For Zuckerberg, Facebook is more than a social networking site. He describes it as a communication tool that facilitates the flow of information between users and their friends, family members, and professional connections.

distracting. Their continual presence can make it hard for employees to concentrate and stay focused. For example, a survey of managers revealed that in 86 percent of meetings, at least some participants checked TM. Finally, because instant messages can be intercepted easily, many organizations are concerned about the security of IM/TM.[33]

One other point: It's important to not let the informality of text messaging ("omg! r u serious? brb") spill over into business emails. Many prefer to keep business communication relatively formal. A survey of employers revealed that 58 percent rate grammar, spelling, and punctuation as "very important" in email messages.[34] By making sure your professional communications are, well, professional, you will show yourself to be mature and serious. That does not mean, of course, that you have to give up TM or IM; you just need to maintain the boundaries between how you communicate with your friends and how you communicate professionally.

Nonverbal Communication

Does body language really make a difference?

Anyone who has ever paid a visit to a singles bar or a nightclub is aware that communication need not be verbal in order to convey a message. A glance, a stare, a smile, a frown, a provocative body movement—they all convey meaning. This example illustrates that no discussion of communication would be complete without a discussion of **nonverbal communication**. This includes body movements, facial expressions, and the physical distance between the sender and the receiver.

nonverbal communication Messages conveyed through body movements, facial expressions, and the physical distance between the sender and the receiver.

kinesics The study of body motions, such as gestures, facial configurations, and other movements of the body.

The academic study of body motions has been labelled **kinesics**. It refers to gestures, facial configurations, and other movements of the body. Because it is a relatively new field, there is not complete agreement on findings. Still, body movement is an important segment of the study of communication.

It has been argued that every body movement has a meaning and that no movement is accidental.[35] Through body language, we can say "Help me, I'm confused," or "Leave me alone, I'm really angry." Rarely do we send our messages consciously. We act out our state of being with nonverbal body language, even if we are not aware of doing so. In North America, we lift one eyebrow for disbelief. We rub our noses for puzzlement. We clasp our arms to isolate ourselves or to protect ourselves. We shrug our shoulders for indifference, wink one eye for intimacy, tap our fingers for impatience, slap our foreheads for forgetfulness.[36] Babies and young children provide another good illustration of effective use of nonverbal communication. Although they lack developed language skills, they often use fairly sophisticated body language to communicate their physical and emotional needs. Such use of body language underscores its importance in communicating needs throughout life.

The two most important messages that body language conveys are (1) the extent to which an individual likes another and is interested in his or her views and (2) the relative perceived status between a sender and receiver.[37] For instance, we are more likely to position ourselves closer to people we like and touch them more often. Similarly, if you feel that you are of higher status than another, you are more likely to display body movements—such as crossed legs or a slouched seated position—that reflect a casual and relaxed manner.[38]

While we may disagree on the specific meaning of certain movements (and different cultures may interpret specific body movements differently), body language adds to and often complicates verbal communication. For instance, if you read the transcript of a meeting, you do not grasp the impact of what was said in the same way you would if you had been there or had seen the meeting on video. Why? There is no record of nonverbal communication. The *intonations,* or emphasis, given to words or phrases is missing.

The *facial expression* of a person also conveys meaning. A snarling face says something different from a smile. Facial expressions, along with intonations, can show arrogance, aggressiveness, fear, shyness, and other characteristics that would never be communicated if you read a transcript of the meeting.

Studies indicate that those who maintain *eye contact* while speaking are viewed with more credibility than those whose eye contact wanders. People who make eye contact are also deemed more competent than those who do not.

The way individuals space themselves in terms of *physical distance*, commonly called **proxemics**, also has meaning. What is considered proper spacing largely depends on cultural norms. For instance, studies have shown that those from "contact" cultures (e.g., Arabs, Latin Americans, southern Europeans) are more comfortable with body closeness and touch than those from "noncontact" cultures (Asians, North Americans, northern Europeans).[39] These differences can lead to confusion. If someone stands closer to you than expected according to your cultural norms, you may interpret the action as an expression of aggressiveness or sexual interest. However, if the person stands farther away than you expect, you might think he or she is displeased with you or uninterested. Someone whose cultural norms differ from yours might be very surprised by your interpretation.

Environmental factors such as seating arrangements or the conditions of the room can also send intended or unintended messages. A person whose desk faces the doorway demonstrates command of his or her physical space, while perhaps also conveying that one should not come too close.

It is important for the receiver to be alert to these nonverbal aspects of communication. You should look for nonverbal cues as well as listen to the literal meaning of a sender's words. In particular, you should be aware of contradictions between the messages. The manager may say that she is free to talk to you about that raise you have been seeking, but you may see nonverbal signals from her (such as looking at her watch) that suggest that this is not the time to discuss the subject. It is not uncommon for people to express one emotion verbally and another nonverbally. These contradictions often suggest that actions speak louder (and more accurately) than words.

We should monitor body language with some care. For instance, while it is often thought that individuals who cross their arms in front of their chests are showing resistance to a message, they might also do this if they are feeling cold, regardless of their reactions to a message.

proxemics The study of physical space in interpersonal relationships.

Silence as Communication

Sherlock Holmes once solved a murder mystery based not on what happened but on what *did not* happen. Holmes remarked to his assistant, Dr. Watson, about "the curious incident of the dog in the nighttime." Watson, surprised, responds, "But the dog did nothing in the nighttime." To which Holmes replied, "That was the curious incident." Holmes concluded the crime had to be committed by someone with whom the dog was familiar because the watchdog did not bark.

The dog that did not bark in the night is often used as a metaphor for an event that is significant by reason of its absence. That story is also an excellent illustration of the importance of silence in communication.

Professors Craig Pinder of the University of Victoria and Karen Harlos of McGill University have noted that silence—defined here as an absence of speech or noise—generally has been ignored as a form of communication in organizational behaviour because it represents *in*action or *non*behaviour. But silence is not necessarily inaction.

Nor is it, as many believe, a failure to communicate. Silence can, in fact, be a powerful form of communication.[40] It can mean someone is thinking or contemplating a response to a question. It can mean a person is anxious and fearful of speaking. It can signal agreement, dissent, frustration, or anger.

In terms of organizational behaviour, we can see several links between silence and work-related behaviour. For instance, silence is a critical element of groupthink because it implies agreement with the majority. It can be a way for employees to express dissatisfaction, as when they "suffer in silence." It can be a sign that someone is upset, as when a typically talkative person suddenly says nothing—"What's the matter with him? Is he all right?" It's a powerful tool used by individuals to signal disfavour by shunning or ignoring someone with "silent insults." As well, it's a crucial element of group decision making, allowing individuals to think over and contemplate what others have said.

Failing to pay close attention to the silent portion of a conversation can result in missing a vital part of the message. Astute communicators watch for gaps, pauses, and hesitations. They hear and interpret silence. They treat pauses, for instance, as analogous to a flashing yellow light at an intersection—they pay attention to what comes next. Is the person thinking, deciding how to frame an answer? Is the person suffering from communication apprehension? Sometimes the real message in a communication is buried in the silence.

Communication Barriers Between Women and Men

Research by Deborah Tannen provides us with important insights into differences in the conversation styles of men and women.[41] In particular, Tannen has been able to explain why gender often creates oral communication barriers. Her research does not suggest that *all* men or *all* women behave the same way in their communication, but she illustrates some important generalizations.

The essence of Tannen's research is that men use talk to emphasize status, while women use it to create connection. According to Tannen, women speak and hear a language of connection and intimacy, while men speak and hear a language of status and independence. So, for many men, conversations are primarily a way to preserve independence and maintain status in a hierarchical social order. For many women, however, conversations are negotiations for closeness in which people try to seek and give confirmation and support. The following examples will illustrate Tannen's thesis.

Men often complain that women talk on and on about their problems. Women criticize men for not listening. What is happening is that when men hear a problem, they often assert their desire for independence and control by offering solutions. Many women, on the other hand, view telling a problem as a means to promote closeness. The women present the problem to gain support and connection, not to get the male's advice. Mutual understanding, as sought by women, is symmetrical. But giving advice is asymmetrical—it sets up the (male) advice giver as more knowledgeable, more reasonable, and more in control; this contributes to distancing men and women in their efforts to communicate.

Men often criticize women for seeming to apologize all the time. Men tend to see the phrase "I'm sorry" as a weakness because they interpret the phrase to mean the woman is accepting blame. However, women typically use "I'm sorry" to express empathy: "I know you must feel bad about this. I probably would too in the same position."

While Tannen has received wide acknowledgment of her work, some suggest that it is anecdotal and/or based on faulty research. Goldsmith and Fulfs argue that men and women have more similarities than differences as communicators, although they acknowledge that when communication difficulties do appear, it is appealing to attribute them to gender.[42] Despite this, Nancy Langton, your Vancouver-based author,

Research indicates that women use language to create connections while men use language to emphasize status and power. The businesswomen conversing here illustrate that women speak and hear a language of connection and intimacy.

has noted, based on evidence from role plays, that men and women make requests for raises differently, and men are more likely to state that men were more effective at making requests, while women are more likely to indicate that it was women who handled the interaction more favourably.[43]

Cross-Cultural Communication

Effective communication is difficult under the best of conditions. Cross-cultural factors clearly create the potential for increased communication problems.

Cultural Barriers

What factors hinder cross-cultural communication?

One author has identified four specific problems related to language difficulties in cross-cultural communications.[44] First, there are *barriers caused by semantics*. As we have noted previously, words mean different things to different people. This is particularly true for people from different national cultures. Some words, for instance, do not translate between cultures. For instance, the new capitalists in Russia may have difficulty communicating with their English-speaking counterparts because English terms such as *efficiency, free market,* and *regulation* cannot be translated directly into Russian.

Second, there are *barriers caused by word connotations*. Words imply different things in different languages. The Japanese word *hai* translates as "yes," but its connotation may be "yes, I am listening," rather than "yes, I agree." Western executives may be hampered in their negotiations if they do not understand this connotation.

Third are *barriers caused by tone differences*. In some cultures language is formal, and in others it's informal. In some cultures, the tone changes depending on the context: People speak differently at home, in social situations, and at work. Using a personal, informal style in a situation where a more formal style is expected can be embarrassing and offensive.

Fourth, there are *barriers caused by differences in perceptions*. People who speak different languages actually view the world in different ways. The Inuit perceive snow differently

Ottawa-based Donna Cona made history when it designed and installed the computer network for the Government of Nunavut. Two-thirds of the firm's software engineers are Aboriginal. Peter Baril, Nunavut's director of informatics services, notes: "Donna Cona's quiet and knowledgeable approach was perhaps the most important skill brought to our project. No other style could have worked in this predominantly Aboriginal environment."

because they have many words for it. They also perceive "no" differently from English speakers because the Inuit have no such word in their vocabulary.

Overcoming Cross-Cultural Difficulties

When communicating with people from a different culture, what can you do to reduce misperceptions, misinterpretations, and misevaluations? Following these four rules can be helpful:[45]

- *Assume differences until similarity is proven.* Most of us assume that others are more similar to us than they actually are. But people from different countries often are very different from us. So you are far less likely to make an error if you assume others are different from you rather than assuming similarity until difference is proven.

- *Emphasize description rather than interpretation or evaluation.* Interpreting or evaluating what someone has said or done, in contrast with describing, is based more on the observer's culture and background than on the observed situation. As a result, delay judgment until you have had sufficient time to observe and interpret the situation from the differing viewpoints of all the cultures involved.

- *Be empathetic.* Before sending a message, put yourself in the recipient's shoes. What are his or her values, experiences, and frames of reference? What do you know about his or her education, upbringing, and background that can give you added insight? Try to see the other person as he or she really is.

- *Treat your interpretations as a working hypothesis.* Once you have developed an explanation for a new situation or think you empathize with someone from a foreign culture, treat your interpretation as a hypothesis that needs further testing rather than as a certainty. Carefully assess the feedback provided by recipients to see if it confirms your hypothesis. For important decisions or communiqués, you can also check with other foreign and home-country colleagues to ensure that your interpretations are on target.

How Communication Breakdown Leads To Conflict

4   What is conflict?

Conflict can be a serious problem in *any* organization. It might not lead to co-CEOs going after each other in court, as happened when brothers Wallace and Harrison McCain battled over command of McCain Foods, the New Brunswick-based french-fry empire they had built together. Still, it can certainly hurt an organization's performance and lead to the loss of good employees.

Conflict Defined

Several common themes underlie most definitions of conflict.[46] Conflict must be *perceived* by the parties to it; if no one is aware of a conflict, it is generally agreed that no conflict exists. Conflict also involves opposition or incompatibility and some form of interaction between the parties.[47] These factors set the conditions that determine the beginning point of the conflict process. We can define **conflict**, then, as a process that begins when one party perceives that another party has negatively affected, or is about to negatively affect, something that the first party cares about.[48]

conflict A process that begins when one party perceives that another party has negatively affected, or is about to negatively affect, something that the first party cares about.

This definition is deliberately broad. It describes that point in any ongoing activity when an interaction "crosses over" to become conflict. It includes the wide range of conflicts that people experience in groups and organizations—incompatibility of goals, differences over interpretations of facts, disagreements based on behavioural expectations, and the like. Finally, our definition is flexible enough to cover the full range of conflict levels—from subtle forms of disagreement to overt and violent acts.

Conflict has positive sides and negative sides, which we will discuss further when we cover functional and dysfunctional conflict. For more on this debate, refer to the *Point/Counterpoint* discussion on page 221.

Functional vs. Dysfunctional Conflict

functional conflict Conflict that supports the goals of the group and improves its performance.

dysfunctional conflict Conflict that hinders group performance.

Not all conflict is bad. Some conflicts support the goals of the group and improve its performance; these are **functional**, or constructive, forms of conflict. But there are conflicts that hinder group performance; these are **dysfunctional**, or destructive, forms of conflict. The criterion that differentiates functional from dysfunctional conflict is group performance. If a group is unable to achieve its goals because of conflict, then the conflict is dysfunctional.

Exhibit 6-5 provides a way of visualizing conflict behaviour. All conflicts exist somewhere along this continuum. At the lower part of the continuum, we have conflicts characterized by subtle, indirect, and highly controlled forms of tension. An illustration might be a student politely objecting to a point the instructor has just made in class. Conflict intensities escalate as they move upward along the continuum, until they become highly destructive. Strikes and lockouts, riots, and wars clearly fall into this upper range. For the most part, you should assume that conflicts that reach the upper ranges of the continuum are almost always dysfunctional. Functional conflicts are typically confined to the lower range of the continuum.

In July 2008, the contract of CUPE local 3903, the union of almost 3400 contract professors, teaching assistants, and research assistants at York University, was coming up for renewal. Union members gathered together to determine what they wanted to achieve in the next round of collective bargaining with the university. Bargaining did not go well, and each side blamed the other for the stalemate. CUPE 3903 and York University were locked in a conflict that led to the cancellation of classes for three months during the 2008–2009 academic year.

RESEARCH FINDINGS: CONFLICT

Research on conflict has yet to clearly identify those situations in which conflict is more likely to be constructive than destructive. However, there is growing evidence that the source of the conflict is a significant factor determining functionality.[49] **Cognitive conflict**, which is task-oriented and occurs because of differences in perspectives and judgments, can often result in identifying potential solutions to problems. Thus it would be regarded as functional conflict. **Affective conflict**, which is emotional and aimed at a person rather than an issue, tends to be dysfunctional conflict.

One study of 53 teams found that cognitive conflict, because it generates more alternatives, led to better decisions, more acceptance of the decisions, and ownership of the decisions. Teams experiencing affective conflict, where members had personality incompatibilities and disputes, showed poorer decisions and lower levels of acceptance of the decisions.[50]

Because conflict can involve our emotions in a variety of ways, it can also lead to stress. You may want to refer to the *OB on the Edge—Stress at Work* on pages 104–111 to get some ideas on how to manage the stress that might arise from conflicts you experience.

cognitive conflict Conflict that is task-oriented and related to differences in perspectives and judgments.

affective conflict Conflict that is emotional and aimed at a person rather than an issue.

Conflict Resolution

Is conflict always bad?

Conflict in the workplace can affect the effectiveness of individuals, teams, and the entire organization.[51] One study found that 20 percent of managers' time is spent managing conflict.[52]

Once conflict arises, what can be done to resolve it? The way a conflict is defined goes a long way toward establishing the sort of outcomes that might settle it. For instance, if I define our salary disagreement as a zero-sum or *win-lose situation*—that is, if you get the increase in pay you want, there will be just that amount less for me—I am going to be far less willing to look for mutual solutions than if I frame the conflict as a potential *win-win situation*. So individual attitudes toward a conflict are important, because attitudes typically define the set of possible settlements.

5 How can conflict be resolved?

Conflict Management Strategies

Conflict researchers often use dual concern theory to describe people's conflict management strategies. Dual concern theory considers how one's degree of *cooperativeness* (the degree to which one tries to satisfy the other person's concerns) and *assertiveness* (the degree to which one tries to satisfy one's own concerns) determine how a conflict is handled.[53] The five conflict-handling strategies identified by the theory are as follows:[54]

- *Forcing.* Imposing one's will on the other party.

- *Problem solving.* Trying to reach an agreement that satisfies both one's own and the other party's aspirations as much as possible.

- *Avoiding.* Ignoring or minimizing the importance of the issues creating the conflict.

- *Yielding.* Accepting and incorporating the will of the other party.

- *Compromising.* Balancing concern for oneself with concern for the other party in order to reach a solution.

| **EXHIBIT 6-5** | Conflict Intensity Continuum |

Annihilatory conflict	Overt efforts to destroy the other party
	Aggressive physical attacks
	Threats and ultimatums
	Assertive verbal attacks
	Overt questioning or challenging of others
No conflict	Minor disagreements or misunderstandings

Sources: Based on S. P. Robbins, *Managing Organizational Conflict: A Nontraditional Approach* (Upper Saddle River, NJ: Prentice Hall, 1974), pp. 93–97; and F. Glasl, "The Process of Conflict Escalation and the Roles of Third Parties," in *Conflict Management and Industrial Relations*, ed. G. B. J. Bomers and R. Peterson (Boston: Kluwer-Nijhoff, 1982), pp. 119–140.

Forcing is a win-lose solution, as is yielding, while problem solving seeks a win-win solution. Avoiding conflict and pretending it does not exist and compromising, so that neither person gets what they want, can yield lose-lose solutions. Exhibit 6-6 illustrates these five strategies, along with specific actions that one might take when using them.

Choosing a particular strategy for resolving conflict depends on a variety of factors. Research shows that while people may choose among the strategies, they have an underlying disposition to handle conflicts in certain ways.[55] In addition, some situations call for particular strategies. For instance, when a small child insists on trying to run into the street, a parent may need a forcing strategy to restrain the child. Co-workers who are having a conflict over setting deadlines to complete a project on time may decide that problem solving is the best strategy to use.

This chapter's *Learning About Yourself Exercise* on pages 222–223 gives you the opportunity to discover your preferred conflict-handling strategy. As well, *OB in Action—Choosing Strategies to Deal With Conflicts* indicates the situations in which each strategy is best used.

What Can Individuals Do to Manage Conflict?

There are a number of conflict resolution techniques that individuals can use to try to defuse conflict inside and outside the workplace. These include the following:[56]

- *Problem solving.* Requesting a face-to-face meeting to identify the problem and resolve it through open discussion.

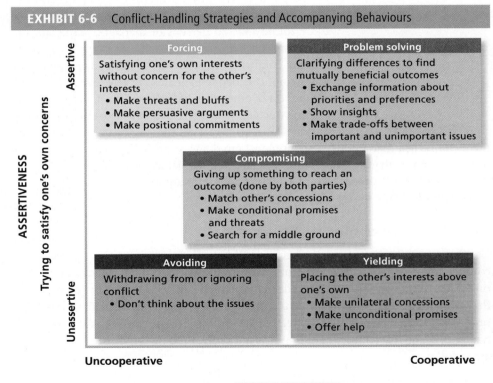

EXHIBIT 6-6   Conflict-Handling Strategies and Accompanying Behaviours

Forcing
Satisfying one's own interests without concern for the other's interests
- Make threats and bluffs
- Make persuasive arguments
- Make positional commitments

Problem solving
Clarifying differences to find mutually beneficial outcomes
- Exchange information about priorities and preferences
- Show insights
- Make trade-offs between important and unimportant issues

Compromising
Giving up something to reach an outcome (done by both parties)
- Match other's concessions
- Make conditional promises and threats
- Search for a middle ground

Avoiding
Withdrawing from or ignoring conflict
- Don't think about the issues

Yielding
Placing the other's interests above one's own
- Make unilateral concessions
- Make unconditional promises
- Offer help

Assertive / Unassertive

ASSERTIVENESS
Trying to satisfy one's own concerns

Uncooperative — Cooperative

COOPERATIVENESS

Trying to satisfy the other person's concerns

Sources: Based on K. W. Thomas, "Conflict and Negotiation Processes in Organizations," in *Handbook of Industrial and Organizational Psychology*, vol. 3, 2nd ed., ed. M. D. Dunnette and L. M. Hough (Palo Alto, CA: Consulting Psychologists Press, 1992), p. 668; C. K. W. De Dreu, A. Evers, B. Beersma, E. S. Kluwer, and A. Nauta, "A Theory-Based Measure of Conflict Management Strategies in the Workplace," *Journal of Organizational Behavior* 22, no. 6 (September 2001), pp. 645–668; and D. G. Pruitt and J. Rubin, *Social Conflict: Escalation, Stalemate and Settlement* (New York: Random House, 1986).

- *Developing superordinate goals.* Creating a shared goal that requires both parties to work together and motivates them to do so.

- *Smoothing.* Playing down differences while emphasizing common interests with the other party.

- *Compromising.* Agreeing with the other party that each will give up something of value to reach an accord.

- *Avoidance.* Withdrawing from, or suppressing, the conflict. The choice of technique may depend on how serious the issue is to you, whether you take a win-win or a win-lose approach, and your preferred conflict management style.

When the conflict is specifically work-related there are additional techniques that might be used:

- *Expansion of resources.* The scarcity of a resource—say, money, promotion opportunities, office space—can create conflict. Expansion of the resource can create a win-win solution.

- *Authoritative command.* Management can use its formal authority to resolve the conflict and then communicate its desires to the parties involved.

- *Altering the human variable.* Behavioural change techniques such as human relations training can alter attitudes and behaviours that cause conflict.

- *Altering the structural variables.* The formal organization structure and the interaction patterns of conflicting parties can be changed through job redesign, transfers, creation of coordinating positions, and the like.

Resolving Personality Conflicts

Personality conflicts are an everyday occurrence in the workplace. While there is no available data for Canada, supervisors in the United States spend about 18 percent of their time handling personality conflicts among employees.[58] A variety of factors leads to personality conflicts, including the following:[59]

- Misunderstandings based on age, race, or cultural differences

- Intolerance, prejudice, discrimination, or bigotry

- Perceived inequities

- Misunderstandings, rumours, or falsehoods about an individual or group

- Blaming for mistakes or mishaps (finger-pointing)

Personality conflicts can result in lowered productivity when people find it difficult to work together. The individuals experiencing the conflict may seek sympathy from other members of the work group, causing co-workers to take sides. The ideal solution

OB in ACTION

Choosing Strategies to Deal With Conflicts

Forcing
→ In emergencies
→ On important but unpopular issues
→ On vital issues when you know you are right
→ Against people who take advantage of noncompetitive behaviour

Problem solving
→ If both sets of concerns are too important to be compromised
→ To merge different perspectives
→ To gain commitment through a consensus
→ To mend a relationship

Avoiding
→ When an issue is trivial
→ When your concerns will not be met
→ When potential disruption outweighs the benefits of resolution
→ To let people cool down and regain perspective

Yielding
→ When you find you are wrong
→ To show your reasonableness
→ When issues are more important to others than to yourself
→ To build social credits for later issues
→ When harmony and stability are especially important

Compromising
→ When goals are important but not worth more assertive approaches
→ When opponents are committed to mutually exclusive goals
→ To achieve temporary settlements to complex issues
→ To arrive at expedient solutions under time pressure[57]

would be for the two people in conflict to work it out between themselves, without involving others, but this does not always happen. However, it is not always possible for people to talk things out, and it may be a Western cultural bias to expect that individuals should generally be able to do so.[60] *OB in Action—Handling Personality Conflicts* suggests ways of dealing with personality conflicts in the workplace.

Negotiation

6 How does one negotiate effectively?

negotiation A process in which two or more parties exchange goods or services and try to agree upon the exchange rate for them.

When parties are potentially in conflict they may choose to negotiate a resolution. Negotiation occurs in the interactions of almost everyone in groups and organizations: Labour bargains with management; managers negotiate with employees, peers, and senior management; salespeople negotiate with customers; purchasing agents negotiate with suppliers; employees agree to answer a colleague's phone for a few minutes in exchange for some past or future benefit. In today's team-based organizations, negotiation skills become critical so that teams can work together effectively.

We define **negotiation** as a process in which two or more parties try to agree on the exchange rate for goods or services they are trading.[62] Note that we use the terms *negotiation* and *bargaining* interchangeably.

Within a negotiation, one should be aware that individuals have *issues, positions,* and *interests. Issues* are items that are specifically placed on the bargaining table for discussion. *Positions* are the individual's stand on the issues. For instance, salary may be an issue for discussion. The salary you hope to receive is your position. Finally, *interests* are the underlying concerns that are affected by the negotiation resolution. For instance, the reason that you might want a six-figure salary is that you are trying to buy a house in Vancouver, and a pay increase is your only hope of being able to make mortgage payments.

Negotiators who recognize the underlying interests of themselves and the other party may have more flexibility in achieving a resolution. For instance, in the example just given, an employer who offers you a mortgage at a lower rate than the bank does, or who provides you with an interest-free loan that can be used against the mortgage, may be able to address your underlying interests without actually meeting your salary position. You may be satisfied with this alternative, if you understand what your interest is.

Interest-based bargaining enabled Vancouver-based NorskeCanada (now Catalyst Paper Corporation) to sign a mutually beneficial five-year contract with the Communications, Energy and Paperworkers Union of Canada in fall 2002, after just nine days of negotiations.[63] While the union and NorkseCanada had experienced bitter conflict in previous negotiations, in this particular situation both sides agreed to focus more on the interests of the parties, rather than on demands and concessions. Both sides were pleased with the outcome.

Bargaining Strategies

There are two general approaches to negotiation—*distributive bargaining* and *integrative bargaining.*[64] These are compared in Exhibit 6-7.

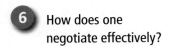

Handling Personality Conflicts

Tips for employees having a personality conflict

→ **Communicate directly** with the other person to resolve the perceived conflict (emphasize problem solving and common objectives, not personalities).

→ **Avoid dragging** co-workers into the conflict.

→ If dysfunctional conflict persists, **seek help** from direct supervisors or human resource specialists.

Tips for third-party observers of a personality conflict

→ **Do not take sides** in someone else's personality conflict.

→ **Suggest the parties work things out** themselves in a constructive and positive way.

→ If dysfunctional conflict persists, **refer the problem to the parties' direct supervisors**.

Tips for managers whose employees are having a personality conflict

→ **Investigate and document** conflict.

→ If appropriate, **take corrective action** (e.g., feedback or behaviour shaping).

→ If necessary, **attempt informal dispute resolution**.

→ **Refer difficult conflicts** to human resource specialists or hired counsellors for formal resolution attempts and other interventions.[61]

EXHIBIT 6-7	Distributive vs. Integrative Bargaining	
Bargaining Characteristic	**Distributive Bargaining**	**Integrative Bargaining**
Available resources	Fixed amount of resources to be divided	Variable amount of resources to be divided
Primary motivations	I win, you lose	I win, you win
Primary interests	Opposed to each other	Convergent or congruent with each other
Focus of relationships	Short-term	Long-term

Source: Based on R. J. Lewicki and J. A. Litterer, *Negotiation* (Homewood, IL: Irwin, 1985), p. 280.

Distributive Bargaining

Should you try to win at any cost when you bargain?

Distributive bargaining is a negotiating strategy that operates under zero-sum (win-lose) conditions. That is, any gain I make is at your expense, and vice versa. Probably the most widely cited example of distributive bargaining is in labour-management negotiations over wages. Typically, management comes to the bargaining table determined to keep its labour costs as low as possible. Since every cent more that labour negotiates increases management's costs, each party bargains aggressively and treats the other as an opponent who must be defeated.

distributive bargaining
Negotiation that seeks to divide up a fixed amount of resources; a win-lose solution.

When engaged in distributive bargaining, a party focuses on trying to get the opponent to agree to a specific target point, or to get as close to it as possible. Examples of such tactics are persuading your opponent of the impossibility of reaching his or her target point and the advisability of accepting a settlement near yours; arguing that your target is fair, while your opponent's is not; and trying to get your opponent to feel emotionally generous toward you and thus accept an outcome close to your target point.

When engaged in distributive bargaining, one of the best things you can do is to make the first offer, and to make it an aggressive one. Research consistently shows that the best negotiators are those who make the first offer and whose initial offer has very favourable terms. Why is this so? One reason is that making the first offer shows power; research shows that individuals in power are much more likely to make initial offers, speak first at meetings, and thereby gain the advantage. Another reason is the anchoring bias (the tendency for people to fixate on initial information). Once that anchoring point is set, people fail to adequately adjust it based on subsequent information. A savvy negotiator sets an anchor with the initial offer, and scores of negotiation studies show that such anchors greatly favour the person who sets it.[65]

Integrative Bargaining

In contrast to distributive bargaining, **integrative bargaining** operates under the assumption that there exists one or more settlements that can create a win-win solution. In terms of intraorganizational behaviour, all things being equal, integrative bargaining is preferable to distributive bargaining. Why? Because the former builds long-term relationships and makes working together in the future easier. It bonds negotiators and allows both sides to leave the bargaining table feeling that they have achieved a victory. For instance, in union-management negotiations, both sides might sit down to figure out other ways to reduce costs within an organization so that it is possible to have greater wage increases. Distributive bargaining, on the other hand, leaves one

integrative bargaining
Negotiation that seeks one or more settlements that can create a win-win solution.

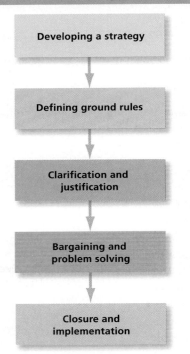

EXHIBIT 6-8   The Negotiation Process

Developing a strategy

Defining ground rules

Clarification and justification

Bargaining and problem solving

Closure and implementation

Source: This model is based on R. J. Lewicki, "Bargaining and Negotiation," *Exchange: The Organizational Behavior Teaching Journal* 6, no. 2 (1981), pp. 39–40.

BATNA The *best* *a*lternative *to* a *n*egotiated *a*greement; the outcome an individual faces if negotiations fail.

bargaining zone The zone between each party's resistance point, assuming there is overlap in this range.

party a loser. It tends to build animosities and deepen divisions when people must work together on an ongoing basis.

Research shows that over repeated bargaining episodes, when the "losing" party feels positive about the negotiation outcome, the party is much more likely to bargain cooperatively in subsequent negotiations. This points to the important advantage of integrative negotiations: Even when you "win," you want your opponent to feel positively about the negotiation.[66]

How to Negotiate

Exhibit 6-8 provides a simplified model of the negotiation process. It views negotiation as made up of five steps: (1) developing a strategy; (2) defining ground rules; (3) clarification and justification; (4) bargaining and problem solving; and (5) closure and implementation.

Developing a Strategy

Before you start negotiating you need to do your homework. What is the nature of the conflict? What is the history leading up to this negotiation? Who is involved and what are their perceptions of the conflict? What do you want from the negotiation? What are *your* goals? It often helps to put your goals in writing and develop a range of outcomes—from "most hopeful" to "minimally acceptable"—to keep your attention focused.

You also want to prepare an assessment of what you think the other party to your negotiation's goals are. What are they likely to ask for? How entrenched are they likely to be in their position? What intangible or hidden interests may be important to them? What might they be willing to settle for? When you can anticipate your opponent's position, you are better equipped to counter his or her arguments with the facts and figures that support your position.

In determining goals, parties are well advised to consider their "target and resistance" points, as well as their *best* *a*lternative *to* a *n*egotiated *a*greement (**BATNA**).[67] The buyer and the seller represent two negotiators. Each has a *target point* that defines what he or she would like to achieve. Each also has a *resistance point*, which marks the lowest outcome that is acceptable—the point below which each would break off negotiations rather than accept a less favourable settlement. The area between these two points makes up each negotiator's aspiration range. As long as there is some overlap between the buyer's and seller's aspiration ranges, there exists a **bargaining zone** where each side's aspirations can be met. Referring to Exhibit 6-9, if the buyer's resistance point is $450 and the seller's resistance point is $500, then the two may not be able to reach agreement because there is no overlap in their aspiration ranges. Recent research suggests that having an attractive BATNA is particularly powerful to a negotiator

EXHIBIT 6-9   Staking Out the Bargaining Zone

$400	$475	$525	$600

←Buyer's aspiration range   Seller's aspiration range →

Bargaining zone

Buyer's target point	Seller's resistance point	Buyer's resistance point	Seller's target point

when the bargaining zone is small.[68] The lengthy and bitter negotiations between the National Hockey League Players' Association and the National Hockey League owners underscored that there was no overlap in the bargaining zone on where the salary cap should be set, as the following *OB in the Workplace* shows.

OB IN THE WORKPLACE

Hockey Union and Management Fail to Score a Goal

How could an entire hockey season be cancelled? In early February 2005, Gary Bettman, National Hockey League (NHL) commissioner, was signalling to hockey fans throughout North America that the 2004–2005 hockey season was about to be called off.[69] Hockey players had been trying to negotiate a new contract with NHL management since 2003, meeting 14 times in 2003, 14 times in 2004, and 9 times by early February 2005 to try to resolve their differences. Little success had been made, despite all of those meetings.

Each side blamed the other for the stalemate and indicated that their BATNA—not playing any hockey at all for an entire season—was more desirable than ending the dispute.

"Their [the hockey players'] outright rejection of our proposal yesterday [February 9, 2005] I think speaks more to the fact that the union is never, ever, ever, ever—under any circumstances—prepared to play under any kind of cost-certain, economic partnership, salary cap—you pick the term—type of system," said Bill Daly, executive vice-president and chief legal officer of the NHL.

Hockey players saw the issue somewhat differently. "They [management] have made it clear they have only one way of doing things, and that's through their hard-cap system," claimed National Hockey League Players' Association (NHLPA) senior director Ted Saskin.

The NHL and the NHLPA settled their differences in July 2005, and the players agreed to a salary cap, something they had said they absolutely would not do throughout most of the negotiations. The 2004–2005 season's 1230 regular-season games were cancelled and there was no Stanley Cup champion for the first time since 1919, when the final between Montreal and Seattle was cancelled because of a flu epidemic.

One's BATNA represents the alternative that an individual will face if negotiations fail. For instance, during the winter 2005 hockey negotiations, for both hockey players and owners, the BATNA was the loss of the 2004–2005 season.

As part of your strategy, you should determine not only your BATNA but some estimate of the other side's as well.[70] If you go into your negotiation having a good idea of what the other party's BATNA is, you will have a better understanding of how far you can press to achieve the results you desire.

You can practise your negotiating skills in the *Working With Others Exercise* on page 224.

Defining Ground Rules

Once you have done your planning and developed a strategy, you are ready to begin defining the ground rules and procedures with the other party over the negotiation itself. Who will do the negotiating? Where will it take place? What time constraints, if any, will apply? To what issues will negotiation be limited? Will there be a specific procedure to follow if an impasse is reached? During this phase, the parties

Gary Bettman (left), the NHL commissioner, shakes hands with former head of the NHLPA, Bob Goodenow, after they finally reached an end to the stalemate that led to the cancellation of the 2004–2005 hockey season. Neither man seemed able to celebrate victory at the end of their lengthy negotiations.

OB in ACTION

Tips for Getting to Yes

R. Fisher and W. Ury present four principles for win-win negotiations in their book *Getting to Yes*:

→ **Separate** the **people from** the **problem**. Work on the issues at hand, rather than getting involved in personality issues between the parties.

→ Focus on **interests, not positions**. Try to identify what each person needs or wants, rather than coming up with an unmovable position.

→ Look for ways to achieve **mutual gains**. Rather than focusing on one "right" solution for your position, brainstorm for solutions that will satisfy the needs of both parties.

→ Use **objective criteria** to achieve a fair solution. Try to focus on fair standards, such as market value, expert opinion, norms, or laws to help guide decision making.[72]

will also exchange their initial proposals or demands. The *Ethical Dilemma Exercise* on page 225 considers whether it is ever appropriate to lie during negotiations.

Clarification and Justification

When initial positions have been exchanged, both you and the other party will explain, amplify, clarify, bolster, and justify your original demands. This part of the process need not be confrontational. Rather, it is an opportunity for educating and informing each other on the issues, why they are important, and how each arrived at their initial demands. This is the point at which you might want to provide the other party with any documentation that helps support your position.

Bargaining and Problem Solving

The essence of the negotiation process is the actual give and take in trying to hash out an agreement. It is here that concessions will undoubtedly need to be made by both parties. *OB in Action—Tips for Getting to Yes* gives you further ideas on how to make negotiating work for you, based on the popular book *Getting to Yes*.[71]

Closure and Implementation

The final step in the negotiation process is formalizing the agreement that has been worked out and developing procedures that are necessary for implementation and monitoring. For major negotiations—which would include everything from labour-management negotiations such as in the National Hockey League situation, to bargaining over lease terms, to buying real estate, to negotiating a job offer for a senior management position—this will require hammering out the specifics in a formal contract. In most cases, however, closing of the negotiation process is nothing more formal than a handshake.

Summary and Implications

1 How does communication work? Findings in this chapter suggest that the goal of perfect communication is unattainable. Yet there is evidence that demonstrates a positive relationship between effective communication (which includes factors such as perceived trust, perceived accuracy, desire for interaction, top-management receptiveness, and upward information requirements) and employee productivity.[73] Therefore, choosing the correct channel, being a good listener, and using feedback well may make for more effective communication.

2 What are the barriers to communication? Human beings will always be subject to errors in communication because of filtering, selective perception, defensiveness, information overload, and language. What is said may not be what is heard. Whatever the sender's expectations, the decoded message in the mind of the receiver represents his or her reality. This "reality" will determine the individual's reactions, including performance, motivation, and degree of satisfaction in the workplace.

3 **What are other issues in communication?** The big topics in communication are electronic communications, the importance of nonverbal communication and silence, gender differences in communication, and cross-cultural differences in communication. As we saw in this chapter, email, among other electronic communications, has become far more prevalent, is causing more stress, and can be misused so that it is not always the most effective means of communication. Nonverbal cues help provide a clearer picture of what someone is trying to say. Silence can be an important communication clue, and failing to pay attention to silence can result in missing some or all of a message. Good communicators hear and interpret silence. We can make some generalizations about differences in the conversational style of men and women; men are more likely to use talk to emphasize status, while women use talk to create connection. We noted that there are a variety of barriers when communicating with someone from a different culture and that it is best to assume differences until similarity is proven, emphasize description rather than *interpretation* or *evaluation*, practise empathy, and treat your interpretations as a working hypothesis.

4 **What is conflict?** Conflict occurs when one person perceives that another person's actions will have a negative effect on something the first party cares about. Many people automatically assume that all conflict is bad. However, conflict can be either functional (constructive) or dysfunctional (destructive) to the performance of a group or unit. An optimal level of conflict encourages communication, prevents stagnation, stimulates creativity, allows tensions to be released, and plants the seeds of change, yet not so much as to be disruptive or to deter activities.

5 **How can conflict be resolved?** The way a conflict is defined goes a long way toward establishing the sort of outcomes that might settle it. One can work toward a *win-lose solution* or a *win-win solution*. Conflict management strategies are determined by the extent to which one wants to cooperate with another party, and the extent to which one asserts his or her own concerns.

6 **How does one negotiate effectively?** Negotiation is a process in which two or more parties try to agree on the exchange rate for goods or services they are trading. Negotiation is an ongoing activity in groups and organizations. Distributive bargaining can resolve disputes, but it often negatively affects one or more negotiators' satisfaction because it is focused on the short term and because it is confrontational. Integrative bargaining, by contrast, tends to provide outcomes that satisfy all parties and build lasting relationships.

SNAPSHOT SUMMARY

1 **The Communication Process**
Encoding and Decoding
The Message
The Channel
The Feedback Loop
The Context

2 **Barriers to Effective Communication**
Filtering
Selective Perception
Defensiveness
Information Overload
Language
Communicating Under Stress

3 **Current Issues in Communication**
Electronic Communications
Nonverbal Communication
Silence as Communication
Communication Barriers Between Women and Men
Cross-Cultural Communication

4 **How Communication Breakdown Leads to Conflict**
Conflict Defined
Functional vs. Dysfunctional Conflict

5 **Conflict Resolution**
Conflict Management Strategies
What Can Individuals Do to Manage Conflict?
Resolving Personality Conflicts

6 **Negotiation**
Bargaining Strategies
How to Negotiate

OB at Work

For Review

1. Describe the communication process and identify its key components. Give an example of how this process operates with both oral and written messages.

2. Contrast encoding and decoding.

3. What are the advantages and disadvantages of email? Of instant messaging?

4. What is nonverbal communication? Does it aid or hinder verbal communication?

5. What does the phrase "sometimes the real message in a communication is buried in the silence" mean?

6. What are the managerial implications from the research contrasting male and female communication styles?

7. List four specific problems related to language difficulties in cross-cultural communication.

8. What is the difference between functional and dysfunctional conflict? What determines functionality?

9. What defines the bargaining zone in distributive bargaining?

10. How can you improve your negotiating effectiveness?

For Critical Thinking

1. "Ineffective communication is the fault of the sender." Do you agree or disagree? Discuss.

2. Using the concept of channel richness, give examples of messages best conveyed by email, in face-to-face communication, and on the company bulletin board.

3. Why do you think so many people are poor listeners?

4. Assume one of your co-workers had to negotiate a contract with someone from China. What problems might he or she face? If the co-worker asked for advice, what suggestions would you make to help facilitate a settlement?

5. From your own experience, describe a situation you were involved in where the conflict was dysfunctional. Describe another example, from your experience, where the conflict was functional. Would the other parties in the conflicts agree with your assessment of what is functional or dysfunctional?

OB for You

- If you are having difficulty communicating with someone, you might consider that both you and the other person are contributing something to that breakdown. This tends to be true even if you are inclined to believe that the other person is the party more responsible for the breakdown.

- Often either selective perception or defensiveness gets in the way of communication. As you work in your groups on student projects, you may want to observe communication flows more critically to help you understand ways that communication can be improved and dysfunctional conflict avoided.

- It may seem easier, but avoiding conflict does not necessarily have a more positive outcome than working with someone to resolve the conflict.

- Trying to achieve a win-win solution in a conflict situation tends to lead to better relationships and greater trust.

Point

Conflict Is Good for an Organization

We have made considerable progress in the last 25 years toward overcoming the negative stereotype given to conflict. Most behavioural scientists and an increasing number of practising managers now accept that the goal of effective management is not to eliminate conflict. Rather, it is to create the right intensity of conflict so as to reap its functional benefits.

Let's briefly review how stimulating conflict can provide benefits to the organization.[74]

- *Conflict is a means by which to bring about radical change.* It is an effective device by which management can drastically change the existing power structure, current interaction patterns, and entrenched attitudes.

- *Conflict facilitates group cohesiveness.* While conflict increases hostility between groups, external threats tend to cause a group to pull together as a unit. Intergroup conflicts raise the extent to which members identify with their own group and increase feelings of solidarity, while, at the same time, internal differences and irritations dissolve.

- *Conflict improves group and organizational effectiveness.* The stimulation of conflict sparks the search for new means and goals and clears the way for innovation. The successful resolution of a conflict leads to greater effectiveness, to more trust and openness, to greater attraction of members for one another, and to the depersonalization of future conflicts. In fact, it has been found that as the number of minor disagreements increases, the number of major clashes decreases.

- *Conflict brings about a slightly higher, more constructive level of tension.* Constructive levels of tension improve the chances of solving the conflicts in a way that is satisfactory to all parties concerned. When the level of tension is very low, the parties are not sufficiently motivated to do something about a conflict.

These points are clearly not comprehensive. As noted in this chapter, conflict provides a number of benefits to an organization. However, groups or organizations that lack conflict are likely to suffer from apathy, stagnation, groupthink, and other debilitating problems. In fact, more organizations probably fail because they have too little conflict rather than too much.

Counterpoint

All Conflicts Are Dysfunctional!

It may be true that conflict is an inherent part of any group or organization. It may not be possible to eliminate it completely. However, just because conflicts exist is no reason to worship them. All conflicts are dysfunctional, and it is one of management's major responsibilities to keep conflict intensity as low as humanly possible. A few points support this case:

- *The negative consequences from conflict can be devastating.* The list of negatives associated with conflict is impressive. Obvious negatives include increased turnover, decreased employee satisfaction, labour grievances and strikes, sabotage, physical aggression, and inefficiencies between work units.

- *Effective managers build teamwork.* A good manager builds a coordinated team. Conflict works against such an objective. A successful work group is like a successful sports team: Each member knows his or her role and supports his or her teammates. When a team works well, the whole becomes greater than the sum of the parts. Management creates teamwork by minimizing internal conflicts and facilitating internal coordination.

- *Competition is good for an organization; conflict is not.* Competition and conflict should not be confused with each other. Conflict is behaviour directed against another party, whereas competition is behaviour aimed at obtaining a goal without interference from another party. Competition is healthy; it is the source of organizational vitality. Conflict, on the other hand, is destructive.

- *Conflict is avoidable.* It may be true that conflict is inevitable when an organization is in a downward spiral, but the goal of good leadership and effective management is to avoid the spiral to begin with. You don't see Warren Buffett getting into a lot of conflicts with his board of directors. It's possible they're complacent, but we think it's more likely because Berkshire Hathaway is a well-run company, doing what it should, and avoiding conflict as a result.

OB *At Work*

What Is Your Primary Conflict-Handling Style?

Indicate how often you rely on each of the following tactics by circling the number you feel is most appropriate.[75]
When I have a conflict at work, I do the following:

	Not at All				Very Much
1. I give in to the wishes of the other party.	1	2	3	4	5
2. I try to realize a middle-of-the-road solution.	1	2	3	4	5
3. I push my own point of view.	1	2	3	4	5
4. I examine issues until I find a solution that really satisfies me and the other party.	1	2	3	4	5
5. I avoid a confrontation about our differences.	1	2	3	4	5
6. I concur with the other party.	1	2	3	4	5
7. I emphasize that we have to find a compromise solution.	1	2	3	4	5
8. I search for gains.	1	2	3	4	5
9. I stand for my own and the other party's goals and interests.	1	2	3	4	5
10. I avoid differences of opinion as much as possible.	1	2	3	4	5
11. I try to accommodate the other party.	1	2	3	4	5
12. I insist we both give in a little.	1	2	3	4	5
13. I fight for a good outcome for myself.	1	2	3	4	5
14. I examine ideas from both sides to find a mutually optimal solution.	1	2	3	4	5
15. I try to make differences loom less large.	1	2	3	4	5
16. I adapt to the other party's goals and interests.	1	2	3	4	5
17. I strive whenever possible toward a 50-50 compromise.	1	2	3	4	5
18. I do everything to win.	1	2	3	4	5
19. I work out a solution that serves my own as well as the other party's interests as well as possible.	1	2	3	4	5
20. I try to avoid a confrontation with the other party.	1	2	3	4	5

Scoring Key

To determine your primary conflict-handling strategy, place the number 1 through 5 that represents your score for each statement next to the number for that statement. Then add up the columns.

OB At Work

Yielding	Compromising	Forcing	Problem solving	Avoiding
1. _____	2. _____	3. _____	4. _____	5. _____
6. _____	7. _____	8. _____	9. _____	10. _____
11. _____	12. _____	13. _____	14. _____	15. _____
16. _____	17. _____	18. _____	19. _____	20. _____
Totals _____	_____	_____	_____	_____

Your primary conflict-handling style is the category with the highest total. Your fallback intention is the category with the second-highest total.

More Learning About Yourself Exercises

Additional self-assessments relevant to this chapter appear on MyOBLab (**www.pearsoned.ca/myoblab**).

II.A.1   What's My Face-to-Face Communication Style?

II.C.5   What's My Preferred Conflict-Handling Style?

II.C.6   What's My Negotiating Style?

IV.E.3   Am I a Gossip?

When you complete the additional assessments, consider the following:

1.   Am I surprised about my score?

2.   Would my friends evaluate me similarly?

BREAKOUT **GROUP** EXERCISES

Form small groups to discuss the following topics, as assigned by your instructor:

1.   Describe a situation in which you ignored someone. What impact did it have on that person's subsequent communication behaviours?

2.   What differences have you observed in the ways that men and women communicate?

3.   You and 2 other students carpool to school every day. The driver has recently taken to playing a new radio station quite loudly. You do not like the music, or the loudness. Using one of the conflict-handling strategies outlined in Exhibit 6-6 on page 212, indicate how you might go about resolving this conflict. Identify a number of BATNAs (*best alternative to a negotiated agreement*) available to you, and then decide whether you should continue carpooling.

OB *At Work*

A Negotiation Role Play

This role play is designed to help you develop your negotiating skills. The class is to break into pairs. One person will play the role of Terry, the department supervisor. The other person will play Dale, Terry's boss.

The Situation: Terry and Dale work for hockey-equipment manufacturer Bauer. Terry supervises a research laboratory. Dale is the manager of research and development (R & D). Terry and Dale are former skaters who have worked for Bauer for more than 6 years. Dale has been Terry's boss for 2 years.

One of Terry's employees has greatly impressed Terry. This employee is Lisa Roland. Lisa was hired 11 months ago. She is 24 years old and holds a master's degree in mechanical engineering. Her entry-level salary was $52 500 a year. She was told by Terry that, in accordance with corporation policy, she would receive an initial performance evaluation at 6 months and a comprehensive review after 1 year. Based on her performance record, Lisa was told she could expect a salary adjustment at the time of the 1-year evaluation.

Terry's evaluation of Lisa after 6 months was very positive. Terry commented on the long hours Lisa was working, her cooperative spirit, the fact that others in the lab enjoyed working with her, and her immediate positive impact on the project to which she had been assigned. Now that Lisa's first anniversary is coming up, Terry has again reviewed Lisa's performance. Terry thinks Lisa may be the best new person the R & D group has ever hired. After only a year, Terry has ranked Lisa third highest in a department of 11.

Salaries in the department vary greatly. Terry, for instance, has a basic salary of $93 800, plus eligibility for a bonus that might add another $7000 to $11 000 a year. The salary range of the 11 department members is $42 500 to $79 000. The lowest salary is a recent hire with a bachelor's degree in physics. The two people that Terry has rated above Lisa earn base salaries of $73 800 and $78 900. They are both 27 years old and have been at Bauer for 3 and 4 years, respectively. The median salary in Terry's department is $65 300.

Terry's Role: You want to give Lisa a big raise. While she is young, she has proven to be an excellent addition to the department. You don't want to lose her. More important, she knows in general what other people in the department are earning, and she thinks she is underpaid. The company typically gives 1-year raises of 5 percent, although 10 percent is not unusual and 20 to 30 percent increases have been approved on occasion. You would like to get Lisa as large an increase as Dale will approve.

Dale's Role: All your supervisors typically try to squeeze you for as much money as they can for their people. You understand this because you did the same thing when you were a supervisor, but your boss wants to keep a lid on costs. He wants you to keep raises for recent hires generally in the range of 5 to 8 percent. In fact, he has sent a memo to all managers and supervisors stating this objective. However, your boss is also very concerned with equity and paying people what they are worth. You feel assured that he will support any salary recommendation you make, as long as it can be justified. Your goal, consistent with cost reduction, is to keep salary increases as low as possible.

The Negotiation: Terry has a meeting scheduled with Dale to discuss Lisa's performance review and salary adjustment. In your role of either Dale or Terry, take a couple of minutes to think through the facts in this exercise and to prepare a strategy. Determine what your target and resistance points are and what your BATNA is. Then you have up to 15 minutes to conduct your negotiation. When your negotiation is complete, the class will compare the various strategies used and the outcomes that resulted.

OB *At Work*

ETHICAL **DILEMMA** EXERCISE

Is It Unethical to Lie and Deceive During Negotiations?

It has been said that the whole notion of negotiation is built on ethical quicksand: To succeed, you must deceive.[76] Is this true? Apparently a lot of people think so. For instance, one study found that 28 percent of negotiators lied about a common interest issue during negotiations, while another study found that 100 percent of negotiators either failed to reveal a problem or actively lied about it during negotiations if they were not directly asked about the issue.

Is it possible for someone to maintain high ethical standards and, at the same time, deal with the daily need to negotiate with bosses, peers, staff, people from other organizations, friends, and even relatives?

We can probably agree that bald-faced lies during negotiation are wrong. At least most ethicists would probably agree. The universal dilemma surrounds the little lies—the omissions, evasions, and concealments that are often necessary to best an opponent.

During negotiations, when is a lie a lie? Is exaggerating benefits, downplaying negatives, ignoring flaws, or saying "I don't know" when in reality you do know considered lying? Is declaring that "this is my final offer and it's nonnegotiable" (even when you are posturing) a lie? Is pretending to bend over backward to make meaningful concessions lying? Rather than being unethical practices, the use of these "lies" is considered by many as indicators that a negotiator is strong, smart, and savvy.

When are evasiveness and deception out of bounds? Is it naive to be completely honest and bare your soul during negotiations? Or are the rules of negotiations unique: Is any tactic that will improve your chance of winning acceptable?

CASE INCIDENT

Emailing "Lazy" Employees

Imagine receiving the following email from your CEO:[77]

We are getting less than 40 hours of work from a large number of our EMPLOYEES. The parking lot is sparsely used at 8 a.m.; likewise at 5 p.m. As managers, you either do not know what your EMPLOYEES are doing or you do not CARE. In either case, you have a problem and you will fix it or I will replace you. :-{{

NEVER in my career have I allowed a team which worked for me to think they had a 40-hour job. I have allowed YOU to create a culture which is permitting this. NO LONGER. :-|

The note (paraphrased) continues: "Hell will freeze over before any more employee benefits are given out. I will be watching the parking lot and expect it to be substantially full at 7:30 a.m. and 6:30 p.m. on weekdays and half full on Saturdays. You have two weeks. Tick, tock. :(''

| :-{{ = very angry :-l = disappointed : (= frowning |

Questions

1. What impact would this message have on you if you received it?

2. Is email the best way to convey such a message?

3. What problems might arise if people outside the organization saw this email?

4. What suggestions, if any, would you make to the CEO to help improve communication effectiveness?

5. What conflict-handling style is this CEO using? What might be a more effective style? Why?

OB *At Work*

VIDEO CASE INCIDENT

CASE 6   Communication at Kluster

Kluster is a web-based company that invites individuals and companies to send in ideas for new products so they can get feedback from others.[78] For example, if a company wanted to develop a new logo, it could ask participants to rate various alternative designs using criteria such as uniqueness, coolness, colour, and so forth. Kluster promotes collaborative decision making that ". . . turns questions into answers, ideas into opportunities, and analysis into action."

Mat Papprocki, the designer at Kluster, says that everyone has ideas, but they generally keep those ideas to themselves and they do not know how to turn the idea into reality. The whole idea at Kluster is to get people to share their ideas and then have many other people in the web-based community comment on the usefulness of the idea.

Tom Pasley, the project manager at Kluster, says that a lot of companies seem to be afraid of what customers think. But the main goal at Kluster is to get feedback from customers. In each part of the development process, ideas are noted, votes are cast, and decisions are made about the idea. The demographic nature of the voter is taken into account and used to create a "weighted vote" that allows educated decisions to be made about the value of new product ideas. This process helps identify a diverse user base that will actually support decisions that a company makes as a result of feedback it gets.

Papprocki says that the Internet allows people to be anonymous and to say what they really think about new product ideas. CEO Ben Kaufman observes that focus groups—the "old faithful" way of doing product testing—pays people for giving opinions, so they may feel obliged to give an opinion about a product or an idea even if they do not have any really strong views about it. But with Kluster's approach, if people say they like the product, it's probably because they really do like it, not because they are trying to avoid hurting someone's feelings.

The Kluster approach yields three important benefits. First, it provides respect. Everyone respects an

individual or a company that admits it does not have all the answers and needs help in getting those answers. Second, opening up the process provides exposure of the new product or idea to thousands of people. Buzz is created for the new product because there is usually a very interesting story to tell about how the product was developed. Third, the process provides education. It gives companies a better idea of where support is coming from, and it helps them understand why certain ideas are better than others.

There are intellectual property issues that arise because of the nature of the Kluster approach, but Kaufman says that if you submit your idea to Kluster, you have a "time and date stamp," and that allows for protection for your idea. As well, when people submit ideas, they control the timing and can stipulate how and where the idea is to be used. If the idea ends up not being used, the person who suggested it retains all rights to the idea. Kaufman recognizes that a big company could steal a good idea from the Kluster website, but if it did so it would incur the wrath of all the people who contributed to assessing the idea. This would create very bad public relations for the big company.

Questions

1. Using Exhibit 6-1, explain how the communication process works in the Illuminator project.

2. What are the benefits of getting customer feedback through the Illuminator project as compared to the traditional focus group? What does this mean for companies?

3. How "rich" is the channel that is used in the Illuminator project? Is the level of richness appropriate for the kind of messages that are being communicated?

4. Briefly describe the barriers to effective communication and indicate which ones might be the most problematic for the Illuminator project.

From *Concepts* to *Skills*

Negotiating

Once you have taken the time to assess your own goals, to consider the other party's goals and interests, and to develop a strategy, you are ready to begin actual negotiations. The following five suggestions should improve your negotiating skills:[79]

1. *Begin with a positive overture.* Studies on negotiation show that concessions tend to be reciprocated and lead to agreements. As a result, begin bargaining with a positive overture—perhaps a small concession—and then reciprocate your opponent's concessions.

2. *Address problems, not personalities.* Concentrate on the negotiation issues, not on the personal characteristics of your opponent. When negotiations get tough, avoid the tendency to attack your opponent. It's your opponent's ideas or position that you disagree with, not him or her personally. Separate the people from the problem, and don't personalize differences.

3. *Pay little attention to initial offers.* Treat an initial offer as merely a point of departure. Everyone has to have an initial position. These initial offers tend to be extreme and idealistic. Treat them as such.

4. *Emphasize win-win solutions.* Inexperienced negotiators often assume that their gain must come at the expense of the other party. As noted with integrative bargaining, that need not be the case. There are often win-win solutions. But assuming a zero-sum game means missed opportunities for trade-offs that could benefit both sides. So if conditions are supportive, look for an integrative solution. Frame options in terms of your opponent's interests, and look for solutions that can allow your opponent, as well as yourself, to declare a victory.

5. *Create an open and trusting climate.* Skilled negotiators are better listeners, ask more questions, focus their arguments more directly, are less defensive, and have learned to avoid words and phrases that can irritate an opponent (for example, "generous offer," "fair price," "reasonable arrangement"). In other words, they are

better at creating the open and trusting climate necessary for reaching an integrative settlement.

Practising Skills

As marketing director for Done Right, a regional home-repair chain, you have come up with a plan you believe has significant potential for future sales. Your plan involves a customer information service designed to help people make their homes more environmentally sensitive. Then, based on homeowners' assessments of their homes' environmental impact, your firm will be prepared to help them deal with problems or concerns they may uncover. You are really excited about the competitive potential of this new service. You envision pamphlets, in-store appearances by environmental experts, as well as contests for consumers and school kids. After several weeks of preparations, you make your pitch to your boss, Nick Castro. You point out how the market for environmentally sensitive products is growing and how this growing demand represents the perfect opportunity for Done Right. Nick seems impressed by your presentation, but he has expressed one major concern: He thinks your workload is already too heavy. He does not see how you are going to have enough time to start this new service and still be able to look after all of your other assigned marketing duties. You really want to start the new service. What strategy will you follow in your negotiation with Nick?

Reinforcing Skills

1. Negotiate with a team member or work colleague to handle a small section of work that you are not going to be able to get done in time for an important deadline.

2. The next time you purchase a relatively expensive item (such as an automobile, apartment lease, appliance, jewellery), attempt to negotiate a better price and gain some concessions such as an extended warranty, smaller down payment, maintenance services, or the like.

Chapter 7 Power and Politics

Can three artistic directors reporting to one general director make an efficient team? Power and politics tell much of the story.

1. What is power?

2. How does one get power?

3. How does dependency affect power?

4. What tactics can be used to increase power?

5. What does it mean to be empowered?

6. How are power and harassment related?

7. Why do people engage in politics?

When the Stratford (Ontario) Festival's artistic director Richard Monette decided to retire after 14 years in the position, the organization was faced with developing a succession plan.[1] Monette and Antoni Cimolino had worked together for years, with Monette responsible for the creative direction of Stratford, and Cimolino, as executive director, responsible for the financial management. Finding someone to replace Monette proved difficult: The organization "had grown too big for just one individual or artistic vision."

Cimolino made a proposal to the board: He would take on a new title, General Director, and three new artistic directors would report to him, rather than to the board. This would consolidate his power in the organization, giving him more authority and responsibility than when he and Monette reported independently to the board.

The board accepted the proposal and announced the new artistic directors, Marti Maraden, Des McAnuff, and Don Shipley, in mid-2006. Less than two years later, however, Maraden and Shipley resigned. Maraden explained her resignation in a long letter to the *Globe and Mail*, indicating that power and politics were at the heart of the discontent. As she explained, "there was no protocol for decision-making, neither written nor spoken" and "a virtually unilateral imposition of [general director Antoni Cimolino's] agenda made it impossible for me to continue."

A major theme throughout this chapter is that power and politics are a natural process in any group or organization. Although you might have heard the saying "Power corrupts, and absolute power corrupts absolutely," power is not always bad. Understanding how to use power and politics effectively makes organizational life more manageable, because it can help you gain the support you need to do your job effectively.

OB Is for Everyone

- Have you ever wondered how you might increase your power?
- Do workplaces empower people?
- Why do some people seem to engage in politics more than others?
- In what situations does impression management work best?

A Definition of Power

1   What is power?

power A capacity that A has to influence the behaviour of B, so that B acts in accordance with A's wishes.

dependency B's relationship to A when A possesses something that B needs.

Power refers to a capacity that A has to influence the behaviour of B, so that B acts in accordance with A's wishes.[2] This definition implies that there is a *potential* for power if someone is dependent on another. But one can have power and not impose it.

Probably the most important aspect of power is that it is a function of **dependency**. The more that B depends on A, the more power A has in the relationship. Dependence, in turn, is based on the alternatives that B perceives and the importance that B places on the alternative(s) that A controls. A person can have power over you only if he or she controls something you desire. If you are attending college or university on funds totally provided by your parents, you probably recognize the power that your parents hold over you. You are dependent on them for financial support. But once you are out of school, have a job, and are making a good income, your parents' power is reduced significantly. Who among us, though, has not known or heard of the rich relative who is able to control a large number of family members merely through the implicit or explicit threat of "writing them out of the will"?

Within larger organizations, the information technology (IT) group often has considerable power, because everyone, right up to the CEO, is dependent on this group to keep computers and networks running. Since few people have the technical expertise to do so, IT personnel end up being viewed as irreplaceable. This gives them a lot of power within the organization.

Power should not be considered a bad thing, however. "Power, if used appropriately, should actually be a positive influence in your organization," says Professor Patricia Bradshaw of the Schulich School of Business at York University. "Having more power doesn't necessarily turn you into a Machiavellian monster. It can help your team and your organization achieve its goals and increase its potential."[3] The positive benefits of power (and politics) have also been explored by Professor Tom Lawrence of SFU Business (at Simon Fraser University) and his colleagues.[4]

Bases of Power

The artistic director of a theatre company often gets more public recognition than the executive director, even though each share management responsibilities. The public can directly see the impact of the artistic director's contribution through the works performed on stage. Antoni Cimolino watched for years as Richard Monette received credit for the growth of the Stratford Festival. When Monette announced his retirement, however, Cimolino did not have the artistic credits to be Monette's replacement. Instead, he suggested that the new artistic directors report to him—making Cimolino the only manager who reported to the board. What bases of power enabled Cimolino to make this proposal to the board?

2   How does one get power?

Where does power come from? What is it that gives an individual or a group influence over others? The answer to these questions was developed by social scientists John French and Bertrand Raven, who first presented a five-category classification scheme of sources or bases of power: coercive, reward, legitimate, expert, and referent.[5] They subsequently added information power to that schema (see Exhibit 7-1).[6]

Coercive Power

coercive power Power that is based on fear.

Coercive power is defined by French and Raven as dependent on fear. One reacts to this power base out of fear of the negative results that might occur if one fails to comply. It rests on the application, or the threat of the application, of physical sanctions such as the infliction of pain, the generation of frustration through restriction of movement, or the controlling by force of basic physiological or safety needs.

EXHIBIT 7-1   Measuring Bases of Power

Does a person have one or more of the six bases of power? These descriptions help identify the person's power base.

Power Base	Statement
Coercive	The person can make things difficult for people, and you want to avoid getting him or her angry.
Reward	The person is able to give special benefits or rewards to people, and you find it advantageous to trade favours with him or her.
Legitimate	The person has the right, considering his or her position and your job responsibilities, to expect you to comply with legitimate requests.
Expert	The person has the experience and knowledge to earn your respect, and you defer to his or her judgment in some matters.
Referent	You like the person and enjoy doing things for him or her.
Information	The person has data or knowledge that you need.

Source: Adapted from G. Yukl and C. M. Falbe, "Importance of Different Power Sources in Downward and Lateral Relations," *Journal of Applied Psychology,* June 1991, p. 417. With permission.

Of all the bases of power available, the power to hurt others is possibly the most often used, most often condemned, and most difficult to control. The state relies on its military and legal resources to intimidate nations, or even its own citizens; businesses rely upon the control of economic resources to request tax reductions; and religious institutions threaten individuals with dire consequences in the afterlife if they do not conduct themselves properly in this life. At the personal level, individuals use coercive power through a reliance on physical strength, words, or the ability to grant or withhold emotional support from others. These bases provide the individual with the means to physically harm, bully, humiliate, or deny love to others.[7]

At the organizational level, A has coercive power over B if A can dismiss, suspend, or demote B, assuming that B values his or her job. Similarly, if A can assign B work activities that B finds unpleasant or treat B in a manner that B finds embarrassing, A possesses coercive power over B.

Reward Power

The opposite of coercive power is **reward power**. People will go along with the wishes or directives of another if doing so produces positive benefits; therefore, one who can distribute rewards that others view as valuable will have power over those others. These rewards can be anything that another person values. In an organizational context, we think of money, favourable performance appraisals, promotions, interesting work assignments, friendly colleagues, important information, and preferred work shifts or sales territories.[8]

As with coercive power, you do not have to be a manager to be able to exert influence through rewards. Rewards such as friendliness, acceptance, and praise are available to everyone in an organization. To the degree that an individual seeks such rewards, your ability to give or withhold them gives you power over that individual.

reward power Power that achieves compliance based on the ability to distribute rewards that others view as valuable.

Legitimate Power

In formal groups and organizations, probably the most frequent access to one or more of the bases of power is through a person's structural position. This is called

In India, Naina Lal Kidwai is a powerful woman in the banking industry. She is the chief executive officer of the Hongkong and Shanghai Banking Corporation (HSBC), India. Kidwai's formal power is based on her position at the bank.

legitimate power Power that a person receives as a result of his or her position in the formal hierarchy of an organization.

expert power Influence based on special skills or knowledge.

legitimate power. It represents the power a person receives as a result of his or her position in the formal hierarchy of an organization.

Positions of authority include coercive and reward powers. Legitimate power, however, is broader than the power to coerce and reward. Specifically, it includes acceptance by members of an organization of the authority of a position. When school principals, bank presidents, or generals speak (assuming that their directives are viewed as within the authority of their positions), teachers, tellers, and privates listen and usually comply. You will note in Exhibit 7-2 that one of the men in the meeting identifies himself as the rule maker, which means that he has legitimate power.

Expert Power

Expert power is influence based on expertise, special skills, or knowledge. Expertise has become one of the most powerful sources of influence as the world has become more technologically oriented. While it is generally acknowledged that physicians have expertise and hence expert power—most of us follow the advice that our doctors give us—you should also recognize that computer specialists, tax accountants, economists, and other specialists can have power as a result of their expertise. Young people may find they have increased power in the workplace these days because of the technical knowledge and expertise that their Baby Boomer managers may not have.

EXHIBIT 7-2

"I was just going to say 'Well, I don't make the rules.' But, of course, I _do_ make the rules."

Source: Drawing by Leo Cullum in *The New Yorker.* Copyright © 1986 *The New Yorker Magazine.* Reprinted by permission.

Expert power relies on trust that all relevant information is given out honestly and completely. Of course, since knowledge is power, the more that information is shared, the less expert power a person has. Thus, some individuals try to protect their power by withholding information.[9] This tactic can result in poor-quality performance by those who need the information.[10] The *Working With Others Exercise* on pages 254–255 gives you the opportunity to explore the effectiveness of different bases of power in changing someone's behaviour.

Referent Power

Referent power develops out of admiration of another and a desire to be like that person. In a sense, then, it is a lot like charisma. If you admire someone to the point of modelling your behaviour and attitudes after him or her, that person possesses referent power over you. Sometimes teachers and coaches have referent power because of our admiration of them. Referent power explains why celebrities are paid millions of dollars to endorse products in commercials. Advertisers such as Toronto-based Roots Canada use pictures on their website of popular Canadians such as actress Amanda Crew (*15/Love* and *Final Destination 3*) and hip-hop artist Kardinal Offishall to convince people to buy specific products.[11] Similarly, Nike has used sports celebrities such as Ottawa Senators' captain Daniel Alfredsson to promote its products.

referent power Influence based on possession by an individual of desirable resources or personal traits.

Information Power

Information power comes from access to and control over information. People in an organization who have data or knowledge that others need can make those others dependent on them. Managers, for instance, because of their access to privileged sales, cost, salary, profit, and similar data, can use this information to control and shape subordinates' behaviour. Similarly, departments that possess information that is critical to a company's performance in times of high uncertainty—for example, the legal department when a firm faces a major lawsuit or the human resource department during critical labour negotiations—will gain increased power in their organizations until those uncertainties are resolved.

information power Power that comes from access to and control over information.

Evaluating the Bases of Power

Generally, people will respond in one of three ways when faced with the people who use the bases of power described above:

- *Commitment.* The person is enthusiastic about the request and shows initiative and persistence in carrying it out.

- *Compliance.* The person goes along with the request grudgingly, puts in minimal effort, and takes little initiative in carrying out the request.

- *Resistance.* The person is opposed to the request and tries to avoid it with such tactics as refusing, stalling, or arguing about it.[12]

A review of the research on the effectiveness of these forms of power finds that they differ in their impact on a person's performance.[13] Exhibit 7-3 on page 234 summarizes some of this research. Coercive power leads to resistance from individuals, decreased satisfaction, and increased mistrust. Reward power results in compliance if the rewards are consistent with what individuals want as rewards, something the *Ethical Dilemma Exercise* on pages 255–256 shows clearly. Legitimate power also results in compliance, but it does not generally result in increased commitment. In other words, legitimate power does not inspire individuals to act beyond the basic level. Expert and referent powers are the most likely to lead to commitment from individuals. Research shows that deadline pressures increase group members' reliance on individuals with expert

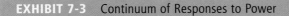

EXHIBIT 7-3   Continuum of Responses to Power

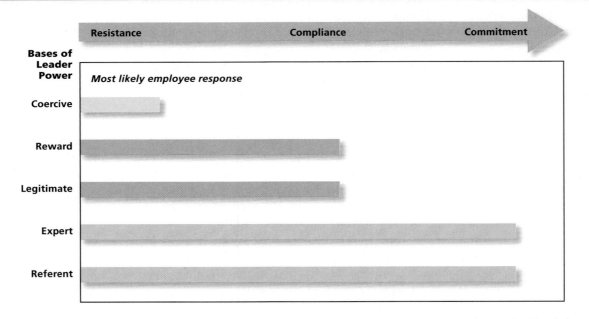

Source: R. M. Steers and J. S. Black, *Organizational Behavior,* 5th ed. (New York: HarperCollins, 1994), p. 487. Reprinted by permission of Pearson Education Inc., Upper Saddle River, New Jersey.

and information power.[14] Ironically, the least effective bases of power for improving commitment—coercive, reward, and legitimate—are the ones most often used by managers, perhaps because they are the easiest to introduce.[15]

Dependency: The Key to Power

> The Canadian arts community was shocked when the general director of the Stratford Festival, Antoni Cimolino, announced in March 2008 that two of his three artistic directors, Marti Maraden and Don Shipley, had resigned.[16] There was widespread speculation about what caused the resignations, but lack of decision-making power likely contributed to their departures. When the three directors (including Des McAnuff) were appointed to work as a team, the understanding was that consensus would determine how they would work with each other. "As a group, that's what we'll be striving to do—to find consensus," said Shipley. "It's never going to be easy but certainly we've been skilled at doing that." Over time, however, consensus became more difficult. Maraden and Shipley would side with each other, while McAnuff had a different viewpoint, which meant that Antoni Cimolino had to make decisions. He often chose McAnuff's views over the other two directors. What factors might lead to one person having greater power over another?

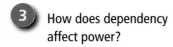

How does dependency affect power?

In this section, we show how an understanding of dependency is central to furthering your understanding of power itself.

The General Dependency Postulate

Let's begin with a general postulate: *The greater B's dependency on A, the greater the power A has over B.* When you possess anything that others require but that you alone control, you make them dependent upon you and therefore you gain power over them.[17] Another way to frame dependency is to think about a relationship in terms of "who needs whom?" The person who has the most need is the one most dependent on the relationship.[18]

Because Xerox Corporation has staked its future on development and innovation, Sophie Vandebroek is in a position of power at Xerox. As the company's chief technology officer, she leads the Xerox Innovation Group of 5000 scientists and engineers at the company's global research centres. The group's mission is "to pioneer high-impact technologies that enable us to lead in our core markets and to create future markets for Xerox." Xerox depends on Vandebroek to make that mission a reality.

Dependency is inversely proportional to the alternative sources of supply. If something is plentiful, possession of it will not increase your power. If everyone is intelligent, intelligence gives no special advantage. Similarly, in the circles of the super rich, money does not result in power. But if you can create a monopoly by controlling information, prestige, or anything that others crave, they become dependent on you. Alternatively, the more options you have, the less power you place in the hands of others. This explains, for example, why most organizations develop multiple suppliers rather than give their business to only one.

What Creates Dependency?

Dependency is increased when the resource you control is important, scarce, and cannot be substituted.[19]

Importance

If nobody wants what you have, there is no dependency. To create dependency, the thing(s) you control must be perceived as important. In some organizations, people who control the budget have a great deal of importance. In other organizations, those who possess the knowledge to keep technology working smoothly are viewed as important. What is important is situational. It varies among organizations and undoubtedly also varies over time within any given organization.

Scarcity

As noted previously, if something is plentiful, possession of it will not increase your power. A resource must be perceived as scarce to create dependency.

Scarcity can help explain how low-ranking employees gain power if they have important knowledge not available to high-ranking employees. Possession of a scarce resource—in this case, important knowledge—makes those who do not have it dependent on those who do. Thus, an individual might refuse to show others how to do a job, or might refuse to share information, thereby increasing his or her importance.

Nonsubstitutability

The fewer substitutes for a resource, the more power comes from control over that resource. At Apple Computer, for example, most observers, as well as the board, have been concerned about how Steve Jobs' health will affect Apple's future, especially after news of his liver transplant broke in spring 2009. In another example, when a union goes on strike and management is not permitted to replace the striking employees, the union has considerable control over the organization's ability to carry out its tasks.

People are often able to ask for special rewards (higher pay or better assignments) because they have skills that others do not.

Influence Tactics

Looking at the controversy surrounding the resignations of two of the Stratford Festival's artistic directors, we can find a number of instances where the various people involved in the controversy used influence tactics to get their way. There is some evidence that Antoni Cimolino and Des McAnuff formed a coalition to ensure that McAnuff would have more say over creative direction than Marti Maraden and Don Shipley. Cimolino used assertiveness to resolve disputes when the three directors could not achieve consensus on artistic direction. He also threatened sanctions such as the "unilateral imposition of his agenda" when the directors could not reach consensus, according to Maraden. So how and why do influence tactics work?

4 What tactics can be used to increase power?

influence tactics Ways that individuals translate power bases into specific actions.

Have you ever wondered how you might increase your power?

How do individuals translate their bases of power into specific, desired actions? Research indicates that people use common tactics to influence outcomes.[20] One study identifies the nine **influence tactics** managers and employees use to increase their power:[21]

1. *Rational persuasion.* Using facts and data to make a logical or rational presentation of ideas.

2. *Inspirational appeals.* Appealing to values, ideals, and goals when making a request.

3. *Consultation.* Getting others involved to support one's objectives.

4. *Ingratiation.* Using flattery, creating goodwill, and being friendly prior to making a request.

5. *Personal appeals.* Appealing to loyalty and friendship when asking for something.

6. *Exchange.* Offering favours or benefits in exchange for support.

7. *Coalition tactics.* Getting the support of other people to provide backing when making a request.

8. *Pressure.* Using demands, threats, and reminders to get someone to do something.

9. *Legitimating tactics.* Claiming the authority or right to make a request, or showing that it supports organizational goals or policies.

Researchers found that there are significant differences in the tactics used to influence actions, depending upon whether people are interacting with someone above or below them in rank. While all individuals favour rational persuasion, those managing upward are even more likely to use it (77 percent vs. 52 percent of those managing downward). Those managing downward are next most likely to use pressure (22 percent) or ingratiation (15 percent). The other favoured choices of those managing upward were coalition tactics (15 percent) and pressure (15 percent).[22]

Some tactics are more effective than others. Specifically, evidence indicates that rational persuasion, inspirational appeals, and consultation tend to be the most effective. On the other hand, pressure tends to frequently backfire and is typically the least effective of the nine tactics.[23] You can also increase your chance of success by using more than one type of tactic at the same time or sequentially, as long as your choices are compatible.[24] For instance, using both ingratiation and legitimacy can lessen the negative reactions that might come from the appearance of being "dictated to" by the boss.

You are more likely to be effective if you begin with "softer" tactics that rely on personal power such as personal and inspirational appeals, rational persuasion, and consultation. If these fail, you can move to "harder" tactics (which emphasize formal power and involve greater costs and risks), such as exchange, coalitions, and pressure.[25] Interestingly, it has been found that using a single soft tactic is more effective than using a single hard tactic, and that combining two soft tactics or a soft tactic and rational persuasion is more effective than any single tactic or a combination of hard tactics.[26]

Empowerment: Giving Power to Employees

Thus far our discussion has implied that—to some extent, at least—power is most likely to rest in the hands of managers, to be used as part of their interaction with employees. However, in today's workplace, there is a movement toward sharing more power with employees by putting them in teams and also by making them responsible for some of the decisions regarding their jobs. With the flattening of organizations, so that there are fewer middle managers, employees also end up with more responsibilities. Organizational specialists refer to this increasing responsibility as *empowerment*. We briefly mention in Chapter 8 that one of the current trends in leadership is empowering employees. Between 1995 and 2005, nearly 50 000 articles about empowerment appeared in the print media in the United States and Canada, with almost 6000 articles appearing in Canadian newspapers during that time.[27]

5 What does it mean to be empowered?

Definition of Empowerment

The definition of **empowerment** that we use here refers to the freedom and the ability of employees to make decisions and commitments.[28] Unfortunately, neither managers nor researchers can agree on the definition of empowerment. Robert E. Quinn and Gretchen M. Spreitzer, in their consulting work with a *Fortune* 500 manufacturing company, found that executives were split about 50-50 in their definition.[29] One group of executives "believed that empowerment was about delegating decision making within a set of clear boundaries." Empowerment would start at the top, specific goals and tasks would be assigned, responsibility would be delegated, and people would be held accountable for their results. The other group believed that empowerment was "a process of risk taking and personal growth." This type of empowerment starts at the bottom, with considering the employees' needs, showing them what empowered behaviour looks like, building teams, encouraging risk-taking, and demonstrating trust in employees' ability to perform.

Much of the press on empowerment has been positive, with both executives and employees applauding the ability of front-line workers to make and execute important

empowerment The freedom and the ability of employees to make decisions and commitments.

Employee empowerment at Good People Company, in Seoul, South Korea, includes a monthly "Pyjamas Day" during which all employees work in the clothing the company designs. Good People managers then hold meetings with employees to solicit their feedback and inspirations about company products, making employees feel that their contributions are important and meaningful.

decisions.[30] However, not all reports are favourable. One management expert noted that much of the talk about empowerment is simply lip service,[31] with organizations telling employees that they have decision-making responsibility but not giving them the authority to carry out their decisions. In order for an employee to be fully empowered, he or she needs access to the information required to make decisions; rewards for acting in appropriate, responsible ways; and the authority to make the necessary decisions. Empowerment means that employees understand how their jobs fit into the organization and that they are able to make decisions regarding job action in light of the organization's purpose and mission. Managers at Montague, PEI-based Durabelt recognize that to be empowered, employees need to have the appropriate skills to handle their jobs. The company sells customized conveyor belts used to harvest some vegetable and fruit crops. Employees need to be responsive to customer concerns when manufacturing the belts. In order to empower employees to manage customer relations successfully, Durabelt created Duraschool, an ongoing training program that provides employees with the skills they need to be more effective.[32]

Empowerment in the Workplace

Do workplaces empower people?

The concept of empowerment has caused much cynicism in many workplaces. Employees are told that they are empowered and yet they do not feel that they have the authority to act, or they feel that their managers still micromanage their performance. Some managers are reluctant to empower their employees because this means sharing or even relinquishing their own power. Other managers worry that empowered employees may decide to work on goals and jobs that are not as closely aligned to organizational goals. Some managers, of course, do not fully understand how to go about empowering their employees.

In some cases, employees do not want to be empowered, and having more power can even make them ill. A study carried out by Professor Jia Lin Xie, of the University of Toronto's Joseph L. Rotman School of Management, and colleagues found that when people are put in charge at work but do not have the confidence to handle their responsibilities, they can become ill.[33] Specifically, people who blame themselves when things go wrong are more likely to suffer colds and infections if they have high levels of control at work. This finding by Professor Xie and her colleagues was somewhat unexpected, as some have hypothesized that greater control at work would lead to less stress. The study showed, instead, that the impact of empowerment depended on personality and job factors. Those who had control, but did not blame themselves when things went wrong, suffered less stress, even if the job was demanding. The study's findings suggest the importance of choosing carefully which employees to empower when doing so. These findings are also consistent with the Hackman-Oldham job characteristics model presented in Chapter 4.[34] Empowerment will be positive if a person has high growth-needs strengths (see Exhibit 4-15 on page 140) but those with low growth-needs strengths may be more likely to experience stress when empowered.

When employees are empowered, it means that they are expected to act, at least in a small way, as owners of the company, rather than just as employees. Ownership is not necessary in the financial sense, but in terms of identifying with the goals and mission of the organization. For employees to be empowered, however, and have an ownership mentality, four conditions need to be met, according to Professor Dan Ondrack at the Rotman School of Management:

- There must be a clear definition of the values and mission of the company.

- The company must help employees gain the relevant skills.

- Employees need to be supported in their decision making and not criticized when they try to do something extraordinary.

- Employees need to be recognized for their efforts.[35]

Exhibit 7-4 outlines what two researchers discovered in studying the characteristics of empowered employees.

Effects of Empowerment

Does empowerment work? Researchers have shown that at both the individual level[36] and the team level,[37] empowerment leads to greater productivity. At Winnipeg-based

---

EXHIBIT 7-4 Characteristics of Empowered People

Robert E. Quinn and Gretchen M. Spreitzer, in their research on the characteristics of empowered people (through both in-depth interviews and survey analysis), found four characteristics that most empowered people have in common:

- Empowered people have a sense of *self-determination* (this means that they are free to choose how to do their work; they are not micromanaged).

- Empowered people have a sense of *meaning* (they feel that their work is important to them; they care about what they are doing).

- Empowered people have a sense of *competence* (this means that they are confident about their ability to do their work well; they know they can perform).

- Empowered people have a sense of *impact* (this means that people believe they can have influence on their work unit; others listen to their ideas).

Source: R. E. Quinn and G. M. Spreitzer, "The Road to Empowerment: Seven Questions Every Leader Should Consider," *Organizational Dynamics,* Autumn 1997, p. 41.

At Vancouver-based Great Little Box Company (GLBC), which designs and manufactures corrugated containers, employees are given the freedom to do whatever they feel is necessary and appropriate to make customers happy. If a customer is dissatisfied with the product, the employee can say, "OK, I'll bring this product back and return it for you" without having to get prior authorization.

Melet Plastics, a manufacturer of plastic components, employees can come in for two extra hours each week (for which they are paid overtime) to work on projects of their choice that help improve the performance of the company. As a result, employees are less likely to see Melet "as a place where they simply arrive, park their brains at the door and do what they're told."[38]

Four US researchers investigated whether empowerment works similarly in different countries.[39] Their findings showed that employees in India gave their supervisors low ratings when empowerment was high, while employees in the United States, Mexico, and Poland rated their supervisors favourably when empowerment was high. In both the United States and Mexico, empowerment had no effect on satisfaction with co-workers. However, satisfaction with co-workers was higher when employees were empowered in Poland. In India, empowerment led to lower satisfaction with co-workers.

Similar findings in a study comparing empowerment in the United States, Brazil, and Argentina indicate that in hierarchical societies, empowerment may need to be introduced with care.[40] Employees in such societies may be more used to working in teams, but they also expect their managers to be the people with all the answers.

Our discussion of empowerment suggests that a number of problems can arise when organizations decide they want to empower employees. First, some managers do not want empowered employees, because this can take away some of their own base of power. Second, some employees have little or no interest in being empowered, and therefore resist any attempts to be empowered. And finally, empowerment is not something that works well in every workplace throughout the world.

The Abuse of Power: Harassment in the Workplace

6 How are power and harassment related?

People who engage in harassment in the workplace are typically abusing their power positions. The manager-employee relationship best characterizes an unequal power relationship, where position power gives the managers the capacity to reward and coerce. Managers give employees their assignments, evaluate their performance, make recommendations for salary adjustments and promotions, and even decide whether employees retain their jobs. These decisions give managers power. Since employees want favourable performance reviews, salary increases, and the like, it is clear that managers control the resources that most employees consider important and scarce. It is also worth noting that individuals who occupy high-status roles (such as management positions) sometimes believe that harassing employees is merely an extension of their right to make demands on lower-status individuals.

Although co-workers do not have position power, they can have influence and use it to harass peers. In fact, although co-workers appear to engage in somewhat less severe forms of harassment than do managers, co-workers are the most frequent perpetrators of harassment, particularly sexual harassment, in organizations. How do co-workers exercise power? Most often they provide or withhold information, cooperation, and support. For example, the effective performance of most jobs requires interaction and support from co-workers. This is especially true these days as work is assigned to teams. By threatening to withhold or delay providing information that is necessary for the successful achievement of your work goals, co-workers can exert power over you.

Some categories of harassment have long been illegal in Canada, including those based on race, religion, and national origin, as well as sexual harassment. Unfortunately, some types of harassment that occur in the workplace are not deemed illegal, even if they create problems for employees and managers. We focus here on two types of harassment that have received considerable attention in the press: workplace bullying and sexual harassment.

Workplace Bullying

Many of us are aware, anecdotally if not personally, of managers who harass employees, demanding overtime without pay or excessive work performance. Further, some of the recent stories of workplace violence have reportedly been the result of an employee's feeling intimidated at work. In research conducted in the private and public sector in southern Saskatchewan, Céleste Brotheridge, a professor at the Université du Québec à Montréal, found that bullying was rather prevalent in the workplace. Forty percent of the respondents noted that they had experienced one or more forms of bullying weekly in the past six months. Ten percent experienced bullying at a much greater level: five or more incidents a week. Brotheridge notes that bullying has a negative effect on the workplace: "Given bullying's [negative] effects on employee health, it is reason for concern."[41]

There is no clear definition of workplace bullying, and Marilyn Noble, a Fredericton-based adult educator, remarks that in some instances there can be a fine line between managing and bullying. However, Noble, who co-chaired a research team on workplace violence and abuse at the University of New Brunswick, notes that "when it becomes a question of shaming people, embarrassing people, holding them up to ridicule, just constantly being on their case for no apparent reason, then [management] is becoming unreasonable." Moreover, "a bully often acts by isolating an individual. And they may be a serial bully, who always has a victim on the go. They may, in fact, have multiple victims on the go, but their strategy is to isolate them from one another."[42]

The effects of bullying can be devastating. Professors Sandy Hershcovis of the University of Manitoba and Julian Barling of Queen's University found that the consequences of bullying were more harmful to its victims than those who suffered sexual harassment. Bullied employees more often quit their jobs, were less satisfied with their jobs, and had more difficult relationships with their supervisors.[43]

Quebec introduced the first anti-bullying labour legislation in North America on June 1, 2004. The legislation defines psychological harassment as "any vexatious behaviour in the form of repeated and hostile or unwanted conduct, verbal comments, actions or gestures that affect an employee's dignity or psychological or physical integrity and that results in a harmful work environment for the employee."[44] Under the Quebec law, bullying allegations will be sent to mediation, where the accuser and the accused will work with an independent third party to try to resolve the problem. If mediation fails, employers who have allowed psychological harassment can be fined up to $10 000 and ordered to pay financial damages to the victim.

Sexual Harassment

The issue of sexual harassment has received increasing attention by corporations and the media because of the growing ranks of female employees, especially in nontraditional work environments, and because of a number of high-profile cases. For example, in March 2006, it was reported that all four female firefighters in the Richmond, BC, fire department had taken a leave of absence, alleging that they had faced repeated sexual harassment and discrimination from male firefighters in the department. The city has since introduced a code of conduct for its firefighters.[45] A survey by York University found that 48 percent of working women in Canada reported they had experienced some form of "gender harassment" in the year before they were surveyed.[46] Sexual harassment is also occurring among young people. A survey of 3000 high school students from eight schools in Toronto, Montreal, and Kingston, Ontario, found that three-quarters of them said they had been sexually harassed at least once by peers.[47]

Barbara Orser, a research affiliate with The Conference Board of Canada, notes that "sexual harassment is more likely to occur in environments that tolerate bullying, intimidation, yelling, innuendo and other forms of discourteous behaviour."[48] Recent research supports this view, finding that within work environments, general incivility, gender harassment, and sexual harassment tended to occur together.[49] These behaviours indicate that one person is trying to use power over another.

The Supreme Court of Canada defines **sexual harassment** as unwelcome behaviour of a sexual nature in the workplace that negatively affects the work environment or leads to adverse job-related consequences for the employee.[50] Despite the legal framework for defining sexual harassment, there continues to be disagreement as to what *specifically* constitutes sexual harassment. Sexual harassment includes unwanted physical touching, recurring requests for dates when it is made clear the person is not interested, and coercive threats that a person will lose her or his job if she or he refuses a sexual proposition. The problems of interpreting sexual harassment often surface around some of its more subtle forms—unwanted looks or comments, off-colour jokes, sexual artifacts such as nude calendars in the workplace, sexual innuendo, or misinterpretations of where the line between "being friendly" ends and "harassment" begins. Most studies confirm that the concept of power is central to understanding sexual harassment.[51] It's about an individual controlling or threatening another individual. This seems to be true whether the harassment comes from a manager, a co-worker, or even an employee.

Because of power inequities, sexual harassment by one's manager typically creates the greatest difficulty for the person being harassed. If there are no witnesses, it is the manager's word against the employee's word. Are there others whom this manager has harassed, and if so, will they come forward? Because of the manager's control over resources, many of those who are harassed are afraid of speaking out for fear of retaliation by the manager.

One of the places where there has been a dramatic increase in the number of sexual harassment complaints is at university campuses across Canada, according to Paddy Stamp, sexual harassment officer at the University of Toronto.[52] However, agreement on what constitutes sexual harassment, and how it should be investigated, is no clearer for universities than for industry.

While nonconsensual sex between professors and students is rape and subject to criminal charges, it is harder to evaluate apparently consensual relationships that occur outside the classroom. There is some argument over whether truly consensual sex is ever possible between students and professors. In an effort to underscore the power discrepancy and potential for abuse of it by professors, in 2003 the University

sexual harassment Unwelcome behaviour of a sexual nature in the workplace that negatively affects the work environment or leads to adverse job-related consequences for the employee.

of California, which includes Berkeley, implemented a policy forbidding romantic relationships between professors and their students as well.[53] Most universities have been unwilling to take such a strong stance. However, this issue is certainly one of concern, because the power distance between professors and students is considerable.

A recent review of the literature shows the damage caused by sexual harassment. As you would expect, individuals who are sexually harassed report more negative job attitudes (lower job satisfaction, diminished organizational commitment) as a result. This review also revealed that sexual harassment undermines the victims' mental and physical health. However, sexual harassment also negatively affects the group in which the victim works, lowering its level of productivity. The authors of this study conclude that sexual harassment "is significantly and substantively associated with a host of harms."[54]

In concluding this discussion, we would like to point out that sexual harassment is about power. It is about an individual controlling or threatening another individual. It is wrong. Moreover, it is illegal. You can understand how sexual harassment surfaces in organizations if you analyze it in power terms. We should also point out that sexual harassment is not something done only by men to women. There have been several cases of males reporting sexual harassment by male managers.[55] While there have been no media reports of women sexually harassing either men or women in Canada, under the framework of the law, it is certainly feasible.

Sexual harassment can include unwanted touching. The woman sitting at her desk is clearly uncomfortable having her colleague's arm draped across her shoulder while he examines something on her computer.

Politics: Power in Action

As speculation about why Marti Maraden and Don Shipley resigned from the Stratford Festival began to appear in the newspapers, Antoni Cimolino tried to control what the public heard about the resignations. His initial statements emphasized that the two had resigned, that they were not asked to quit. However, about a week later, Maraden published a letter in the *Globe and Mail* to give her side of the story. She said that she had urged that the announcement of the resignations wait until later in the season, so as to avoid disruption to the planned performances. Yet in a meeting on March 12, Maraden reports, "Antoni told me that Don's and my resignation would be announced the next day, and that settlement papers had already been drawn up." When Cimolino drew up the papers for Maraden and Shipley to sign, it may have been less about making the "right" decision and more about making a political decision to silence dissent. So why is politics so prevalent? Is it merely a fact of life?

Organizational behaviour researchers have learned a lot in recent years about how people gain and use power in organizations. Part of using power in organizations is engaging in organizational politics to influence others to help you achieve your personal objectives. Lobbying others to get them to vote with you on a particular decision is engaging in organizational politics.

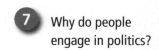

7 Why do people engage in politics?

When people get together in groups, power will be exerted. People want to carve out niches from which to exert influence, to earn rewards, and to advance their careers.[56] When employees in organizations convert their power into action, we describe them as engaged in politics. Those with good political skills have the ability to use their bases of power effectively.[57] Below we cover the types of political activity people use to try to influence others as well as impression management. Political skills are not confined to adults, of course. When your Vancouver author's six-year-old nephew wanted the latest Game Boy, knowing full well his parents did not approve, he waged a careful, deliberate campaign to wear them down, explaining how he would use the toy only at assigned times, etc. His politicking paid off: Within six weeks he succeeded in getting the toy.

Definition of Political Behaviour

There has been no shortage of definitions for organizational politics. One clever definition of *politics* comes from Tom Jakobek, Toronto's former budget chief, who said, "In politics, you may have to go from A to C to D to E to F to G and then to B."[58]

For our purposes, we will define **political behaviour** in organizations as those activities that are outside one's formal role (i.e., not part of one's specific job duties), and that influence, or try to influence, the distribution of advantages and disadvantages within the organization.[59]

This definition encompasses key elements from what most people mean when they talk about organizational politics. Political behaviour is *outside* one's specified job requirements. The behaviour attempts to use one's *bases of power.* Our definition also encompasses efforts to influence the goals, criteria, or processes used for decision making when we state that politics is concerned with "the distribution of advantages and disadvantages within the organization." Our definition is broad enough to include such varied political behaviours as whistle-blowing, spreading rumours, withholding key information from decision makers, leaking confidential information about organizational activities to the media, exchanging favours with others in the organization for mutual benefit, and lobbying on behalf of or against a particular individual or decision alternative. Exhibit 7-5 provides a quick measure to help you assess how political your workplace is.

Now that you have learned a bit about political behaviour, you may want to assess your own political behaviour in our *Learning About Yourself Exercise* on page 253.

Political behaviour is not confined to just individual hopes and goals. Politics might also be used to achieve organizational goals.[60] For instance, if a CEO wants to change the way employees are paid, say from salaries to commissions, this might not be a popular choice to the employees. While it might make good organizational sense to make this change (perhaps the CEO believes this will increase productivity), simply imposing the change through the use of power (go along with this or you're fired) might not be very popular. Instead, the CEO may try to pitch the reasons for the change to sympathetic managers and employees, trying to get them to understand the necessity for the change. Burnaby, BC-based TELUS used a direct approach with its employees after four and a half years of unsuccessful bargaining with union leaders. Management became frustrated with the impasse and explained their wage and benefit offer directly to employees in the hopes of getting the employees to side with management rather than their union leaders. The union was outraged by this behaviour, and it took several more months for union members and management to finally complete a new collective agreement in fall 2005.

The Reality of Politics

Why, you may wonder, must politics exist? Isn't it possible for an organization to be politics-free? It's *possible*, but most unlikely. Organizations are made up of individuals and groups with different values, goals, and interests.[61] This sets up the potential for

political behaviour Those activities that influence, or attempt to influence, the distribution of advantages and disadvantages within the organization.

EXHIBIT 7-5   A Quick Measure of How Political Your Workplace Is

How political is your workplace? Answer the 12 questions using the following scale:

SD = Strongly disagree
D = Disagree
U = Uncertain
A = Agree
SA = Strongly agree

1. Managers often use the selection system to hire only people who can help them in their future. _____

2. The rules and policies concerning promotion and pay are fair; it's how managers carry out the policies that is unfair and self-serving. _____

3. The performance ratings people receive from their managers reflect more of the managers' "own agenda" than the actual performance of the employee. _____

4. Although a lot of what my manager does around here appears to be directed at helping employees, it's actually intended to protect my manager. _____

5. There are cliques or "in-groups" that hinder effectiveness around here. _____

6. My co-workers help themselves, not others. _____

7. I have seen people deliberately distort information requested by others for purposes of personal gain, either by withholding it or by selectively reporting it. _____

8. If co-workers offer to lend some assistance, it is because they expect to get something out of it. _____

9. Favouritism rather than merit determines who gets ahead around here. _____

10. You can usually get what you want around here if you know the right person to ask. _____

11. Overall, the rules and policies concerning promotion and pay are specific and well-defined. _____

12. Pay and promotion policies are generally clearly communicated in this organization. _____

This questionnaire taps the three salient dimensions that have been found to be related to perceptions of politics: manager behaviour; co-worker behaviour; and organizational policies and practices. To calculate your score for items 1–10, give yourself 1 point for Strongly disagree; 2 points for Disagree; and so forth (through 5 points for Strongly agree). For items 11 and 12, reverse the score (that is, 1 point for Strongly agree, etc.). Sum up the total: The higher the total score, the greater the degree of perceived organizational politics.

Source: G. R. Ferris, D. D. Frink, D. P. S. Bhawuk, J. Zhou, and D. C. Gilmore, "Reactions of Diverse Groups to Politics in the Workplace," *Journal of Management* 22, no. 1 (1996), pp. 32–33.

conflict over resources. The allocation of departmental budgets, space, project responsibilities, and bonuses are the kind of resource issues about which organizational members will disagree.

Resources in organizations are also limited, which often turns potential conflict into real conflict. If resources were abundant, then all the various constituencies within the organization could satisfy their goals. Because they are limited, not everyone's interests can be provided for. Moreover, whether true or not, gains by one individual or group are often *perceived* as being at the expense of others within the organization. These forces create competition among members for the organization's limited resources.

Maybe the most important factor behind politics within organizations is the realization that most of the "facts" that are used to allocate the limited resources are open to interpretation. What, for instance, is *good* performance? What is an *adequate*

President and CEO Aris Kaplanis of Toronto-based high-tech firm Teranet (shown here at far right with his senior management group) discourages negative office politics among his employees. The company employs the Golden Rule, "Do unto others as you would have others do unto you." He tells his employees, "If you're here to play a game, you're in the wrong business."

improvement? What constitutes an *unsatisfactory* job? It is in this large and ambiguous middle ground of organizational life—where the facts *do not* speak for themselves—that politics flourish.

Finally, because most decisions must be made in a climate of ambiguity—where facts are rarely fully objective and thus are open to interpretation—people within organizations will use whatever influence they can to taint the facts to support their goals and interests. That, of course, creates the activities we call *politicking*. For more about how one engages in politicking, see *From Concepts to Skills* on pages 258–259.

Therefore, to answer the earlier question of whether it is possible for an organization to be politics-free, we can say "yes"—but only if all the members of that organization hold the same goals and interests, organizational resources are not scarce, and performance outcomes are completely clear and objective. However, that does not describe the organizational world that most of us live in!

RESEARCH FINDINGS: POLITICKING

Our earlier discussion focused on the favourable outcomes for individuals who successfully engage in politicking. But for most people—who have modest political skills or are unwilling to play the politics game—outcomes tend to be mainly negative.[62] There is, for instance, very strong evidence indicating that perceptions of organizational politics are negatively related to job satisfaction.[63] The perception of politics also tends to increase job anxiety and stress. This seems to be because of the belief that, by not engaging in politics, a person may be losing ground to others who are active politickers, or, conversely, because of the additional pressures individuals feel of having entered into and competing in the political arena.[64] Not surprisingly, when politicking becomes too much to handle, it can lead employees to quit.[65] Finally, there is preliminary evidence suggesting that politics leads to self-reported declines in employee performance.[66] Perceived organizational politics appears to have a demotivating effect on individuals, and thus leads to decreased performance levels.

Types of Political Activity

Why do some people seem to engage in politics more than others?

Within organizations, we can find a variety of political activities in which people engage. These include the following:[67]

- *Attacking or blaming others.* Used when trying to avoid responsibility for failure.

- *Using information.* Withholding or distorting information, particularly to hide negative information.

- *Managing impressions.* Bringing positive attention to one's self or taking credit for the positive accomplishments of others.

- *Building support for ideas.* Making sure that others will support one's ideas before they are presented.

- *Praising others.* Making important people feel good.

- *Building coalitions.* Joining with other people to create a powerful group.

- *Associating with influential people.* Building support networks.

- *Creating obligations.* Doing favours for others so they will owe you favours later.

Individuals will use these political activities for different purposes, as this chapter's *Case Incident—The Politics of Backstabbing* on pages 256–257 illustrates. Some of these activities are more likely to be used to defend one's position (such as attacking or blaming others), while other activities are meant to enhance one's image (such as building support for ideas and managing impressions).

Impression Management

In what situations does impression management work best?

The process by which individuals attempt to control the impression others form of them is called **impression management**.[68] Being perceived positively by others should have benefits for people in organizations. It might, for instance, help them initially to get the jobs they want in an organization and, once hired, to get favourable evaluations, superior salary increases, and more rapid promotions. In a political context, it might help bring more advantages their way. Impression management is a subject that has gained more attention of OB researchers recently.[69]

Impression management does not imply that the impressions people convey are necessarily false (although, of course, they sometimes are).[70] Some activities may be done with great sincerity. For instance, you may *actually* believe that ads contribute little to sales in your region or that you are the key to the tripling of your division's sales. However, if the image claimed is false, you may be discredited.[71] The impression manager must be cautious not to be perceived as insincere or manipulative.[72] This chapter's *Point/Counterpoint* on page 252 considers the ethics of managing impressions.

impression management The process by which individuals attempt to control the impression others form of them.

RESEARCH FINDINGS: IMPRESSION MANAGEMENT TECHNIQUES

Most of the studies undertaken to test the effectiveness of impression management techniques have related it to two criteria: interview success and performance evaluations. Let's consider each of these.

The evidence indicates that most job applicants use impression management techniques in interviews[73] and that, when impression management behaviour is used, it works.[74] In one study, for instance, interviewers felt that applicants for a position as a customer-service representative who used impression management techniques performed better in the interview, and they seemed somewhat more inclined to hire these people.[75] Moreover, when the researchers considered applicants' credentials, they concluded that it was the impression management techniques alone that influenced the interviewers. That is, it did not seem to matter if applicants were well or poorly qualified. If they used impression management techniques, they did better in the interview.

Research indicates that some impression management techniques work better than others in the interview. Researchers have compared applicants who used techniques that focused on promoting one's accomplishments (called *self-promotion*) to applicants who used techniques that focused on complimenting the interviewer and finding areas of agreement (referred to as *ingratiation*). In general, applicants appear to use self-promotion more than ingratiation.[76] What is more, self-promotion tactics may be more important to interviewing success. Applicants who work to create an appearance of competence by enhancing their accomplishments, taking credit for successes, and explaining away failures do better in interviews. These effects reach beyond the interview: Applicants who use more self-promotion tactics also seem to get more follow-up job-site visits, even after adjusting for grade-point average, gender, and job type. Ingratiation also works well in interviews, meaning that applicants who compliment the interviewer, agree with his or her opinions, and emphasize areas of fit do better than those who do not.[77]

In terms of performance ratings, the picture is quite different. Ingratiation is positively related to performance ratings, meaning that those who ingratiate with their supervisors get higher performance evaluations. However, self-promotion appears to backfire: Those who self-promote actually seem to receive *lower* performance evaluations.[78] Another study of 760 boards of directors found that individuals who ingratiate themselves to current board members (express agreement with the director, point out shared attitudes and opinions, compliment the director) increase their chances of landing on a board.[79] What explains these results? If you think about them, they make sense. Ingratiating always works because everyone—both interviewers and supervisors—likes to be treated nicely. However, self-promotion may work only in interviews and backfire on the job because, whereas the interviewer has little idea whether you are blowing smoke about your accomplishments, the supervisor knows because it's his or her job to observe you. Thus, if you are going to self-promote, remember that what works in an interview will not always work once you are on the job.

Making Office Politics Work

One thing to be aware of is that extreme office politics can have a negative effect on employees. Researchers have found that organizational politics is associated with less organizational commitment,[80] lower job satisfaction,[81] and decreased job performance.[82] Individuals who experience greater organizational politics are more likely to report higher levels of job anxiety,[83] and they are more likely to consider leaving the organization.[84]

Is there an effective way to engage in office politics that is less likely to be disruptive or negative? We discussed different negotiation strategies in Chapter 6, including a *win-lose* strategy, which means that if I win, you lose, and a *win-win* strategy, which means creating situations in which both of us can win. *Fast Company*, a business magazine, identifies several rules that may help you make your way through the office politics maze:[85]

- *Nobody wins unless everybody wins.* The most successful proposals look for ways to acknowledge, if not include, the interests of others. This requires building support for your ideas across the organization. "Real political skill isn't about campaign tactics," says Lou DiNatale, a veteran political consultant at the University of Massachusetts. "It's about pulling people toward your ideas and then pushing those ideas through to other people." When ideas are packaged to look as if they are best for the organization as a whole and will help others, it is harder for others to counteract your proposal.

- *Don't just ask for opinions—change them.* It is helpful to find out what people think and then, if necessary, set out to change their opinions so that they can see what you want to do. It is also important to seek out the opinions of those you do not know well, or who are less likely to agree with you. Gathering together people who always support you is often not enough to build an effective coalition.

- *Everyone expects to be paid back.* In organizations, as in life, we develop personal relationships with those around us. It is those personal relationships that affect much of the behaviour in organizations. By building good relationships with colleagues, supporting them in their endeavours, and showing appreciation for what they accomplish, you are building a foundation of support for your own ideas.

- *Success can create opposition.* As part of the office politics, success can be viewed as a *win-lose* strategy, which we identified above. Some people may feel that your success comes at their expense. So, for instance, your higher profile may mean that a project of theirs will be received less favourably. You have to be prepared to deal with this opposition.

Summary and Implications

1 **What is power?** Power refers to a capacity that A has to influence the behaviour of B, so that B acts in accordance with A's wishes.

2 **How does one get power?** There are six bases or sources of power: coercive, reward, legitimate, expert, referent, and information. These forms of power differ in their ability to improve a person's performance. *Coercive power* tends to result in negative performance responses from individuals; it decreases satisfaction, increases mistrust, and creates fear. *Reward power* may improve performance, but it can also lead to unethical behaviour. *Legitimate power* does not have a negative effect, but does not generally stimulate employees to improve their attitudes or performance, and it does not generally result in increased commitment. Ironically, the least effective bases of power—coercive, legitimate, and reward—are the ones most likely to be used by managers, perhaps because they are the easiest to implement. By contrast, effective leaders use *expert* and/or *referent power*; these forms of power are not derived from the person's position. *Information power* comes from access to and control over information and can be used in both positive (sharing) and negative (withholding) ways in the organization.

3 **How does dependency affect power?** To maximize your power, you will want to increase others' dependence on you. You can, for instance, increase your power in relation to your employer by developing knowledge or a skill that he or she needs and for which there is no ready substitute. However, you will not be alone in trying to build your bases of power. Others, particularly employees and peers, will seek to make you dependent on them. While you try to maximize others' dependence on you, you will be trying to minimize your dependence on others. Of course, others you work with will be trying to do the same. The result is a continual struggle for power.

4 **What tactics can be used to increase power?** One particular study identified nine tactics, or strategies, that managers and employees use to increase their power: rational persuasion, inspirational appeals, consultation, ingratiation, personal appeals, exchange, coalition tactics, pressure, and legitimating tactics.[86]

5 **What does it mean to be empowered?** Empowerment refers to the freedom and the ability of employees to make decisions and commitments. There is a lot of positive press on empowerment. However, much of the talk of empowerment in organizations does not result in employees being empowered. Some managers do not fully understand how to go about empowering their employees, and others find it difficult to share their power with employees. As well, some employees have little or no interest in being empowered, and empowerment is not something that works well in every culture.

6 **How are power and harassment related?** People who engage in harassment in the workplace are typically abusing their power position. Harassment can come in many forms, from gross abuse of power toward anyone of lower rank, to abuse of individuals because of their personal characteristics, such as race, religion, national origin, and gender.

7 **Why do people engage in politics?** People use politics to influence others to help them achieve their personal objectives. Whenever people get together in groups, power will be exerted. People also use impression management to influence people. Impression management is the process by which individuals attempt to control the impression others form of them. Though politics is a natural occurrence in organizations, when it is carried to an extreme it can damage relationships among individuals.

OB at Work

For Review

1. What is power? How do you get it?

2. Contrast the bases of power and influence tactics.

3. What are some of the key contingency variables that determine which tactic a power holder is likely to use?

4. Which of the six bases of power lie with the individual? Which are derived from the organization?

5. State the general dependency postulate. What does it mean?

6. What creates dependency? Give an applied example.

7. Identify the range of empowerment that might be available to employees.

8. Define *sexual harassment.* Who is most likely to harass an employee: a boss, a co-worker, or a subordinate? Explain.

9. How are power and politics related?

10. Define *political behaviour.* Why is politics a fact of life in organizations?

For Critical Thinking

1. Based on the information presented in this chapter, if you were a recent graduate entering a new job, what would you do to maximize your power and accelerate your career progress?

2. "Politics isn't inherently bad. It is merely a way to get things accomplished within organizations." Do you agree or disagree? Defend your position.

3. You are a sales representative for an international software company. After four excellent years, sales in your territory are off 30 percent this year. Describe three impression management techniques you might use to convince your manager that your sales record is better than one could have expected under the circumstances.

4. "Sexual harassment should not be tolerated in the workplace." "Workplace romances are a natural occurrence in organizations." Are both of these statements true? Can they be reconciled?

5. Which impression management techniques have you used? What ethical implications, if any, are there in using impression management?

OB for You

- There are a variety of ways to increase your power in an organization. As an example, you could acquire more knowledge about a situation and then use that information to negotiate a bonus with your employer. Even if you do not get the bonus, the knowledge may help you in other ways.

- To increase your power, consider how dependent others are on you. Dependency is affected by your importance, substitutability, and scarcity options. If you have needed skills that no one else has, you will have more power.

- You can develop political skills. Remembering to take time to join in an office birthday celebration for someone is part of developing the skill of working with others effectively.

Point

Managing Impressions Is Unethical

Managing impressions is wrong for both ethical and practical reasons. First, managing impressions is just another name for lying. Don't we have a responsibility, both to ourselves and to others, to present ourselves as we really are? Australian philosopher Tony Coady wrote, "Dishonesty has always been perceived in our culture, and in all cultures but the most bizarre, as a central human vice." Immanuel Kant's categorical imperative asks us to consider the following: If you want to know whether telling a lie on a particular occasion is justifiable, you must try to imagine what would happen if everyone were to lie. Surely, you would agree that a world in which no one lies is preferable to one in which lying is common, because in such a world we could never trust anyone. Thus, we should try to present the truth as best we can. Impression management goes against this virtue.

Practically speaking, impression management generally backfires in the long run. Remember Sir Walter Scott's quote, "Oh what a tangled web we weave, when first we practise to deceive!" Once we start to distort the facts, where do we stop? When George O'Leary was hired as the football coach for Notre Dame University (in Indiana), he said on his résumé that 30 years before, he had obtained a degree from Stony Brook University, which he never earned. Obviously, this information was unimportant to his football accomplishments, and ironically, he had written it on his résumé 20 years earlier when hired for a job at Syracuse University; he had simply never corrected the inaccuracy. But when the truth came out, O'Leary was out of a job.

People are most satisfied with their jobs when their values match the culture of the organizations. If either side misrepresents itself in the interview process, then odds are people will not fit in the organizations they choose. What is the benefit in this?

This does not imply that a person should not put his or her best foot forward. But that means exhibiting qualities that are good no matter the context—being friendly, being positive and self-confident, being qualified and competent, while still being honest.

Counterpoint

There Is Nothing Wrong with Managing Impressions

Oh, come on. Get off your high horse. Everybody fudges to some degree in the process of applying for a job. If you really told the interviewer what your greatest weakness or worst mistake was, you would never get hired. What if you answered, "I find it hard to get up in the morning and get to work"?

These sorts of "white lies" are expected and act as a kind of social lubricant. If we really knew what people where thinking, we would go crazy. Moreover, you can quote all the philosophy you want, but sometimes it's necessary to lie. You mean you would not lie to save the life of a family member? It's naive to think we can live in a world without lying.

Sometimes a bit of deception is necessary to get a job. I know a gay applicant who was rejected from a job he really wanted because he told the interviewer he had written two articles for gay magazines. What if he had told the interviewer a little lie? Would harm really have been done? At least he would have a job.

As another example, when an interviewer asks you what you earned on your previous job, that information will be used against you, to pay you a salary lower than you deserve. Is it wrong to boost your salary a bit? Or would it be better to disclose your actual salary and be taken advantage of?

The same goes for complimenting interviewers, agreeing with their opinions, and so forth. If an interviewer tells you, "We believe in community involvement," are you supposed to tell the interviewer you have never volunteered for anything?

Of course, you can go too far. We are not advocating that people totally fabricate their backgrounds. What we are talking about here is a reasonable amount of enhancement. If we can help ourselves without doing any real harm, then impression management is not the same as lying and actually is something we should teach others.

OB At Work

How Political Are You?

To determine your political tendencies, please review the following statements.[87] Check the answer that best represents your behaviour or belief, even if that particular behaviour or belief is not present all the time.

		True	False
1.	You should make others feel important through an open appreciation of their ideas and work.	____	____
2.	Because people tend to judge you when they first meet you, always try to make a good first impression.	____	____
3.	Try to let others do most of the talking, be sympathetic to their problems, and resist telling people that they are totally wrong.	____	____
4.	Praise the good traits of the people you meet, and always give people an opportunity to save face if they are wrong or make a mistake.	____	____
5.	Spreading false rumours, planting misleading information, and backstabbing are necessary, if somewhat unpleasant, methods of dealing with your enemies.	____	____
6.	Sometimes it is necessary to make promises that you know you will not or cannot keep.	____	____
7.	It is important to get along with everybody, even with those who are generally recognized as windbags, abrasive, or constant complainers.	____	____
8.	It is vital to do favours for others so that you can call in these IOUs at times when they will do you the most good.	____	____
9.	Be willing to compromise, particularly on issues that are minor to you but major to others.	____	____
10.	On controversial issues, it is important to delay or avoid your involvement if possible.	____	____

Scoring Key

According to the author of this instrument, a complete organizational politician will answer "true" to all 10 questions. Organizational politicians with fundamental ethical standards will answer "false" to questions 5 and 6, which deal with deliberate lies and uncharitable behaviour. Individuals who regard manipulation, incomplete disclosure, and self-serving behaviour as unacceptable will answer "false" to all or almost all of the questions.

More Learning About Yourself Exercises

Additional self-assessments relevant to this chapter appear on my MyOBLab (**www.pearsoned.ca/myoblab**).

IV.F.1   Is My Workplace Political?

II.C.3   How Good Am I at Playing Politics?

When you complete the additional assessments, consider the following:

1. Am I surprised about my score?
2. Would my friends evaluate me similarly?

OB *At Work*

BREAKOUT **GROUP** EXERCISES

Form small groups to discuss the following topics, as assigned by your instructor:

1. Describe an incident in which you tried to use political behaviour in order to get something you wanted. What influence tactics did you use?

2. In thinking about the incident described above, were your influence tactics effective? Why?

3. Describe an incident in which you saw someone engaging in politics. What was your reaction to observing the political behaviour? Under what circumstances do you think political behaviour is appropriate?

WORKING WITH **OTHERS** EXERCISE

Understanding Bases of Power

Step 1:   Your instructor will divide the class into groups of about 5 or 6 (making sure there are at least 5 groups).[88] Each group will be assigned 1 of the following bases of power: (1) coercive, (2) reward, (3) legitimate, (4) expert, (5) referent, (6) information. Refer to your text for discussion of these terms.

Step 2:   Each group is to develop a role play that highlights the use of the power assigned. The role play should be developed using the following scenario:

> You are the leader of a group that is trying to develop a website for a new client. One of your group members, who was assigned the task of researching and analyzing the websites of your client's competition, has twice failed to bring the analysis to scheduled meetings, even though the member knew the assignment was due. Consequently, your group is falling behind in getting the website developed. As leader of the group, you have decided to speak with this team member and to use your specific brand of power to influence the individual's behaviour.

Step 3:   Each group should select 1 person to play the group leader and another to play the member who has not done the assignment. You have 10 minutes to prepare an influence plan.

Step 4:   Each group will conduct its role play. In the event of multiple groups being assigned the same power base, 1 of the groups may be asked to volunteer. While you are watching the other groups' role plays, try to put yourself in the place of the person being influenced to see whether that type of influence would cause you to change your behaviour.

Immediately after each role play, while the next one is being set up, you should pretend that you were the person being influenced, and then record your reaction using the questionnaire below. To do this, take out a sheet of paper and tear it into 5 (or 6) pieces. At the top of each piece of paper, write the type of influence that was used. Then write the letters *A, B, C,* and *D* in a column, and indicate which number on the scale (see below) reflects the influence attempt.

OB *At Work*

Reaction to Influence Questionnaire

For each role play, think of yourself being on the receiving end of the influence attempt described and record your own reaction.

Type of power used _____

A. As a result of the influence attempt, I will . . .

| **definitely not comply** | 1 | 2 | 3 | 4 | 5 | **definitely comply** |

B. Any change that does come about will be . . .

| **temporary** | 1 | 2 | 3 | 4 | 5 | **long-lasting** |

C. My own personal reaction is . . .

| **resistant** | 1 | 2 | 3 | 4 | 5 | **accepting** |

D. As a result of this influence attempt, my relationship with my group leader will probably be . . .

| **worse** | 1 | 2 | 3 | 4 | 5 | **better** |

Step 5: For each influence type, 1 member of each group will take the pieces of paper from group members and calculate the average group score for each of the 4 questions. For efficiency, this should be done while the role plays are being conducted.

Step 6: Your instructor will collect the summaries from each group, and then lead a discussion based on these results.

Step 7: Discussion.

1. Which kind of influence is most likely to result immediately in the desired behaviour?

2. Which will have the longest-lasting effects?

3. What effect will using a particular base of power have on the ongoing relationship?

4. Which form of power will others find most acceptable? Least acceptable? Why?

5. Are there some situations in which a particular type of influence strategy might be more effective than others?

ETHICAL **DILEMMA** EXERCISE

Swapping Personal Favours?

Jack Grubman was a powerful man on Wall Street.[89] As a star analyst of telecom companies for the Salomon Smith Barney unit of Citigroup, his recommendations carried a lot of weight with investors.

For years, Grubman had been negative about the stock of AT&T. But in November 1999, he upgraded his opinion on the stock. According to email evidence, it appears that Grubman's decision to upgrade AT&T was not based on the stock's fundamentals. There were other factors involved.

At the time, his boss at Citigroup, Sanford Weill, was in the midst of a power struggle with co-CEO John Reed to become the single head of the company. Meanwhile, Salomon was looking for additional business to increase its revenues. Getting investment banking business fees from AT&T would be a big plus toward improving revenues. Salomon's efforts at getting

(Continued)

OB *At Work*

that AT&T business would definitely be improved if Grubman would upgrade his opinion on the stock. Furthermore, Weill sought Grubman's upgrade to win favour with AT&T CEO Michael Armstrong, who sat on Citigroup's board. Weill wanted Armstrong's backing in his efforts to oust Reed.

Grubman had his own concerns. Although he was earning tens of millions a year in his job, he was a man of modest background. He was the son of a city employee in Philadelphia. He wanted the best for his twin daughters, which included entry to an exclusive New York City nursery school—a school that a year earlier had reportedly turned down Madonna's daughter. Weill made a call on Grubman's behalf to the school and pledged a $1 million donation from Citigroup.

At approximately the same time, Weill also asked Grubman to "take a fresh look" at his neutral rating on AT&T. Shortly after being asked to review his rating, Grubman turned positive, raised his rating, and AT&T awarded Salomon an investment-banking job worth nearly $45 million.

Did Sanford Weill do anything unethical? How about Jack Grubman? What do you think?

CASE INCIDENT

The Politics of Backstabbing

Scott Rosen believed that he was making progress as an assistant manager of a financial-services company—until he noticed that his colleague, another assistant manager, was attempting to push him aside.[90] On repeated occasions, Rosen would observe his colleague speaking with their manager behind closed doors. During these conversations, Rosen's colleague would attempt to persuade the supervisor that Rosen was incompetent and mismanaging his job, a practice that Rosen found out after the fact. Rosen recounts one specific instance of his colleague's backstabbing efforts: When a subordinate asked Rosen a question to which Rosen did not know the answer, his colleague would say to their supervisor, "I can't believe he didn't know something like that." On other occasions, after Rosen instructed a subordinate to complete a specific task, Rosen's colleague would say to the same subordinate, "I wouldn't make you do something like that." What was the end result of such illegitimate political tactics? Rosen was demoted, an action that led him to resign shortly after, while his colleague was promoted. "Whatever I did, I lost," recounts Rosen.

What leads individuals to behave this way? According to Judith Briles, a management consultant who has extensively studied the practice of backstabbing, a tight job market is often a contributing factor. Fred Nader, another management consultant, believes that backstabbing is the result of "some kind of character disorder."

One executive at a technology company admits that blind ambition was responsible for the backstabbing he did. In 1999, he was assigned as an external sales representative, partnered with a colleague who worked internally at their client's office. The executive wanted the internal sales position for himself. To reach this goal, he systematically engaged in backstabbing to shatter his colleague's credibility. Each time he heard a complaint, however small, from the client, he would ask for it in an email and then forward the information to his boss. He would include a short message about his colleague, such as: "I'm powerless to deal with this. She's not being responsive and the customer is beating on me." In addition, he would fail to share important information with her before presentations with their boss, to convey the impression that she did not know what she was talking about. He even went so far as to schedule meetings with their boss on an electronic calendar, but then altered her version so that she was late. Eventually, he convinced his boss that she was overworked. He was transferred to the client's office, while his colleague was moved back to the main office.

Incidents such as these may not be uncommon in the workplace. Given today's competitive work environment, employees may be using political games to move ahead. To guard against backstabbing, Bob McDonald, a management consultant, recommends that backstabbing victims tell supervisors and other key personnel that the backstabber is not a friend. He states that this may be effective because backstabbers often claim to be friends of their victims, and then act as if they are hesitant about sharing negative information with others because of this

OB At Work

professed friendship. In any event, it is clear that employees in organizations need to be aware of illegitimate political behaviour. Companies may need to adopt formal policies to safeguard employees against such behaviour; however, it may be the case that behaviours such as backstabbing and spreading negative rumours are difficult to detect. Thus, both employees and managers should try to verify information to avoid the negative repercussions that can come from backstabbing and other illegitimate behaviours.

Questions

1. What factors, in addition to those cited here, do you believe lead to illegitimate political behaviours such as backstabbing?

2. Imagine that a colleague is engaging in illegitimate political behaviour toward you. What steps might you take to reduce or eliminate this behaviour? Do you believe that it is ever justifiable to engage in illegitimate political behaviours such as backstabbing? If so, what are some conditions that might justify such behaviour?

3. In addition to the obvious negative effects of illegitimate political behaviour on victims, such as those described in this case, what might be some negative effects on the perpetrators? On the organization as a whole?

VIDEO CASE INCIDENT

CASE 7   Whistle-blowers at the RCMP

CBC

In 2007, four members of the RCMP went public with charges of fraud, misrepresentation, corruption, and nepotism against the leadership of the RCMP.[91] The most senior member of the group was Fraser Macauley, a career Mountie who had worked his way up through the ranks to become a senior human resource officer. He said he had tried to alert his bosses to problems at the RCMP, but that he was lied to, shunned, and eventually pushed out of his job for his whistle-blowing activity.

While it is very unusual to see Mounties talking publicly about fraud, nepotism, and other criminal allegations, the four Mounties testified that a senior group of managers at the RCMP had breached the organization's core values *and* the criminal code. Macauley recognizes that the RCMP is taking a hit in its reputation, but he came forward because he felt that doing so would eventually make the organization a better place.

Many Canadians are wondering how something like this could happen in our national police force. Macauley says that a small group of top managers used the RCMP pension fund to hire people who were related to senior members of the force and who were not even doing pension fund work. The four Mounties who testified said that when they reported this unacceptable activity to senior management, they were stonewalled and punished.

When the allegations first emerged, an internal investigation was launched by the RCMP, but then cancelled by Commissioner Giuliano Zaccardelli. The Ottawa city police then conducted its own investigation, but no formal charges were laid. The Auditor General eventually confirmed much of what Macauley was saying, but by that time Macauley had been transferred to the Department of National Defence (DND). Macauley says the DND was known as the "penalty box." He is certain that he was transferred because he had been looking into pension fund irregularities. He also received a reduced performance bonus from his boss, Assistant Commissioner Barbara George. He was told that happened because he did not support the commissioner.

During his last conversation with Commissioner Zaccardelli, Macauley was told "it was time to go." This was an emotional conversation and Macauley felt terrible. He told Zaccardelli that he (Macauley) had never lied to the commissioner before, so why did Zaccardelli think he would start now? Zaccardelli called the accusations Macauley was making "baseless" and said that the pension fund was not at risk. Macauley points out that he never said that the pension fund was at risk, but that funds were being used in an unacceptable manner and relatives

(*Continued*)

OB *At Work*

of top managers were being paid for work that was not pension fund–related. Macauley says that now it's about accountability for decisions that top managers made.

After the public investigation, Macauley was reinstated in his former job. His boss, Barbara George, was suspended from her job for allegedly misleading the parliamentary committee that was looking into the allegations. Commissioner Zaccardelli is no longer with the RCMP.

Questions

1. List and briefly describe the bases of power that are available in organizations. Which bases were being used by the top managers at the RCMP?

2. Why were individuals like Macauley dependent on people like Barbara George and Commissioner Zaccardelli?

3. What is political behaviour? To what extent was it evident at the RCMP?

From *Concepts* to *Skills*

Politicking

Forget, for a moment, the ethics of politicking and any negative impressions you may have of people who engage in organizational politics.[92] If you wanted to be more politically adept in your organization, what could you do? The following eight suggestions are likely to improve your political effectiveness.

1. *Frame arguments in terms of organizational goals.* Effective politicking requires camouflaging your self-interest. No matter that your objective is self-serving; all the arguments you marshal in support of it must be framed in terms of the benefits that the organization will gain. People whose actions appear to blatantly further their own interests at the expense of the organization's are almost universally denounced, are likely to lose influence, and often suffer the ultimate penalty of being expelled from the organization.

2. *Develop the right image.* If you know your organization's culture, you understand what the organization wants and values from its employees—in terms of dress; associates to cultivate, and those to avoid; whether to appear risk-taking or risk-aversive; the preferred leadership style; the importance placed on getting along well with others; and so forth. Then you are equipped to project the appropriate image. Because the assessment of your performance is not a fully objective process, both style and substance must be addressed.

3. *Gain control of organizational resources.* The control of organizational resources that are scarce and important is a source of power. Knowledge and expertise are particularly effective resources to control. They make you more valuable to the organization and therefore more likely to gain security, advancement, and a receptive audience for your ideas.

4. *Make yourself appear indispensable.* Because we are dealing with appearances rather than objective facts, you can enhance your power by appearing to be indispensable. That is, you do not have to really be indispensable as long as key people in the organization believe that you are. If the organization's prime decision makers believe there is no ready substitute for what you are giving the organization, they are likely to go to great lengths to ensure that your desires are satisfied.

5. *Be visible.* Because performance evaluation has a substantial subjective component, it is important that your manager and those in power in the organization be made aware of your contribution. If you are fortunate enough to have a job that brings your accomplishments to the attention of others, it may not be necessary to take direct measures to increase your visibility. But your job may require you to handle activities that are low in visibility, or your specific contribution may be indistinguishable because you are part of a team endeavour. In such cases—without appearing to toot your own horn or create the image of a braggart—you will want to call attention to yourself by highlighting your successes in routine reports, having satisfied customers relay their appreciation to senior executives in your organization, being seen at social functions, being active in your

professional associations, developing powerful allies who speak positively about your accomplishments, and similar tactics. Of course, the skilled politician actively and successfully lobbies to get those projects that will increase his or her visibility.

6. *Develop powerful allies.* It helps to have powerful people in your camp. Cultivate contacts with potentially influential people above you, at your own level, and in the lower ranks. They can provide you with important information that may not be available through normal channels. There will be times, too, when decisions will be made in favour of those with the greatest support. Having powerful allies can provide you with a coalition of support if and when you need it.

7. *Avoid "tainted" members.* In almost every organization, there are fringe members whose status is questionable. Their performance and/or loyalty is suspect. Keep your distance from such individuals. Given the reality that effectiveness has a large subjective component, your own effectiveness might be called into question if you are perceived as too closely associated with tainted members.

8. *Support your manager.* Your immediate future is in the hands of your current manager. Since he or she evaluates your performance, you will typically want to do whatever is necessary to have your manager on your side. You should make every effort to help your manager succeed, make her look good, support her if she is under siege, and spend the time to find out what criteria she will be using to assess your effectiveness. Do not undermine your manager, and do not speak negatively of her to others.

Practising Skills

You used to be the star marketing manager for Hilton Electronics Corporation. But for the past year, you have been outpaced again and again by Sean, a new manager in the design department who has been accomplishing everything expected of him and more. Meanwhile, your best efforts to do your job well have been sabotaged and undercut by Maria—your and Sean's manager. For example, before last year's international consumer electronics show, Maria moved $30 000 from your budget to Sean's. Despite your best efforts, your marketing team could not complete all the marketing materials normally developed to showcase all of your organization's new products at this important industry show. Also, Maria has chipped away at your staff and budget ever since. Although you have been able to meet most of your goals with fewer staff and less budget, Maria has continued to slice away resources from your group. Just last week, she eliminated two positions in your team of eight marketing specialists to make room for a new designer and some extra equipment for Sean. Maria is clearly taking away your resources while giving Sean whatever he wants and more. You think it's time to do something or soon you will not have any team or resources left. What do you need to do to make sure your division has the resources to survive and grow?

Reinforcing Skills

1. Keep a one-week journal of your behaviour describing incidents when you tried to influence others around you. Assess each incident by asking: Were you successful at these attempts to influence them? Why or why not? What could you have done differently?

2. Outline a specific action plan, based on concepts in this module, that would improve your career progression in the organization in which you currently work or an organization in which you think you would like to be employed.

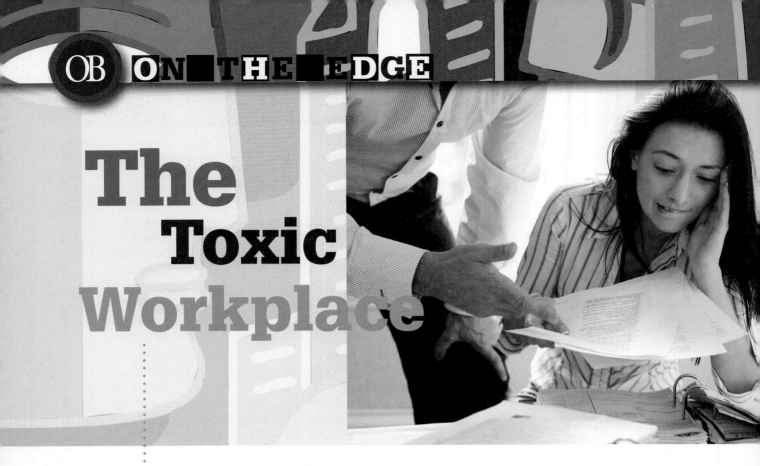

The Toxic Workplace

It's not unusual to find the following employee behaviours in today's workplace:

> *Answering the phone with a "yeah," neglecting to say thank you or please, using voice mail to screen calls, leaving a half-cup of coffee behind to avoid having to brew the next pot, standing uninvited but impatiently over the desk of someone engaged in a telephone conversation, dropping trash on the floor and leaving it for the maintenance crew to clean up, and talking loudly on the phone about personal matters.[1]*

Some employers or managers fit the following descriptions:

> *In the months since [the new owner of the pharmacy] has been in charge [he] has made it clear that he is at liberty to fire employees at will . . . change their positions, decrease their bonus percentages, and refuse time-off and vacation choices. Furthermore, he has established an authoritarian work structure characterized by distrust, cut-backs on many items deemed essential to work comfort, disrespect, rigidity and poor to no communication.[2]*

> *He walked all over people. He made fun of them; he intimidated them. He criticized work for no reason, and he changed his plans daily.[3]*

What Is Happening in Our Workplaces?

Workplaces today are receiving highly critical reviews, being called everything from "uncivil" to "toxic."

Lynne Anderson and Christine Pearson, two management professors from St. Joseph's University and the University of North Carolina, respectively, note that "Historians may view the dawn of the twenty-first century as a time of thoughtless acts and rudeness: We tailgate, even in the slow lane; we dial wrong numbers and then slam the receiver on the innocent respondent; we break appointments with nonchalance."[4] The workplace has often been seen as one of the places where civility still ruled, with co-workers treating each other with a mixture of formality and friendliness, distance and politeness. However, with downsizing, re-engineering, budget cuts, pressures for increased productivity, autocratic work environments, and the use of part-time employees, there has been an increase in "uncivil and aggressive workplace behaviours."[5]

What does civility in the workplace mean? A simple definition of workplace civility is behaviour "involving politeness and regard for others in the workplace, within workplace norms for respect."[6] Workplace incivility, then, "involves acting with disregard for others in the workplace, in violation of workplace norms for respect."[7] Of course, different workplaces will have different norms for what determines mutual respect. For instance, in most restaurants, if the staff were rude to you when you were there for dinner, you would be annoyed, and perhaps even complain to the manager. However, at The Elbow Room in downtown Vancouver, if customers complain they are in a hurry, manager Patrick Savoie might well say, "If you're in a hurry, you should have gone to McDonald's."[8] Such a comeback is acceptable to the diners at The Elbow Room, because rudeness is its trademark.

Most work environments are not expected to be characterized by such rudeness. However, this has been changing in recent years. Robert Warren, a University of Manitoba marketing professor, notes that "simple courtesy has gone by the board."[9]

There is documented evidence of the rise of violence and threats of violence at work.[10] However, several studies have found that there is persistent negative behaviour in the workplace that is not of a violent nature.[11] For instance, a survey of 603 Toronto nurses found that 33 percent had experienced verbal abuse during the five previous days of work.[12]

Another study found that 78 percent of employees interviewed think that workplace incivility has increased in the past 10 years.[13] The researchers found that men are mostly to blame for this change: "Although men and women are targets of disrespect and rudeness in equal numbers . . . men instigate the rudeness 70 percent of the time."[14]

Rude behaviour is not confined to men, however. Professor André Roberge at Laval University suggests that some of the rudeness is generational. He finds that "young clerks often lack both knowledge and civility. Employers are having to train young people in simple manners because that is not being done at home."[15] Professor Warren backs this up: "One of the biggest complaints I hear from businesses when I go to talk about graduates is the lack of interpersonal skills."[16]

Workplace Violence

Recently, researchers have suggested that incivility may be the beginning of more negative behaviours in the workplace, including aggression and violence.[17]

Pierre Lebrun chose a deadly way to exhibit the anger he had stored up from his workplace.[18] He took a hunting rifle to Ottawa-Carleton–based OC Transpo and killed four public transit co-workers on April 6, 1999, before turning the gun on himself. Lebrun felt that he had been the target of harassment by his co-workers for years because of his stuttering. If this sounds like an unusual response for an irate employee, consider the circumstances at OC Transpo. "Quite apart from what's alleged or otherwise with Mr. Lebrun's situation, we know [OC Transpo has] had a very unhappy work environment for a long time," Al Loney, former chair of Ottawa-Carleton's transit commission, noted. A consultant's report produced the year before the shooting found a workplace with "rock-bottom morale and poor management." It was not uncommon for fights to break out in the unit where the four men were killed.

Workplace violence, according to the International Labour Organization (ILO), includes

any incident in which a person is abused, threatened or assaulted in circumstances relating to [his or her] work. These behaviours would originate from customers or co-workers at any level of the organization. This definition would include all forms of harassment, bullying, intimidation, physical threats, assaults, robbery and other intrusive behaviour.[19]

No Canadian statistics on anger at work are available, although 53 percent of women and 47 percent of men reported experiencing workplace violence in 2004.[20] Studies show that anger pervades the US workplace. A 2000 Gallup poll conducted in the United States found that 25 percent of the working adults surveyed felt like screaming or shouting because of job stress, 14 percent had considered hitting a co-worker, and 10 percent worry about colleagues becoming violent. Almost half of US workers experienced yelling and verbal abuse on the job in 2008, and about 2.5 percent report that they have pushed, slapped, or hit someone at work.[21] Twenty employees are murdered each week in the United States.[22]

Canadian workplaces are not murder-free, either. Between 2001 and 2005, an average of 14 workers were killed each year while "on-the-job."[23] Most of these workplace incidents were carried out by male spouses and partners of female employees. Surprisingly, Canada scores higher than the United States on workplace violence. In an ILO study involving 130 000 workers in 32 countries, Argentina was ranked the most violent. Romania was second, France third, and Canada fourth. The United States placed ninth.[24]

Sixty-four percent of union representatives who were surveyed reported an increase in workplace aggression, based on their review of incident reports, grievance files, and other solid evidence.[25] To understand the seriousness of this situation, consider that one-quarter of Nova Scotia teachers surveyed reported that they faced physical violence at work during the 2001–2002 school year.[26]

What Causes Incivility (and Worse) in the Workplace?

If employers and employees are acting with less civility toward each other, what is causing this to happen?

Managers and employees often have different views of the employee's role in the organization. Jeffrey Pfeffer, a professor of organizational behaviour at the Graduate School of Business at Stanford University, notes that many companies do not really value their employees: "Most managers, if they're being honest with themselves, will admit it: When they look at their people, they see costs, they see salaries, they see benefits, they see overhead. Very few companies look at their people and see assets."[27]

Most employees, however, like to think that they are assets to their

FactBox

- In 2008, 52% of working Canadians reported a strong sense of loyalty to their employer. In 1991, the level of commitment was 62%.

- 72% of Canadian workers would leave their employers if offered a better-paying comparable job.

- Of those who experience rudeness, 12% quit their jobs in response, 22% decrease their work effort, and 52% lose work time worrying about it.

- Employees over the age of 55 express the highest degree of commitment to their employers.[28]

organization. The realization that they are simply costs and not valued members of an organization can cause frustration for employees.

In addition, "employers' excessive demands and top-down style of management are contributing to the rise of 'work rage,'" claims Gerry Smith, vice-president of organizational health and training at Toronto-based Shepell•fgi and author of *Work Rage*.[29] He cites demands coming from a variety of sources: "overtime, downsizing, rapid technological changes, company restructuring and difficulty balancing the demands of job and home."[30] Smith worries about the consequences of these demands: "If you push people too hard, set unrealistic expectations and cut back their benefits, they're going to strike back."[31]

Smith's work supports the findings of a study that reported the most common cause of anger is the actions of supervisors or managers.[32] Other common causes of anger identified by the researchers include lack of productivity by co-workers and others; tight deadlines; heavy workload; interaction with the public; and poor treatment.

The Psychological Contract

Some researchers have looked at this frustration in terms of a breakdown of the psychological contract formed between employees and employers. Employers and employees begin to develop psychological contracts as they are first introduced to each other in the hiring process.[33] These continue over time as the employer and the employee come to understand each other's expectations about the amounts and quality of work to be performed and the types of rewards to be given. For instance, when an employee is continually asked to work late and/or be available at all hours through pagers and email, the employee may assume that doing so will result in greater rewards or faster promotion down the line. The employer may have had no such intention, and may even be thinking that the employee should be grateful simply to have a job. Later, when the employee does not get expected (though never promised) rewards, he or she is disappointed.

Sandra Robinson, an organizational behaviour professor at the Sauder School of Business at the University of British Columbia, and her colleagues have found that when a psychological contract is violated (perceptually or actually), the relationship between the employee and the employer is damaged. This can result in the loss of trust.[34] The breakdown in trust can cause employees to be less ready to accept decisions or obey rules.[35] The erosion of trust can also lead employees to take revenge on the employer. So they do not carry out their end of a task, or they refuse to pass on messages. They engage in any number of subtle and not-so-subtle behaviours that affect the way work gets done—or prevents work from getting done.

The Toxic Organization

Pfeffer suggests that companies have become "toxic places to work."[36] He notes that companies, particularly in Silicon Valley, ask their employees to sign contracts on the first day of work indicating the employee's understanding that the company has the right to fire at will and for any reason. Some employers also ask their employees to choose between having a life and having a career. Pfeffer relates a joke people used to tell about Microsoft: "We offer flexible time—you can work any 18 hours you want."[37] This kind of attitude can be toxic to employees, though this does not imply that Microsoft is a toxic employer.

What does it mean to be a toxic organization? The late professor Peter Frost of the Sauder School of Business at the University of British Columbia noted that there will always be pain in organizations, but that sometimes it becomes so intense or prolonged that conditions within the organization begin to break down. In other words, the situation becomes toxic. This is not dissimilar to what the liver or kidneys do when toxins become too intense in a human body.[38]

What causes organizations to be toxic? Like Pfeffer, professors Frost and Robinson identify a number of factors. Downsizing and organizational change are two main factors, particularly in recent years. Sometimes organizations experience unexpected events—such as the sudden death of a key manager, an unwise move by senior management, strong competition from a start-up company—that lead to toxicity. Other organizations are toxic throughout their system due to policies and practices that create distress. Such factors as unreasonable stretch goals or performance targets, or unrelenting internal competition, can create toxicity. There are also toxic managers who lead through insensitivity, vindictiveness, and failure to take responsibility, or they are control freaks or are unethical. The inset *Do You Have a Toxic Manager?* on page 264 lists some types of toxic managers and the workplace culture that fosters their behaviour.

What Are the Effects of Incivility and Toxicity in the Workplace?

In general, researchers have found that the effects of workplace anger are sometimes subtle: a hostile work environment and the tendency to do only enough work to get by.[39]

Those who feel chronic anger in the workplace are more likely to report "feelings of betrayal by the organization, decreased feelings of loyalty, a decreased sense that respondent values and the organization's values are similar, a decreased sense that the employer treated the respondent with dignity and respect, and a decreased sense that employers had fulfilled promises made to respondents."[40] So do these feelings make a difference? Apparently so. Researchers have found that those who felt angry with their employers were less likely to put forth their best effort, more likely to be competitive toward other employees, and less likely to suggest "a quicker and better way to do their job."[41] All of these actions tend to decrease the productivity possible in the workplace.

It's not just those who work for an organization who are affected by incivility and toxicity. Poor service, from indifference to rudeness to outright hostility, characterizes many transactions in Canadian businesses. "Across the country, better business bureaus, provincial government consumer-help agencies

Do You Have a Toxic Manager?

Below are some of the toxic behaviours of managers and the workplace cultures that allow these behaviours to thrive.[42]

Managerial Toxic Behaviour

- *Actor behaviour.* These managers act out anger rather than discuss problems. They slam doors, sulk, and make it clear they are angry, but refuse to talk about it.

- *Fragmentor behaviour.* These managers see no connection between what they do and the outcome, and take no responsibility for their behaviour.

- *Me-first behaviour.* These managers make decisions based on their own convenience.

- *Mixed-messenger behaviour.* These managers present themselves one way, but their behaviour does not match what they say.

- *Wooden-stick behaviour.* These managers are extremely rigid and controlling.

- *Escape-artist behaviour.* These managers don't deal with reality; they often lie or, at the extreme, escape through drugs or alcohol.

Workplace Culture That Fosters This Behaviour

- *Macho culture.* People don't discuss problems. The emphasis is to "take it like a man."

- *Specialist culture.* Employees who are technically gifted or great in their fields don't have to consider how their behaviour or work impacts anyone.

- *Elitist culture.* Promotions and rewards are not based on your work but on who your buddies are.

- *Office-politics culture.* Promotions and rewards are based on flattery and positioning.

- *Change-resistant culture.* Upper management struggles to maintain the status quo regardless of the outcome.

- *Workaholic culture.* Employees are forced to spend more time at the office than necessary.

and media ombudsmen report a lengthening litany of complaints about contractors, car dealers, repair shops, moving companies, airlines and department stores."[43] This suggests that customers and clients may well be feeling the impact of internal workplace dynamics.

The Toxin Handler

Employees of toxic organizations suffer pain from their experiences in a toxic environment. In some organizations, mechanisms, often informal, are set up to deal with the results of toxicity.

Frost and Robinson identified a special role that some employees play in trying to relieve the toxicity within an organization: the toxin handler. This person tries to mitigate the pain by softening the blow of downsizing, or change, or the behaviour of the toxic leader. Essentially, the toxin handler helps others around him or her deal with the strains of the organization by counselling, advising, shielding employees from the wrath of angry managers, reinterpreting the managers' messages to make them less harsh, and so on.

So who takes on this role? Certainly no organization to date has a line on its organizational chart for "the toxin handler." Often the role emerges as part of an individual's position in an organization; for instance, a manager in the human resource department may take on this role. In many cases, however, handlers are pulled into the role "bit by bit—by their colleagues, who turn to them because they are trustworthy, calm, kind and nonjudgmental."[44]

Frost and Robinson, in profiling these individuals, suggest that toxin handlers are predisposed to say yes, have a high tolerance for pain, a surplus of empathy, and when they notice people in pain, they have a need to make the situation right. But these are not individuals who thrive simply on dealing with the emotional needs of others. Quoting one of the managers in their study, Frost and Robinson cite the full range of activities of most toxin handlers: "These people are usually relentless in their drive to accomplish organizational targets and rarely lose focus on business issues. Managing emotional pain is one of their means."[45]

How Toxin Handlers Alleviate Organizational Pain

- They listen empathetically.

- They suggest solutions.

- They work behind the scenes to prevent pain.

- They carry the confidences of others.

- They reframe difficult messages.[46]

The inset *How Toxin Handlers Alleviate Organizational Pain* identifies the many tasks that toxin handlers take on in an organization. Frost and Robinson suggest that these tasks will probably need to be handled forever, and they recommend that organizations take steps to actively support people performing this role.

Research Exercises

1. Look for data on violence and anger in the workplace in other countries. How do these data compare with the Canadian and American data presented here? What might you conclude about how violence and anger in the workplace are expressed in different cultures?

2. Identify three Canadian organizations that are trying to foster better and/or less toxic environments for their employees. What kind of effect is this having on the organizations' bottom lines?

Your Perspective

1. Is it reasonable to suggest, as some researchers have, that young people today have not learned to be civil to others or do not place a high priority on doing so? Do you see this as one of the causes of incivility in the workplace?

2. What should be done about managers who create toxicity in the workplace while being rewarded because they achieve bottom-line results? Should bottom-line results justify their behaviour?

Want to Know More?

If you would like to read more on this topic, see Peter Frost, *Toxic Emotions at Work* (Cambridge, MA: Harvard Business School Press, 2003); P. Frost and S. Robinson, "The Toxic Handler: Organizational Hero—and Casualty," *Harvard Business Review,* July–August 1999, pp. 96–106 (Reprint 99406); and K. Macklem, "The Toxic Workplace: A Poisoned Work Environment Can Wreak Havoc on a Company's Culture and Its Employees," *Macleans.ca,* January 31, 2005. You can find the latter article at **www.macleans.ca/article.jsp?content= 20050131_99562_99562&source=srch.**

FACEOFF

Manners are an over-romanticized concept. The big issue is not that employees need to be concerned about their manners. Rather, employers should be paying better wages.

The Golden Rule, "Do unto others as you would have others do unto you," should still have a role in today's workplace. Being nice pays off.

A major sporting equipment retailer wants to be as eco-friendly as possible. What kinds of leadership skills are needed to inspire and motivate employees to think about the environment?

1 What is the difference between a manager and a leader?

2 Are there specific traits, behaviours, and situations that affect how one leads?

3 How does a leader lead with vision?

4 Are there leadership roles for nonmanagers?

5 What are some of the contemporary issues in leadership?

Conventional wisdom suggests that visionary leaders are optimists.[1] Patagonia's founder, Yvon Chouinard, whose parents were French-Canadian, is living proof that that conventional wisdom is not always right.

Patagonia is famous for its outdoor gear. But it is also famous for its eco-friendly ethic. Much of the credit for this balance goes to Chouinard, who has embraced the idea presented by the late environmentalist David Brower: "There is no business to be done on a dead planet." Chouinard is known for informality, favouring environmentalism, and a love of the outdoors.

Despite Chouinard's positive values, he is also a pessimist. He says, "I don't think we're going to be here 100 years from now as a society, or maybe even as a species." In another forum, he wrote, "Patagonia will never be completely socially responsible. It will never make a totally sustainable, nondamaging product."

Chouinard's business model may seem a little strange, but that's how his vision works. By portraying the future in its darkest terms, Patagonia builds the case for its way of doing business. If humans are on the verge of extinguishing themselves, then it becomes all the more important to buy from environmentally conscious companies.

In this chapter, we examine the various studies on leadership to determine what makes an effective leader. We first consider the traits, behaviours, and situations that affect one's ability to lead, and then we consider visionary leadership. We then look at how leadership is being spread throughout the organization, and how you might lead yourself, through self-management. Finally, we consider contemporary issues in leadership.

OB Is for Everyone

- Have you ever wondered if there was one right way to lead?
- Is a leader always necessary?
- Can anyone be a leader?
- How do you manage yourself?

Are Managers and Leaders the Same?

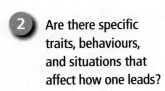

1 What is the difference between a manager and a leader?

Leadership and *management* are two terms that are often confused. What is the difference between them?

John Kotter of the Harvard Business School argues that "managers promote stability while leaders press for change and only organizations that embrace both sides of the contradiction can survive in turbulent times."[2]

Professor Rabindra Kanungo at McGill University sees a growing consensus emerging "among management scholars that the concept of 'leadership' must be distinguished from the concept of 'supervision/management.'"[3] Exhibit 8-1 illustrates Kanungo's distinctions between management and leadership. Leaders establish direction by developing a vision of the future; then they align people by communicating this vision and inspiring them to overcome hurdles. Managers implement the vision and strategy provided by leaders, coordinate and staff the organization, and handle day-to-day problems.

In our discussion of leadership, we will focus on two major tasks of those who lead in organizations: managing those around them to get the day-to-day tasks done (leadership as supervision) and inspiring others to do the extraordinary (leadership as vision).

Leadership as Supervision

> Patagonia's Yvon Chouinard is a very different style of manager.[4] He believes in the M.B.A. theory of management—"management by absence." He spends nearly half the year surfing or water skiing, because he does not believe that being a leader should require sacrificing one's lifestyle. He does not want to be in the office every day.
>
> So what kind of employees do best under Chouinard's style of leadership? He explains: "Our employees are so independent, we've been told by psychologists, that they would be considered unemployable in a typical company." He values employees who are independent thinkers, and who will question what they think are bad decisions.
>
> Patagonia managers lead by example. There are no special parking places: "The best spots are reserved for fuel-efficient cars." Employees are able to inspect the financial records to see how the company is being run. The company runs on "flextime"—employees can choose their hours. Chouinard's philosophy is "let my people go surfing," which means that if the surf is good, employees can take some time out of the work day to go surfing. He trusts his employees to get their work done, even if they do take a surf break. Are Chouinard's views of employees and management unusual? How much supervision is needed if employees are guided by a vision?

2 Are there specific traits, behaviours, and situations that affect how one leads?

In this section we discuss theories of leadership that were developed before 1980. These early theories focused on the supervisory nature of leadership—that is, how leaders managed the day-to-day functioning of employees. The three general types of theories that emerged were (1) trait theories, which propose that leaders have a particular set of traits that makes them different from nonleaders; (2) behavioural theories, which propose that particular behaviours make for better leaders; and (3) contingency theories, which propose that the situation has an effect on leaders. When you think about these theories, remember that although they have been considered "theories of leadership," they rely on an older understanding of what "leadership" means, and they do not convey Kanungo's distinction between leadership and supervision.

Trait Theory: Are Leaders Different From Others?

trait theories of leadership
Theories proposing that traits—personality, social, physical, or intellectual—differentiate leaders from nonleaders.

Have you ever wondered whether there is some fundamental personality difference that makes some people "born leaders"? **Trait theories of leadership** emerged in the hope that if it were possible to identify the traits of leaders, it would be easier to select people to fill leadership roles. Being able to select good leaders is important because not all people know how to be good leaders.

EXHIBIT 8-1	Distinguishing Leadership From Management	
Management		**Leadership**
1. Engages in day-to-day caretaker activities: Maintains and allocates resources		Formulates long-term objectives for reforming the system: Plans strategy and tactics
2. Exhibits supervisory behaviour: Acts to make others maintain standard job behaviour		Exhibits leading behaviour: Acts to bring about change in others congruent with long-term objectives
3. Administers subsystems within organizations		Innovates for the entire organization
4. Asks how and when to engage in standard practice		Asks what and why to change standard practice
5. Acts within established culture of the organization		Creates vision and meaning for the organization
6. Uses transactional influence: Induces compliance in manifest behaviour using rewards, sanctions, and formal authority		Uses transformational influence: Induces change in values, attitudes, and behaviour using personal examples and expertise
7. Relies on control strategies to get things done by subordinates		Uses empowering strategies to make followers internalize values
8. Status quo supporter and stabilizer		Status quo challenger and change creator

Source: R. N. Kanungo, "Leadership in Organizations: Looking Ahead to the 21st Century," *Canadian Psychology* 39, no. 1–2 (1998), p. 77.

Trait theories of leadership differentiate leaders from nonleaders by focusing on personal qualities and characteristics. Individuals such as Pierre Trudeau, Barack Obama, South Africa's Nelson Mandela, Virgin Group CEO Richard Branson, and Apple co-founder Steve Jobs are recognized as leaders and described in terms such as *charismatic*, *enthusiastic*, and *courageous*. The search for personality, social, physical, or intellectual attributes that would describe leaders and differentiate them from non-leaders goes back to the earliest stages of leadership research.

Research efforts at isolating leadership traits resulted in a number of dead ends. For instance, a review in the late 1960s of 20 studies identified nearly 80 leadership traits, but only 5 of these traits were common to 4 or more of the investigations.[5] By the 1990s, after numerous studies and analyses, about the best thing that could be said was that most "leaders are not like other people," but the particular traits that were isolated varied a great deal from review to review.[6] It was a pretty confusing state of affairs.

A breakthrough, of sorts, came when researchers began organizing traits around the Big Five Personality Model (see Chapter 2).[7] What became clear was that most of the dozens of traits that emerged in various leadership reviews could be subsumed under one of the Big Five factors, and that this approach resulted in consistent and strong support for traits as predictors of leadership. For instance, ambition and energy—two common traits of leaders—are part of extraversion. Rather than focus on these two specific traits, it is better to think of them in terms of the more general trait of extraversion.

Comprehensive reviews of the leadership literature, when organized around the Big Five, have found that extraversion is the most important trait of effective leaders.[8] But results show that extraversion is more strongly related to leader emergence than to leader effectiveness. This is not totally surprising, since sociable and dominant people are more likely to assert themselves in group situations. While the assertive nature of extraverts is a positive, leaders need to make sure they are not too assertive—one study found that leaders who scored very high on assertiveness were less effective than those who scored moderately high.[9]

Conscientiousness and openness to experience also showed strong and consistent relationships to leadership, but not as strong as extraversion. The traits of agreeableness and emotional stability do not appear to offer much help in predicting leadership. Overall, it does appear that the trait approach does have something to offer. Leaders who are extraverted (individuals who like being around people and are able to assert themselves), conscientious (individuals who are disciplined and keep commitments they make), and open (individuals who are creative and flexible) do seem to have an advantage when it comes to leadership, suggesting that good leaders do have key traits in common.

Based on the latest findings, we offer two conclusions. First, traits can predict leadership. Twenty years ago, the evidence suggested otherwise. But this was probably because of the lack of a valid framework for classifying and organizing traits. The Big Five Personality Model seems to have fixed that. Second, traits do a better job at predicting the emergence of leaders and the appearance of leadership than in actually distinguishing between *effective* and *ineffective* leaders.[10] The fact that an individual exhibits the traits and others consider that person to be a leader does not necessarily mean that the leader is successful at getting his or her group to achieve its goals.

This chapter's *Point/Counterpoint* on page 295 raises further issues on whether leaders are born or made. *Case Incident—The Kinder, Gentler Leader?* on pages 298–299 looks at the trend toward leaders who have a sensitive and caring style.

Emotional Intelligence and Leadership

Recent studies are indicating that another trait that may indicate effective leadership is emotional intelligence (EI), which we discussed in Chapter 2. Advocates of EI argue that, without it, a person can have outstanding training, a highly analytical mind, a compelling vision, and an endless supply of terrific ideas, but still not make a great leader. This may be especially true as individuals move up in an organization.[11] But why is EI so critical to effective leadership? A core component of EI is empathy. Empathetic leaders can sense others' needs, listen to what followers say (and do not say), and are able to read the reactions of others. As one leader noted, "The caring part of empathy, especially for the people with whom you work, is what inspires people to stay with a leader when the going gets rough. The mere fact that someone cares is more often than not rewarded with loyalty."[12]

Despite these claims for its importance, the link between EI and leadership effectiveness is much less investigated than other traits. One reviewer noted, "Speculating about the practical utility of the EI construct might be premature." Despite such warnings, EI is being viewed as a panacea for many organizational malaises, with recent suggestions that EI is essential for leadership effectiveness.[13] But until more rigorous evidence accumulates, we cannot be confident about the connection.

Sally Jewell, CEO of Recreational Equipment, Inc. (REI), is an employee-oriented leader. During her tenure as CEO, Jewell has turned a struggling company into one with record sales. But she credits REI's success to the work of employees, stating that she does not believe in "hero CEOs." Jewell respects each employee's contribution to the company and includes in her leadership people who are very different from herself. Described as a leader high in consideration, she listens to employees' ideas and empowers them in performing their jobs.

Behavioural Theories: Do Leaders Behave in Particular Ways?

Limited success in the study of traits led researchers to look at the behaviours that specific leaders exhibit. They wondered if there was something unique in the way that effective leaders behave. They also wondered if it was possible to *train* people to be leaders.

The three best-known **behavioural theories of leadership** are the Ohio State University studies that were conducted starting in the late 1940s, the University of Michigan studies conducted at about the same time, and Blake and Mouton's Leadership Grid, which reflects the behavioural definitions of both the Ohio and Michigan studies. All three approaches consider two main dimensions by which managers can be characterized: attention to production and attention to people.

The Ohio State Studies

In the Ohio State studies, these two dimensions are known as *initiating structure* and *consideration*.[14] **Initiating structure** refers to the extent to which a leader is likely to define and structure his or her role and the roles of employees in order to attain goals; it includes behaviour that tries to organize work, work relationships, and goals. For instance, leaders using this style may develop specific output goals or deadlines for employees.

Consideration is defined as the extent to which a leader is likely to have job relationships characterized by mutual trust, respect for employees' ideas, and regard for their feelings. A leader who is high in consideration shows concern for followers' comfort, well-being, status, and satisfaction. For instance, leaders using this style may create more flexible hours, or flextime, to make it easier for employees to manage family issues during work hours.

The Michigan Studies

Researchers at the University of Michigan, whose work is referred to as "the Michigan studies," also developed two dimensions of leadership behaviour, which they labelled *employee oriented* and *production oriented*.[15] **Employee-oriented leaders** emphasize interpersonal relations. They take a personal interest in the needs of their subordinates and accept individual differences among members. **Production-oriented leaders**, in contrast, tend to emphasize the technical or task aspects of the job. They are mainly concerned with making sure the group accomplishes its tasks, and the group members are simply a means to that end.

The Leadership Grid

Blake and Mouton developed a graphic portrayal of a two-dimensional view of leadership style.[16] They proposed a **Leadership Grid** based on the styles of "concern for people" and "concern for production," which essentially represent the Ohio State dimensions of consideration and initiating structure, or the Michigan dimensions of employee orientation and production orientation.

The grid, shown in Exhibit 8-2 on page 272, has 9 possible positions along each axis, creating 81 different positions in which the leader's style may fall, but emphasis has been placed on 5: impoverished management (1,1); authority-obedience management (9,1); middle-of-the-road management (5,5); country club management (1,9); and team management (9,9). The grid shows the dominating factors in a leader's thinking with respect to how to get results from people, without focusing on what the specific results are.

RESEARCH FINDINGS: BEHAVIOURAL THEORIES OF LEADERSHIP

A lengthy review of the results of behavioural studies supports the idea that people-oriented behaviour by leaders is related to employee satisfaction and motivation and leader effectiveness; meanwhile, production-oriented behaviour by leaders is slightly more strongly related to performance by the leader, the

---

behavioural theories of leadership Theories that propose that specific behaviours differentiate leaders from nonleaders.

initiating structure The extent to which a leader is likely to define and structure his or her role and the roles of employees in order to attain goals.

consideration The extent to which a leader is likely to have job relationships characterized by mutual trust, respect for employees' ideas, and regard for their feelings.

employee-oriented leader A leader who emphasizes interpersonal relations.

production-oriented leader A leader who emphasizes the technical or task aspects of the job.

Leadership Grid A two-dimensional grid outlining 81 different leadership styles.

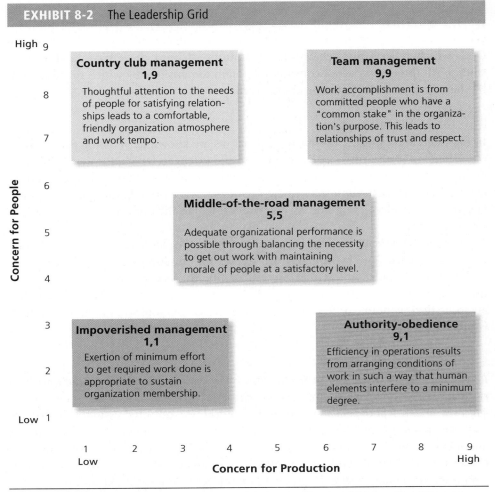

EXHIBIT 8-2   The Leadership Grid

Country club management 1,9
Thoughtful attention to the needs of people for satisfying relationships leads to a comfortable, friendly organization atmosphere and work tempo.

Team management 9,9
Work accomplishment is from committed people who have a "common stake" in the organization's purpose. This leads to relationships of trust and respect.

Middle-of-the-road management 5,5
Adequate organizational performance is possible through balancing the necessity to get out work with maintaining morale of people at a satisfactory level.

Impoverished management 1,1
Exertion of minimum effort to get required work done is appropriate to sustain organization membership.

Authority-obedience 9,1
Efficiency in operations results from arranging conditions of work in such a way that human elements interfere to a minimum degree.

Concern for People (vertical axis, High 9 to Low 1)
Concern for Production (horizontal axis, Low 1 to High 9)

group, and the organization.[17] The research also provides some insights into when leaders should be production oriented and when they should be people oriented:[18]

- When subordinates experience a lot of pressure because of deadlines or unclear tasks, leaders who are people oriented will increase employee satisfaction and performance.

- When the task is interesting or satisfying, there is less need for leaders to be people oriented.

- When it's clear how to perform the task and what the goals are, leaders who are people oriented will increase employee satisfaction, while those who are task oriented will increase dissatisfaction.

- When people do not know what to do or individuals do not have the knowledge or skills to do the job, it's more important for leaders to be production oriented than people oriented.

The followers of leaders who were high on people orientation were more satisfied with their jobs and more motivated and also had more respect for their leader. Leaders who were high on task orientation showed higher levels of group and organization productivity and more positive performance evaluations.

Contingency Theories: Does the Situation Matter?

Have you ever wondered if there was one right way to lead?

As research on leadership developed, it became clear that predicting leadership success was more complex than simply isolating a few traits or preferable behaviours. Starting in the 1960s, leadership theories began to examine the situational factors that affect a leader's ability to act. This research pointed out that not all leaders can lead in every situation.[19]

Situational, or contingency, theories of leadership try to isolate critical situational factors that affect leadership effectiveness. The theories consider the degree of structure in the task being performed, the quality of leader-member relations, the leader's position power, group norms, information availability, employee acceptance of leader's decisions, employee maturity, and the clarity of the employee's role.[20]

We discuss four situational theories below: the Fiedler contingency model, Hersey and Blanchard's situational leadership theory, path-goal theory, and substitutes for leadership. All of these theories focus on the relationship of the leader to followers, and there is broad support for the idea that this relationship is important.[21]

situational, or contingency, theories Theories that propose that leadership effectiveness depends on the situation.

Fiedler Contingency Model

The first comprehensive contingency model for leadership was developed by Fred Fiedler.[22] The **Fiedler contingency model** proposes that effective group performance depends on the proper match between the leader's style and the degree to which the situation gives control to the leader.

Fiedler created the *least preferred co-worker (LPC) questionnaire* to determine whether individuals were mainly interested in good personal relations with co-workers, and thus were *relationship oriented*, or mainly interested in productivity, and thus were *task oriented*. Fiedler assumed that an individual's leadership style is fixed. Therefore, if a situation requires a task-oriented leader and the person in that leadership position is relationship oriented, either the situation has to be modified or the leader must be removed and replaced for optimum effectiveness to be achieved.

Fiedler identified three contingency dimensions that together define the situation a leader faces:

Fiedler contingency model A theory that proposes that effective group performance depends on the proper match between the leader's style and the degree to which the situation gives control to the leader.

- *Leader-member relations.* The degree of confidence, trust, and respect members have in their leader.

- *Task structure.* The degree to which the job assignments are procedurized (that is, structured or unstructured).

- *Position power.* The degree of influence a leader has over power variables such as hiring, firing, discipline, promotions, and salary increases.

Fiedler stated that the better the leader-member relations, the more highly structured the job, and the stronger the position power, the more control the leader has. He suggested that task-oriented leaders perform best in situations of high and low control, while relationship-oriented leaders perform best in moderate control situations.[23] In a high-control situation, a leader can "get away" with task orientation, because the relationships are good and followers are easily influenced.[24] In a low-control situation (which is marked by poor relations, ill-defined tasks, and low influence), task orientation may be the only thing that makes it possible to get something done. In a moderate-control situation, the leader's relationship orientation may smooth the way to getting things done.

Hersey and Blanchard's Situational Leadership Theory®

Paul Hersey and Ken Blanchard have developed a leadership model that has gained a strong following among management development specialists.[25] This model—called **situational leadership® (SL)**—has been incorporated into the leadership training of more than 700 of the *Fortune* 1000 companies, and more than a million managers a year from a wide variety of organizations are being taught its basic elements.[26]

SL views the leader-follower relationship as similar to that of a parent and child. Just as a parent needs to give up control as a child becomes more mature and responsible, so too should leaders. Hersey and Blanchard identify four specific leader behaviours— from highly directive to highly laissez-faire. The most effective behaviour depends on a follower's ability and motivation. This is illustrated in Exhibit 8-3. SL says that if a follower is *unable and unwilling* to do a task, the leader needs to give clear and specific directions (in other words, be highly directive). If a follower is *unable and willing*, the leader needs to display high task orientation to compensate for the follower's lack of ability, and high relationship orientation to get the follower to "buy into" the leader's desires (in other words, "sell" the task). If the follower is *able and unwilling*, the leader needs to adopt a supportive and participative style. Finally, if the employee is both *able and willing*, the leader does not need to do much (in other words, a laissez-faire approach will work).

Both the Fiedler contingency model and Hersey and Blanchard's SL have some intuitive appeal. Blanchard's work, for instance, is widely applied in the workplace. However, both theories have received far less empirical support, and Fiedler's theory has been found more difficult to apply in the work situation than the next model we consider, path-goal theory.[27]

Path-Goal Theory

Currently, one of the most respected approaches to leadership is **path-goal theory**. Developed by University of Toronto professor Martin Evans in the late 1960s, it was later expanded on by Robert House (formerly at the University of Toronto, but now at

situational leadership® (SL) A theory that proposes that effective leaders adapt their leadership style according to how willing and able a follower is to perform tasks.

path-goal theory A theory that says it is the leader's job to assist followers in attaining their goals and to provide the necessary direction and/or support to ensure that their individual goals are compatible with the overall goals of the group or organization.

EXHIBIT 8-3 Hersey and Blanchard's Situational Leadership®

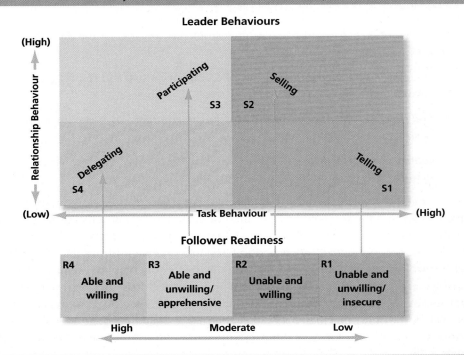

the Wharton School of Business at the University of Pennsylvania). Path-goal theory is a contingency model of leadership that extracts key elements from the Ohio State leadership research on initiating structure and consideration and from the expectancy theory of motivation (discussed in Chapter 4).[28]

The essence of the theory is that it is the leader's job to assist followers in attaining their goals and to provide the necessary direction and/or support to ensure that their individual goals are compatible with the overall goals of the group or organization. The term *path-goal* derives from the belief that effective leaders both clarify the path to help their followers achieve their work goals and make the journey along the path easier by removing roadblocks and pitfalls.

According to this theory, leaders should follow three guidelines to be effective:[29]

- *Determine the outcomes subordinates want.* These might include good pay, job security, interesting work, and the autonomy to do one's job.

- *Reward individuals with their desired outcomes* when they perform well.

- *Let individuals know what they need to do to receive rewards* (that is, the path to the goal), remove any barriers that would prevent a high level of performance, and express confidence that individuals have the ability to perform well.

Path-goal theory identifies four leadership behaviours that might be used in different situations to motivate individuals:

- The *directive leader* lets followers know what is expected of them, schedules work to be done, and gives specific guidance as to how to accomplish tasks. This closely parallels the Ohio State dimension of initiating structure. This behaviour is best used when individuals have difficulty doing tasks or the tasks are ambiguous. It would not be very helpful when used with individuals who are already highly motivated, have the skills and abilities to do the task, and understand the requirements of the task.

- The *supportive leader* is friendly and shows concern for the needs of followers. This is essentially synonymous with the Ohio State dimension of consideration. This behaviour is often recommended when individuals are under stress or otherwise show that they need to be supported.

- The *participative leader* consults with followers and uses their suggestions before making a decision. This behaviour is most appropriate when individuals need to buy in to decisions.

- The *achievement-oriented leader* sets challenging goals and expects followers to perform at their highest level. This behaviour works well with individuals who like challenges and are highly motivated. It would be less effective with less capable individuals or those who are highly stressed from overwork.

As Exhibit 8-4 on page 276 illustrates, path-goal theory proposes two types of contingency variables that affect the leadership behaviour–outcome relationship: environmental variables that are outside the control of the employee and variables that are part of the personal characteristics of the employee. House assumes that leaders are flexible and can display any or all of these behaviours, depending on the situation. Some situations may in fact need more than one style from the leader. The theory proposes that employee performance and satisfaction are likely to be positively influenced when the leader compensates for things lacking in either the employee or the work setting. However, the leader who spends time explaining tasks when those tasks are already clear or when the employee has the ability and experience to handle them without interference is likely to be ineffective because the employee will see such

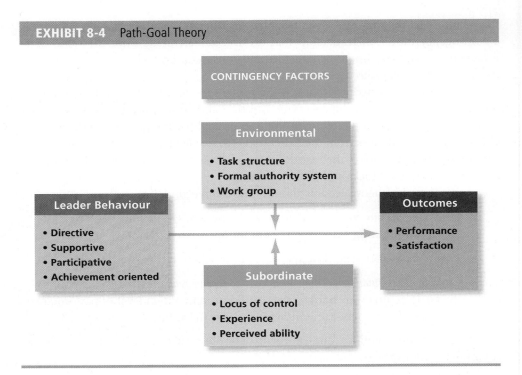

EXHIBIT 8-4 Path-Goal Theory

CONTINGENCY FACTORS

Environmental
- Task structure
- Formal authority system
- Work group

Leader Behaviour
- Directive
- Supportive
- Participative
- Achievement oriented

Subordinate
- Locus of control
- Experience
- Perceived ability

Outcomes
- Performance
- Satisfaction

directive behaviour as redundant or even insulting. Research generally supports path-goal theory.[30]

One question that arises from contingency theories is whether leaders can actually adjust their behaviour to various situations. As we know, individuals differ in their behavioural flexibility. Some people show considerable ability to adjust their behaviour to external, situational factors; they are adaptable. Others, however, exhibit high levels of consistency regardless of the situation. High self-monitors are usually able to adjust their leadership styles to suit changing situations better than low self-monitors.[31] Clearly, if an individual's leadership style range is very narrow and he or she cannot or will not adjust (that is, the person is a low self-monitor), that individual will be successful only in very specific situations suitable to his or her style.

Substitutes for Leadership

Is a leader always necessary?

The previous three theories argue that leaders are needed, but that leaders should consider the situation in determining the style of leadership to adopt. However, numerous studies collectively demonstrate that, in many situations, leaders' actions are irrelevant. Certain individual, job, and organizational variables can act as *substitutes* for leadership or *neutralize* the leader's ability to influence his or her followers.[32]

If employees have appropriate experience, training, or "professional" orientation or if employees are indifferent to organizational rewards, the effect of leadership can be replaced or neutralized. Experience and training, for instance, can replace the need for a leader's support or ability to create structure and reduce task ambiguity. Jobs that are inherently unambiguous and routine, provide their own feedback, or are intrinsically satisfying generally require less hands-on leadership. Organizational characteristics such as explicit formalized goals, rigid rules and procedures, and cohesive work groups can replace formal leadership (see Exhibit 8-5). Recent research has supported the importance of ability and intrinsic satisfaction in considering performance outcomes.[33]

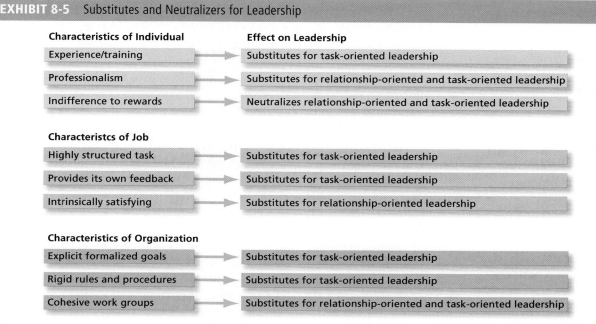

EXHIBIT 8-5 Substitutes and Neutralizers for Leadership

Characteristics of Individual	Effect on Leadership
Experience/training	Substitutes for task-oriented leadership
Professionalism	Substitutes for relationship-oriented and task-oriented leadership
Indifference to rewards	Neutralizes relationship-oriented and task-oriented leadership

Characteristcs of Job	
Highly structured task	Substitutes for task-oriented leadership
Provides its own feedback	Substitutes for task-oriented leadership
Intrinsically satisfying	Substitutes for relationship-oriented leadership

Characteristics of Organization	
Explicit formalized goals	Substitutes for task-oriented leadership
Rigid rules and procedures	Substitutes for task-oriented leadership
Cohesive work groups	Substitutes for relationship-oriented and task-oriented leadership

Source: Based on S. Kerr and J. M. Jermier, "Substitutes for Leadership: Their Meaning and Measurement," *Organizational Behavior and Human Performance,* December 1978, p. 378.

Inspirational Leadership

Patagonia's mission statement, featured prominently on its website, is "Build the best product, do no unnecessary harm, use business to inspire and implement solutions to the environmental crisis."[34] The company continues to grow, and Yvon Chouinard regularly declines offers to buy the firm ("I don't want some Wall Street greaseball running my company," he says). Patagonia receives 900 applications for every position it fills. Although Patagonia is not as large as some retailers, its use of environmentalism to its advantage has influenced other retailers—such as The Gap, Levi Strauss, and, most recently, Walmart—to follow in its footsteps. You would think all this would make Chouinard optimistic about the future. Not a chance. "I know everything's going to hell," he says.

Although he's uncharacteristic of leaders in some ways, Chouinard has the qualities of an inspirational leader—that is, he has a vision, sticks with it, and inspires followers to go beyond their own self-interests in pursuing it. What does it take for a person to lead with vision?

The leadership theories that we have discussed were developed at a time when most organizations were structured in traditional hierarchies where there were classic lines of command. Today, organizations are trying to be innovative, faster moving, and more responsive to employees who are highly educated and intelligent, and who want more say in the workplace. Thus, new styles of leadership are evolving to meet the demands of these organizations. The more recent approaches to leadership move away from the supervisory tasks of leaders and focus on vision-setting activities. Today, leadership theories also try to explain how certain leaders can inspire extraordinary levels of performance among their followers, and they stress symbolic and emotionally appealing leadership behaviours.[35] In what follows, we consider transactional leadership, transformational leadership, and charismatic leadership.

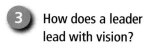

3 How does a leader lead with vision?

From Transactional to Transformational Leadership

transactional leaders Leaders who guide or motivate their followers in the direction of established goals by clarifying role and task requirements.

Most of the leadership theories presented thus far in this chapter have concerned **transactional leaders**. Such leaders guide or motivate their followers in the direction of established goals by clarifying role and task requirements. In some styles of transactional leadership, the leader uses rewarding and recognizing behaviours. This approach results in performance that meets expectations, though rarely does one see results that exceed expectations.[36] In other styles of transactional leadership, the leader emphasizes correction and possible punishment rather than rewards and recognition. This style "results in performance below expectations, and discourages innovation and initiative in the workplace."[37] Of course, leaders should not ignore poor performance, but effective leaders emphasize how to achieve expectations rather than dwell on mistakes.

transformational leaders Leaders who inspire followers to go beyond their own self-interests for the good of the organization and have a profound and extraordinary effect on their followers.

Some leaders inspire followers to transcend their own self-interests for the good of the organization and have a profound and extraordinary effect on their followers. These are **transformational leaders**, such as Matthew Barrett, former chair of Barclays PLC, Britain's second-largest bank, and former CEO of Bank of Montreal; Frank Stronach, chair of Aurora, Ontario-based Magna International; and Mogens Smed, CEO of Calgary-based DIRTT (Doing It Right This Time) and former CEO of SMED International. Other Canadians who have frequently been cited as charismatic leaders include René Lévesque, the late Quebec premier; Lucien Bouchard, former Bloc Québécois leader; Michaëlle Jean, Governor General; Pierre Trudeau, the late prime minister; and Craig Kielburger, the Canadian teenager who founded Free The Children to promote children's rights and combat exploitation of child labour. What links these individuals is that they pay attention to the concerns and developmental needs of individual followers. Transformational leaders change followers' awareness of issues by helping them look at old problems in new ways, and they are able to excite, arouse, and inspire followers to exert extra effort to achieve group goals.[38]

charismatic leadership Leadership that critically examines the status quo with a view to developing and articulating future strategic goals or vision for the organization, and then leading organizational members to achieve these goals through empowering strategies.

Transformational leadership is sometimes identified separately from **charismatic leadership** in the literature, although McGill's Kanungo notes that the two formulations do not differ in that charismatic leaders are also transformational leaders. Relying on his judgment, we use the two concepts interchangeably. As Kanungo notes, the charismatic leader "critically examines the status quo with a view to developing and articulating future strategic goals or vision for the organization and then leading organizational members to achieve these goals through empowering strategies."[39] While not all transformational leaders are charismatic in personality, both transformational and charismatic leaders work to empower their followers to reach higher goals.

Full Range of Leadership Model

Transactional and transformational leadership should not be viewed as opposing approaches to getting things done.[40] Transformational leadership is built *on top of* transactional leadership—it produces levels of employee effort and performance that go beyond what would occur with a transactional approach alone. You should be aware, though, that if you are a good transactional leader but do not have transformational qualities, you will likely only be a mediocre leader. The best leaders are transactional *and* transformational.

Exhibit 8-6 shows the full range of leadership model. The lower three styles represent aspects of transactional leadership. Laissez-faire is the most passive and therefore the least effective of the leader behaviours. Leaders using this style are rarely viewed as effective. Management by exception—regardless of whether it is active or passive—is slightly better than laissez-faire, but it's still considered ineffective leadership. Leaders who practise management by exception leadership tend to be available only when there is a problem, which is often too late. Contingent reward leadership can be an

The inspiring vision of Apple's charismatic co-founder and CEO, Steve Jobs, is to make state-of-the-art technology easy for people to use. Through this vision, Jobs inspires, motivates, and leads employees to develop products such as Macintosh computers, iPod music players, and iPhones. "The iPhone is like having your life in your pocket," says Jobs; Apple's entry into the mobile phone market includes an iPod, a camera, an alarm clock, and Internet communication capabilities with an easy-to-use touch-screen design.

EXHIBIT 8-6   Full Range of Leadership Model

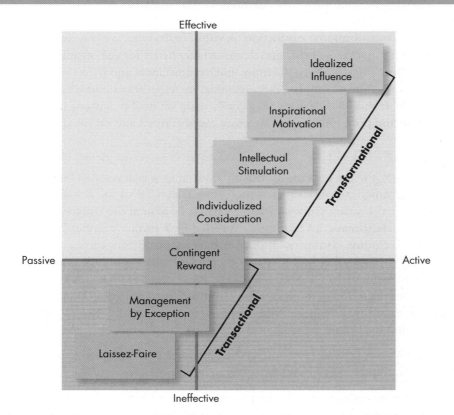

effective style of leadership. However, leaders will not get their employees to go above and beyond the call of duty when practising this style of leadership.

Only with the four remaining leadership styles—which are all aspects of transformational leadership—are leaders able to motivate followers to perform above expectations and transcend their own self-interest for the sake of the organization. Using these transformational styles results in extra effort from employees, higher productivity, higher morale and satisfaction, higher organizational effectiveness, lower turnover, lower absenteeism, and greater organizational adaptability. Based on this model, leaders are generally most effective when they regularly use each of the four transformational behaviours.

Can transformational and charismatic leadership be learned? One study of Canadian bank managers found that those managers who underwent transformational leadership training had bank branches that performed significantly better than branches with managers who did not undergo training. Other studies show similar results.[41] Would you be able to be a charismatic leader? We give you tips in this chapter's *From Concepts to Skills* on pages 300–301.

Sharing a Vision

Perhaps one of the key components of charismatic leadership and transformational leadership is the ability to articulate a vision. A review of various definitions finds that a vision differs from other forms of direction setting in several ways:

> *A vision has clear and compelling imagery that offers an innovative way to improve, which recognizes and draws on traditions, and connects to actions that people can take to realize change. Vision taps people's emotions and energy. Properly articulated, a vision creates the enthusiasm that people have for sporting events and other leisure-time activities, bringing the energy and commitment to the workplace.*[42]

The key properties of a vision seem to be inspirational possibilities that are value-centred and realizable, with superior imagery and articulation.[43] Visions should be able to create possibilities that are inspirational and unique, and offer a new order that can produce organizational distinction. A vision is likely to fail if it does not offer a view of the future that is clearly and demonstrably better for the organization and its members. Desirable visions fit the times and circumstances and reflect the uniqueness of the organization. People in the organization must also believe that the vision is attainable. It should be perceived as challenging yet doable. Visions that have clear articulation and powerful imagery are more easily grasped and accepted.

RESEARCH FINDINGS: CHARISMATIC LEADERSHIP

While the idea of charismatic leadership was developed based on North American observations, professors Dale Carl of the School of Business Management at Ryerson University and Mansour Javidan at the University of Calgary suggest that charismatic leadership is expressed in a similar manner in a variety of countries, including Hungary, India, Turkey, Austria, Singapore, Sweden, and Venezuela.[44] This finding indicates that there may be some universal aspects of this style of leadership.

A number of studies demonstrate the effectiveness of charismatic and transformational leadership.[45] We consider the impact of this leadership style on company performance and individual performance.

Company Performance Do vision and charismatic leadership really make a difference? Several studies provide positive evidence that they do:

- One study contrasted 18 visionary companies with 18 comparable nonvisionary firms over a 65-year period.[46] The visionary companies performed 6 times better than the comparison group, based on standard financial criteria, and their stocks performed 15 times better than the general market.

- In a study of 250 executives and managers at a major financial services company, Jane Howell (at the Richard Ivey School of Business at the University of Western Ontario) and her colleagues found that "transformational leaders had 34 percent higher business unit performance results than other types of leaders."[47]

- An unpublished study by Robert House and some colleagues of 63 American and 49 Canadian companies (including Nortel Networks, Molson, Gulf Canada [now ConocoPhillips], and Manulife Financial) found that "between 15 and 25 percent of the variation in profitability among the companies was accounted for by the leadership qualities of their CEO."[48] That is, charismatic leaders led more profitable companies in the 1990s. This may explain the high compensation packages for CEOs that we discussed in Chapter 4.

Individual Performance An increasing body of research shows that people working for charismatic leaders are motivated to exert extra work effort and, because they like their leaders, they express greater satisfaction.[49]

The evidence supporting the superiority of transformational leadership over the transactional variety is overwhelmingly impressive. For instance, a number of studies of US, Canadian, and German military officers found, at every level, that transformational leaders were evaluated as more effective than their transactional counterparts.[50] Managers at FedEx who were rated by their followers as exhibiting more transformational leadership were evaluated by their immediate supervisors as higher performers and more promotable.[51] Nevertheless, transformational leadership should be used with some caution in non–North American contexts, because its effectiveness may be affected by cultural values concerning leadership.[52]

In summary, the overall evidence indicates that transformational leadership correlates more strongly than transactional leadership with lower turnover rates, higher productivity, and higher employee satisfaction.[53] One caveat to this research is a study by Professor Timothy DeGroot of McMaster University and his colleagues. They found that charismatic leadership had a greater impact on team performance than on individual performance, and they suggest that the positive findings of previous studies are the result of charismatic leaders providing a better team environment for everyone, which then resulted in higher performance.[54] To learn more about how to be transformational/charismatic yourself, see the *Working With Others Exercise* on page 297.

The Dark Side of Charismatic Leadership
When organizations are in need of great change, charismatic leaders are often able to inspire their followers to meet the challenges of change. Be aware that a charismatic leader may become a liability to an organization once the crisis is over and the need for dramatic change subsides.[55] Why? Because then the charismatic leader's overwhelming self-confidence can be a liability. He or she is unable to listen to others, becomes uncomfortable when challenged by aggressive employees, and begins to hold an unjustifiable belief in his or her "rightness" on issues. Some would argue that Jean Chrétien's behaviour leading up to his decision to announce that he would eventually step down as prime minister, thus preventing a divisive leadership review in February 2003, would fit this description.

Harvard Business School professor Rakesh Khurana argues that many of today's chief executives have been "chosen for their ability to articulate messianic 'visions' for their companies; inspire employees to do whatever it takes to realize these grand designs; and imbue investors with faith in their own talents."[56] These traits, however, might have led to the corporate scandals that unfolded in recent years. Charismatic leadership, by its very nature, silences criticism. Thus, employees follow the lead of their visionary CEOs unquestioningly. Professor David Leighton, of the Richard Ivey School of Business at the University of Western Ontario, notes that even the boards of directors and auditors were reluctant to challenge these CEOs. He also suggests that Canada's "more balanced culture," which is less likely to turn CEOs into heroes, may help protect the country from some of the scandals that the United States faced.[57]

Is Charismatic Leadership Always Necessary?

A recent study of 29 companies that went from good to great (their cumulative stock returns were all at least three times better than the general stock market over 15 years) found that a key difference in successful charismatic leaders may be the fact that they are not *ego-driven*.[58] Although the leaders of these firms were fiercely ambitious and driven, their ambition was directed toward their company rather than themselves. They generated extraordinary results, but with little fanfare or hoopla. They took responsibility for mistakes and poor results but gave credit for successes to other people. They also prided themselves on developing strong leaders inside the firm who could direct the company to greater heights after they were gone. These individuals have been called **level 5 leaders** because they have four basic leadership qualities—individual capability, team skills, managerial competence, and the ability to stimulate others to high performance—plus a fifth dimension: a paradoxical blend of personal humility and professional will. Level 5 leaders channel their ego needs away from themselves and into the goal of building a great company.

level 5 leaders Leaders who are fiercely ambitious and driven, whose ambition is directed toward their company rather than themselves.

Contemporary Leadership Roles

Patagonia helps its employees develop their leadership skills, particularly in the area of environmentalism.[59] Each year, 40 of the company's employees can take a two-month internship with an environmental group, while still collecting their paycheque. Patagonia also gives training to individuals who want to participate in environmental protests by sponsoring civil disobedience workshops.

Chouinard believes his employees are well-suited for engaging in self-leadership. "Hire the people you trust, people who are passionate about their job, passionate about what they're doing. Just leave them alone, and they'll get the job done," he says. What are the different ways that people who are not officially in charge can also be effective leaders?

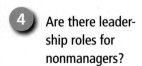

4 Are there leadership roles for nonmanagers?

Can anyone be a leader?

People who are not in formal positions of leadership often wonder if there is any chance of being a leader without a formal role.[60] The following sections aim to explain how leadership can be spread throughout an organization through mentoring, self-leadership, team leadership, online leadership, and leading without authority. Even if you are not a manager or someone thinking about leadership in a corporate situation, this discussion offers important insights into how you can take on a leadership role in an organization.

As you consider the ways that roles can spread to people who are not managers, be aware that not all organizations engage in this practice, and even within organizations, not all managers are happy with sharing their power with those under them. Gifted leaders often recognize that they actually have more power if they share power. That is, sharing power enables them to build coalitions and teams that work together for the overall good of the organization. There are other managers, though, who fear the loss of any power.

Mentoring

Many leaders create mentoring relationships. A **mentor** is often a senior employee who sponsors and supports a less-experienced employee (a protégé). The mentoring role includes coaching, counselling, and sponsorship.[61] As a coach, mentors help develop their protégés' skills. As counsellors, mentors provide support and help bolster protégés' self-confidence. And as sponsors, mentors actively intervene on behalf of their protégés, lobby to get their protégés visible assignments, and politic to get their protégés rewards such as promotions and salary increases.

Successful mentors are good teachers. They can present ideas clearly, listen well, and empathize with the problems of their protégés. They also share experiences with the protégés, act as role models, share contacts, and provide guidance through the political maze of the organization. They provide advice on how to survive and get ahead in the organization and act as a sounding board for ideas that protégés may be hesitant to share with their direct supervisors. Mentors vouch for their protégés, answer for them in the highest circles within the organization, and make appropriate introductions.

Some organizations have formal mentoring programs, in which mentors are officially assigned to new or high-potential employees. For instance, Montreal-based Bell Canada introduced Mentor Match in late 2002 to bring together senior and junior employees. The mentors meet one-on-one for about an hour a month to build a stronger understanding of leadership and organizational knowledge for the younger employees.[62] However, in contrast to Bell Canada's formal system, most organizations rely on informal mentoring—with senior managers personally selecting employees as protégés or junior employees asking senior employees to mentor them.

The most effective mentoring relationships exist outside the immediate boss-subordinate interface.[63] The boss-subordinate context has an inherent conflict of interest and tension, mostly attributable to managers' direct evaluation of the performance of subordinates, that limits openness and meaningful communication.

Why would a leader want to be a mentor? There are personal benefits to the leader as well as benefits for the organization. The mentor-protégé relationship gives the mentor unfiltered access to the attitudes and feelings of lower-ranking employees. Protégés can be an excellent source of information on potential problems; they can provide early warning signals to upper managers because they short-circuit the formal channels. So the mentor-protégé relationship is a valuable communication channel that allows mentors to learn about problems before they become common knowledge to others in upper management. In addition, in terms of leader self-interest, mentoring can provide personal satisfaction to senior executives. It gives them the opportunity to share with others the knowledge and experience that they have developed over many years.

From the organization's standpoint, mentoring provides a support system for high-potential employees. Where mentors exist, protégés are often more motivated, better grounded politically, and less likely to quit. A recent comprehensive review of the research, for instance, found that mentoring provided substantial benefits to protégés.[64] Specifically, mentored employees had higher compensation, a larger number of promotions, and were more satisfied with their careers than their nonmentored counterparts.

Are all employees in an organization equally likely to participate in a mentoring relationship? Unfortunately the answer is no.[65] The evidence indicates that minorities

mentor A senior employee who sponsors and supports a less-experienced employee.

Narayana Murthy (right in photo), one of the founders of Infosys Technologies in Bangalore, India, stepped down as CEO to serve the firm as chief mentor. In this role, Murthy shares his experiences, knowledge, and lessons learned while he built the company he started in 1981 and grew to 75 000 employees with sales of $3 billion. In mentoring Infosys's core management team, he wants to provide next-generation leadership for the firm. His goal is to build leadership qualities among Infosys employees by spending time at various corporate campuses and discussing issues that add value to the company. Murthy is shown here mentoring the new Infosys CEO, Nandan Nilekani.

and women are less likely to be chosen as protégés than are white males and thus they are less likely to accrue the benefits of mentorship. Mentors tend to select protégés who are similar to themselves in criteria such as background, education, gender, race, ethnicity, and religion. "People naturally move to mentor and can more easily communicate with those with whom they most closely identify."[66]

In a twist to the typical mentoring-down idea, Procter & Gamble introduced a Mentoring Up program to help senior managers become more aware of what female managers can contribute to the organization. In its program, mid-level female managers mentor senior-level male executives. The program has led to fewer departures of female managers and has exposed women to top decision makers.[67]

Coaching

A number of organizations have introduced coaching, which is different from mentoring. "Mentoring, at its best, involves a longer term relationship in which there is an emotional attachment between mentor and protégé."[68] By contrast, coaching is often more task oriented and short term. Coaching is used by senior and middle managers in particular, although other managers use coaching as part of their leadership style. A good coach

- Emphasizes self-development and self-discovery of the person being coached

- Offers the person being coached constructive feedback on how to improve

- Meets regularly with the person being coached

- Is a good listener

- Challenges the person being coached to perform
- Sets realistic standards for the person being coached to achieve.[69]

Self-Leadership (or Self-Management)

How do you manage yourself?

A growing trend in organizations is the focus on self-leadership, or self-management.[70] (Recall our discussion of self-managed teams in Chapter 5.) With self-leadership, individuals and teams set goals, plan and implement tasks, evaluate performance, solve their own problems, and motiv-ate themselves.

Several factors call for self-leadership: reduced levels of supervision; offices in the home; teamwork; and growth in service and professional employment in which individuals are often required to make decisions on the spot.

Despite the lack of studies of self-management techniques in organizational settings, self-management strategies have been shown to be successful in nonorganizational settings.[71] Those who practise self-management look for opportunities to be more effective in the workplace and improve their career success. Their behaviour is self-reinforced; that is, they provide their own sense of reward and feedback after carrying out their tasks. Moreover, self-reinforced behaviour is often maintained at a higher rate than behaviour that is externally regulated.[72] *OB in Action—Engaging in Self-Leadership* indicates ways in which you can practise effective self-leadership.

How do leaders create self-leaders? The following approaches have been suggested:[73]

> ### OB in ACTION
>
> ## Engaging in Self-Leadership
> To engage in effective self-leadership:[74]
>
> → **Think horizontally, not vertically**. Vertical relationships in the organization matter, but peers can become trusted colleagues and have a great impact on your work.
>
> → Focus on **influence, not control**. Work with your colleagues, not for them. Be collaborative and share credit.
>
> → **Create opportunities**, do not wait for them. Rather than look for the right time, be more action oriented.

- *Model self-leadership.* Practise self-observation, setting challenging personal goals, self-direction, and self-reinforcement. Then display these behaviours, and encourage others to rehearse and then produce them.

- *Encourage employees to create self-set goals.* Support employees in developing quantitative, specific goals; having such goals is the most important part of self-leadership.

- *Encourage the use of self-rewards to strengthen and increase desirable behaviours.* By contrast, limit self-punishment only to occasions when the employee has been dishonest or destructive.

- *Create positive thought patterns.* Encourage employees to use mental imagery and self-talk to further stimulate self-motivation.

- *Create a climate of self-leadership.* Redesign the work to increase the natural rewards of a job and focus on these naturally rewarding features of work to increase motivation.

- *Encourage constructive self-criticism.* Encourage individuals to be critical of their own performance to find ways to improve.

The underlying assumptions behind self-leadership are that people are responsible, capable, and able to exercise initiative without the external constraints of bosses, rules, or regulations. Given the proper support, individuals can monitor and control their own behaviour. The *Learning About Yourself Exercise* on page 296 provides further examples of how to engage in self-leadership.

Providing Team Leadership

Increasingly, leadership is taking place within a team context. As teams grow in popularity, the role of the leader in guiding team members takes on more importance.[75] Also, because of its more collaborative nature, the role of team leader differs from the traditional leadership role performed by front-line supervisors.

Many leaders are not equipped to handle the move to team leader. As one prominent consultant noted, "Even the most capable managers have trouble making the transition because all the command-and-control type things they were encouraged to do before are no longer appropriate. There's no reason to have any skill or sense of this."[76] This same consultant estimated that "probably 15 percent of managers are natural team leaders; another 15 percent could never lead a team because it runs counter to their personality. [They are unable to put aside their dominating style for the good of the team.] Then there's that huge group in the middle: team leadership doesn't come naturally to them, but they can learn it."[77]

Effective team leaders need to build commitment and confidence, remove obstacles, create opportunities, and be part of the team.[78] They have to learn skills such as the patience to share information, the willingness to trust others, the ability to give up authority, and an understanding of when to intervene. New team leaders may try to retain too much control at a time when team members need more autonomy, or they may abandon their teams at times when the teams need support and help.[79]

Exhibit 8-7 gives a lighthearted look at what it means to be a team leader.

Roles of Team Leaders

A recent study of 20 organizations that reorganized themselves around teams found certain common responsibilities that all leaders had to assume. These included coaching, facilitating, handling disciplinary problems, reviewing team/individual performance, training, and communicating.[80] Many of these responsibilities apply to managers in general. A more meaningful way to describe the team leader's job is to focus on two priorities: managing the team's relations with outsiders and facilitating the team process.[81] We have divided these priorities into four specific roles that team leaders play:

- *Liaisons with outsiders.* Outsiders include upper management, other internal teams, customers, and suppliers. The leader represents the team to other

EXHIBIT 8-7

Source: DILBERT reprinted by permission of United Features Syndicate, Inc.

constituencies, secures needed resources, clarifies others' expectations of the team, gathers information from the outside, and shares this information with team members.

- *Troubleshooters.* When the team has problems and asks for assistance, team leaders sit in on meetings and try to help resolve the problems. This rarely relates to technical or operational issues because the team members typically know more about the tasks being done than does the team leader. The leader contributes by asking penetrating questions, by helping the team discuss problems, and by getting needed resources from external constituencies. For instance, when a team in an aerospace firm found itself short-handed, its team leader took responsibility for getting more staff. He presented the team's case to upper management and got the approval through the company's human resource department.

- *Conflict managers.* When disagreements surface, team leaders help process the conflict. What is the source of the conflict? Who is involved? What are the issues? What resolution options are available? What are the advantages and disadvantages of each? By getting team members to address questions such as these, the leader minimizes the disruptive aspects of intrateam conflicts.

- *Coaches.* They clarify expectations and roles, teach, offer support, cheerlead, and do whatever else is necessary to help team members improve their work performance.

Online Leadership

How do you lead people who are physically separated from you and for whom interactions are basically reduced to written digital communications? This is a question that, to date, has not received as much attention from organizational behaviour researchers as face-to-face leadership.[82] Despite the fact that interacting face-to-face is generally a better way of doing business, the reality is that today's managers and their employees are increasingly being linked by electronic networks rather than geographical proximity; many employees are interacting with individuals who are on the other side of the globe.

In face-to-face communications, harsh *words* can be softened by nonverbal action. A smile and comforting gestures, for instance, can lessen the blow behind strong words like *disappointed*, *unsatisfactory*, *inadequate*, or *below expectations*. That nonverbal component does not exist with online interactions. The *structure* of words in a digital communication has the power to motivate or demotivate the receiver.

Leaders need to be sure the *tone* of their email correctly reflects the emotions they want to send. Is the message formal or informal? Does it match the verbal style of the sender? Does it convey the appropriate level of importance or urgency? The fact that many people's writing style is very different from their interpersonal style is certainly a potential problem.

Jane Howell at the Richard Ivey School of Business, University of Western Ontario, and one of her students, Kate Hall-Merenda, considered the issues of leading from a distance.[83] They noted that physical distance has the potential to create many problems, with team members feeling isolated, forgotten, and perhaps not cared about. It may result in lowered productivity. Their study of 109 business leaders and 371 followers in a large financial institution found that physical distance makes it more difficult to develop high-quality relationships.

Howell and Hall-Merenda suggest that some of the same characteristics of transformational leaders are appropriate for long-distance managing. In particular, they emphasize the need to articulate a compelling vision and to communicate that vision in an inspiring way. Encouraging employees to think about ways to strive toward that vision is another important task of the leader.

Online leaders confront unique challenges, the greatest of which appears to be developing and maintaining trust. Identification-based trust, for instance, is particularly difficult to achieve when there is a lack of intimacy and face-to-face interaction.[84] Online negotiations have also been found to be hindered because parties express lower levels of trust.[85] It's not clear whether it's even possible for employees to identify with or trust leaders with whom they only communicate electronically.[86]

This discussion leads us to the tentative conclusion that, for an increasing number of managers, good interpersonal skills may include the abilities to communicate support and leadership through written words on a computer screen and to read emotions in others' messages. With the increased emphasis on electronic communication, writing skills are likely to become an extension of interpersonal skills.

Leading Without Authority

What if your goal is to be a leader, even if you do not have the authority (or formal appointment) to be one? For instance, what if you wanted to convince the dean of your school to introduce new business courses that were more relevant, or you wanted to convince the president of the company where you work that she should start thinking about more environmentally friendly strategies in dealing with waste? How do you effectively lead in a student group, when everyone is a peer?

Leadership at the grassroots level in organizations does happen. Rosabeth Moss Kanter, in her book *The Change Masters*,[87] discusses examples of people who saw something in their workplace that needed changing and took the responsibility to do so upon themselves. Employees were more likely to do this when organizations permitted initiative at all levels of the organization, rather than making it a tool of senior executives only.

Leading without authority simply means exhibiting leadership behaviour even though you do not have a formal position or title that might encourage others "to obey." Neither Martin Luther King Jr. nor Nelson Mandela operated from a position of authority, yet each was able to inspire many to follow him in the quest for social justice. The workplace can be an opportunity for leading without authority as well. As Ronald Heifetz of Harvard's Kennedy School of Government notes, "Leadership means taking responsibility for hard problems beyond anyone's expectations."[88] It also means not waiting for the coach's call.[89]

What are the benefits of leading without authority? Heifetz has identified three:[90]

- *Latitude for creative deviance.* When a person does not have authority, and the trappings that go with authority, it's easier to raise harder questions and look for less traditional solutions.

- *Issue focus.* Leading without authority means that individuals can focus on a single issue, rather than be concerned with the myriad issues that those in authority face.

- *Front-line information.* Leading without authority means that an individual is closer to the detailed experiences of some of the stakeholders. Thus, more information is available to this kind of leader.

Not all organizations will support this type of leadership, and some have been known to actively suppress it. Still others will look aside, not encouraging, but not discouraging either. Nevertheless, you may want to reflect on the possibility of engaging in leadership behaviour because you see a need, rather than because you are required to act.

Contemporary Issues in Leadership

Yvon Chouinard believes in responsible leadership that promotes a better environment for the world.[91] He is not yet satisfied with the changes that Patagonia has made to create environmentally friendly clothing. "We have to dig deeper and try to make products that close the loop—clothing that can be recycled infinitely into similar or equal products, which is something we continue to strive for," he says.

Chouinard believes that doing the right thing for the environment is the right thing for company practice. "We've found that every time we've elected to do the right thing, even when it costs twice as much, it's turned out to be more profitable," he explains.

Chouinard believes that Patagonia will never be able to be a completely environmentally friendly company, no matter how hard it tries to do so. But he is pleased that other companies (Clif Bar, the Gap, and Levi Strauss) are now starting to follow Patagonia's lead. How does moral leadership relate to the company's bottom line?

What is authentic leadership? Is there a moral dimension to leadership? Do men and women rely on different leadership styles, and if so, is one style inherently superior to the other? In this section, we briefly address these contemporary issues in leadership.

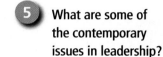

5 What are some of the contemporary issues in leadership?

Authentic Leadership

Authentic leaders know who they are, know what they believe in and value, and act on those values and beliefs openly and candidly. Their followers would consider them to be ethical people. The primary quality, therefore, produced by authentic leadership is trust. How does authentic leadership build trust? Authentic leaders share information, encourage open communication, and stick to their ideals. The result: People come to have faith in authentic leaders.

Because the concept is so recent, there has not been a lot of research on authentic leadership. However, we believe it's a promising way to think about ethics and trust in leadership because it focuses on the moral aspects of being a leader. Transformational or charismatic leaders can have a vision and communicate it persuasively, but sometimes the vision is wrong (as in the case of Hitler), or the leader is more concerned with his own needs or pleasures, as in the case of business leader Bernie Madoff (ex-chair of Bernard L. Madoff Investment Securities).[92]

authentic leaders Leaders who know who they are, know what they believe in and value, and act on these values and beliefs openly and candidly. Their followers would consider them to be ethical people.

Is There a Moral Dimension to Leadership?

Only recently have ethicists and leadership researchers begun to consider the ethical implications in leadership.[93] Why now? One reason may be the growing general interest in ethics throughout the field of management. Another reason may be that, these days, it seems that ethical lapses by business leaders are never absent from the headlines.

Ethics touches on leadership in a number of ways. Transformational leaders, for instance, have been described by one authority as encouraging moral virtue when they try to change the attitudes and behaviours of followers.[94] Charisma, too, has an ethical component. Unethical leaders are more likely to use their charisma to enhance power over followers, directed toward self-serving ends. We prefer to believe that ethical leaders use their charisma in a socially constructive way to serve others.[95] Consider, too, the issue of abuse of power by leaders—for example, when they give themselves large salaries and bonuses while also trying to cut costs by laying off long-time employees. Because top executives set the moral tone for an organization, they need to set high ethical standards, demonstrate those standards through their own behaviour, and encourage and reward integrity in others.

socialized charismatic leadership A leadership concept that states that leaders model ethical conduct and convey values that are other-centred vs. self-centred.

Leadership effectiveness needs to address the means that a leader uses in trying to achieve goals, as well as the content of those goals. Recently, scholars have tried to integrate ethical and charismatic leadership by advancing the idea of **socialized charismatic leadership**—leadership that models ethical conduct and conveys values that are other-centred versus self-centred.[96] Before we judge any leader to be effective, we should consider both the means used by the leader to achieve goals and the moral content of those goals.

Professor James Clawson of the Darden Graduate School of Business, University of Virginia, suggests that there are four cornerstones to a "moral foundation of leadership".[97]

- *Truth telling.* Leaders who tell the truth as they see it allow for a mutual, fair exchange to occur.

- *Promise keeping.* Leaders need to be careful about the commitments they make, and then careful to keep those commitments.

- *Fairness.* Leaders who are equitable ensure that followers get their fair share for their contributions to the organization.

- *Respect for the individual.* Leaders who tell the truth, keep promises, and are fair show respect for followers. Respect means treating people with dignity.

Moral leadership comes from within the individual, and in general means treating people well and with respect. This chapter's *Ethical Dilemma Exercise* on page 298 raises some provocative issues about whether we should consider just the ends toward which a leader strives, or the means as well.

Gender: Do Men and Women Lead Differently?

An extensive review of the literature suggests two conclusions.[98] First, the similarities between male and female leaders tend to outweigh the differences. Second, what differences there are seem to be that women fall back on a more democratic leadership style while men feel more comfortable with a directive style.

The similarities among men and women leaders should not be completely surprising. Almost all the studies looking at this issue have treated managerial positions as synonymous with leadership roles. Both male and female managers have characteristics that set them apart from the general population. Just as people who choose careers in law enforcement or civil engineering have a lot in common, so do individuals who choose managerial careers. People with traits associated with leadership—such as intelligence, confidence, and sociability—are more likely to be perceived as leaders and encouraged to pursue careers where they can exert leadership. This is true regardless of gender. Similarly, organizations tend to recruit and promote people who project leadership attributes into leadership positions. The result is that, regardless of gender, those who achieve formal leadership positions in organizations tend to be more alike than different.

Despite the previous conclusion, studies indicate some differences in the inherent leadership styles of women and men. A recent Conference Board of Canada study found that "women are particularly strong in managing interpersonal relationships and their approach is more consensual."[99] Other studies have shown that women tend to adopt a style of shared leadership. They encourage participation, share power and information, and try to enhance followers' self-worth. They prefer to lead through inclusion and rely on their charisma, expertise, contacts,

Bill Young created Toronto-based Social Capital Partners to help businesses hire the hard to employ: youths, single mothers, Aboriginal people, new immigrants, and those with disabilities or problems with substance abuse. His goal is to help people who are struggling get back into the economic mainstream.

and interpersonal skills to influence others. Men, on the other hand, are more likely to use a directive command-and-control style. They rely on the formal authority of their position for their influence base.

Given that men have historically held the great majority of leadership positions in organizations, it is tempting to assume that the differences noted between men and women would automatically work to favour men. They do not. In today's organizations, flexibility, teamwork, trust, and information sharing are replacing rigid structures, competitive individualism, control, and secrecy. The best leaders listen, motivate, and provide support to their people. Many women seem to do those things better than men. As a specific example, the expanded use of cross-functional teams in organizations means that effective leaders must become skilled negotiators. The leadership styles women typically use can make them better at negotiating, as they are less likely than men to focus on wins, losses, and competition. They tend to treat negotiations in the context of a continuing relationship—trying hard to make the other party a winner in his or her own and others' eyes.

Although it's interesting to see how men's and women's leadership styles differ, a more important question is whether they differ in effectiveness. Although some researchers have shown that men and women tend to be equally effective as leaders,[100] an increasing number of studies have shown that women executives, when rated by their peers, employees, and bosses, score higher than their male counterparts in a wide variety of measures, including getting extra effort from subordinates and overall effectiveness in leading. Subordinates also report more satisfaction with the leadership given by women.[101] See Exhibit 8-8 on page 292 for a scorecard on where female managers do better, based on a summary of five studies. Why these differences? One possible explanation is that in today's organizations, flexibility, teamwork and partnering, trust, and information sharing are rapidly replacing rigid structures, competitive individualism, control, and secrecy. In these types of workplaces, effective managers must use more social and interpersonal behaviours. They must listen, motivate, and provide support to their people. They must inspire and influence rather than control. Women seem to do those things better than men.[102]

George Cooke, CEO of Toronto-based Dominion of Canada General Insurance, believes in promoting women to senior positions. He is noteworthy for this: Dominion is well above the national average in the percentage of women who have made it to the executive ranks of Canada's top companies.

EXHIBIT 8-8   Where Female Managers Do Better: A Scorecard

None of the five studies set out to find gender differences. They stumbled on them while compiling and analyzing performance evaluations.

Skill (Each check mark denotes which group scored higher on the respective studies.)	MEN	WOMEN
Motivating others		✓ ✓ ✓ ✓ ✓
Fostering communication		✓ ✓ ✓ ✓ *
Producing high-quality work		✓ ✓ ✓ ✓ ✓
Strategic planning	✓ ✓	✓ ✓ *
Listening to others		✓ ✓ ✓ ✓ ✓
Analyzing issues	✓ ✓	✓ ✓ *

* In one study, women's and men's scores in these categories were statistically even.

Data: Hagberg Consulting Group, Management Research Group, Lawrence A. Pfaff, Personnel Decisions International Inc., Advanced Teamware Inc.

Source: R. Sharpe, "As Leaders, Women Rule," *BusinessWeek,* November 20, 2000, p. 75. Reprinted by permission of BusinessWeek.

Summary and Implications

1 **What is the difference between a manager and a leader?** Managers promote stability, while leaders press for change. Leaders provide vision and strategy; managers implement that vision and strategy, coordinate and staff the organization, and handle day-to-day problems.

2 **Are there specific traits, behaviours, and situations that affect how one leads?** Early leadership theories were concerned with supervision and sought to find out if there were ways to identify leaders. Trait theories examined whether any traits were universal among leaders. While there are some common traits, leaders are more different than the same in terms of traits. Emotional intelligence is one of the few traits that has been found to be extremely important for leadership success. Other research has tried to discover whether some behaviours create better leaders than others. The findings were mixed, suggesting that leaders need to be both task oriented and people oriented. The mixed findings led researchers to contingency theories that consider the effect of the situations in which leadership is applied. This research tells us that leaders need to adjust their behaviours depending on the situation and the needs of employees. Contingency theories were an important contribution to the study of leadership.

3 **How does a leader lead with vision?** The more recent approaches to leadership move away from the supervisory tasks of leaders and focus on vision-setting activities. These theories try to explain how certain leaders can achieve extraordinary performance levels from their followers, and they stress symbolic and emotionally appealing leadership behaviours. These leaders, known as *charismatic* or *transformational leaders,* inspire followers to go beyond their own self-interests for the good of the organization.

4 **Are there leadership roles for nonmanagers?** There are several approaches to being a leader even if one does not have a formal position of leadership. Mentoring is one way to be an informal leader. Mentors sponsor and support less-experienced

employees, coaching and counselling them about their jobs. With self-leadership, individuals and teams set goals, plan and implement tasks, evaluate performance, solve their own problems, and motivate themselves. The supervisor plays a much reduced role. A person can also act as an informal leader on a team. Providing leadership online to telecommuting and physically distant employees is another leadership role available to many people. Keeping online teams motivated can be a challenging role. Leading without authority means exhibiting leadership behaviour even though you do not have a formal position or title that might encourage others to obey.

5 **What are some of the contemporary issues in leadership?** One leadership challenge today is how to be an authentic leader. Authentic leaders know who they are, know what they believe in and value, and act on those values and beliefs openly and candidly. Leaders also face the demand to be moral in their leadership. Moral leadership comes from within the individual, and, in general, means treating people well and with respect. Another hot issue in leadership is the question of whether men and women use different leadership styles, and, if that is the case, whether one style is inherently superior to the other. The literature suggests two conclusions. First, the similarities between men and women tend to outweigh the differences. Second, what differences there are seem to relate to women's falling back on a more democratic leadership style and men's feeling more comfortable with a directive style. Yet another interesting issue in leadership is providing leadership online. Leadership demands are different when one does not have the opportunity for face-to-face interaction. For an increasing number of leaders, good interpersonal skills may include the ability to communicate support and leadership through written words on a computer screen and to read emotions in others' messages.

OB at Work

For Review

1. Trace the development of leadership research.

2. Describe the strengths and weaknesses of trait theories of leadership.

3. What is the Leadership Grid? Contrast its approach to leadership with the approaches of the Ohio State and Michigan studies.

4. What are the contingency variables in path-goal theory?

5. When might leaders be irrelevant?

6. What characteristics define an effective follower?

7. What are the differences between transactional and transformational leaders?

8. Describe the strengths and weaknesses of a charismatic leader.

9. What is moral leadership?

10. Why do you think effective female and male managers often exhibit similar traits and behaviours?

For Critical Thinking

1. Reconcile path-goal theory and substitutes for leadership.

2. What kind of activities could a full-time college or university student pursue that might lead to the perception that he or she is a charismatic leader? In pursuing those activities, what might the student do to enhance this perception?

3. Based on the low representation of women in upper management, to what extent do you think that organizations should actively promote women into the senior ranks of management?

4. Is there an ethical problem if leaders focus more on looking like leaders than actually being leaders? Discuss.

5. "Leaders make a real difference in an organization's performance." Build an argument in support of this statement. Then build an argument against this statement.

OB for You

- It is easy to imagine that theories of leadership are more important to those who are leaders or who plan in the near future to become leaders. However, leadership opportunities occur throughout an organization. You have no doubt seen student leaders who did not necessarily have any formal authority be extremely successful.

- Leaders are not born. They learn how to lead by paying attention to situations and what needs to be done.

- There is no one best way to lead. It is important to consider the situation and the needs of the people who will be led.

- Sometimes no leader is needed—the individuals in the group simply work well enough together that each takes turns at leadership without appointing a formal leader.

Point

Leaders Are Born

In North America, people are socialized to believe they can be whoever they want to be—and that includes being a leader.[103] While that makes for a nice children's tale (think *The Little Engine That Could*—"I think I can, I think I can"), the world's affairs and people's lives are not always wrapped in pretty little packages, and this is one example. Being an effective leader has more to do with what you are born with than what you do with what you have.

That leaders are born, not made, is not a new idea. Victorian-era historian Thomas Carlyle wrote, "History is nothing but the biography of a few great men." Although today we should modify this to include women, his point still rings true: Great leaders are what make teams, companies, and even countries great. Can anyone disagree that people like Lester Pearson and Pierre Trudeau were gifted political leaders? Or that Joan of Arc and George Patton were brilliant and courageous military leaders? Or that Henry Ford, Jack Welch, Steve Jobs, and Rupert Murdoch are, or were, gifted business leaders? As one reviewer of the literature put it, "Leaders are not like other people." These leaders are great leaders because they have the right stuff—stuff the rest of us don't have, or have in lesser quantities.

If you are not yet convinced, there is new evidence to support this position. A recent study of several hundred identical twins separated at birth found an amazing correlation in their ascendance into leadership roles. These twins were raised in totally different environments—some rich, some poor, some by educated parents, others by relatively uneducated parents, some in cities, others in small towns. But the researchers found that, despite their different environments, each pair of twins had striking similarities in terms of whether they became leaders.

Other research has found that shared environment—being raised in the same household, for example—has very little influence on leadership emergence. Despite what we might like to believe, the evidence is clear: A substantial part of leadership is a product of our genes. If we have the right stuff, we are destined to be effective leaders. If we have the wrong stuff, we are unlikely to excel in that role. Leadership cannot be for everyone, and we make a mistake in thinking that everyone is equally capable of being a good leader.

Counterpoint

Leaders Are Made

Of course, personal qualities and characteristics matter to leadership, as they do to most other behaviours.[104] But the real key is what you do with what you have.

First, if great leadership were merely the possession of a few key traits—say, intelligence and personality—we could simply give people a test and select the most intelligent, extraverted, and conscientious people to be leaders. But that would be a disaster. It helps to have these traits, but leadership is much too complex to be reduced to a simple formula of traits. As smart as Steve Jobs is, there are smarter and more extraverted people out there—thousands of them. That is not the essence of what makes him, or political or military leaders, great. It is a combination of factors—upbringing, early business experiences, learning from failure, and driving ambition. Second, great leaders tell us that the key to their leadership success is not the characteristics they had at birth, but what they learned along the way.

Take Warren Buffett, who is admired not only for his investing prowess but also as a leader and boss. Being a great leader, according to Buffett, is a matter of acquiring the right habits. "The chains of habit are too light to be noticed until they are too heavy to be broken," he says. Buffett argues that characteristics or habits such as intelligence, trustworthiness, and integrity are the most important to leadership—and at least the latter two can be developed. He says, "You need integrity, intelligence, and energy to succeed. Integrity is totally a matter of choice—and it is habit-forming."

Finally, this focus on "great men and great women" is not very productive. Even if it were true that great leaders were born, it's a very impractical approach to leadership. People need to believe in something, and one of those things is that they can improve themselves. If we walked around thinking we were just some accumulation of genetic markers and our entire life was just a stage in which our genes played themselves out, who would want to live that way? People like the optimistic story of *The Little Engine That Could* because we have a choice to think positively (we can become good leaders) or negatively (leaders are predetermined), and it's better to be positive.

OB *At Work*

Are You a Self-Manager?

To determine your self-management initiative, rate each of the following items, from 1 ("Never Do This") to 7 ("Always Do This").[105]

	Never Do This				Always Do This		
Planning							
1. I plan out my day before beginning to work.	1	2	3	4	5	6	7
2. I try to schedule my work in advance.	1	2	3	4	5	6	7
3. I plan my career carefully.	1	2	3	4	5	6	7
4. I come to work early to plan my day.	1	2	3	4	5	6	7
5. I use lists and agendas to structure my workday.	1	2	3	4	5	6	7
6. I set specific job goals on a regular basis.	1	2	3	4	5	6	7
7. I set daily goals for myself.	1	2	3	4	5	6	7
8. I try to manage my time.	1	2	3	4	5	6	7
Access Management							
1. I control the access subordinates have to me in order to get my work done.	1	2	3	4	5	6	7
2. I use a special place at work where I can work uninterrupted.	1	2	3	4	5	6	7
3. I hold my telephone calls when I need to get things done.	1	2	3	4	5	6	7
Catch-up Activities							
1. I come in early or stay late at work to prevent distractions from interfering with my work.	1	2	3	4	5	6	7
2. I take my work home with me to make sure it gets done.	1	2	3	4	5	6	7
3. I come in on my days off to catch up on my work.	1	2	3	4	5	6	7
Emotions Management							
1. I have learned to manage my aggressiveness with my subordinates.	1	2	3	4	5	6	7
2. My facial expression and conversational tone are important in dealing with subordinates.	1	2	3	4	5	6	7
3. It's important for me to maintain a "professional" manager-subordinate relationship.	1	2	3	4	5	6	7
4. I try to keep my emotions under control.	1	2	3	4	5	6	7

Scoring Key

Higher scores mean a higher degree of self-management. For the overall scale, scores of 100 or higher represent high scores. For each area, the following represent high scores: planning, scores of 48 or higher; access management, scores of 18 or higher; catch-up activities, scores of 18 or higher; and emotions management, scores of 24 or higher.

OB At Work

More Learning About Yourself Exercises

Additional self-assessments relevant to this chapter appear on MyOBLab (**www.pearsoned.ca/myoblab**).

II.B.1 What's My Leadership Style?

IV.E.5 What Is My LPC Score?

II.B.2 How Charismatic Am I?

IV.E.4 Am I an Ethical Leader?

When you complete the additional assessments, consider the following:

1. Am I surprised about my score?

2. Would my friends evaluate me similarly?

BREAKOUT **GROUP** EXERCISES

Form small groups to discuss the following topics, as assigned by your instructor:

1. Identify an example of someone you think of as a good leader (currently or in the past). What traits did he or she have? How did these traits differ from someone you identify as a bad leader?

2. Identify a situation in which you were in a leadership position (in a group, in the workplace, within your family, etc.). To what extent were you able to use a contingency approach to leadership? What made that easier or more difficult for you?

3. When you have worked in student groups, how frequently have leaders emerged in the group? What difficulties occur when leaders are leading peers? Are there ways to overcome these difficulties?

WORKING WITH **OTHERS** EXERCISE

Being Charismatic

From Concepts to Skills on pages 300–301 suggests how to become charismatic. In this exercise, you will use that information to practise projecting charisma.[106]

  a. The class should break into pairs.

  b. Student A's task is to "lead" Student B through a new-student orientation to your college or university. The orientation should last about 10 to 15 minutes. Assume Student B is new to your college or university and is unfamiliar with the campus. Student A should try to project himself or herself as charismatic.

  c. Roles now reverse and Student B's task is to "lead" Student A in a 10- to 15-minute program on how to study more effectively for college or university exams. Take a few minutes to think about what has worked well for you, and assume that Student A is a new student interested in improving his or her study habits. This time, Student B should try to project himself or herself as charismatic.

  d. When both role plays are complete, each pair should assess how well it did in projecting charisma and how it might improve.

ETHICAL **DILEMMA** EXERCISE

Do the Ends Justify the Means?

The power that comes from being a leader can be used for evil as well as for good.[107] When you assume the benefits of leadership, you also assume ethical burdens. But many highly successful leaders have relied on questionable tactics to achieve their ends. These include manipulation, verbal attacks, physical intimidation, lying, fear, and control. Consider a few examples:

- Bill Clinton was viewed as a charismatic US president. Yet he lied when necessary and "managed" the truth.

- Former Prime Minister Jean Chrétien successfully led Canada through 10 years of economic change. Those close to him were committed and loyal followers. Yet concerns were raised that he might have been willing to quietly spend millions of dollars in sponsorship money to manage the Quebec situation.

- Apple CEO Steve Jobs received backdated stock options: He was allowed to purchase shares of Apple at prices well below their market price at the time he was given the options. In fact, the options were backdated so that he could buy the shares at the lowest possible price. Former Apple CFO Fred Anderson argues that he warned Jobs about the accounting problems produced by backdating, but says he (Anderson) is the one who took the fall.

Should leaders be judged solely on their end achievements? Or do the means they choose also reflect on their leadership qualities? Are employees, shareholders, and society too quick to excuse leaders who use questionable means if they are successful in achieving their goals? Is it impossible for leaders to be ethical *and* successful?

CASE INCIDENT

The Kinder, Gentler Leader?

The stereotypical view of a CEO—tough-minded, dominant, and hyper-aggressive—may be giving way to a more sensitive image.[108] Nowhere is this shifting standard more apparent than at General Electric. There may be no CEO more revered for his leadership style than former CEO Jack Welch, a "tough guy," in his own words. Yet his handpicked successor, Jeff Immelt, is remarkable for his very different leadership style. Whereas Welch was intense, brash, and directive, Immelt was described by *Financial Times* as "unshakably polite, self-deprecating and relaxed."

Of course, Immelt is only one leader, and his success at GE is hardly assured. But he is far from alone in the set of seemingly sensitive CEOs. Colgate-Palmolive CEO Reuben Mark says of his leadership credo, "I have made it my business to be sure that nothing important or creative at Colgate-Palmolive is perceived as my idea." In an interesting contrast to former Chrysler CEO Bob

Nardelli, Chrysler deputy CEO Jim Press (formerly president of Toyota of America) embraces "servant leadership" and says one of his main functions is to "get out of the way" and support those who work with him.

A recent study of CEOs seems to suggest that this trend is spreading. The CEOs in its sample scored, on average, 12 points below average on tough-mindedness. Yes, that is below average. As one observer of the corporate world concludes, "The Jack Welch approach appears to be on the wane."

You might think a kinder, gentler approach works only for *Fortune* 500 CEOs, whose very job security might rely on glowing press coverage. However, consider the meteoric rise of Barack Obama—all the way from state senator to president in just five years. While a student at Harvard Law School, Obama was famous attorney Laurence Tribe's research assistant. Tribe said of Obama, "I've known senators, presidents. I've never known anyone with what seems to me more raw political talent. He just seems to have the surest way of calmly reaching across what are impenetrable barriers to many people."

Although some have argued that Obama's behaviour represents an emphasis of style over substance, it may be that after years of acrimonious political wars, people have started to consider the *how* as important as the *what*. It seems clear that part of Obama's popularity reflects people's desire for a kinder, gentler leader.

Questions

1. Do you think the kinder, gentler leader image is just a fad?

2. Do you think the kinder, gentler leadership approach works better in some situations than others? It is possible that Welch and Immelt are *both* effective leaders?

3. Do you think the leadership style of people like Immelt and Obama is a result of nature, nurture, or both? What factors can you think of to support your answer?

VIDEO CASE INCIDENT

CASE 8

Leadership at Kluster

Ben Kaufman is the CEO of Kluster, a web-based company that invites individuals and companies to send in ideas for new products.[109] At age 17, Kaufman started his career as a web designer, but soon became bored with that. At 18, he came up with a new idea for a lanyard with integrated headphones to be used with the iPod, and that was the start of mophie, a company that makes a line of iPod accessories.

At Macworld 2007, Kaufman tried something new: a community-based decision-making process he calls "the Illuminator project." At the show, he handed out sketch pads to attendees and invited them to design new products for mophie. Within three days, the company had three new products, and released them two months later. Although Kaufman considered that he was heading up a product development company, he eventually had to admit that all of his products were iPod accessories, and he did not want to be that limited. Kaufman sold the mophie brand in 2007 and launched Kluster.

Kluster gives consumers the opportunity to influence new products and marketing strategies using the approach established in the Illuminator project. At Kluster, instead of a bunch of marketing people trying to figure out new products and how to market new products, consumers are invited to share their ideas and give feedback, which brings them into the product development cycle.

Andres Arango is the design coordinator at Kluster. He coordinates the activity of Kaufman and the top designers at the company. Arango says that Kaufman has weird charisma and vision. When Kaufman originally told Arango about the Illuminator idea, Arango thought it was a little crazy. But he also thought the project was revolutionary, and that is why he joined the company.

Peter Wadsworth, an engineer at Kluster, says that Kaufman realizes that he is not a manager, and that is why Kaufman demoted himself to bring in a seasoned leader. The company needed good management in order to get venture capital and to make sales. Wadsworth says that Kaufman is confident, but Kaufman realized that other people just saw a teenage kid running amok with other people's money. Kaufman gets a lot of praise, but he does not have a big head about it. At the same time, he is not intimidated about meeting with celebrities or CEOs because he thinks everyone is equal.

Kaufman does not strive for consensus, and being popular is not a concern of his. He knows his limitations and skills. He will not tell someone else what to do with their skill set. His communication ability is not always the best, and he does not often praise employees for good work, but he does give them a lot of leeway to work on projects when he sees that they are doing a good job.

Kaufman does not hesitate when he makes decisions, and he is prepared to live with the consequences of his decisions. Wadsworth says he would not trust Kaufman to take care of his dog, but he does trust him to make good decisions on the big issues that affect the company.

(Continued)

OB At Work

Kaufman says that he closely supervises people in the company. He says he is a "madman." He wants to make sure that his employees are happy (or at least sort of happy). He does not know whether or not he is a good leader. He leaves that judgment to others.

Questions

1. What is the difference between leadership and management? Is Kaufman a leader? A manager? Both? Neither? Explain your reasoning.

2. Describe the leadership style of Ben Kaufman in terms of the behavioural theories of leadership described in this chapter. What are his leadership strengths and weaknesses?

3. Using a contingency theory of your choice, determine which style of leadership Ben Kaufman should be using.

4. What is the difference between transformational leaders and transactional leaders? What kind of leader is Kaufman? Explain your reasoning.

From Concepts to Skills

Practising to Be Charismatic

In order to be charismatic in your leadership style, you need to engage in the following behaviours:[110]

1. *Project a powerful, confident, and dynamic presence.* This has both verbal and nonverbal components. Use a captivating and engaging tone of voice. Convey confidence. Talk directly to people, maintain direct eye contact, and hold your body posture in a way that says you are sure of yourself. Speak clearly, avoid stammering, and avoid sprinkling your sentences with noncontent phrases such as "ahhh" and "you know."

2. *Articulate an overarching goal.* You need to share a vision for the future, develop an unconventional way of achieving the vision, and have the ability to communicate the vision to others.

   The vision is a clear statement of where you want to go and how you are going to get there. You need to persuade others that the achievement of this vision is in their self-interest.

   You need to look for fresh and radically different approaches to problems. The road to achieving your vision should be seen as novel but also appropriate to the context.

   Charismatic individuals not only have a vision; they are also able to get others to buy into it. The real power of Martin Luther King Jr. was not that he had a dream but that he could articulate it in terms that made it accessible to millions.

3. *Communicate high performance expectations and confidence in others' ability to meet these expectations.* You need to demonstrate your confidence in people by stating ambitious goals for them individually and as a group. You then convey absolute belief that they will achieve their expectations.

4. *Be sensitive to the needs of followers.* Charismatic leaders get to know their followers individually. You need to understand their individual needs and develop intensely personal relationships with each. This is done by encouraging them to express their points of view, being approachable, genuinely listening to and caring about their concerns, and asking questions so that followers can learn what is really important to them.

Practising Skills

You recently graduated from college with your degree in business administration. You have spent the past two summers working at London Mutual Insurance (LMI), filling in as an intern on a number of different jobs while employees took their vacations. You have received and accepted an offer to join LMI full time as supervisor of the policy-renewal department.

LMI is a large insurance company. In the headquarters office alone, where you will be working, there are more than 1500 employees. The company believes strongly in the personal development of its employees. This translates into a philosophy, emanating from the top executive offices, of trust and respect for all LMI employees. The company is also regularly at the top of most lists of "best companies to work for," largely because of its progressive work/life programs and strong commitment to minimizing layoffs.

In your new job, you will direct the activities of 18 policy-renewal clerks. Their jobs require little training and are highly routine. A clerk's responsibility is to ensure that renewal notices are sent on current policies, to tabulate any changes in premiums, to advise the sales division if a policy is to be cancelled as a result of nonresponse to renewal notices, and to answer questions and solve problems related to renewals.

The people in your work group range in age from 19 to 62, with a median age of 25. For the most part, they are high school graduates with little previous working experience. They earn between $1850 and $2400 a month. You will be replacing a long-time LMI employee, Jan Allison. Jan is retiring after 37 years with LMI, the past 14 spent as a policy-renewal supervisor. Because you spent a few weeks in Jan's group last summer, you are familiar with Jan's style and are acquainted with most of the department members. But people don't know you very well and are suspicious of the fact that you are fresh out of university and have little experience in the department. And the reality is that you got this job because management wanted someone with a post-secondary degree to oversee the department.

Your most vocal critic is Lillian Lantz. Lillian is well into her 50s, has been a policy-renewal clerk for over 12 years, and—as the person who has worked the longest in the department—carries a lot of weight with group members. It will be very hard to lead this department without Lillian's support.

Using your knowledge of leadership concepts, which leadership style would you choose and why?

Reinforcing Skills

1. Think of a group or team to which you currently belong or of which you have been a part. What type of leadership style did the leader of this group appear to exhibit? Give some specific examples of the types of leadership behaviours he or she used. Evaluate the leadership style. Was it appropriate for the group? Why or why not? What would you have done differently? Why?

2. Observe two sports teams (either college or professional—one that you consider successful and the other unsuccessful). What leadership styles appear to be used in these teams? Give some specific examples of the types of leadership behaviours you observe. How would you evaluate the leadership style? Was it appropriate for the team? Why or why not? To what degree do you think leadership style influenced the team's outcomes?

9 Decision Making, Creativity, and Ethics

When word went out that food poisoning might be linked to a Maple Leaf Foods meat processing plant, the company's CEO had to make a decision. Did Michael McCain act fast enough to alert the public, and were his actions socially responsible?

1 Is there a right way to make decisions?

2 How do people actually make decisions?

3 What factors affect group decision making?

4 How can we get more creative decisions?

5 What is ethics, and how can it be used for better decision making?

6 What is corporate social responsibility?

O n August 7, 2008, officials of Toronto-based Maple Leaf Foods were notified that there was a public health inquiry into some of its products.[1] On August 12, the Canadian Food Inspection Agency (CFIA) told the company it was launching a formal investigation into some products produced at its Toronto meat plant. Maple Leaf's distributors were told to take the questionable products off the market, but the public was not alerted to any potential problems.

It was not until four days later that the company's CEO, Michael McCain, was first notified that there was a problem, and by that time the CFIA had confirmed bacterial contamination in some Maple Leaf products. It took another week for Maple Leaf, through its CEO, to announce a massive product recall to the public.

McCain's decision about what to say to the public about the listeria contamination is just one example of the many decisions companies face every day. By acting quickly, he was praised for being honest with the public about what the company was doing to protect public health.

In this chapter, we describe how decisions in organizations are made, as well as how creativity is linked to decision making. We also look at the ethical and socially responsible aspects of decision making as part of our discussion. Decision making affects people at all levels of the organization, and it is engaged in by both individuals and groups. Therefore, we also consider the special characteristics of group decision making.

OB *Is for Everyone*

- Do people really consider every alternative when making a decision?
- Is it okay to use intuition when making decisions?
- Why is it that we sometimes make bad decisions?
- Why are some people more creative than others?
- Why do some people make more ethical decisions than others?

How Should Decisions Be Made?

decision The choice made from two or more alternatives.

problem A discrepancy between some current state of affairs and some desired state.

opportunity An occasion that gives rise to thoughts about new ways of proceeding.

rational Refers to choices that are consistent and value-maximizing within specified constraints.

rational decision-making model A six-step decision-making model that describes how individuals should behave in order to maximize some outcome.

A **decision** is the choice made from two or more alternatives. Decision making occurs as a reaction to a problem or an opportunity. A **problem** is a discrepancy between some current state of affairs and some desired state, requiring consideration of alternative courses of action.[2] An **opportunity** occurs when something unplanned happens, giving rise to thoughts about new ways of proceeding.

Whenever any of us make a decision, we have a process that we go through to help us arrive at that decision. Some of us take a very rational approach, with specific steps by which we analyze parts of the decision, others rely on intuition, and some just decide to put two or more alternatives into a hat and pull one out.

Knowing how to make decisions is an important part of everyday life. Below we consider various decision-making models that apply to both individual and group choices. (Later in the chapter, we discuss special aspects of group decision making.) We start with the *rational model*, which describes decision making in the ideal world, a situation that rarely exists. We then look at alternatives to the rational model and how decisions actually get made.

The Rational Decision-Making Process

The **rational** decision maker makes consistent, high-quality choices within specified constraints.[3] These choices are made following a six-step **rational decision-making model**.[4]

The Rational Model

The six steps in the rational decision-making model are listed in Exhibit 9-1.

First, the decision maker must *define the problem*. If you calculate your monthly expenses and find you are spending $50 more than your monthly earnings, you have defined a problem. Many poor decisions can be traced to the decision maker overlooking a problem or defining the wrong problem.

Once a decision maker has defined the problem, he or she needs to *identify the criteria* that will be important in solving the problem. In this step, the decision maker determines what is relevant in making the decision. This step brings the decision maker's interests, values, and personal preferences into the process. Identifying criteria is important because people can have different ideas about what is relevant. Also keep in mind that any factors not identified in this step are considered irrelevant to the decision maker.

To understand the types of criteria that might be used to make a decision, consider the many sponsorship requests the Toronto-based Canadian Imperial Bank of Commerce (CIBC) receives each year. In making a decision about whether or not to support a request, the bank considers the following criteria:[5]

- Strategic fit with CIBC's overall goals and objectives

- Ability to achieve youth customer–segment marketing objectives

- Tangible and intangible benefits of the proposal, such as goodwill, reputation, and cost/potential revenue

- Organizational impact

- Business risks (if any)

EXHIBIT 9-1   Steps in the Rational Decision-Making Model

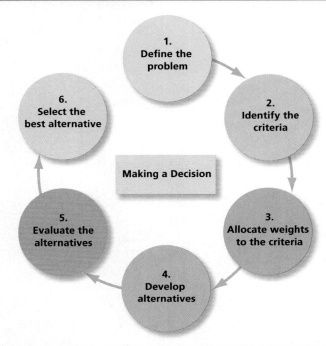

If the sponsorship request does not meet these criteria, it is not funded.

The criteria identified are rarely all equal in importance. So the third step requires the decision maker to *allocate weights to the criteria* in order to give them the correct priority in the decision.

The fourth step requires the decision maker to *develop alternatives* that could succeed in resolving the problem. No attempt is made in this step to appraise these alternatives, only to list them.

Once the alternatives are listed, the decision maker must *evaluate the alternatives*. The strengths and weaknesses of each alternative become evident as they are compared with the criteria and weights established in the second and third steps.

The final step in this model requires the decision maker to *select the best alternative*. This is done by evaluating each alternative against the weighted criteria and selecting the alternative with the highest total score.

Assumptions of the Model

The rational decision-making model we just described contains a number of assumptions.[6] Let's briefly outline those assumptions.

- *Problem clarity.* The problem is clear and unambiguous. The decision maker is assumed to have complete information regarding the decision situation.

- *Known options.* It is assumed the decision maker can identify all the relevant criteria and list all the workable alternatives. The decision maker is also aware of all possible implications of each alternative.

- *Clear preferences.* Rationality assumes that the criteria and alternatives can be ranked and weighted to reflect their importance.

- *Constant preferences.* It is assumed that the specific decision criteria are constant and that the weights assigned to them are stable over time.

- *No time or cost constraints.* The decision maker can obtain full information about criteria and alternatives because it is assumed that there are no time or cost constraints.

- *Maximum payoff.* The decision maker will choose the alternative that yields the highest perceived value.

Symantec CEO John Thompson made a decision in reaction to the problem of an explosion of Internet viruses. Thompson said, "About every 15 to 18 months, there's a new form of attack that makes old technologies less effective." So he decided to acquire 13 companies that specialize in products such as personal firewalls, intrusion detection, and early warning systems that protect everything from corporate intranets to consumer email inboxes.

How Do Individuals Actually Make Decisions?

When Michael McCain pondered what to say to the public about Maple Leaf's contaminated meat products, he carefully considered where to get advice.[7] "Going through the crisis, there are two advisers I've paid no attention to," he told reporters. "The first are the lawyers, and the second are the accountants. It's not about money or legal liability—this is about our being accountable for providing consumers with safe food."

McCain's actions suggest that he had genuine concern for public safety, and he apologized profusely to those who had been victims of the contamination. In putting consumers ahead of money and legal liability, he was seen to be doing the right thing for the public. When making a decision, how many different constituents should a CEO consider before taking action? Should shareholders have a say in the decision when public safety is at issue?

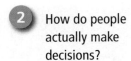
How do people actually make decisions?

Do decision makers actually follow the rational model? Do they carefully assess problems, identify all relevant criteria, use their creativity to identify all workable alternatives, and painstakingly evaluate every alternative to find an optimizing choice? When decision makers are faced with a simple problem and few alternative courses of action, and when the cost of searching out and evaluating alternatives is low, the rational model provides a fairly accurate description of the decision process.[8] However, such situations are the exception. Most decisions in the real world do not follow the rational model. For instance, people are usually content to find an acceptable or reasonable solution to their problem rather than an optimizing one. As such, decision makers generally make limited use of their creativity. Choices tend to be confined to the problem symptom and to the current alternative. As one expert in decision making has concluded: "Most significant decisions are made by judgment, rather than by a defined prescriptive model."[9] What's more, people are remarkably unaware of making suboptimal decisions.[10]

In the following sections, we identify areas where the reality of decision making conflicts with the rational model.[11] None of these ways of making decisions should be considered *irrational*; they are simply departures from the rational model that occur when information is unavailable or too costly to collect.

Problem Identification

Most of the decisions that get made reflect only the problems that decision makers see. Problems do not arrive with flashing neon lights to identify themselves. One person's *problem* may even be another person's *acceptable status quo*. So how do decision makers identify and select problems?

Problems that are visible tend to have a higher probability of being selected than ones that are important.[12] Why? We can offer at least two reasons. First, it's easier to recognize visible problems. They are more likely to catch a decision maker's attention. This explains why politicians are more likely to talk about the "crime problem" than the "illiteracy problem." Second, remember that we are concerned with decision making in organizations. Decision makers want to appear competent and "on top of problems." This motivates them to focus attention on problems that are visible to others.

Do not ignore the decision maker's self-interest. If a decision maker faces a conflict between selecting a problem that is important to the organization and one that is important to the decision maker, self-interest tends to win out.[13] This also ties in with the issue of visibility. It is usually in a decision maker's best interest to attack high-profile problems. It conveys to others that things are under control. Moreover, when the decision maker's performance is later reviewed, the evaluator is more likely to give a high rating to someone who has been aggressively attacking visible problems than to someone whose actions have been less obvious.

Bounded Rationality in Considering Alternatives

Do people really consider every alternative when making a decision?

When you considered which college or university to attend, did you look at every possible alternative? Did you carefully identify all the criteria that were important to your decision? Did you evaluate each alternative against the criteria in order to find the school that is best for you? The answer to these questions is probably "no." But don't feel bad, because few people select their educational institution this way.

It is difficult for individuals to identify and consider every possible alternative available to them. Realistically speaking, people are limited by their ability to interpret, process, and act on information. This is called **bounded rationality**.[14]

bounded rationality Limitations on a person's ability to interpret, process, and act on information.

Because of bounded rationality, individuals are not able to discover and consider every alternative for a decision. Instead, they identify a limited list of the most obvious choices. In most cases, these will include familiar criteria and previously tested solutions. Rather than carefully reviewing and evaluating each alternative in great detail, individuals will settle on an alternative that is "good enough"—one that meets an acceptable level of performance. The first alternative that meets the "good enough" criterion ends the search. So decision makers choose a final solution that **satisfices** rather than optimizes; that is, they seek a solution that is both satisfactory and sufficient. In practice this might mean that rather than interviewing 10 job candidates for a position, a manager interviews one at a time until one that is "good enough" is interviewed—that is, the first job candidate encountered who meets the minimum criteria for the job. The federal government has proposed this rule for its own hiring, as *OB in the Workplace* shows.

satisfice To provide a solution that is both satisfactory and sufficient.

IN THE WORKPLACE

Ottawa May Stop Hiring "Best Qualified"

Is hiring the "best-qualified" person too much work? Executives and middle managers working in the federal government seem to think so.[15] They argue that "being qualified and competent for a particular job should be enough" even though the person may not be the best possible candidate.

Public servants asked for the rules on hiring to be loosened so that they could actually start hiring and filling positions rather than spending so much time finding the "best-qualified" person. They find those searches excruciating and exhausting. When managers follow the federal guidelines for hiring, it can take six months or more to fill a position.

Steve Hindle, former president of the Professional Institute of the Public Service of Canada, explains why hiring someone who is qualified is probably good enough: "If people are honest, what they want is someone who is qualified, but the idea of finding the best? Do we have the time, tools and money needed to find the very best? You want someone competent and good and if they're the best, that's great."

However, not everyone agrees that changing the rules for hiring is a good idea. The public sector unions worry that favouritism may become more common. But they do agree that the current system has too much red tape.

Intuition

Is it okay to use intuition when making decisions?

Perhaps the least rational way of making decisions is to rely on intuition. **Intuitive decision making** is a nonconscious process created from distilled experience.[16] Its defining qualities are that it occurs outside conscious thought; it relies on holistic associations, or links between disparate pieces of information; it's fast; and it's affectively charged, meaning that it usually engages the emotions.[17]

intuitive decision making A nonconscious decision-making process created out of a person's many experiences.

Intuition is not rational, but that does not necessarily make it wrong. It does not necessarily operate in opposition to rational analysis; rather, the two can complement each other. Intuition can be a powerful force in decision making. Research on chess playing provides an excellent illustration of how intuition works.[18]

Novice chess players and grand masters were shown an actual, but unfamiliar, chess game with about 25 pieces on the board. After 5 or 10 seconds, the pieces were removed, and each subject was asked to reconstruct the pieces by position. On average, the grand master could put 23 or 24 pieces in their correct squares, while the novice was able to replace only 6. Then the exercise was changed. This time, the pieces were placed randomly on the board. Again, the novice got only about 6 correct, but so did the grand master! The second exercise demonstrated that the grand master did not have a better memory than the novice. What the grand master *did* have was the ability, based on the experience of having played thousands of chess games, to recognize patterns and clusters of pieces that occur on chessboards in the course of games. Studies also show that decisions made in seconds exhibit only a moderately lower level of skill than decisions made when playing a game under tournament conditions, where decisions can take half an hour or longer. The expert's experience allows him or her to recognize the pattern in a situation and draw on previously learned information associated with that pattern to arrive at a decision quickly. The result is that the intuitive decision maker can decide rapidly based on what appears to be very limited information.

For most of the twentieth century, experts believed that decision makers' use of intuition was irrational or ineffective. That is no longer the case.[19] There is growing recognition that rational analysis has been overemphasized and that, in certain instances, relying on intuition can improve decision making.[20] Those who use intuition effectively often rely on their experiences to help guide and assess their intuitions. That is why many managers are able to rely on intuition.

A study of 60 experienced professionals holding high-level positions in major US organizations found that many of them used intuition to help them make workplace decisions.[21] Twelve percent said they always used it, while 47 percent said they often used intuition. Only 10 percent said they rarely or seldom used intuition. More than 90 percent of managers said they were likely to use a mix of intuition and data analysis when making decisions.

When asked the types of decisions for which they most often used intuition, 40 percent reported that they used it to make people-related decisions such as hiring, performance appraisal, harassment complaints, and safety issues. The managers said they also used intuition for quick or unexpected decisions so they could avoid delays. They also were more likely to rely on intuition in novel situations that had a lot of uncertainty.

The results from this study suggest that intuitive decisions are best applied when time is short, when policies, rules, and guidelines do not give clear-cut advice, when there is a great deal of uncertainty, and when detailed numerical analysis needs a check and balance.

While intuition can be invaluable in making good decisions, we cannot rely on it too much. Because it is so unquantifiable, it's hard to know when our hunches are right or wrong. The key is not to either abandon or rely solely on intuition, but to supplement it with evidence and good judgment.

Judgment Shortcuts

Why is it that we sometimes make bad decisions?

Decision makers engage in bounded rationality, but an accumulating body of research tells us that decision makers also allow systematic biases and errors to creep into their judgments.[22] These come from attempts to find shortcuts in the decision process. To minimize effort and avoid difficult trade-offs, people tend to rely too heavily on experience, impulses, gut feelings, and convenient rules of thumb. In many instances, these shortcuts are helpful. However, they can lead to distortions of rationality, as *OB in the Street* shows.

OB IN THE STREET

Penalty Kick Decisions

Should you stand still or leap into action? This is the classic question facing a goalie in a faceoff against a midfielder for a penalty kick.[23] Ofer H. Azar, a lecturer in the School of Management at Ben-Gurion University in Israel, finds that goalies often make the wrong decision.

Why? The goalie tries to anticipate where the ball will go after the kick. There is only a split second to do anything after the kick, so anticipating and acting seem like a good decision.

Azar became interested in studying goalie behaviour after realizing that the "incentives are huge" for the goalie to get it right. "Goalkeepers face penalty kicks regularly, so they are not only high-motivated decision makers, but also very experienced ones," he explains. That said, 80 percent of penalty kicks score, so goalies are in a difficult situation at that instant when the kick goes off.

Azar's study found that goalies rarely stayed in the centre of the net as the ball was fired (just 6.3 percent of the time). But staying in the centre is actually the best strategy. Goalies halted penalty kicks when staying in the centre 33.3 percent of the time. They were successful only 14.2 percent of the time when they moved left and only 12.6 percent of the time when they moved right.

Azar argues that the results show that there is a "bias for action," explaining that goalies think they will feel worse if they do *nothing* and miss, than if they do *something* and miss. This bias then clouds their judgment, encouraging them to move to one side or the other, rather than just staying in the centre, where the odds are actually more in their favour.

In what follows, we discuss some of the most common judgment shortcuts to alert you to mistakes that are often made when making decisions.

Overconfidence Bias

It's been said that "no problem in judgment and decision making is more prevalent and more potentially catastrophic than overconfidence."[24]

When we are given factual questions and asked to judge the probability that our answers are correct, we tend to be far too optimistic. This is known as **overconfidence bias**. For instance, studies have found that when people say they are 65 to 70 percent confident that they are right, they are actually correct only about 50 percent of the time.[25] And when they say they are 100 percent sure, they tend to be right about 70 to 85 percent of the time.[26]

overconfidence bias Error in judgment that arises from being far too optimistic about one's own performance.

From an organizational standpoint, one of the most interesting findings related to overconfidence is that those individuals whose intellectual and interpersonal abilities are *weakest* are most likely to overestimate their performance and ability.[27] So as managers and employees become more knowledgeable about an issue, they become less likely to display overconfidence.[28] Overconfidence is most likely to surface when organizational members are considering issues or problems that are outside their area of expertise.[29]

Anchoring Bias

The **anchoring bias** is a tendency to fixate on initial information and fail to adequately adjust for subsequent information.[30] The anchoring bias occurs because our mind appears to give a disproportionate amount of emphasis to the first information

anchoring bias A tendency to fixate on initial information and fail to adequately adjust for subsequent information.

it receives.[31] Anchors are widely used by people in professions where persuasion skills are important—such as advertising, management, politics, real estate, and law. For instance, in a mock jury trial, the plaintiff's attorney asked one set of jurors to make an award in the range of $15 million to $50 million. The plaintiff's attorney asked another set of jurors for an award in the range of $50 million to $150 million. Consistent with the anchoring bias, the median awards were $15 million and $50 million, respectively.[32]

Consider the role of anchoring in negotiations. Any time a negotiation takes place, so does anchoring. As soon as someone states a number, your ability to ignore that number has been compromised. For instance, when a prospective employer asks how much you were making in your prior job, your answer typically anchors the employer's offer. You may want to keep this in mind when you negotiate your salary, but remember to set the anchor only as high as you realistically can.

Confirmation Bias

confirmation bias The tendency to seek out information that reaffirms past choices and to discount information that contradicts past judgments.

The rational decision-making process assumes that we objectively gather information. But we do not. We *selectively* gather it. The **confirmation bias** represents a specific case of selective perception. We seek out information that reaffirms our past choices, and we discount information that contradicts them.[33] We also tend to accept at face value information that confirms our preconceived views, while we are critical and skeptical of information that challenges these views. Therefore, the information we gather is typically biased toward supporting views we already hold. This confirmation bias influences where we go to collect evidence because we tend to seek out sources most likely to tell us what we want to hear. It also leads us to give too much weight to supporting information and too little to contradictory information.

Availability Bias

availability bias The tendency for people to base their judgments on information that is readily available to them rather than on complete data.

The **availability bias** is the tendency for people to base their judgments on information that is readily available to them rather than on complete data. Events that evoke emotions, that are particularly vivid, or that have occurred more recently tend to be more available in our memories. As a result, we tend to overestimate unlikely events such as an airplane crash, compared with more likely events such as car crashes. The availability bias can also explain why managers, when doing annual performance appraisals, tend to give more weight to recent behaviours of an employee than to those behaviours of six or nine months ago.

Escalation of Commitment

escalation of commitment An increased commitment to a previous decision despite clear evidence suggesting that decision may have been incorrect.

Some decision makers escalate commitment to a failing course of action.[34] **Escalation of commitment** refers to staying with a decision even when there is clear evidence that it's wrong. For example, a friend has been working for the same employer for four years. Although she admits that things are not going too well at work, she is determined to stay, rather than find another job. When asked to explain this seemingly nonrational choice of action, she responds: "I put a lot of time and effort into learning how to do this job."

Individuals escalate commitment to a failing course of action when they view themselves as responsible for the failure. That is, they "throw good money after bad" to demonstrate that their initial decision was not wrong and to avoid having to admit they made a mistake.

Many organizations have suffered large losses because a manager was determined to prove his or her original decision was right by continuing to commit resources to what was a lost cause from the beginning.

Randomness Error

Human beings have a lot of difficulty dealing with chance. Most of us like to believe we have some control over our world and our destiny. Although we undoubtedly can control a good part of our future through rational decision making, the truth is that the world will always contain random events. Our tendency to believe we can predict the outcome of random events is the **randomness error**.

Decision making becomes impaired when we try to create meaning out of random events. One of the most serious impairments occurs when we turn imaginary patterns into superstitions.[35] These can be completely contrived ("I never make important decisions on Friday the 13th") or evolve from a certain pattern of behaviour that has been reinforced previously (Tiger Woods often wears a red shirt during the final round of a golf tournament because he won many junior golf tournaments while wearing red shirts). Although many of us engage in some superstitious behaviour, it can be debilitating when it affects daily judgments or biases major decisions. At the extreme, some decision makers become controlled by their superstitions—making it nearly impossible for them to change routines or objectively process new information.

> **randomness error** The tendency of individuals to believe that they can predict the outcome of random events.

Winner's Curse

The **winner's curse** describes the tendency for the winning participants in a competitive auction to pay too much for the item won. Some buyers will underestimate the value of an item, and others will overestimate it, and the highest bidder (the winner) will be the one who overestimated the most. Therefore, unless the bidders dramatically undervalue, there is a good chance that the "winner" will pay too much.

Logic predicts that the winner's curse gets stronger as the number of bidders increases. The more bidders there are, the more likely that some of them have greatly overestimated the good's value. So, beware of auctions with an unexpectedly large number of bidders.

> **winner's curse** The tendency for the winning participants in an auction to pay too much for the item won.

Hindsight Bias

The **hindsight bias** is the tendency to believe falsely, after the outcome of an event is actually known, that we could have accurately predicted that outcome.[36] When something happens and we have accurate feedback on the outcome, we seem to be pretty good at concluding that the outcome was relatively obvious. As Malcolm Gladwell, author of *Blink*, *Outliers*, and *The Tipping Point*, writes, "What is clear in hindsight is rarely clear before the fact. It's an obvious point, but one that nonetheless bears repeating."[37]

The hindsight bias reduces our ability to learn from the past. It permits us to think that we are better at making predictions than we really are and can result in our being more confident about the accuracy of future decisions than we have a right to be. If, for instance, your actual predictive accuracy is only 40 percent, but you think it's 90 percent, you are likely to become falsely overconfident and less vigilant in questioning your predictive skills.

OB in Action—Reducing Biases and Errors in Decision Making provides you with some ideas for improving your decision making. To learn more about your decision-making style, refer to the *Learning About Yourself Exercise* on pages 334–335.

> **hindsight bias** The tendency to believe falsely, after the outcome of an event is actually known, that one could have accurately predicted that outcome.

OB in ACTION

Reducing Biases and Errors in Decision Making

→ **Focus on goals**. Clear goals make decision making easier and help you eliminate options that are inconsistent with your interests.

→ **Look for information that disconfirms** your **beliefs**. When we deliberately consider various ways we could be wrong, we challenge our tendencies to think we are smarter than we actually are.

→ **Don't create meaning** out of random events. Ask yourself if patterns can be meaningfully explained or whether they are merely coincidence. Don't attempt to create meaning out of coincidence.

→ **Increase** your **options**. The more alternatives you can generate, and the more diverse those alternatives, the greater your chance of finding an outstanding one.[38]

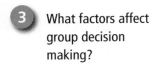

What factors affect group decision making?

Group Decision Making

While a variety of decisions in both life and organizations are made at the individual level, the belief—as shown by the use of juries—that two heads are better than one has long been accepted as a basic component of North America's and many other countries' legal systems. This belief has expanded to the point that, today, many decisions in organizations are made by groups, teams, or committees. In this section, we will review group decision making and compare it with individual decision making.

Groups vs. the Individual

Decision-making groups may be widely used in organizations, but does that mean group decisions are preferable to those made by an individual alone? The answer to this question depends on a number of factors we consider below.[39] See Exhibit 9-2 for a summary of our major points.

Strengths of Group Decision Making

Groups generate *more complete information and knowledge.* By combining the resources of several individuals, groups bring more input into the decision process. Groups can bring an *increased diversity of views* to the decision process, and, thus, the opportunity to consider more approaches and alternatives. In terms of decision outcomes, the evidence indicates that a group will almost always outperform even the best individual. So groups generate *higher-quality decisions.*[40] Group decisions also tend to be more *accurate.* If *creativity* is important, groups tend to be more creative in their decisions than individuals.[41] Groups also lead to *increased acceptance of a solution.* Many decisions fail after the final choice is made because people do not accept them. Group members who participated in making a decision are likely to support the decision enthusiastically and encourage others to accept it.

Weaknesses of Group Decision Making

Despite the advantages noted, group decisions involve certain drawbacks. First, they are *time-consuming.* Groups typically take more time to reach a solution than an individual would. Thus, group decisions are not always efficient. Second, there are *conformity pressures* in groups. The desire of group members to be accepted and considered an asset to the group can result in quashing any overt disagreement. Third, group discussion can be *dominated by one or a few members.* If this dominant coalition is composed of low- and medium-ability members, the group's overall effectiveness will diminish. Finally, group decisions suffer from *ambiguous responsibility.* In an individual

EXHIBIT 9-2 Group vs. Individual Decision Making		
Criteria of Effectiveness	**Groups**	**Individuals**
More complete information	✔	
Diversity of views	✔	
Decision quality	✔	
Accuracy	✔	
Creativity	✔	
Degree of acceptance	✔	
Speed		✔
Efficiency		✔

decision, it is clear who is accountable for the final outcome. In a group decision, the responsibility of any single member is watered down.

Effectiveness and Efficiency

Whether groups are more effective than individuals depends on the criteria you use to define effectiveness. In terms of *accuracy*, group decisions are generally more accurate than the decisions of the average individual in a group, but they are less accurate than the judgments of the most accurate group member.[42] If decision effectiveness is defined in terms of *speed*, individuals are superior. If *creativity* is important, groups tend to be more effective than individuals. And if effectiveness means the degree of *acceptance* the final solution achieves, the nod again goes to the group.[43]

But effectiveness cannot be considered without also assessing efficiency. In terms of efficiency, groups almost always stack up as a poor second to the individual decision maker. With few exceptions, group decision making consumes more work hours than if an individual were to tackle the same problem alone. The exceptions tend to be the instances in which, to achieve comparable quantities of diverse input, the single decision maker must spend a great deal of time reviewing files and talking to people. Because groups can include members from diverse areas, the time spent searching for information can be reduced. However, as we noted, these advantages in efficiency tend to be the exception. Groups are generally less efficient than individuals. In deciding whether to use groups, then, consideration should be given to assessing whether increases in effectiveness are more than enough to offset the reductions in efficiency. This chapter's *Working With Others Exercise* on pages 336–337 gives you an opportunity to assess the effectiveness and efficiency of group decision making versus individual decision making.

Groupthink and Groupshift

Two by-products of group decision making have received a considerable amount of attention by organizational behaviour (OB) researchers: groupthink and groupshift. As we will show, these two phenomena have the potential to affect the group's ability to appraise alternatives objectively and arrive at quality solutions.

Groupthink

Have you ever felt like speaking up in a meeting, classroom, or informal group, but decided against it? One reason might have been shyness. On the other hand, you might have been a victim of **groupthink**, a phenomenon in which group pressures for conformity prevent the group from critically appraising unusual, minority, or unpopular views. It describes a deterioration in an individual's mental efficiency, reality testing, and moral judgment as a result of group pressures.[44]

We have all seen the symptoms of the groupthink phenomenon:[45]

groupthink A phenomenon in which group pressures for conformity prevent the group from critically appraising unusual, minority, or unpopular views.

- *Illusion of invulnerability.* Group members become overconfident among themselves, allowing them to take extraordinary risks.

- *Assumption of morality.* Group members believe highly in the moral rightness of the group's objectives and do not feel the need to debate the ethics of their actions.

- *Rationalization.* Group members rationalize any resistance to the assumptions they have made. No matter how strongly the evidence may contradict their basic assumptions, members behave so as to reinforce those assumptions continually.

- *Stereotyping outgroups.* People outside the group who criticize decisions and actions are viewed as "enemies" who do not know what they are talking about.

- *Minimized doubts.* Group members who have doubts or hold differing points of view seek to avoid deviating from what appears to be group consensus by keeping silent about misgivings and even minimizing to themselves the importance of their doubts.

- *Illusion of unanimity.* If someone does not speak, it's assumed that he or she is in full agreement. In other words, abstention becomes viewed as a yes vote.

- *Mindguards.* One or more members of the team become self-appointed guardians to make sure that negative or inconsistent information does not reach team members.

- *Peer pressure.* Group members apply direct pressure on those who momentarily express doubts about any of the group's shared views or who question the alternative favoured by the majority.

One place where groupthink has been shown to happen is among jurors, as *OB in the Street* shows.

OB IN THE STREET

Groupthink in an Enron Jury

Can pressure cause people to change their decision? Although most of us view Enron as the very symbol of corporate corruption, not every Enron employee behaved unethically.[46] Twenty former Enron employees—most notably Ken Lay, Jeff Skilling, and Andrew Fastow—were either convicted of or pleaded guilty to fraudulent behaviour. The conviction of another Enron executive you have probably never heard of—former broadband finance chief Kevin Howard—provides a fascinating, and disturbing, glimpse into how juries use group pressure to reach decisions.

Howard's first trial ended in a hung jury. In the second trial, he was found guilty of conspiracy, fraud, and falsifying records. However, shortly after his conviction, two jurors and two alternate jurors said they were pressured by other jurors to reach a unanimous decision even though they believed Howard was innocent. Juror Ann Marie Campbell said, in a sworn statement, "There was just so much pressure to change my vote that I felt like we had to compromise and give in to the majority because I felt like there was no other choice." Campbell said that at one point a male juror tried to "grab her by the shoulders" to convince her, and another "banged his fist on the table during deliberations." Another jury member said, "There was an atmosphere of 'Let's fry them.'"

On appeal, a judge threw out Howard's conviction, based, in part, on the earlier judge's instruction to the convicting jury that pressured them to reach a unanimous decision. The Kevin Howard case shows how strong groupthink pressures can be, and the degree to which individuals can be pressured to give in to the majority.

Does groupthink attack all groups? No. It seems to occur most often where there is a clear group identity, where members hold a positive image of their group, which they want to protect, and where the group perceives a collective threat to this positive image.[47] So groupthink is less a way to suppress dissenters than a means for a group to protect its positive image. This chapter's *Case Incident—The Dangers of Groupthink* on pages 338–339 provides instances when groupthink proved to be harmful.

What can managers do to minimize groupthink?[48]

- *Monitor group size.* People grow more intimidated and hesitant as group size increases, and, although there is no magic number that will eliminate group-think, individuals are likely to feel less personal responsibility when groups get larger than about 10.

- *Encourage group leaders to play an impartial role.* Leaders should actively seek input from all members and avoid expressing their own opinions, especially in the early stages of deliberation.

- *Appoint one group member to play the role of devil's advocate.* This member's role is to overtly challenge the majority position and offer divergent perspectives.

- *Stimulate active discussion of diverse alternatives* to encourage dissenting views and more objective evaluations.

While considerable anecdotal evidence indicates the negative implications of groupthink in organizational settings, not much actual empirical work has been con-ducted in organizations in this area.[49] In fact, researchers of groupthink have been criti-cized for suggesting that its effect is uniformly negative[50] and for overestimating the link between the decision-making process and its outcome.[51] A study of groupthink using 30 teams from five large corporations suggests that elements of groupthink may affect decision making differently. For instance, the illusion of invulnerability, belief in inherent group morality, and the illusion of unanimity were positively associated with team performance.[52] The most recent research suggests that we should be aware of groupthink conditions that lead to poor decisions, while realizing that not all group-think symptoms harm decision making.

Groupshift

Evidence suggests that there are differences between the decisions groups make and the decisions that might be made by individual members within the group.[53] In some cases, group decisions are more conservative than individual decisions. More often, group decisions are riskier than individual decisions.[54] In either case, participants have engaged in **groupshift**, a phenomenon in which the initial positions of individual group members become exaggerated because of the interactions of the group.

What appears to happen in groups is that the discussion leads to a significant shift in the positions of members toward a more extreme position in the direction in which they were already leaning before the discussion. So conservative types become more cautious and more aggressive types assume more risk. The group discussion tends to exaggerate the initial position of individual members.

Groupshift can be viewed as a special case of groupthink. The group's decision reflects the dominant decision-making norm that develops during the group's discus-sion. Whether the shift in the group's decision is toward greater caution or more risk depends on the dominant pre-discussion norm.

The greater shift toward risk has generated several explanations for the phenomenon.[55] It has been argued, for instance, that the discussion creates familiarity among the members. As they become more comfortable with each other, they also become bolder and more daring. Another argument is that our society values risk, that we admire individuals who are willing to take risks, and that group discussion motivates members to show that they are at least as willing as their peers to take risks. The most plausible explanation of the shift toward risk, however, seems to be that the group diffuses responsibility. Group decisions free any single member from accountability for the group's final choice. Greater risk can be taken because even if the decision fails, no one member can be held wholly responsible.

groupshift A phenomenon in which the initial positions of individual group members become exaggerated because of the interactions of the group.

How should you use the findings on groupshift? You should recognize that group decisions exaggerate the initial position of the individual members, that the shift has been shown more often to be toward greater risk, and that whether a group will shift toward greater risk or caution is a function of the members' pre-discussion inclinations.

Group Decision-Making Techniques

Groups can use a variety of techniques to stimulate decision making. We outline four of them below.

Interacting Groups

interacting groups Typical groups, in which members interact with each other face to face.

The most common form of group decision making takes place in **interacting groups**. In these groups, members meet face to face and rely on both verbal and nonverbal interaction to communicate with each other. All kinds of groups use this technique frequently, from groups organized to develop a class project, to a work team, to a senior management team. But as our discussion of groupthink demonstrates, interacting groups often censor themselves and pressure individual members toward conformity of opinion. *Brainstorming*, the *nominal group technique*, and *electronic meetings* have been proposed as ways to reduce many of the problems inherent in the traditional interacting group.

Brainstorming

brainstorming An idea-generation process that specifically encourages any and all alternatives while withholding any criticism of those alternatives.

Brainstorming is meant to overcome pressures for conformity within the interacting group that prevent the development of creative alternatives.[56] It achieves this by using an idea-generation process that specifically encourages any and all alternatives while withholding any criticism of those alternatives.

You have no doubt engaged in brainstorming when you have tried to come up with ideas for how to present a project for class. In a typical brainstorming session, a half-dozen to a dozen people sit around a table. The group leader, or even another team member, states the problem in a clear manner so that all participants understand it. Members then "freewheel" as many alternatives as they can in a given period of time. No criticism is allowed, and all the alternatives are recorded for later discussion and analysis. With one idea stimulating others and judgments of even the most bizarre suggestions withheld until later, group members are encouraged to "think the unusual."

A more recent variant of brainstorming is electronic brainstorming, which is done by people interacting on computers to generate ideas. For example, Calgary-based Jerilyn Wright & Associates uses electronic brainstorming to help clients design their workspaces through software that has been adapted for office-space design.[57]

Brainstorming may indeed generate ideas—but not in a very efficient manner. Research consistently shows that individuals working alone generate more ideas than a group in a brainstorming session. Why? One of the primary reasons is because of "production blocking." In other words, when people are generating ideas in a group, there are many people talking at once, which blocks the thought process and eventually impedes the sharing of ideas.[58] Brainstorming, we should also note, is merely a process for generating ideas. The following two techniques go further by offering methods of actually arriving at a preferred solution.[59]

Nominal Group Technique

nominal group technique A group decision-making method in which individual members meet face to face to pool their judgments in a systematic but independent fashion.

The **nominal group technique** restricts discussion or interpersonal communication during the decision-making process; thus the term *nominal* (which means "in name only"). Group members are all physically present, as in a traditional committee meeting, but members operate independently. Specifically, a problem is presented and then the following steps take place:

- Members meet as a group, but before any discussion takes place each member independently writes down his or her ideas about the problem.

- After this silent period, each member presents one idea to the group. Group members take turns presenting a single idea until all ideas have been presented and recorded. No discussion takes place until all ideas have been recorded.

- The group then discusses the ideas for clarity and evaluates them.

- Each group member silently and independently ranks the ideas. The idea with the highest overall ranking determines the final decision.

The steps of the nominal group technique are illustrated in Exhibit 9-3. The chief advantage of this technique is that it permits the group to meet formally but does not restrict independent thinking as the interacting group does.

A number of studies suggest that brainstorming by nominal groups is more effective than brainstorming by interacting groups. However, recent research suggests that nominal groups generate more ideas and more original ideas, but not necessarily more quality ideas.[60] Research generally shows that nominal groups outperform brainstorming groups.[61]

Electronic Meetings

The most recent approach to group decision making blends the nominal group technique with sophisticated computer technology.[62] It's called the computer-assisted group, or **electronic meeting**. Once the technology is in place, the concept is simple. As many as 50 people sit around a horseshoe-shaped table, which is empty except for a series of computer terminals. Issues are presented to the participants, and they type their responses onto their computer monitors. Individual comments, as well as total votes, are displayed on a projection screen in the room.

The major advantages of the electronic meeting are anonymity, honesty, and speed. Participants can anonymously type any messages they want, and they flash on the screen for all to see at the push of buttons on participants' keyboards. This type of meeting also allows people to be brutally honest without penalty. In addition, it is fast because chit-chat is eliminated, discussions do not digress, and many participants can "talk" at once without stepping on one another's toes. The future of group meetings undoubtedly will include extensive use of this technology.

The early evidence, however, indicates that electronic meetings do not achieve most of their proposed benefits. Evaluations of numerous studies found that electronic meetings actually led to *decreased* group effectiveness, required *more* time to complete tasks, and resulted in *reduced* member satisfaction compared with face-to-face groups.[63]

electronic meeting A meeting in which members interact on computers, allowing for anonymity of comments and aggregation of votes.

EXHIBIT 9-3 Nominal Group Technique

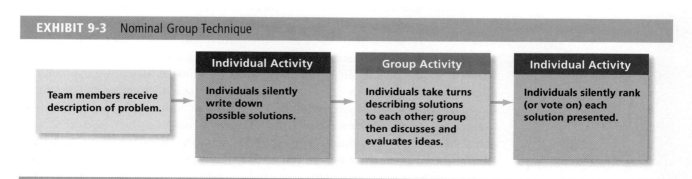

| Team members receive description of problem. | **Individual Activity** Individuals silently write down possible solutions. | **Group Activity** Individuals take turns describing solutions to each other; group then discusses and evaluates ideas. | **Individual Activity** Individuals silently rank (or vote on) each solution presented. |

EXHIBIT 9-4 Evaluating Group Effectiveness				
	Type of Group			
Effectiveness Criteria	**Interacting**	**Brainstorming**	**Nominal**	**Electronic**
Number and quality of ideas	Low	Moderate	High	High
Social pressure	High	Low	Moderate	Low
Money costs	Low	Low	Low	High
Speed	Moderate	Moderate	Moderate	Moderate
Task orientation	Low	High	High	High
Potential for interpersonal conflict	High	Low	Moderate	Low
Commitment to solution	High	Not applicable	Moderate	Moderate
Development of group cohesiveness	High	High	Moderate	Low

Source: Based on J. K. Murnighan, "Group Decision Making: What Strategies Should You Use?" *Academy of Management Review,* February 1981, p. 61.

Nevertheless, current enthusiasm for computer-mediated communications suggests that this technology is here to stay and is likely to increase in popularity in the future.

Each of these four group decision techniques has its own strengths and weaknesses. The choice of one technique over another depends on what criteria you want to emphasize and the cost–benefit trade-off. For instance, as Exhibit 9-4 indicates, an interacting group is good for achieving commitment to a solution, brainstorming develops group cohesiveness, the nominal group technique is an inexpensive means for generating a large number of ideas, and electronic meetings minimize social pressures and conflicts.

Creativity in Organizational Decision Making

④ How can we get more creative decisions?

creativity The ability to produce novel and useful ideas.

Although following the steps of the rational decision-making model will often improve decisions, a rational decision maker also needs **creativity**; that is, the ability to produce novel and useful ideas.[64] These are ideas that are different from what has been done before but that are appropriate to the problem or opportunity presented.

Why is creativity important to decision making? It allows the decision maker to more fully appraise and understand the problem, including seeing problems others cannot see. Such thinking is becoming more important.

Creative Potential

Most people have creative potential they can use when confronted with a decision-making problem. But to unleash that potential, they have to get out of the psychological ruts many of us fall into and learn how to think about a problem in divergent ways.

People differ in their inherent creativity, and exceptional creativity is scarce. Albert Einstein, Marie Curie, Pablo Picasso, and Wolfgang Amadeus Mozart were individuals of exceptional creativity. In more recent times, Canadian artist Emily Carr, legendary Canadian concert pianist Glenn Gould, and Canadian author Margaret Atwood have been noted for the creative contributions they have made to their fields. But what about the typical individual? People who score high on openness to experience (see Chapter 2), for example, are more likely than others to be creative. Intelligent people also are more likely than others to be creative.[65] Other traits associated with creative people include independence, self-confidence, risk-taking, a positive core

Unleashing the creative potential of employees is crucial to the continued success of video game maker Electronic Arts in developing innovative entertainment software. Designed to stimulate employees' creativity, EA's work environment is casual and fun, and employees are given the freedom to manage their own work time. To recharge their creativity, they can take a break from their projects and relax at a serenity pool, work out in a state-of-the-art fitness centre, play pool or table tennis in a games room, or play basketball, soccer, or beach volleyball in an outdoor recreation area.

self-evaluation, tolerance for ambiguity, a low need for structure, and perseverance in the face of frustration.[66] A study of the lifetime creativity of 461 men and women found that fewer than 1 percent were exceptionally creative.[67] However, 10 percent were highly creative and about 60 percent were somewhat creative. This suggests that most of us have creative potential; we just need to learn to unleash it.

From Concepts to Skills on pages 340–341 provides suggestions on how you can become more effective at solving problems creatively.

Three-Component Model of Creativity

Why are some people more creative than others?

Given that most people have the capacity to be at least somewhat creative, what can individuals and organizations do to stimulate employee creativity? The best answer to this question lies in the **three-component model of creativity**.[68] Based on an extensive body of research, this model proposes that individual creativity essentially requires expertise, creative-thinking skills, and intrinsic task motivation (see Exhibit 9-5 on page 320). Studies confirm that the higher the level of each of these three components, the higher the creativity.

three-component model of creativity The proposition that individual creativity requires expertise, creative-thinking skills, and intrinsic task motivation.

Expertise is the foundation for all creative work. Film writer, producer, and director Quentin Tarantino spent his youth working in a video rental store, where he built up an encyclopedic knowledge of movies. The potential for creativity is enhanced when individuals have abilities, knowledge, proficiencies, and similar expertise in their field of endeavour. For example, you would not expect someone with a minimal knowledge of programming to be very creative as a software engineer.

The second component is *creative-thinking skills*. This encompasses personality characteristics associated with creativity, the ability to use analogies, and the talent to see the familiar in a different light.

Research suggests that we are more creative when we are in a good mood, so if we need to be creative, we should do things that make us happy, such as listening to music we enjoy, eating foods we like, watching funny movies, or socializing with others.[69]

Evidence also suggests that being around others who are creative can actually make us more inspired, especially if we are creatively "stuck."[70] One study found that "weak ties"

EXHIBIT 9-5   The Three Components of Creativity

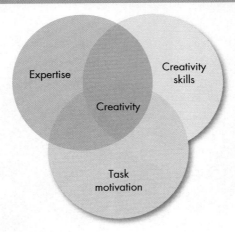

Source: Copyright © 1997, by The Regents of the University of California. Reprinted from *The California Management Review* 40, no. 1. By permission of The Regents.

to creative people—knowing creative people but not all that closely—facilitates creativity because the people are there as a resource if we need them, but they are not so close as to stunt our own independent thinking.[71]

The effective use of analogies allows decision makers to apply an idea from one context to another. One of the most famous examples in which analogy resulted in a creative breakthrough was Alexander Graham Bell's observation that it might be possible to apply the way the ear operates to his "talking box." He noticed that the bones in the ear are operated by a delicate, thin membrane. He wondered why, then, a thicker and stronger piece of membrane should not be able to move a piece of steel. From that analogy, the telephone was conceived.

Some people have developed their creative skills because they are able to see problems in a new way. They are able to make the strange familiar and the familiar strange.[72] For instance, most of us think of hens laying eggs. But how many of us have considered that a hen is only an egg's way of making another egg?

The final component in the three-component model of creativity is *intrinsic task motivation*. This is the desire to work on something because it's interesting, involving, exciting, satisfying, or personally challenging. This motivational component turns creativity *potential* into *actual* creative ideas. It determines the extent to which individuals fully engage their expertise and creative skills.

Creative people often love their work, to the point of seeming obsession. Our work environment can have a significant effect on intrinsic motivation. Stimulants that foster creativity include a culture that encourages the flow of ideas; fair and constructive judgment of ideas; rewards and recognition for creative work; sufficient financial, material, and information resources; freedom to decide what work is to be done and how to do it; a supervisor who communicates effectively, shows confidence in others, and supports the work group; and work group members who support and trust each other.[73]

Organizational Factors That Affect Creativity

In two decades of research analyzing the link between the work environment and creativity, six organizational factors have been found to positively affect creativity:[74]

- *Challenge*. When people are matched up with the right assignments, their expertise and skills can be brought to the task of creative thinking. Individuals should be stretched, but not overwhelmed.

- *Freedom.* To be creative, once a person is given a project, he or she needs the freedom to determine the process. In other words, let the person decide how to tackle the problem. This heightens intrinsic motivation.

- *Resources.* Time and money are the two main resources that affect creativity. Thus, managers need to allot these resources carefully.

- *Work-group features.* In Chapter 5, our discussion of group composition and diversity concluded that diverse groups were likely to come up with more creative solutions. In addition to ensuring a diverse group of people, team members need to share excitement about the goal, must be willing to support each other through difficult periods, and must recognize one another's unique knowledge and perspectives.

- *Supervisory encouragement.* To sustain passion, most people need to feel that what they are doing matters to others. Managers can reward, collaborate, and communicate to nurture the creativity of individuals and teams.

- *Organizational support.* Creativity-supporting organizations reward creativity, and also make sure that there is information sharing and collaboration. They make sure that negative political problems do not get out of control.

Five organizational factors have been found to block your creativity at work:[75]

- *Expected evaluation.* Focusing on how your work is going to be evaluated.

- *Surveillance.* Being watched while you are working.

- *External motivators.* Focusing on external, tangible rewards.

- *Competition.* Facing win-lose situations with peers.

- *Constrained choice.* Being given limits on how you can do your work.

Canadian Tire built a better tent by giving people an environment that encouraged them to think creatively, as this *OB in the Workplace* shows.

OB IN THE WORKPLACE

Canadian Tire's "Innovation Room" Unleashes Creativity

Can playing with crayons help produce a better tent? Managers at Toronto-based Canadian Tire want better decisions than the kind that come from sitting around a boardroom table.[76] So they built an "innovation room" that is "a cross between a kindergarten classroom and a fantasy land."

To get new ideas for camping gear, they invited friends and family with an interest in camping to meet in the innovation room. The room has LEGO sets, crayons, a canoe, and a sundeck.

Managers were trying to create a new product—a tent with lighting—but were not sure how to develop a product that would sell. They left it to friends and family to get it right. By getting people together in the innovation room, where they could play and brainstorm, the idea emerged for a solar-lit tent. The tent is now a big seller.

"It's really about unlocking and unleashing creativity and getting people to just let loose and dream a little and have fun," says Glenn Butt, a senior vice-president at Canadian Tire. "It's a process that usually ends up with some very unique and different products and concepts."

What About Ethics in Decision Making?

When Michael McCain was first notified that some of Maple Leaf's meat products were being investigated for bacterial contamination, he did not immediately notify the public.[77] He did inform distributors to stop distributing the questionable products, but those packages already purchased could still be eaten by consumers. McCain faced a dilemma: At the time that he was notified of the problem, Maple Leaf products were only suspected of contamination, not found to be contaminated. What is the ethical thing to do in a situation like this?

5 **What is ethics, and how can it be used for better decision making?**

ethics The study of moral values or principles that guide our behaviour and inform us whether actions are right or wrong.

No contemporary discussion of decision making would be complete without the inclusion of ethics, because ethical considerations should be an important criterion in organizational decision making. **Ethics** is the study of moral values or principles that guide our behaviour and inform us whether actions are right or wrong. Ethical principles help us "do the right thing." In this section, we present four ways to frame decisions ethically and examine the factors that shape an individual's ethical decision-making behaviour. We also examine organizational responses to the demand for ethical behaviour, as well as consideration of ethical decisions when doing business in other cultures. To learn more about your ethical decision-making approach, see the *Ethical Dilemma Exercise* on page 338.

Four Ethical Decision Criteria

utilitarianism A decision focused on outcomes or consequences that emphasizes the greatest good for the greatest number.

An individual can use four different criteria in making ethical choices.[78] The first is the *utilitarian* criterion, in which decisions are made solely on the basis of their outcomes or consequences. The goal of **utilitarianism** is to provide the greatest good for the greatest number. This view tends to dominate business decision making. It is consistent with goals such as efficiency, productivity, and high profits. By maximizing profits, for instance, a business executive can argue that he or she is securing the greatest good for the greatest number—as he or she hands out dismissal notices to 15 percent of the employees.

A second ethical criterion is *rights*. This criterion calls on individuals to make decisions consistent with fundamental liberties and privileges as set forth in documents such as the Canadian Charter of Rights and Freedoms. An emphasis on rights in decision making means respecting and protecting the basic rights of individuals, such as the rights to privacy, free speech, and due process. For instance, this criterion would be used to protect **whistle-blowers** when they report unethical or illegal practices by their organizations to the media or to government agencies on the grounds of their right to free speech.

whistle-blowers Individuals who report unethical practices by their employers to outsiders.

A third ethical criterion is *justice*. This criterion requires individuals to impose and enforce rules fairly and impartially so there is an equitable distribution of benefits and costs. Union members typically favour this criterion. It justifies paying people the same wage for a given job, regardless of performance differences, and it uses seniority as the primary determination in making layoff decisions. A focus on justice protects the interests of the underrepresented and less powerful, but it can encourage a sense of entitlement that reduces risk-taking, innovation, and productivity.

A fourth ethical criterion is *care*. The ethics of care can be stated as follows: "The morally correct action is the one that expresses care in protecting the special relationships that individuals have with each other."[79] Care as an ethical criterion came out of feminist literature[80] to address the idea that the male-dominated view of ethics was too impersonal and ignored the relationships among individuals.[81] The care criterion suggests that individuals should be aware of the needs, desires, and well-being of those to whom they are closely connected. Recent research does not suggest that men and women differ in their use of justice versus care in making decisions.[82] However, this criterion does remind us of the difficulty of being impartial in all decisions.

Decision makers, particularly in for-profit organizations, tend to feel safe and comfortable when they use utilitarianism. Many questionable actions can be justified when framed as being in the best interests of "the organization" and stockholders. But many critics of business decision makers argue that this perspective should change because it can result in ignoring the rights of some individuals, particularly those with minority representation in the organization.[83] Increased concern in society about individual rights and social justice suggests the need for managers to develop ethical standards based on nonutilitarian criteria. This presents a solid challenge to today's managers because making decisions using criteria such as individual rights and social justice involves far more ambiguities than using utilitarian criteria such as effects on efficiency and profits. This helps to explain why managers are increasingly criticized for their actions. Raising prices, selling products with questionable effects on consumer health, closing down inefficient plants, laying off large numbers of employees, moving production overseas to cut costs, and similar decisions can be justified in utilitarian terms. But that may no longer be the single criterion by which good decisions should be judged.

Factors That Influence Ethical Decision-Making Behaviour

Why do some people make more ethical decisions than others?

What accounts for unethical behaviour in organizations? Is it immoral individuals or work environments that promote unethical activity? The answer is *both!* The evidence indicates that ethical or unethical actions are largely a function of both the individual's characteristics and the environment in which he or she works.[84] The model in Exhibit 9-6 illustrates factors affecting ethical decision making and emphasizes three factors: stage of moral development, locus of control, and the organizational environment.

Stages of Moral Development

Stages of moral development assess a person's capacity to judge what is morally right.[85] Research suggests that there are three levels of moral development, and each level has two stages.[86] The higher one's moral development, the less dependent he or she is on outside influences and thus the more he or she will be predisposed to behave ethically. The first level is the preconventional level, the second is the conventional level, and the highest level is the principled level. These levels and their stages are described in Exhibit 9-7 on page 324.

The research indicates that people proceed through the stages one step at a time, though they do not necessarily reach the highest stage.[87] Most adults are at a mid-level

stages of moral development The developmental stages that explain a person's capacity to judge what is morally right.

EXHIBIT 9-6   Factors Affecting Ethical Decision-Making Behaviour

Stewart Leibl, president of Perth's, a Winnipeg dry-cleaning chain, is a founding sponsor of the Koats for Kids program. The company's outlets are a drop-off point for no-longer-needed children's coats, which Perth's cleans free of charge before distributing them to children who have no winter coats. Leibl is going beyond utilitarian criteria when he says, "We all have a responsibility to contribute to the society that we live in." He is also looking at social justice.

of moral development—they are strongly influenced by peers and will follow an organization's rules and procedures. Those individuals who have progressed to the higher stages place increased value on the rights of others, regardless of the majority's opinion, and are likely to challenge organizational practices they personally believe are wrong. Those at the higher stages are most likely to make ethical decisions using the criteria of rights, justice, and care, which we discussed earlier.

Locus of Control

Research indicates that people with an external *locus of control* (that is, they believe their lives are controlled by outside forces, such as luck or chance) are less likely to

---

EXHIBIT 9-7   Stages of Moral Development

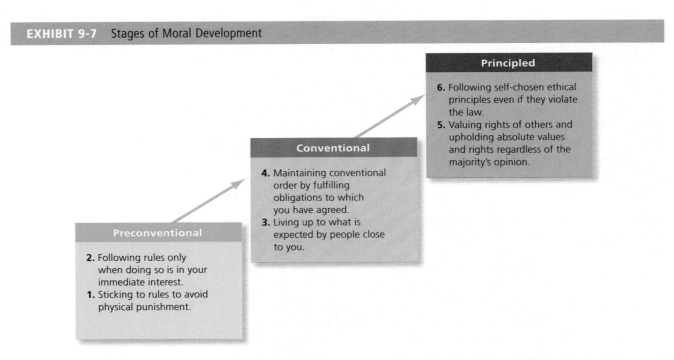

Source: Based on L. Kohlberg, "Moral Stages and Moralization: The Cognitive-Developmental Approach," in *Moral Development and Behaviour: Theory, Research, and Social Issues,* ed. T. Lickona (New York: Holt, Rinehart and Winston, 1976), pp. 34–35.

take responsibility for the consequences of their behaviour and are more likely to rely on external influences to determine their behaviour. Those with an internal locus of control (they believe they are responsible for their destinies), on the other hand, are more likely to rely on their own internal standards of right and wrong to guide their behaviour.

Organizational Environment

The *organizational environment* refers to an employee's perception of organizational expectations. Does the organizational culture encourage and support ethical behaviour by rewarding it or discourage unethical behaviour by punishing it? Characteristics of an organizational environment that are likely to foster high levels of ethical decision making include written codes of ethics; high levels of moral behaviour by senior management; realistic performance expectations; performance appraisals that evaluate means as well as ends; visible recognition and promotions for individuals who display high levels of moral behaviour; and visible punishment for those who act unethically. An organization that has policies to protect whistle-blowers— individuals who report unethical practices to the press or government agencies—also makes it possible for people to speak out if they observe questionable activities. West-Jet, for example, introduced a whistle-blowing policy after being taken to court by Air Canada and Jetsgo for questionable practices. Unfortunately, many people who speak out against irregularities end up being punished for doing so, which is why strong company policies are necessary.

In summary, people who lack a strong moral sense are much less likely to make unethical decisions if they are constrained by an organizational environment that frowns on such behaviours. Conversely, righteous individuals can be corrupted by an organizational environment that permits or encourages unethical practices. In the next section, we consider how to formulate an ethical decision.

Making Ethical Decisions

While there are no clear-cut ways to differentiate ethical from unethical decision making, there are some questions you should consider.

Exhibit 9-8 on page 326 illustrates a decision tree to guide ethical decision making. This tree is built on three of the ethical decision criteria—utilitarianism, rights, and justice—presented earlier. The first question you need to answer addresses self-interest versus organizational goals.

The second question concerns the rights of other parties. If the decision violates the rights of someone else (his or her right to privacy, for instance), then the decision is unethical.

The final question that needs to be addressed relates to whether the decision conforms to standards of equity and justice. The department head who raises the performance evaluation of a favoured employee and lowers the evaluation of a disfavoured employee—and then uses these evaluations to justify giving the former a big raise and nothing to the latter—has treated the disfavoured employee unfairly.

Unfortunately, the answers to the questions in Exhibit 9-8 are often argued in ways to make unethical decisions seem ethical. Powerful people, for example, can become very adept at explaining self-serving behaviours in terms of the organization's best interests. Similarly, they can persuasively argue that unfair actions are really fair and just. Our point is that immoral people can justify almost any behaviour. Those who are powerful, articulate, and persuasive are the most likely to be able to get away with unethical actions successfully. When faced with an ethical dilemma, try to answer the questions in Exhibit 9-8 truthfully.

EXHIBIT 9-8   Is a Decision Ethical?

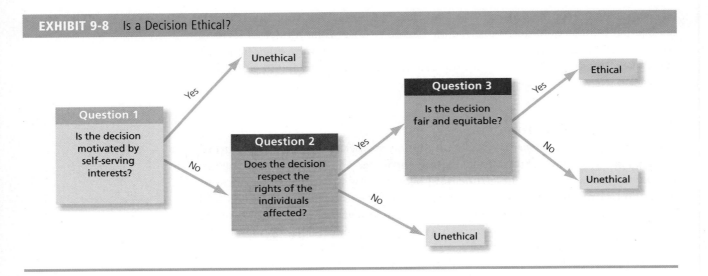

Organizational Response to Demands for Ethical Behaviour

During the 1990s, an explosion in the demand for more ethics occurred in Canada and the United States. A second explosion occurred in 2002, after the Enron, World-Com, and other accounting scandals. In Canada, more than 120 ethics specialists now offer services as in-house moral arbitrators, mediators, watchdogs, and listening posts. Some work at Canada's largest corporations, including the CIBC, Canada Post, Magna International, RBC, and McDonald's Canada. These corporate ethics officers hear about issues such as colleagues making phone calls on company time, managers yelling at their employees, product researchers being asked to fake data to meet a deadline, or a company wanting to terminate a contract because the costs are higher than anticipated. Ethics professor Wayne Norman of the Université de Montréal believes that ethics officers are a positive trend, noting, "all sorts of studies show the companies that take ethics seriously tend to be more successful."[88]

Many corporations are also developing codes of ethics. For example, about 60 percent of Canada's 650 largest corporations have some sort of ethics code,[89] and nearly all of the companies in the *Fortune* 500 index have codes of ethics available on their websites.[90] Having a corporate ethics policy is not enough, however; employees must be instructed in how to follow the policy. While no comparable Canadian data are available, a survey of employees in US businesses with ethics codes found that 75 percent of those surveyed had observed ethical or legal violations in the previous 12 months, including deceptive sales practices, unsafe working conditions, sexual harassment, conflicts of interest, and environmental violations.[91] Companies with codes of ethics may not do enough monitoring. For instance, David Nitkin, president of Toronto-based EthicScan Canada, an ethics consultancy, notes that "only about 15% of [larger Canadian corporations with codes of ethics] have designated an ethics officer or ombudsman" or provide an ethics hotline, and that less than 10 percent offer whistle-blower protection.[92] *OB in Action—Developing a Meaningful Code of Ethics* shows how to implement codes of ethics in organizations.

OB in ACTION

Developing a Meaningful Code of Ethics

→ Clearly **state basic principle**s and expectations.

→ Realistically **focus on potential ethical dilemmas** that employees face.

→ **Distribute** the **code** to all employees.

→ **Train individuals** so that they understand the code.

→ **Enforce penalties** for violating the code.[93]

A small group of companies is even starting a new trend in monitoring ethical practices, hiring an ethical auditor, much as they would hire a financial auditor. The ethical auditor is hired to "double-check an organization's perception of its own morals."[94] Vancouver City Savings Credit Union (Vancity), Bell Canada, Tetra Pak, British Telecom, the University of Toronto, and The Body Shop have all brought in ethical auditors.

Another way to encourage ethical behaviour is to create mechanisms that encourage employees to speak up when they see wrongdoing. Toronto-based BBDO Canada encourages "candour moments." Employees are empowered "to call each other on behaviour that goes against company values, even junior employees who want to be candid with managers," says the ad agency's president and CEO, Gerry Frascione.[95]

What About National Culture?

We have already shown that there are differences between Canada and the United States in the legal treatment of ethics violations and the creation of an ethical corporate culture. However, it is important to note that what is considered unethical in one country may not be viewed similarly in another country. The reason is that there are no global ethical standards. Contrasts between Asia and the West provide an illustration.[96] In Japan, people doing business together often exchange gifts, even expensive ones. This is part of Japanese tradition. When North American and European companies started doing business in Japan, most North American executives were not aware of the Japanese tradition of exchanging gifts and wondered whether this was a form of bribery. Most have come to accept this tradition now and have even set different limits on gift giving in Japan from other countries.[97]

In another instance illustrating the differences between Asia and North America, a manager of a large US company that operates in China caught an employee stealing. Following company policy, she fired the employee and turned him over to the local

Paul Nielsen (shown with his wife, Dayle), owns Calgary-based DumpRunner Waste Systems, a specialty garbage and debris removal company. He encourages an ethical approach to dealing with both clients and employees. He notes that in Calgary, business is built on handshakes and being true to your word, and people are expected to act ethically. Ethical behaviour may be easier for Nielsen than for some others. He says he is guided by his passion for being in business, rather than a "quest for money."

authorities for his act. Later she discovered, much to her horror, that the former employee had been executed for the theft.[98] These examples indicate that standards for ethical behaviour and the consequences of particular acts are not universally similar. The fact that standards for ethical behaviour and the consequences of particular acts are not universal presents a variety of problems for those doing business in other countries.

Companies operating branches in foreign countries are faced with tough decisions about how to conduct business under ethical standards that differ from those in Canada. For instance, Canadian companies must decide whether they want to operate in countries such as China, Burma, and Nigeria, which abuse human rights. Although the Canadian government permits investing in these countries, it also encourages companies to act ethically.

While ethical standards may seem ambiguous in the West, criteria defining right and wrong are actually much clearer in the West than in Asia. John McWilliams, senior vice-president, general counsel, and secretary for Calgary-based Nexen, notes that requests for bribes are not necessarily direct: "Usually, they don't say, 'Give me X thousands of dollars and you've got the deal.' It's a lot more subtle than that."[99] Michael Davies, vice-president and general counsel for Mississauga-based General Electric Canada, offers an example: "A payment [is] made to an administrative official to do the job that he's supposed to do. In other words, you pay a fellow over the counter $10 when you're in the airport in Saudi Arabia to get on the flight you're supposed to get on, because, otherwise, he's going to keep you there for two days."

The need for global organizations to establish ethical principles for decision makers in all countries may be critical if high standards are to be upheld and if consistent practices are to be achieved. Having agreements among countries to create and enforce anti-bribery laws may not be enough, however. The 34 countries of the OECD (Organisation for Economic Co-operation and Development) entered into an agreement to tackle corporate bribery in 1997. However, a study by Berlin-based Transparency International in 2008 found that 18 of the OECD countries are "doing little or nothing" to enforce the agreement. Canada, along with the United Kingdom and Japan, came under strong criticism. The three countries filed a total of four cases in 2007 and 2008, compared with a total of 245 cases filed by the United States, Germany, and France. "Canada is the only OECD country to bar its tax inspectors from reporting suspicions of foreign bribery to law enforcement authorities," Transparency International noted.[100]

Corporate Social Responsibility

When Maple Leaf Foods CEO Michael McCain realized that meat contamination occurring in the company's Toronto meat processing plant had caused a number of deaths, he was faced with a possible public-relations disaster.[101] People might stop buying Maple Leaf products, perhaps forever. He chose to act in a socially responsible way. "The core principle here was to first do what's in the interest of public health, and second to be open and transparent in taking accountability," McCain said.

Many found McCain's willingness to take responsibility for the food contamination a bit unusual, but reassuring, particularly when considering the massive bonuses many financial executives received in 2008, even though a number of financial institutions in the US faced collapse.

"His candour at a time when his contemporaries would have scurried behind spin doctors and legal eagles was a refreshing way to address a potentially devastating mistake. I actually trust the man!" said Peter Lapinskie of the *Daily Observer* in Pembroke, Ontario. "It's so rare to see a white-collar executive descend from the ivory tower, apologize and reach out to the public in such plain language," said Ruth Davenport of CJNI radio in Halifax. To what extent should companies be socially responsible?

Corporate social responsibility is defined as an organization's responsibility to consider the impact of its decisions on society. Thus, organizations may try to better society through such things as charitable contributions or providing better wages to employees working in offshore factories. Organizations may engage in these practices because they feel pressured by society to do so, or they may seek ways to improve society because they feel it is the right thing to do.

Eighty percent of Canadians feel that Ottawa should establish standards for corporate social responsibility and require corporations to report on how they are meeting guidelines, according to a recent survey.[102] Many Canadian companies are feeling the pressure to demonstrate social responsibility as well. For example, a poll by Environics found that 9 out of 10 Canadian shareholders want environmental and social performance taken into account when companies are valued. In another survey, done by GlobeScan, 71 percent of respondents believe that consumers can have an impact on whether companies behave responsibly.[103]

Not everyone agrees with the position of organizations assuming social responsibility. For example, economist Milton Friedman remarked in *Capitalism and Freedom* that "few trends could so thoroughly undermine the very foundations of our free society as the acceptance by corporate officials of a social responsibility other than to make as much money for their stockholders as possible."[104]

Joel Bakan, professor of law at the University of British Columbia, author of *The Corporation*,[105] and co-director of the documentary of the same name, is more critical of organizations than Friedman, though he finds that current laws support corporate behaviour that some might find troubling. Bakan suggests that today's corporations have many of the same characteristics as a psychopathic personality (self-interested, lacking empathy, manipulative, and reckless in their disregard of others). Bakan notes

6 What is corporate social responsibility?

corporate social responsibility
An organization's responsibility to consider the impact of its decisions on society.

Mark Trang, an employee of Salesforce.com, teaches business basics to grade 5 students at an elementary school. Salesforce.com encourages every employee to donate 1 percent of his or her working time to the community. Through volunteer work, Salesforce.com gives employees the opportunity to experience the joy and satisfaction that comes from helping others. Employees give to the community by feeding the homeless, tutoring kids, gardening in community parks, lending computer expertise to nonprofit organizations, and providing disaster relief.

that even though companies have a tendency to act psychopathically, this is not why they are fixated on profits. Rather, the only legal responsibility corporations have is to maximize organizational profits for stockholders. He suggests more laws and more restraints need to be put in place if corporations are to behave with more social responsibility, as current laws direct corporations to be responsible to their shareholders and make little mention of responsibility toward other stakeholders.

A recent survey at 110 MBA programs in the US and Canada conducted by Net Impact found that MBA students are very interested in the subject of corporate social responsibility. While students who were involved in Net Impact gave even more favourable responses, 81 percent of respondents not part of the club "believed business professionals should take into account social and environmental impacts when making decisions." Almost two-thirds of these respondents felt that corporate social responsibility should be part of core MBA classes and 60 percent said "they would seek socially responsible employment."[106]

For more on the debate about social responsibility versus concentrating on the bottom line, see this chapter's *Point/Counterpoint* on page 333.

SNAPSHOT SUMMARY

Summary and Implications

1 Is there a right way to make decisions? The rational decision-making model describes the six steps individuals take to make decisions: (1) Define the problem, (2) identify the criteria, (3) allocate weights to the criteria, (4) develop alternatives, (5) evaluate the alternatives, and (6) select the best alternative. This is an ideal model, and not every decision follows these steps thoroughly .

2 How do people actually make decisions? Most decisions in the real world do not follow the rational model. For instance, people are usually content to find an acceptable or reasonable solution to their problem rather than an optimizing one. Thus, decision makers may rely on bounded rationality, satisficing, and intuition in making decisions. They may also rely on judgment shortcuts, such as overconfidence bias, anchoring bias, confirmation bias, availability bias, escalation of commitment, randomness error, winner's curse, and hindsight bias.

3 What factors affect group decision making? Groups generate more complete information and knowledge, they offer increased diversity of views, they generate higher-quality decisions, and they lead to increased acceptance of a solution. However, group decisions are time-consuming. They also lead to conformity pressures, and the group discussion can be dominated by one or a few members. Finally, group decisions suffer from ambiguous responsibility, and the responsibility of any single member is watered down.

4 How can we get more creative decisions? While there is some evidence that individuals vary in their ability to be creative, research shows that individuals are more creative when they have expertise at the task at hand, creative-thinking skills, and are motivated by intrinsic interest. Five organizational factors have been found that can block creativity at work: (1) *expected evaluation*—focusing on how work is going to be evaluated; (2) *surveillance*—being watched while working; (3) *external motivators*—emphasizing external, tangible rewards; (4) *competition*—facing win-lose situations with peers; and (5) *constrained choice*—being given limits on how to do the work.

5 **What is ethics, and how can it be used for better decision making?** Ethics is the study of moral values or principles that guide our behaviour and inform us whether actions are right or wrong. Ethical principles help us "do the right thing." An individual can use four different criteria in making ethical choices. The first is the *utilitarian* criterion, in which decisions are made solely on the basis of their outcomes or consequences. The second is *rights*; this ethical criterion focuses on respecting and protecting the basic rights of individuals. The third is *justice*; this ethical criterion requires individuals to impose and enforce rules fairly and impartially so there is an equitable distribution of benefits and costs. The fourth is *care*; this ethical criterion suggests that we should be aware of the needs, desires, and well-being of those to whom we are closely connected. There are advantages and disadvantages to each of these criteria.

6 **What is corporate social responsibility?** Corporate social responsibility is defined as an organization's responsibility to consider the impact of its decisions on society. Thus, organizations may try to better society through such things as charitable contributions or providing better wages to employees working in off-shore factories. Organizations may engage in these practices because they feel pressured by society to do so, or they may seek ways to improve society because they feel it is the right thing to do.

OB at Work

For Review

1. What is the rational decision-making model? Under what conditions is it applicable?

2. Describe organizational factors that might constrain decision makers.

3. What role does intuition play in effective decision making?

4. What is groupthink? What is its effect on decision-making quality?

5. What is groupshift? What is its effect on decision-making quality?

6. Identify five organizational factors that block creativity at work.

7. Describe the four criteria that individuals can use in making ethical decisions.

8. Are unethical decisions more a function of the individual decision maker or the decision maker's work environment? Explain.

9. What is corporate social responsibility, and why do companies engage in it?

For Critical Thinking

1. "For the most part, individual decision making in organizations is an irrational process." Do you agree or disagree? Discuss.

2. What factors do you think differentiate good decision makers from poor ones? Relate your answer to the six-step rational decision-making model.

3. Have you ever increased your commitment to a failed course of action? If so, analyze the follow-up decision to increase your commitment and explain why you behaved as you did.

4. If group decisions consistently achieve better-quality outcomes than those achieved by individuals, how did the phrase "a camel is a horse designed by a committee" become so popular and ingrained in our culture?

OB for You

- In some decision situations, you might consider following the rational decision-making model. This will ensure that you examine a wider variety of options before committing to a particular decision.

- Analyze decision situations and be aware of your biases. We all bring biases to the decisions we make. Combine rational analysis with intuition. As you gain experience, you should feel increasingly confident in using your intuition with your rational analysis.

- Use creativity-stimulation techniques. You can improve your overall decision-making effectiveness by searching for innovative solutions to problems. This can be as basic as telling yourself to think creatively and to look specifically for unique alternatives.

- When making decisions, you should consider their ethical implications. A quick way to do this is to ask yourself: Would I be embarrassed if this action were printed on the front page of the local newspaper?

Point

Organizations Should Just Stick to the Bottom Line

The major goals of organizations are and should be efficiency, productivity, and high profits. By maximizing profits, businesses ensure that they will survive and thus make it possible to provide employment. Doing so is in the best interests of the organization, employees, and stockholders. Moreover, it is up to individuals to show that they are concerned about the environment through their investment and purchasing activities, not for corporations to lead the way.

Let's examine some of the reasons why it is not economically feasible to place all of the burden of protecting the environment on the shoulders of big business.

Studies show that environmental regulations are too costly. The Conference Board of Canada has suggested that environmental regulations cost Canadian companies $580 million to $600 million a year.[107] The Fraser Institute in Vancouver reported that all regulations, including those designed to protect the environment, cost Canadian industry $103 billion a year.[108] Environmental regulations can also be harmful to jobs. In British Columbia, the Forest Practices Code is said to have added $1 billion a year to harvesting costs and resulted in a number of job cuts.

While businesses are concerned with the high cost that results from environmental regulations, the general public is not completely supportive of protecting the environment either, particularly if it will inconvenience them.[109]

Companies would be better off sticking to the bottom line, and governments should stay away from imposing costly environmental regulations on business. Stringent environmental standards cause trade distortions, and governments rarely consider the cost of complying with regulations. Companies should be allowed to take their lead from shareholders and customers. If these constituencies want businesses to pay for environmental protection, they will indicate this by investing in firms that do so. Until they do, the cost of environmental legislation is simply too high.

Counterpoint

Environmental Responsibility Is Part of the Bottom Line

Going green makes good economic sense. The studies reported in the *Point* argument tend to overstate the cost of environmental regulations.[110] They do not consider the benefits to society of those regulations.

A closer look at a few companies that have devoted efforts to being more environmentally friendly will illustrate the benefits of this approach. When the Quaker Oats Company of Canada started working toward a "greener" work environment, its plant in Peterborough, Ontario, saved more than $1 million in three years through various environmental initiatives.[111] As another example, Toronto-based Inco spent $600 million to change the way it produces nickel at its Sudbury, Ontario, operations in order to be less destructive to the local environment. Its smelting process is one of the most energy efficient and environmentally friendly in the world. Inco continues to work to restore the appearance of Sudbury, which had been devastated by Inco's older smelting process. Trees have grown back, the wildlife has returned, and the air is clean. Sudbury has even been listed as one of the 10 most desirable places to live in Canada. While Inco invested a lot of money to change its production process, Doug Hamilton, controller at Inco's Ontario division in Sudbury, has said, "Our Sulphur Dioxide Abatement Program was an awesome undertaking. Not only did this investment allow us to capture 90 percent of the sulphur in the ore we mine, but the new processes save the company $90 million a year in production costs. That strikes me as a pretty smart investment."[112] London, Ontario-based 3M Canada started a Pollution Prevention Pays (3P) program more than 20 years ago.[113] The program emphasizes stopping pollution at the source to avoid the expense and effort of cleaning it up or treating it after the fact. The recycling program at 3M Canada's tape plant in Perth, Ontario, reduced its waste by 96 percent and saved the company about $650 000 annually. The capital cost for the program was only $30 000.

The examples of Quaker Oats, Inco, and 3M show that companies that are environmentally friendly have an advantage over their competitors. If organizations control their pollution costs better than their competitors, they will use their resources more efficiently and therefore increase profitability.

OB *At Work*

Decision-Making Style Questionnaire

Circle the response that comes closest to the way you usually feel or act. There are no right or wrong responses to any of these items.[114]

1. I am more careful about
    a. people's feelings   **b.** their rights

2. I usually get along better with
    a. imaginative people   **b.** realistic people

3. It is a higher compliment to be called
    a. a person of real feeling   **b.** a consistently reasonable person

4. In doing something with other people, it appeals more to me
    a. to do it in the accepted way   **b.** to invent a way of my own

5. I get more annoyed at
    a. fancy theories   **b.** people who do not like theories

6. It is higher praise to call someone
    a. a person of vision   **b.** a person of common sense

7. I more often let
    a. my heart rule my head   **b.** my head rule my heart

8. I think it is a worse fault
    a. to show too much warmth   **b.** to be unsympathetic

9. If I were a teacher, I would rather teach
    a. courses involving theory   **b.** factual courses

Which word in the following pairs appeals to you more? Circle *a* or *b*.

10. a. Compassion   **b.** Foresight

11. a. Justice   **b.** Mercy

12. a. Production   **b.** Design

13. a. Gentle   **b.** Firm

14. a. Uncritical   **b.** Critical

15. a. Literal   **b.** Figurative

16. a. Imaginative   **b.** Matter-of-fact

Scoring Key

Mark each of your responses on the following scales. Then use the point value column to arrive at your score. For example, if you answered *a* to the first question, you would check *1a* in the Feeling column. This response receives zero points when you add up the point value column. Instructions for classifying your scores are indicated following the scales.

OB *At Work*

Sensation	Point Value	Intuition	Point Value	Thinking	Point Value	Feeling	Point Value
2b _____	1	2a _____	2	1b _____	1	1a _____	0
4a _____	1	4b _____	1	3b _____	2	3a _____	1
5a _____	1	5b _____	1	7b _____	1	7a _____	1
6b _____	1	6a _____	0	8a _____	0	8b _____	1
9b _____	2	9a _____	2	10b _____	2	10a _____	1
12a _____	1	12b _____	0	11a _____	2	11b _____	1
15a _____	1	15b _____	1	13b _____	1	13a _____	1
16b _____	2	16a _____	0	14b _____	0	14a _____	1
Maximum Point Value	(10)		(7)		(9)		(7)

Circle *Intuition* if your Intuition score is equal to or greater than your Sensation score. Circle *Sensation* if your Sensation score is greater than your Intuition score. Circle *Feeling* if your Feeling score is greater than your Thinking score. Circle *Thinking* if your Thinking score is greater than your Feeling score.

A high score on *Intuition* indicates you see the world in holistic terms. You tend to be creative. A high score on *Sensation* indicates that you are realistic and see the world in terms of facts. A high score on *Feeling* means you make decisions based on gut feeling. A high score on *Thinking* indicates a highly logical and analytical approach to decision making.

More Learning About Yourself Exercises

Additional self-assessments relevant to this chapter appear at MyOBLab (**www.pearsoned.ca/myoblab**).

IV.A.2 Am I a Deliberate Decision Maker?

I.A.5 How Creative Am I?

When you complete the additional assessments, consider the following:

1. Am I surprised about my score?

2. Would my friends evaluate me similarly?

BREAKOUT **GROUP** EXERCISES

Form small groups to discuss the following topics, as assigned by your instructor:

1. Apply the rational decision-making model to deciding where your group might eat dinner this evening. How closely were you able to follow the rational model in making this decision?

2. The company that makes your favourite snack product has been accused of being weak in its social responsibility efforts. What impact will this have on your purchase of any more products from that company?

3. You have seen a classmate cheat on an exam or an assignment. Do you do something about this or ignore it?

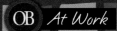

Wilderness Survival Exercise

You are a member of a hiking party. After reaching base camp on the first day, you decide to take a quick sunset hike by yourself. After a few exhilarating miles, you decide to return to camp. On your way back, you realize that you are lost. You have shouted for help to no avail. It is now dark and getting cold.

Your Task

Without communicating with anyone else in your group, read the following scenarios and choose the best answer. Keep track of your answers on a sheet of paper. You have 10 minutes to answer the 10 questions.

1. The first thing you decide to do is to build a fire. However, you have no matches, so you use the bow and drill method. What is the bow and drill method?

    a. A dry, soft stick is rubbed between one's hands against a board of supple green wood.

    b. A soft green stick is rubbed between one's hands against a hardwood board.

    c. A straight stick of wood is quickly rubbed back-and forth against a dead tree.

    d. Two sticks (one being the bow, the other the drill) are struck to create a spark.

2. It occurs to you that you can also use the fire as a distress signal. When signalling with fire, how do you form the international distress signal?

    a. 2 fires   **b.** 4 fires in a square

    c. 4 fires in a cross   **d.** 3 fires in a line

3. You are very thirsty. You go to a nearby stream and collect some water in the small metal cup you have in your backpack. How long should you boil the water?

    a. 15 minutes   **b.** A few seconds

    c. 1 hour   **d.** It depends on the altitude.

4. You are very hungry, so you decide to eat what appear to be edible berries. When performing the universal edibility test, what should you do?

    a. Do not eat for 2 hours before the test.

    b. If the plant stings your lip, confirm the sting by holding it under your tongue for 15 minutes.

    c. If nothing bad has happened 2 hours after digestion, eat half a cup of the plant and wait again.

    d. Separate the plant into its basic components and eat each component, one at a time.

5. Next, you decide to build a shelter for the evening. In selecting a site, what do you *not* have to consider?

    a. It must contain material to make the type of shelter you need.

    b. It must be free of insects, reptiles, and poisonous plants.

    c. It must be large enough and level enough for you to lie down comfortably.

    d. It must be on a hill so you can signal rescuers and keep an eye on your surroundings.

6. In the shelter that you built, you notice a spider. You heard from a fellow hiker that black widow spiders populate the area. How do you identify a black widow spider?

    a. Its head and abdomen are black; its thorax is red.

    b. It is attracted to light.

    c. It runs away from light.

    d. It is a dark spider with a red or orange marking on the female's abdomen.

7. After getting some sleep, you notice that the night sky has cleared, so you decide to try to find your way back to base camp. You believe you should travel north and can use the North Star for navigation. How do you locate the North Star?

   a. Hold your right hand up as far as you can and look between your index and middle fingers.

   b. Find Sirius and look 60 degrees above it and to the right.

   c. Look for the Big Dipper and follow the line created by its cup end.

   d. Follow the line of Orion's belt.

8. You come across a fast-moving stream. What is the best way to cross it?

   a. Find a spot downstream from a sandbar, where the water will be calmer.

   b. Build a bridge.

   c. Find a rocky area, as the water will be shallow and you will have hand- and footholds.

   d. Find a level stretch where it breaks into a few channels.

9. After walking for about an hour, you feel several spiders in your clothes. You don't feel any pain, but you know some spider bites are painless. Which of these spider bites is painless?

   a. Black widow   **b.** Brown recluse

   c. Wolf spider   **d.** Harvestman (daddy longlegs)

10. You decide to eat some insects. Which insects should you avoid?

   a. Adults that sting or bite   **b.** Caterpillars and insects that have a pungent odour

   c. Hairy or brightly coloured ones   **d.** All of the above

Group Task

Break into groups of 5 or 6 people. Now imagine that your whole group is lost. Answer each question as a group, employing a consensus approach to reach each decision. Once the group comes to an agreement, write the decision down on the same sheet of paper that you used for your individual answers. You will have approximately 20 minutes for the group task.

Scoring Your Answers

Your instructor will provide you with the correct answers, which are based on expert judgments in these situations. Once you have received the answers, calculate (A) your individual score; (B) your group's score; (C) the average individual score in the group; and (D) the best individual score in the group. Write these down and consult with your group to ensure that these scores are accurate.

(A) Your individual score _____   (C) Average individual score in group _____

(B) Your group's score _____   (D) Best individual score in group _____

Discussion Questions

1. How did your group (B) perform relative to yourself (A)?

2. How did your group (B) perform relative to the average individual score in the group (C)?

3. How did your group (B) perform relative to the best individual score in the group (D)?

4. Compare your results with those of other groups. Did some groups do a better job of outperforming individuals than others?

5. What do these results tell you about the effectiveness of group decision making?

6. What can groups do to make group decision making more effective?

OB *At Work*

ETHICAL **DILEMMA** EXERCISE

Five Ethical Decisions: What Would You Do?

Assume you are a middle manager in a company with about 1000 employees. How would you respond to each of the following situations?[115]

1. You are negotiating a contract with a potentially very large customer whose representative has hinted that you could almost certainly be assured of getting his business if you gave him and his wife an all-expenses-paid cruise to the Caribbean. You know the representative's employer would not approve of such a "payoff," but you have the discretion to authorize such an expenditure. What would you do?

2. You have the opportunity to steal $100 000 from your company with absolute certainty that you would not be detected or caught. Would you do it?

3. Your company policy on reimbursement for meals while travelling on company business is that you will be repaid for your out-of-pocket costs, which are not to exceed $50 a day. You do not need receipts for these expenses—the company will take your word. When travelling, you tend to eat at fast-food places and rarely spend more than $15 a day. Most of your colleagues submit reimbursement requests in the range of $45 to $50 a day regardless of what their actual expenses are. How much would you request for your meal reimbursements?

4. Assume that you're the manager at a gaming company, and you're responsible for hiring a group to outsource the production of a highly anticipated new game. Because your company is a giant in the industry, numerous companies are trying to get the bid. One of them offers you some kickbacks if you give that firm the bid, but ultimately, it is up to your bosses to decide on the company. You don't mention the incentive, but you push upper management to give the bid to the company that offered you the kickback. Is withholding the truth as bad as lying? Why or why not?

5. You have discovered that one of your closest friends at work has stolen a large sum of money from the company. Would you do nothing? Go directly to an executive to report the incident before talking about it with the offender? Confront the individual before taking action? Make contact with the individual with the goal of persuading that person to return the money?

CASE INCIDENT

The Dangers of Groupthink

Sometimes, the desire to maintain group harmony overrides the importance of making sound decisions. When that occurs, team members are said to engage in groupthink. Here are three examples:[116]

- A civilian worker at a large US Air Force base recalls a time that groupthink overcame her team's decision-making ability. She was a member of a process improvement team that an Air Force general had formed to develop a better way to handle the base's mail, which included important letters from high-ranking military individuals. The team was composed mostly of civilians, and it took almost a month to come up with a plan. The problem: The plan was not a process improvement. Recalls the civilian worker, "I was horrified. What used to be 8 steps; now there were 19." The team had devised a new system that resulted in each piece of mail being read by several middle managers before reaching its intended recipient. The team's new plan slowed down the mail considerably, with an average delay of two weeks. Even though the team members all knew that the new system was worse than its predecessor, no one wanted to question the team's solidarity. The problems lasted for almost an entire year. It was not until the general who formed the team complained about the mail that the system was changed.

- Virginia Turezyn, managing director of Infinity Capital, states that during the dot-com boom of the late 1990s, she was a victim of groupthink. At first, Turezyn was skeptical about the stability of the boom. But after continually reading about start-ups turning into multimillion-dollar payoffs, she began to feel differently. Turezyn decided to invest millions in several dot-coms, including I-drive, a company that provided electronic data storage. The problem was that I-drive was giving the storage away for free, and as a result, the company was losing money. Turezyn recalls one board meeting at I-drive where she spoke up to no avail. "We're spending way too much money," she screamed. The younger executives shook their heads and replied that if they charged for storage they would lose their customers. Says Turezyn, "I started to think, 'Maybe I'm just too old. Maybe I really don't get it.'" Unfortunately, Turezyn did get it. I-drive later filed for bankruptcy.

- Steve Blank, an entrepreneur, also fell victim to groupthink. Blank was a dot-com investor, and he participated on the advisory boards of several Internet start-ups. During meetings for one such start-up, a web photo finisher, Blank tried to persuade his fellow board members to change the business model to be more traditional. Recalls Blank, "I went to those meetings and started saying things like, 'Maybe you should spend that $10 million you just raised on acquiring a customer base rather than building a brand.' The CEO told me, 'Steve, you just don't get it—all the rules have changed.'" The team did not take Blank's advice, and Blank says that he lost hundreds of thousands of dollars on the deal.

According to Michael Useem, a professor at the University of Pennsylvania's Wharton School of Business, one of the main reasons that groupthink occurs is a lack of conflict. "A single devil's advocate or whistle-blower faces a really uphill struggle," he states. "But if you [the naysayer] have one ally, that is enormously strengthening."

Questions

1. What are some factors that led to groupthink in the cases described here? What can teams do to attempt to prevent groupthink from occurring?

2. How might differences in status among group members contribute to groupthink? For example, how might lower-status members react to a group's decision? Are lower-status members more or less likely to be dissenters? Why might higher-status group members be more effective dissenters?

3. Microsoft CEO Steve Ballmer says that he encourages dissent. Can such norms guard against the occurrence of groupthink? As a manager, how would you try to cultivate norms that prevent groupthink?

4. How might group characteristics such as size and cohesiveness affect groupthink?

VIDEO CASE INCIDENT

CASE 9   The "Feel-Better" Bracelet   CBC

Q-Ray advertisements say that its "Serious Performance Bracelet" is designed to help people play, work, and live better."[117] The advertisements say that the $200 bracelet—which supposedly makes people feel better by balancing positive and negative forces—is ionized using a special secret process.

Golfers claim that the bracelet reduces their pain, so *Marketplace* went looking for answers at the golf course. Sandra Post, a champion golfer, is a paid spokesperson for the bracelet. When Wendy Mesley of *Marketplace* interviews her, Post emphasizes the jewellery aspect of the Q-Ray, not its pain-relief qualities. Mesley also interviews golfers Frank and Sam. Frank tells her that the bracelet has reduced his arthritis pain, but Sam (who also wears one of the bracelets) thinks the pain relief is mostly in peoples' heads.

Advertising that a product provides pain relief is a tricky business. Until 2006, people in Q-Ray ads said that the bracelet had cured their pain. But now they cannot say that because the US Federal Trade Commission ruled that such advertising is deceptive. There are no medical studies to back this claim.

(Continued)

OB *At Work*

Andrew Park is the man who brought the Q-Ray to North America, and his son Charles is marketing the product in Canada. Park says that 150 000 Q-Rays have been sold in Canada at a price of $200 each. In an interview with Mesley, Park claims that the company does not make pain-relief claims for the product in its advertisements. Mesley shows Park a hidden-camera film clip where he makes a pain-relief claim during the shooting of an infomercial. Park says that he believes that the product reduces pain, and that if a person believes the bracelet will relieve pain, it will. Mesley also plays a hidden-camera clip showing retail salespeople telling customers that the Q-Ray reduces arthritic pain. Park says he cannot control what retailers tell their customers.

Marketplace asked Christopher Yip, an engineer at the University of Toronto, to test a Q-Ray bracelet to determine if it was ionized. Yip found that it did not hold an electrical charge and was therefore not ionized. When Park is confronted with this evidence, he says that he never claimed that the bracelet would hold an electrical charge. Rather, he simply says that the bracelet is ionized using an "exclusive ionization process." Hidden-camera video of retail sales-people shows them explaining ionization by saying things like "it picks up the iron in your blood and speeds up circulation" and "negative ions are collected in the ends of the bracelet." Retail salespeople say they are not sure what ionization is.

Mesley also shows Park a hidden-camera interview with the Q-Ray sales coordinator. The coordinator mentions several types of pain that Q-Ray bracelets relieve—migraine, carpal tunnel, and arthritis. Park says that he will have to meet with the sales coordinator and inform her that she cannot make these pain-relief claims.

Questions

1. What is ethics? How is the concept relevant for the Q-ray bracelet situation?
2. List and briefly describe the four criteria that a person might use when trying to make an ethical choice. Which criterion do you think Q-ray used in the marketing of its bracelet? Which criterion do you think should be used?
3. Do you think that individuals at Q-ray are behaving in an ethical or unethical way? Use Exhibit 9-8 to analyze the situation and help you make a decision. Do you see any problems with Exhibit 9-8? Explain.
4. What is social responsibility? Is Q-ray acting in a socially responsible fashion? Defend your answer.

From *Concepts* to *Skills*

Solving Problems Creatively

You can be more effective at solving problems creatively if you use the following 10 suggestions:[118]

1. *Think of yourself as creative.* Research shows that if you think you can't be creative, you won't be. Believing in your ability to be creative is the first step to becoming more creative.

2. *Pay attention to your intuition.* Every individual has a subconscious mind that works well. Sometimes answers will come to you when you least expect them. Listen to that "inner voice." In fact, most creative people will keep notepads near their beds and write down ideas when the thoughts come to them.

3. *Move away from your comfort zone.* Every individual has a comfort zone in which certainty exists. But creativity and the known often do not mix. To be creative, you need to move away from the status quo and focus your mind on something new.

4. *Determine what you want to do.* This includes such things as taking time to understand a problem before beginning to try to resolve it, getting all the facts in mind, and trying to identify the most important facts.

5. *Think outside the box.* Use analogies whenever possible (e.g., could you approach your problem like a fish out of water and look at what the fish does to cope? Or can you use the things you have to do to find your way when it's foggy to help you solve your problem?). Use different problem-solving strategies, such as verbal, visual, mathematical, or theatrical. Look at your problem from a different perspective or ask yourself what someone else, like your grandmother, might do if faced with the same situation.

6. *Look for ways to do things better.* This may involve trying consciously to be original, not worrying about looking foolish, keeping an open mind, being alert to odd or puzzling facts, thinking of unconventional ways to use objects and the environment, discarding usual or habitual ways of doing things, and striving for objectivity by being as critical of your own ideas as you would be of someone else's.

7. *Find several right answers.* Being creative means continuing to look for other solutions even when you think you have solved the problem. A better, more creative solution just might be found.

8. *Believe in finding a workable solution.* Like believing in yourself, you also need to believe in your ideas. If you don't think you can find a solution, you probably won't.

9. *Brainstorm with others.* Creativity is not an isolated activity. Bouncing ideas off of others creates a synergistic effect.

10. *Turn creative ideas into action.* Coming up with creative ideas is only part of the process. Once the ideas are generated, they must be implemented. Keeping great ideas in your mind, or on papers that no one will read, does little to expand your creative abilities.

Practising Skills

Every time the phone rings, your stomach clenches and your palms start to sweat. And it's no wonder! As sales manager for Brinkers, a machine tool parts manufacturer, you are besieged by calls from customers who are upset about late deliveries. Your boss, Carter Hererra, acts as both production manager and scheduler. Every time your sales representatives negotiate a sale, it's up to Carter to determine whether production can actually meet the delivery date the customer specifies. Carter invariably says, "No problem." The good thing about this is that you make a lot of initial sales. The bad news is that production hardly ever meets the shipment dates that Carter authorizes. He doesn't seem to be all that concerned about the aftermath of late deliveries. He says, "Our customers know they're getting outstanding quality at a great price. Just let them try to match that anywhere. It can't be done. So even if they have to wait a couple of extra days or weeks, they're still getting the best deal they can." Somehow the customers do not see it that way, and they let you know about their unhappiness. Then it's up to you to try to smooth over the relationship. You know this problem has to be taken care of, but what possible solutions are there? After all, how are you going to keep from making your manager angry or making the customers angry? Use your knowledge of creative problem solving to come up with solutions.

Reinforcing Skills

1. Take 20 minutes to list as many medical or health-care-related jobs as you can that begin with the letter *r* (for instance, radiologist, registered nurse). If you run out of listings before time is up, it's OK to quit early. But try to be as creative as you can.

2. List on a piece of paper some common terms that apply to both *water* and *finance*. How many were you able to come up with?

10

Organizational Culture and Change

How does a pizza franchise business ensure quality control across the country? Developing a strong culture is part of the answer.

1 What is the purpose of organizational culture?

2 How do you create and maintain organizational culture?

3 Can organizational culture have a downside?

4 How do organizations manage change?

5 Why do people and organizations resist change?

When you walk into a Boston Pizza restaurant in BC, Ontario, or Quebec, you will find many similarities, but a few differences too.[1] The Quebec restaurants carry poutine, while the Ontario restaurants have a meatball sub on the menu and use a different type of pepperoni on the pizzas than those made in BC and Quebec.

Despite these menu differences, the similarity that binds the Richmond, BC-based Boston Pizza restaurants throughout Canada and the United States is the strong organizational culture created by the company's founders and co-chairs, Jim Treliving and George Melville. The two men believe that a strong culture makes for a strong organization, and they emphasize the importance of finding the right people, having good systems in place, training employees, and communicating effectively.

The emphasis on a strong culture seems to be paying off for Boston Pizza. In 2008, it was named one of Canada's 10 Most Admired Corporate Cultures, and its three-year average revenue growth far exceeded industry standards and the TSX 60 Composite index.

In this chapter, we show that every organization has a culture. We examine how that culture reveals itself and the it has on the attitudes and behaviours of members of that organization. An understanding of what makes up an organization's culture and how culture is , sustained, and learned enhances our ability to explain and predict the behaviour of people at work. We also look at different approaches organizations take to managing change.

OB *Is for Everyone*

- What does organizational culture do?
- Is culture the same as rules?
- What kind of organizational culture would work best for you?
- Are there positive approaches to change?
- How do you respond to change?
- What makes organizations resist change?

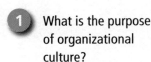

What is the purpose of organizational culture?

What Is Organizational Culture?

When Henry Mintzberg, professor at McGill University and one of the world's leading management experts, was asked to compare organizational structure and corporate culture, he said, "Culture is the soul of the organization—the beliefs and values, and how they are manifested. I think of the structure as the skeleton, and as the flesh and blood. And culture is the soul that holds the thing together and gives it life force."[2]

Mintzberg's metaphor provides a clear image of how to think about culture. Culture provides stability to an organization and gives employees a clear understanding of "the way things are done around here." Culture sets the tone for how organizations operate and how individuals within the organization interact. Think of the different impressions you have when a receptionist tells you that "Ms. Dettweiler" will be available in a moment, while at another organization you are told that "Emma" will be with you as soon as she gets off the phone. It's clear that in one organization the rules are more formal than in the other.

As we discuss organizational culture, you may want to remember that organizations differ considerably in the cultures they adopt. Consider the different cultures of Calgary-based WestJet Airlines and Montreal-based Air Canada. WestJet is viewed as having a "young, spunky, can-do environment, where customers will have more fun."[3] Air Canada, by contrast, is considered less helpful and friendly. One analyst even suggested that Air Canada staff "tend to make their customers feel stressed" by their confrontational behaviour.[4] Our discussion of culture should help you understand how these differences across organizations occur.

As you start to think about different organizations where you might work, you will want to consider their cultures. An organization that expects employees to work 15 hours a day may not be one in which you would like to work. An understanding of culture might help you discover the firm's expectations before you accept a job, or it might help you understand why you like (or do not like) the college or university you attend. Some organizations' cultures are admired more than others: Toronto-based Four Seasons Hotels and Resorts, Edmonton-based Intuit Canada, Calgary-based WestJet, and Montreal-based Yellow Pages Group are 4 of the 10 companies named "Most Admired Corporate Cultures of 2008."

Below, we propose a specific definition of organizational culture and review several issues that revolve around this definition. *From Concepts to Skills* on pages 373–375 tells you how to read an organization's culture. You may want to complete the *Learning About Yourself Exercise* on page 369, which assesses whether you would be more comfortable in a formal, rule-oriented culture or a more informal, flexible culture.

Definition of Organizational Culture

organizational culture The pattern of shared values, beliefs, and assumptions considered appropriate for thinking and acting within an organization.

Organizational culture is the pattern of shared values, beliefs, and assumptions considered appropriate for thinking and acting within an organization. The key features of culture are as follows:

- Culture is shared by the members of the organization.

- Culture helps members of the organization solve and understand the things that the organization encounters, both internally and externally.

- Because the assumptions, beliefs, and expectations that make up culture have worked over time, members of the organization believe they are valid. Therefore, they are taught to people who join the organization.

- These assumptions, beliefs, and expectations strongly influence how people perceive, think, feel, and behave within the organization.[5]

Not every group develops a culture, although any group that has existed for a while and has shared learnings will likely have a culture. Groups that experience high turnover (so that learnings are not passed down to new members very effectively) and groups that have not experienced any challenging events may not develop cultures.

Levels of Culture

Because organizational culture has multiple levels,[6] the metaphor of an iceberg has often been used to describe it.[7] However, a simmering volcano may better represent the layers of culture: beliefs, values, and assumptions bubble below the surface, producing observable aspects of culture at the surface. Exhibit 10-1 reminds us that culture is very visible at the level of **artifacts**. These are what you see, hear, and feel when you encounter an organization's culture. You may notice, for instance, that employees in two offices have very different dress policies, or one office displays great works of art while another posts company mottos on the wall.

Exhibit 10-1 also shows us that beliefs, values, and assumptions, unlike artifacts, are not always readily observable. Instead, we rely on the visible artifacts (material symbols, special language used, rituals carried out, and stories told to others) to help us uncover the organization's beliefs, values, and assumptions. **Beliefs** are the understandings of how objects and ideas relate to each other. **Values** are the stable, long-lasting beliefs about what is important. For instance, Winnipeg-based Palliser Furniture, a manufacturer of wooden and upholstered furniture, promotes the following corporate values: "demonstrate integrity in all relationships," "promote the dignity and value of each other," and strive for excellence."[8] **Assumptions** are the taken-for-granted notions of how something should be. When basic assumptions are held by the entire group, members will have difficulty conceiving of another way of doing things. For instance, in Canada, some students hold a basic assumption that universities should not consider costs when setting tuition but that they should keep tuition low for greater access by students. Beliefs, values, and assumptions, if we can uncover them, help us understand why organizations do the things that we observe.

artifacts Aspects of an organization's culture that an individual can see, hear, and feel.

beliefs The understandings of how objects and ideas relate to each other.

values The stable, long-lasting beliefs about what is important.

assumptions The taken-for-granted notions of how something should be.

EXHIBIT 10-1   Layers of Culture

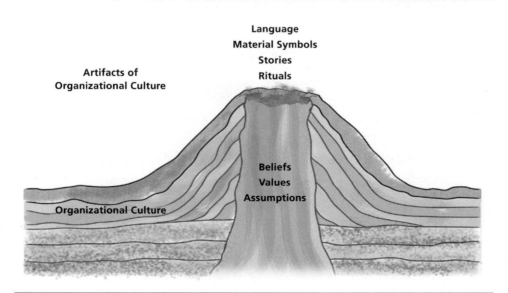

Language
Material Symbols
Stories
Rituals

Artifacts of Organizational Culture

Beliefs
Values
Assumptions

Organizational Culture

Vancouver-based Playland amusement park hires hundreds of young people each summer to run the rides, sell tickets, and manage the games booths. Managers want to make sure that new employees will fit into the "fun culture" of the environment. Instead of one-on-one interviews, applicants are put into teams where they solve puzzles together while managers watch the group dynamics. Amy Nguyen (left) and Chloe Wong are two of the teens hired after they did well in the group interview.

Characteristics of Culture

Research suggests that seven primary characteristics capture the essence of an organization's culture:[9]

- *Innovation and risk-taking.* The degree to which employees are encouraged to be innovative and take risks.

- *Attention to detail.* The degree to which employees are expected to work with precision, analysis, and attention to detail.

- *Outcome orientation.* The degree to which management focuses on results, or outcomes, rather than on the techniques and processes used to achieve these outcomes.

- *People orientation.* The degree to which management decisions take into consideration the effect of outcomes on people within the organization.

- *Team orientation.* The degree to which work activities are organized around teams rather than individuals.

- *Aggressiveness.* The degree to which people are aggressive and competitive rather than easygoing and supportive.

- *Stability.* The degree to which organizational activities emphasize maintaining the status quo in contrast to growth.

Each of these characteristics exists on a continuum from low to high. For instance, Boston Pizza, discussed in this chapter's opening vignette, is high on innovation and risk-taking, and high on people orientation and team orientation.

When individuals consider their organizations according to these seven characteristics, they get a composite picture of the organizations' culture. This picture becomes the basis for feelings of shared understanding that members have about the organization, how things are done in it, and the way members are supposed to behave. Exhibit 10-2 demonstrates how these characteristics can be mixed to create highly diverse organizations.

EXHIBIT 10-2   Contrasting Organizational Cultures

Organization A	Organization B
• Managers must fully document all decisions.	• Management encourages and rewards risk-taking and change.
• Creative decisions, change, and risks are not encouraged.	• Employees are encouraged to "run with" ideas, and failures are treated as "learning experiences."
• Extensive rules and regulations exist for all employees.	• Employees have few rules and regulations to follow.
• Productivity is valued over employee morale.	• Productivity is balanced with treating its people right.
• Employees are encouraged to stay within their own department.	• Team members are encouraged to interact with people at all levels and functions.
• Individual effort is encouraged.	• Many rewards are team-based.

Functions of Culture

What does organizational culture do?

Culture performs a number of functions within an organization:

- It has a boundary-defining role because it creates distinction between one organization and others.

- It conveys a sense of identity to organization members.

- It helps create commitment to something larger than an individual's self-interest.

- It enhances stability; it is the social glue that helps hold the organization together by providing appropriate standards for what employees should say and do.

- It serves as a control mechanism that guides and shapes the attitudes and behaviour of employees, and helps them make sense of the organization.

This last function is of particular interest to us.[10] As the following quotation makes clear, culture defines the rules of the game:

Culture by definition is elusive, intangible, implicit, and taken for granted. But every organization develops a core set of assumptions, understandings, and implicit rules that govern day-to-day behaviour in the workplace. Until newcomers learn the rules, they are not accepted as full-fledged members of the organization. Transgressions of the rules on the part of high-level executives or front-line employees result in universal disapproval and powerful penalties. Conformity to the rules becomes the primary basis for reward and upward mobility.[11]

The role of culture in influencing employee behaviour appears to be increasingly important in today's workplace.[12] As organizations widen spans of control, flatten structures, introduce teams, reduce formalization, and empower employees, the *shared meaning* provided by a strong culture ensures that everyone is pointed in the same direction. Geoffrey Relph, IBM Canada's former marketing director of professional services (now an associate at Ottawa, Ontario-based Strata, an executive management firm), compared the culture of his previous company (GE Appliances in Louisville, Kentucky) with that of IBM: "The priorities in GE are: Make the financial commitments. Make the financial commitments. Make the financial commitments.' At IBM, the company's attention is divided among customer satisfaction, employee morale, and positive financial results."[13] These two cultures give employees and managers different messages about where they should direct their attention. Recent research suggests, moreover, that employees are more likely to behave appropriately when there are clear norms about behaviour, rather than general guidelines, such as "be honest."[14]

Culture can also influence people's ethical behaviour. When lower-level employees see their managers padding expense reports, this sends a signal that the firm tolerates such dishonest behaviour. Firms that emphasize individual sales records may encourage unhealthy competition among sales staff, including "misplacing" phone messages and not being helpful to someone else's client. Toronto-based GMP Securities, on the other hand, emphasizes the importance of a teamwork culture so that individuals are not competing against one another and engaging in questionable activities. Founding partner Brad Griffiths notes that "the corporate culture is to make an environment where everybody feels they're involved. We want to be successful, but not at the expense of the individual."[15] For further discussion of the effect of culture on ethical behaviour, see this chapter's *Ethical Dilemma Exercise* on page 371.

Do Organizations Have Uniform Cultures?

Organizational culture represents a common perception held by the organization's members. This was made explicit when we defined culture as a system of *shared* meaning. We should expect, therefore, that individuals with different backgrounds or at different levels in the organization will tend to describe the organization's culture in similar terms.[16]

However, the fact that organizational culture has common properties does not mean that there cannot be subcultures within it. Most large organizations have a dominant culture and numerous sets of subcultures.[17]

dominant culture A system of shared meaning that expresses the core values shared by a majority of the organization's members.

subcultures Mini-cultures within an organization, typically defined by department designations and geographical separation.

core values The primary, or dominant, values that are accepted throughout the organization.

A **dominant culture** expresses the core values that are shared by a majority of the organization's members. When we talk about an *organization's culture,* we are referring to its dominant culture. It is this macro view of culture that gives an organization its distinct personality.[18] **Subcultures** tend to develop in large organizations to reflect common problems, situations, or experiences that members face. These subcultures are likely to be defined by department designations and geographical separation.

An organization's purchasing department, for example, can have a subculture that is unique to the members of that department. It will include the **core values**—the primary, or dominant, values in the organization—plus additional values unique to members of the purchasing department. Similarly, an office or unit of the organization that is physically separated from the organization's main operations may take on a different personality. Again, the core values are essentially retained but modified to reflect the distinct situation of the separated unit.

If organizations had no dominant culture and were composed only of numerous subcultures, the value of organizational culture as an independent variable would be significantly lessened. This is because there would be no uniform interpretation of what represented appropriate and inappropriate behaviour. It is the "shared

Organizational culture guides and shapes the attitudes of employees at New Zealand Air. One of the airline's guiding principles is to champion and promote New Zealand and its national heritage, both within the country and overseas. In this photo, a cabin crew member dressed in traditional Maori clothing and a pilot touch noses to represent the sharing of a single breath following a ceremony for the airline's purchase of a Boeing airplane in Everett, Washington. Such expressions of representing their country with pride create a strong bond among employees.

meaning" aspect of culture that makes it such a potent device for guiding and shaping behaviour. That is what allows us to say that Microsoft's culture values aggressiveness and risk-taking,[19] and then to use that information to better understand the behaviour of Microsoft executives and employees. But we cannot ignore the reality that as well as a dominant culture, many organizations have subcultures that can influence the behaviour of members. Some strong subcultures can even make it difficult for managers to introduce organizational change. This sometimes happens in unionized environments and can occur in nonunionized environments as well. To learn more about how to identify the culture of an organization, see *From Concepts to Skills* on pages 373–375.

Creating and Sustaining an Organization's Culture

One of the challenges Boston Pizza founders Jim Treliving and George Melville face in managing the 305 restaurants across Canada and more than 28 000 employees is making sure that everyone is on the same page.[20] The individual restaurants in the chain are not owned by the company. Instead, franchisees invest a considerable amount of money in order to gain the right to own a Boston Pizza restaurant. Thus, there could be a conflict between what the founders want done and what a franchisor feels is best for his or her investment.

Treliving and Melville try to prevent this conflict by carefully vetting franchise candidates. Potential franchisees are informed of the initial $60 000 fee and start-up costs that could run between $1.6 million and $2.4 million. Despite the size of their investment, franchisees must demonstrate a "willingness to adhere to the Boston Pizza system." Franchisees are given a lot of help in starting out, however.

When Hank Van Poelgeest opened up the first Boston Pizza restaurant in St. John's, Newfoundland, in January 2006, he naturally worried. A lot of preparation had gone into the opening, months of planning, careful choice of location, and a team of nine people had been sent from head office to help hire and train staff. The new staff did a dress rehearsal of the grand-opening four times to make sure nothing went wrong.

The preparation was so thorough that the opening exceeded all expectations. "We wanted to use the first couple of weeks as a slow beginning," says Van Poelgeest, "but we've never had a slow beginning." What role does culture play in creating high-performing employees?

An organization's culture does not pop out of thin air. Once established, it rarely fades away. Exhibit 10-3 summarizes how an organization's culture is established and sustained. The original culture derives from the founder's philosophy. This in turn strongly influences the criteria used in hiring. The actions of the current top management set the general climate of what is acceptable behaviour and what is not. How employees are to be socialized will depend both on the degree of success an organization achieves in matching new employees' values to its own in the selection process and on top management's preference for socialization methods. We describe each part of this process on the next page.

2 How do you create and maintain organizational culture?

EXHIBIT 10-3 How Organizational Cultures Form

How a Culture Begins

Is culture the same as rules?

An organization's current customs, traditions, and general way of doing things owe a great deal to what it has done before and how successful those previous endeavours have been. This leads us to the ultimate source of an organization's culture: its founders.[21]

The founders traditionally have a major impact on that organization's early culture. They have a vision of what the organization should be. They are not constrained by previous customs or ideologies. Because new organizations are typically small, it is possible for the founders to impose their vision on all organizational members.

A culture can be created in three ways.[22] First, founders hire and keep only employees who think and feel the way they do. Second, they indoctrinate and socialize these employees to their way of thinking and feeling. Finally, the founders' behaviour acts as a role model, encouraging employees to identify with the founders and internalize those beliefs, values, and assumptions. When the organization succeeds, the founders' vision is seen as a primary determinant of that success. At that point, the founders' entire personality becomes embedded in the culture of the organization.

The culture at Edmonton-based PCL, the largest general contracting organization in Canada, is still strongly influenced by the vision of Ernest Poole, who founded the company in 1906. "Poole's rules," which include "Employ highest grade people obtainable" and "Encourage integrity, loyalty and efficiencies," still influence the way the company hires and trains its employees long after the founder's death.[23] Other contemporary examples of founders who have had an immeasurable impact on their organizations' cultures are Ted Rogers of Toronto-based Rogers Communications, Frank Stronach of Aurora, Ontario-based Magna International, and Richard Branson of the Virgin Group.

Keeping a Culture Alive

Once a culture is in place, human resource practices within the organization act to maintain it by giving employees a set of similar experiences.[24] For example, the selection process, performance evaluation criteria, training and career development activities, and promotion procedures ensure that new employees fit in with the culture, rewarding those who support it and penalizing (even expelling) those who challenge it. Three forces play a particularly important part in sustaining a culture: *selection* practices, the actions of *top management*, and *socialization* methods. Let's take a closer look at each.

Selection

The explicit goal of the selection process is to identify and hire individuals who have the knowledge, skills, and abilities to perform the jobs within the organization successfully. Typically, more than one candidate will meet any given job's requirements. The final decision as to who is hired is significantly influenced by the decision maker's judgment of how well each candidate will fit into the organization. This attempt to ensure a proper match, either deliberately or inadvertently, results in the hiring of people who have values consistent with those of the organization, or at least a good portion of those values.[25]

At the same time, the selection process provides information about the organization to applicants. If they perceive a conflict between their values and those of the organization, they can remove themselves from the applicant pool. Selection, therefore, becomes a two-way street, allowing the employer or applicant to look elsewhere if there appears to be a mismatch. In this way, the selection process sustains an organization's culture by selecting out those individuals who might attack or undermine its core values. *OB in the Workplace* shows how one company's method of interviewing ensures that applicants are right for the job.

OB IN THE WORKPLACE

Playland's Interviews Are More Than Fun and Games

How does a company make sure an applicant is right for the job? At Playland, Vancouver's largest amusement park, applicants for a summer job do not do one-on-one interviews with managers or the human resource department.[26] Instead, they are asked to deconstruct a JENGA tower with a group of nine other applicants and answer a variety of "interesting questions." When an applicant removes a block from the tower, they answer a question printed on it.

Amy Nguyen, a 15-year-old high school student applying for her first job, had the following question: "There's a customer who had to line up a long time for food and he was very upset by the time he got to the front of the line. What would you do?"

"I said I would apologize, look cute and tell him, 'Let me see if my manager can do anything for you,'" says Nguyen. This answer got her a second interview, and she eventually got the job.

Jennifer Buensuceso, a PNE gaming manager at Playland, thinks the new way of hiring is much better than when she faced a one-on-one question and answer format when she was hired. She says the new method helps managers learn about the applicant's "team-building and individuality. You get to see them think out of the box."

This format is also good for nervous teens and those whose first language is not English. Getting them to play relaxes them and helps managers to see "who shows natural leadership skills, who's outgoing, who works well on a team and who's good at problem-solving."[27]

Top Management

The actions of top management also have a major impact on the organization's culture.[28] Through what they say and how they behave, senior executives establish norms that filter down through the organization. These norms establish whether risk-taking is desirable; how much freedom managers should give their employees; what is appropriate dress; what actions will pay off in terms of pay raises, promotions, and other rewards; and the like. Apple's culture of secrecy stems from how private Steve Jobs is, as shown in *OB in the Workplace*.

OB IN THE WORKPLACE

Private CEO Leads by Example

When Steve Jobs, founder and figurehead of Apple Computer, took a leave of absence from the company in January 2009, few details were given about the reason for the leave.[29] Jobs' reportedly had a "hormonal imbalance" and needed some time off. In mid-June, word leaked that Jobs' had had a liver transplant sometime in the spring.

Apple's culture of secrecy is not limited to Jobs' health. The company is known for trying to keep all sorts of information secret, from product information to release dates. The company sometimes gives misleading information not only to reporters, but even to its employees to prevent premature leaks about product development. "I was at the iPod launch," said Edward Eigerman, a former systems engineer at Apple. "No one that I worked with saw that coming."

How does the company maintain such a high level of secrecy? Mainly through its culture and norms. Employees sign nondisclosure agreements, and they are fired if it's determined they have leaked information to the press or other parties. "They make everyone super, super paranoid about security," said Mark Hamblin, a former Apple employee. "I have never seen anything else like it at another company."

Apple's culture of secrecy may be more a reflection of Jobs' personality rather than simply a business strategy. Regis McKenna, a Silicon Valley marketing veteran who has advised Apple in the past, notes that "what most people don't understand is that Steve has always been very personal about his life. He has always kept things close to the vest since I've known him, and only confided in relatively few people."

Socialization

What kind of organizational culture would work best for you?

No matter how effectively the organization recruits and selects new employees, they are not fully trained in the organization's culture when they start their jobs. Because they are unfamiliar with the organization's culture, new employees may disturb the beliefs and customs that are in place. The organization will, therefore, want to help new employees adapt to its culture. This adaptation process is called **socialization**.[30]

socialization The process by which new employees adapt to an organization's culture.

New employees at the Japanese electronics company Sanyo are socialized through a particularly long training program. At their intensive

The source of Cranium's culture is co-founder and CEO Richard Tait, shown here at a toy fair demonstrating the toys and games his company makes. Tait created a culture of fun and collaboration at Cranium so employees can work in an environment that stimulates creativity and innovation in developing new products. At Cranium, employees choose their own titles. Tait chose Grand Poo Bah, and the chief financial officer selected Professor Profit. The office walls at Cranium are painted in bright primary colours, and music plays everywhere.

five-month course, trainees eat and sleep together in company-subsidized dorms and are required to vacation together at company-owned resorts. They learn the Sanyo way of doing everything—from how to speak to managers to proper grooming and dress.[31] The company considers this program essential for transforming young employees, fresh out of school, into dedicated *kaisha senshi*, or corporate warriors.

As we discuss socialization, keep in mind that the new employee's entry into the organization is the most critical stage. This is when the organization seeks to mould the outsider into an employee "in good standing." Those employees who fail to learn the essential role behaviours risk being labelled "nonconformists" or "rebels," which often leads to their being fired. The organization continues to socialize every employee, though maybe not as explicitly, throughout his or her career in the organization. This further contributes to sustaining the culture. (Sometimes, however, employees are not fully socialized. For instance, you will note in Exhibit 10-4 that the cartoon employees had learned they were supposed to wear checkerboard caps to work, but clearly did not know why.)

EXHIBIT 10-4

"I don't know how it started, either. All I know is that it's part of our corporate culture."

Source: Drawing by Mick Stevens in *The New Yorker*, October 3, 1994. Copyright © 1994 by The New Yorker Magazine, Inc. Reprinted by permission.

The Liabilities of Organizational Culture

We have treated organizational culture in a nonjudgmental manner thus far. We have not said that it is good or bad, only that it exists. Many of its functions, as outlined, are valuable for both the organization and the employee. Culture enhances organizational commitment and increases the consistency of employee behaviour. These are clearly benefits to an organization. From an employee's standpoint, culture is valuable because it reduces ambiguity. It tells employees how things are done and what is important. However, we should not ignore the potentially dysfunctional aspects of culture, especially of a strong culture, on an organization's effectiveness. As recent research suggests, cultures that strongly emphasize competition can lead to negative organizational consequences.[32]

We now consider culture's impact on change, diversity, and mergers and acquisitions.

 Can organizational culture have a downside?

Culture as a Barrier to Change

Culture is a liability when the shared values do not agree with those that will further the organization's effectiveness. Employees are less likely to have shared values when the organization's environment is dynamic. When the environment is undergoing rapid change, the organization's entrenched culture may no longer be appropriate. Consistency of behaviour is an asset to an organization when it faces a stable environment. However, it may burden the organization and make it difficult to respond to changes in the environment. For many organizations with strong cultures, practices that led to previous successes can lead to failure when those practices no longer match up well with environmental needs.[33] When employees at the Royal Canadian Mint failed to act rapidly to create a commemorative coin for Canadian golfer Mike Weir, then-president and CEO David Dingwall felt this underscored the Mint's reluctance to respond to a competitive environment. Consistent with this, research shows that overly friendly cultures may prevent managers from making important strategic decisions for fear of harming relationships.[34] This chapter's *Point/Counterpoint* on page 368 further explores the question of whether a culture can change.

Culture as a Barrier to Diversity

Hiring new employees who, because of race, gender, disability, or other differences, are not like the majority of the organization's members creates a paradox.[35] Management wants the new employees to accept the organization's core cultural values. Otherwise, these employees are unlikely to fit in or be accepted. But at the same time, management wants to openly acknowledge and demonstrate support for the differences that these employees bring to the workplace.

Strong cultures put considerable pressure on employees to conform. They limit the range of values and styles that are acceptable. It is no coincidence that employees at Disney theme parks appear to be almost universally attractive, clean, and wholesome looking with bright smiles. That's the image the Walt Disney Company seeks. It selects employees who will maintain that image. Once the theme-park employees are on the job, a strong culture—supported by formal rules and regulations—ensures that they will act in a relatively uniform and predictable way.

Organizations seek out and hire diverse individuals because of the new strengths they bring to the workplace. Yet these diverse behaviours and strengths are likely to diminish in strong cultures as people try to fit in. Strong cultures, therefore, can be liabilities when they effectively eliminate the unique strengths that people of different backgrounds bring to the organization. Moreover, strong cultures can also be liabilities when they support institutional bias or become insensitive to people who are different.

Culture as a Barrier to Mergers and Acquisitions

Historically, the key factors that management looked at in making merger or acquisition decisions were related to financial advantages or product synergy. In recent years, cultural compatibility has become the primary concern.[36] While a favourable financial statement or product line may be the initial attraction of an acquisition candidate, whether the acquisition actually works seems to have more to do with how well the two organizations' cultures match up. Daimler-Benz and Chrysler struggled to make their 1998 merger work, as *OB Around the Globe* shows.

OB AROUND THE GLOBE

Mergers Across National Borders Are Challenging

What happens when two companies with very different cultures merge? When Daimler-Benz and Chrysler merged in 1998 to form DaimlerChrysler, some called it a "marriage made in heaven."[37] The merger was supposed to create a global automaker out of two respected companies. Instead, the merger has been a disaster, with the US-based Chrysler arm becoming a money loser in the years since the merger. In spring 2002, DaimlerChrysler's stock was worth half of what it had been on the day the merger was announced. By 2005, DaimlerChrysler was still not doing as well financially as analysts and shareholders had hoped, although there had been slight improvements in overall profitability.

The Germans and the Americans blame each other for the failure, and the very different cultures of the two organizations no doubt led to many of the problems. Daimler-Benz was extremely hierarchical, while Chrysler, with its "cowboy culture," was more egalitarian. Chrysler's managers were independent, and its middle managers were empowered. While this structure led to a lot of infighting, it also resulted in much creativity—for example, the development of the popular PT Cruiser.

Employees at Chrysler were very slow to trust the German management that took over the company in what was billed as a merger of equals. Jürgen Schrempp, chair of the merged companies until 2005, admitted that he intended for the merger to be a takeover. Thus, to North American employees, it's no surprise that he slashed thousands of jobs in Canada and the United States after the merger.

Distrust went both ways: German management did not trust the American senior managers at Chrysler, and eventually Schrempp let them go. They were viewed as overpaid and lazy, unwilling to work overtime or miss their golf games by flying on weekends. These images of one another did not make it easy for managers from the two companies to work together and created much uncertainty for the employees at Chrysler. In 2007, this "marriage made in heaven" came to an end. Daimler sold Chrysler to a private equity firm, enabling both car manufacturers to get back to basics without the challenges created by conflicting cultures.

As the Daimler-Benz and Chrysler merger and divorce suggests, bringing employees from two different companies together is likely to cause friction. Chrysler employees were subjected to another cultural change with the merger of Fiat and Chrysler in June 2009, and the installation of Fiat's CEO, Sergio Marchionne, as the head of both operations.

Strategies for Merging Cultures

Organizations can use several strategies when considering how to merge the cultures of two organizations:[38]

- *Assimilation.* The entire new organization is determined to take on the culture of one of the merging organizations. This strategy works best when one of the organizations has a relatively weak culture. However, if a culture is simply imposed on an organization, it rarely works.

- *Separation.* The organizations remain separate and keep their individual cultures. This strategy works best when the organizations have little overlap in the industries in which they operate.

- *Integration.* A new culture is formed by merging parts of each of the organizations. This strategy works best when aspects of each organization's culture need to be improved.

Approaches to Managing Change

Our discussion of organizational culture as well as the issues that arise when organizations merge leads to a fundamental question for all organizations: How can change be managed? In what follows, we consider several approaches to managing change: Lewin's classic three-step model of the change process, Kotter's eight-step plan for implementing change, action research, and appreciative inquiry. We should also note that recent research emphasizes the need in change processes to manage the "hard stuff" as well as the "soft," or people, issues in order to be successful.[39]

Who is responsible for managing change in an organization? The answer is change agents.[40] **Change agents** can be managers or nonmanagers, employees of the organization, or outside consultants.

Lewin's Three-Step Model

Assuming that an organization has uncovered a need for change, how does it engage in the change process? Kurt Lewin argued that successful change in organizations should follow three steps, which are illustrated in Exhibit 10-5 on page 356: **unfreezing** the status quo, **moving** to a new state, and **refreezing** the new change to make it

4   How do organizations manage change?

change agents People who act as catalysts and assume the responsibility for managing change.

unfreezing Change efforts to overcome the pressures of both individual resistance and group conformity.

moving Efforts to get employees involved in the change process.

refreezing Stabilizing a change intervention by balancing driving and restraining forces.

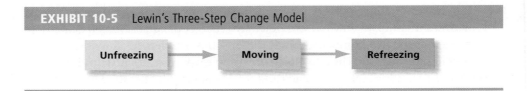

EXHIBIT 10-5   Lewin's Three-Step Change Model

Unfreezing → Moving → Refreezing

permanent.[41] The value of this model can be seen in the following example, where the management of a large oil company decided to reorganize its marketing function in Western Canada.

The oil company had three regional offices in the West, located in Winnipeg, Calgary, and Vancouver. The decision was made to consolidate the marketing divisions of the three regional offices into a single regional office to be located in Calgary. The reorganization meant transferring more than 150 employees, eliminating some duplicate managerial positions, and instituting a new hierarchy of command. As you might guess, such a huge move was difficult to keep secret. The rumours preceded the announcement by several months. The decision itself was made unilaterally. It came from the executive offices in Toronto. Those people affected had no say whatsoever in the choice. For anyone in Vancouver or Winnipeg who might have disliked the decision and its consequences—the problems involved in transferring to another city, pulling youngsters out of school, making new friends, having new co-workers, undergoing the reassignment of responsibilities—the only recourse was to quit. The status quo was about to change.

driving forces Forces that direct behaviour away from the status quo.

restraining forces Forces that hinder movement away from the status quo.

The status quo can be considered an equilibrium state. To move from this equilibrium—to overcome the pressures of both individual resistance and group conformity—unfreezing is necessary. Exhibit 10-6 shows that unfreezing can occur in one of three ways. The **driving forces**, which direct behaviour away from the status quo, can be increased. The **restraining forces**, which hinder movement from the existing equilibrium, can be decreased. A third alternative is to *combine the first two approaches*. Companies that have been successful in the past are likely to encounter restraining forces because people question the need for change.[42] Similarly, research shows that companies with strong cultures excel at incremental change but are overcome by restraining forces against radical change.[43]

The oil company's management expected employee resistance to the consolidation and outlined its alternatives. Management could use positive incentives to encourage employees to accept the change. For instance, the company could offer pay increases to those who accepted the transfer. It could also offer to pay all moving expenses. Management might offer low-cost mortgage funds to allow employees to buy new homes in Calgary. Of course, management might also consider unfreezing acceptance of the status quo by removing restraining forces. Employees could be counselled individually. Each employee's concerns and apprehensions could be heard and specifically clarified. Assuming that most of the fears are unjustified, the counsellor could assure the employees that there was nothing to fear and then demonstrate, through tangible evidence, that restraining forces are unwarranted. If resistance is extremely high, management may have to resort to both reducing resistance and increasing the attractiveness of the alternative so the unfreezing can succeed.

Research on organizational change has shown that, to be effective, change has to happen quickly.[44] Organizations that build up to change do less well than those that get to and through the movement stage quickly.

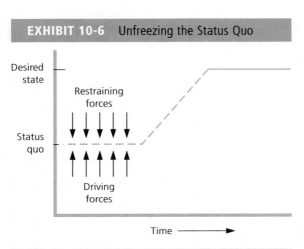

EXHIBIT 10-6   Unfreezing the Status Quo

Desired state

Restraining forces

Status quo

Driving forces

Time →

Once the consolidation change has been implemented, if it is to be successful, the new situation must be refrozen so that it can be sustained over time. Unless this last step is taken, there is a very good chance that the change will be short-lived and that employees will try to revert to the previous state of equilibrium. The objective of refreezing, then, is to stabilize the new situation by balancing the driving and restraining forces.

How could the oil company's management refreeze its consolidation change? It could systematically replace temporary forces with permanent ones. For instance, management might impose a new bonus system tied to the specific changes desired. The formal rules and regulations governing the behaviour of those affected by the change could also be revised to reinforce the new situation. Over time, of course, the work group's own norms will evolve to sustain the new equilibrium. But until that point is reached, management will have to rely on more formal mechanisms. The *Working With Others Exercise* on pages 370–371 gives you the opportunity to identify driving and restraining forces for another company experiencing problems with change and to make some recommendations for change.

A key feature of Lewin's three-step model is its conception of change as an episodic activity, with a beginning, a middle, and an end. However, the structure of today's workplaces requires change to take place as an ongoing, if not chaotic, process. Certainly the adjustment that companies have made to the realities of e-commerce indicates a more chaotic change, rather than a controlled and planned change.

Kotter's Eight-Step Plan for Implementing Change

John Kotter, professor of leadership at Harvard Business School, built on Lewin's three-step model to create a more detailed approach for implementing change.[45]

Kotter began by listing common failures that occur when managers try to initiate change. These include the inability to create a sense of urgency about the need for change; failure to create a coalition for managing the change process; the absence of a vision for change and to effectively communicate that vision; not removing obstacles that could impede the achievement of the vision; failure to provide short-term and achievable goals; the tendency to declare victory too soon; and not anchoring the changes in the organization's culture.

Kotter then established eight sequential steps to overcome these problems. These steps are listed in Exhibit 10-7.

EXHIBIT 10-7   Kotter's Eight-Step Plan for Implementing Change
1. Establish a sense of urgency by creating a compelling reason for why change is needed.
2. Form a coalition with enough power to lead the change.
3. Create a new vision to direct the change and strategies for achieving the vision.
4. Communicate the vision throughout the organization.
5. Empower others to act on the vision by removing barriers to change and encouraging risk-taking and creative problem solving.
6. Plan for, create, and reward short-term "wins" that move the organization toward the new vision.
7. Consolidate improvements, reassess changes, and make necessary adjustments in the new programs.
8. Reinforce the changes by demonstrating the relationship between new behaviours and organizational success.

Source: Based on J. P. Kotter, *Leading Change* (Boston: Harvard Business School Press, 1996).

Notice how Exhibit 10-7 builds on Lewin's model. Kotter's first four steps essentially represent the "unfreezing" stage. Steps 5 through 7 represent "moving." The final step works on "refreezing." Kotter's contribution lies in providing managers and change agents with a more detailed guide for implementing change successfully.

Action Research

action research A change process based on the systematic collection of data and then selection of a change action based on what the analyzed data indicate.

Action research refers to a change process based on the systematic collection of data and then selection of a change action based on what the analyzed data indicate.[46] The importance of this approach is that it provides a scientific method for managing planned change.

The process of action research, carried out by a change agent, consists of five steps:

1. *Diagnosis.* The change agent gathers information about problems, concerns, and needed changes from members of the organization by asking questions, reviewing records, and listening to the concerns of employees.

2. *Analysis.* The change agent organizes the information gathered into primary concerns, problem areas, and possible actions.

3. *Feedback.* The change agent shares with employees what has been found during diagnosis and analysis. The employees, with the help of the change agent, develop action plans for bringing about any needed change.

4. *Action.* The employees and the change agent carry out the specific actions to correct the problems that have been identified.

5. *Evaluation.* The change agent evaluates the action plan's effectiveness, using the data gathered initially as a benchmark.

Action research provides at least two specific benefits for an organization. First, it is problem-focused. The change agent objectively looks for problems and the type of problem determines the type of change action. While this may seem intuitively obvious, a lot of change activities are not done this way. Rather, they are solution-centred. The change agent has a favourite solution—for example, implementing flextime, teams, or a process re-engineering program—and then seeks out problems that his or her solution fits. Second, because action research so heavily involves employees in the process, resistance to change is reduced. In fact, once employees have actively participated in the feedback stage, the change process typically takes on a momentum of its own. The employees and groups that have been involved become an internal source of sustained pressure to bring about the change.

Appreciative Inquiry

appreciative inquiry An approach to change that seeks to identify the unique qualities and special strengths of an organization, which can then be built on to improve performance.

Are there positive approaches to change?

Most organizational change approaches start from a negative perspective: The organization has problems that need solutions. **Appreciative inquiry** accentuates the positive.[47] Rather than looking for problems to fix, this approach seeks to identify the unique qualities and special strengths of an organization, which can then be built on to improve performance. That is, it focuses on an organization's successes rather than on its problems.

Advocates of appreciative inquiry argue that problem-solving approaches always ask people to look backward at yesterday's failures, to focus on shortcomings, and they rarely result in new visions. Instead of creating a climate for positive change, action research and organizational development (OD) techniques such as survey feedback and process consultation end up placing blame and generating

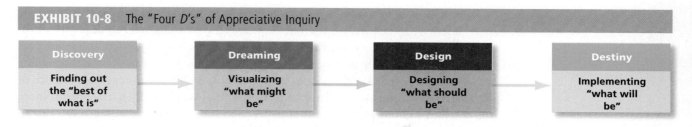

EXHIBIT 10-8 The "Four *D*'s" of Appreciative Inquiry

Discovery	Dreaming	Design	Destiny
Finding out the "best of what is"	Visualizing "what might be"	Designing "what should be"	Implementing "what will be"

Source: Based on D. L. Cooperrider and D. Whitney, *Collaborating for Change: Appreciative Inquiry* (San Francisco: Berrett-Koehler, 2000).

defensiveness. Proponents of appreciative inquiry claim it makes more sense to refine and enhance what the organization is already doing well. This allows the organization to change by playing to its strengths and competitive advantages.

The appreciative inquiry process (see Exhibit 10-8) essentially consists of four steps, or "Four *D*'s," often played out in a large-group meeting over a two- or three-day time period, and overseen by a trained change agent:

- *Discovery.* The idea is to find out what people think are the strengths of the organization. For instance, employees are asked to recount times they felt the organization worked best or when they specifically felt most satisfied with their jobs.

- *Dreaming.* The information from the discovery phase is used to speculate on possible futures for the organization. For instance, people are asked to envision the organization in five years and to describe what is different.

- *Design.* Based on the dream articulation, participants focus on finding a common vision of how the organization will look and agree on its unique qualities.

- *Destiny.* In this final step, participants discuss how the organization is going to fulfill its dream. This typically includes the writing of action plans and the development of implementation strategies.

Appreciative inquiry has proven an effective change strategy in organizations such as Toronto-based Orchestras Canada, Ajax, Ontario-based Nokia Canada, Burnaby, BC-based TELUS, Calgary-based EnCana, and Toronto-based CBC.

The use of appreciative inquiry in organizations is relatively recent, and it has not yet been determined when it is most appropriately used for organizational change.[48] However, it does give us the opportunity of viewing change from a much more positive perspective.

Resistance to Change

One of the most well-documented findings from studies of individual and organizational behaviour is that organizations and their members resist change. One recent study showed that even when employees are shown data that suggests they need to change, they latch onto whatever data they can find that suggests they are okay and do not need to change. Our egos are fragile, and we often see change as threatening.[49]

In some ways, resistance to change is positive. It provides a degree of stability and predictability to behaviour. If there were not some resistance, organizational behaviour would take on the characteristics of chaotic randomness. Resistance to change can also be a source of functional conflict. For example, resistance to a reorganization plan or a change in a product line can stimulate a healthy debate over the merits of the idea and result in a better decision. But there is a definite downside to resistance to change. It hinders adaptation and progress.

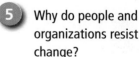

5 Why do people and organizations resist change?

Resistance to change does not necessarily surface in standard ways. Resistance can be overt, implicit, immediate, or deferred. It is easiest for management to deal with resistance when it is overt and immediate. For instance, a change is proposed, and employees respond immediately by voicing complaints, engaging in work slowdowns, threatening to go on strike, or the like. The greater challenge is managing resistance that is implicit or deferred. Implicit resistance efforts are more subtle—loss of loyalty to the organization, loss of motivation to work, increased errors or mistakes, increased absenteeism due to "sickness"—and hence more difficult to recognize. Similarly, deferred actions cloud the link between the source of resistance and the reaction to it. A change may produce what appears to be only a minimal reaction at the time it is initiated, but then resistance surfaces weeks, months, or even years later. Or a single change that in and of itself might have little impact becomes the straw that breaks the camel's back. Reactions to change can build up and then explode in some response that seems totally out of proportion to the change action it follows. The resistance, of course, has merely been deferred and stockpiled. What surfaces is a response to the accumulation of previous changes.

Let's look at the sources of resistance. For analytical purposes, we have categorized them as individual and organizational sources. In the real world, the sources often overlap.

Individual Resistance

How do you respond to change?

Individual sources of resistance to change reside in basic human characteristics such as perceptions, personalities, and needs. This chapter's *Case Incident—GreyStar Art & Greetings Makes Technological Changes* on pages 371–372 looks at an individual who resists change in the workplace. Exhibit 10-9 summarizes four reasons why individuals may resist change:[50]

- *Self-interest.* People worry that they will lose something of value if change happens. Thus, they look after their own self-interests rather than those of the total organization.

EXHIBIT 10-9   Sources of Individual Resistance to Change

Source: Based on J. P. Kotter and L. A. Schlesinger, "Choosing Strategies for Change," *Harvard Business Review*, July–August 2008, pp. 107–109.

- *Misunderstanding and lack of trust.* People resist change when they do not understand the nature of the change and fear that the cost of change will outweigh any potential gains for them. This often occurs when they do not trust those initiating the change.

- *Different assessments.* People resist change when they see it differently than their managers do and think the costs outweigh the benefits, even for the organization. Managers may assume that employees have the same information that they do, but this is not always the case.

- *Low tolerance for change.* People resist change because they worry that they do not have the skills and behaviour required of the new situation. They may feel that they are being asked to do too much, too quickly.

In addition to the above, individuals sometimes worry that being asked to change may indicate that what they have been doing in the past was somehow wrong. Managers should not overlook the effects of peer pressure on an individual's response to change. As well, the manager's attitude (positive or negative) toward the change and his or her relationship with employees will affect an individual's response to change.

Cynicism

Employees often feel cynical about the change process, particularly if they have been through several rounds of change and nothing appears (to them) to have changed. One study identified sources of cynicism in the change process of a large unionized manufacturing plant.[51] The major elements contributing to the cynicism were as follows:

- Feeling uninformed about what was happening
- Lack of communication and respect from one's manager
- Lack of communication and respect from one's union representative
- Lack of opportunity for meaningful participation in decision making

The researchers also found that employees with negative personalities were more likely to be cynical about change. While organizations might not be able to change an individual's personality, they certainly have the ability to provide greater communication and respect, as well as opportunities to take part in decision making. The researchers found that cynicism about change led to such outcomes as lower commitment, less satisfaction, and reduced motivation to work hard. Exhibit 10-10 illustrates why some employees, particularly Dilbert, may have reason to feel cynical about organizational change.

EXHIBIT 10-10

Source: Dilbert, by Scott Adams. August 3, 1996. DILBERT reprinted by permission of United Feature Syndicate, Inc.

Organizational Resistance

What makes organizations resist change?

Organizations, by their very nature, are conservative.[52] They actively resist change. You do not have to look far to see evidence of this phenomenon. Government agencies want to continue doing what they have been doing for years, whether the need for their service changes or remains the same. Organized religions are deeply entrenched in their history. Attempts to change church doctrine require great persistence and patience. Educational institutions, which exist to open minds and challenge established ways of thinking, are themselves extremely resistant to change. Most school systems are using essentially the same teaching technologies today that they were 50 years ago. Similarly, most business firms appear highly resistant to change. Half of the 309 human resource executives of Canadian firms who took part in a 1998 survey rated their companies' ability to manage change as "fair."[53] One-third of them said that their ability to manage change was their weakest skill, and only 25 percent of the companies made a strong effort to train leaders in the change process. When organizations refuse to change with the times, they can face catastrophic results, as can be seen with the Big Three US automakers (Ford, Chrysler, and General Motors) who in late 2008 were begging for the US and Canadian governments to bail them out financially. Chrysler and Ford asked for even more money in 2009, but this came with strict restructuring guidelines from the Obama administration, so that the companies would finally make some needed changes to their financial situation.

Six major sources of organizational resistance to change (shown in Exhibit 10-11) have been identified:[54]

- *Structural inertia.* Organizations have built-in mechanisms—such as their selection processes and formal regulations—to produce stability. When an organization is confronted with change, this structural inertia acts as a counterbalance to sustain stability.

- *Limited focus of change.* Organizations are made up of a number of interdependent subsystems. One cannot be changed without affecting the others. So limited changes in subsystems tend to be nullified by the larger system.

EXHIBIT 10-11   Sources of Organizational Resistance to Change

- *Group inertia.* Even if individuals want to change their behaviour, group norms may act as a constraint.

- *Threat to expertise.* Changes in organizational patterns may threaten the expertise of specialized groups.

- *Threat to established power relationships.* Any redistribution of decision-making authority can threaten long-established power relationships within the organization.

- *Threat to established resource allocations.* Groups in the organization that control sizable resources often see change as a threat. They tend to be content with the way things are.

Overcoming Resistance to Change

Before we move on to ways to overcome resistance to change, it's important to note that not all change is good. Research has shown that sometimes an emphasis on making speedy decisions can lead to bad decisions. Sometimes the line between resisting needed change and falling into a "speed trap" is a fine one indeed. What is more, sometimes in the "fog of change," those who are initiating change fail to realize the full magnitude of the effects they are causing or to estimate their true costs to the organization. Thus, although the perspective generally taken is that rapid, transformational change is good, this is not always the case. Change agents need to carefully think through the full implications.

Seven tactics can be used by change agents to deal with resistance to change.[55] Let's review them briefly.

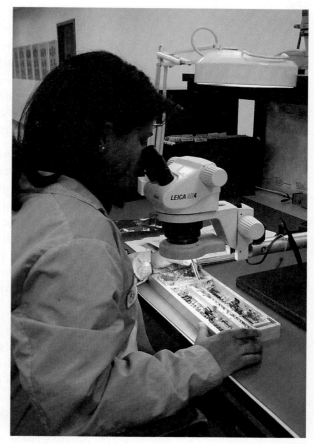

Though most people and organizations resist change, at Advantech AMT, located in Dorval, Quebec, change is the norm. Françoise Binette, chief finance officer, says that "Managing change forms an intrinsic part of our corporate DNA and it is this environment that has allowed us to consistently develop unique and innovative products."

- *Education and communication.* Resistance can be reduced through communicating with employees to help them see the logic of a change. Communication can reduce resistance on two levels. First, it fights the effects of misinformation and poor communication: If employees receive the full facts and get any misunderstandings cleared up, resistance should subside. Second, communication can be helpful in "selling" the need for change. Research shows that the way the need for change is sold matters—change is more likely when the necessity of changing is packaged properly.[56] A study of German companies revealed that changes are most effective when a company communicates its rationale, balancing various stakeholder (shareholders, employees, community, customers) interests, versus a rationale based on shareholder interests only.[57]

- *Participation and involvement.* It's difficult for individuals to resist a change decision in which they participated. Before making a change, those opposed can be brought into the decision process. Assuming that the participants have the expertise to make a meaningful contribution, their involvement can reduce resistance, obtain commitment, and increase the quality of the change decision.

- *Building support and commitment.* Change agents can offer a range of supportive efforts to reduce resistance. When employees' fear and anxiety are high, employee counselling and therapy, new-skills training, or a short paid leave of absence may facilitate adjustment. Research on middle managers has shown that when managers or employees have low emotional commitment to change, they favour the status quo and resist it.[58] So building support with employees can also help them emotionally commit to the change rather than embrace the status quo.

- *Implementing changes fairly.* Try as managers might to have employees see change positively, most workers tend to react negatively. Most people simply do not like change. But one way organizations can minimize the negative impact of change, even when employees frame it as a negative, is to makes sure the change is implemented fairly. As we learned in Chapter 4, procedural fairness becomes especially important when employees perceive an outcome as negative, so when implementing changes, it's crucial that organizations bend over backwards to make sure employees see the reason for the change, and perceive that the changes are being implemented consistently and fairly.[59]

- *Manipulation and co-optation. Manipulation* refers to covert influence attempts. Twisting and distorting facts to make them appear more attractive, withholding undesirable information, and creating false rumours to get employees to accept a change are all examples of manipulation. *Co-optation*, on the other hand, is a form of both manipulation and participation. It seeks to "buy off" the leaders of a resistance group by giving them a key role in the change decision.

- *Selecting people who accept change.* Research suggests that the ability to easily accept and adapt to change is related to personality—some people simply have more positive attitudes about change than others.[60] It appears that people who adjust best to change are those who are open to experience, take a positive attitude toward change, are willing to take risks, and are flexible in their behaviour. One study of managers in the United States, Europe, and Asia found that those with a positive self-concept and high risk tolerance coped better with organizational change. The study authors suggested that organizations could facilitate the change process by selecting people who score high on these characteristics. Another study found that selecting people based on a resistance-to-change scale worked well in eliminating those who tended to react emotionally to change or to be rigid.[61]

- *Explicit and implicit coercion.* Coercion is the application of direct threats or force upon the resisters. If the corporate management is determined to close a manufacturing plant should employees not acquiesce to a pay cut, then coercion would be the label attached to its change tactic. Other examples of coercion are threats of transfer, loss of promotions, negative performance evaluations, and a poor letter of recommendation.

Michael Adams, president of Environics Research Group in Toronto, has noted that Canadians may have become more resistant to change in recent years.[62] Between 1983 and the mid-1990s, Canadians increasingly reported that they "felt confident in their ability to cope with change." This trend has reversed in recent years. Half of Canadians aged 15 to 33 now "feel left behind and overwhelmed by the pace of life and the prevalence of technology." Those who feel left behind tend to be those who are not college- or university-educated, highly skilled, or adaptive.

The Politics of Change

No discussion of resistance to change would be complete without a brief mention of the politics of change. Because change invariably threatens the status quo, it inherently implies political activity.[63]

Politics suggests that the demand for change is more likely to come from employees who are new to the organization (and have less invested in the status quo) or managers who are slightly removed from the main power structure. Those managers who have spent their entire careers with a single organization and eventually achieve a senior position in the hierarchy are often major impediments to change. Change itself is a very real threat to their status and position. Yet they may be expected to implement changes to demonstrate that they are not merely caretakers.

By trying to bring about change, senior managers can symbolically convey to various constituencies—stockholders, suppliers, employees, customers—that they are on top of problems and adapting to a dynamic environment. Of course, as you might guess, when forced to introduce change, these long-time power holders tend to introduce changes that do not fundamentally challenge the status quo. Radical change is too threatening. This, incidentally, explains why boards of directors that recognize the need for the rapid introduction of fundamental, radical change in their organizations often turn to outside candidates for new leadership.[64]

You may remember that we discussed politics in Chapter 7 and gave some suggestions on how to more effectively encourage people to go along with your ideas. That chapter also indicated how individuals acquire power, which provides further insight into the ability of some individuals to resist change.

Summary and Implications

1 **What is the purpose of organizational culture?** Organizational culture is the pattern of shared values, beliefs, and assumptions considered to be the appropriate way to think and act within an organization. Culture provides stability to an organization and gives employees a clear understanding of "the way things are done around here."

2 **How do you create and maintain organizational culture?** The original culture of an organization is derived from the founder's philosophy. That philosophy then influences what types of employees are hired. The culture of the organization is then reinforced by top management, who signal what is acceptable behaviour and what is not.

3 **Can organizational culture have a downside?** Many of culture's functions are valuable for both the organization and the employee. Culture enhances organizational commitment and increases the consistency of employee behaviour. Culture also reduces ambiguity for employees by telling them what is important and how things are done. However, a strong culture can have a negative effect, such as Enron's pressure-cooker culture, which led to the company's ultimate collapse. Culture can act as a barrier to change, it can make it difficult to create an inclusive environment, and it can hinder the success of mergers and acquisitions.

4 **How do organizations manage change?** Kurt Lewin argued that successful change in organizations should follow three steps: *unfreezing* the status quo, *moving* to a new state, and *refreezing* the new change to make it permanent. John Kotter built on Lewin's three-step model to create a more detailed eight-step plan for implementing change. Another approach to managing change is action research. *Action research* refers to a change process based on the systematic collection of data and the selection of a change action based on what the analyzed data indicate. Some organizations use appreciative inquiry to manage change. *Appreciative inquiry* seeks to identify the unique qualities and special strengths of an organization, which can then be built on to improve performance.

5 **Why do people and organizations resist change?** Individuals resist change because of basic human characteristics such as perceptions, personalities, and needs. Organizations resist change because they are conservative and because change is difficult. The status quo is often preferred by those who feel they have the most to lose if change goes ahead.

OB at Work

For Review

1. How can an outsider assess an organization's culture?

2. What defines an organization's subcultures?

3. Can an employee survive in an organization if he or she rejects its core values? Explain.

4. What benefits can socialization provide for the organization? For the new employee?

5. How can culture be a liability to an organization?

6. How does Lewin's three-step model of change deal with resistance to change?

7. How does Kotter's eight-step plan for implementing change deal with resistance to change?

8. What are the factors that lead individuals to resist change?

9. What are the factors that lead organizations to resist change?

For Critical Thinking

1. Is socialization brainwashing? Explain.

2. Can you identify a set of characteristics that describes your college's or university's culture? Compare them with several of your peers' lists. How closely do they agree?

3. "Resistance to change is an irrational response." Do you agree or disagree? Explain.

OB for You

■ Carefully consider the culture of any organization at which you are thinking of being employed. You will feel more comfortable in cultures that share your values and expectations.

■ When you work in groups on student projects, the groups create mini-cultures of their own. Be aware of the values and norms that are being supported early on in the group's life, as these will greatly influence the group's culture.

■ Be aware that change is a fact of life. If you need to change something in yourself, be aware of the importance of creating new systems to replace the old. Saying you want to be healthier, without specifying that you intend to go to the gym three times a week, or eat five servings of fruits and vegetables a day, means that change likely will not occur. It's important to specify goals and behaviours as part of that change.

Point

Organizational Culture Does Not Change

An organization's culture develops over many years and is rooted in deeply held values to which employees are strongly committed. In addition, there are a number of forces continually operating to maintain a given culture. These would include written statements about the organization's mission and philosophy, the design of physical spaces and buildings, the dominant leadership style, hiring criteria, past promotion practices, entrenched rituals, popular stories about key people and events, the organization's historical performance evaluation criteria, and the organization's formal structure.

Selection and promotion policies are particularly important devices that work against cultural change. Employees chose the organization because they perceived their values as a "good fit" with those of the organization. They become comfortable with that fit and will strongly resist efforts to disturb the equilibrium.

Those in control in organizations will also select senior managers who will continue the current culture. Even attempts to change a culture by going outside the organization to hire a new chief executive are unlikely to be effective. The evidence indicates that the culture is more likely to change the executive than the other way around. Why? It's too entrenched, and change becomes a potential threat to member self-interest. In fact, a more pragmatic view of the relationship between an organization's culture and its chief executive would be to note that the practice of filling senior-level management positions from the ranks of current managerial employees ensures that those who run the organization have been fully indoctrinated in the organization's culture. Promoting from within provides stability and lessens uncertainty. When a company's board of directors selects as a new chief executive officer an individual who has spent 30 years in the company, it virtually guarantees that the culture will continue unchanged.

Our argument, however, should not be viewed as saying that culture can never be changed. In the unusual case when an organization confronts a survival-threatening crisis—a crisis universally acknowledged as a true life-or-death situation—members of the organization will be responsive to efforts at cultural change. However, anything less than a crisis is unlikely to be effective in bringing about cultural change.

Counterpoint

How to Change an Organization's Culture

Changing an organization's culture is extremely difficult, but cultures can be changed. The evidence suggests that cultural change is most likely to occur when most or all of the following conditions exist:

- *A dramatic crisis.* This is the shock that undermines the status quo and calls into question the relevance of the current culture. Examples of these crises might be a surprising financial setback, the loss of a major customer, or a dramatic technological breakthrough by a competitor. The *Columbia* space-shuttle disaster was a dramatic crisis for NASA. A $7-million deficit was a dramatic crisis for the Royal Canadian Mint.

- *Turnover in leadership.* New top leadership, which can provide an alternative set of key values, may be perceived as more capable of responding to the crisis. This would definitely be the organization's chief executive, but also might need to include all senior management positions. The recent rush to hire outside CEOs after the Enron and WorldCom scandals illustrates attempts to create more ethical climates through the introduction of new leadership. At NASA, some of the top leadership was moved to other positions after the *Columbia* disaster. A new CEO at the Royal Canadian Mint, who was determined to turn around a deficit situation, brought about many changes to that organization.

- *Young and small organization.* The younger the organization is, the less entrenched its culture will be. Similarly, it's easier for management to communicate its new values when the organization is small. This point helps explain the difficulty that multibillion-dollar corporations have in changing their cultures.

- *Weak culture.* The more widely held a culture is and the higher the agreement among members on its values, the more difficult it will be to change. A strong culture has been one of the problems facing NASA. Conversely, weak cultures are more open to change than strong ones.

Efforts directed at changing organizational culture do not usually yield immediate or dramatic results. For, in the final analysis, cultural change is a lengthy process—measured in years, not months. But we can ask the question "Can culture be changed?" and the answer is "Yes!"

OB *At Work*

What Kind of Organizational Culture Fits You Best?

For each of the following statements, circle the level of agreement or disagreement that you personally feel:

SA	=	**Strongly agree**
A	=	**Agree**
U	=	**Uncertain**
D	=	**Disagree**
SD	=	**Strongly disagree**

1. I like being part of a team and having my performance assessed in terms of my contribution to the team. SA A U D SD

2. No person's needs should be compromised in order for a department to achieve its goals. SA A U D SD

3. I like the thrill and excitement of taking risks. SA A U D SD

4. If a person's job performance is inadequate, it's irrelevant how much effort he or she made. SA A U D SD

5. I like things to be stable and predictable. SA A U D SD

6. I prefer managers who provide detailed and rational explanations for their decisions. SA A U D SD

7. I like to work where there isn't a great deal of pressure and where people are essentially easygoing. SA A U D SD

Scoring Key

For items 1, 2, 3, 4, and 7, score as follows: Strongly Agree = +2, Agree = +1, Uncertain = 0, Disagree = –1, Strongly Disagree = –2.

For items 5 and 6, reverse the score (Strongly Agree = –2, and so on).

Add up your total. Your score will fall somewhere between +14 and –14.

What does your score mean? The lower your score, the more comfortable you will be in a formal, mechanistic, rule-oriented, and structured culture. This is often associated with large corporations and government agencies. Positive scores indicate a preference for informal, humanistic, flexible, and innovative cultures, which are more likely to be found in research units, advertising firms, high-tech companies, and small businesses.

More Learning About Yourself Exercises

Additional self-assessments relevant to this chapter appear on MyOBLab (**www.pearsoned.ca/myoblab**).

III.B.2 How Committed Am I to My Organization?

III.C.2 How Stressful Is My Life?

When you complete the additional assessments, consider the following:

1. Am I surprised about my score?
2. Would my friends evaluate me similarly?

OB *At Work*

BREAKOUT **GROUP** EXERCISES

Form small groups to discuss the following topics, as assigned by your instructor:

1.   Identify artifacts of culture in your current or previous workplace. From these artifacts, would you conclude that the organization has a strong or weak culture?

2.   Have you or someone you know worked somewhere where the culture was strong? What was your reaction to that strong culture? Did you like that environment, or would you prefer to work where there is a weaker culture? Why?

3.   Reflect on either the culture of one of your classes or the culture of the organization where you work, and identify characteristics of that culture that could be changed. How might these changes be made?

WORKING WITH OTHERS EXERCISE

The Beacon Aircraft Company

Objectives[65]

1.   To illustrate how forces for change and stability must be managed in organizational change programs.

2.   To illustrate the effects of alternative change techniques on the relative strength of forces for change and forces for stability.

The Situation

The marketing division of the Beacon Aircraft Company has undergone two reorganizations in the past two years. Initially, its structure changed from a functional one, in which employees were organized within departments, to a matrix form, in which employees from several different functions reported both to their own manager and to a project manager. But the matrix structure did not satisfy some functional managers. They complained that the structure confused the authority and responsibility relationships.

In reaction to these complaints, the marketing manager revised Beacon's structure back to the functional form. This new structure had a marketing group and several project groups. The project groups were managed by project managers with a few general staff members, but no functional specialists, such as people from marketing, were assigned to these groups.

After the change, some problems began to surface. Project managers complained that they could not obtain adequate assistance from functional staff members. It not only took more time to obtain necessary assistance, but it also created problems in establishing stable relationships with functional staff members. Since these problems affected their services to customers, project managers demanded a change in the organizational structure— probably again toward a matrix structure. Faced with these complaints and demands from project managers, the vice-president is pondering another reorganization. He has requested an outside consultant to help him in the reorganization plan.

The Procedure

1.   Divide yourselves into groups of 5 to 7 and take the role of consultants.

2.   Each group identifies the driving and restraining forces found in the firm. List these forces.

The Driving Forces

_____

_____

_____

_____

The Restraining Forces

_____

_____

_____

_____

3. Each group develops a set of strategies for increasing the driving forces and another set for reducing the restraining forces.

4. Each group prepares a list of changes it wants to introduce.

5. The class reassembles and hears each group's recommendations.

ETHICAL **DILEMMA** EXERCISE

Is There Room for Snooping in an Organization's Culture?

Although some of the spying Hewlett-Packard performed on some members of its board of directors appeared to violate California law, much of it was legal. Moreover, many companies spy on their employees—sometimes with and sometimes without their knowledge or consent. Organizations differ in their culture of surveillance. Some differences are due to the type of business. A US Department of Defense contractor has more reason—perhaps even an obligation—to spy on its employees than does an orange juice producer.

However, surveillance in most industries is on the upswing. There are several reasons for this, including the huge growth of two sectors with theft and security problems (services and information technology, respectively) and the increased availability of surveillance technology.

Consider the following surveillance actions and, for each action, decide whether it would never be ethical (mark N), would sometimes be ethical (mark S), or would always be ethical (mark A). For those you mark S, indicate what factors your judgment would depend on.

1. Sifting through an employee's trash for evidence of wrongdoing

2. Periodically reading email messages for disclosure of confidential information or inappropriate use

3. Conducting video surveillance of workspace

4. Monitoring websites visited by employees and determining the appropriateness and work-relatedness of those visited

5. Taping phone conversations

6. Posing as a job candidate, an investor, a customer, or a colleague (when the real purpose is to solicit information)

Would you be less likely to work for an employer that engaged in some of these methods? Why or why not? Do you think use of surveillance says something about an organization's culture?

CASE INCIDENT

GreyStar Art & Greetings Makes Technological Changes

Tammy Reinhold didn't believe the rumours. Now that the rumours were confirmed, she was in denial. "I can't believe it," she said. "I've worked as a greeting-card artist here for over 15 years. I love what I do. Now they tell me that I'm going to have to do all my work on a computer."

Tammy was not alone in her fear. The company's other two artists, Mike Tomaski and Maggie Lyall, were just as concerned. Each had graduated from art school near the top of his or her class. They came to work for GreyStar Art & Greetings right out of school—Mike in 1985, Tammy in 1991, and Maggie in 1997. They chose the company, which had been around for more than 50 years, because of its reputation as a good place to work. The company also had never had a layoff.

GreyStar Art & Greetings is a small maker of greeting cards and specialty wrapping paper. It has

(Continued)

modest resources and modest ambitions. Management has always pursued progress slowly. Artists do much of their work by hand. Today, however, the company installed three high-powered Mac computers equipped with the latest graphics and photo-manipulation software, including Photoshop, Quark, and Illustrator.

Courtland Grey, the company's owner, called Tammy, Mike, and Maggie into his office this morning. He told them about the changes that were going to be made. Grey acknowledged that the three were going to have a lot to learn to be able to do all their work on computers. But he stressed that the changes would dramatically speed up the art-production and photo-layout processes and eventually result in significant cost savings. He offered to send the three to a one-week course specifically designed to train artists in the new technology and software. He also said he expected all of

the company's art and photo operations to be completely digitalized within three months.

Tammy is not stupid. She has been following the trends in graphic art. More and more work is being done on computers. She just thought, as did Mike and Maggie, that she might escape having to learn these programs. After all, GreyStar Art & Greetings is not Hallmark. But Tammy was wrong. Technology is coming to GreyStar Art & Greetings and there isn't much she can do about it. Other than complain or look for another job!

Questions

1. Explain Tammy's resistance.
2. Evaluate the way Courtland Grey handled this change.
3. What, if anything, would you have done differently if you had been Grey?

VIDEO CASE INCIDENT

CASE 10

Organizational Culture at TerraCycle

TerraCycle—a company co-founded by Canadian entrepreneurs Tom Szaky and Jon Beyer—makes a wide range of eco-friendly products from garbage.[66] Szaky observes that the primary purpose of business has always been to make a profit. Early in the last century, some businesses engaged in unreasonable activities—such as the use of child labour—in pursuit of profit. About 30 years ago, a new type of business emerged, one that was concerned about the environment. But it simply passed on the cost of being green to its customers. An even newer approach is called *eco-capitalism*, where the goal is to do the best thing for the environment *and* for society, and to do so while making more money than the big, traditional companies. In eco-capitalism, the goods drive the money instead of the money driving the goods.

When TerraCycle started out, it was financed on business plan contest winnings and the credit cards of its co-founders. Eventually, a few investors were found who were willing to put a large amount of money into the business. But Szaky felt that they wanted to move the company away from its eco-focus, and he was not willing to do that because it would not be consistent

with the vision and culture that he wanted to establish at TerraCycle.

Albe Zakes is the company's director of public relations, and he says that TerraCycle is actually "making a difference." The company is not just riding the eco-friendly wave. It is making products that are useful and environmentally sound. Its culture is the new face of business. It is young, hip, eco-friendly, and socially responsible and has a good relationship with the local community in which it operates. Most of the workers are in their 20s, and the action is fast and furious. There is so much going on that there is no time to really organize. The culture is one of "let's get this job done and then move on to the next one."

The external walls of the company's factory—which are covered with graffiti—give a hint about what the company's culture is like inside. Zakes says that TerraCycle has the most colourful headquarters in the country. A "graffiti jam" is held every year, where up to 50 artists paint original graffiti on TerraCycle's external factory walls. It is a community event, and includes kids from different summer programs in the area. One advantage for TerraCycle is that the factory gets repainted every year.

Zakes says that the company is very aggressive and takes a lot of risks. It does not move slowly through research and development like a lot of big companies do. Rather, at TerraCycle, employees figure out what works and run as fast as possible with it. In that kind of culture, everyone must be very flexible and willing to change direction quickly. The work is very demanding, and people are given a lot of responsibility. Because everyone is on a first-name basis, they feel very close and can bond together to overcome challenges.

Questions

1. Describe the organizational culture at TerraCycle. How is it different from what you might find at a more traditional organization? How is it similar?

2. Is the way TerraCycle's culture developed consistent with what is proposed in Exhibit 10-3 on page 349? Explain.

3. The walls at TerraCycle are covered in graffiti, the company holds graffiti jams, and now the company is selling graffiti-covered plant pots. Explain why graffiti is such a large part of the organization's culture.

4. Being socially responsible and eco-friendly are top priorities at TerraCycle. Explain how these values flow through the organization.

5. Each of the seven primary characteristics of culture can range from low to high. Rate each of the seven characteristics at TerraCycle. Explain your ratings.

From *Concepts* to *Skills*

How to "Read" an Organization's Culture

The ability to read and assess an organization's culture can be a valuable skill.[67] If you are looking for a job, you will want to choose an employer whose culture is compatible with your values and in which you will feel comfortable. If you can accurately assess a prospective employer's culture before you make your decision, you may be able to save yourself a lot of grief and reduce the likelihood of making a poor choice. Similarly, you will undoubtedly have business transactions with numerous organizations during your professional career. You will be trying to sell a product or service, negotiate a contract, arrange a joint venture, or you may merely be seeking out which individual in an organization controls certain decisions. The ability to assess another organization's culture can be a definite plus in successfully completing these pursuits.

For the sake of simplicity, we will approach the problem of reading an organization's culture from that of a job applicant. We will assume you are interviewing for a job.

Here is a list of things you can do to help learn about a potential employer's culture:

- Observe the physical surroundings. Pay attention to signs, pictures, style of dress, length of hair, degree of openness between offices, and office furnishings and arrangements.

- With whom are you meeting? Just the person who would be your immediate manager? Or potential colleagues, managers from other departments, or senior executives? Afterwards, based on what they revealed, to what degree do people other than the immediate manager have input into hiring decisions?

- How would you characterize the style of the people you met? Formal? Casual? Serious? Jovial?

- Does the organization have formal rules and regulations printed in a human resource policy manual? If so, how detailed are these policies?

(Continued)

- Ask questions of the people you meet. The most valid and reliable information tends to come from asking the same questions of many people (to see how closely their responses align) and by talking with boundary spanners. *Boundary spanners* are employees whose work links them to the external environment. This includes jobs such as human resource interviewer, salesperson, purchasing agent, labour negotiator, public relations specialist, and company lawyer.

Questions that will give you insights into organizational processes and practices might include the following:

- What is the background of the founders?

- What is the background of current senior managers? What are their functional specializations? Were they promoted from within or hired from outside?

- How does the organization integrate new employees? Is there an orientation program? Training? If so, could you describe these features?

- How does your manager define his or her job success? (Amount of profit? Serving customers? Meeting deadlines? Acquiring budget increases?)

- How would you define fairness in terms of reward allocations?

- Can you identify some people here who are on the "fast track"? What do you think has put them on the fast track?

- Can you identify someone who seems to be considered a deviant in the organization? How has the organization responded to this person?

- Can you describe a decision that someone made here that was well received?

- Can you describe a decision that did not work out well? What were the consequences for the decision maker?

- Could you describe a crisis or critical event that has occurred recently in the organization? How did top management respond? What was learned from this experience?

Practising Skills

You are the nursing supervisor at a community hospital employing both emergency-room and floor nurses. Each of these teams of nurses tends to work almost exclusively with others doing the same job. In your professional reading, you have come across the concept of cross-training nursing teams and giving them more varied responsibilities, which in turn has been shown to both improve patient care and lower costs. You call the two team leaders, Sue and Scott, into your office to explain that you want the nursing teams to move to this approach. To your surprise, they are both opposed to the idea. Sue says she and the other emergency-room nurses feel they are needed in the ER, where they fill the most vital role in the hospital. They work special hours when needed, do whatever tasks are required, and often work in difficult and stressful circumstances. They think the floor nurses have relatively easy jobs for the pay they receive. Scott, the leader of the floor nurse team, tells you that his group believes the ER nurses lack the special training and extra experience that the floor nurses bring to the hospital. The floor nurses claim they have the heaviest responsibilities and do the most exacting work. Because they have ongoing contact with patients and families, they believe they should not be called away from vital floor duties to help the ER nurses complete their tasks. Now that you are faced with this resistance, how can you most effectively introduce the cross-training model?

Reinforcing Skills

1. Choose two courses that you are taking this term, ideally in different faculties, and describe the culture of the classroom in each. What are the similarities and differences? What values about learning might you infer from your observations of culture?

2. Compare the atmosphere or feeling you get from various organizations. Because of the number and wide variety that you will find, it will probably be easiest for you to do this exercise using restaurants, retail stores, or banks. Based on the atmosphere that you observe, what type of organizational culture do you think these organizations might have? If you can, interview three employees at each organization for their descriptions of their organization's culture.

3. Think about changes (major and minor) that you have dealt with over the past year. Perhaps these changes involved other people and perhaps they were personal. Did you resist the change? Did others resist the change? How did you overcome your resistance or the resistance of others to the change?

4. Interview a manager at three different organizations about a change he or she has introduced. What was the manager's experience in bringing in the change? How did the manager manage resistance to the change?

Endnotes

Chapter 1

1 E. Beaton, "Managing Growth: Rapid Recovery." *Profit* 27, no. 3 (June 2008), pp. 92–93.

2 C. R. Farquhar and J. A. Longair, *Creating High-Performance Organizations With People*, Report # R164–96 (Ottawa: The Conference Board of Canada, 1996).

3 Cited in R. Alsop, "Playing Well with Others," *Wall Street Journal*, September 9, 2002.

4 See, for instance, C. Penttila, "Hiring Hardships," *Entrepreneur*, October 2002, pp. 34–35.

5 James T. Bond with Cindy Thompson, Ellen Galinsky, and David Prottas, *The 2002 National Study of the Changing Workforce* (New York: Families and Work Institute, 2002).

6 I. S. Fulmer, B. Gerhart, and K. S. Scott, "Are the 100 Best Better? An Empirical Investigation of the Relationship Between Being a 'Great Place to Work' and Firm Performance," *Personnel Psychology*, Winter 2003, pp. 965–993.

7 T. Belford, "Strategy for the New Economy," *Financial Post* (*National Post*), March 14, 2005, p. FP9.

8 Based on E. Beaton, "Managing Growth: Rapid Recovery." *Profit* 27, no. 3 (June 2008), pp. 92–93.

9 See, for example, M. J. Driver, "Cognitive Psychology: An Interactionist View"; R. H. Hall, "Organizational Behavior: A Sociological Perspective"; and C. Hardy, "The Contribution of Political Science to Organizational Behavior," all in J. W. Lorsch, ed., *Handbook of Organizational Behavior* (Englewood Cliffs, NJ: Prentice Hall, 1987), pp. 62–108.

10 Based on W. Chuang and B. Lee, "An Empirical Evaluation of the Overconfidence Hypothesis," *Journal of Banking and Finance*, September 2006, pp. 2489–2515; and A. R. Drake, J. Wong, and S. B. Salter, "Empowerment, Motivation, and Performance: Examining the Impact of Feedback and Incentives on Nonmanagement Employees," *Behavioral Research in Accounting* 19 (2007), pp. 71–89.

11 D. M. Rousseau and S. McCarthy, "Educating Managers from an Evidence-Based Perspective," *Academy of Management Learning & Education* 6, no. 1 (2007), pp. 84–101.

12 K. Holland, "Inside the Minds of Your Employees," *New Yorker*, January 28, 2007.

13 S. Brearton and J. Daly, "The 50 Best Companies to Work for in Canada," *Report on Business*, March 21, 2009, www.theglobeandmail.com/report-on-business/rob-magazine/the-fifty-best-companies-to-work-for-in-canada/article503896/ (accessed September 23, 2009).

14 R. T. Mowday, L. W. Porter, and R. M. Steers, *Employee Organization Linkages: The Psychology of Commitment, Absenteeism, and Turnover* (New York: Academic Press, 1982).

15 C. R. Farquhar and J. A. Longair, *Creating High-Performance Organizations With People*, Report # R164–96 (Ottawa: The Conference Board of Canada, 1996).

16 C. R. Farquhar and J. A. Longair, *Creating High-Performance Organizations With People*, Report # R164–96 (Ottawa: The Conference Board of Canada, 1996).

17 "People Power," *Canadian Business Review*, Spring 1996, p. 42.

18 Based on E. Beaton, "Managing Growth: Rapid Recovery." *Profit* 27, no. 3 (June 2008), pp. 92–93.

19 W. Marsden, "Ad Exec Brault Gets 2H Years in Jail," *Gazette* (Montreal), May 6, 2006.

20 T. A. Wright, R. Cropanzano, P. J. Denney, and G. L. Moline, "When a Happy Worker Is a Productive Worker: A Preliminary Examination of Three Models," *Canadian Journal of Behavioural Science* 34, no. 3 (July 2002), pp. 146–150.

21 R. O'Flanagan, "Sears Employees Consider Joining Steelworkers," *Sudbury Star*, July 8, 2005, p. A3.

22 S. Findlay, "Employee Loyalty Takes a Nasty Fall," *Macleans.ca*, July 30, 2009.

23 B. Dumaine, "The New Non-Manager Managers," *Fortune*, February 22, 1993, pp. 80–84.

24 "Wanted: Teammates, Crew Members, and Cast Members: But No Employees," *Wall Street Journal*, April 30, 1996, p. A1.

25 S. Ross, "U.S. Managers Fail to Fit the Bill in New Workplace: Study," *Reuters News Agency*, November 19, 1999.

26 "Ask the Legends: Clive Beddoe," *PROFIT*, November 2007; C. Wells, "Secret to WestJet's Success Lies in Its People, Culture: Durfy," *Western Star*, May 16, 2007; "WestJet Tops List of Canada's 10 Most Admired Corporate Cultures," *CNW Group*, January 16, 2008, www.newswire.ca; and P. Verburg, "Prepare for Takeoff," *Canadian Business*, December 25, 2000, pp. 94–96+.

27 The Conference Board of Canada, *Employability Skills Profile*, 1998.

28 T. Belford, "Strategy for the New Economy," *Financial Post* (*National Post*), March 14, 2005, p. FP9.

29 D. Nebenzahl, "People Skills Matter Most," *Gazette* (Montreal), September 20, 2004, p. B1.

30 See, for instance, R. R. Thomas Jr., "From Affirmative Action to Affirming Diversity," *Harvard Business Review*, March–April

1990, pp. 107–117; B. Mandrell and S. Kohler-Gray, "Management Development That Values Diversity," *Personnel*, March 1990, pp. 41–47; J. Dreyfuss, "Get Ready for the New Work Force," *Fortune*, April 23, 1990, pp. 165–181; and I. Wielawski, "Diversity Makes Both Dollars and Sense," *Los Angeles Times*, May 16, 1994, p. I1–3.

31 Based on K.-A. Riess, "SGI among Top 100 Diversity Employers," *StarPhoenix*, April 5, 2008, p. F12.

32 See, for instance, E. E. Kossek and S. A. Lobel, eds., *Managing Diversity* (Cambridge, MA: Blackwell, 1996); J. A. Segal, "Diversify for Dollars," *HR Magazine*, April 1997, pp. 134–140; and "Strength Through Diversity for Bottom-Line Success," *Working Women*, March 1999, pp. 67–77.

33 E. Beauchesne, "Stats Can Misjudges Canada's Productivity," *CanWest News*, April 27, 2006, p. 1; and K. Beckman, P. M. Darby, D. Lemaire, and Y. St-Maurice, *Death by a Thousand Paper Cuts: The Effect of Barriers to Competition on Canadian Productivity* (Ottawa: The Conference Board of Canada, April 2006).

34 P. Drucker, *Management: Tasks, Responsibilities, Practices* (New York: Harper & Row, 1974).

35 D. W. Organ, *Organizational Citizenship Behavior: The Good Soldier Syndrome* (Lexington, MA: Lexington Books, 1988), p. 4.

36 M. G. Ehrhart and S. E. Naumann, "Organizational Citizenship Behavior in Work Groups: A Group Norms Approach," *Journal of Applied Psychology* 89, no. 6 (December 1, 2004), pp. 960–974.

37 "Corporate Culture," *Canadian HR Reporter* 17, no. 21 (December 6, 2004), pp. 7–11.

38 See, for example, P. M. Podsakoff and S. B. MacKenzie, "Organizational Citizenship Behavior and Sales Unit Effectiveness," *Journal of Marketing Research*, August 1994, pp. 351–363; P. M. Podsakoff, M. Ahearne, and S. B. MacKenzie, "Organizational Citizenship Behavior and the Quantity and Quality of Work Group Performance," *Journal of Applied Psychology*, April 1997, pp. 262–270; L. A. Bettencourt, K. Gwinner, and M. L. Meuter, "A Comparison of Attitude, Personality, and Knowledge Predictors of Service-Oriented Organizational Citizenship Behaviors," *Journal of Applied Psychology* 86, 2001, pp. 29–41; and E. W. Morrison, "Organizational Citizenship Behavior as a Critical Link Between HRM Practices and Service Quality," *Human Resource Management* 35, 1996, pp. 493–512.

39 See, for instance, V. S. Major, K. J. Klein, and M. G. Ehrhart, "Work Time, Work Interference with Family, and Psychological Distress," *Journal of Applied Psychology*, June 2002, pp. 427–436; D. Brady, "Rethinking the Rat Race," *BusinessWeek*, August 26, 2002, pp. 142–143; J. M. Brett and L. K. Stroh, "Working 61 Plus Hours a Week: Why Do Managers Do It?" *Journal of Applied Psychology*, February 2003, pp. 67–78.

40 See, for instance, *The 2002 National Study of the Changing Workforce* (New York: Families and Work Institute, 2002).

41 Cited in S. Armour, "Workers Put Family First Despite Slow Economy, Jobless Fears," *USA Today*, June 2, 2002, p. B3.

42 S. Shellenbarger, "What Job Candidates Really Want to Know: Will I Have a Life?" *Wall Street Journal*, November 17, 1999, p. B1; and "U.S. Employers Polish Image to Woo a Demanding New Generation," *Manpower Argus*, February 2000, p. 2.

43 F. Luthans and C. M. Youssef, "Emerging Positive Organizational Behavior," *Journal of Management*, June 2007, pp. 321–349; and J. E. Dutton and S. Sonenshein, "Positive Organizational Scholarship," in *Encyclopedia of Positive Psychology*, ed. C. Cooper and J. Barling, (Thousand Oaks, CA: Sage, 2007).

44 L. M. Roberts, G. Spreitzer, J. Dutton, R. Quinn, E. Heaphy, and B. Barker, "How to Play to Your Strengths," *Harvard Business Review*, January 2005, pp. 1–6; and L. M. Roberts, J. E. Dutton, G. M. Spreitzer, E. D. Heaphy, and R. E. Quinn, "Composing the Reflected Best-Self Portrait: Becoming Extraordinary in Work Organizations," *Academy of Management Review* 30, no. 4 (2005), pp. 712–736.

45 M. Kaeter, "The Age of the Specialized Generalist," *Training*, December 1993, pp. 48–53; and N. Templin, "Auto Plants, Hiring Again, Are Demanding Higher-Skilled Labor," *Wall Street Journal*, March 11, 1994, p. A1.

46 Created based on material from R. E. Quinn, S. R. Faerman, M. P. Thompson, and M. R. McGrath, *Becoming a Master Manager: A Competency Framework* (New York: John Wiley & Sons, 1990), Chapter 1.

47 Based on M. J. Critelli, "Striking a Balance," *IndustryWeek*, November 20, 2000, pp. 26–36.

48 Based on K. H. Hammonds, "Handle With Care," *Fast Company*, August 2002, pp. 103–107.

49 Based on "Foundations of Control at TerraCycle," *Organizational Behavior Video Library*, 2008. Copyrighted by Prentice-Hall.

50 R. E. Quinn, *Beyond Rational Management: Mastering the Paradoxes and Competing Demands of High Performance* (San Francisco: Jossey-Bass, 1991); R. E. Quinn, S. R. Faerman, M. P. Thompson, and M. R. McGrath, *Becoming a Master Manager: A Competency Framework* (New York: John Wiley & Sons, 1990); K. Cameron and R. E. Quinn, *Diagnosing and Changing Organizational Culture: Based on the Competing Values Framework* (Reading, MA: Addison Wesley Longman, 1999).

51 R. E. Quinn, S. R. Faerman, M. P. Thompson, and M. R. McGrath, *Becoming a Master Manager: A Competency Framework* (New York: John Wiley & Sons, 1990).

52 D. Maley, "Canada's Top Women CEOs," *Maclean's*, October 20, 1997, pp. 52+.

53 Written by Nancy Langton and Joy Begley © 1999. (The events described are based on an actual situation, although the participants, as well as the centre, have been disguised.)

Chapter 2

1 Based on www.walmart.ca/wps-portal/storelocator/Canada-About_Walmart.jsp; "Wal-Mart Canada's Mario Pilozzi Awarded with Retail Industry's Highest Honour 'Distinguished Retailer of the Year,'" www.retailcouncil.org/news/media/press/2007/pr20070516.asp; and "Wal-Mart Canada Named One of Canada's Best Employers," news release, January 2, 2007, www.newswire.ca.

2 T. Cole, "Who Loves Ya?" *Report on Business Magazine*, April 1999, pp. 44–60.

3   Based on S. Thomas, "COPE Council Delivers 'Stunning' Blow to Big Box Giant," *Vancouver Courier*, July 3, 2005, p. 13; and "Green Wal-Mart Should Be Given the Green Light," *Vancouver Sun*, June 13, 2005, p. A10.

4   H. H. Kelley, "Attribution in Social Interaction," in *Attribution: Perceiving the Causes of Behavior*, ed. E. Jones et al. (Morristown, NJ: General Learning Press, 1972).

5   See L. Ross, "The Intuitive Psychologist and His Shortcomings," in *Advances in Experimental Social Psychology*, vol. 10, ed. L. Berkowitz (Orlando, FL: Academic Press, 1977), pp. 174–220; and A. G. Miller and T. Lawson, "The Effect of an Informational Option on the Fundamental Attribution Error," *Personality and Social Psychology Bulletin*, June 1989, pp. 194–204.

6   M. L. A. Hayward, V. P. Rindova, and T. G. Pollock, "Believing One's Own Press: The Causes and Consequences of CEO Celebrity," *Strategic Management Journal* 25, no. 7 (July 2004), pp. 637–653.

7   N. Epley and D. Dunning, "Feeling 'Holier Than Thou': Are Self-Serving Assessments Produced by Errors in Self- or Social Predictions?" *Journal of Personality and Social Psychology*, March 2001.

8   M. Goerke, J. Moller, and S. Schulz-Hardt, "'It's Not My Fault—but Only I Can Change It': Counterfactual and Prefactual Thoughts of Managers," *Journal of Applied Psychology* 89, no. 2 (April 2004), pp. 279–292.

9   B. McKenna, "Modern Suicides Hold Little Glory," *Globe and Mail*, June 2, 1998, p. A14.

10 S. Nam, "Cultural and Managerial Attributions for Group Performance" (PhD diss., University of Oregon), cited in R. M. Steers, S. J. Bischoff, and L. H. Higgins, "Cross-Cultural Management Research," *Journal of Management Inquiry*, December 1992, pp. 325–326.

11 *Focus on Diversity* based on A. Kerr, "Illness Can Be a Workplace Handicap," *Globe and Mail*, July 15, 2002.

12 S. E. Asch, "Forming Impressions of Personality," *Journal of Abnormal and Social Psychology*, July 1946, pp. 258–290.

13 A. Parducci, "Category Judgment: A Range-Frequency Model," *Psychological Review* 72, no. 6 (November 1965), pp. 407–418; D. M. O'Reilly, R. A. Leitch, and D. H. Wedell, "The Effects of Immediate Context on Auditors' Judgments of Loan Quality," *Auditing* 23, no. 1 (2004), pp. 89–105; and J. DeCoster and H. M. Claypool, "A Meta-Analysis of Priming Effects on Impression Formation Supporting a General Model of Information Biases," *Personality & Social Psychology Review* 8, no. 1 (2004), pp. 2–27.

14 See, for example, G. N. Powell, "The Good Manager: Business Students' Stereotypes of Japanese Managers Versus Stereotypes of American Managers," *Group & Organizational Management*, March 1992, pp. 44–56; W. C. K. Chiu, A. W. Chan, E. Snape, and T. Redman, "Age Stereotypes and Discriminatory Attitudes Towards Older Workers: An East–West Comparison," *Human Relations*, May 2001, pp. 629–661; C. Ostroff and L. E. Atwater, "Does Whom You Work with Matter? Effects of Referent Group Gender and Age Composition on Managers' Compensation," *Journal of Applied Psychology*, August 2003, pp. 725–740; and M. E. Heilman, A. S. Wallen, D. Fuchs, and M. M. Tamkins, "Penalties for Success: Reactions to Women Who Succeed at Male Gender-Typed Tasks," *Journal of Applied Psychology*, June 2004, pp. 416–427.

15 J. L. Eberhardt, P. G. Davies, V. J. Purdic-Vaughns, and S. L. Johnson, "Looking Deathworthy: Perceived Stereotypicality of Black Defendants Predicts Capital-Sentencing Outcomes," *Psychological Science* 17, no. 5 (2006), pp. 383–386.

16 J. T. Jost and A. C. Kay, "Complementary Justice: Effects of 'Poor but Happy' and 'Poor but Honest' Stereotype Exemplars on System Justification and Implicit Activation of the Justice Motive," *Journal of Personality and Social Psychology* 85, no. 5 (2003), pp. 823–837.

17 J. C. Ziegert and P. J. Hanges, "Employment Discrimination: The Role of Implicit Attitudes, Motivation, and a Climate for Racial Bias," *Journal of Applied Psychology* 90, no. 3 (May 2005), pp. 553–562; and D. Pager and L. Quillian, "Walking the Talk? What Employers Say Versus What They Do," *American Sociological Review* 70, no. 3 (June 2005), pp. 355–380.

18 "Wal-Mart Canada Named One of Canada's Best Employers," news release, January 2, 2007, www.newswire.ca; "Wal-Mart Makes Green Pledge for All Its Stores; Not Just Hopping on a Bandwagon," *Province* (Vancouver), August 27, 2008, p. A35; and G. Scotton, "Shopping Boom Follows Wal-Mart," *Calgary Herald*, August 22, 2006, p. B1.

19 See, for example, E. C. Webster, *Decision Making in the Employment Interview* (Montreal: McGill University, Industrial Relations Centre, 1964).

20 See, for example, R. D. Bretz Jr., G. T. Milkovich, and W. Read, "The Current State of Performance Appraisal Research and Practice: Concerns, Directions, and Implications," *Journal of Management*, June 1992, pp. 323–324; and P. M. Swiercz, M. L. Icenogle, N. B. Bryan, and R. W. Renn, "Do Perceptions of Performance Appraisal Fairness Predict Employee Attitudes and Performance?" in *Proceedings of the Academy of Management*, ed. D. P. Moore (Atlanta: Academy of Management, 1993), pp. 304–308.

21 J. Schaubroeck and S. S. K. Lam, "How Similarity to Peers and Supervisor Influences Organizational Advancement in Different Cultures," *Academy of Management Journal* 45, no. 6 (2002), pp. 1120–1136.

22 K. A. Martin, A. R. Sinden, J. C. Fleming, "Inactivity May Be Hazardous to Your Image: The Effects of Exercise Participation on Impression Formation," *Journal of Sport & Exercise Psychology* 22, no. 4 (December 2000), pp. 283–291.

23 See, for example, D. Eden, *Pygmalion in Management* (Lexington, MA: Lexington, 1990); D. Eden, "Leadership and Expectations: Pygmalion Effects and Other Self-Fulfilling Prophecies," *Leadership Quarterly*, Winter 1992, pp. 271–305; D. B. McNatt, O. B. Davidson and D. Eden, "Remedial Self-Fulfilling Prophecy: Two Field Experiments to Prevent Golem Effects Among Disadvantaged Women," *Journal of Applied Psychology*, June 2000, pp. 386–398; and D. B. McNatt, "Ancient Pygmalion Joins Contemporary Management: A Meta-Analysis of the Result," *Journal of Applied Psychology* 85, no. 2 (April 2000), pp. 314–322.

24 D. Eden and A. B. Shani, "Pygmalion Goes to Boot Camp: Expectancy, Leadership, and Trainee Performance," *Journal of Applied Psychology*, April 1982, pp. 194–199.

25 G. W. Allport, *Personality: A Psychological Interpretation* (New York: Holt, Rinehart and Winston, 1937), p. 48.

26 K. I. van der Zee, J. N. Zaal, and J. Piekstra, "Validation of the Multicultural Personality Questionnaire in the Context of Personnel Selection," *European Journal of Personality* 17 (2003), pp. S77–S100.

27 T. A. Judge, C. A. Higgins, C. J. Thoresen, and M. R. Barrick, "The Big Five Personality Traits, General Mental Ability, and Career Success Across the Life Span," *Personnel Psychology* 52, no. 3 (1999), pp. 621–652.

28 S. Srivastava, O. P. John, and S. D. Gosling, "Development of Personality in Early and Middle Adulthood: Set Like Plaster or Persistent Change?" *Journal of Personality and Social Psychology*, May 2003, pp. 1041–1053.

29 See A. H. Buss, "Personality as Traits," *American Psychologist*, November 1989, pp. 1378–1388; and D. G. Winter, O. P. John, A. J. Stewart, E. C. Klohnen, and L. E. Duncan, "Traits and Motives: Toward an Integration of Two Traditions in Personality Research," *Psychological Review*, April 1998, pp. 230–250.

30 R. R. McCrae and A. Terracciano, "Universal Features of Personality Traits from the Observer's Perspective: Data from 50 Cultures," *Journal of Personality and Social Psychology* 88, no. 3 (2005), pp. 547–561.

31 See, for instance, G. W. Allport and H. S. Odbert, "Trait Names, A Psycholexical Study," *Psychological Monographs* 47, no. 211 (1936); and R. B. Cattell, "Personality Pinned Down," *Psychology Today*, July 1973, pp. 40–46.

32 R. B. Kennedy and D. A. Kennedy, "Using the Myers-Briggs Type Indicator in Career Counseling," *Journal of Employment Counseling*, March 2004, pp. 38–44.

33 G. N. Landrum, *Profiles of Genius* (New York: Prometheus, 1993).

34 See, for instance, D. J. Pittenger, "Cautionary Comments Regarding the Myers-Briggs Type Indicator," *Consulting Psychology Journal: Practice and Research*, Summer 2005, pp. 210–221; L. Bess and R. J. Harvey, "Bimodal Score Distributions and the Myers-Briggs Type Indicator: Fact or Artifact?" *Journal of Personality Assessment*, February 2002, pp. 176–186; R. M. Capraro and M. M. Capraro, "Myers-Briggs Type Indicator Score Reliability Across Studies: A Meta-Analytic Reliability Generalization Study," *Educational and Psychological Measurement*, August 2002, pp. 590–602; and R. C. Arnau, B. A. Green, D. H. Rosen, D. H. Gleaves, and J. G. Melancon, "Are Jungian Preferences Really Categorical? An Empirical Investigation Using Taxometric Analysis," *Personality and Individual Differences*, January 2003, pp. 233–251.

35 See, for example, J. M. Digman, "Personality Structure: Emergence of the Five-Factor Model," in *Annual Review of Psychology*, vol. 41, ed. M. R. Rosenzweig and L. W. Porter (Palo Alto, CA: Annual Reviews, 1990), pp. 417–440; R. R. McCrae and O. P. John, "An Introduction to the Five-Factor Model and Its Applications," *Journal of Personality*, June 1992, pp. 175–215; L. R. Goldberg, "The Structure of Phenotypic Personality Traits," *American Psychologist*, January 1993, pp. 26–34; P. H. Raymark, M. J. Schmit, and R. M. Guion, "Identifying Potentially Useful Personality Constructs for Employee Selection," *Personnel Psychology*, Autumn 1997, pp. 723–736; and O. Behling, "Employee Selection: Will Intelligence and Conscientiousness Do the Job?" *Academy of Management Executive*, 12, 1998, pp. 77–86.

36 D. J. Ozer and V. Benet-Martinez, "Personality and the Prediction of Consequential Outcomes," *Annual Review of Psychology* 57, no. 1 (2006), pp. 401–421.

37 See, for instance, M. R. Barrick and M. K. Mount, "The Big Five Personality Dimensions and Job Performance: A Meta-Analysis," *Personnel Psychology*, Spring 1991, pp. 1–26; G. M. Hurtz and J. J. Donovan, "Personality and Job Performance: The Big Five Revisited," *Journal of Applied Psychology*, December 2000, pp. 869–879; J. Hogan and B. Holland, "Using Theory to Evaluate Personality and Job-Performance Relations: A Socioanalytic Perspective," *Journal of Applied Psychology*, February 2003, pp. 100–112; and M. R. Barrick and M. K. Mount, "Select on Conscientiousness and Emotional Stability," in *Handbook of Principles of Organizational Behavior*, ed. E. A. Locke (Malden, MA: Blackwell, 2004), pp. 15–28.

38 M. K. Mount, M. R. Barrick, and J. P. Strauss, "Validity of Observer Ratings of the Big Five Personality Factors," *Journal of Applied Psychology*, April 1994, p. 272. Additionally confirmed by G. M. Hurtz and J. J. Donovan, "Personality and Job Performance: The Big Five Revisited," *Journal of Applied Psychology* 85, 2000, pp. 869–879; and M. R. Barrick, M. K. Mount, and T. A. Judge, "The FFM Personality Dimensions and Job Performance: Meta-Analysis of Meta-Analyses," *International Journal of Selection and Assessment* 9, 2001, pp. 9–30.

39 F. L. Schmidt and J. E. Hunter, "The Validity and Utility of Selection Methods in Personnel Psychology: Practical and Theoretical Implications of 85 Years of Research Findings," *Psychological Bulletin*, September 1998, p. 272.

40 T. A. Judge and J. E. Bono, "A Rose by Any Other Name... Are Self-Esteem, Generalized Self-Efficacy, Neuroticism, and Locus of Control Indicators of a Common Construct?" in *Personality Psychology in the Workplace*, ed. B. W. Roberts and R. Hogan (Washington, DC: American Psychological Association), pp. 93–118.

41 A. Erez and T. A. Judge, "Relationship of Core Self-Evaluations to Goal Setting, Motivation, and Performance," *Journal of Applied Psychology* 86, no. 6 (2001), pp. 1270–1279.

42 U. Malmendier and G. Tate, "CEO Overconfidence and Corporate Investment," *Journal of Finance* 60, no. 6 (December 2005), pp. 2661–2700.

43 R. Sandomir, "Star Struck," *New York Times*, January 12, 2007, pp. C10, C14.

44 R. G. Vleeming, "Machiavellianism: A Preliminary Review," *Psychological Reports*, February 1979, pp. 295–310.

45 R. Christie and F. L. Geis, *Studies in Machiavellianism* (New York: Academic Press, 1970), p. 312; and N. V. Ramanaiah, A. Byravan, and F. R. J. Detwiler, "Revised Neo Personality Inventory Profiles of Machiavellian and Non-Machiavellian People," *Psychological Reports*, October 1994, pp. 937–938.

46 R. Christie and F. L. Geis, *Studies in Machiavellianism* (New York: Academic Press, 1970).

47 C. Sedikides, E. A. Rudich, A. P. Gregg, M. Kumashiro, and C. Rusbult, "Are Normal Narcissists Psychologically Healthy?

Self-Esteem Matters," *Journal of Personality and Social Psychology* 87, no. 3 (2004), pp. 400–416, reviews some of the literature on narcissism.

48 P. T. Costa, and R. R. McCrae, "Domains and Factors: Hierarchical Personality Assessment Using the NEO Personality Inventory," *Journal of Personality Assessment* 64, 1995, pp. 21–50; and D. L. Paulhus, "Normal Narcissism: Two Minimalist Accounts," *Psychological Inquiry* 12, 2001, pp. 228–230.

49 M. Maccoby, "Narcissistic Leaders: The Incredible Pros, the Inevitable Cons," *Harvard Business Review*, January–February 2000, pp. 69–77, www.maccoby.com/Articles/NarLeaders.shtml (accessed August 1, 2009).

50 W. K. Campbell and C. A. Foster, "Narcissism and Commitment in Romantic Relationships: An Investment Model Analysis," *Personality and Social Psychology Bulletin* 28, no. 4 (2002), pp. 484–495.

51 T. A. Judge, J. A. LePine, and B. L. Rich, "The Narcissistic Personality: Relationship with Inflated Self-Ratings of Leadership and with Task and Contextual Performance," *Journal of Applied Psychology* 91, no. 4 (2006), pp. 762–776.

52 See M. Snyder, *Public Appearances/Private Realities: The Psychology of Self-Monitoring* (New York: W. H. Freeman, 1987).

53 See M. Snyder, *Public Appearances/Private Realities: The Psychology of Self-Monitoring* (New York: W. H. Freeman, 1987).

54 M. Kilduff and D. V. Day, "Do Chameleons Get Ahead? The Effects of Self-Monitoring on Managerial Careers," *Academy of Management Journal*, August 1994, pp. 1047–1060.

55 D. V. Day, D. J. Schleicher, A. L. Unckless, and N. J. Hiller, "Self-Monitoring Personality at Work: A Meta-Analytic Investigation of Construct Validity," *Journal of Applied Psychology*, April 2002, pp. 390–401.

56 R. N. Taylor and M. D. Dunnette, "Influence of Dogmatism, Risk-Taking Propensity, and Intelligence on Decision-Making Strategies for a Sample of Industrial Managers," *Journal of Applied Psychology*, August 1974, pp. 420–423.

57 I. L. Janis and L. Mann, *Decision Making: A Psychological Analysis of Conflict, Choice, and Commitment* (New York: Free Press, 1977); W. H. Stewart Jr. and L. Roth, "Risk Propensity Differences Between Entrepreneurs and Managers: A Meta-Analytic Review," *Journal of Applied Psychology*, February 2001, pp. 145–153; J. B. Miner and N. S. Raju, "Risk Propensity Differences Between Managers and Entrepreneurs and Between Low- and High-Growth Entrepreneurs: A Reply in a More Conservative Vein," *Journal of Applied Psychology* 89, no. 1 (2004), pp. 3–13; and W. H. Stewart Jr. and P. L. Roth, "Data Quality Affects Meta-Analytic Conclusions: A Response to Miner and Raju (2004) Concerning Entrepreneurial Risk Propensity," *Journal of Applied Psychology* 89, no. 1 (2004), pp. 14–21.

58 N. Kogan and M. A. Wallach, "Group Risk Taking as a Function of Members' Anxiety and Defensiveness," *Journal of Personality*, March 1967, pp. 50–63.

59 M. Friedman and R. H. Rosenman, *Type A Behavior and Your Heart* (New York: Alfred A. Knopf, 1974), p. 84.

60 M. Friedman and R. H. Rosenman, *Type A Behavior and Your Heart* (New York: Alfred A. Knopf, 1974), pp. 84–85.

61 K. A. Matthews, "Assessment of Type A Behavior, Anger, and Hostility in Epidemiological Studies of Cardiovascular Disease," in *Measuring Psychological Variables in Epidemiologic Studies of Cardiovascular Disease*, NIH Publication No. 85-2270, ed. A. M. Ostfield and E. D. Eaker (Washington, DC: US Department of Health and Human Services, 1985).

62 M. Friedman and R. H. Rosenman, *Type A Behavior and Your Heart* (New York: Alfred A. Knopf, 1974), p. 86.

63 J. Schaubroeck, D. C. Ganster, and B. E. Kemmerer, "Job Complexity, 'Type A' Behavior, and Cardiovascular Disorder," *Academy of Management Journal* 37, April 1994, pp. 426–439.

64 J. M. Crant, "Proactive Behavior in Organizations," *Journal of Management* 26, no. 3 (2000), p. 436.

65 S. E. Seibert, M. L. Kraimer, and J. M. Crant, "What Do Proactive People Do? A Longitudinal Model Linking Proactive Personality and Career Success," *Personnel Psychology*, Winter 2001, p. 850; and J. A. Thompson, "Proactive Personality and Job Performance: A Social Capital Perspective," *Journal of Applied Psychology* 90, no. 5 (2005), pp. 1011–1017.

66 T. S. Bateman and J. M. Crant, "The Proactive Component of Organizational Behavior: A Measure and Correlates," *Journal of Organizational Behavior*, March 1993, pp. 103–118; A. L. Frohman, "Igniting Organizational Change from Below: The Power of Personal Initiative," *Organizational Dynamics*, Winter 1997, pp. 39–53; and J. M. Crant and T. S. Bateman, "Charismatic Leadership Viewed from Above: The Impact of Proactive Personality," *Journal of Organizational Behavior*, February 2000, pp. 63–75.

67 J. M. Crant, "Proactive Behavior in Organizations," *Journal of Management* 26, no. 3 (2000), p. 436.

68 See, for instance, R. C. Becherer and J. G. Maurer, "The Proactive Personality Disposition and Entrepreneurial Behavior Among Small Company Presidents," *Journal of Small Business Management*, January 1999, pp. 28–36.

69 S. E. Seibert, J. M. Crant, and M. L. Kraimer, "Proactive Personality and Career Success," *Journal of Applied Psychology*, June 1999, pp. 416–427; and S. E. Seibert, M. L. Kraimer, and J. M. Crant, "What Do Proactive People Do? A Longitudinal Model Linking Proactive Personality and Career Success," *Personnel Psychology*, Winter 2001, p. 850.

70 F. Kluckhohn and F. L. Strodtbeck, *Variations in Value Orientations* (Evanston, IL: Row Peterson, 1961).

71 J. Pickard, "Misuse of Tests Leads to Unfair Recruitment," *People Management* 2, no. 25 (1996), p. 7.

72 J. Pickard, "Misuse of Tests Leads to Unfair Recruitment," *People Management* 2, no. 25 (1996), p. 7.

73 Based on S. Thomas, "Wal-Mart Reluctant Star of Documentary," *Vancouver Courier*, November 13, 2005, p. 9.

74 See N. H. Frijda, "Moods, Emotion Episodes and Emotions," in *Handbook of Emotions*, ed. M. Lewis and J. M. Haviland (New York: Guildford Press, 1993), pp. 381–403.

75 N. H. Frijda, "Moods, Emotion Episodes and Emotions," in *Handbook of Emotions*, ed. M. Lewis and J. M. Haviland (New York: Guildford Press, 1993), p. 381. This point is further explored in L. J. Barclay, D. P. Skarlicki, and S. D. Pugh, "Exploring the Role of Emotions in Injustice Perceptions and Retaliation," *Journal of Applied Psychology* 90, no. 4 (2005), pp. 629–643, who find that the experience of injustice can result in varied emotions.

76 See, for example, P. Ekman, "An Argument for Basic Emotions," *Cognition and Emotion*, May/July 1992, pp. 169–200; C. E. Izard, "Basic Emotions, Relations Among Emotions, and Emotion–Cognition Relations," *Psychological Bulletin*, November 1992, pp. 561–565; and J. L. Tracy and R.W. Robins, "Emerging Insights into the Nature and Function of Pride," *Current Directions in Psychological Science* 16, no. 3 (2007), pp. 147–150.

77 R. C. Solomon, "Back to Basics: On the Very Idea of 'Basic Emotions,'" *Journal for the Theory of Social Behaviour* 32, no. 2 (June 2002), pp. 115–144.

78 P. Ekman, *Emotions Revealed: Recognizing Faces and Feelings to Improve Communication and Emotional Life* (New York: Times Books/Henry Holt and Co., 2003).

79 P. R. Shaver, H. J. Morgan, and S. J. Wu, "Is Love a 'Basic' Emotion?" *Personal Relationships* 3, no. 1 (March 1996), pp. 81–96.

80 R. C. Solomon, "Back to Basics: On the Very Idea of 'Basic Emotions,'" *Journal for the Theory of Social Behaviour* 32, no. 2 (June 2002), pp. 115–144.

81 H. M. Weiss and R. Cropanzano, "Affective Events Theory: A Theoretical Discussion of the Structure, Causes and Consequences of Affective Experiences at Work," in B. M. Staw and L. L. Cummings (eds.), *Research in Organizational Behavior*, vol. 18 (Greenwich, CT: JAI Press, 1996), pp. 17–19.

82 Cited in R. D. Woodworth, *Experimental Psychology* (New York: Holt, 1938).

83 See J. A. Morris and D. C. Feldman, "Managing Emotions in the Workplace," *Journal of Managerial Issues* 9, no. 3 (1997), pp. 257–274; S. Mann, *Hiding What We Feel, Faking What We Don't: Understanding the Role of Your Emotions at Work* (New York: HarperCollins, 1999); and S. M. Kruml and D. Geddes, "Catching Fire without Burning Out: Is There an Ideal Way to Perform Emotion Labor?" in *Emotions in the Workplace*, ed. N. M. Ashkansay, C. E. J. Hartel, and W. J. Zerbe (New York: Quorum Books, 2000), pp. 177–188.

84 Based on S. Treleaven "Cry, Baby; Demonstrating Fragility Could Work to Your Advantage," *National Post*, January 12, 2008, p. FW7; P. Kitchen, "Experts: Crying at Work on the Rise," *Newsday*, June 10, 2007; and S. Shellenbarger, "Read This and Weep," *Wall Street Journal*, April 26, 2007, p. D1.

85 P. Ekman, W. V. Friesen, and M. O'Sullivan, "Smiles When Lying," in *What the Face Reveals: Basic and Applied Studies of Spontaneous Expression Using the Facial Action Coding System (FACS)*, ed. P. Ekman and E. L. Rosenberg (London: Oxford University Press, 1997), pp. 201–216.

86 A. Grandey, "Emotion Regulation in the Workplace: A New Way to Conceptualize Emotional Labor," *Journal of Occupational Health Psychology* 5, no. 1 (2000), pp. 95–110; and R. Cropanzano, D. E. Rupp, and Z. S. Byrne, "The Relationship of Emotional Exhaustion to Work Attitudes, Job Performance, and Organizational Citizenship Behavior," *Journal of Applied Psychology*, February 2003, pp. 160–169.

87 A. R. Hochschild, "Emotion Work, Feeling Rules, and Social Structure," *American Journal of Sociology*, November 1979, pp. 551–575; W.-C. Tsai, "Determinants and Consequences of Employee Displayed Positive Emotions," *Journal of Management* 27, no. 4 (2001), pp. 497–512; M. W. Kramer and J. A. Hess, "Communication Rules for the Display of Emotions in Organizational Settings," *Management Communication Quarterly*, August 2002, pp. 66–80; and J. M. Diefendorff and E. M. Richard, "Antecedents and Consequences of Emotional Display Rule Perceptions," *Journal of Applied Psychology*, April 2003, pp. 284–294.

88 B. M. DePaulo, "Nonverbal Behavior and Self-Presentation," *Psychological Bulletin*, March 1992, pp. 203–243.

89 C. S. Hunt, "Although I Might Be Laughing Loud and Hearty, Deep Inside I'm Blue: Individual Perceptions Regarding Feeling and Displaying Emotions at Work" (paper presented at the Academy of Management Conference, Cincinnati, August 1996), p. 3.

90 R. C. Solomon, "Back to Basics: On the Very Idea of 'Basic Emotions,'" *Journal for the Theory of Social Behaviour* 32, no. 2 (2002), pp. 115–144.

91 C. M. Brotheridge and R. T. Lee, "Development and Validation of the Emotional Labour Scale," *Journal of Occupational & Organizational Psychology* 76, no. 3 (September 2003), pp. 365–379.

92 A. A. Grandey, "When 'the Show Must Go On': Surface Acting and Deep Acting as Determinants of Emotional Exhaustion and Peer-Rated Service Delivery," *Academy of Management Journal*, February 2003, pp. 86–96; and A. A. Grandey, D. N. Dickter, and H. Sin, "The Customer Is Not Always Right: Customer Aggression and Emotion Regulation of Service Employees," *Journal of Organizational Behavior* 25, no. 3 (May 2004), pp. 397–418.

93 N. M. Ashkanasy, and C. S. Daus, "Emotion in the Workplace: The New Challenge for Managers," *Academy of Management Executive* 16, no. 1 (2002), pp. 76–86.

94 This section is based on Daniel Goleman, *Emotional Intelligence* (New York: Bantam, 1995); J. D. Mayer and G. Geher, "Emotional Intelligence and the Identification of Emotion," *Intelligence*, March–April 1996, pp. 89–113; J. Stuller, "EQ: Edging Toward Respectability," *Training*, June 1997, pp. 43–48; R. K. Cooper, "Applying Emotional Intelligence in the Workplace," *Training & Development*, December 1997, pp. 31–38; "HR Pulse: Emotional Intelligence," *HR Magazine*, January 1998, p. 19; M. Davies, L. Stankov, and R. D. Roberts, "Emotional Intelligence: In Search of an Elusive Construct," *Journal of Personality and Social Psychology*, October 1998, pp. 989–1015; and D. Goleman, *Working With Emotional Intelligence* (New York: Bantam, 1999).

95 T. Sy, S. Cote, and R. Saavedra, "The Contagious Leader: Impact of the Leader's Mood on the Mood of Group Members, Group Affective Tone, and Group Processes," *Journal of Applied Psychology* 90, no. 2 (March 2005), pp. 295–305.

96 Based on D. R. Caruso, J. D. Mayer, and P. Salovey, "Emotional Intelligence and Emotional Leadership," in *Multiple Intelligences and Leadership*, ed. R. E. Riggio, S. E. Murphy, and F. J. Pirozzolo (Mahwah, NJ: Lawrence Erlbaum, 2002), p. 70.

97 This section is based on Daniel Goleman, *Emotional Intelligence* (New York: Bantam, 1995); P. Salovey and D. Grewal, "The Science of Emotional Intelligence," *Current Directions in Psychological Science* 14, no. 6 (2005), pp. 281–285; M. Davies, L. Stankov, and R. D. Roberts, "Emotional Intelligence: In Search of an

Elusive Construct," *Journal of Personality and Social Psychology*, October 1998, pp. 989–1015; D. Geddes and R. R. Callister, "Crossing the Line(s): A Dual Threshold Model of Anger in Organizations," *Academy of Management Review* 32, no. 3 (2007), pp. 721–746; and J. Ciarrochi, J. P. Forgas, and J. D. Mayer, eds., *Emotional Intelligence in Everyday Life* (Philadelphia: Psychology Press, 2001).

98 F. I. Greenstein, *The Presidential Difference: Leadership Style from FDR to Clinton* (Princeton, NJ: Princeton University Press, 2001).

99 M. Maccoby, "To Win the Respect of Followers, Leaders Need Personality Intelligence," *Ivey Business Journal* 72, no. 3 (May–June 2008); J. Reid, "The Resilient Leader: Why EQ Matters," *Business Journal* 72, no. 3 (May–June 2008); and P. Wieand, J. Birchfield, and M. C. Johnson III, "The New Leadership Challenge: Removing the Emotional Barriers to Sustainable Performance in a Flat World," *Ivey Business Journal* 72, no. 4 (July–August 2008).

100 J. Rowlands, "Soft Skills Give Hard Edge," *Globe and Mail*, June 9, 2004, p. C8.

101 P. Wieand, J. Birchfield, and M. C. Johnson III, "The New Leadership Challenge: Removing the Emotional Barriers to Sustainable Performance in a Flat World," *Ivey Business Journal* 72, no. 4 (July–August 2008).

102 C. Cherniss, "The Business Case for Emotional Intelligence," *Consortium for Research on Emotional Intelligence in Organizations*, 1999, www.eiconsortium.org/reports/business_case_for_ei.html (accessed August 1, 2009).

103 K. S. Law, C. Wong, and L. J. Song, "The Construct and Criterion Validity of Emotional Intelligence and Its Potential Utility for Management Studies," *Journal of Applied Psychology* 89, no. 3 (2004), pp. 483–496.

104 H. A. Elfenbein and N. Ambady, "Predicting Workplace Outcomes from the Ability to Eavesdrop on Feelings," *Journal of Applied Psychology* 87, no. 5 (October 2002), pp. 963–971.

105 D. L. Van Rooy and C. Viswesvaran, "Emotional Intelligence: A Meta-Analytic Investigation of Predictive Validity and Nomological Net," *Journal of Vocational Behavior* 65, no. 1 (August 2004), pp. 71–95.

106 R. Bar-On, D. Tranel, N. L. Denburg, and A. Bechara, "Exploring the Neurological Substrate of Emotional and Social Intelligence," *Brain* 126, no. 8 (August 2003), pp. 1790–1800.

107 E. A. Locke, "Why Emotional Intelligence Is an Invalid Concept," *Journal of Organizational Behavior* 26, no. 4 (June 2005), pp. 425–431.

108 J. M. Conte, "A Review and Critique of Emotional Intelligence Measures," *Journal of Organizational Behavior* 26, no. 4 (June 2005), pp. 433–440; and M. Davies, L. Stankov, and R. D. Roberts, "Emotional Intelligence: In Search of an Elusive Construct," *Journal of Personality and Social Psychology* 75, no. 4 (1998), pp. 989–1015.

109 T. Decker, "Is Emotional Intelligence a Viable Concept?" *Academy of Management Review* 28, no. 2 (April 2003), pp. 433–440; and M. Davies, L. Stankov, and R. D. Roberts, "Emotional Intelligence: In Search of an Elusive Construct," *Journal of Personality and Social Psychology* 75, no. 4 (1998), pp. 989–1015.

110 F. J. Landy, "Some Historical and Scientific Issues Related to Research on Emotional Intelligence," *Journal of Organizational Behavior* 26, no. 4 (June 2005), pp. 411–424.

111 S. L. Robinson and R. J. Bennett, "A Typology of Deviant Workplace Behaviors: A Multidimensional Scaling Study," *Academy of Management Journal*, April 1995, p. 556.

112 S. L. Robinson and R. J. Bennett, "A Typology of Deviant Workplace Behaviors: A Multidimensional Scaling Study," *Academy of Management Journal*, April 1995, pp. 555–572.

113 Based on A. G. Bedeian, "Workplace Envy," *Organizational Dynamics*, Spring 1995, p. 50.

114 A. G. Bedeian, "Workplace Envy," *Organizational Dynamics*, Spring 1995, p. 54.

115 K. Lee and N. J. Allen, "Organizational Citizenship Behavior and Workplace Deviance: The Role of Affect and Cognition," *Journal of Applied Psychology* 87, no. 1 (2002), pp. 131–142; and T. A. Judge, B. A. Scott, and R. Ilies, "Hostility, Job Attitudes, and Workplace Deviance: Test of a Multilevel Model," *Journal of Applied Psychology* 91, no. 1 (2006) 126–138.

116 H. M. Weiss and R. Cropanzano, "Affective Events Theory," in *Research in Organizational Behavior*, vol. 18, ed. B. M. Staw and L. L. Cummings (Greenwich, CT: JAI Press, 1996), p. 55.

117 H. Liao and A. Chuang, "A Multilevel Investigation of Factors Influencing Employee Service Performance and Customer Outcomes," *Academy of Management Journal* 47, no. 1 (2004), pp. 41–58.

118 D. J. Beal, J. P. Trougakos, H. M. Weiss, and S. G. Green, "Episodic Processes in Emotional Labor: Perceptions of Affective Delivery and Regulation Strategies," *Journal of Applied Psychology* 91, no. 5 (2006), pp. 1057–1065.

119 Cited in S. W. Floyd, J. Roos, F. Kellermanns, *Innovating Strategy Process* (Blackwell Publishing, 2005), p. 66.

120 D. Zapf and M. Holz, "On the Positive and Negative Effects of Emotion Work in Organizations," *European Journal of Work and Organizational Psychology* 15, no. 1 (2006), pp. 1–28.

121 D. Zapf, "Emotion Work and Psychological Well-Being: A Review of the Literature and Some Conceptual Considerations," *Human Resource Management Review* 12, no. 2 (2002), pp. 237–268.

122 J. E. Bono and M. A. Vey, "Toward Understanding Emotional Management at Work: A Quantitative Review of Emotional Labor Research," in *Emotions in Organizational Behavior*, ed. C. E. Härtel and W. J. Zerbe (Mahwah, NJ: Lawrence Erlbaum, 2005), pp. 213–233.

123 R. Christie and F. L. Geis, *Studies in Machiavellianism* (New York: Academic Press, 1970).

124 R. D. Lennox and R. N. Wolfe, "Revision of the Self-Monitoring Scale," *Journal of Personality and Social Psychology*, June 1984, p. 1361. Copyright 1984 by the American Psychological Association. Reprinted by permission.

125 Adapted from N. Kogan and M. A. Wallach, *Risk Taking: A Study in Cognition and Personality* (New York: Holt, Rinehart and Winston, 1964), pp. 256–261. Reprinted with permission of Wadsworth, a division of Thomson Learning: www.thomsonrights.com. Fax 800-730-2215.

126 Adapted from R. W. Bortner, "Short Rating Scale as a Potential Measure of Pattern A Behavior," *Journal of Chronic Diseases,* June 1969, pp. 87–91. With permission from Elsevier.

127 A. Fisher, "Success Secret: A High Emotional IQ," *Fortune,* October 26, 1998, p. 298. Reprinted with permission of Time Warner Inc.

128 This dilemma is based on R. R. Hastings, "Survey: The Demographics of Tattoos and Piercings," *HR Week,* February 2007, www.shrm.org; and H. Wessel, "Taboo of Tattoos in the Workplace," *Orlando (Florida) Sentinel,* May 28, 2007, www.tmcnet.com/usubmit/2007/05/28/2666555.htm (accessed August 1, 2009); S. O'Donnell, "Popularity of Piercing Pokes Holes in Traditional Workplace Standards," *Edmonton Journal,* March 12, 2006, p. A1; K. Dedyna, "Picture-Perfect Workers? TATTOOS: Inky Designs Gain Acceptance with Bosses, Clients," *Province* (Vancouver), August 28, 2005, p. A50.

129 Based on M. Blombert, "Cultivating a Career," *Gainesville (Florida) Sun,* May 9, 2005, p. D1.

130 Based on "How Bad Is Your Boss?" *CBC Venture,* January 15, 2006.

131 Based on V. P. Richmond, J. C. McCroskey, and S. K. Payne, *Nonverbal Behavior in Interpersonal Relations,* 2nd ed. (Englewood Cliffs, NJ: Prentice Hall, 1991), pp. 117–138; and L. A. King, "Ambivalence Over Emotional Expression and Reading Emotions in Situations and Faces," *Journal of Personality and Social Psychology,* March 1998, pp. 753–762.

Chapter 3

1 Based on S. Klie, "Hail the New Chief," *Canadian HR Reporter,* July 14, 2008, p. 13.

2 M. Rokeach, *The Nature of Human Values* (New York: Free Press, 1973), p. 5.

3 See, for instance, B. Meglino and E. Ravlin, "Individual Values in Organizations," *Journal of Management* 24, no. 3 (1998), pp. 351–389.

4 M. Rokeach and S. J. Ball-Rokeach, "Stability and Change in American Value Priorities, 1968–1981," *American Psychologist,* May 1989, pp. 775–784.

5 M. Rokeach, *The Nature of Human Values* (New York: Free Press, 1973), p. 6.

6 J. M. Munson and B. Z. Posner, "The Factorial Validity of a Modified Rokeach Value Survey for Four Diverse Samples," *Educational and Psychological Measurement,* Winter 1980, pp. 1073–1079; and W. C. Frederick and J. Weber, "The Values of Corporate Managers and Their Critics: An Empirical Description and Normative Implications," in *Business Ethics: Research Issues and Empirical Studies.* ed. W. C. Frederick and L. E. Preston (Greenwich, CT: JAI Press, 1990), pp. 123–144.

7 W. C. Frederick and J. Weber, "The Values of Corporate Managers and Their Critics: An Empirical Description and Normative Implications," in *Business Ethics: Research Issues and Empirical Studies,* ed. W. C. Frederick and L. E. Preston (Greenwich, CT: JAI Press, 1990), pp. 123–144.

8 W. C. Frederick and J. Weber, "The Values of Corporate Managers and Their Critics: An Empirical Description and Normative Implications," in *Business Ethics: Research Issues and Empirical Studies,* ed. W. C. Frederick and L. E. Preston (Greenwich, CT: JAI Press, 1990), p. 132.

9 K. Hodgson, *A Rock and a Hard Place: How to Make Ethical Business Decisions When the Choices Are Tough* (New York: AMACOM, 1992), pp. 66–67.

10 K. Hodgson, "Adapting Ethical Decisions to a Global Marketplace," *Management Review* 81, no. 5 (May 1992), pp. 53–57. Reprinted by permission.

11 *KPMG Code of Conduct,* www.kpmg.ca/en/about/documents/KPMGCodeofConduct.pdf (accessed August 4, 2009).

12 G. Hofstede, *Culture's Consequences: International Differences in Work-Related Values* (Beverly Hills, CA: Sage, 1980); G. Hofstede, *Cultures and Organizations: Software of the Mind* (London: McGraw-Hill, 1991); G. Hofstede, "Cultural Constraints in Management Theories," *Academy of Management Executive* 7, no. 1 (1993), pp. 81–94; G. Hofstede and M. F. Peterson, "National Values and Organizational Practices," in *Handbook of Organizational Culture and Climate,* ed. N. M. Ashkanasy, C. M. Wilderom, and M. F. Peterson (Thousand Oaks, CA: Sage, 2000), pp. 401–416; and G. Hofstede, *Culture's Consequences: Comparing Values, Behaviors, Institutions, and Organizations Across Nations,* 2nd ed. (Thousand Oaks, CA: Sage, 2001). For criticism of this research, see B. McSweeney, "Hofstede's Model of National Cultural Differences and Their Consequences: A Triumph of Faith—A Failure of Analysis," *Human Relations* 55, no. 1 (2002), pp. 89–118.

13 G. Hofstede and M. H. Bond, "The Confucius Connection: From Cultural Roots to Economic Growth," *Organizational Dynamics,* Spring 1988, pp. 12–13.

14 M. H. Bond, "Reclaiming the Individual from Hofstede's Ecological Analysis—A 20-Year Odyssey: Comment on Oyserman et al. (2002)," *Psychological Bulletin* 128, no. 1 (2002), pp. 73–77; G. Hofstede, "The Pitfalls of Cross-National Survey Research: A Reply to the Article by Spector et al. on the Psychometric Properties of the Hofstede Values Survey Module 1994," *Applied Psychology: An International Review* 51, no. 1 (2002), pp. 170–178; and T. Fang, "A Critique of Hofstede's Fifth National Culture Dimension," *International Journal of Cross-Cultural Management* 3, no. 3 (2003), pp. 347–368.

15 The five usual criticisms and Hofstede's responses (in parentheses) are: 1. Surveys are not a suitable way to measure cultural differences (answer: they should not be the only way); 2. Nations are not the proper units for studying cultures (answer: they are usually the only kind of units available for comparison); 3. A study of the subsidiaries of one company cannot provide information about entire national cultures (answer: what was measured were differences among national cultures. Any set of functionally equivalent samples can supply information about such differences); 4. The IBM data are old and therefore obsolete (answer: the dimensions found are assumed to have century-old roots; they have been validated against all kinds of external measurements; recent replications show no loss of validity); 5. Four or five dimensions are not enough (answer: additional dimensions should be statistically independent of the dimensions defined earlier; they should be valid on the basis of correlations with external measures; candidates are welcome to apply). See A. Harzing and G. Hofstede, "Planned

Change in Organizations: The Influence of National Culture," in *Research in the Sociology of Organizations, Cross Cultural Analysis of Organizations*, vol. 14, ed. P. A. Bamberger, M. Erez, and S. B. Bacharach (Greenwich, CT: JAI Press, 1996), pp. 297–340.

16 M. Javidan and R. J. House, "Cultural Acumen for the Global Manager: Lessons from Project GLOBE," *Organizational Dynamics* 29, no. 4 (2001), pp. 289–305; and R. J. House, P. J. Hanges, M. Javidan, and P. W. Dorfman, eds., *Leadership, Culture, and Organizations: The GLOBE Study of 62 Societies* (Thousand Oaks, CA: Sage, 2004).

17 P. C. Early, "Leading Cultural Research in the Future: A Matter of Paradigms and Taste," *Journal of International Business Studies*, September 2006, pp. 922–931; G. Hofstede, "What Did GLOBE Really Measure? Researchers' Minds versus Respondents' Minds," *Journal of International Business Studies*, September 2006, pp. 882–896; and M. Javidan, R. J. House, P. W. Dorfman, P. J. Hanges, and M. S. de Luque, "Conceptualizing and Measuring Cultures and Their Consequences: A Comparative Review of GLOBE's and Hofstede's Approaches," *Journal of International Business Studies*, September 2006, pp. 897–914.

18 B. Meglino, E. C. Ravlin, and C. L. Adkins, "A Work Values Approach to Corporate Culture: A Field Test of the Value Congruence Process and Its Relationship to Individual Outcomes," *Journal of Applied Psychology* 74, 1989, pp. 424–432.

19 B. Z. Posner, J. M. Kouzes, and W. H. Schmidt, "Shared Values Make a Difference: An Empirical Test of Corporate Culture," *Human Resource Management* 24, 1985, pp. 293–310; and A. L. Balazas, "Value Congruency: The Case of the 'Socially Responsible' Firm," *Journal of Business Research* 20, 1990, pp. 171–181.

20 C. A. O'Reilly, J. Chatman, and D. Caldwell, "People and Organizational Culture: A Q-Sort Approach to Assessing Person-Organizational Fit," *Academy of Management Journal* 34, 1991, pp. 487–516.

21 C. Enz and C. K. Schwenk, "Performance and Sharing of Organizational Values" (paper presented at the annual meeting of the Academy of Management, Washington, DC, 1989).

22 Statistics Canada, "2006 Census: Immigration, Citizenship, Language, Mobility and Migration," *The Daily*, December 4, 2007; and "2006 Census: Ethnic Origin, Visible Minorities, Place of Work and Mode of Transportation," *The Daily*, April 2, 2008.

23 Statistics Canada, "Immigration in Canada: A Portrait of the Foreign-born Population, 2006 Census: Immigrants in Metropolitan Areas," www12.statcan.ca/english/census06/analysis/immcit/city_life.cfm (accessed August 4, 2009).

24 K. Young, "Language: Allophones on the Rise," *National Post*, December 4, 2007.

25 K. Young, "Language: Allophones on the Rise," *National Post*, December 4, 2007.

26 Statistics Canada, "Ethnic Diversity Survey, 2002," *The Daily*, September 29, 2003.

27 The Pew Research Center for the People & the Press, *Views of a Changing World 2003* (Washington, DC: The Pew Research Center for the People & the Press, June 2003).

28 M. Adams, *Fire and Ice: The United States, Canada and the Myth of Converging Values* (Toronto: Penguin Canada, 2003).

29 M. Adams, *Fire and Ice: The United States, Canada and the Myth of Converging Values* (Toronto: Penguin Canada, 2003).

30 R. N. Kanungo and J. K. Bhatnagar, "Achievement Orientation and Occupational Values: A Comparative Study of Young French and English Canadians," *Canadian Journal of Behavioural Science* 12, 1978, pp. 384–392; M. W. McCarrey, S. Edwards, and R. Jones, "The Influence of Ethnolinguistic Group Membership, Sex and Position Level on Motivational Orientation of Canadian Anglophone and Francophone Employees," *Canadian Journal of Behavioural Science* 9, 1977, pp. 274–282; M. W. McCarrey, S. Edwards, and R. Jones, "Personal Values of Canadian Anglophone and Francophone Employees and Ethnolinguistic Group Membership, Sex and Position Level," *Journal of Psychology* 104, 1978, pp. 175–184; S. Richer and P. Laporte, "Culture, Cognition and English-French Competition," in *Readings in Social Psychology: Focus on Canada*, ed. D. Koulack and D. Perlman (Toronto: Wiley & Sons, 1973); and L. Shapiro and D. Perlman, "Value Differences Between English and French Canadian High School Students," *Canadian Ethnic Studies* 8, 1976, pp. 50–55.

31 R. N. Kanungo and J. K. Bhatnagar, "Achievement Orientation and Occupational Values: A Comparative Study of Young French and English Canadians," *Canadian Journal of Behavioural Science* 12, 1978, pp. 384–392.

32 V. Mann-Feder and V. Savicki, "Burnout in Anglophone and Francophone Child and Youth Workers in Canada: A Cross-Cultural Comparison," *Child & Youth Care Forum* 32, no. 6 (December 2003), p. 345.

33 R. N. Kanungo and J. K. Bhatnagar, "Achievement Orientation and Occupational Values: A Comparative Study of Young French and English Canadians," *Canadian Journal of Behavioural Science* 12, 1978, pp. 384–392.

34 V. Mann-Feder and V. Savicki, "Burnout in Anglophone and Francophone Child and Youth Workers in Canada: A Cross-Cultural Comparison," *Child & Youth Care Forum* 32, no. 6 (December 2003), pp. 337–354.

35 A. Stalikas, E. Casas, and A. D. Carson, "In the Shadow of the English: English and French Canadians Differ by Psychological Type," *Journal of Psychological Type* 38, 1996, pp. 4–12.

36 K. L. Gibson, S. J. Mckelvie, A. F. De Man, "Personality and Culture: A Comparison of Francophones and Anglophones in Québec," *Journal of Social Psychology* 148, no. 2 (2008), pp. 133–165.

37 H. C. Jain, J. Normand, and R. N. Kanungo, "Job Motivation of Canadian Anglophone and Francophone Hospital Employees," *Canadian Journal of Behavioural Science*, April 1979, pp. 160–163; R. N. Kanungo, G. J. Gorn, and H. J. Dauderis, "Motivational Orientation of Canadian Anglophone and Francophone Managers," *Canadian Journal of Behavioural Science*, April 1976, pp. 107–121.

38 M. Major, M. McCarrey, P. Mercier, and Y. Gasse, "Meanings of Work and Personal Values of Canadian Anglophone and Francophone Middle Managers," *Canadian Journal of Administrative Sciences*, September 1994, pp. 251–263.

39 G. Bouchard, F. Rocher, and G. Rocher, *Les Francophones Québécois* (Montreal, PQ: Bowne de Montréal, 1991).

40 K. L. Gibson, S. J. Mckelvie, A. F. De Man, "Personality and Culture: A Comparison of Francophones and Anglophones in Québec," *Journal of Social Psychology* 148, no. 2 (2008), pp. 133–165.

41   A. Derfel, "Boy, Are We Stressed Out! Quebec Has Highest Rate of Work Absenteeism," *Gazette* (Montreal), May 29, 2003, p. A1.

42   P. La Novara, "Culture Participation: Does Language Make a Difference?" *Focus on Culture* 13, no. 3, Catalogue no. 87-004-XIE (Ottawa: Statistics Canada, 2002).

43   Statistics Canada, *2001 Census.* Cited in Treasury Board of Canada Secretariat, "Canada's Performance Report 2005—Annex 3—Indicators and Additional Information: Aboriginal Peoples," www.tbs-sct.gc.ca/report/govrev/05/ann304-eng.asp#a3business (accessed October 5, 2009).

44   C. Howes, "The New Native Tycoons: Armed With a New Sense of Entrepreneurialism, Aboriginals Across Canada Have Begun Cashing in on Energy, Forestry, Mining and Other Sectors, and Are Creating Businesses at a Rate Faster Than the National Average," *Financial Post* (*National Post*), January 27, 2001, p. D5.

45   L. Redpath and M. O. Nielsen, "A Comparison of Native Culture, Non-Native Culture and New Management Ideology," *Canadian Journal of Administrative Sciences* 14, no. 3 (1997), p. 327.

46   G. C. Anders and K. K. Anders, "Incompatible Goals in Unconventional Organizations: The Politics of Alaska Native Corporations," *Organization Studies* 7, 1986, pp. 213–233; G. Dacks, "Worker-Controlled Native Enterprises: A Vehicle for Community Development in Northern Canada?" *Canadian Journal of Native Studies* 3, 1983, pp. 289–310; L. P. Dana, "Self-Employment in the Canadian Sub-Arctic: An Exploratory Study," *Canadian Journal of Administrative Sciences* 13, 1996, pp. 65–77.

47   L. Redpath and M. O. Nielsen, "A Comparison of Native Culture, Non-Native Culture and New Management Ideology," *Canadian Journal of Administrative Sciences* 14, no. 3 (1997), p. 327.

48   R. B. Anderson, "The Business Economy of the First Nations in Saskatchewan: A Contingency Perspective," *Canadian Journal of Native Studies* 2, 1995, pp. 309–345.

49   E. Struzik, "'Win-Win Scenario' Possible for Resource Industry, Aboriginals," *Edmonton Journal*, April 6, 2003, p. A12.

50   D. C. Natcher and C. G. Hickey, "Putting the Community Back into Community-Based Resource Management: A Criteria and Indicators Approach to Sustainability," *Human Organization* 61, no. 4 (2002), pp. 350–363.

51   www.highlevelwoodlands.com.

52   Discussion based on L. Redpath and M. O. Nielsen, "A Comparison of Native Culture, Non-Native Culture and New Management Ideology," *Canadian Journal of Administrative Sciences* 14, no. 3 (1997), pp. 327–339.

53   Discussion based on L. Redpath and M. O. Nielsen, "A Comparison of Native Culture, Non-Native Culture and New Management Ideology," *Canadian Journal of Administrative Sciences* 14, no. 3 (1997), pp. 327–339.

54   D. Grigg and J. Newman, "Five Ways to Foster Bonds, Win Trust in Business," *Ottawa Citizen*, April 23, 2003, p. F12.

55   T. Chui, K. Tran, and J. Flanders, "Chinese Canadians: Enriching the Cultural Mosaic," *Canadian Social Trends* 76, Spring 2005.

56   Statistics Canada, "Canada's Visible Minority Population in 2017," *The Daily*, March 22, 2005.

57   I. Y. M. Yeung and R. L. Tung, "Achieving Business Success in Confucian Societies: The Importance of Guanxi (Connections)," *Organizational Dynamics: Special Report*, 1998, pp. 72–83.

58   I. Y. M. Yeung and R. L. Tung, "Achieving Business Success in Confucian Societies: The Importance of Guanxi (Connections)," *Organizational Dynamics: Special Report*, 1998, p. 73.

59   Material in this section based on the work of M. Adams, *Sex in the Snow* (Toronto: Penguin Books, 1997); and M. Adams, *Fire and Ice: The United States, Canada and the Myth of Converging Values* (Toronto: Penguin Canada, 2003).

60   N. A. Hira, "You Raised Them, Now Manage Them," *Fortune*, May 28, 2007, pp. 38–46; R. R. Hastings, "Surveys Shed Light on Generation Y Career Goals," *SHRM Online*, March 2007, www.shrm.org; and S. Jayson, "The 'Millennials' Come of Age," *USA Today*, June 29, 2006, pp. 1D, 2D.

61   Statistics Canada, "Census of Population," *The Daily*, February 11, 2003.

62   Based on P. Krivel, "Culture of Openness Boosts Productivity; Accounting Firm Knows Welcoming Atmosphere Has a Positive Impact on the Bottom Line," *Toronto Star*, April 3, 2008, p. R5; S. Klie, "Hail the New Chief," *Canadian HR Reporter*, July 14, 2008, p. 13; and Lesley Young, "Diversity Drives KPMG to Top," *Canadian HR Reporter*, March 24, 2008, p. 15.

63   Based on C. Ricketts, "When in London, Do as the Californians Do," *Wall Street Journal*, January 23, 2007, p. B5.

64   G. Shaw, "Canada Lags World on Job Quality," *Vancouver Sun*, September 18, 2004, p. F5.

65   J. Barling, E. K. Kelloway, and R. D. Iverson, "High-Quality Work, Job Satisfaction, and Occupational Injuries," *Journal of Applied Psychology* 88, no. 2 (2003), pp. 276–283; and F. W. Bond and D. Bunce, "The Role of Acceptance and Job Control in Mental Health, Job Satisfaction, and Work Performance," *Journal of Applied Psychology* 88, no. 6 (2003), pp. 1057–1067.

66   E. Diener, E. Sandvik, L. Seidlitz, and M. Diener, "The Relationship Between Income and Subjective Well-Being: Relative or Absolute?" *Social Indicators Research* 28 (1993), pp. 195–223.

67   T. A. Judge and C. Hurst, "The Benefits and Possible Costs of Positive Core Self-Evaluations: A Review and Agenda for Future Research," in *Positive Organizational Behavior*, ed. D. Nelson & C. L. Cooper (London, UK: Sage Publications, 2007), pp. 159–174.

68   M. T. Iaffaldano and M. Muchinsky, "Job Satisfaction and Job Performance: A Meta-Analysis," *Psychological Bulletin*, March 1985, pp. 251–273.

69   T. A. Judge, C. J. Thoresen, J. E. Bono, and G. K. Patton, "The Job Satisfaction–Job Performance Relationship: A Qualitative and Quantitative Review," *Psychological Bulletin*, May 2001, pp. 376–407; and T. Judge, S. Parker, A. E. Colbert, D. Heller, and R. Ilies, "Job Satisfaction: A Cross-Cultural Review," in *Handbook of Industrial, Work, & Organizational Psychology*, vol. 2, ed. N. Anderson, D. S. Ones, H. K. Sinangil, and C. Viswesvaran (Thousand Oaks, CA: Sage, 2001), p. 41.

70   C. N. Greene, "The Satisfaction–Performance Controversy," *Business Horizons*, February 1972, pp. 31–41; E. E. Lawler III,

Motivation in Organizations (Monterey, CA: Brooks/Cole, 1973); and M. M. Petty, G. W. McGee, and J. W. Cavender, "A Meta-Analysis of the Relationship Between Individual Job Satisfaction and Individual Performance," *Academy of Management Review*, October 1984, pp. 712–721.

71   C. Ostroff, "The Relationship Between Satisfaction, Attitudes, and Performance: An Organizational Level Analysis," *Journal of Applied Psychology*, December 1992, pp. 963–974; A. M. Ryan, M. J. Schmit, and R. Johnson, "Attitudes and Effectiveness: Examining Relations at an Organizational Level," *Personnel Psychology*, Winter 1996, pp. 853–882; and J. K. Harter, F. L. Schmidt, and T. L. Hayes, "Business-Unit Level Relationship Between Employee Satisfaction, Employee Engagement, and Business Outcomes: A Meta-Analysis," *Journal of Applied Psychology*, April 2002, pp. 268–279.

72   D. W. Organ, *Organizational Citizenship Behavior: The Good Soldier Syndrome* (Lexington, MA: Lexington Books, 1988), p. 4.

73   D. W. Organ, *Organizational Citizenship Behavior: The Good Soldier Syndrome* (Lexington, MA: Lexington Books, 1988); C. A. Smith, D. W. Organ, and J. P. Near, "Organizational Citizenship Behavior: Its Nature and Antecedents," *Journal of Applied Psychology*, 1983, pp. 653–663.

74   J. Farh, C. Zhong, and D. W. Organ, "Organizational Citizenship Behavior in the People's Republic of China," *Organization Science* 15, no. 2 (2004), pp. 241–253.

75   J. M. George and A. P. Brief, "Feeling Good–Doing Good: A Conceptual Analysis of the Mood at Work—Organizational Spontaneity Relationship," *Psychological Bulletin* 112, 2002, pp. 310–329; and S. Wagner and M. Rush, "Altruistic Organizational Citizenship Behavior: Context, Disposition and Age," *Journal of Social Psychology* 140, 2002, pp. 379–391.

76   S. D. Salamon and Y. Deutsch, "OCB as a Handicap: An Evolutionary Psychological Perspective," *Journal of Organizational Behavior* 27, no. 2 (2006), pp. 185–199.

77   P. E. Spector, *Job Satisfaction: Application, Assessment, Causes, and Consequences* (Thousand Oaks, CA: Sage, 1997), pp. 57–58.

78   P. M. Podsakoff, S. B. MacKenzie, J. B. Paine, and D. G. Bachrach, "Organizational Citizenship Behaviors: A Critical Review of the Theoretical and Empirical Literature and Suggestions for Future Research," *Journal of Management* 26, no. 3 (2000), pp. 513–563.

79   See T. S. Bateman and D. W. Organ, "Job Satisfaction and the Good Soldier: The Relationship Between Affect and Employee 'Citizenship,'" *Academy of Management Journal*, December 1983, pp. 587–595; C. A. Smith, D. W. Organ, and J. P. Near, "Organizational Citizenship Behavior: Its Nature and Antecedents," *Journal of Applied Psychology*, October 1983, pp. 653–663; and A. P. Brief, *Attitudes in and Around Organizations* (Thousand Oaks, CA: Sage, 1998), pp. 44–45.

80   D. W. Organ and R. H. Moorman, "Fairness and Organizational Citizenship Behavior: What Are the Connections?" *Social Justice Research* 6, no. 1 (March 1993), pp. 5–18.

81   D. W. Organ and K. Ryan, "A Meta-Analytic Review of Attitudinal and Dispositional Predictors of Organizational Citizenship Behavior," *Personnel Psychology*, Winter 1995, p. 791.

82   J. Farh, P. M. Podsakoff, and D. W. Organ, "Accounting for Organizational Citizenship Behavior: Leader Fairness and Task

Scope versus Satisfaction," *Journal of Management*, December 1990, pp. 705–722; R. H. Moorman, "Relationship Between Organizational Justice and Organizational Citizenship Behaviors: Do Fairness Perceptions Influence Employee Citizenship?" *Journal of Applied Psychology*, December 1991, pp. 845–855; and M. A. Konovsky and D. W. Organ, "Dispositional and Contextual Determinants of Organizational Citizenship Behavior," *Journal of Organizational Behavior*, May 1996, pp. 253–266.

83   D. W. Organ, "Personality and Organizational Citizenship Behavior," *Journal of Management*, Summer 1994, p. 466.

84   J. L. Farh, C. B. Zhong, and D. W. Organ, "Organizational Citizenship Behavior in the People's Republic of China," *Organization Science* 15, no. 2 (March–April 2004), pp. 241–253.

85   See, for instance, E. Naumann and D. W. Jackson Jr., "One More Time: How Do You Satisfy Customers?" *Business Horizons*, May–June 1999, pp. 71–76; D. J. Koys, "The Effects of Employee Satisfaction, Organizational Citizenship Behavior, and Turnover on Organizational Effectiveness: A Unit-Level, Longitudinal Study," *Personnel Psychology*, Spring 2001, pp. 101–114; and J. Griffith, "Do Satisfied Employees Satisfy Customers? Support-Services Staff Morale and Satisfaction Among Public School Administrators, Students, and Parents," *Journal of Applied Social Psychology*, August 2001, pp. 1627–1658.

86   M. J. Bitner, B. H. Booms, and L. A. Mohr, "Critical Service Encounters: The Employee's Viewpoint," *Journal of Marketing*, October 1994, pp. 95–106.

87   E. A. Locke, "The Nature and Causes of Job Satisfaction," in *Handbook of Industrial and Organizational Psychology*, ed. M. D. Dunnette (Chicago: Rand McNally, 1976), p. 1331; S. L. McShane, "Job Satisfaction and Absenteeism: A Meta-Analytic Re-Examination," *Canadian Journal of Administrative Science*, June 1984, pp. 61–77; R. D. Hackett and R. M. Guion, "A Reevaluation of the Absenteeism–Job Satisfaction Relationship," *Organizational Behavior and Human Decision Processes*, June 1985, pp. 340–381; K. D. Scott and G. S. Taylor, "An Examination of Conflicting Findings on the Relationship Between Job Satisfaction and Absenteeism: A Meta-Analysis," *Academy of Management Journal*, September 1985, pp. 599–612; R. D. Hackett, "Work Attitudes and Employee Absenteeism: A Synthesis of the Literature" (paper presented at the 1988 National Academy of Management Conference, Anaheim, CA, August 1988); and R. P. Steel and J. R. Rentsch, "Influence of Cumulation Strategies on the Long-Range Prediction of Absenteeism," *Academy of Management Journal*, December 1995, pp. 1616–1634.

88   J. L. Cotton and J. M. Tuttle, "Employee Turnover: A Meta-Analysis and Review With Implications for Research," *Academy of Management Review* 11, 1986, pp. 55–70; R. W. Griffeth and P. W. Hom, "The Employee Turnover Process," *Research in Personnel and Human Resources Management* 13, 1995, pp. 245–293; P. W. Hom, F. Caranikas-Walker, G. E. Prussia, and R. W. Griffeth, "A Meta-Analytical Structural Equations Analysis of a Model of Employee Turnover," *Journal of Applied Psychology* 77, 1992, pp. 890–909; P. W. Hom and R. W. Griffeth, *Employee Turnover* (Cincinnati, OH: South-Western College, 1995); W. H. Mobley, R. W. Griffeth, H. H. Hand, and B. Meglino, "Review and Conceptual Analysis of the Employee Turnover Process," *Psychological Bulletin* 86, 1979, pp. 493–522; J. L. Price, *The Study of Turnover* (Ames, IA: Iowa State University Press, 1977); R. P. Steel and N. K. Ovalle, "A Review and Meta-Analysis of Research on the Relationship Between Behavioral Intentions

and Employee Turnover," *Journal of Applied Psychology* 69, 1984, pp. 673–686; and R. P. Tett and J. P. Meyer, "Job Satisfaction, Organizational Commitment, Turnover Intention, and Turnover: Path Analyses Based on Meta-Analytical Findings," *Personnel Psychology* 46, 1993, pp. 259–293.

89 T. A. Judge, "Does Affective Disposition Moderate the Relationship Between Job Satisfaction and Voluntary Turnover?" *Journal of Applied Psychology*, June 1993, pp. 395–401.

90 S. M. Puffer, "Prosocial Behavior, Noncompliant Behavior, and Work Performance Among Commission Salespeople," *Journal of Applied Psychology*, November 1987, pp. 615–621; J. Hogan and R. Hogan, "How to Measure Employee Reliability," *Journal of Applied Psychology*, May 1989, pp. 273–279; and C. D. Fisher and E. A. Locke, "The New Look in Job Satisfaction Research and Theory," in *Job Satisfaction*, ed. C. J. Cranny, P. C. Smith, and E. F. Stone (New York: Lexington Books, 1992), pp. 165–194.

91 K. A. Hanisch, C. L. Hulin, and M. Roznowski, "The Importance of Individuals' Repertoires of Behaviors: The Scientific Appropriateness of Studying Multiple Behaviors and General Attitudes," *Journal of Organizational Behavior* 19, no. 5 (1998), pp. 463–480.

92 S. M. Puffer, "Prosocial Behavior, Noncompliant Behavior, and Work Performance Among Commission Salespeople," *Journal of Applied Psychology*, November 1987, pp. 615–621; J. Hogan and R. Hogan, "How to Measure Employee Reliability," *Journal of Applied Psychology*, May 1989, pp. 273–279; and C. D. Fisher and E. A. Locke, "The New Look in Job Satisfaction Research and Theory," in *Job Satisfaction*, ed. C. J. Cranny, P. C. Smith, and E. F. Stone (New York: Lexington Books, 1992), pp. 165–194.

93 R. B. Freeman, "Job Satisfaction as an Economic Variable," *American Economic Review*, January 1978, pp. 135–141.

94 G. J. Blau and K. R. Boal, "Conceptualizing How Job Involvement and Organizational Commitment Affect Turnover and Absenteeism," *Academy of Management Review*, April 1987, p. 290.

95 N. J. Allen and J. P. Meyer, "The Measurement and Antecedents of Affective, Continuance, and Normative Commitment to the Organization," *Journal of Occupational Psychology* 63, 1990, pp. 1–18; and J. P Meyer, N. J. Allen, and C. A. Smith, "Commitment to Organizations and Occupations: Extension and Test of a Three-Component Conceptualization," *Journal of Applied Psychology* 78, 1993, pp. 538–551.

96 M. Riketta, "Attitudinal Organizational Commitment and Job Performance: A Meta-Analysis," *Journal of Organizational Behavior*, March 2002, pp. 257–266.

97 T. A. Wright and D. G. Bonett, "The Moderating Effects of Employee Tenure on the Relation Between Organizational Commitment and Job Performance: A Meta-Analysis," *Journal of Applied Psychology*, December 2002, pp. 1183–1190.

98 See, for instance, W. Hom, R. Katerberg, and C. L. Hulin, "Comparative Examination of Three Approaches to the Prediction of Turnover," *Journal of Applied Psychology*, June 1979, pp. 280–290; H. Angle and J. Perry, "Organizational Commitment: Individual and Organizational Influence," *Work and Occupations*, May 1983, pp. 123–146; J. L. Pierce and R. B. Dunham, "Organizational Commitment: Pre-Employment Propensity and Initial Work Experiences," *Journal of Management*, Spring 1987, pp. 163–178; and T. Simons and Q. Roberson, "Why Managers Should Care About Fairness: The Effects of Aggregate Justice Perceptions on Organizational Outcomes," *Journal of Applied Psychology* 88, no. 3 (2003), pp. 432–443.

99 K. Bentein, R. Vandenberg, C. Vandenberghe, and F. Stinglhamber, "The Role of Change in the Relationship Between Commitment and Turnover: A Latent Growth Modeling Approach," *Journal of Applied Psychology* 90, no. 3 (2005), pp. 468–482.

100 J. P. Meyer, S. V. Paumonen, I. R. Gellatly, R. D. Goffin, and D. N. Jackson, "Organizational Commitment and Job Performance: It's the Nature of the Commitment That Counts," *Journal of Applied Psychology* 74, 1989, pp. 152–156; L. M. Shore and S. J. Wayne, "Commitment and Employee Behavior: Comparison of Affective and Continuance Commitment With Perceived Organizational Support," *Journal of Applied Psychology* 78, 1993, pp. 774–780.

101 D. M. Rousseau, "Organizational Behavior in the New Organizational Era," in *Annual Review of Psychology* 48, ed. J. T. Spence, J. M. Darley, and D. J. Foss (Palo Alto, CA: Annual Reviews, 1997), p. 523.

102 "Do as I Do," *Canadian Business*, March 12, 1999, p. 35.

103 J. R. Katzenback and J. A. Santamaria, "Firing up the Front Line," *Harvard Business Review*, May–June 1999, p. 109.

104 C. Hult, "Organizational Commitment and Person-Environment Fit in Six Western Countries," *Organization Studies* 26, no. 2 (2005), pp. 249–270.

105 D. R. May, R. L. Gilson, and L. M. Harter, "The Psychological Conditions of Meaningfulness, Safety and Availability and the Engagement of the Human Spirit at Work," *Journal of Occupational and Organizational Psychology* 77, no. 1 (2004), pp. 11–37.

106 J. K. Harter, F. L. Schmidt, and T. L. Hayes, "Business-Unit-Level Relationship Between Employee Satisfaction, Employee Engagement, and Business Outcomes: A Meta-Analysis," *Journal of Applied Psychology* 87, no. 2 (2002), pp. 268–279.

107 E. A. Locke, "The Nature and Causes of Job Satisfaction," in *Handbook of Industrial and Organizational Psychology*, ed. M. D. Dunnette (Chicago: Rand McNally, 1976), pp. 1319–1328.

108 See, for instance, T. A. Judge and S. Watanabe, "Another Look at the Job Satisfaction–Life Satisfaction Relationship," *Journal of Applied Psychology*, December 1993, pp. 939–948; R. D. Arvey, B. P. McCall, T. J. Bouchard Jr., and P. Taubman, "Genetic Influences on Job Satisfaction and Work Values," *Personality and Individual Differences*, July 1994, pp. 21–33; and D. Lykken and A. Tellegen, "Happiness Is a Stochastic Phenomenon," *Psychological Science*, May 1996, pp. 186–189.

109 R. N. Lussier, *Human Relations in Organizations: A Skill Building Approach*, 2nd ed. (Homewood, IL: Richard D. Irwin, 1993). Reprinted by permission of the McGraw-Hill Companies, Inc.

110 This exercise is based on M. Allen, "Here Comes the Bribe," *Entrepreneur*, October 2000, p. 48.

111 Based on M. Burke, "The Guru in the Vegetable Bin," *Forbes*, March 3, 2003, pp. 56–58.

112 Based on "Flair Bartending," *CBC Venture's Dreamers and Schemers*, November 8, 2006.

OB on the Edge: Stress at Work

1   P. McGuire, "An Old Family Recipe for Success; Business Like His Father and Grandfather Before Him, Moosehead President Andrew Oland Has Managed to Remain Grounded," *Telegraph-Journal*, August 4, 2008, p. E2; and M. Dunne, "Demand for Wellness Programs Growing; Employment Workers Increasingly Seek Employers Who Offer Assistance, Conference Told," *Telegraph-Journal*, June 16, 2007, p. E1.

2   Paragraph based on D. Hansen, "Worker Who Felt 'Thrown Away' Wins," *Vancouver Sun*, August 16, 2006.

3   Statistics Canada, "Life Stress, by Sex, Household Population Aged 18 and Over, Canada, Provinces, Territories, Health Regions and Peer Groups, 2005," www.statcan.ca/english/freepub/82-221-XIE/2006001/tables/t004b.htm (accessed August 14, 2009).

4   Table compiled using data from Statistics Canada, "Life Stress, by Sex, Household Population Aged 18 and Over, Canada, Provinces, Territories, Health Regions and Peer Groups, 2005," www.statcan.ca/english/freepub/82-221-XIE/2006001/tables/t004b.htm (accessed August 14, 2009).

5   K. MacQueen, "Workplace Stress Costs Us Dearly, and Yet Nobody Knows What It Is or How to Deal with It," *Maclean's*, October 15, 2007.

6   K. MacQueen, "Workplace Stress Costs Us Dearly, and Yet Nobody Knows What It Is or How to Deal with It," *Maclean's*, October 15, 2007.

7   L. Duxbury and C. Higgins, "2001 National Work-Life Conflict Study," as reported in J. Campbell, "'Organizational Anorexia' Puts Stress on Employees," *Ottawa Citizen*, July 4, 2002.

8   K. Harding, "Balance Tops List of Job Desires," *Globe and Mail*, May 7, 2003, pp. C1, C6.

9   V. Galt, "Productivity Buckling under the Strain of Stress, CEOs Say," *Globe and Mail*, June 9, 2005, p. B1.

10 "Canadian Workers among Most Stressed," *Worklife Report* 14, no. 2 (2002), pp. 8–9.

11 N. Ayed, "Absenteeism Up Since 1993," *Canadian Press Newswire*, March 25, 1998.

12 N. Ayed, "Absenteeism Up Since 1993," *Canadian Press Newswire*, March 25, 1998.

13 Adapted from R. S. Schuler, "Definition and Conceptualization of Stress in Organizations," *Organizational Behavior and Human Performance*, April 1980, p. 189. For an updated review of definitions, see C. L. Cooper, P. J. Dewe, and M. P. O'Driscoll, *Organizational Stress: A Review and Critique of Theory, Research, and Applications* (Thousand Oaks, CA: Sage, 2002).

14 *Health* magazine as appearing in Centers for Disease Control and Prevention, US Department of Health and Human Services, "*Helicobacter pylori* and Peptic Ulcer Disease—Myths," www.cdc.gov/ulcer/myth.htm (accessed August 14, 2009).

15 See, for instance, M. A. Cavanaugh, W. R. Boswell, M. V. Roehling, and J. W. Boudreau, "An Empirical Examination of Self-Reported Work Stress among U.S. Managers," *Journal of Applied Psychology*, February 2000, pp. 65–74.

16 N. P. Podsakoff, J. A. LePine, and M. A. LePine, "Differential Challenge-Hindrance Stressor Relationships with Job Attitudes, Turnover Intentions, Turnover, and Withdrawal Behavior: A Meta-Analysis," *Journal of Applied Psychology* 92, no. 2 (2007), pp. 438–454; J. A. LePine, M. A. LePine, and C. L. Jackson, "Challenge and Hindrance Stress: Relationships with Exhaustion, Motivation to Learn, and Learning Performance," *Journal of Applied Psychology*, October 2004, pp. 883–891.

17 J. de Jonge and C. Dormann, "Stressors, Resources, and Strain at Work: A Longitudinal Test of the Triple-Match Principle," *Journal of Applied Psychology* 91, no. 5 (2006), pp. 1359–1374.

18 N. W. Van Yperen and O. Janssen, "Fatigued and Dissatisfied or Fatigued but Satisfied? Goal Orientations and Responses to High Job Demands," *Academy of Management Journal*, December 2002, pp. 1161–1171; N. W. Van Yperen and M. Hagedoorn, "Do High Job Demands Increase Intrinsic Motivation or Fatigue or Both? The Role of Job Control and Job Social Support," *Academy of Management Journal*, June 2003, pp. 339–348; K. Daniels, N. Beesley, A. Cheyne, and V. Wimalasiri, "Coping Processes Linking the Demands-Control-Support Model, Affect and Risky Decisions at Work," *Human Relations* 61, no. 6, (2008), pp. 845–874; and M. van den Tooren and J. de Jonge "Managing Job Stress in Nursing: What Kind of Resources Do We Need?" *Journal of Advanced Nursing* 63, no. 1 (2008), pp. 75–84.

19 This section is adapted from C. L. Cooper and R. Payne, *Stress at Work* (London: Wiley, 1978); S. Parasuraman and J. A. Alutto, "Sources and Outcomes of Stress in Organizational Settings: Toward the Development of a Structural Model," *Academy of Management Journal* 27, no. 2 (June 1984), pp. 330–350; and P. M. Hart and C. L. Cooper, "Occupational Stress: Toward a More Integrated Framework," in *Handbook of Industrial, Work and Organizational Psychology*, vol. 2, ed. N. Anderson, D. S. Ones, H. K. Sinangil, and C. Viswesvaran (London: Sage, 2001), pp. 93–114.

20 E. A. Rafferty and M. A. Griffin, "Perceptions of Organizational Change: A Stress and Coping Perspective," *Journal of Applied Psychology* 71, no. 5 (2007), pp. 1154–1162.

21 See, for example, M. L. Fox, D. J. Dwyer, and D. C. Ganster, "Effects of Stressful Job Demands and Control of Physiological and Attitudinal Outcomes in a Hospital Setting," *Academy of Management Journal*, April 1993, pp. 289–318.

22 G. W. Evans and D. Johnson, "Stress and Open-Office Noise," *Journal of Applied Psychology*, October 2000, pp. 779–783.

23 T. M. Glomb, J. D. Kammeyer-Mueller, and M. Rotundo, "Emotional Labor Demands and Compensating Wage Differentials," *Journal of Applied Psychology*, August 2004, pp. 700–714; and A. A. Grandey, "When 'The Show Must Go On': Surface Acting and Deep Acting as Determinants of Emotional Exhaustion and Peer-Rated Service Delivery," *Academy of Management Journal*, February 2003, pp. 86–96.

24 V. S. Major, K. J. Klein, and M. G. Ehrhart, "Work Time, Work Interference with Family, and Psychological Distress," *Journal of Applied Psychology*, June 2002, pp. 427–436; see also P. E. Spector, C. L. Cooper, S. Poelmans, T. D. Allen, M. O'Driscoll, J. I. Sanchez, O. L. Siu, P. Dewe, P. Hart, L. Lu, L. F. R. De Moreas, G. M. Ostrognay, K. Sparks, P. Wong, and S. Yu, "A Cross-National Comparative Study of Work-Family Stressors, Working Hours, and Well-Being: China and Latin America versus the Anglo World," *Personnel Psychology*, Spring 2004, pp. 119–142.

25 S. McKay, "The Work-Family Conundrum," *Financial Post Magazine*, December 1997, pp. 78–81; and A. Davis, "Respect Your Elders: Pressure on the Healthcare System Means Elderly Patients Aren't

Staying in Hospitals as Long as They Used to," *Benefits Canada* 26, no. 8 (2002), p. 13.

26 L. T. Thomas and D. C. Ganster, "Impact of Family-Supportive Work Variables on Work-Family Conflict and Strain: A Control Perspective," *Journal of Applied Psychology* 80, 1995, pp. 6–15.

27 D. L. Nelson and C. Sutton, "Chronic Work Stress and Coping: A Longitudinal Study and Suggested New Directions," *Academy of Management Journal*, December 1990, pp. 859–869.

28 FactBox based on A. Picard, "The Working Wounded," *Globe and Mail*, June 22, 2008; S. McGovern, "No Rest for the Weary," *Gazette* (Montreal), August 19, 2003, p. B1; and D. McMurdy, "People Get Stress Relief Express-Style," *Financial Post* (*National Post*), January 15, 2005, p. IN1.

29 H. Selye, *The Stress of Life* (New York: McGraw-Hill, 1976).

30 R. S. Schuler, "Definition and Conceptualization of Stress in Organizations," *Organizational Behavior and Human Performance*, April 1980, p. 191; and R. L. Kahn and P. Byosiere, "Stress in Organizations," *Organizational Behavior and Human Performance*, April 1980, pp. 604–610.

31 KPMG Canada, compensation letter, July 1998.

32 B. D. Steffy and J. W. Jones, "Workplace Stress and Indicators of Coronary-Disease Risk," *Academy of Management Journal* 31, 1988, p. 687.

33 C. L. Cooper and J. Marshall, "Occupational Sources of Stress: A Review of the Literature Relating to Coronary Heart Disease and Mental Ill Health," *Journal of Occupational Psychology* 49, no. 1 (1976), pp. 11–28.

34 J. R. Hackman and G. R. Oldham, "Development of the Job Diagnostic Survey," *Journal of Applied Psychology*, April 1975, pp. 159–170.

35 J. L. Xie and G. Johns, "Job Scope and Stress: Can Job Scope Be Too High?" *Academy of Management Journal*, October 1995, pp. 1288–1309.

36 S. J. Motowidlo, J. S. Packard, and M. R. Manning, "Occupational Stress: Its Causes and Consequences for Job Performance," *Journal of Applied Psychology*, November 1987, pp. 619–620.

37 See, for instance, R. C. Cummings, "Job Stress and the Buffering Effect of Supervisory Support," *Group & Organization Studies*, March 1990, pp. 92–104; M. R. Manning, C. N. Jackson, and M. R. Fusilier, "Occupational Stress, Social Support, and the Cost of Health Care," *Academy of Management Journal*, June 1996, pp. 738–750; and P. D. Bliese and T. W. Britt, "Social Support, Group Consensus and Stressor-Strain Relationships: Social Context Matters," *Journal of Organizational Behavior*, June 2001, pp. 425–436.

38 R. Williams, *The Trusting Heart: Great News About Type A Behavior* (New York: Times Books, 1989).

39 T. H. Macan, "Time Management: Test of a Process Model," *Journal of Applied Psychology*, June 1994, pp. 381–391.

40 See, for example, G. Lawrence-Ell, *The Invisible Clock: A Practical Revolution in Finding Time for Everyone and Everything* (Seaside Park, NJ: Kingsland Hall, 2002).

41 J. Kiely and G. Hodgson, "Stress in the Prison Service: The Benefits of Exercise Programs," *Human Relations*, June 1990, pp. 551–572.

42 E. J. Forbes and R. J. Pekala, "Psychophysiological Effects of Several Stress Management Techniques," *Psychological Reports*, February 1993, pp. 19–27; and G. Smith, "Meditation, the New Balm for Corporate Stress," *BusinessWeek*, May 10, 1993, pp. 86–87.

43 J. Lee, "How to Fight That Debilitating Stress in Your Workplace," *Vancouver Sun*, April 5, 1999, p. C3. Reprinted with permission.

44 H. Staseson, "Can Perk Help Massage Bottom Line? On-Site Therapeutic Sessions Are Used by an Increasingly Diverse Group of Employers Hoping to Improve Staff Performance," *Globe and Mail*, July 3, 2002, p. C1.

45 Health Canada, "Wellness Programs Offer Healthy Return, Study Finds," *Report Bulletin*, #224, October 2001, p. 1.

46 H. Staseson, "Can Perk Help Massage Bottom Line? On-Site Therapeutic Sessions Are Used by an Increasingly Diverse Group of Employers Hoping to Improve Staff Performance," *Globe and Mail*, July 3, 2002, p. C1.

47 B. Bouw, "Employers Embrace Wellness at Work: Fitness Programs Gaining Popularity as Companies Look to Boost Productivity with Healthier Staff," *Globe and Mail*, April 10, 2002, p. C1.

48 P. M. Wright, "Operationalization of Goal Difficulty as a Moderator of the Goal Difficulty-Performance Relationship," *Journal of Applied Psychology*, June 1990, pp. 227–234; E. A. Locke and G. P. Latham, "Building a Practically Useful Theory of Goal Setting and Task Motivation: A 35-Year Odyssey," *American Psychologist* 57, no. 9 (2002), pp. 705–717; K. L. Langeland, C. M. Johnson, and T. C. Mawhinney, "Improving Staff Performance in a Community Mental Health Setting: Job Analysis, Training, Goal Setting, Feedback, and Years of Data," *Journal of Organizational Behavior Management*, 1998, pp. 21–43.

49 J. Lee, "How to Fight That Debilitating Stress in Your Workplace," *Vancouver Sun*, April 5, 1999, p. C3. Reprinted with permission.

50 See, for instance, R. A. Wolfe, D. O. Ulrich, and D. F. Parker, "Employee Health Management Programs: Review, Critique, and Research Agenda," *Journal of Management*, Winter 1987, pp. 603–615; D. L. Gebhardt and C. E. Crump, "Employee Fitness and Wellness Programs in the Workplace," *American Psychologist*, February 1990, pp. 262–272; and C. E. Beadle, "And Let's Save 'Wellness.' It Works," *New York Times*, July 24, 1994, p. F9.

51 J. Lee, "How to Fight That Debilitating Stress in Your Workplace," *Vancouver Sun*, April 5, 1999, p. C3.

Chapter 4

1 Opening vignette based on M. Beamish, "Lions Know Practice Makes Perfect," *Nanaimo Daily News*, August 23, 2005, p. B3; M. Sekeres, "Two Sides to Buono," *Kamloops Daily News*, September 8, 2005, p. A13; and J. Morris, "Still Feeling the Passion, Wally Buono Agrees to Contract Extension with Lions," *Canadian Press*, March 31, 2008.

2 G. P. Latham and C. C. Pinder, "Work Motivation Theory and Research at the Dawn of the Twenty-First Century," *Annual Review of Psychology* 56, no. 1 (2005), pp. 485–516; and C. C. Pinder, *Work Motivation in Organizational Behavior* (Upper

Saddle River, NJ: Prentice Hall, 1998), p. 11. See also E. A. Locke and G. P. Latham, "What Should We Do About Motivation Theory? Six Recommendations for the Twenty-First Century," *Academy of Management Review* 29, no. 3 (July 1, 2004), pp. 388–403.

3   D. McGregor, *The Human Side of Enterprise* (New York: McGraw-Hill, 1960). For an updated analysis of Theory X and Theory Y constructs, see R. J. Summers and S. F. Cronshaw, "A Study of McGregor's Theory X, Theory Y and the Influence of Theory X, Theory Y Assumptions on Causal Attributions for Instances of Worker Poor Performance," in *Organizational Behavior*, ed. S. L. McShane, ASAC 1988 Conference Proceedings, 9, part 5, Halifax, 1988, pp. 115–123.

4   K. W. Thomas, *Intrinsic Motivation at Work* (San Francisco: Berrett-Koehler, 2000); and K. W. Thomas, "Intrinsic Motivation and How It Works," *Training*, October 2000, pp. 130–135.

5   S. E. DeVoe and S. S. Iyengar, "Managers' Theories of Subordinates: A Cross-cultural Examination of Manager Perceptions of Motivation and Appraisal of Performance," *Organizational Behavior and Human Decision Processes* 93, no. 1 (January 2004), pp. 47–61.

6   C. P. Alderfer, "An Empirical Test of a New Theory of Human Needs," *Organizational Behavior and Human Performance*, May 1969, pp. 142–175.

7   D. C. McClelland, *The Achieving Society* (New York: Van Nostrand Reinhold, 1961); J. W. Atkinson and J. O. Raynor, *Motivation and Achievement* (Washington, DC: Winston, 1974); D. C. McClelland, *Power: The Inner Experience* (New York: Irvington, 1975); M. J. Stahl, *Managerial and Technical Motivation: Assessing Needs for Achievement, Power, and Affiliation* (New York: Praeger, 1986); and D. G. Winter, "The Motivational Dimensions of Leadership: Power, Achievement, and Affiliation," in *Multiple Intelligences and Leadership*, ed. R. E. Riggio, S. E. Murphy, and F. J. Pirozzolo (Mahwah, NJ: Lawrence Erlbaum, 2002), pp. 119–138.

8   A. H. Maslow, *Motivation and Personality* (New York: Harper and Row, 1954).

9   G. P. Latham and C. C. Pinder, "Work Motivation Theory and Research at the Dawn of the Twenty-First Century," *Annual Review of Psychology* 56, no. 1 (2005), pp. 485–516.

10   R. Hogan and R. Warremfeltz, "Educating the Modern Manager," *Academy of Management Journal*, 2003, pp. 74–84.

11   K. Korman, J. H. Greenhaus, and I. J. Badin, "Personnel Attitudes and Motivation," in *Annual Review of Psychology*, ed. M. R. Rosenzweig and L. W. Porter (Palo Alto, CA: Annual Reviews, 1977), p. 178; and M. A. Wahba and L. G. Bridwell, "Maslow Reconsidered: A Review of Research on the Need Hierarchy Theory," *Organizational Behavior and Human Performance*, April 1976, pp. 212–240.

12   C. P. Alderfer, "An Empirical Test of a New Theory of Human Needs," *Organizational Behavior and Human Performance*, May 1969, pp. 142–175.

13   C. P. Schneider and C. P. Alderfer, "Three Studies of Measures of Need Satisfaction in Organizations," *Administrative Science Quarterly*, December 1973, pp. 489–505; and I. Borg and M. Braun, "Work Values in East and West Germany: Different Weights, but Identical Structures," *Journal of Organizational Behavior* 17, special issue (1996), pp. 541–555.

14   J. P. Wanous and A. Zwany, "A Cross-Sectional Test of Need Hierarchy Theory," *Organizational Behavior and Human Performance*, May 1977, pp. 78–97.

15   D. C. McClelland, *The Achieving Society* (New York: Van Nostrand Reinhold, 1961); J. W. Atkinson and J. O. Raynor, *Motivation and Achievement* (Washington, DC: Winston, 1974); D. C. McClelland, *Power: The Inner Experience* (New York: Irvington, 1975); and M. J. Stahl, *Managerial and Technical Motivation: Assessing Needs for Achievement, Power, and Affiliation* (New York: Praeger, 1986).

16   D. C. McClelland, *The Achieving Society* (New York: Van Nostrand Reinhold, 1961).

17   D. C. McClelland, *Power: The Inner Experience* (New York: Irvington, 1975); D. C. McClelland and D. H. Burnham, "Power Is the Great Motivator," *Harvard Business Review*, March–April 1976, pp. 100–110; and R. E. Boyatzis, "The Need for Close Relationships and the Manager's Job," in *Organizational Psychology: Readings on Human Behavior in Organizations*, 4th ed., ed. D. A. Kolb, I. M. Rubin, and J. M. McIntyre (Upper Saddle River, NJ: Prentice Hall, 1984), pp. 81–86.

18   D. G. Winter, "The Motivational Dimensions of Leadership: Power, Achievement, and Affiliation," in *Multiple Intelligences and Leadership*, ed. R. E. Riggio, S. E. Murphy, and F. J. Pirozzolo (Mahwah, NJ: Lawrence Erlbaum, 2002), pp. 119–138.

19   F. Herzberg, B. Mausner, and B. Snyderman, *The Motivation to Work* (New York: Wiley, 1959).

20   R. J. House and L. A. Wigdor, "Herzberg's Dual-Factor Theory of Job Satisfaction and Motivations: A Review of the Evidence and Criticism," *Personnel Psychology*, Winter 1967, pp. 369–389; D. P. Schwab and L. L. Cummings, "Theories of Performance and Satisfaction: A Review," *Industrial Relations*, October 1970, pp. 403–430; R. J. Caston and R. Braito, "A Specification Issue in Job Satisfaction Research," *Sociological Perspectives*, April 1985, pp. 175–197; and J. Phillipchuk and J. Whittaker, "An Inquiry into the Continuing Relevance of Herzberg's Motivation Theory," *Engineering Management Journal* 8, 1996, pp. 15–20.

21   Based on L. Ullrich, "Anything but Glamorous at 4 a.m.: No Security, Insane Hours, No Pension and Zero Benefits," *Province* (Vancouver), August 3, 2005, p. A40.

22   V. H. Vroom, *Work and Motivation* (New York: John Wiley, 1964).

23   J. Choudhury, "The Motivational Impact of Sales Quotas on Effort," *Journal of Marketing Research*, February 1993, pp. 28–41; and C. C. Pinder, *Work Motivation* (Glenview, IL: Scott Foresman, 1984), Chapter 7.

24   A. Grimes, "Lessons from the Locker Room: Vancouver's Top Coaches Share Their Keys to Success With Business Leaders," Vancouver Board of Trade, April 6, 2006, www.boardoftrade.com/vbot_speech.asp?pageID=174&speechID=914&offset=&speechfind (accessed August 10, 2009).

25   "Workplace 2000: Working Toward the Millennium," *Angus Reid Group*, Fall 1997, p. 14.

26   See www.radical.ca.

27   See, for example, H. G. Heneman III and D. P. Schwab, "Evaluation of Research on Expectancy Theory Prediction of Employee Performance," *Psychological Bulletin*, July 1972, pp. 1–9; T. R.

Mitchell, "Expectancy Models of Job Satisfaction, Occupational Preference and Effort: A Theoretical, Methodological and Empirical Appraisal," *Psychological Bulletin*, November 1974, pp. 1053–1077; and L. Reinharth and M. A. Wahba, "Expectancy Theory as a Predictor of Work Motivation, Effort Expenditure, and Job Performance," *Academy of Management Journal*, September 1975, pp. 502–537.

28 See, for example, L. W. Porter and E. E. Lawler III, *Managerial Attitudes and Performance* (Homewood, IL: Richard D. Irwin, 1968); D. F. Parker and L. Dyer, "Expectancy Theory as a Within-Person Behavioral Choice Model: An Empirical Test of Some Conceptual and Methodological Refinements," *Organizational Behavior and Human Performance*, October 1976, pp. 97–117; H. J. Arnold, "A Test of the Multiplicative Hypothesis of Expectancy-Valence Theories of Work Motivation," *Academy of Management Journal*, April 1981, pp. 128–141; J. P. Wanous, T. L. Keon, and J. C. Latack, "Expectancy Theory and Occupational/Organizational Choices: A Review and Test," *Organizational Behaviour and Human Performance*, August 1983, pp. 66–86; and W. Van Eerde and H. Thierry, "Vroom's Expectancy Models and Work-Related Criteria: A Meta-Analysis," *Journal of Applied Psychology* 81, October 1996, pp. 575–586.

29 P. C. Earley, *Face, Harmony, and Social Structure: An Analysis of Organizational Behavior Across Cultures* (New York: Oxford University Press, 1997); R. M. Steers and C. Sanchez-Runde, "Culture, Motivation, and Work Behavior," in *Handbook of Cross-Cultural Management*, ed. M. Gannon and K. Newman (London: Blackwell, 2001), pp. 190–215; and H. C. Triandis, "Motivation and Achievement in Collectivist and Individualistic Cultures," in *Advances in Motivation and Achievement*, vol. 9, ed. M. Maehr and P. Pintrich (Greenwich, CT: JAI Press, 1995), pp. 1–30.

30 J. Brown, "Quitters Never Win: The (Adverse) Incentive Effects of Competing with Superstars," University of California, Berkeley, unpublished paper, April 2008.

31 E. A. Locke, "Toward a Theory of Task Motivation and Incentives," *Organizational Behavior and Human Performance*, May 1968, pp. 157–189; and G. H. Seijts, G. P. Latham, K. Tasa, and B. Latham, "Goal Setting and Goal Orientation: An Integration of Two Different yet Related Literatures," *Academy of Management Journal* 47, no. 2 (2004), pp. 227–239.

32 E. A. Locke, K. N. Shaw, L. M. Saari, and G. P. Latham, "Goal Setting and Task Performance: 1969–1980," *Psychological Bulletin*, July 1981, p. 126.

33 P. C. Earley, P. Wojnaroski, and W. Prest, "Task Planning and Energy Expended: Exploration of How Goals Influence Performance," *Journal of Applied Psychology*, February 1987, pp. 107–114.

34 "KEY Group Survey Finds Nearly Half of All Employees Have No Set Performance Goals," *IPMA-HR Bulletin*, March 10, 2006, p. 1; S. Hamm, "SAP Dangles a Big, Fat Carrot," *BusinessWeek*, May 22, 2006, pp. 67–68; and "P&G CEO Wields High Expectations but No Whip," *USA Today*, February 19, 2007, p. 3B.

35 See, for instance, S. J. Carroll and H. L. Tosi, *Management by Objectives: Applications and Research* (New York: Macmillan, 1973); and R. Rodgers and J. E. Hunter, "Impact of Management by Objectives on Organizational Productivity," *Journal of Applied Psychology*, April 1991, pp. 322–336.

36 E. A. Locke and G. P. Latham, *A Theory of Goal Setting and Task Performance* (Englewood Cliffs, NJ: Prentice Hall, 1980).

37 R. Ilies and T. A. Judge, "Goal Regulation Across Time: The Effects of Feedback and Affect," *Journal of Applied Psychology* 90, no. 3 (May 2005), pp. 453–467.

38 A. Bandura, *Self-Efficacy: The Exercise of Control* (New York: Freeman, 1997).

39 A. D. Stajkovic and F. Luthans, "Self-Efficacy and Work-Related Performance: A Meta-Analysis," *Psychological Bulletin*, September 1998, pp. 240–261; and A. Bandura, "Cultivate Self-Efficacy for Personal and Organizational Effectiveness," in *Handbook of Principles of Organizational Behavior*, ed. E. Locke (Malden, MA: Blackwell, 2004), pp. 120–136.

40 A. Bandura and D. Cervone, "Differential Engagement in Self-Reactive Influences in Cognitively-Based Motivation," *Organizational Behavior and Human Decision Processes*, August 1986, pp. 92–113.

41 J. R. Hollenbeck, C. R. Williams, and H. J. Klein, "An Empirical Examination of the Antecedents of Commitment to Difficult Goals," *Journal of Applied Psychology*, February 1989, pp. 18–23. See also J. C. Wofford, V. L. Goodwin, and S. Premack, "Meta-Analysis of the Antecedents of Personal Goal Level and of the Antecedents and Consequences of Goal Commitment," *Journal of Management*, September 1992, pp. 595–615; and M. E. Tubbs, "Commitment as a Moderator of the Goal-Performance Relation: A Case for Clearer Construct Definition," *Journal of Applied Psychology*, February 1993, pp. 86–97.

42 See R. E. Wood, A. J. Mento, and E. A. Locke, "Task Complexity as a Moderator of Goal Effects: A Meta-Analysis," *Journal of Applied Psychology*, August 1987, pp. 416–425; R. Kanfer and P. L. Ackerman, "Motivation and Cognitive Abilities: An Integrative/Aptitude-Treatment Interaction Approach to Skill Acquisition," *Journal of Applied Psychology* 74, monograph (1989), pp. 657–690; T. R. Mitchell and W. S. Silver, "Individual and Group Goals When Workers Are Interdependent: Effects on Task Strategies and Performance," *Journal of Applied Psychology*, April 1990, pp. 185–193; and A. M. O'Leary-Kelly, J. J. Martocchio, and D. D. Frink, "A Review of the Influence of Group Goals on Group Performance," *Academy of Management Journal*, October 1994, pp. 1285–1301.

43 Based on L. Little, "Lions Lock up Clermont," *Times-Colonist*, September 12, 2007, p. D9; M. Beamish, "Simon's Work Day: Hair Cuts, Extensions," *Vancouver Sun*, May 26, 2006, p. G5; "B.C. Lions Sign Geroy Simon to Contract Extension through 2009," *Daily Townsman*, May 26, 2006, p. 7; "B.C. Lions Face 'Unbearable' Contract Pressures: Wally Buono's Challenge," *National Post*, April 26, 2006, p. S9; and S. Petersen, "Esks Re-Sign Tucker for Big 'Chunk of Change,'" *Edmonton Journal*, February 17, 2006, p. C8.

44 J. S. Adams, "Inequity in Social Exchanges," in *Advances in Experimental Social Psychology*, ed. L. Berkowitz (New York: Academic Press, 1965), pp. 267–300.

45 See, for example, E. Walster, G. W. Walster, and W. G. Scott, *Equity: Theory and Research* (Boston: Allyn and Bacon, 1978); and J. Greenberg, "Cognitive Reevaluation of Outcomes in Response to Underpayment Inequity," *Academy of Management Journal*, March 1989, pp. 174–184.

46 P. S. Goodman and A. Friedman, "An Examination of Adams' Theory of Inequity," *Administrative Science Quarterly*, September 1971, pp. 271–288; R. P. Vecchio, "An Individual-Differences Interpretation of the Conflicting Predictions Generated by

Equity Theory and Expectancy Theory," *Journal of Applied Psychology*, August 1981, pp. 470–481; J. Greenberg, "Approaching Equity and Avoiding Inequity in Groups and Organizations," in *Equity and Justice in Social Behavior*, ed. J. Greenberg and R. L. Cohen (New York: Academic Press, 1982), pp. 389–435; E. W. Miles, J. D. Hatfield, and R. C. Huseman, "The Equity Sensitive Construct: Potential Implications for Worker Performance," *Journal of Management*, December 1989, pp. 581–588; R. T. Mowday, "Equity Theory Predictions of Behavior in Organizations," in *Motivation and Work Behavior*, 5th ed., ed. R. Steers and L. W. Porter (New York: McGraw-Hill, 1991), pp. 111–131; and R. T. Mowday and K. A. Colwell, "Employee Reactions to Unfair Outcomes in the Workplace: The Contributions of Adams' Equity Theory to Understanding Work Motivation," in *Motivation and Work Behavior*, 7th ed., ed. L. W. Porter, G. A. Bigley, and R. M. Steers (Burr Ridge, IL: Irwin/McGraw-Hill, 2003), pp. 65–82.

47   See, for example, K. S. Sauley and A. G. Bedeian, "Equity Sensitivity: Construction of a Measure and Examination of Its Psychometric Properties," *Journal of Management* 26, no. 5 (2000), pp. 885–910; and M. N. Bing and S. M. Burroughs, "The Predictive and Interactive Effects of Equity Sensitivity in Teamwork-Oriented Organizations," *Journal of Organizational Behavior*, May 2001, pp. 271–290.

48   J. Greenberg and S. Ornstein, "High Status Job Title as Compensation for Underpayment: A Test of Equity Theory," *Journal of Applied Psychology*, May 1983, pp. 285–297; and J. Greenberg, "Equity and Workplace Status: A Field Experiment," *Journal of Applied Psychology*, November 1988, pp. 606–613.

49   P. S. Goodman, "Social Comparison Process in Organizations," in *New Directions in Organizational Behavior*, ed. B. M. Staw and G. R. Salancik (Chicago: St. Clair, 1977), pp. 97–132; and J. Greenberg, "A Taxonomy of Organizational Justice Theories," *Academy of Management Review*, January 1987, pp. 9–22.

50   See, for instance, J. Greenberg, *The Quest for Justice on the Job* (Thousand Oaks, CA: Sage, 1996); R. Cropanzano and J. Greenberg, "Progress in Organizational Justice: Tunneling Through the Maze," in *International Review of Industrial and Organizational Psychology*, vol. 12, ed. C. L. Cooper and I. T. Robertson (New York: Wiley, 1997); and J. A. Colquitt, D. E. Conlon, M. J. Wesson, C. O. L. H. Porter, and K. Y. Ng, "Justice at the Millennium: A Meta-Analytic Review of the 25 Years of Organizational Justice Research," *Journal of Applied Psychology*, June 2001, pp. 425–445.

51   R. J. Bies and J. S. Moag, "Interactional Justice: Communication Criteria for Fairness," in *Research on Negotiation in Organizations*, vol. 1, ed. B. H. Sheppard (Greenwich, CT: JAI Press, 1986), pp. 43–55.

52   D. P. Skarlicki and R. Folger, "Retaliation in the Workplace: The Roles of Distributive, Procedural, and Interactional Justice," *Journal of Applied Psychology* 82, no. 3 (1997), pp. 434–443.

53   R. Cropanzano, C. A. Prehar, and P. Y. Chen, "Using Social Exchange Theory to Distinguish Procedural from Interactional Justice," *Group & Organization Management* 27, no. 3 (2002), pp. 324–351; and S. G. Roch and L. R. Shanock, "Organizational Justice in an Exchange Framework: Clarifying Organizational Justice Dimensions," *Journal of Management*, April 2006, pp. 299–322.

54   J. A. Colquitt, D. E. Conlon, M. J. Wesson, C. O. L. H. Porter, and K. Y. Ng, "Justice at the Millennium: A Meta-Analytic

Review of the 25 Years of Organizational Justice Research," *Journal of Applied Psychology*, June 2001, pp. 425–445.

55   D. P. Skarlicki and R. Folger, "Retaliation in the Workplace: The Roles of Distributive, Procedural and Interactional Justice," *Journal of Applied Psychology* 82, 1997, pp. 434–443.

56   R. de Charms, *Personal Causation: The Internal Affective Determinants of Behavior* (New York: Academic Press, 1968).

57   E. L. Deci, R. Koestner, and R. M. Ryan, "A Meta-Analytic Review of Experiments Examining the Effects of Extrinsic Rewards on Intrinsic Motivation," *Psychological Bulletin* 125, no. 6 (November 1999), pp. 627–668.

58   A. Kohn, *Punished by Rewards* (Boston: Houghton Mifflin, 1993).

59   J. B. Miner, *Theories of Organizational Behavior* (Hinsdale, IL: Dryden Press, 1980), p. 157; and A. Kohn, *Punished by Rewards* (Boston: Houghton Mifflin, 1993).

60   A. Kohn, *Punished by Rewards* (Boston: Houghton Mifflin, 1993).

61   B. Nelson, "Dump the Cash, Load on the Praise," *Personnel Journal* 75, July 1996, pp. 65–66.

62   J. Pfeffer, *The Human Equation: Building Profits by Putting People First* (Boston: Harvard Business School Press, 1998).

63   K. W. Thomas, E. Jansen, and W. G. Tymon Jr., "Navigating in the Realm of Theory: An Empowering View of Construct Development," in *Research in Organizational Change and Development*, vol. 10, ed. W. A. Pasmore and R. W. Woodman (Greenwich, CT: JAI Press, 1997), pp. 1–30.

64   Our definition of a formal recognition system is based on S. E. Markham, K. D. Scott, and G. H. McKee, "Recognizing Good Attendance: A Longitudinal, Quasi-Experimental Field Study," *Personnel Psychology*, Autumn 2002, p. 641.

65   Hewitt Associates, "Employers Willing to Pay for High Performance," news release, September 8, 2004.

66   J. Buckstein, "In Praise of Praise in the Workplace," *Globe and Mail*, June 15, 2005, p. C1.

67   J. Buckstein, "In Praise of Praise in the Workplace," *Globe and Mail*, June 15, 2005, p. C1.

68   Based on S. Baille-Ruder, "Sweet Devotion: How Chocolatier R.C. Purdy Developed the Perfect Recipe for a Superstar Workforce," *Profit*, December 2004, pp. 44–51; L. Pratt, "Management Tip from the Top," *National Post*, July 26, 2004, p. FP9; B. Constantineau, "Staff Discounts Can Make a Good Employer Great," *Vancouver Sun*, July 16, 2005, p. A1; and www.purdys.com/Content/Employer-of-Choice.

69   "Praise Beats Raise as Best Motivator, Survey Shows," *Vancouver Sun*, September 10, 1994.

70   S. L. Rynes, B. Gerhart, and L. Parks, "Personnel Psychology: Performance Evaluation and Pay for Performance," *Annual Review of Psychology* 56, no. 1 (2005), p. 572.

71   Based on S. E. Gross and J. P. Bacher, "The New Variable Pay Programs: How Some Succeed, Why Some Don't," *Compensation & Benefits Review*, January–February 1993, p. 51; and J. R. Schuster and P. K. Zingheim, "The New Variable Pay: Key Design Issues," *Compensation & Benefits Review*, March–April 1993, p. 28.

72. Peter Brieger, "Variable Pay Packages Gain Favour: Signing Bonuses, Profit Sharing Taking Place of Salary Hikes," *Financial Post (National Post)*, September 13, 2002, p. FP5; and Hewitt Associates, "Calgary Salary Increases Reach New Heights, According to Hewitt," news release, September 6, 2007, www.hewittassociates.com/Intl/NA/en-CA/AboutHewitt/Newsroom/PressReleaseDetail.aspx?cid=4428 (accessed August 10, 2009).

73. L. Wiener, "Paycheck Plus," *U.S. News & World Report*, February 24–March 3, 2003, p. 58.

74. Cited in "Pay Programs: Few Employees See the Pay-for-Performance Connection," *Compensation & Benefits Report*, June 2003, p. 1.

75. C. Hallamore, "Merit Pay in Unionized Environments," *The Conference Board of Canada*, December 2005.

76. "Bonus Pay in Canada," *Manpower Argus*, September 1996, p. 5.

77. "Higher Salaries and Bonuses Key to Retaining Employees, Survey Finds," *Edmonton Journal*, April 15, 2006, p. F2.

78. See, for instance, S. C. Hanlon, D. G. Meyer, and R. R. Taylor, "Consequences of Gainsharing," *Group & Organization Management*, March 1994, pp. 87–111; J. G. Belcher Jr., "Gainsharing and Variable Pay: The State of the Art," *Compensation & Benefits Review*, May–June 1994, pp. 50–60; and T. M. Welbourne and L. R. Gomez Mejia, "Gainsharing: A Critical Review and a Future Research Agenda," *Journal of Management* 21, no. 3 (1995), pp. 559–609.

79. D. Beck, "Implementing a Gainsharing Plan: What Companies Need to Know," *Compensation & Benefits Review*, January–February 1992, p. 23.

80. T. M. Welbourne and L. R. Gomez-Mejia, "Gainsharing: A Critical Review and a Future Research Agenda," *Journal of Management* 21, no. 3 (1995), pp. 559–609.

81. M. Byfield, "Ikea's Boss Gives Away the Store for a Day," *Report Newsmagazine*, October 25, 1999, p. 47.

82. K. Cox, "Power Struggle Cost FPI Millions," *Globe and Mail*, February 21, 2002, p. B3.

83. See K. M. Young, ed., *The Expanding Role of ESOPs in Public Companies* (New York: Quorum, 1990); J. L. Pierce and C. A. Furo, "Employee Ownership: Implications for Management," *Organizational Dynamics*, Winter 1990, pp. 32–43; J. Blasi and D. L. Druse, *The New Owners: The Mass Emergence of Employee Ownership in Public Companies and What It Means to American Business* (Champaign, IL: Harper Business, 1991); F. T. Adams and G. B. Hansen, *Putting Democracy to Work: A Practical Guide for Starting and Managing Worker-Owned Businesses* (San Francisco: Berrett-Koehler, 1993); and A. A. Buchko, "The Effects of Employee Ownership on Employee Attitudes: An Integrated Causal Model and Path Analysis," *Journal of Management Studies*, July 1993, pp. 633–656.

84. A. Toulin, "Lowly Staff Join Bosses in Receiving Stock Options," *National Post*, March 1, 2001, pp. C1, C12.

85. K. Vermond, "Worker as Shareholder: Is It Worth It?" *Globe and Mail*, March 29, 2008, p. B21.

86. A. A. Buchko, "The Effects of Employee Ownership on Employee Attitudes: An Integrated Causal Model and Path Analysis," *Journal of Management Studies*, July 1993, pp. 633–656.

87. C. M. Rosen and M. Quarrey, "How Well Is Employee Ownership Working?" *Harvard Business Review*, September–October 1987, pp. 126–132.

88. W. N. Davidson and D. L. Worrell, "ESOP's Fables: The Influence of Employee Stock Ownership Plans on Corporate Stock Prices and Subsequent Operating Performance," *Human Resource Planning*, 1994, pp. 69–85.

89. J. L. Pierce and C. A. Furo, "Employee Ownership: Implications for Management," *Organizational Dynamics*, Winter 1990, pp. 32–43; and S. Kaufman, "ESOPs' Appeal on the Increase," *Nation's Business*, June 1997, p. 43.

90. G. D. Jenkins Jr., N. Gupta, A. Mitra, and J. D. Shaw, "Are Financial Incentives Related to Performance? A Meta-Analytic Review of Empirical Research," *Journal of Applied Psychology*, October 1998, pp. 777–787.

91. T. Coupé, V. Smeets, and F. Warzynski, "Incentives, Sorting and Productivity along the Career: Evidence from a Sample of Top Economists," *Journal of Law, Economics, & Organization* 22, no. 1 (April 2006), pp. 137–167.

92. A. Kauhanen and H. Piekkola, "What Makes Performance-Related Pay Schemes Work? Finnish Evidence," *Journal of Management and Governance* 10, no. 2 (2006), pp. 149–177.

93. J. S. Ang, A.-S. Chen, and J. W. Lin, "Ascertaining the Effects of Employee Bonus Plans," *Applied Economics* 37, no. 12 (July 10, 2005), pp. 1439–1448; C. G. Hanson and W. D. Bell, *Profit Sharing and Profitability: How Profit Sharing Promotes Business Success* (London: Kogan Page Ltd., 1987); E. M. Doherty, W. R. Nord, and J. L. McAdams, "Gainsharing and Organizational Development: A Productive Synergy," *Journal of Applied Behavioral Science*, August 1989, pp. 209–230; and T. C. McGrath, "How Three Screw Machine Companies Are Tapping Human Productivity Through Gainsharing," *Employment Relations Today* 20, no. 4 (1994), pp. 437–447.

94. P. A. Siegel and D. C. Hambrick, "Pay Disparities Within Top Management Groups: Evidence of Harmful Effects on Performance of High-Technology Firms," *Organization Science* 16, no. 3 (May–June 2005), pp. 259–276; S. Kerr, "Practical, Cost-Neutral Alternatives That You May Know, but Don't Practice," *Organizational Dynamics* 28, no. 1 (1999), pp. 61–70; E. E. Lawler, *Strategic Pay* (San Francisco: Jossey Bass, 1990); and J. Pfeffer, *The Human Equation: Building Profits by Putting People First* (Boston: Harvard Business School Press, 1998).

95. A. D. Stajkovic and F. Luthans, "Differential Effects of Incentive Motivators on Work Performance," *Academy of Management Journal*, June 2001, pp. 580–590; and A. M. Dickinson, "Are We Motivated by Money? Some Results from the Laboratory," *Performance Improvement* 44, no. 3 (March 2005), pp. 18–24.

96. S. L. Rynes, B. Gerhart, and L. Parks, "Personnel Psychology: Performance Evaluation and Pay for Performance," *Annual Review of Psychology* 56, no. 1 (2005), p. 572.

97. E. Beauchesne, "Pay Bonuses Improve Productivity, Study Shows," *Vancouver Sun*, September 13, 2002, p. D5.

98. E. Beauchesne, "Pay Bonuses Improve Productivity, Study Shows," *Vancouver Sun*, September 13, 2002, p. D5.

99. V. Sanderson, "Sweetening Their Slice: More Hardware and Lumberyard Dealers Are Investing in Profit-Sharing Programs as

a Way to Promote Employee Loyalty," *Hardware Merchandising*, May–June 2003, p. 66.

100 J. Pfeffer and N. Langton, "The Effects of Wage Dispersion on Satisfaction, Productivity, and Working Collaboratively: Evidence from College and University Faculty," *Administrative Science Quarterly* 38, no. 3 (1983), pp. 382–407.

101 "Risk and Reward: More Canadian Companies Are Experimenting With Variable Pay," *Maclean's*, January 8, 1996, pp. 26–27.

102 "Risk and Reward: More Canadian Companies Are Experimenting With Variable Pay," *Maclean's*, January 8, 1996, pp. 26–27.

103 P. K. Zingheim and J. R. Schuster, "Introduction: How Are the New Pay Tools Being Deployed?" *Compensation & Benefits Review*, July–August 1995, pp. 10–11.

104 *OB in the Street* based on "In Pursuit of Level Playing Fields," *Globe and Mail*, March 9, 2002, p. S1.

105 T. Denison, "Formula for Success," August 13, 2004, www.collegecolours.com/columns/004.html.

106 J. R. Hackman and G. R. Oldham, "Motivation Through the Design of Work: Test of a Theory," *Organizational Behavior and Human Performance*, August 1976, pp. 250–279.

107 J. R. Hackman and G. R. Oldham, *Work Redesign* (Reading, MA: Addison Wesley, 1980).

108 J. R. Hackman, "Work Design," in *Improving Life at Work*, ed. J. R. Hackman and J. L. Suttle (Santa Monica, CA: Goodyear, 1977), pp. 132–133.

109 J. R. Hackman, "Work Design," in *Improving Life at Work*, ed. J. R. Hackman and J. L. Suttle (Santa Monica, CA: Goodyear, 1977), p. 129.

110 S. Kerr, "On the Folly of Rewarding A, While Hoping for B," *Academy of Management Executive* 9, no. 1 (1995), pp. 7–14.

111 "More on the Folly," *Academy of Management Executive* 9, no. 1 (1995), pp. 15–16.

112 J. S. Lublin, "It's Shape-up Time for Performance Reviews," *Wall Street Journal*, October 3, 1994, p. B1.

113 Much of this section is based on H. H. Meyer, "A Solution to the Performance Appraisal Feedback Enigma," *Academy of Management Executive*, February 1991, pp. 68–76.

114 T. D. Schelhardt, "It's Time to Evaluate Your Work, and All Involved Are Groaning," *Wall Street Journal*, November 19, 1996, p. A1.

115 R. J. Burke, "Why Performance Appraisal Systems Fail," *Personnel Administration*, June 1972, pp. 32–40.

116 B. D. Cawley, L. M. Keeping, and P. E. Levy, "Participation in the Performance Appraisal Process and Employee Reactions: A Meta-Analytic Review of Field Investigations," *Journal of Applied Psychology*, August 1998, pp. 615–633; and P. E. Levy, and J. R. Williams, "The Social Context of Performance Appraisal: A Review and Framework for the Future," *Journal of Management* 30, no. 6 (2004), pp. 881–905.

117 A. Kohn, *Punished by Rewards* (Boston: Houghton Mifflin, 1993), p. 181.

118 List directly quoted from R. Kreitner and A. Kinicki, *Organizational Behavior*, 6th ed. (New York: McGraw-Hill/Irwin, 2004), p. 335.

119 A. Kohn, *Punished by Rewards* (Boston: Houghton Mifflin, 1993), p. 181.

120 A. Kohn, *Punished by Rewards* (Boston: Houghton Mifflin, 1993), p. 186. See also P. R. Scholtes, "An Elaboration of Deming's Teachings on Performance Appraisal," in *Performance Appraisal: Perspectives on a Quality Management Approach*, ed. G. N. McLean, S. R. Damme, and R. A. Swanson (Alexandria, VA: American Society for Training and Development, 1990); and H. H. Meyer, E. Kay, and J. R. P. French Jr., "Split Roles in Performance Appraisal," *Harvard Business Review*, 1965, excerpts reprinted in "HBR Retrospect," *Harvard Business Review*, January–February 1989, p. 26; W.-U. Meyer, M. Bachmann, U. Biermann, M. Hempelmann, F.-O. Ploeger, and H. Spiller, "The Informational Value of Evaluative Behavior: Influences of Praise and Blame on Perceptions of Ability," *Journal of Educational Psychology* 71, 1979, pp. 259–268; A. Halachmi and M. Holzer, "Merit Pay, Performance Targeting, and Productivity," *Review of Public Personnel Administration* 7, 1987, pp. 80–91.

121 A. S. Blinder, "Introduction," in *Paying for Productivity: A Look at the Evidence*, ed. A. S. Blinder (Washington, DC: Brookings Institution, 1990).

122 A. Kohn, *Punished by Rewards* (Boston: Houghton Mifflin, 1993), p. 187.

123 D. Tjosvold, *Working Together to Get Things Done: Managing for Organizational Productivity* (Lexington, MA: Lexington Books, 1986); P. R. Scholtes, *The Team Handbook: How to Use Teams to Improve Quality* (Madison, WI: Joiner Associates, 1988); and A. Kohn, *No Contest: The Case Against Competition*, rev. ed. (Boston: Houghton Mifflin, 1992).

124 E. L. Deci, "Applications of Research on the Effects of Rewards," in *The Hidden Costs of Rewards: New Perspectives on the Psychology of Human Motivation*, ed. M. R. Lepper and D. Green (Hillsdale, NJ: Erlbaum, 1978).

125 S. E. Perry, *San Francisco Scavengers: Dirty Work and the Pride of Ownership* (Berkeley: University of California Press, 1978).

126 A. Kohn, *Punished by Rewards* (Boston: Houghton Mifflin, 1993), p. 192.

127 T. H. Naylor, "Redefining Corporate Motivation, Swedish Style," *Christian Century*, May 30–June 6, 1990, pp. 566–570; R. A. Karasek, T. Thorell, J. E. Schwartz, P. L. Schnall, C. F. Pieper, and J. L. Michela, "Job Characteristics in Relation to the Prevalence of Myocardial Infarction in the US Health Examination Survey (HES) and the Health and Nutrition Examination Survey (HANES)," *American Journal of Public Health* 78, 1988, pp. 910–916; D. P. Levin, "Toyota Plant in Kentucky Is Font of Ideas for the U.S.," *New York Times*, May 5, 1992, pp. A1, D8.

128 M. Bosquet, "The Prison Factory," reprinted from *Le Nouvel Observateur* in *Working Papers for a New Society*, Spring 1973, pp. 20–27; J. Holusha, "Grace Pastiak's 'Web of Inclusion,'" *New York Times*, May 5, 1991, pp. F1, F6; J. Simmons and W. Mares, *Working Together: Employee Participation in Action* (New York: New York University Press, 1985); D. I. Levine and L. D'Andrea Tyson, "Participation, Productivity, and the Firm's Environment," in *Paying for Productivity: A Look at the Evidence*, ed. A. S. Blinder (Washington, DC: Brookings Institution, 1990); and

W. F. Whyte, "Worker Participation: International and Historical Perspectives," *Journal of Applied Behavioral Science* 19, 1983, pp. 395–407.

129 J. A. Ross, "Japan: Does Money Motivate?" *Harvard Business Review,* September–October 1997. See also R. B. Money and J. L. Graham, "Salesperson Performance, Pay, and Job Satisfaction: Tests of a Model Using Data Collected in the U.S. and Japan" (working paper, University of South Carolina, 1997).

130 N. J. Adler, *International Dimensions of Organizational Behavior,* 3rd ed. (Cincinnati, OH: South Western, 1997), p. 158.

131 A. Kohn, *Punished by Rewards* (Boston: Houghton Mifflin, 1993).

132 W. G. Ouchi, *Theory Z* (New York: Avon Books, 1982); "Bosses' Pay," *Economist,* February 1, 1992, pp. 19–22; and W. Edwards Deming, *Out of the Crisis* (Cambridge: MIT Center for Advanced Engineering Study, 1986).

133 J. Pfeffer, *The Human Equation: Building Profits by Putting People First* (Boston: Harvard Business School Press, 1998).

134 G. Hofstede, "Motivation, Leadership, and Organization: Do American Theories Apply Abroad?" *Organizational Dynamics,* Summer 1980, p. 55.

135 J. K. Giacobbe-Miller, D. J. Miller, and V. I. Victorov, "A Comparison of Russian and U.S. Pay Allocation Decisions, Distributive Justice Judgments, and Productivity Under Different Payment Conditions," *Personnel Psychology,* Spring 1998, pp. 137–163.

136 S. L. Mueller and L. D. Clarke, "Political-Economic Context and Sensitivity to Equity: Differences Between the United States and the Transition Economies of Central and Eastern Europe," *Academy of Management Journal,* June 1998, pp. 319–329.

137 J. Zaslow, "Losing Well: How a Successful Man Deals with a Rare and Public Failure," *Wall Street Journal,* March 2, 2006, p. D1.

138 E. Biyalogorsky, W. Boulding, and R. Staelin, "Stuck in the Past: Why Managers Persist with New Product Failures," *Journal of Marketing,* April 2006, pp. 108–121.

139 Based on R. Steers and D. Braunstein, "A Behaviorally Based Measure of Manifest Needs in Work Settings," *Journal of Vocational Behavior,* October 1976, p. 254; and R. N. Lussier, *Human Relations in Organizations: A Skill Building Approach* (Homewood, IL: Richard D. Irwin, 1990), p. 120.

140 Exercise developed by Steve Robbins, with special thanks to Professor Penny Wright (San Diego State University) for her suggestions during the development of this exercise. Exercise modified by Nancy Langton.

141 E. Church, "Market Recovery Delivers Executive Payout Bonanza," *Globe and Mail,* May 4, 2005, pp. B1, B9; "Gimme Gimme: Greed, the Most Insidious of Sins, Has Once Again Embraced a Decade," *Financial Post,* September 28/30, 1996, pp. 24–25; and I. McGugan, "A Crapshoot Called Compensation," *Canadian Business,* July 1995, pp. 67–70.

142 H. Mackenzie, "The Great CEO Pay Race: Over Before It Begins," *Canadian Centre for Policy Alternatives,* December 2007.

143 Based on C. Benedict, "The Bullying Boss," *New York Times,* June 22, 2004, p. F1.

144 Based on "Human Resources at KPMG," Organizational Behavior Video Library, 2008. Copyrighted by Prentice-Hall.

145 Based on S. P. Robbins and D. A. DeCenzo, *Fundamentals of Management,* 4th ed. (Upper Saddle River, NJ: Prentice Hall, 2004), p. 85.

Chapter 5

1 Based on "Emery 'Don't Take Responsibility' for Playoff Loss," *Province* (Vancouver), April 18, 2008, p. A62; and "Ducks Destroy Senators to Win Stanley Cup," *cbcsports.ca,* June 7, 2007, www.cbc.ca/sports/hockey/story/2007/06/06/nhl-senators-ducks.html (accessed August 12, 2009).

2 J. R. Katzenbach and D. K. Smith, *The Wisdom of Teams: Creating the High-Performance Organization* (New York: Harper Business, 1999), p. 45.

3 J. R. Katzenbach and D. K. Smith, *The Wisdom of Teams: Creating the High-Performance Organization* (New York: Harper Business, 1999), p. 214.

4 See, for example, D. Tjosvold, *Team Organization: An Enduring Competitive Advantage* (Chichester, UK: Wiley, 1991); S. A. Mohrman, S. G. Cohen, and A. M. Mohrman Jr., *Designing Team-Based Organizations* (San Francisco: Jossey-Bass, 1995); P. MacMillan, *The Performance Factor: Unlocking the Secrets of Teamwork* (Nashville, TN: Broadman and Holman, 2001); and E. Salas, C. A. Bowers, and E. Edens, eds., *Improving Teamwork in Organizations: Applications of Resource Management Training* (Mahwah, NJ: Lawrence Erlbaum, 2002).

5 K. Warren, "A Team Under Construction: The Senators, Much Like the Queensway, Are Undergoing Major Changes as Training Camp for the '08–09 Season Begins Today," *Ottawa Citizen,* September 17, 2008, p. B3.

6 B. W. Tuckman, "Developmental Sequences in Small Groups," *Psychological Bulletin,* June 1965, pp. 384–399; B. W. Tuckman and M. C. Jensen, "Stages of Small-Group Development Revisited," *Group and Organizational Studies,* December 1977, pp. 419–427; and M. F. Maples, "Group Development: Extending Tuckman's Theory," *Journal for Specialists in Group Work,* Fall 1988, pp. 17–23.

7 R. C. Ginnett, "The Airline Cockpit Crew," in *Groups That Work (and Those That Don't),* ed. J. R. Hackman (San Francisco: Jossey-Bass, 1990).

8 C. J. G. Gersick, "Time and Transition in Work Teams: Toward a New Model of Group Development," *Academy of Management Journal,* March 1988, pp. 9–41; C. J. G. Gersick, "Marking Time: Predictable Transitions in Task Groups," *Academy of Management Journal,* June 1989, pp. 274–309; E. Romanelli and M. L. Tushman, "Organizational Transformation as Punctuated Equilibrium: An Empirical Test," *Academy of Management Journal,* October 1994, pp. 1141–1166; B. M. Lichtenstein, "Evolution or Transformation: A Critique and Alternative to Punctuated Equilibrium," in *Academy of Management Best Paper Proceedings,* ed. D. P. Moore (National Academy of Management Conference, Vancouver, 1995), pp. 291–295; and A. Seers and S. Woodruff, "Temporal Pacing in Task Forces: Group Development or Deadline Pressure?" *Journal of Management* 23, no. 2 (1997), pp. 169–187.

9 C. J. G. Gersick, "Time and Transition in Work Teams: Toward a New Model of Group Development," *Academy of Management*

Journal, March 1988, pp. 9–41; M. J. Waller, J. M. Conte, C. B. Gibson, and M. A. Carpenter, "The Effect of Individual Perceptions of Deadlines on Team Performance," *Academy of Management Review*, October 2001, pp. 586–600; G. A. Okhuysen and M. J. Waller, "Focusing on Midpoint Transitions: An Analysis of Boundary Conditions," *Academy of Management Journal* 45, 2002, pp. 1056–1065; and M. J. Waller, M. E. Zellmer-Bruhn, and R. C. Giambatista, "Watching the Clock: Group Pacing Behavior Under Dynamic Deadlines," *Academy of Management Journal* 45, 2002, pp. 1046–1055.

10　A. Chang, P. Bordia, and J. Duck, "Punctuated Equilibrium and Linear Progression: Toward a New Understanding of Group Development," *Academy of Management Journal* 46, no. 1 (2003), pp. 106–117.

11　K. L. Bettenhausen, "Five Years of Groups Research: What We Have Learned and What Needs to Be Addressed," *Journal of Management* 17, 1991, pp. 345–381; and R. A. Guzzo and G. P. Shea, "Group Performance and Intergroup Relations in Organizations," in *Handbook of Industrial and Organizational Psychology*, 2nd ed., vol. 3, ed. M. D. Dunnette and L. M. Hough (Palo Alto, CA: Consulting Psychologists Press, 1992), pp. 269–313.

12　A. Chang, P. Bordia, and J. Duck, "Punctuated Equilibrium and Linear Progression: Toward a New Understanding of Group Development," *Academy of Management Journal* 46, no. 1 (2003), pp. 106–117; and S. G. S. Lim and J. K. Murnighan, "Phases, Deadlines, and the Bargaining Process," *Organizational Behavior and Human Decision Processes* 58, 1994, pp. 153–171.

13　K. Warren, "All-For-One, One-For-All; New Senators Coach Craig Hartsburg Says Stars and Role Players Alike Must All Buy into the Team-First Program," *Ottawa Citizen*, September 10, 2008, p. B1.

14　See, for instance, D. L. Gladstein, "Groups in Context: A Model of Task Group Effectiveness," *Administrative Science Quarterly*, December 1984, pp. 499–517; J. R. Hackman, "The Design of Work Teams," in *Handbook of Organizational Behavior*, ed. J. W. Lorsch (Englewood Cliffs, NJ: Prentice Hall, 1987), pp. 315–342; M. A. Campion, G. J. Medsker, and C. A. Higgs, "Relations Between Work Group Characteristics and Effectiveness: Implications for Designing Effective Work Groups," *Personnel Psychology*, 1993; and R. A. Guzzo and M. W. Dickson, "Teams in Organizations: Recent Research on Performance and Effectiveness," in *Annual Review of Psychology*, vol. 47, ed. J. T. Spence, J. M. Darley, and D. J. Foss, 1996, pp. 307–338.

15　D. E. Hyatt and T. M. Ruddy, "An Examination of the Relationship Between Work Group Characteristics and Performance: Once More into the Breach," *Personnel Psychology*, Autumn 1997, p. 555.

16　This model is based on D. R. Ilgen, J. R. Hollenbeck, M. Johnson, and D. Jundt, "Teams in Organizations: From Input-Process-Output Models to IMOI Models," *Annual Review of Psychology* 56, no. 1 (2005), pp. 517–543; M. A. Campion, E. M. Papper, and G. J. Medsker, "Relations Between Work Team Characteristics and Effectiveness: A Replication and Extension," *Personnel Psychology*, Summer 1996, pp. 429–452; D. E. Hyatt and T. M. Ruddy, "An Examination of the Relationship Between Work Group Characteristics and Performance: Once More into the Breach," *Personnel Psychology*, Autumn 1997, pp. 553–585; S. G. Cohen and D. E. Bailey, "What Makes Teams Work: Group Effectiveness Research from the Shop Floor to the Executive Suite," *Journal of Management* 23, no. 3 (1997), pp. 239–290; G. A. Neuman and J. Wright, "Team Effectiveness: Beyond Skills and Cognitive Ability," *Journal of Applied Psychology*, June 1999, pp. 376–389; and L. Thompson, *Making the Team* (Upper Saddle River, NJ: Prentice Hall, 2000), pp. 18–33.

17　*OB in the Street* based on J. Mc Intosh, "On The Road to the 2010 Olympics," thestar.com, February 10, 2008; M. Petrie, "Canada's Skeleton Crew Made Peace to Improve," CanWest News Service, February 21, 2005; and B. Graveland, "Pain Credits Team for Win," *Edmonton Journal*, February 22, 2005, p. D3.

18　M. Petrie, "Canada's Skeleton Crew Made Peace to Improve," CanWest News Service, February 21, 2005.

19　B. Graveland, "Pain Credits Team for Win," *Edmonton Journal*, February 22, 2005, p. D3.

20　See M. Mattson, T. V. Mumford, and G. S. Sintay, "Taking Teams to Task: A Normative Model for Designing or Recalibrating Work Teams" (paper presented at the National Academy of Management Conference, Chicago, August 1999); and G. L. Stewart and M. R. Barrick, "Team Structure and Performance: Assessing the Mediating Role of Intrateam Process and the Moderating Role of Task Type," *Academy of Management Journal*, April 2000, pp. 135–148.

21　Based on W. G. Dyer, R. H. Daines, and W. C. Giauque, *The Challenge of Management* (New York: Harcourt Brace Jovanovich, 1990), p. 343.

22　E. M. Stark, "Interdependence and Preference for Group Work: Main and Congruence Effects on the Satisfaction and Performance of Group Members," *Journal of Management* 26, no. 2 (2000), pp. 259–279; and J. W. Bishop, K. D. Scott, and S. M. Burroughs, "Support, Commitment, and Employee Outcomes in a Team Environment," *Journal of Management* 26, no. 6 (2000), pp. 1113–1132.

23　J. R. Hackman, *Leading Teams* (Boston: Harvard Business School Press, 2002).

24　P. Balkundi and D. A. Harrison, "Ties, Leaders, and Time in Teams: Strong Inference About Network Structure's Effects on Team Viability and Performance," *Academy of Management Journal* 49, no. 1 (2006), pp. 49–68; G. Chen, B. L. Kirkman, R. Kanfer, D. Allen, and B. Rosen, "A Multilevel Study of Leadership, Empowerment, and Performance in Teams," *Journal of Applied Psychology* 92, no. 2 (2007), pp. 331–346; L. A. DeChurch and M. A. Marks, "Leadership in Multiteam Systems," *Journal of Applied Psychology* 91, no. 2 (2006), pp. 311–329; A. Srivastava, K. M. Bartol, and E. A. Locke, "Empowering Leadership in Management Teams: Effects on Knowledge Sharing, Efficacy, and Performance," *Academy of Management Journal* 49, no. 6 (2006), pp. 1239–1251; and J. E. Mathieu, K. K. Gilson, and T. M. Ruddy, "Empowerment and Team Effectiveness: An Empirical Test of an Integrated Model," *Journal of Applied Psychology* 91, no. 1 (2006), pp. 97–108.

25　W. Immen, "The More Women in Groups, the Better," *Globe and Mail*, April 27, 2005, p. C3.

26　J. L. Berdahl and C. Anderson, "Men, Women, and Leadership Centralization in Groups Over Time," *Group Dynamics: Theory, Research, and Practice* 9, no. 1 (2005), pp. 45–57.

27　R. Wageman, J. R. Hackman, and E. V. Lehman, "Development of the Team Diagnostic Survey" (working paper, Tuck School, Dartmouth College, Hanover, NH, 2004).

28　J. R. Hackman and R. Wageman, "A Theory of Team Coaching," *Academy of Management Review* 30, no. 2 (April 2005), pp. 269–287.

29 R. I. Beekun, "Assessing the Effectiveness of Sociotechnical Interventions: Antidote or Fad?" *Human Relations*, October 1989, pp. 877–897.

30 S. G. Cohen, G. E. Ledford, and G. M. Spreitzer, "A Predictive Model of Self-Managing Work Team Effectiveness," *Human Relations*, May 1996, pp. 643–676.

31 D. R. Ilgen, J. R. Hollenbeck, M. Johnson, and D. Jundt, "Teams in Organizations: From Input-Process-Output Models to IMOI Models," *Annual Review of Psychology* 56, no. 1 (2005), pp. 517–543.

32 K. T. Dirks, "Trust in Leadership and Team Performance: Evidence from NCAA Basketball," *Journal of Applied Psychology*, December 2000, pp. 1004–1012; and M. Williams, "In Whom We Trust: Group Membership as an Affective Context for Trust Development," *Academy of Management Review*, July 2001, pp. 377–396.

33 P. L. Schindler and C. C. Thomas, "The Structure of Interpersonal Trust in the Workplace," *Psychological Reports*, October 1993, pp. 563–573.

34 See S. T. Johnson, "Work Teams: What's Ahead in Work Design and Rewards Management," *Compensation & Benefits Review*, March–April 1993, pp. 35–41; and A. M. Saunier and E. J. Hawk, "Realizing the Potential of Teams Through Team-Based Rewards," *Compensation & Benefits Review*, July–August 1994, pp. 24–33.

35 D. L. Ferrin and K. T. Dirks, "The Use of Rewards to Increase and Decrease Trust: Mediating Processes and Differential Effects," *Organization Science* 14, no. 1 (January–February 2003), pp. 18–31.

36 J. Pfeffer and N. Langton, "The Effect of Wage Dispersion on Satisfaction, Productivity, and Working Collaboratively: Evidence from College and University Faculty," *Administrative Science Quarterly* 38, 1993, pp. 382–407.

37 M. Bloom, "The Performance Effects of Pay Dispersion on Individuals and Organizations," *Academy of Management Journal* 42, 1999, pp. 25–40.

38 For a more detailed breakdown on team skills, see M. J. Stevens and M. A. Campion, "The Knowledge, Skill, and Ability Requirements for Teamwork: Implications for Human Resource Management," *Journal of Management*, Summer 1994, pp. 503–530.

39 S. T. Bell, "Deep-Level Composition Variables as Predictors of Team Performance: A Meta-Analysis," *Journal of Applied Psychology* 92, no. 3 (2007), pp. 595–615; and M. R. Barrick, G. L. Stewart, M. J. Neubert, and M. K. Mount, "Relating Member Ability and Personality to Work-Team Processes and Team Effectiveness," *Journal of Applied Psychology*, June 1998, pp. 377–391.

40 A. Ellis, J. R. Hollenbeck, and D. R. Ilgen, "Team Learning: Collectively Connecting the Dots," *Journal of Applied Psychology* 88, no. 5 (2003), pp. 821–835; C. O. L. H. Porter, J. R. Hollenbeck, and D. R. Ilgen, "Backing Up Behaviors in Teams: The Role of Personality and Legitimacy of Need," *Journal of Applied Psychology* 88, no. 3 (June 2003), pp. 391–403; A. Colquitt, J. R. Hollenbeck, and D. R. Ilgen, "Computer-Assisted Communication and Team Decision-Making Performance: The Moderating Effect of Openness to Experience," *Journal of Applied Psychology* 87, no. 2 (April 2002), pp. 402–410; J. A. LePine, J. R. Hollenbeck, D. R. Ilgen, and J. Hedlund, "The Effects of Individual Differences on the Performance of Hierarchical Decision Making Teams: Much More Than G," *Journal of Applied Psychology* 82, no. 5 (1997), pp. 803–811; C. Jackson and J. LePine, "Peer Responses to a Team's Weakest Link," *Journal of Applied Psychology* 88, no. 3 (2003), pp. 459–475; and J. LePine, "Team Adaptation and Postchange Performance," *Journal of Applied Psychology* 88, no. 1 (2003), pp. 27–39.

41 E. Sundstrom, K. P. Meuse, and D. Futrell, "Work Teams: Applications and Effectiveness," *American Psychologist*, February 1990, pp. 120–133.

42 See M. F. Peterson, P. B. Smith, A. Akande, S. Ayestaran, S. Bochner, V. Callan, N. Guk Cho, J. Correia Jesuino, M. D'Amorim, P.-H. François, K. Hofmann, P. L. Koopman, K. Leung, T. K. Lim, S. Mortazavi, J. Munene, M. Radford, A. Ropo, G. Savage, B. Setiadi, T. N. Sinha, R. Sorenson, and C. Viedge, "Role Conflict, Ambiguity, and Overload: A 21-Nation Study," *Academy of Management Journal*, April 1995, pp. 429–452.

43 See, for instance, M. Sashkin and K. J. Kiser, *Putting Total Quality Management to Work* (San Francisco: Berrett-Koehler, 1993); and J. R. Hackman and R. Wageman, "Total Quality Management: Empirical, Conceptual and Practical Issues," *Administrative Science Quarterly*, June 1995, pp. 309–342.

44 D. van Knippenberg, C. K. W. De Dreu, and A. C. Homan, "Work Group Diversity and Group Performance: An Integrative Model and Research Agenda," *Journal of Applied Psychology* 89, no. 6 (December 2004), pp. 1008–1022.

45 R. J. Ely and D. A. Thomas, "Cultural Diversity at Work: The Effects of Diversity Perspectives on Work Group Processes and Outcomes," *Administrative Science Quarterly* 46, 2001, pp. 229–273; K. A. Jehn, G. B. Northcraft, and M. A. Neale, "Why Some Differences Make a Difference: A Field Study of Diversity, Conflict, and Performance in Workgroups," *Administrative Science Quarterly* 44, 1999, pp. 741–763; and W. E. Watson, K. Kumar, and L. K. Michaelsen, "Cultural Diversity's Impact on Interaction Process and Performance: Comparing Homogeneous and Diverse Task Groups," *Academy of Management Journal* 36, 1993, pp. 590–602.

46 For a review, see K. Y. Williams and C. A. O'Reilly, "Demography and Diversity in Organizations: A Review of 40 Years of Research," in *Research in Organizational Behavior*, vol. 20, ed. B. M. Staw and L. L. Cummings (Greenwich, CT: JAI Press, 1998), pp. 77–140.

47 See, for instance, J. M. Sacco and N. Schmitt, "A Dynamic Multilevel Model of Demographic Diversity and Misfit Effects," *Journal of Applied Psychology* 90, no. 2 (March 2005), pp. 203–231.

48 E. Peterson, "Negotiation Teamwork: The Impact of Information Distribution and Accountability on Performance Depends on the Relationship Among Team Members," *Organizational Behavior and Human Decision Processes* 72, 1997, pp. 364–384.

49 J. Labianca, "The Ties That Blind," *Harvard Business Review* 82, no. 10 (October 2004), p. 19.

50 D. A. Harrison, K. H. Price, J. H. Gavin, and A. T. Florey, "Time, Teams, and Task Performance: Changing Effects of Surface- and Deep-Level Diversity on Group Functioning," *Academy of Management Journal* 45, no. 5 (2002), pp. 1029–1045; and J. S. Bunderson and K. M. Sutcliffe, "Comparing Alternative Conceptualizations of Functional Diversity in Management Teams: Process and Performance Effects," *Academy of Management Journal* 45, no. 5 (2002), pp. 875–893.

51   M. A. Neale, G. B. Northcraft, and K. A. Jehn, "Exploring Pandora's Box: The Impact of Diversity and Conflict on Work Group Performance," *Performance Improvement Quarterly* 12, no. 1 (1999), pp. 113–126.

52   See, for instance, M. Sashkin and K. J. Kiser, *Putting Total Quality Management to Work* (San Francisco: Berrett-Koehler, 1993); and J. R. Hackman and R. Wageman, "Total Quality Management: Empirical, Conceptual and Practical Issues," *Administrative Science Quarterly*, June 1995, pp. 309–342.

53   J. S. Bunderson and K. M. Sutcliffe, "Comparing Alternative Conceptualizations of Functional Diversity in Management Teams: Process and Performance Effects," *Academy of Management Journal* 45, no. 5 (2002), pp. 875–893, discusses some of the recent work in this area.

54   G. S. Van der Vegt, and J. S. Bunderson, "Learning and Performance in Multidisciplinary Teams: The Importance of Collective Team Identification," *Academy of Management Journal* 48, no. 3 (2005), pp. 532–547.

55   R. J. Ely and D. A. Thomas, "Cultural Diversity at Work: The Effects of Diversity Perspectives on Work Group Processes and Outcomes," *Administrative Science Quarterly* 46, 2001, pp. 229–273.

56   J. T. Polzer, L. P. Milton, and W. B. Swann Jr., "Capitalizing on Diversity: Interpersonal Congruence in Small Work Groups," *Administrative Science Quarterly* 47, no. 2 (2002), pp. 296–324.

57   *Focus on Diversity* based on B. L. Kelsey, "Increasing Minority Group Participation and Influence Using a Group Support System," *Canadian Journal of Administrative Sciences* 17, no. 1 (2000), pp. 63–75.

58   See D. R. Comer, "A Model of Social Loafing in Real Work Groups," *Human Relations*, June 1995, pp. 647–667.

59   E. Sundstrom, K. P. Meuse, and D. Futrell, "Work Teams: Applications and Effectiveness," *American Psychologist*, February 1990, pp. 120–133.

60   D. E. Hyatt and T. M. Ruddy, "An Examination of the Relationship Between Work Group Characteristics and Performance: Once More into the Breach," *Personnel Psychology*, Autumn 1997, p. 555; and J. D. Shaw, M. K. Duffy, and E. M. Stark, "Interdependence and Preference for Group Work: Main and Congruence Effects on the Satisfaction and Performance of Group Members," *Journal of Management* 26, no. 2 (2000), pp. 259–279.

61   R. Wageman, "Critical Success Factors for Creating Superb Self-Managing Teams," *Organizational Dynamics*, Summer 1997, p. 55.

62   M. A. Campion, E. M. Papper, and G. J. Medsker, "Relations Between Work Team Characteristics and Effectiveness: A Replication and Extension," *Personnel Psychology*, Summer 1996, p. 430.

63   M. A. Campion, E. M. Papper, and G. J. Medsker, "Relations Between Work Team Characteristics and Effectiveness: A Replication and Extension," *Personnel Psychology*, Summer 1996, p. 430.

64   K. Hess, *Creating the High-Performance Team* (New York: Wiley, 1987); J. R. Katzenbach and D. K. Smith, *The Wisdom of Teams* (Boston: Harvard Business School Press, 1993), pp. 43–64; and K. D. Scott and A. Townsend, "Teams: Why Some Succeed and Others Fail," *HR Magazine*, August 1994, pp. 62–67.

65   J. E. Mathieu and W. Schulze, "The Influence of Team Knowledge and Formal Plans on Episodic Team Process–Performance Relationships," *Academy of Management Journal* 49, no. 3 (2006), pp. 605–619.

66   A. Gurtner, F. Tschan, N. K. Semmer, and C. Nagele, "Getting Groups to Develop Good Strategies: Effects of Reflexivity Interventions on Team Process, Team Performance, and Shared Mental Models," *Organizational Behavior and Human Decision Processes* 102 (2007), pp. 127–142; M. C. Schippers, D. N. Den Hartog, and P. L. Koopman, "Reflexivity in Teams: A Measure and Correlates," *Applied Psychology: An International Review* 56, no. 2 (2007), pp. 189–211; and C. S. Burke, K. C. Stagl, E. Salas, L. Pierce, and D. Kendall, "Understanding Team Adaptation: A Conceptual Analysis and Model," *Journal of Applied Psychology* 91, no. 6 (2006), pp. 1189–1207.

67   E. Weldon and L. R. Weingart, "Group Goals and Group Performance," *British Journal of Social Psychology*, Spring 1993, pp. 307–334.

68   R. A. Guzzo, P. R. Yost, R. J. Campbell, and G. P. Shea, "Potency in Groups: Articulating a Construct," *British Journal of Social Psychology*, March 1993, pp. 87–106; S. J. Zaccaro, V. Blair, C. Peterson, and M. Zazanis, "Collective Efficacy," in *Self-Efficacy, Adaptation and Adjustment: Theory, Research and Application*, ed. J. E. Maddux (New York: Plenum, 1995), pp. 308–330; and D. L. Feltz and C. D. Lirgg, "Perceived Team and Player Efficacy in Hockey," *Journal of Applied Psychology*, August 1998, pp. 557–564.

69   For some of the controversy surrounding the definition of cohesion, see J. Keyton and J. Springston, "Redefining Cohesiveness in Groups," *Small Group Research*, May 1990, pp. 234–254.

70   C. R. Evans and K. L. Dion, "Group Cohesion and Performance: A Meta-Analysis," *Small Group Research*, May 1991, pp. 175–186; B. Mullen and C. Cooper, "The Relation Between Group Cohesiveness and Performance: An Integration," *Psychological Bulletin*, March 1994, pp. 210–227; S. M. Gully, D. J. Devine, and D. J. Whitney, "A Meta-Analysis of Cohesion and Performance: Effects of Level of Analysis and Task Interdependence," *Small Group Research*, 1995, pp. 497–520; and P. M. Podsakoff, S. B. MacKenzie, and M. Ahearne, "Moderating Effects of Goal Acceptance on the Relationship Between Group Cohesiveness and Productivity," *Journal of Applied Psychology*, December 1997, pp. 974–983.

71   A. Chang and P. Bordia, "A Multidimensional Approach to the Group Cohesion–Group Performance Relationship," *Small Group Research*, August 2001, pp. 379–405.

72   Submitted by Don Miskiman, Chair, Department of Management, and U-C Professor of Management, Malaspina University-College, Nanaimo, BC. With permission.

73   Paragraph based on R. Kreitner and A. Kinicki, *Organizational Behavior*, 6th ed. (New York: Irwin, 2004), pp. 459–461.

74   R. Kreitner and A. Kinicki, *Organizational Behavior*, 6th ed. (New York: Irwin, 2004), p. 460. Reprinted by permission of McGraw Hill Education.

75   K. M. Eisenhardt, J. L. Kahwajy, and L. J. Bourgeois III, "How Management Teams Can Have a Good Fight," *Harvard Business Review*, July–August 1997, p. 78.

76   K. Jehn, "A Multimethod Examination of the Benefits and Detriments of Intragroup Conflict," *Administrative Science Quarterly*, June 1995, pp. 256–282.

77 K. M. Eisenhardt, J. L. Kahwajy, and L. J. Bourgeois III, "How Management Teams Can Have a Good Fight," *Harvard Business Review,* July–August 1997, p. 78.

78 Based on K. M. Eisenhardt, J. L. Kahwajy, and L. J. Bourgeois III, "How Management Teams Can Have a Good Fight," *Harvard Business Review,* July–August 1997, p. 78.

79 K. Hess, *Creating the High-Performance Team* (New York: Wiley, 1987).

80 See, for example, C. M. Fiol and E. J. O'Connor, "Identification in Face-to-Face, Hybrid, and Pure Virtual Teams: Untangling the Contradictions," *Organization Science* 16, no. 1 (January–February 2005), pp. 19–32; L. L. Martins, L. L. Gilson, and M. T. Maynard, "Virtual Teams: What Do We Know and Where Do We Go from Here?" *Journal of Management* 30, no. 6 (December 2004), pp. 805–835; D. Duarte and N. T. Snyder, *Mastering Virtual Teams: Strategies, Tools, and Techniques* (San Francisco: Jossey-Bass, 1999); M. L. Maznevski and K. M. Chudoba, "Bridging Space Over Time: Global Virtual Team Dynamics and Effectiveness," *Organization Science,* September–October 2000, pp. 473–492; and J. Katzenbach and D. Smith, "Virtual Teaming," *Forbes,* May 21, 2001, pp. 48–51.

81 K. Kiser, "Working on World Time," *Training,* March 1999, p. 30.

82 B. B. Baltes, M. W. Dickson, M. P. Sherman, C. C. Bauer, and J. S. LaGanke, "Computer-Mediated Communication and Group Decision Making: A Meta-Analysis," *Organizational Behaviour and Human Decision Processes* 87, no. 1 (2002), pp. 156–179.

83 J. M. Wilson, S. G. Straus, and B. McEvily, "All in Due Time: The Development of Trust in Computer-Mediated and Face-to-Face Teams," *Organizational Behavior and Human Decision Processes* 99, no. 1 (2006), pp. 16–33; and S. L. Jarvenpaa, K. Knoll, and D. E. Leidner, "Is Anybody Out There? Antecedents of Trust in Global Virtual Teams," *Journal of Management Information Systems,* Spring 1998, pp. 29–64.

84 This section based on A. Majchrzak, A. Malhotra, J. Stamps, and J. Lipnack, "Can Absence Make a Team Grow Stronger?" *Harvard Business Review* 82, no. 5 (May 2004), pp. 131–136.

85 B. L. Kirkman, B. Rosen, C. B. Gibson, P. E. Tesluk, and S. O. McPherson, "Five Challenges to Virtual Team Success: Lessons from Sabre, Inc.," *Academy of Management Executive* 16, no. 3 (2002), pp. 67–79.

86 P. J. Hinds and M. Mortensen. "Understanding Conflict in Geographically Distributed Teams: The Moderating Effects of Shared Identity, Shared Context, and Spontaneous Communication," *Organization Science* 16, no. 3 (2005), pp. 290–307.

87 C. Joinson, "Managing Virtual Teams," *HR Magazine,* June 2002, p. 71. Reprinted with the permission of *HR Magazine,* published by the Society for Human Resource Management, Alexandria, VA.

88 D. Brown, "Innovative HR Ineffective in Manufacturing Firms," *Canadian HR Reporter,* April 7, 2003, pp. 1–2.

89 A. B. Drexler and R. Forrester, "Teamwork—Not Necessarily the Answer," *HR Magazine,* January 1998, pp. 55–58.

90 R. Forrester and A. B. Drexler, "A Model for Team-Based Organization Performance," *Academy of Management Executive,* August

1999, p. 47. See also S. A. Mohrman, with S. G. Cohen and A. M. Mohrman Jr., *Designing Team-Based Organizations* (San Francisco: Jossey-Bass, 1995); and J. H. Shonk, *Team-Based Organizations* (Homewood, IL: Business One Irwin, 1992).

91 Based on N. Katz, "Sports Teams as a Model for Workplace Teams: Lessons and Liabilities," *Academy of Management Executive,* August 2001, pp. 56–67.

92 Based on N. Katz, "Sports Teams as a Model for Workplace Teams: Lessons and Liabilities," *Academy of Management Executive,* August 2001, pp. 56–67.

93 Adapted from D. A. Whetten and K. S. Cameron, *Developing Management Skills,* 3rd ed. © 1995, pp. 534–535. Adapted by permission of Pearson Education, Inc., Upper Saddle River, NJ.

94 This exercise is based on "The Paper Tower Exercise: Experiencing Leadership and Group Dynamics" by Phillip L. Hunsaker and Johanna S. Hunsaker, unpublished manuscript. A brief description is included in "Exchange," *The Organizational Behavior Teaching Journal* 4, no. 2 (1979), p. 49. Reprinted by permission of the authors. The materials listed was suggested by Prof. Sally Maitlis, Sauder School of Business, UBC.

95 Based on C. Stapells, "Business Executives Bullish About Spa Time," *Toronto Star,* July 6, 2006, p. H3; C. Dahle, "How to Avoid a Rout at the Company Retreat," *New York Times,* October 31, 2004, p. 10; S. Max, "Seagate's Morale-athon," *BusinessWeek,* April 3, 2006, pp. 110–112; M. C. White, "Doing Good on Company Time," *New York Times,* May 8, 2007, p. C6; and N. H. Woodward, "Making the Most of Team Building," *HR Magazine,* September 2006, pp. 73–76.

96 Based on "Groups and Teams at Kluster," Organizational Behavior Video Library, 2008. Copyrighted by Prentice-Hall.

97 Based on S. P. Robbins and P. L. Hunsaker, *Training in Interpersonal Skills,* 2nd ed. (Upper Saddle River, NJ: Prentice Hall, 1996), pp. 168–184.

Chapter 6

1 Based on B. Erskine, "Oil Sands: The Next Generation Sessions," submission to International Association of Business Communicators, www.iabc.com/awards/gq/WPMgt.htm.

2 See, for example, K. W. Thomas and W. H. Schmidt, "A Survey of Managerial Interests With Respect to Conflict," *Academy of Management Journal,* June 1976, p. 317.

3 L. Ramsay, "Communication Key to Workplace Happiness," *Financial Post,* December 6/8, 1997, p. 58.

4 "Employers Cite Communication Skills, Honesty/Integrity as Key for Job Candidates," *IPMA-HR Bulletin* (March 23, 2007), p. 1.

5 D. K. Berlo, *The Process of Communication* (New York: Holt, Rinehart and Winston, 1960), p. 54.

6 J. C. McCroskey, J. A. Daly, and G. Sorenson, "Personality Correlates of Communication Apprehension," *Human Communication Research,* Spring 1976, pp. 376–380.

7 See R. L. Daft and R. H. Lengel, "Information Richness: A New Approach to Managerial Behavior and Organization Design," in *Research in Organizational Behavior,* vol. 6, ed. B. M. Staw and

L. L. Cummings (Greenwich, CT: JAI Press, 1984), pp. 191–233; R. E. Rice and D. E. Shook, "Relationships of Job Categories and Organizational Levels to Use of Communication Channels, Including Electronic Mail: A Meta-Analysis and Extension," *Journal of Management Studies,* March 1990, pp. 195–229; R. E. Rice, "Task Analyzability, Use of New Media, and Effectiveness," *Organization Science,* November 1992, pp. 475–500; S. G. Straus and J. E. McGrath, "Does the Medium Matter? The Interaction of Task Type and Technology on Group Performance and Member Reaction," *Journal of Applied Psychology,* February 1994, pp. 87–97; J. Webster and L. K. Trevino, "Rational and Social Theories as Complementary Explanations of Communication Media Choices: Two Policy-Capturing Studies," *Academy of Management Journal,* December 1995, pp. 1544–1572; and L. K. Trevino, J. Webster, and E. W. Stein, "Making Connections: Complementary Influences on Communication Media Choices, Attitudes, and Use," *Organization Science,* March–April 2000, pp. 163–182.

8   I. Austen, "Telling Tales Out of School, on YouTube," *New York Times,* November 27, 2006; and D. Rogers, "Quebec Students Suspended for Posting Teacher's Outburst Online," *Ottawa Citizen,* November 25, 2006.

9   R. L. Daft, R. H. Lengel, and L. K. Trevino, "Message Equivocality, Media Selection, and Manager Performance: Implications for Information Systems," *MIS Quarterly,* September 1987, pp. 355–368.

10   "Virtual Pink Slips Start Coming Online," *Vancouver Sun,* July 3, 1999, p. D15.

11   Thanks are due to an anonymous reviewer for providing this elaboration.

12   Based on S. Klie, "Dawning of a New Day at Suncor," *Canadian HR Reporter,* October 22, 2007, p. 21.

13   M. Richtel, "Lost in E-Mail, Tech Firms Face Self-Made Beast," *New York Times,* June 14, 2008.

14   S. I. Hayakawa, *Language in Thought and Action* (New York: Harcourt Brace Jovanovich, 1949), p. 292.

15   H. Weeks, "Taking the Stress Out of Stressful Conversations," *Harvard Business Review,* July–August 2001, pp. 112–119.

16   Based on S. Klie, "Dawning of a New Day at Suncor," *Canadian HR Reporter,* October 22, 2007, p. 21; and B. Erskine, "Oil Sands: The Next Generation Sessions," submission to International Association of Business Communicators, www.iabc.com/awards/gq/WPMgt.htm.

17   See, for instance, R. Hotch, "Communication Revolution," *Nation's Business,* May 1993, pp. 20–28; G. Brockhouse, "I Have Seen the Future," *Canadian Business,* August 1993, pp. 43–45; R. Hotch, "In Touch Through Technology," *Nation's Business,* January 1994, pp. 33–35; and P. LaBarre, "The Other Network," *IndustryWeek,* September 19, 1994, pp. 33–36.

18   "Email Brings Costs and Fatigue," *Western News* (UWO), July 9, 2004, http://communications.uwo.ca/com/western_news/stories/email_brings_costs_and_fatigue_20040709432320/ (accessed August 16, 2009).

19   K. Macklem, "You've Got Too Much Mail," *Maclean's,* January 30, 2006, pp. 20–21.

20   "Overloaded Canadians Trash 42% of All E-Mails: Study," *Ottawa Citizen,* June 26, 2008, p. D5.

21   D. Brady, "*!#?@ the E-mail. Can We Talk?" *BusinessWeek,* December 4, 2006, p. 109.

22   E. Binney, "Is E-mail the New Pink Slip?" *HR Magazine,* November 2006, pp. 32–33; and R. L. Rundle, "Critical Case: How an Email Rant Jolted a Big HMO," *Wall Street Journal,* April 24, 2007, pp. A1, A16.

23   "Some Email Recipients Say 'Enough Already,'" *Gainesville* (Florida) *Sun,* June 3, 2007, p. 1G.

24   D. Goleman, "Flame First, Think Later: New Clues to E-mail Misbehavior," *New York Times,* February 20, 2007, p. D5; and E. Krell, "The Unintended Word," *HR Magazine,* August 2006, pp. 50–54.

25   R. Zeidner, "Keeping E-mail in Check," *HR Magazine,* June 2007, pp. 70–74; "E-mail May Be Hazardous to Your Career," *Fortune,* May 14, 2007, p. 24; "More Firms Fire Employees for E-mail Violations," *Gainesville* (Florida) *Sun,* June 6, 2006, p. B1.

26   Based on S. Proudfoot, "1 in 3 Workers Admit to Improper E-mail; Stories of Career-Killing Gaffes Leave Many Unfazed, Study Finds," *Edmonton Journal,* June 25, 2008, p. A1; E. Church, "Employers Read E-mail as Fair Game," *Globe and Mail,* April 14, 1998, p. B16; and J. Kay, "Someone Will Watch Over Me: Think Your Office E-mails Are Private? Think Again," *National Post Business,* January 2001, pp. 59–64.

27   J. Kay, "Someone Will Watch Over Me: Think Your Office E-Mails Are Private? Think Again," *National Post Business,* January 2001, pp. 59–64.

28   E. Church, "Employers Read E-Mail as Fair Game," *Globe and Mail,* April 14, 1998, p. B16.

29   Based on "At Many Companies, Hunt for Leakers Expands Arsenal of Monitoring Tactics," *Wall Street Journal,* September 11, 2006, pp. B1, B3; and B. J. Alge, G. A. Ballinger, S. Tangirala, and J. L. Oakley, "Information Privacy in Organizations: Empowering Creative and Extra-Role Performance," *Journal of Applied Psychology* 91, no. 1 (2006), pp. 221–232.

30   A. Harmon, "Appeal of Instant Messaging Extends into the Workplace," *New York Times,* March 11, 2003, p. A1.

31   Report released by the Canadian Wireless Telecommunications Association, as reported in P. Wilson, "Record Growth of Text Messaging Continues in Canada," *Vancouver Sun,* March 23, 2005, p. D2; and J. Bow, "Business Jumps on Text-Messaging Wave, *Business Edge,* April 5, 2007, p. 12.

32   J. Bow, "Business Jumps on Text-Messaging Wave," *Business Edge,* April 5, 2007, p. 12.

33   "Survey Finds Mixed Reviews on Checking E-mail During Meetings," *IPMA-HR Bulletin,* April 27, 2007, p. 1.

34   K. Gurchiek, "Shoddy Writing Can Trip Up Employees, Organizations," *SHRM Online,* April 27, 2006, pp. 1–2.

35   R. L. Birdwhistell, *Introduction to Kinesics* (Louisville, KY: University of Louisville Press, 1952).

36   J. Fast, *Body Language* (Philadelphia: M. Evans, 1970), p. 7.

37   A. Mehrabian, *Nonverbal Communication* (Chicago: Aldine-Atherton, 1972).

38 N. M. Henley, "Body Politics Revisited: What Do We Know Today?" in P. J. Kalbfleisch and M. J. Cody (eds.), *Gender, Power, and Communication in Human Relationships* (Hillsdale, NJ: Erlbaum, 1995), pp. 27–61.

39 E. T. Hall, *The Hidden Dimension*, 2nd ed. (Garden City, NY: Anchor Books/Doubleday, 1966).

40 This section largely based on C. C. Pinder and K. P. Harlos, "Employee Silence: Quiescence and Acquiescence as Responses to Perceived Injustice," in *Research in Personnel and Human Resource Management*, ed. G. R. Ferris (Greenwich, CT: JAI, 2002), pp. 331–369; and P. Mornell, "The Sounds of Silence," *Inc.*, February 2001, pp. 117–118.

41 See D. Tannen, *You Just Don't Understand: Women and Men in Conversation* (New York: Ballantine Books, 1991); and D. Tannen, *Talking from 9 to 5* (New York: William Morrow, 1995).

42 D. Goldsmith and P. Fulfs, "You Just Don't Have the Evidence: An Analysis of Claims and Evidence in Deborah Tannen's *You Just Don't Understand*," in *Communications Yearbook*, vol. 22, ed. M. Roloff (Thousand Oaks, CA: Sage, 1999).

43 N. Langton, "Differences in Communication Styles: Asking for a Raise," in *Organizational Behavior: Experiences and Cases*, 4th ed., ed. D. Marcic (St. Paul, MN: West Publishing, 1995).

44 See M. Munter, "Cross-Cultural Communication for Managers," *Business Horizons*, May–June 1993, pp. 75–76.

45 N. Adler, *International Dimensions of Organizational Behavior*, 4th ed. (Cincinnati, OH: South Western, 2002), p. 94.

46 See, for instance, C. F. Fink, "Some Conceptual Difficulties in Theory of Social Conflict," *Journal of Conflict Resolution*, December 1968, pp. 412–460. For an updated review of the conflict literature, see J. A. Wall Jr. and R. R. Callister, "Conflict and Its Management," *Journal of Management* 21, no. 3 (1995), pp. 515–558.

47 L. L. Putnam and M. S. Poole, "Conflict and Negotiation," in *Handbook of Organizational Communication: An Inter-disciplinary Perspective*, ed. F. M. Jablin, L. L. Putnam, K. H. Roberts, and L. W. Porter (Newbury Park, CA: Sage, 1987), pp. 549–599.

48 K. W. Thomas, "Conflict and Negotiation Processes in Organizations," in *Handbook of Industrial and Organizational Psychology*, vol. 3, 2nd ed., ed. M. D. Dunnette and L. M. Hough (Palo Alto, CA: Consulting Psychologists Press, 1992), pp. 651–717.

49 K. Jehn, "A Multimethod Examination of the Benefits and Detriments of Intragroup Conflict," *Administrative Science Quarterly*, June 1995, pp. 256–282; K. A. Jehn, "A Qualitative Analysis of Conflict Types and Dimensions in Organizational Groups," *Administrative Science Quarterly*, September 1997, pp. 530–557; K. A. Jehn and E. A. Mannix, "The Dynamic Nature of Conflict: A Longitudinal Study of Intragroup Conflict and Group Performance," *Academy of Management Journal*, April 2001, pp. 238–251; C. K. W. De Dreu and A. E. M. Van Vianen, "Managing Relationship Conflict and the Effectiveness of Organizational Teams," *Journal of Organizational Behavior*, May 2001, pp. 309–328; and K. A. Jehn and C. Bendersky, "Intragroup Conflict in Organizations: A Contingency Perspective on the Conflict-Outcome Relationship," in *Research in Organizational Behavior*, vol. 25, ed. R. M. Kramer and B. M. Staw (Oxford, UK: Elsevier, 2003), pp. 199–210.

50 A. C. Amason, "Distinguishing the Effects of Functional and Dysfunctional Conflict on Strategic Decision Making: Resolving a Paradox for Top Management Teams," *Academy of Management Journal* 39, no. 1 (1996), pp. 123–148.

51 D. Tjosvold, "Cooperative and Competitive Goal Approach to Conflict: Accomplishments and Challenges," *Applied Psychology: An International Review* 47, no. 3 (1998), pp. 285–342.

52 K. W. Thomas, "Conflict and Negotiation Processes in Organizations," in *Handbook of Industrial and Organizational Psychology*, vol. 3, 2nd ed., ed. M. D. Dunnette and L. M. Hough (Palo Alto, CA: Consulting Psychologists Press, 1992), pp. 651–717.

53 C. K. W. De Dreu, A. Evers, B. Beersma, E. S. Kluwer, and A. Nauta, "A Theory-Based Measure of Conflict Management Strategies in the Workplace," *Journal of Organizational Behavior* 22, no. 6 (September 2001), pp. 645–668. See also D. G. Pruitt and J. Rubin, *Social Conflict: Escalation, Stalemate and Settlement* (New York: Random House, 1986).

54 C. K. W. De Dreu, A. Evers, B. Beersma, E. S. Kluwer, and A. Nauta, "A Theory-Based Measure of Conflict Management Strategies in the Workplace," *Journal of Organizational Behavior* 22, no. 6 (September 2001), pp. 645–668.

55 R. A. Baron, "Personality and Organizational Conflict: Effects of the Type A Behavior Pattern and Self-Monitoring," *Organizational Behavior and Human Decision Processes*, October 1989, pp. 281–296; A. Drory and I. Ritov, "Effects of Work Experience and Opponent's Power on Conflict Management Styles," *International Journal of Conflict Management* 8, 1997, pp. 148–161; R. J. Sternberg and L. J. Soriano, "Styles of Conflict Resolution," *Journal of Personality and Social Psychology*, July 1984, pp. 115–126; and R. J. Volkema and T. J. Bergmann, "Conflict Styles as Indicators of Behavioral Patterns in Interpersonal Conflicts," *Journal of Social Psychology*, February 1995, pp. 5–15.

56 These ideas are based on S. P. Robbins, *Managing Organizational Conflict: A Nontraditional Approach* (Upper Saddle River, NJ: Prentice Hall, 1974), pp. 59–89.

57 Based on K. W. Thomas, "Toward Multidemensional Values in Teaching: The Example of Conflict Behaviours," *Academy of Management Review*, July 1977, p. 487; and C. K. W. De DDreu, A. Evers, B. Beersma, E. S. Kluwer, and A. Nauta, "A Theory-Based Measure of Conflllict Management Strategies in the Workplace," *Journal of Organizational Behaviour* 22, no. 6 (September 2001). pp. 645–688.

58 R. D. Ramsey, "Interpersonal Conflicts," *SuperVision* 66, no. 4 (April 2005), pp. 14–17.

59 R. D. Ramsey, "Interpersonal Conflicts," *SuperVision* 66, no. 4 (April 2005), pp. 14–17.

60 M. A. Von Glinow, D. L. Shapiro, and J. M. Brett, "Can We Talk, and Should We? Managing Emotional Conflict in Multicultural Teams," *Academy of Management Review* 29, no. 4 (October 2004), pp. 578–592.

61 R. Kreitner and A. Kinicki, *Organizational Behavior*, 6th ed. (New York: McGraw Hill, 2004), p. 492, Table 14-1. Reprinted by permission of McGraw Hill Education.

62 J. A. Wall Jr., *Negotiation: Theory and Practice* (Glenview, IL: Scott Foresman, 1985).

63   K. Harding, "A New Language, a New Deal," *Globe and Mail*, October 30, 2002, pp. C1, C10.

64   This model is based on R. J. Lewicki, "Bargaining and Negotiation," *Exchange: The Organizational Behavior Teaching Journal* 6, no. 2 (1981), pp. 39–40; and B. S. Moskal, "The Art of the Deal," *IndustryWeek*, January 18, 1993, p. 23.

65   J. C. Magee, A. D. Galinsky, and D. H. Gruenfeld, "Power, Propensity to Negotiate, and Moving First in Competitive Interactions," *Personality and Social Psychology Bulletin*, February 2007, pp. 200–212.

66   J. R. Curhan, H. A. Elfenbein, and H. Xu, "What Do People Value When They Negotiate? Mapping the Domain of Subjective Value in Negotiation," *Journal of Personality and Social Psychology* 91, no. 3 (2007), pp. 493–512.

67   R. Fisher and W. Ury, *Getting to Yes: Negotiating Agreement Without Giving In*, 2nd ed. (New York: Penguin Books, 1991).

68   P. H. Kim and A. R. Fragale, "Choosing the Path to Bargaining Power: An Empirical Comparison of BATNAs and Contributions in Negotiation," *Journal of Applied Psychology* 90, no. 2 (March 2005), pp. 373–381.

69   P. LeBrun, "Talks End Badly Thursday in Toronto," *Canadian Press*, February 10, 2005; A. Woods, "Season Down to Final Hours," *National Post*, February 11, 2005, pp. B8, B11.

70   M. H. Bazerman and M. A. Neale, *Negotiating Rationally* (New York: Free Press, 1992), pp. 67–68.

71   R. Fisher and W. Ury, *Getting to Yes: Negotiating Agreement Without Giving In*, 2nd ed. (New York: Penguin Books, 1991).

72   R. Fisher and W. Ury, *Getting to Yes* (New York: Penguin Books, 1991).

73   S. A. Hellweg and S. L. Phillips, "Communication and Productivity in Organizations: A State-of-the-Art Review," in *Proceedings of the 40th Annual Academy of Management Conference*, Detroit, 1980, pp. 188–192.

74   The points presented here were influenced by E. Van de Vliert, "Escalative Intervention in Small-Group Conflicts," *Journal of Applied Behavioral Science*, Winter 1985, pp. 19–36.

75   C. K. W. De Dreu, A. Evers, B. Beersma, E. S. Kluwer, and A. Nauta, "A Theory-Based Measure of Conflict Management Strategies in the Workplace," *Journal of Organizational Behavior* 22, no. 6 (September 2001), pp. 645–668. Copyright © John Wiley & Sons Limited. Reproduced with permission.

76   Based on M. E. Schweitzer, "Deception in Negotiations," in *Wharton on Making Decisions*, ed. S. J. Hoch and H. C. Kunreuther (New York: Wiley, 2001), pp. 187–200; and M. Diener, "Fair Enough," *Entrepreneur*, January 2002, pp. 100–102.

77   Based on E. Wong, "Stinging Office E-Mail Lights 'Firestorm,'" *Globe and Mail*, April 9, 2001, p. M1; P. D. Broughton, "Boss's Angry Email Sends Shares Plunging," *Daily Telegraph of London*, April 6, 2001; D. Stafford, "Shattering the Illusion of Respect," *Kansas City Star*, March 29, 2001, p. C1.

78   Based on "Communication and IT at Kluster," Organizational Behavior Video Library, 2008. Copyrighted by Prentice-Hall.

79   These suggestions are based on J. A. Wall Jr. and M. W. Blum, "Negotiations," *Journal of Management*, June 1991, pp. 278–282;

and J. S. Pouliot, "Eight Steps to Success in Negotiating," *Nation's Business*, April 1999, pp. 40–42.

Chapter 7

1   Opening vignette based on R. Ouzounian, "Stratford's Fantastic Four," *thestar.com*, August 18, 2007 (accessed February 3, 2009); K. Taylor, "When Too Many Cooks Can Be Poison," *Globe and Mail*, March 29, 2008, p. R15; R. Ouzounian, "Similarities May Have Torn Stratford Trio Apart," *thestar.com*, March 25, 2008 (accessed February 3, 2009).

2   Based on B. M. Bass, *Bass & Stogdill's Handbook of Leadership*, 3rd ed. (New York: Free Press, 1990).

3   S. Prashad, "Fill Your Power Gap," *Globe and Mail*, July 23, 2003, p. C3.

4   T. B. Lawrence, M. K. Mauws, B. Dyck, and R. F. Kleysen, "The Politics of Organizational Learning: Integrating Power into the 4I Framework," *Academy of Management Review* 30, no. 1 (January 2005), pp. 180–191.

5   J. R. P. French Jr. and B. Raven, "The Bases of Social Power," in *Studies in Social Power*, ed. D. Cartwright (Ann Arbor: University of Michigan, Institute for Social Research, 1959), pp. 150–167. For an update on French and Raven's work, see D. E. Frost and A. J. Stahelski, "The Systematic Measurement of French and Raven's Bases of Social Power in Workgroups," *Journal of Applied Social Psychology*, April 1988, pp. 375–389; T. R. Hinkin and C. A. Schriesheim, "Development and Application of New Scales to Measure the French and Raven (1959) Bases of Social Power," *Journal of Applied Psychology*, August 1989, pp. 561–567; and G. E. Littlepage, J. L. Van Hein, K. M. Cohen, and L. L. Janiec, "Evaluation and Comparison of Three Instruments Designed to Measure Organizational Power and Influence Tactics," *Journal of Applied Social Psychology*, January 16–31, 1993, pp. 107–125.

6   B. H. Raven, "Social Influence and Power," in *Current Studies in Social Psychology*, ed. I. D. Steiner and M. Fishbein (New York: Holt, Rinehart and Winston, 1965), pp. 371–382.

7   D. Kipnis, *The Powerholders* (Chicago: University of Chicago Press, 1976), pp. 77–78.

8   E. A. Ward, "Social Power Bases of Managers: Emergence of a New Factor," *Journal of Social Psychology*, February 2001, pp. 144–147.

9   D. Hickson, C. Hinings, C. Lee, R. Schneck, and J. Pennings, "A Strategic Contingencies Theory of Intra-Organizational Power," *Administrative Science Quarterly* 16, 1971, pp. 216–229.

10   J. W. Dean Jr. and J. R. Evans, *Total Quality: Management, Organization, and Strategy* (Minneapolis-St. Paul, MN: West, 1994).

11   M. Folb, "Cause Celeb: From Deborah Cox to Maestro, Homegrown Talent Is Hocking Retail Fashion," *Marketing Magazine*, April 5, 1999, p. 13.

12   G. Yukl, H. Kim, and C. M. Falbe, "Antecedents of Influence Outcomes," *Journal of Applied Psychology* 81, no. 3 (June 1, 1996), pp. 309–317.

13   P. P. Carson, K. D. Carson, and C. W. Roe, "Social Power Bases: A Meta-Analytic Examination of Interrelationships and Outcomes," *Journal of Applied Social Psychology* 23, no. 14 (1993), pp. 1150–1169.

14 Cited in J. R. Carlson, D. S. Carlson, and L. L. Wadsworth, "The Relationship Between Individual Power Moves and Group Agreement Type: An Examination and Model," *S.A.M. Advanced Management Journal* 65, no. 4 (2000), pp. 44–51.

15 C. M. Falbe and G. Yukl, "Consequences for Managers of Using Single Tactics and Combinations of Tactics," *Academy of Management Journal* 35, 1992, pp. 638–652.

16 Vignette based on R. Ouzounian, "Resignations a Blow to Stratford," *thestar.com*, March 13, 2008 (accessed February 4, 2009); and R. Ouzounian, "Similarities May Have Torn Stratford Trio Apart," *thestar.com*, March 25, 2008 (accessed February 4, 2009).

17 R. E. Emerson, "Power-Dependence Relations," *American Sociological Review* 27, 1962, pp. 31–41.

18 Thanks are due to an anonymous reviewer for supplying this insight.

19 H. Mintzberg, *Power in and Around Organizations* (Englewood Cliffs, NJ: Prentice Hall, 1983), p. 24.

20 See, for example, D. Kipnis, S. M. Schmidt, C. Swaffin-Smith, and I. Wilkinson, "Patterns of Managerial Influence: Shotgun Managers, Tacticians, and Bystanders," *Organizational Dynamics*, Winter 1984, pp. 58–67; T. Case, L. Dosier, G. Murkison, and B. Keys, "How Managers Influence Superiors: A Study of Upward Influence Tactics," *Leadership and Organization Development Journal* 9, no. 4 (1988), pp. 25–31; D. Kipnis and S. M. Schmidt, "Upward-Influence Styles: Relationship With Performance Evaluations, Salary, and Stress," *Administrative Science Quarterly*, December 1988, pp. 528–542; G. Yukl and C. M. Falbe, "Influence Tactics and Objectives in Upward, Downward, and Lateral Influence Attempts," *Journal of Applied Psychology*, April 1990, pp. 132–140; G. Yukl, H. Kim, and C. M. Falbe, "Antecedents of Influence Outcomes," *Journal of Applied Psychology*, June 1996, pp. 309–317; K. E. Lauterbach and B. J. Weiner, "Dynamics of Upward Influence: How Male and Female Managers Get Their Way," *Leadership Quarterly*, Spring 1996, pp. 87–107; K. R. Xin and A. S. Tsui, "Different Strokes for Different Folks? Influence Tactics by Asian-American and Caucasian-American Managers," *Leadership Quarterly*, Spring 1996, pp. 109–132; S. J. Wayne, R. C. Liden, I. K. Graf, and G. R. Ferris, "The Role of Upward Influence Tactics in Human Resource Decisions," *Personnel Psychology*, Winter 1997, pp. 979–1006; and C. A. Higgins and T. A. Judge, "The Effect of Applicant Influence Tactics on Recruiter Perceptions of Fit and Hiring Recommendations: A Field Study," *Journal of Applied Psychology* 89, no. 4 (August 2004), pp. 622–632.

21 This section adapted from G. Yukl, C. M. Falbe, and J. Y. Youn, "Patterns of Influence Behavior for Managers," *Group & Organization Studies* 18, no. 1 (March 1993), p. 7.

22 This section adapted from G. Yukl, C. M. Falbe, and J. Y. Youn, "Patterns of Influence Behavior for Managers," *Group & Organization Studies* 18, no. 1 (March 1993), p. 7.

23 G. Yukl, *Leadership in Organizations*, 5th ed. (Upper Saddle River, NJ: Prentice Hall, 2002), pp. 141–174; G. R. Ferris, W. A. Hochwarter, C. Douglas, F. R. Blass, R. W. Kolodinsky, and D. C. Treadway, "Social Influence Processes in Organizations and Human Resource Systems," in *Research in Personnel and Human Resources Management*, vol. 21, ed. G. R. Ferris and J. J. Martocchio (Oxford, UK: JAI Press/Elsevier, 2003), pp. 65–127; and C. A. Higgins, T. A. Judge, and G. R. Ferris, "Influence Tactics and Work Outcomes: A Meta-Analysis," *Journal of Organizational Behavior*, March 2003, pp. 89–106.

24 C. M. Falbe and G. Yukl, "Consequences for Managers of Using Single Influence Tactics and Combinations of Tactics," *Academy of Management Journal*, July 1992, pp. 638–653.

25 G. Yukl, *Leadership in Organizations*, 5th ed. (Upper Saddle River, NJ: Prentice Hall, 2002), pp. 141–174.

26 C. M. Falbe and G. Yukl, "Consequences for Managers of Using Single Influence Tactics and Combinations of Tactics," *Academy of Management Journal*, July 1992, pp. 638–653.

27 Search of *Business Source Premier* and *Canadian Newsstand* articles conducted by Nancy Langton, September 2005.

28 This is the definition given by R. Forrester, "Empowerment: Rejuvenating a Potent Idea," *The Academy of Management Executive*, August 2000, pp. 67–80.

29 R. E. Quinn and G. M. Spreitzer, "The Road to Empowerment: Seven Questions Every Leader Should Consider," *Organizational Dynamics*, Autumn 1997, p. 38.

30 S. Wetlaufer, "Organizing for Empowerment: An Interview With AES's Roger Sant and Dennis Bakke," *Harvard Business Review*, January–February 1999, pp. 110–123.

31 C. Argyris, "Empowerment: The Emperor's New Clothes," *Harvard Business Review*, May–June 1998.

32 K. Kitagawa, *Empowering Employee–Learners With Essential Skills at Durabelt Inc.* (Ottawa: The Conference Board of Canada, March 2005).

33 J. Schaubroeck, J. R. Jones, and J. L. Xie, "Individual Differences in Utilizing Control to Cope With Job Demands: Effects on Susceptibility to Infectious Disease," *Journal of Applied Psychology*, April 2001, pp. 265–278.

34 Thanks are due to an anonymous reviewer for this insight.

35 "Delta Promotes Empowerment," *Globe and Mail*, May 31, 1999, Advertising Supplement, p. C5.

36 G. M. Spreitzer, "Psychological Empowerment in the Workplace: Dimensions, Measurement, and Validation," *Academy of Management Journal* 38, 1995, pp. 1442–1465; G. M. Spreitzer, M. A. Kizilos, and S. W. Nason, "A Dimensional Analysis of the Relationship Between Psychological Empowerment and Effectiveness, Satisfaction, and Strain," *Journal of Management* 23, 1997, pp. 679–704; and K. W. Thomas and W. G. Tymon, "Does Empowerment Always Work: Understanding the Role of Intrinsic Motivation and Personal Interpretation," *Journal of Management Systems* 6, 1994, pp. 39–54.

37 D. E. Hyatt and T. M. Ruddy, "An Examination of the Relationship Between Work Group Characteristics and Performance: Once More Into the Breach," *Personnel Psychology* 50, 1997, pp. 553–585; B. L. Kirkman and B. Rosen, "Beyond Self-Management: Antecedents and Consequences of Team Empowerment," *Academy of Management Journal* 42, 1999, pp. 58–74; P. E. Tesluck, D. J. Brass, and J. E. Mathieu, "An Examination of Empowerment Processes at Individual and Group Levels" (paper presented at the 11th annual conference of the Society of Industrial and Organizational Psychology, San Diego, 1996).

38   D. Kivell, "Support Employees' Efforts to Sustain Gains," *Plant*, February 20, 2006, p. 32.

39   C. Robert, T. M. Probst, J. J. Martocchio, and F. Drasgow, and J. J. Lawler, "Empowerment and Continuous Improvement in the United States, Mexico, Poland, and India: Predicting Fit on the Basis of the Dimensions of Power Distance and Individualism," *Journal of Applied Psychology* 85, no. 5 (2000), pp. 643–658.

40   W. A. Randolph and M. Sashkin, "Can Organizational Empowerment Work in Multinational Settings?" *Academy of Management Executive*, February 2002, pp. 102–115.

41   T. Lee and C. M. Brotheridge, "When the Prey Becomes the Predator: Bullying as Predictor of Reciprocal Bullying, Coping, and Well-Being" (working paper, University of Regina, 2005).

42   "More and More Workplaces Have Bullies," *Leader-Post* (Regina), December 14, 2004, p. A1.

43   M. S. Hershcovis and J. Barling, "Comparing the Outcomes of Sexual Harassment and Workplace Aggression: A Meta-Analysis" (paper presented at the Seventh International Conference on Work, Stress and Health, Washington, DC, March 8, 2008).

44   Quebec Labour Standards, s. 81.18, *Psychological Harassment at Work*.

45   M. Bridge, "Female Firefighters Claim Harassment," *Vancouver Sun*, March 22, 2006, p. A1.

46   "Employers Underestimate Extent of Sexual Harassment, Report Says," *Vancouver Sun*, March 8, 2001, p. D6.

47   N. Alcoba, "Students Face Sexual Harassment," *Vancouver Sun*, November 30, 2005, p. A8.

48   "Employers Underestimate Extent of Sexual Harassment, Report Says," *Vancouver Sun*, March 8, 2001, p. D6.

49   S. Lim and L. M. Cortina, "Interpersonal Mistreatment in the Workplace: The Interface and Impact of General Incivility and Sexual Harassment," *Journal of Applied Psychology* 90, no. 3 (2005), pp. 483–496.

50   *Janzen v. Platy Enterprises Ltd.* [1989] 10 C.H.R.R. D/6205 SCC.

51   The following section is based on J. N. Cleveland and M. E. Kerst, "Sexual Harassment and Perceptions of Power: An Under-Articulated Relationship," *Journal of Vocational Behavior*, February 1993, pp. 49–67.

52   J. Goddu, "Sexual Harassment Complaints Rise Dramatically," *Canadian Press Newswire*, March 6, 1998.

53   K. Von Hoffmann, "Forbidden Fruit: Student-Faculty Relationships," *Yale Herald*, October 17, 2003, p. 1.

54   C. R. Willness, P. Steel, and K. Lee, "A Meta-Analysis of the Antecedents and Consequences of Workplace Sexual Harassment," *Personnel Psychology* 60 (2007), pp. 127–162.

55   See, for instance, "Car Dealership Settles Same Sex Harassment Lawsuit," *Associated Press*, June 28, 1999.

56   S. A. Culbert and J. J. McDonough, *The Invisible War: Pursuing Self-Interest at Work* (New York: John Wiley, 1980), p. 6.

57   H. Mintzberg, *Power in and Around Organizations* (Englewood Cliffs, NJ: Prentice Hall, 1983), p. 26.

58   T. Cole, "Who Loves Ya?" *Report on Business Magazine*, April 1999, p. 54.

59   D. Farrell and J. C. Petersen, "Patterns of Political Behavior in Organizations," *Academy of Management Review*, July 1982, p. 405. For a thoughtful analysis of the academic controversies underlying any definition of organizational politics, see A. Drory and T. Romm, "The Definition of Organizational Politics: A Review," *Human Relations*, November 1990, pp. 1133–1154.

60   P. Dawson and D. Buchanan, "The Way It Really Happened: Competing Narratives in the Political Process of Technological Change," *Human Relations* 58, no. 7 (2005), pp. 845–865; A. Spicer, "The Political Process of Inscribing a New Technology," *Human Relations* 58, no. 7 (2005), pp. 867–890; and J. Swan and H. Scarbrough, "The Politics of Networked Innovation," *Human Relations* 58, no. 7 (2005), pp. 913–943.

61   J. Pfeffer, *Power in Organizations* (Marshfield, MA: Pittman, 1981).

62   G. R. Ferris, G. S. Russ, and P. M. Fandt, "Politics in Organizations," in *Impression Management in Organizations*, ed. R. A. Giacalone and P. Rosenfeld (Newbury Park, CA: Sage, 1989), pp. 143–170; and K. M. Kacmar, D. P. Bozeman, D. S. Carlson, and W. P. Anthony, "An Examination of the Perceptions of Organizational Politics Model: Replication and Extension," *Human Relations*, March 1999, pp. 383–416.

63   K. M. Kacmar and R. A. Baron, "Organizational Politics: The State of the Field, Links to Related Processes, and an Agenda for Future Research," in *Research in Personnel and Human Resources Management*, vol. 17, ed. G. R. Ferris (Greenwich, CT: JAI Press, 1999); and M. Valle and L. A. Witt, "The Moderating Effect of Teamwork Perceptions on the Organizational Politics–Job Satisfaction Relationship," *Journal of Social Psychology*, June 2001, pp. 379–388.

64   G. R. Ferris, D. D. Frink, M. C. Galang, J. Zhou, K. M. Kacmar, and J. L. Howard, "Perceptions of Organizational Politics: Prediction, Stress-Related Implications, and Outcomes," *Human Relations*, February 1996, pp. 233–266; K. M. Kacmar, D. P. Bozeman, D. S. Carlson, and W. P. Anthony, "An Examination of the Perceptions of Organizational Politics Model; Replication and Extension," *Human Relations*, March 1999, p. 388; and J. M. L. Poon, "Situational Antecedents and Outcomes of Organizational Politics Perceptions," *Journal of Managerial Psychology* 18, no. 2 (2003), pp. 138–155.

65   C. Kiewitz, W. A. Hochwarter, G. R. Ferris, and S. L. Castro, "The Role of Psychological Climate in Neutralizing the Effects of Organizational Politics on Work Outcomes," *Journal of Applied Social Psychology*, June 2002, pp. 1189–1207; and J. M. L. Poon, "Situational Antecedents and Outcomes of Organizational Politics Perceptions," *Journal of Managerial Psychology* 18, no. 2 (2003), pp. 138–155.

66   K. M. Kacmar and R. A. Baron, "Organizational Politics: The State of the Field, Links to Related Processes, and an Agenda for Future Research," in *Research in Personnel and Human Resources Management*, vol. 17, ed. G. R. Ferris (Greenwich, CT: JAI Press, 1999); and M. Valle and L. A. Witt, "The Moderating Effect of Teamwork Perceptions on the Organizational Politics–Job Satisfaction Relationship," *Journal of Social Psychology*, June 2001, pp. 379–388.

67   R. W. Allen, D. L. Madison, L. W. Porter, P. A. Renwick, and B. T. Mayes, "Organizational Politics: Tactics and Characteristics of Its Actors," *California Management Review*, Fall 1979, pp. 77–83.

68   W. L. Gardner and M. J. Martinko, "Impression Management in Organizations," *Journal of Management*, June 1988, pp. 321–338; D. C. Gilmore and G. R. Ferris, "The Effects of Applicant Impression Management Tactics on Interviewer Judgments," *Journal of Management*, December 1989, pp. 557–564; M. R. Leary and R. M. Kowalski, "Impression Management: A Literature Review and Two-Component Model," *Psychological Bulletin*, January 1990, pp. 34–47; S. J. Wayne and K. M. Kacmar, "The Effects of Impression Management on the Performance Appraisal Process," *Organizational Behavior and Human Decision Processes*, February 1991, pp. 70–88; E. W. Morrison and R. J. Bies, "Impression Management in the Feedback-Seeking Process: A Literature Review and Research Agenda," *Academy of Management Review*, July 1991, pp. 522–541; S. J. Wayne and R. C. Liden, "Effects of Impression Management on Performance Ratings: A Longitudinal Study," *Academy of Management Journal*, February 1995, pp. 232–260; and C. K. Stevens and A. L. Kristof, "Making the Right Impression: A Field Study of Applicant Impression Management During Job Interviews," *Journal of Applied Psychology*, October 1995, pp. 587–606.

69   See, for instance, M. C. Bolino and W. H. Turnley, "More Than One Way to Make an Impression: Exploring Profiles of Impression Management," *Journal of Management* 29, no. 2 (2003), pp. 141–160; S. Zivnuska, K. M. Kacmar, L. A. Witt, D. S. Carlson, and V. K. Bratton, "Interactive Effects of Impression Management and Organizational Politics on Job Performance," *Journal of Organizational Behavior*, August 2004, pp. 627–640; and W.-C. Tsai, C.-C. Chen, and S.-F. Chiu, "Exploring Boundaries of the Effects of Applicant Impression Management Tactics in Job Interviews," *Journal of Management*, February 2005, pp. 108–125.

70   M. R. Leary and R. M. Kowalski, "Impression Management: A Literature Review and Two-Component Model," *Psychological Bulletin*, January 1990, p. 40.

71   W. L. Gardner and M. J. Martinko, "Impression Management in Organizations," *Journal of Management*, June 1988, p. 333.

72   R. A. Baron, "Impression Management by Applicants During Employment Interviews: The 'Too Much of a Good Thing' Effect," in *The Employment Interview: Theory, Research, and Practice*, ed. R. W. Eder and G. R. Ferris (Newbury Park, CA: Sage, 1989), pp. 204–215.

73   A. P. J. Ellis, B. J. West, A. M. Ryan, and R. P. DeShon, "The Use of Impression Management Tactics in Structural Interviews: A Function of Question Type?" *Journal of Applied Psychology*, December 2002, pp. 1200–1208.

74   R. A. Baron, "Impression Management by Applicants During Employment Interviews: The 'Too Much of a Good Thing' Effect," in *The Employment Interview: Theory, Research, and Practice*, ed. R. W. Eder and G. R. Ferris (Newbury Park, CA: Sage, 1989); D. C. Gilmore and G. R. Ferris, "The Effects of Applicant Impression Management Tactics on Interviewer Judgments," *Journal of Management*, December 1989, pp. 557–564; C. K. Stevens and A. L. Kristof, "Making the Right Impression: A Field Study of Applicant Impression Management During Job Interviews," *Journal of Applied Psychology* 80, 1995, pp. 587–606; and L. A. McFarland, A. M. Ryan, and S. D. Kriska, "Impression Management Use and Effectiveness Across Assessment Methods," *Journal of Management* 29, no. 5 (2003), pp. 641–661; and W.-C. Tsai, C.-C. Chen, and S.-F. Chiu, "Exploring Boundaries of the Effects of Applicant Impression Management Tactics in Job Interviews," *Journal of Management*, February 2005, pp. 108–125.

75   D. C. Gilmore and G. R. Ferris, "The Effects of Applicant Impression Management Tactics on Interviewer Judgments," *Journal of Management*, December 1989, pp. 557–564.

76   C. K. Stevens and A. L. Kristof, "Making the Right Impression: A Field Study of Applicant Impression Management During Job Interviews," *Journal of Applied Psychology* 80, 1995, pp. 587–606.

77   C. A. Higgins, T. A. Judge, and G. R. Ferris, "Influence Tactics and Work Outcomes: A Meta-Analysis," *Journal of Organizational Behavior*, March 2003, pp. 89–106.

78   C. A. Higgins, T. A. Judge, and G. R. Ferris, "Influence Tactics and Work Outcomes: A Meta-Analysis," *Journal of Organizational Behavior*, March 2003, pp. 89–106.

79   J. D. Westphal and I. Stern, "Flattery Will Get You Everywhere (Especially if You Are a Male Caucasian): How Ingratiation, Boardroom Behavior, and Demographic Minority Status Affect Additional Board Appointments of U.S. Companies," *Academy of Management Journal* 50, no. 2 (2007), pp. 267–288.

80   J. M. Maslyn and D. B. Fedor, "Perceptions of Politics: Does Measuring Different Foci Matter?" *Journal of Applied Psychology* 84, 1998, pp. 645–653; and L. G. Nye and L. A. Witt, "Dimensionality and Construct Validity of the Perceptions of Organizational Politics Scale," *Educational and Psychological Measurement* 53, 1993, pp. 821–829.

81   G. R. Ferris, D. D. Frink, D. I. Bhawuk, J. Zhou, and D. C. Gilmore, "Reactions of Diverse Groups to Politics in the Workplace," *Journal of Management* 22, 1996, pp. 23–44; K. M. Kacmar, D. P. Bozeman, D. S. Carlson, and W. P. Anthony, "An Examination of the Perceptions of Organizational Politics Model: Replication and Extension," *Human Relations* 52, 1999, pp. 383–416.

82   T. P. Anderson, "Creating Measures of Dysfunctional Office and Organizational Politics: The DOOP and Short-Form DOOP Scales," *Psychology: A Journal of Human Behavior* 31, 1994, pp. 24–34.

83   G. R. Ferris, D. D. Frink, D. I. Bhawuk, J. Zhou, and D. C. Gilmore, "Reactions of Diverse Groups to Politics in the Workplace," *Journal of Management* 22, 1996, pp. 23–44; K. M. Kacmar, D. P. Bozeman, D. S. Carlson, and W. P. Anthony, "An Examination of the Perceptions of Organizational Politics Model: Replication and Extension," *Human Relations* 52, 1999, pp. 383–416.

84   K. M. Kacmar, D. P. Bozeman, D. S. Carlson, and W. P. Anthony, "An Examination of the Perceptions of Organizational Politics Model: Replication and Extension," *Human Relations* 52, 1999, pp. 383–416; J. M. Maslyn and D. B. Fedor, "Perceptions of Politics: Does Measuring Different Foci Matter?" *Journal of Applied Psychology* 84, 1998, pp. 645–653.

85   M. Warshaw, "The Good Guy's (and Gal's) Guide to Office Politics," *Fast Company*, April 1998, p. 156.

86   G. Yukl, C. M. Falbe, and J. Y. Youn, "Patterns of Influence Behavior for Managers," *Group & Organization Studies* 18, no. 1 (March 1993), p. 7.

87   J. F. Byrnes, "The Political Behavior Inventory." Reprinted by permission of Dr. Joseph F. Byrnes, Bentley College, Waltham, Massachusetts.

88 This exercise was inspired by one found in Judith R. Gordon, *Organizational Behavior*, 2nd ed. (Englewood Cliffs, NJ: Prentice Hall, 1992), pp. 499–502.

89 Based on D. Kadlec, "Did Sandy Play Dirty?" *Time Online Edition*, November 25, 2002.

90 Based on J. Sandberg, "Sabotage 101: The Sinister Art of Backstabbing," *Wall Street Journal*, February 11, 2004, p. B1.

91 Based on "Whistleblower," *CBC News: Sunday*, April 1, 2007.

92 *From Concepts to Skills* based on S. P. Robbins and P. L. Hunsaker, *Training in Interpersonal Skills: Tips for Managing People at Work*, 2nd ed. (Upper Saddle River, NJ: Prentice Hall, 1996), pp. 131–134.

OB on the Edge: The Toxic Workplace

1 L. M. Anderson and C. M. Pearson, "Tit for Tat? The Spiraling Effect of Incivility in the Workplace," *Academy of Management Review* 24, no. 3 (1999), p. 453.

2 The source of this quotation is N. Giarrusso, "An Issue of Job Satisfaction," unpublished undergraduate term paper, Concordia University, Montreal, 1990. It is cited in B. E. Ashforth, "Petty Tyranny in Organizations: A Preliminary Examination of Antecedents and Consequences," *Canadian Journal of Administrative Sciences* 14, no. 2 (1997), pp. 126–140.

3 P. Frost and S. Robinson, "The Toxic Handler: Organizational Hero—and Casualty," *Harvard Business Review*, July–August 1999, p. 101 (Reprint 99406).

4 L. M. Anderson and C. M. Pearson, "Tit for Tat? The Spiraling Effect of Incivility in the Workplace," *Academy of Management Review* 24, no. 3 (1999), pp. 452–471.

5 L. M. Anderson and C. M. Pearson, "Tit for Tat? The Spiraling Effect of Incivility in the Workplace," *Academy of Management Review* 24, no. 3 (1999), pp. 452–471. For further discussion of this, see R. A. Baron and J. H. Neuman, "Workplace Violence and Workplace Aggression: Evidence on Their Relative Frequency and Potential Causes," *Aggressive Behavior* 22, 1996, pp. 161–173; C. C. Chen and W. Eastman, "Towards a Civic Culture for Multicultural Organizations," *Journal of Applied Behavioral Science* 33, 1997, pp. 454–470; J. H. Neuman and R. A. Baron, "Aggression in the Workplace," in *Antisocial Behavior in Organizations*, ed. R. A. Giacalone and J. Greenberg (Thousand Oaks, CA: Sage, 1997), pp. 37–67.

6 L. M. Anderson and C. M. Pearson, "Tit for Tat? The Spiraling Effect of Incivility in the Workplace," *Academy of Management Review* 24, no. 3 (1999), pp. 452–471.

7 L. M. Anderson and C. M. Pearson, "Tit for Tat? The Spiraling Effect of Incivility in the Workplace," *Academy of Management Review* 24, no. 3 (1999), pp. 452–471.

8 R. Corelli, "Dishing Out Rudeness: Complaints Abound as Customers Are Ignored, Berated," *Maclean's*, January 11, 1999, p. 44.

9 R. Corelli, "Dishing Out Rudeness: Complaints Abound as Customers Are Ignored, Berated," *Maclean's*, January 11, 1999, p. 44.

10 See, for example, "The National Labour Survey," *The Canadian Initiative on Workplace Violence*, March 2000, www. workplace-violence.ca/research/survey1.pdf (accessed August 23, 2009).

11 R. A. Baron and J. H. Neuman, "Workplace Violence and Workplace Aggression: Evidence on Their Relative Frequency and Potential Causes," *Aggressive Behavior* 22, 1996, pp. 161–173; K. Bjorkqvist, K. Osterman, and M. Hjelt-Back, "Aggression Among University Employees," *Aggressive Behavior* 20, 1986, pp. 173–184; and H. J. Ehrlich and B. E. K. Larcom, *Ethnoviolence in the Workplace* (Baltimore, MD: Center for the Applied Study of Ethnoviolence, 1994).

12 J. Graydon, W. Kasta, and P. Khan, "Verbal and Physical Abuse of Nurses," *Canadian Journal of Nursing Administration*, November–December 1994, pp. 70–89.

13 C. M. Pearson and C. L. Porath, "Workplace Incivility: The Target's Eye View" (paper presented at the annual meetings of The Academy of Management, Chicago, August 10, 1999).

14 "Men More Likely to Be Rude in Workplace, Survey Shows," *Vancouver Sun*, August 16, 1999, p. B10.

15 R. Corelli, "Dishing Out Rudeness: Complaints Abound as Customers Are Ignored, Berated," *Maclean's*, January 11, 1999, p. 44.

16 R. Corelli, "Dishing Out Rudeness: Complaints Abound as Customers Are Ignored, Berated," *Maclean's*, January 11, 1999, p. 44.

17 R. A. Baron and J. H. Neuman, "Workplace Violence and Workplace Aggression: Evidence on Their Relative Frequency and Potential Causes," *Aggressive Behavior* 22, 1996, pp. 161–173; C. MacKinnon, *Only Words* (New York: Basic Books, 1994); J. Marks, "The American Uncivil Wars," *U.S. News & World Report*, April 22, 1996, pp. 66–72; and L. P. Spratlen, "Workplace Mistreatment: Its Relationship to Interpersonal Violence," *Journal of Psychosocial Nursing* 32, no. 12 (1994), pp. 5–6.

18 Information in this paragraph based on B. Branswell, "Death in Ottawa: The Capital Is Shocked by a Massacre That Leaves Five Dead," *Maclean's*, April 19, 1999, p. 18; "Four Employees Killed by Former Co-worker," *Occupational Health & Safety*, June 1999, pp. 14, 16; and "Preventing Workplace Violence," *Human Resources Advisor Newsletter*, Western Edition, May–June 1999, pp. 1–2.

19 W. M. Glenn, "An Employee's Survival Guide: An ILO Survey of Workplaces in 32 Countries Ranked Argentina the Most Violent, Followed by Romania, France and Then, Surprisingly, Canada," *Occupational Health & Safety*, April–May 2002, p. 28 passim.

20 D. Flavelle, "Managers Cited for Increase in 'Work Rage,'" *Vancouver Sun*, April 11, 2000, pp. D1, D11; and "Profile of Workplace Victimization Incidents," *Statistics Canada*, 2007, www.statcan.ca/english/research/85F0033MIE/2007013/findings/profile.htm (accessed August 23, 2009).

21 E. Wulfhorst, "Desk Rage Spoils Workplace for Many Americans," *Reuters*, July 10, 2008, www.reuters.com/article/newsOne/idUSN0947145320080710 (accessed August 23, 2009).

22 S. James, "Long Hours Linked to Rising Toll from Stress," *Financial Post* (*National Post*), August 6, 2003, p. FP12.

23 "Profile of Workplace Victimization Incidents," *Statistics Canada*, 2007, www.statcan.ca/english/research/85F0033MIE/ 2007013/findings/profile.htm (accessed August 23, 2009).

24 W. M. Glenn, "An Employee's Survival Guide: An ILO Survey of Workplaces in 32 Countries Ranked Argentina the Most Violent, Followed by Romania, France and Then, Surprisingly, Canada," *Occupational Health & Safety*, April–May 2002, p. 28 passim.

25 W. M. Glenn, "An Employee's Survival Guide: An ILO Survey of Workplaces in 32 Countries Ranked Argentina the Most Violent, Followed by Romania, France and Then, Surprisingly, Canada," *Occupational Health & Safety*, April–May 2002, p. 28 passim.

26 "A Quarter of Nova Scotia Teachers Who Responded to a Recent Survey Said They Faced Physical Violence at Work During the 2001–02 School Year," *Canadian Press Newswire*, February 14, 2003.

27 A. M. Webber, "Danger: Toxic Company," *Fast Company*, November 1998, pp. 152–157.

28 Information for FactBox based on "Breeding Loyalty Pays for Employers," *Vancouver Sun*, April 22, 2000, p. D14; and P. Mackenzie, "Loyalty a Moving Target," *Toronto Star*, March 8, 2008, www.thestar.com/article/309355 (accessed August 23, 2009).

29 D. Flavelle, "Managers Cited for Increase in 'Work Rage,'" *Vancouver Sun*, April 11, 2000, pp. D1, D11; and G. Smith, *Work Rage* (Toronto: HarperCollins Canada, 2000).

30 "Work Rage," *BCBusiness Magazine*, January 2001, p. 23.

31 D. Flavelle, "Managers Cited for Increase in 'Work Rage,'" *Vancouver Sun*, April 11, 2000, pp. D1, D11.

32 D. E. Gibson and S. G. Barsade, "The Experience of Anger at Work: Lessons from the Chronically Angry" (paper presented at the annual meetings of the Academy of Management, Chicago, August 11, 1999).

33 H. Levinson, *Emotional Health in the World of Work* (Boston: South End Press, 1964); and E. Schein, *Organizational Psychology* (Englewood Cliffs, NJ: Prentice Hall, 1980).

34 E. W. Morrison and S. L. Robinson, "When Employees Feel Betrayed: A Model of How Psychological Contract Violation Develops," *Academy of Management Journal* 22, 1997, pp. 226–256; S. L. Robinson, "Trust and Breach of the Psychological Contract," *Administrative Science Quarterly* 41, 1996, pp. 574–599; and S. L. Robinson, M. S. Kraatz, and D. M. Rousseau, "Changing Obligations and the Psychological Contract: A Longitudinal Study," *Academy of Management Journal* 37, 1994, pp. 137–152.

35 T. R. Tyler and P. Dogoey, "Trust in Organizational Authorities: The Influence of Motive Attributions on Willingness to Accept Decisions," in *Trust in Organizations*, ed. R. M. Kramer and T. R. Tyler (Thousand Oaks, CA: Sage, 1996), pp. 246–260.

36 A. M. Webber, "Danger: Toxic Company," *Fast Company*, November 1998, pp. 152–157.

37 A. M. Webber, "Danger: Toxic Company," *Fast Company*, November 1998, pp. 152–157.

38 P. Frost, *Toxic Emotions at Work* (Cambridge, MA: Harvard Business School Press, 2003).

39 "Men More Likely to Be Rude in Workplace, Survey Shows," *Vancouver Sun*, August 16, 1999, p. B10.

40 D. E. Gibson and S. G. Barsade, "The Experience of Anger at Work: Lessons from the Chronically Angry" (paper presented at the annual meetings of the Academy of Management, Chicago, August 11, 1999).

41 D. E. Gibson and S. G. Barsade, "The Experience of Anger at Work: Lessons from the Chronically Angry" (paper presented at the annual meetings of the Academy of Management, Chicago, August 11, 1999).

42 L. McClure, *Risky Business* (Binghamton, NY: Haworth Press, 1996).

43 R. Corelli, "Dishing Out Rudeness: Complaints Abound as Customers Are Ignored, Berated," *Maclean's*, January 11, 1999, p. 44.

44 P. Frost and S. Robinson, "The Toxic Handler: Organizational Hero—and Casualty," *Harvard Business Review*, July–August 1999, p. 101 (Reprint 99406).

45 P. Frost and S. Robinson, "The Toxic Handler: Organizational Hero—and Casualty," *Harvard Business Review*, July–August 1999, p. 101 (Reprint 99406).

46 P. Frost and S. Robinson, "The Toxic Handler: Organizational Hero—and Casualty," *Harvard Business Review*, July–August 1999, p. 101 (Reprint 99406).

Chapter 8

1 Opening vignette based on "Endless Summer," *Fortune*, April 2, 2007, pp. 63–70; and Y. Chouinard, *Let My People Go Surfing*, (New York: Penguin Books, 2005).

2 J. P. Kotter, "What Leaders Really Do," *Harvard Business Review*, May–June 1990, pp. 103–111.

3 R. N. Kanungo, "Leadership in Organizations: Looking Ahead to the 21st Century," *Canadian Psychology* 39, no. 1–2 (1998), p. 77. For more evidence of this consensus, see N. Adler, *International Dimensions of Organizational Behavior*, 3rd ed. (Cincinnati, OH: South-Western College Publishing, 1997); R. J. House, "Leadership in the Twenty-First Century," in *The Changing Nature of Work*, ed. A. Howard (San Francisco: Jossey-Bass, 1995), pp. 411–450; R. N. Kanungo and M. Mendonca, *Ethical Dimensions of Leadership* (Thousand Oaks, CA: Sage Publications, 1996); and A. Zaleznik, "The Leadership Gap," *Academy of Management Executive* 4, no. 1 (1990), pp. 7–22.

4 Vignette based on "Endless Summer," *Fortune*, April 2, 2007, pp. 63–70; and Y. Chouinard, *Let My People Go Surfing*, (New York: Penguin Books, 2005).

5 J. G. Geier, "A Trait Approach to the Study of Leadership in Small Groups," *Journal of Communication*, December 1967, pp. 316–323.

6 S. A. Kirkpatrick and E. A. Locke, "Leadership: Do Traits Matter?" *Academy of Management Executive*, May 1991, pp. 48–60; and S. J. Zaccaro, R. J. Foti, and D. A. Kenny, "Self-Monitoring and Trait-Based Variance in Leadership: An Investigation of Leader Flexibility Across Multiple Group Situations," *Journal of Applied Psychology*, April 1991, pp. 308–315.

7 See T. A. Judge, J. E. Bono, R. Ilies, and M. Werner, "Personality and Leadership: A Review" (paper presented at the 15th Annual Conference of the Society for Industrial and Organizational Psychology, New Orleans, 2000); and T. A. Judge, J. E. Bono, R. Ilies, and M. W. Gerhardt, "Personality and Leadership: A Qualitative and Quantitative Review," *Journal of Applied Psychology*, August 2002, pp. 765–780.

8 T. A. Judge, J. E. Bono, R. Ilies, and M. Werner, "Personality and Leadership: A Review" (paper presented at the 15th Annual

Conference of the Society for Industrial and Organizational Psychology, New Orleans, 2000).

9 D. R. Ames and F. J. Flynn, "What Breaks a Leader: The Curvilinear Relation Between Assertiveness and Leadership," *Journal of Personality and Social Psychology* 92, no. 2 (2007), pp. 307–324.

10 T. A. Judge, J. E. Bono, R. Ilies, and M. Werner, "Personality and Leadership: A Review" (paper presented at the 15th Annual Conference of the Society for Industrial and Organizational Psychology, New Orleans, 2000); R. G. Lord, C. L. DeVader, and G. M. Alliger, "A Meta-Analysis of the Relation Between Personality Traits and Leadership Perceptions: An Application of Validity Generalization Procedures," *Journal of Applied Psychology,* August 1986, pp. 402–410; and J. A. Smith and R. J. Foti, "A Pattern Approach to the Study of Leader Emergence," *Leadership Quarterly,* Summer 1998, pp. 147–160.

11 This section is based on D. Goleman, "What Makes a Leader?" *Harvard Business Review,* November–December 1998, pp. 93–102; J. M. George, "Emotions and Leadership: The Role of Emotional Intelligence," *Human Relations,* August 2000, pp. 1027–1055; C. S. Wong and K. S. Law, "The Effects of Leader and Follower Emotional Intelligence on Performance and Attitude: An Exploratory Study," *Leadership Quarterly,* June 2002, pp. 243–274; and D. R. Caruso, and C. J. Wolfe, "Emotional Intelligence and Leadership Development" in *Leader Development for Transforming Organizations: Growing Leaders for Tomorrow,* ed. D. David and S. J. Zaccaro (Mahwah, NJ: Lawrence Erlbaum, 2004) pp. 237–263.

12 J. Champy, "The Hidden Qualities of Great Leaders," *Fast Company,* November 2003, p. 135.

13 T. A. Judge, J. A. LePine, and B. L. Rich, "Loving Yourself Abundantly: Relationship of the Narcissistic Personality to Self- and Other Perceptions of Workplace Deviance, Leadership, and Task and Contextual Performance," *Journal of Applied Psychology* 91, no. 4 (2006), pp. 762–776.

14 R. M. Stogdill and A. E. Coons, eds., *Leader Behavior: Its Description and Measurement,* Research Monograph no. 88 (Columbus: Ohio State University, Bureau of Business Research, 1951). This research is updated in S. Kerr, C. A. Schriesheim, C. J. Murphy, and R. M. Stogdill, "Toward a Contingency Theory of Leadership Based Upon the Consideration and Initiating Structure Literature," *Organizational Behavior and Human Performance,* August 1974, pp. 62–82; and C. A. Schriesheim, C. C. Cogliser, and L. L. Neider, "Is It 'Trustworthy'? A Multiple-Levels-of-Analysis Reexamination of an Ohio State Leadership Study, With Implications for Future Research," *Leadership Quarterly,* Summer 1995, pp. 111–145.

15 R. Kahn and D. Katz, "Leadership Practices in Relation to Productivity and Morale," in *Group Dynamics: Research and Theory,* 2nd ed., ed. D. Cartwright and A. Zander (Elmsford, NY: Row, Paterson, 1960).

16 R. R. Blake and A. A. McCanse, *Leadership Dilemmas—Grid Solutions* (Houston: Gulf Publishing Company, 1991); R. R. Blake and J. S. Mouton, "Management by Grid Principles or Situationalism: Which?" *Group and Organization Studies* 7 (1982), pp. 207–210.

17 T. A. Judge, R. F. Piccolo, and R. Ilies, "The Forgotten Ones? The Validity of Consideration and Initiating Structure in Leadership Research," *Journal of Applied Psychology* 89, no. 1 (February 2004), pp. 36–51; and R. T. Keller, "Transformational Leadership, Initiating Structure, and Substitutes for Leadership: A Longitudinal Study of Research and Development Project Team

Performance," *Journal of Applied Psychology* 91, no. 1 (2006), pp. 202–210.

18 Based on G. Johns and A. M. Saks, *Organizational Behaviour,* 5th ed. (Toronto: Pearson Education Canada, 2001), p. 276.

19 A. J. Mayo and N. Nohria, "Zeitgeist Leadership," *Harvard Business Review* 83, no. 10 (2005), pp. 45–60.

20 See, for instance, P. M. Podsakoff, S. B. MacKenzie, M. Ahearne, and W. H. Bommer, "Searching for a Needle in a Haystack: Trying to Identify the Illusive Moderators of Leadership Behavior," *Journal of Management* 1, no. 3 (1995), pp. 422–470.

21 H. Wang, K. S. Law, R. D. Hackett, D. Wang, and Z. X. Chen, "Leader-Member Exchange as a Mediator of the Relationship Between Transformational Leadership and Followers' Performance and Organizational Citizenship Behavior," *Academy of Management Journal* 48, no. 3 (June 2005), pp. 420–432.

22 F. E. Fiedler, *A Theory of Leadership Effectiveness* (New York: McGraw-Hill, 1967).

23 Cited in R. J. House and R. N. Aditya, "The Social Scientific Study of Leadership: Quo Vadis?" *Journal of Management* 23, no. 3 (1997), p. 422.

24 G. Johns and A. M. Saks, *Organizational Behaviour,* 5th ed. (Toronto: Pearson Education Canada, 2001), pp. 278–279.

25 P. Hersey and K. H. Blanchard, "So You Want to Know Your Leadership Style?" *Training and Development Journal,* February 1974, pp. 1–15; and P. Hersey, K. H. Blanchard, and D. E. Johnson, *Management of Organizational Behavior: Leading Human Resources,* 8th ed. (Upper Saddle River, NJ: Prentice Hall, 2001).

26 Cited in C. F. Fernandez and R. P. Vecchio, "Situational Leadership Theory Revisited: A Test of an Across-Jobs Perspective," *Leadership Quarterly* 8, no. 1 (1997), p. 67.

27 For controversy surrounding the Fiedler LPC scale, see A. Bryman, "Leadership in Organizations," in *Handbook of Organization Studies,* ed. S. R. Clegg, C. Hardy, and W. R. Nord (London: Sage Publications, 1996), pp. 279–280; A. Bryman, *Leadership and Organizations* (London: Routledge & Kegan Paul, 1986); and T. Peters and N. Austin, *A Passion for Excellence* (New York: Random House, 1985). For supportive evidence on the Fiedler model, see L. H. Peters, D. D. Hartke, and J. T. Pohlmann, "Fiedler's Contingency Theory of Leadership: An Application of the Meta-Analysis Procedures of Schmidt and Hunter," *Psychological Bulletin,* March 1985, pp. 274–285; C. A. Schriesheim, B. J. Tepper, and L. A. Tetrault, "Least Preferred Co-Worker Score, Situational Control, and Leadership Effectiveness: A Meta-Analysis of Contingency Model Performance Predictions," *Journal of Applied Psychology,* August 1994, pp. 561–573; and R. Ayman, M. M. Chemers, and F. Fiedler, "The Contingency Model of Leadership Effectiveness: Its Levels of Analysis," *Leadership Quarterly,* Summer 1995, pp. 147–167. For evidence that LPC scores are not stable, see, for instance, R. W. Rice, "Psychometric Properties of the Esteem for the Least Preferred Coworker (LPC) Scale," *Academy of Management Review,* January 1978, pp. 106–118; C. A. Schriesheim, B. D. Bannister, and W. H. Money, "Psychometric Properties of the LPC Scale: An Extension of Rice's Review," *Academy of Management Review,* April 1979, pp. 287–290; and J. K. Kennedy, J. M. Houston, M. A. Korgaard, and D. D. Gallo, "Construct Space of the Least Preferred Co-Worker (LPC) Scale," *Educational & Psychological Measurement,* Fall 1987, pp. 807–814. For difficulty in applying Fiedler's model, see E. H. Schein, *Organizational Psychology,* 3rd ed. (Englewood

Cliffs, NJ: Prentice Hall, 1980), pp. 116–117; and B. Kabanoff, "A Critique of Leader Match and Its Implications for Leadership Research," *Personnel Psychology*, Winter 1981, pp. 749–764. **For evidence that Hersey and Blanchard's model has received little attention from researchers, see** R. K. Hambleton and R. Gumpert, "The Validity of Hersey and Blanchard's Theory of Leader Effectiveness," *Group & Organizational Studies*, June 1982, pp. 225–242; C. L. Graeff, "The Situational Leadership Theory: A Critical View," *Academy of Management Review*, April 1983, pp. 285–291; R. P. Vecchio, "Situational Leadership Theory: An Examination of a Prescriptive Theory," *Journal of Applied Psychology*, August 1987, pp. 444–451; J. R. Goodson, G. W. McGee, and J. F. Cashman, "Situational Leadership Theory: A Test of Leadership Prescriptions," *Group & Organization Studies*, December 1989, pp. 446–461; W. Blank, J. R. Weitzel, and S. G. Green, "A Test of the Situational Leadership Theory," *Personnel Psychology*, Autumn 1990, pp. 579–597; and W. R. Norris and R. P. Vecchio, "Situational Leadership Theory: A Replication," *Group & Organization Management*, September 1992, pp. 331–342. **For evidence of partial support for the theory, see** R. P. Vecchio, "Situational Leadership Theory: An Examination of a Prescriptive Theory," *Journal of Applied Psychology*, August 1987, pp. 444–451; and W. R. Norris and R. P. Vecchio, "Situational Leadership Theory: A Replication," *Group & Organization Management*, September 1992, pp. 331–342. **For evidence of no support for Hersey and Blanchard, see** W. Blank, J. R. Weitzel, and S. G. Green, "A Test of the Situational Leadership Theory," *Personnel Psychology*, Autumn 1990, pp. 579–597.

28. M. G. Evans, "The Effects of Supervisory Behavior on the Path-Goal Relationship," *Organizational Behavior and Human Performance* 5, 1970, pp. 277–298; M. G. Evans, "Leadership and Motivation: A Core Concept," *Academy of Management Journal* 13, 1970, pp. 91–102; R. J. House, "A Path-Goal Theory of Leader Effectiveness," *Administrative Science Quarterly*, September 1971, pp. 321–338; R. J. House and T. R. Mitchell, "Path-Goal Theory of Leadership," *Journal of Contemporary Business*, Autumn 1974, p. 86; M. G. Evans, "Leadership," in *Organizational Behavior*, ed. S. Kerr (Columbus, OH: Grid Publishing, 1979); R. J. House, "Retrospective Comment," in *The Great Writings in Management and Organizational Behavior*, 2nd ed., ed. L. E. Boone and D. D. Bowen (New York: Random House, 1987), pp. 354–364; and M. G. Evans, "Fuhrungstheorien, Weg-ziel-theorie," in *Handworterbuch Der Fuhrung*, 2nd ed., ed. A. Kieser, G. Reber, and R. Wunderer, trans. G. Reber (Stuttgart, Germany: Schaffer Poeschal Verlag, 1995), pp. 1075–1091.

29. G. R. Jones, J. M. George, C. W. L. Hill, and N. Langton, *Contemporary Management* (Toronto: McGraw-Hill Ryerson, 2002), p. 392.

30. See J. C. Wofford and L. Z. Liska, "Path-Goal Theories of Leadership: A Meta-Analysis," *Journal of Management*, Winter 1993, pp. 857–876; M. G. Evans, "R.J. House's 'A Path-Goal Theory of Leader Effectiveness,'" *Leadership Quarterly*, Fall 1996, pp. 305–309; C. A. Schriesheim and L. L. Neider, "Path-Goal Leadership Theory: The Long and Winding Road," *Leadership Quarterly*, Fall 1996, pp. 317–321; A. Somech, "The Effects of Leadership Style and Team Process on Performance and Innovation in Functionally Heterogeneous Teams," *Journal of Management* 32, no. 1 (2006), pp. 132–157; and S. Yun, S. Faraj, and H. P. Sims, "Contingent Leadership and Effectiveness of Trauma Resuscitation Teams," *Journal of Applied Psychology* 90, no. 6 (2005), pp. 1288–1296.

31. L. R. Anderson, "Toward a Two-Track Model of Leadership Training: Suggestions from Self-Monitoring Theory," *Small Group Research*, May 1990, pp. 147–167; G. H. Dobbins, W. S. Long,

E. J. Dedrick, and T. C. Clemons, "The Role of Self-Monitoring and Gender on Leader Emergence: A Laboratory and Field Study," *Journal of Management*, September 1990, pp. 609–618; and S. J. Zaccaro, R. J. Foti, and D. A. Kenny, "Self-Monitoring and Trait-Based Variance in Leadership: An Investigation of Leader Flexibility Across Multiple Group Situations," *Journal of Applied Psychology*, April 1991, pp. 308–315.

32. S. Kerr and J. M. Jermier, "Substitutes for Leadership: Their Meaning and Measurement," *Organizational Behavior and Human Performance*, December 1978, pp. 375–403; J. P. Howell and P. W. Dorfman, "Substitutes for Leadership: Test of a Construct," *Academy of Management Journal*, December 1981, pp. 714–728; J. P. Howell, P. W. Dorfman, and S. Kerr, "Leadership and Substitutes for Leadership," *Journal of Applied Behavioral Science* 22, no. 1 (1986), pp. 29–46; J. P. Howell, D. E. Bowen, P. W. Dorfman, S. Kerr, and P. M. Podsakoff, "Substitutes for Leadership: Effective Alternatives to Ineffective Leadership," *Organizational Dynamics*, Summer 1990, pp. 21–38; P. M. Podsakoff, B. P. Niehoff, S. B. MacKenzie, and M. L. Williams, "Do Substitutes for Leadership Really Substitute for Leadership? An Empirical Examination of Kerr and Jermier's Situational Leadership Model," *Organizational Behavior and Human Decision Processes*, February 1993, pp. 1–44; P. M. Podsakoff and S. B. MacKenzie, "An Examination of Substitutes for Leadership Within a Levels-of-Analysis Framework," *Leadership Quarterly*, Fall 1995, pp. 289–328; P. M. Podsakoff, S. B. MacKenzie, and W. H. Bommer, "Transformational Leader Behaviors and Substitutes for Leadership as Determinants of Employee Satisfaction, Commitment, Trust, and Organizational Citizenship Behaviors," *Journal of Management* 22, no. 2 (1996), pp. 259–298; P. M. Podsakoff, S. B. MacKenzie, and W. H. Bommer, "Meta-Analysis of the Relationships Between Kerr and Jermier's Substitutes for Leadership and Employee Attitudes, Role Perceptions, and Performance," *Journal of Applied Psychology*, August 1996, pp. 380–399; and J. M. Jermier and S. Kerr, "'Substitutes for Leadership: Their Meaning and Measurement'—Contextual Recollections and Current Observations," *Leadership Quarterly* 8, no. 2 (1997), pp. 95–101.

33. R. T. Keller, "Transformational Leadership, Initiating Structure, and Substitutes for Leadership: A Longitudinal Study of Research and Development Project Team Performance," *Journal of Applied Psychology* 91, no. 1 (2006), pp. 202–210.

34. Vignette based on "Endless Summer," *Fortune*, April 2, 2007, pp. 63–70; and Y. Chouinard, *Let My People Go Surfing*, (New York: Penguin Books, 2005).

35. A. Bryman, "Leadership in Organizations," in *Handbook of Organization Studies*, ed. S. R. Clegg, C. Hardy, and W. R. Nord (London: Sage Publications, 1996), pp. 276–292.

36. J. M. Howell and B. J. Avolio, "The Leverage of Leadership," in *Leadership: Achieving Exceptional Performance*, A Special Supplement Prepared by the Richard Ivey School of Business, *Globe and Mail*, May 15, 1998, pp. C1, C2.

37. J. M. Howell and B. J. Avolio, "The Leverage of Leadership," in *Leadership: Achieving Exceptional Performance*, A Special Supplement Prepared by the Richard Ivey School of Business, *Globe and Mail*, May 15, 1998, pp. C1, C2.

38. J. M. Howell and B. Shamir, "The Role of Followers in the Charismatic Leadership Process: Relationships and Their Consequences," *Academy of Management Review* 30, no. 1 (2005), pp. 96–112.

39   R. N. Kanungo, "Leadership in Organizations: Looking Ahead to the 21st Century," *Canadian Psychology* 39, no. 1–2 (1998), p. 78.

40   B. M. Bass, "Leadership: Good, Better, Best," *Organizational Dynamics,* Winter 1985, pp. 26–40; and J. Seltzer and B. M. Bass, "Transformational Leadership: Beyond Initiation and Consideration," *Journal of Management,* December 1990, pp. 693–703.

41   See, for instance, J. Barling, T. Weber, and E. K. Kelloway, "Effects of Transformational Leadership Training on Attitudinal and Financial Outcomes: A Field Experiment," *Journal of Applied Psychology,* December 1996, pp. 827–832; and T. Dvir, D. Eden, and B. J. Avolio, "Impact of Transformational Leadership on Follower Development and Performance: A Field Experiment," *Academy of Management Journal,* August 2002, pp. 735–744.

42   P. C. Nutt and R. W. Backoff, "Crafting Vision," *Journal of Management Inquiry,* December 1997, p. 309.

43   P. C. Nutt and R. W. Backoff, "Crafting Vision," *Journal of Management Inquiry,* December 1997, pp. 312–314.

44   D. E. Carl and M. Javidan, "Universality of Charismatic Leadership: A Multi-Nation Study," *Academy of Management Proceedings,* 2001, pp. IM: B1–B6.

45   For an overview of this research, see T. A. Judge and R. F. Piccolo, "Transformational and Transactional Leadership: A Meta-Analytic Test of Their Relative Validity," *Journal of Applied Psychology* 89, no. 5 (October 2004), pp. 755–768.

46   J. C. Collins and J. I. Porras, *Built to Last: Successful Habits of Visionary Companies* (New York: HarperBusiness, 1994).

47   J. M. Howell and B. J. Avolio, "The Leverage of Leadership," in *Leadership: Achieving Exceptional Performance,* A Special Supplement Prepared by the Richard Ivey School of Business, *Globe and Mail,* May 15, 1998, p. C2.

48   "Building a Better Boss," *Maclean's,* September 30, 1996, p. 41.

49   H. Wang, K. S. Law, R. D. Hackett, D. Wang, and Z. X. Chen, "Leader-Member Exchange as a Mediator of the Relationship Between Transformational Leadership and Followers' Performance and Organizational Citizenship Behavior," *Academy of Management Journal* 48, no. 3 (June 2005), pp. 420–432; T. Dvir, D. Eden, B. J. Avolio, and B. Shamir, "Impact of Transformational Leadership on Follower Development and Performance: A Field Experiment," *Academy of Management Journal* 45, no. 4 (2002), pp. 735–744; R. J. House, J. Woycke, and E. M. Fodor, "Charismatic and Noncharismatic Leaders: Differences in Behavior and Effectiveness," in *Charismatic Leadership in Organizations,* ed. J. A. Conger and R. N. Kanungo (Thousand Oaks, CA: Sage, 1998), pp. 103–104; and S. A. Kirkpatrick and E. A. Locke, "Direct and Indirect Effects of Three Core Charismatic Leadership Components on Performance and Attitudes," *Journal of Applied Psychology,* February 1996, pp. 36–51.

50   Cited in B. M. Bass and B. J. Avolio, "Developing Transformational Leadership: 1992 and Beyond," *Journal of European Industrial Training,* January 1990, p. 23.

51   J. J. Hater and B. M. Bass, "Supervisors' Evaluation and Subordinates' Perceptions of Transformational and Transactional Leadership," *Journal of Applied Psychology,* November 1988, pp. 695–702.

52   G. M. Spreitzer, K. H. Perttula, and K. Xin, "Traditionality Matters: An Examination of the Effectiveness of Transformational Leadership in the United States and Taiwan," *Journal of Organizational Behavior* 26, no. 3 (2005), pp. 205–227.

53   B. M. Bass and B. J. Avolio, "Developing Transformational Leadership: 1992 and Beyond," *Journal of European Industrial Training,* January 1990, p. 23; and J. M. Howell and B. J. Avolio, "The Leverage of Leadership," in *Leadership: Achieving Exceptional Performance,* A Special Supplement Prepared by the Richard Ivey School of Business, *Globe and Mail,* May 15, 1998, pp. C1, C2.

54   T. DeGroot, D. S. Kiker, and T. C. Cross, "A Meta-Analysis to Review Organizational Outcomes Related to Charismatic Leadership," *Canadian Journal of Administrative Sciences* 17, no. 4 (2000), pp. 356–371.

55   J. A. Conger, *The Charismatic Leader: Behind the Mystique of Exceptional Leadership* (San Francisco: Jossey-Bass, 1989); R. Hogan, R. Raskin, and D. Fazzini, "The Dark Side of Charisma," in *Measures of Leadership,* ed. K. E. Clark and M. B. Clark (West Orange, NJ: Leadership Library of America, 1990); D. Sankowsky, "The Charismatic Leader as Narcissist: Understanding the Abuse of Power," *Organizational Dynamics,* Spring 1995, pp. 57–71; and J. O'Connor, M. D. Mumford, T. C. Clifton, T. L. Gessner, and M. S. Connelly, "Charismatic Leaders and Destructiveness: An Historiometric Study," *Leadership Quarterly,* Winter 1995, pp. 529–555.

56   R. Khurana, "Toward More Rational CEO Succession," *Chief Executive,* April 2003, p. 16.

57   G. Pitts, "Scandals Part of Natural Cycles of Excess," *Globe and Mail,* June 28, 2002, pp. B1, B5.

58   J. Collins, "Level 5 Leadership: The Triumph of Humility and Fierce Resolve," *Harvard Business Review,* January 2001, pp. 67–76; R. A. Minde and J. Groebel, eds., *Cooperation and Prosocial Behaviour* (Cambridge, UK: Cambridge University Press, 1991), p. 194; D. J. McAllister, "Affect- and Cognition-Based Trust as Foundations for Interpersonal Cooperation in Organizations," *Academy of Management Journal,* February 1995, p. 25; and D. M. Rousseau, S. B. Sitkin, R. S. Burt, and C. Camerer, "Not So Different After All: A Cross-Discipline View of Trust," *Academy of Management Review,* July 1998, pp. 393–404.

59   Vignette based on "Endless Summer," *Fortune,* April 2, 2007, pp. 63–70; and Y. Chouinard, *Let My People Go Surfing,* (New York: Penguin Books, 2005).

60   S. Greenhouse, "Working Life (High and Low)," *New York Times,* April 20, 2008, pp. BU1, 4.

61   See, for example, L. J. Zachary, *The Mentor's Guide: Facilitating Effective Learning Relationships* (San Francisco: Jossey-Bass, 2000); M. Murray, *Beyond the Myths and Magic of Mentoring: How to Facilitate an Effective Mentoring Process,* rev. ed. (New York: Wiley, 2001); and F. Warner, "Inside Intel's Mentoring Movement," *Fast Company,* April 2002, pp. 116–120.

62   *Mentoring: Finding a Perfect Match for People Development Briefing* (Ottawa: The Conference Board of Canada, June 2003).

63   J. A. Wilson and N. S. Elman, "Organizational Benefits of Mentoring," *Academy of Management Executive,* November 1990, p. 90; and J. Reingold, "Want to Grow as a Leader? Get a Mentor!" *Fast Company,* January 2001, pp. 58–60.

64   T. D. Allen, L. T. Eby, M. L. Poteet, E. Lentz, and L. Lima, "Career Benefits Associated With Mentoring for Protégés: A

Meta-Analysis," *Journal of Applied Psychology*, February 2004, pp. 127–136.

65   See, for example, D. A. Thomas, "The Impact of Race on Managers' Experiences of Developmental Relationships: An Intra-Organizational Study," *Journal of Organizational Behavior*, November 1990, pp. 479–492; K. E. Kram and D. T. Hall, "Mentoring in a Context of Diversity and Turbulence," in *Managing Diversity*, ed. E. E. Kossek and S. A. Lobel (Cambridge, MA: Blackwell, 1996), pp. 108–136; M. N. Ruderman and M. W. Hughes-James, "Leadership Development Across Race and Gender," in *The Center for Creative Leadership Handbook of Leadership Development*, ed. C. D. McCauley, R. S. Moxley, and E. Van Velsor (San Francisco: Jossey-Bass, 1998), pp. 291–335; and B. R. Ragins and J. L. Cotton, "Mentor Functions and Outcomes: A Comparison of Men and Women in Formal and Informal Mentoring Relationships," *Journal of Applied Psychology*, August 1999, pp. 529–550.

66   J. A. Wilson and N. S. Elman, "Organizational Benefits of Mentoring," *Academy of Management Executive*, November 1990, p. 90.

67   D. Zielinski, "Mentoring Up," *Training* 37, no. 10 (October 2000), pp. 136–141.

68   J. M. Hunt and J. R. Weintraub, "Learning Developmental Coaching," *Journal of Management Education* 28, no. 1 (February 2004), pp. 39–61.

69   J. Mills, "Subordinate Perceptions of Managerial Coaching Practices," *Proceedings*, Academy of Management, Chicago, 1986, pp. 113–116.

70   C. C. Manz and H. P. Sims Jr., *The New SuperLeadership: Leading Others to Lead Themselves* (San Francisco: Berrett-Koehler Publishers, 2001).

71   A. Bandura, "Self-Reinforcement: Theoretical and Methodological Considerations," *Behaviorism* 4, 1976, pp. 135–155; P. W. Corrigan, C. J. Wallace, and M. L. Schade, "Learning Medication Self-Management Skills in Schizophrenia; Relationships With Cognitive Deficits and Psychiatric Symptom," *Behavior Therapy*, Winter, 1994, pp. 5–15; A. S. Bellack, "A Comparison of Self-Reinforcement and Self-Monitoring in a Weight Reduction Program," *Behavior Therapy* 7, 1976, pp. 68–75; T. A. Eckman, W. C. Wirshing, and S. R. Marder, "Technique for Training Schizophrenic Patients in Illness Self-Management: A Controlled Trial," *American Journal of Psychiatry* 149, 1992, pp. 1549–1555; J. J. Felixbrod and K. D. O'Leary, "Effect of Reinforcement on Children's Academic Behavior as a Function of Self-Determined and Externally Imposed Contingencies," *Journal of Applied Behavior Analysis* 6, 1973, pp. 141–150; A. J. Litrownik, L. R. Franzini, and D. Skenderian, "The Effects of Locus of Reinforcement Control on a Concept Identification Task," *Psychological Reports* 39, 1976, pp. 159–165; P. D. McGorry, "Psychoeducation in First-Episode Psychosis: A Therapeutic Process," *Psychiatry*, November, 1995, pp. 313–328; G. S. Parcel, P. R. Swank, and M. J. Mariotto, "Self-Management of Cystic Fibrosis: A Structural Model for Educational and Behavioral Variables," *Social Science and Medicine* 38, 1994, pp. 1307–1315; G. E. Speidel, "Motivating Effect of Contingent Self-Reward," *Journal of Experimental Psychology* 102, 1974, pp. 528–530.

72   D. B. Jeffrey, "A Comparison of the Effects of External Control and Self-Control on the Modification and Maintenance of Weight," *Journal of Abnormal Psychology* 83, 1974, pp. 404–410.

73   C. C. Manz and H. P. Sims Jr., *The New SuperLeadership: Leading Others to Lead Themselves* (San Francisco: Berrett-Koehler, 2001).

74   J. Kelly and S. Nadler, "Leading From Below," *Wall Street Journal*, March 3, 2007, pp. R4, R10.

75   See, for instance, J. H. Zenger, E. Musselwhite, K. Hurson, and C. Perrin, *Leading Teams: Mastering the New Role* (Homewood, IL: Business One Irwin, 1994); and M. Frohman, "Nothing Kills Teams Like Ill-Prepared Leaders," *IndustryWeek*, October 2, 1995, pp. 72–76.

76   M. Frohman, "Nothing Kills Teams Like Ill-Prepared Leaders," *IndustryWeek*, October 2, 1995, p. 93.

77   M. Frohman, "Nothing Kills Teams Like Ill-Prepared Leaders," *IndustryWeek*, October 2, 1995, p. 100.

78   J. R. Katzenbach and D. K. Smith, *The Wisdom of Teams: Creating the High-Performance Organization* (Boston, MA: Harvard Business School, 1993).

79   N. Steckler and N. Fondas, "Building Team Leader Effectiveness: A Diagnostic Tool," *Organizational Dynamics*, Winter 1995, p. 20.

80   R. S. Wellins, W. C. Byham, and G. R. Dixon, *Inside Teams* (San Francisco: Jossey-Bass, 1994), p. 318.

81   N. Steckler and N. Fondas, "Building Team Leader Effectiveness: A Diagnostic Tool," *Organizational Dynamics*, Winter 1995, p. 21.

82   B. J. Avolio, S. Kahai, and G. E. Dodge, "E-Leadership: Implications for Theory, Research, and Practice," *Leadership Quarterly*, Winter 2000, pp. 615–668; and B. J. Avolio and S. S. Kahai, "Adding the 'E' to E-Leadership: How It May Impact Your Leadership," *Organizational Dynamics* 31, no. 4 (2003), 325–338.

83   J. Howell and K. Hall-Merenda, "Leading From a Distance," in *Leadership: Achieving Exceptional Performance*, A Special Supplement Prepared by the Richard Ivey School of Business, *Globe and Mail*, May 15, 1998, pp. C1, C2.

84   S. J. Zaccaro and P. Bader, "E-Leadership and the Challenges of Leading E-Teams: Minimizing the Bad and Maximizing the Good," *Organizational Dynamics* 31, no. 4 (2003), pp. 381–385.

85   C. E. Naquin and G. D. Paulson, "Online Bargaining and Interpersonal Trust," *Journal of Applied Psychology*, February 2003, pp. 113–120.

86   B. Shamir, "Leadership in Boundaryless Organizations: Disposable or Indispensable?" *European Journal of Work and Organizational Psychology* 8, no. 1 (1999), pp. 49–71.

87   R. M. Kanter, *The Change Masters: Innovation and Entrepreneurship in the American Corporation* (New York: Simon and Schuster, 1983).

88   R. A. Heifetz, *Leadership Without Easy Answers* (Cambridge, MA: Harvard University Press, 1996), p. 205.

89   R. A. Heifetz, *Leadership Without Easy Answers* (Cambridge, MA: Harvard University Press, 1996), p. 205.

90   R. A. Heifetz, *Leadership Without Easy Answers* (Cambridge, MA: Harvard University Press, 1996), p. 188.

91   Vignette based on S. Casey, "Patagonia: Blueprint for Green Business," *Fortune*, May 29, 2007; and Y. Chouinard, *Let My People Go Surfing*, (New York: Penguin Books, 2005).

92   R. Ilies, F. P. Morgeson, and J. D. Nahrgang, "Authentic Leadership and Eudaemonic Wellbeing: Understanding Leader-Follower Outcomes," *Leadership Quarterly* 16, 2005, pp. 373–394.

93   This section is based on E. P. Hollander, "Ethical Challenges in the Leader–Follower Relationship," *Business Ethics Quarterly*, January 1995, pp. 55–65; J. C. Rost, "Leadership: A Discussion About Ethics," *Business Ethics Quarterly*, January 1995, pp. 129–142; L. K. Treviño, M. Brown, and L. P. Hartman, "A Qualitative Investigation of Perceived Executive Ethical Leadership: Perceptions From Inside and Outside the Executive Suite," *Human Relations*, January 2003, pp. 5–37; and R. M. Fulmer, "The Challenge of Ethical Leadership," *Organizational Dynamics* 33, no. 3 (2004), pp. 307–317.

94   J. M. Burns, *Leadership* (New York: Harper & Row, 1978).

95   J. M. Howell and B. J. Avolio, "The Ethics of Charismatic Leadership: Submission or Liberation?" *Academy of Management Executive*, May 1992, pp. 43–55.

96   M. E. Brown and L. K. Treviño, "Socialized Charismatic Leadership, Values Congruence, and Deviance in Work Groups," *Journal of Applied Psychology* 91, no. 4 (2006), pp. 954–962.

97   J. G. Clawson, *Level Three Leadership* (Upper Saddle River, NJ: Prentice Hall, 1999), pp. 46–49.

98   The material in this section is based on J. Cliff, N. Langton, and H. Aldrich, "Walking The Talk? Gendered Rhetoric vs. Action in Small Firms," *Organizational Studies* 26, no. 1 (2005), pp. 63–91; S. Helgesen, *The Female Advantage: Women's Ways of Leadership* (New York: Doubleday, 1990); A. H. Eagly and B. T. Johnson, "Gender and Leadership Style: A Meta-Analysis," *Psychological Bulletin*, September 1990, pp. 233–256; A. H. Eagly and S. J. Karau, "Gender and the Emergence of Leaders: A Meta-Analysis," *Journal of Personality and Social Psychology*, May 1991, pp. 685–710; J. B. Rosener, "Ways Women Lead," *Harvard Business Review*, November–December 1990, pp. 119–125; A. H. Eagly, M. G. Makhijani, and B. G. Klonsky, "Gender and the Evaluation of Leaders: A Meta-Analysis," *Psychological Bulletin*, January 1992, pp. 3–22; A. H. Eagly, S. J. Karau, and B. T. Johnson, "Gender and Leadership Style Among School Principals: A Meta-Analysis," *Educational Administration Quarterly*, February 1992, pp. 76–102; L. R. Offermann and C. Beil, "Achievement Styles of Women Leaders and Their Peers," *Psychology of Women Quarterly*, March 1992, pp. 37–56; R. L. Kent and S. E. Moss, "Effects of Size and Gender Role on Leader Emergence," *Academy of Management Journal*, October 1994, pp. 1335–1346; C. Lee, "The Feminization of Management," *Training*, November 1994, pp. 25–31; H. Collingwood, "Women as Managers: Not Just Different: Better," *Working Woman*, November 1995, p. 14; J. B. Rosener, *America's Competitive Secret: Women Managers* (New York: Oxford University Press, 1995).

99   B. Orser, *Creating High Performance Organizations: Leveraging Women's Leadership* (Ottawa: The Conference Board of Canada, 2000).

100   J. M. Norvilitis and H. M. Reid, "Evidence for an Association Between Gender-Role Identity and a Measure of Executive Function," *Psychological Reports*, February 2002, pp. 35–45; W. H. Decker and D. M. Rotondo, "Relationships Among Gender, Type of Humor, and Perceived Leader Effectiveness," *Journal of Managerial Issues*, Winter 2001, pp. 450–465; H. Aguinis and S. K. R. Adams, "Social-Role Versus Structural Models of Gender and Influence Use in Organizations: A Strong Inference Approach," *Group & Organization Management*, December 1998, pp. 414–446; and A. H. Eagly, S. J. Karau, and M. G. Makhijani, "Gender and the Effectiveness of Leaders: A Meta-Analysis," *Psychological Bulletin* 117, 1995, pp. 125–145.

101   A. H. Eagly, M. C. Johannesen-Schmidt, and M. L. van Engen, "Transformational, Transactional, and Laissez-Faire Leadership Styles: A Meta-Analysis Comparing Women and Men," *Psychological Bulletin* 129, no. 4 (July 2003), pp. 569–591; K. M. Bartol, D. C. Martin, and J. A. Kromkowski, "Leadership and the Glass Ceiling: Gender and Ethnic Influences on Leader Behaviors at Middle and Executive Managerial Levels," *Journal of Leadership & Organizational Studies*, Winter 2003, pp. 8–19; and R. Sharpe, "As Leaders, Women Rule," *BusinessWeek*, November 20, 2000, pp. 74–84.

102   K. M. Bartol, D. C. Martin, and J. A. Kromkowski, "Leadership and the Glass Ceiling: Gender and Ethnic Influences on Leader Behaviors at Middle and Executive Managerial Levels," *Journal of Leadership & Organizational Studies*, Winter 2003, pp. 8–19.

103   Based on R. D. Arvey, Z. Zhang, and B. J. Avolio, "Developmental and Genetic Determinants of Leadership Role Occupancy Among Women," *Journal of Applied Psychology*, May 2007, pp. 693–706.

104   M. Pandya, "Warren Buffett on Investing and Leadership: I'm Wired for This Game," *Wharton Leadership Digest* 3, no. 7 (April 1999), http://leadership.wharton.upenn.edu/digest/04-99.shtml (accessed August 19, 2009).

105   M. Castaneda, T. A. Kolenko, and R. J. Aldag, "Self-Management Perceptions and Practices: A Structural Equations Analysis," *Journal of Organizational Behavior* 20, 1999. Table 4, pp. 114–115. Copyright © John Wiley & Sons, Inc. Reproduced with permission.

106   This exercise is based on J. M. Howell and P. J. Frost, "A Laboratory Study of Charismatic Leadership," *Organizational Behavior and Human Decision Processes*, April 1989, pp. 243–269.

107   Based on C. E. Johnson, *Meeting the Ethical Challenges in Leadership* (Thousand Oaks, CA: Sage, 2001), pp. 4–5.

108   Based on J. Hollon, "Leading Well Is Simple," *Workforce Management*, November 6, 2006, p. 50; A. Pomeroy, "CEOs Show Sensitive Side," *HR Magazine*, August 2006, p. 14; P. Bacon, Jr., "Barack Obama," *Time*, April 18, 2005, p. 60–61; J. Marquez, "Kindness Pays... Or Does It?" *Workforce Management*, June 25, 2007, pp. 40–41; and C. Woodyard, "Press: 'I Was in Love with Cars Every Second,'" *USA Today*, January 23, 2006, p. 5B.

109   Based on "Leadership at Kluster," Organizational Behavior Video Library, 2008. Copyrighted by Prentice-Hall.

110   Based on J. M. Howell and P. J. Frost, "A Laboratory Study of Charismatic Leadership," *Organizational Behavior and Human Decision Processes*, April 1989, pp. 243–269.

Chapter 9

1   Opening vignette based on G. Pitts, "The Testing of Michael McCain," *Report on Business Magazine*, November 2008, p. 60ff.

2   W. Pounds, "The Process of Problem Finding," *Industrial Management Review*, Fall 1969, pp. 1–19.

3   See H. A. Simon, "Rationality in Psychology and Economics," *Journal of Business*, October 1986, pp. 209–224; and A. Langley,

"In Search of Rationality: The Purposes Behind the Use of Formal Analysis in Organizations," *Administrative Science Quarterly*, December 1989, pp. 598–631.

4   For a review of the rational model, see E. F. Harrison, *The Managerial Decision Making Process*, 5th ed. (Boston: Houghton Mifflin, 1999), pp. 75–102.

5   T. Barry, "Smart Cookies: Why CIBC Said Yes to the Girl Guides," *Marketing Magazine*, May 31, 1999, pp. 11, 14.

6   J. G. March, *A Primer on Decision Making* (New York: Free Press, 1994), pp. 2–7.

7   Based on G. Pitts, "The Testing of Michael McCain," *Report on Business Magazine*, November 2008, p. 60ff.

8   D. L. Rados, "Selection and Evaluation of Alternatives in Repetitive Decision Making," *Administrative Science Quarterly*, June 1972, pp. 196–206.

9   M. Bazerman, *Judgment in Managerial Decision Making*, 3rd ed. (New York: Wiley, 1994), p. 5.

10 J. E. Russo, K. A. Carlson, and M. G. Meloy, "Choosing an Inferior Alternative," *Psychological Science* 17, no. 10 (2006), pp. 899–904.

11 See, for instance, L. R. Beach, *The Psychology of Decision Making* (Thousand Oaks, CA: Sage, 1997).

12 See, for example, M. D. Cohen, J. G. March, and J. P. Olsen, "A Garbage Can Model of Organizational Choice," *Administrative Science Quarterly*, March 1972, pp. 1–25.

13 See J. G. Thompson, *Organizations in Action* (New York: McGraw-Hill, 1967), p. 123.

14 See H. A. Simon, *Administrative Behavior*, 4th ed. (New York: Free Press, 1997); and M. Augier, "Simon Says: Bounded Rationality Matters," *Journal of Management Inquiry*, September 2001, pp. 268–275. Individuals may also be constrained by time, which makes them focus their deliberations on fewer aspects of alternatives. For further discussion of this point, see J. W. Payne, J. R. Bettman, and E. J. Johnson, "Behavioral Decision Research: A Constructive Processing Perspective," *Annual Review of Psychology* 43, no. 1 (1992), pp. 87–131.

15 *OB in the Workplace* based on K. May, "Ottawa May Stop Hiring Best Qualified," *National Post*, March 4, 2002, p. A4.

16 See T. Gilovich, D. Griffin, and D. Kahneman, *Heuristics and Biases: The Psychology of Intuitive Judgment* (New York: Cambridge University Press, 2002).

17 E. Dane and M. G. Pratt, "Exploring Intuition and Its Role in Managerial Decision Making," *Academy of Management Review* 32, no. 1 (2007), pp. 33–54.

18 As described in H. A. Simon, "Making Management Decisions: The Role of Intuition and Emotion," *Academy of Management Executive*, February 1987, pp. 59–60.

19 N. Khatri and H. A. Ng, "The Role of Intuition in Strategic Decision Making," *Human Relations*, January 2000, pp. 57–86; J. A. Andersen, "Intuition in Managers: Are Intuitive Managers More Effective?" *Journal of Managerial Psychology* 15, no. 1–2 (2000), pp. 46–63; D. Myers, *Intuition: Its Powers and Perils* (New Haven, CT: Yale University Press, 2002); and L. Simpson, "Basic Instincts," *Training*, January 2003, pp. 56–59.

20 See, for instance, L. A. Burke and M. K. Miller, "Taking the Mystery Out of Intuitive Decision Making," *Academy of Management Executive*, November 1999, pp. 91–99.

21 L. A. Burke and M. K. Miller, "Taking the Mystery Out of Intuitive Decision Making," *Academy of Management Executive*, November 1999, pp. 91–99.

22 S. P. Robbins, *Decide & Conquer: Making Winning Decisions and Taking Control of Your Life* (Upper Saddle River, NJ: Financial Times/Prentice Hall, 2004), p. 13.

23 Based on P. Cohen, "Stand Still: Use Penalty-Kick Wisdom to Make Your Decisions," *National Post*, March 8, 2008, p. FW9.

24 S. Plous, *The Psychology of Judgment and Decision Making* (New York: McGraw-Hill, 1993), p. 217.

25 S. Lichtenstein and B. Fischhoff, "Do Those Who Know More Also Know More About How Much They Know?" *Organizational Behavior and Human Performance*, December 1977, pp. 159–183.

26 B. Fischhoff, P. Slovic, and S. Lichtenstein, "Knowing With Certainty: The Appropriateness of Extreme Confidence," *Journal of Experimental Psychology: Human Perception and Performance*, November 1977, pp. 552–564.

27 J. Kruger and D. Dunning, "Unskilled and Unaware of It: How Difficulties in Recognizing One's Own Incompetence Lead to Inflated Self-Assessments," *Journal of Personality and Social Psychology*, November 1999, pp. 1121–1134.

28 B. Fischhoff, P. Slovic, and S. Lichtenstein, "Knowing with Certainty: The Appropriateness of Extreme Confidence," *Journal of Experimental Psychology* 3 (1977), pp. 552–564.

29 J. Kruger and D. Dunning, "Unskilled and Unaware of It: How Difficulties in Recognizing One's Own Incompetence Lead to Inflated Self-Assessments," *Journal of Personality and Social Psychology*, November 1999, pp. 1121–1134.

30 See, for instance, A. Tversky and D. Kahneman, "Judgment Under Uncertainty: Heuristics and Biases," *Science*, September 1974, pp. 1124–1131.

31 J. S. Hammond, R. L. Keeney, and H. Raiffa, *Smart Choices* (Boston: HBS Press, 1999), p. 191.

32 R. Hastie, D. A. Schkade, and J. W. Payne, "Juror Judgments in Civil Cases: Effects of Plaintiff's Requests and Plaintiff's Identity on Punitive Damage Awards," *Law and Human Behavior*, August 1999, pp. 445–470.

33 See R. S. Nickerson, "Confirmation Bias: A Ubiquitous Phenomenon in Many Guises," *Review of General Psychology*, June 1998, pp. 175–220; and E. Jonas, S. Schultz-Hardt, D. Frey, and N. Thelen, "Confirmation Bias in Sequential Information Search After Preliminary Decisions," *Journal of Personality and Social Psychology*, April 2001, pp. 557–571.

34 See B. M. Staw, "The Escalation of Commitment to a Course of Action," *Academy of Management Review*, October 1981, pp. 577–587; and H. Moon, "Looking Forward and Looking Back: Integrating Completion and Sunk-Cost Effects Within an Escalation-of-Commitment Progress Decision," *Journal of Applied Psychology*, February 2001, pp. 104–113.

35 See, for instance, A. James and A. Wells, "Death Beliefs, Superstitious Beliefs and Health Anxiety," *British Journal of Clinical Psychology*, March 2002, pp. 43–53.

36 R. L. Guilbault, F. B. Bryant, J. H. Brockway, and E. J. Posavac, "A Meta-Analysis of Research on Hindsight Bias," *Basic and Applied Social Psychology*, September 2004, pp. 103–117; and L. Werth, F. Strack, and J. Foerster, "Certainty and Uncertainty: The Two Faces of the Hindsight Bias," *Organizational Behavior and Human Decision Processes*, March 2002, pp. 323–341.

37 M. Gladwell, "Connecting the Dots," *New Yorker*, March 10, 2003.

38 S. P. Robbins, *Decide & Conquer: Making Winning Decisions and Taking Control of Your Life* (Upper Saddle River, NJ: Financial Times/ Prentice Hall, 2004), pp. 164–168.

39 See N. R. F. Maier, "Assets and Liabilities in Group Problem Solving: The Need for an Integrative Function," *Psychological Review*, April 1967, pp. 239–249; G. W. Hill, "Group Versus Individual Performance: Are N+1 Heads Better Than One?" *Psychological Bulletin*, May 1982, pp. 517–539; and A. E. Schwartz and J. Levin, "Better Group Decision Making," *Supervisory Management*, June 1990, p. 4.

40 See, for example, R. A. Cooke and J. A. Kernaghan, "Estimating the Difference Between Group Versus Individual Performance on Problem-Solving Tasks," *Group & Organization Studies*, September 1987, pp. 319–342; and L. K. Michaelsen, W. E. Watson, and R. H. Black, "A Realistic Test of Individual Versus Group Consensus Decision Making," *Journal of Applied Psychology*, October 1989, pp. 834–839.

41 See, for example, W. C. Swap and Associates, *Group Decision Making* (Newbury Park, CA: Sage, 1984).

42 D. Gigone and R. Hastie "Proper Analysis of the Accuracy of Group Judgments," *Psychological Bulletin*, 121(1), January 1997, pp. 149–167; and B. L. Bonner, S. D. Sillito, and M. R. Baumann, "Collective Estimation: Accuracy, Expertise, and Extroversion as Sources of Intra-Group Influence," *Organizational Behavior and Human Decision Processes* 103, 2007, pp. 121–133.

43 See, for example, W. C. Swap and Associates, *Group Decision Making* (Newbury Park, CA: Sage, 1984).

44 I. L. Janis, *Groupthink* (Boston: Houghton Mifflin, 1982); W. Park, "A Review of Research on Groupthink," *Journal of Behavioral Decision Making*, July 1990, pp. 229–245; C. P. Neck and G. Moorhead, "Groupthink Remodeled: The Importance of Leadership, Time Pressure, and Methodical Decision Making Procedures," *Human Relations*, May 1995, pp. 537–558; and J. N. Choi and M. U. Kim, "The Organizational Application of Groupthink and Its Limits in Organizations," *Journal of Applied Psychology*, April 1999, pp. 297–306.

45 Based on I. L. Janis, *Groupthink: Psychological Studies of Policy Decisions and Fiascoes*, 2nd ed. (Boston: Houghton Mifflin, 1982), p. 244.

46 K. Hays, "Judge Dismisses Enron Convictions," *Houston (Texas) Chronicle*, February 1, 2007.

47 M. E. Turner and A. R. Pratkanis, "Mitigating Groupthink by Stimulating Constructive Conflict," in *Using Conflict in Organizations*, ed. C. De Dreu and E. Van de Vliert (London: Sage, 1997), pp. 53–71.

48 See N. R. F. Maier, *Principles of Human Relations* (New York: John Wiley, 1952); I. L. Janis, *Groupthink: Psychological Studies of Policy Decisions and Fiascoes*, 2nd ed. (Boston: Houghton Mifflin, 1982); and C. R. Leana, "A Partial Test of Janis' Groupthink Model: Effects of Group Cohesiveness and Leader Behavior on Defective Decision Making," *Journal of Management*, Spring 1985, pp. 5–17.

49 J. N. Choi and M. U. Kim, "The Organizational Application of Groupthink and Its Limitations in Organizations," *Journal of Applied Psychology* 84, 1999, pp. 297–306.

50 J. Longley and D. G. Pruitt, "Groupthink: A Critique of Janis' Theory," in *Review of Personality and Social Psychology*, ed. L. Wheeler (Newbury Park, CA: Sage, 1980), pp. 507–513; and J. A. Sniezek, "Groups Under Uncertainty: An Examination of Confidence in Group Decision Making," *Organizational Behavior and Human Decision Processes* 52, 1992, pp. 124–155.

51 C. McCauley, "The Nature of Social Influence in Groupthink: Compliance and Internalization," *Journal of Personality and Social Psychology* 57, 1989, pp. 250–260; P. E. Tetlock, R. S. Peterson, C. McGuire, S. Chang, and P. Feld, "Assessing Political Group Dynamics: A Test of the Groupthink Model," *Journal of Personality and Social Psychology* 63, 1992, pp. 781–796; S. Graham, "A Review of Attribution Theory in Achievement Contexts," *Educational Psychology Review* 3, 1991, pp. 5–39; and G. Moorhead and J. R. Montanari, "An Empirical Investigation of the Groupthink Phenomenon," *Human Relations* 39, 1986, pp. 399–410.

52 J. N. Choi and M. U. Kim, "The Organizational Application of Groupthink and Its Limitations in Organizations," *Journal of Applied Psychology* 84, 1999, pp. 297–306.

53 See D. J. Isenberg, "Group Polarization: A Critical Review and Meta-Analysis," *Journal of Personality and Social Psychology*, December 1986, pp. 1141–1151; J. L. Hale and F. J. Boster, "Comparing Effect Coded Models of Choice Shifts," *Communication Research Reports*, April 1988, pp. 180–186; and P. W. Paese, M. Bieser, and M. E. Tubbs, "Framing Effects and Choice Shifts in Group Decision Making," *Organizational Behavior and Human Decision Processes*, October 1993, pp. 149–165.

54 See, for example, N. Kogan, and M. A. Wallach, "Risk Taking as a Function of the Situation, the Person, and the Group," in *New Directions in Psychology*, vol. 3 (New York: Holt, Rinehart and Winston, 1967); and M. A. Wallach, N. Kogan, and D. J. Bem, "Group Influence on Individual Risk Taking," *Journal of Abnormal and Social Psychology* 65, 1962, pp. 75–86.

55 R. D. Clark III, "Group-Induced Shift Toward Risk: A Critical Appraisal," *Psychological Bulletin*, October 1971, pp. 251–270.

56 A. F. Osborn, *Applied Imagination: Principles and Procedures of Creative Thinking* (New York: Scribner's, 1941). See also P. B. Paulus, M. T. Dzindolet, G. Poletes, and L. M. Camacho, "Perception of Performance in Group Brainstorming: The Illusion of Group Productivity," *Personality and Social Psychology Bulletin*, February 1993, pp. 78–89.

57 I. Edwards, "Office Intrigue: By Design, Consultants Have Workers Conspire to Create Business Environments Tailored to Getting the Job Done," *Financial Post Daily*, December 16, 1997, p. 25.

58 N. L. Kerr and R. S. Tindale, "Group Performance and Decision-Making," *Annual Review of Psychology* 55 (2004), pp. 623–655.

59 See A. L. Delbecq, A. H. Van deVen, and D. H. Gustafson, *Group Techniques for Program Planning: A Guide to Nominal and Delphi Processes* (Glenview, IL: Scott, Foresman, 1975); and W. M. Fox, "Anonymity and Other Keys to Successful Problem-Solving Meetings," *National Productivity Review*, Spring 1989, pp. 145–156.

60 E. F. Rietzschel, B. A. Nijstad, and W. Stroebe, "Productivity Is Not Enough: A Comparison of Interactive and Nominal

Brainstorming Groups on Idea Generation and Selection," *Journal of Experimental Social Psychology* 42, no. 2 (2006), pp. 244–251.

61 C. Faure, "Beyond Brainstorming: Effects of Different Group Procedures on Selection of Ideas and Satisfaction With the Process," *Journal of Creative Behavior* 38 (2004), pp. 13–34.

62 See, for instance, A. R. Dennis and J. S. Valacich, "Computer Brainstorms: More Heads Are Better Than One," *Journal of Applied Psychology*, August 1993, pp. 531–537; R. B. Gallupe and W. H. Cooper, "Brainstorming Electronically," *Sloan Management Review*, Fall 1993, pp. 27–36; and A. B. Hollingshead and J. E. McGrath, "Computer-Assisted Groups: A Critical Review of the Empirical Research," in *Team Effectiveness and Decision Making in Organizations*, ed. R. A. Guzzo and E. Salas (San Francisco: Jossey-Bass, 1995), pp. 46–78.

63 B. B. Baltes, M. W. Dickson, M. P. Sherman, C. C. Bauer, and J. LaGanke, "Computer-Mediated Communication and Group Decision Making: A Meta-Analysis," *Organizational Behavior and Human Decision Processes*, January 2002, pp. 156–179.

64 T. M. Amabile, "A Model of Creativity and Innovation in Organizations," in *Research in Organizational Behavior*, vol. 10, ed. B. M. Staw and L. L. Cummings (Greenwich, CT: JAI Press, 1988), p. 126; and J. E. Perry-Smith and C. E. Shalley, "The Social Side of Creativity: A Static and Dynamic Social Network Perspective," *Academy of Management Review*, January 2003, pp. 89–106.

65 G. J. Feist and F. X. Barron, "Predicting Creativity from Early to Late Adulthood: Intellect, Potential, and Personality," *Journal of Research in Personality*, April 2003, pp. 62–88.

66 R. W. Woodman, J. E. Sawyer, and R. W. Griffin, "Toward a Theory of Organizational Creativity," *Academy of Management Review*, April 1993, p. 298; J. M. George and J. Zhou, "When Openness to Experience and Conscientiousness Are Related to Creative Behavior: An Interactional Approach," *Journal of Applied Psychology*, June 2001, pp. 513–524; and E. F. Rietzschel, C. K. W. de Dreu, and B. A. Nijstad, "Personal Need for Structure and Creative Performance: The Moderating Influence of Fear of Invalidity," *Personality and Social Psychology Bulletin*, June 2007, pp. 855–866.

67 Cited in C. G. Morris, *Psychology: An Introduction*, 9th ed. (Upper Saddle River, NJ: Prentice Hall, 1996), p. 344.

68 This section is based on T. M. Amabile, "Motivating Creativity in Organizations: On Doing What You Love and Loving What You Do," *California Management Review* 40, no. 1 (Fall 1997), pp. 39–58.

69 A. M. Isen, "Positive Affect," in *Handbook of Cognition and Emotion*, ed. T. Dalgleish and M. J. Power (New York: Wiley, 1999), pp. 521–539.

70 J. Zhou, "When the Presence of Creative Coworkers Is Related to Creativity: Role of Supervisor Close Monitoring, Developmental Feedback, and Creative Personality," *Journal of Applied Psychology* 88, no. 3 (June 2003), pp. 413–422.

71 J. E. Perry-Smith, "Social Yet Creative: The Role of Social Relationships in Facilitating Individual Creativity," *Academy of Management Journal* 49, no. 1 (2006), pp. 85–101.

72 W. J. J. Gordon, *Synectics* (New York: Harper & Row, 1961).

73 See T. M. Amabile, *KEYS: Assessing the Climate for Creativity* (Greensboro, NC: Center for Creative Leadership, 1995);

N. Madjar, G. R. Oldham, and M. G. Pratt, "There's No Place Like Home? The Contributions of Work and Nonwork Creativity Support to Employees' Creative Performance," *Academy of Management Journal*, August 2002, pp. 757–767; and C. E. Shalley, J. Zhou, and G. R. Oldham, "The Effects of Personal and Contextual Characteristics on Creativity: Where Should We Go from Here?" *Journal of Management*, November 2004, pp. 933–958.

74 M. Amabile, "How to Kill Creativity," *Harvard Business Review*, September–October 1998, pp. 76–87; H.-S. Choi and L. Thompson, "Old Wine in a New Bottle: Impact of Membership Change on Group Creativity," *Organizational Behavior and Human Decision Processes* 98, no. 2 (2005), pp. 121–132; R. Florida and J. Goodnight, "Managing for Creativity," *Harvard Business Review* 83, no. 7 (2005), pp. 124+; L. L. Gilson, J. E. Mathieu, C. E. Shalley, and T. R. Ruddy, "Creativity and Standardization: Complementary or Conflicting Drivers of Team Effectiveness?" *Academy of Management Journal* 48, no. 3 (2005), pp. 521–531; and K. G. Smith, C. J. Collins, and K. D. Clark, "Existing Knowledge, Knowledge Creation Capability, and the Rate of New Product Introduction in High-Technology Firms," *Academy of Management Journal* 48, no. 2 (2005), pp. 346–357.

75 Cited in T. Stevens, "Creativity Killers," *IndustryWeek*, January 23, 1995, p. 63.

76 M. Strauss, "Retailers Tap into War-Room Creativity of Employees," *Globe and Mail*, March 12, 2007, p. B1.

77 Based on G. Pitts, "The Testing of Michael McCain," *Report on Business Magazine*, November 2008, p. 60ff.

78 G. F. Cavanagh, D. J. Moberg, and M. Valasquez, "The Ethics of Organizational Politics," *Academy of Management Journal*, June 1981, pp. 363–374.

79 P. L. Schumann, "A Moral Principles Framework for Human Resource Management Ethics," *Human Resource Management Review* 11, Spring–Summer 2001, pp. 93–111.

80 See, for instance, R. S. Dillon, "Care and Respect," in *Explorations in Feminist Ethics: Theory and Practice*, ed. E. Browning Cole and S. Coultrap-McQuin (Bloomington, IN: Indiana University Press, 1992), pp. 69–81; C. Gilligan, *In a Different Voice: Psychological Theory and Women's Development* (Cambridge, MA: Harvard University Press, 1982); and M. C. Raugust, "Feminist Ethics and Workplace Values," in *Explorations in Feminist Ethics: Theory and Practice*, ed. E. Browning Cole and S. Coultrap-McQuin (Bloomington, IN: Indiana University Press, 1992), pp. 69–81.

81 P. L. Schumann, "A Moral Principles Framework for Human Resource Management Ethics," *Human Resource Management Review* 11, Spring–Summer 2001, pp. 93–111.

82 S. Jaffee and J. Hyde, "Gender Differences in Moral Orientation: A Meta-Analysis," *Psychological Bulletin*, September 2000, pp. 703–726.

83 See, for example, T. Machan, ed., *Commerce and Morality* (Totowa, NJ: Rowman and Littlefield, 1988).

84 L. K. Trevino, "Ethical Decision Making in Organizations: A Person-Situation Interactionist Model," *Academy of Management Review*, July 1986, pp. 601–617; and L. K. Trevino and S. A. Youngblood, "Bad Apples in Bad Barrels: A Causal Analysis of Ethical Decision Making Behavior," *Journal of Applied Psychology*, August 1990, pp. 378–385.

85   See L. Kohlberg, *Essays in Moral Development: The Philosophy of Moral Development*, vol. 1 (New York: Harper & Row, 1981); L. Kohlberg, *Essays in Moral Development: The Psychology of Moral Development*, vol. 2 (New York: Harper & Row, 1984); and R. S. Snell, "Complementing Kohlberg: Mapping the Ethical Reasoning Used by Managers for Their Own Dilemma Cases," *Human Relations*, January 1996, pp. 23–50.

86   L. Kohlberg, *Essays in Moral Development: The Philosophy of Moral Development*, vol. 1 (New York: Harper & Row, 1981); L. Kohlberg, *Essays in Moral Development: The Philosophy of Moral Development*, vol. 2 (New York: Harper & Row, 1984); and R. S. Snell, "Complementing Kohlberg: Mapping the Ethical Reasoning Used by Managers for Their Own Dilemma Cases," *Human Relations*, January 1996, pp. 23–49.

87   J. Weber, "Managers' Moral Reasoning: Assessing Their Responses to Three Moral Dilemmas," *Human Relations*, July 1990, pp. 687–702; and S. B. Knouse and R. A. Giacalone, "Ethical Decision-Making in Business: Behavioral Issues and Concerns," *Journal of Business Ethics*, May 1992, pp. 369–377.

88   D. Todd, "Business Responds to Ethics Explosion," *Vancouver Sun*, April 27, 1998, pp. A1, A7.

89   L. Bogomolny, "Good Housekeeping," *Canadian Business*, March 1, 2004, pp. 87–88; and L. Ramsay, "A Matter of Principle," *Financial Post* (*National Post*), February 26, 1999, p. C18.

90   M. McCann, "Despite Costs, There Are Profits in Ethically Produced Products," *Telegraph-Journal*, May 30, 2008, p. B4.

91   "Ethics Programs Aren't Stemming Employee Misconduct," *Wall Street Journal*, May 11, 2000, p. A1.

92   L. Bogomolny, "Good Housekeeping," *Canadian Business*, March 1, 2004, pp. 87–88.

93   Based on W. E. Stead, D. L. Worrell, and J. G. Stead, "An Integrative Model for Understanding and Managing Ethical Behavior in Business Organizations," *Journal of Business Ethics* 9, no. 3 (March 1990), pp. 233–242.

94   D. Todd, "Ethics Audit: Credit Union Reveals All," *Vancouver Sun*, October 19, 1998, p. A5.

95   "Corporate Culture," *Canadian HR Reporter* 17, no. 21 (December 6, 2004), pp. 7–11.

96   W. Chow Hou, "To Bribe or Not to Bribe?" *Asia, Inc.*, October 1996, p. 104; and T. Jackson, "Cultural Values and Management Ethics: A 10-Nation Study," *Human Relations*, October 2001, pp. 1267–1302.

97   T. Donaldson, "Values in Tension: Ethics Away from Home," *Harvard Business Review*, September–October 1996, pp. 48–62.

98   P. Digh, "Shades of Gray in the Global Marketplace," *HR Magazine*, April 1997, pp. 91–98.

99   McWilliams and Davies quotations from A. Gillis, "How Can You Do Business in a Country Where Crooked Cops Will Kill You for a Song?" *Report on Business Magazine*, March 1998, p. 60.

100   N. Roland, "U.K., Japan and Canada Failing to Crack Down on Foreign Bribes, Says Watchdog Group," *Financial Week*, June 25, 2008, www.financialweek.com/apps/pbcs.dll/article?AID=/20080625/REG/814229098/1036 (accessed August 20, 2009).

101   Vignette based on G. Pitts, "The Testing of Michael McCain," *Report on Business Magazine*, November 2008, p. 60ff; and K. Owram, "Maple Leaf Foods CEO Michael McCain Named Business Newsmaker of the Year," *Canadian Press*, January, 1, 2009.

102   "Many Canadian Businesses and Citizens Want to See Tougher Federal Rules Governing Corporate Responsibility and It's Time for the Government to Take Action, Says a Social Justice Coalition," *Canadian Press Newswire*, January 24, 2002.

103   Per 2003 Environics and 2004 GlobeScan polls, as reported in "Corporate Responsibility An Implementation Guide for Canadian Business" www.ic.gc.ca/epic/site/csr-rse.nsf/vwapj/CSR_mar2006.pdf/$FILE/CSR_mar2006.pdf (accessed August 20, 2009).

104   M. Friedman, *Capitalism and Freedom* (Chicago: University of Chicago Press, 1962).

105   J. Bakan, *The Corporation* (Toronto: Big Picture Media Corporation, 2003).

106   www.greenbiz.com/news/2006/10/25/survey-shows-mba-students-believe-business-should-be-agent-social-change (accessed August 20, 2009).

107   A. Howatson, *Lean Green: Benefits from a Streamlined Canadian Environmental Regulatory System* (Ottawa: The Conference Board of Canada, April 1996).

108   L. Jones and S. Graf, "Canada's Regulatory Burden: How Many Regulations? At What Cost?" *Fraser Forum*, August 2001.

109   R. Brunet, "To Survive and Thrive: Bled Dry by the NDP, BC Business Plots a New Course for the 21st Century," *British Columbia Report*, February 9, 1998, pp. 18–22.

110   G. Gallon, "Bunk Behind the Backlash: Highly Publicized Reports Exaggerate the Costs of Environmental Regulation," *Alternatives*, Fall 1997, pp. 14–15.

111   J. K. Grant, "Whatever Happened to Our Concern About the Environment?" *Canadian Speeches*, April 1997, pp. 37–42.

112   "The Business of Being Green," advertising supplement, *Canadian Business*, January 1996, pp. 41–56.

113   Minnesota Mining and Manufacturing Company (3M), "Pollution Prevention Pays: Moving Toward Environmental Sustainability," Brochure #78-6900-3343-2, St. Paul, MN, 1998; and J. K. Grant, "Whatever Happened to Our Concern About the Environment?" *Canadian Speeches*, April 1997, pp. 37–42.

114   Based on a personality scale developed by D. Hellriegel, J. Slocum, and R. W. Woodman, *Organizational Behavior*, 3rd ed. (St. Paul, MN: West Publishing, 1983), pp. 127–141, and reproduced in J. M. Ivancevich and M. T. Matteson, *Organizational Behavior and Management*, 2nd ed. (Homewood, IL: BPI/Irwin, 1990), pp. 538–539.

115   Several of these scenarios are based on D. R. Altany, "Torn Between Halo and Horns," *IndustryWeek*, March 15, 1993, pp. 15–20.

116   Based on C. Hawn, "Fear and Posing," *Forbes*, March 25, 2002, pp. 22–25; and J. Sandberg, "Some Ideas Are So Bad That Only Team Efforts Can Account for Them," *Wall Street Journal*, September 29, 2004, p. B1.

117 "Buyer Belief," *CBC Marketplace*, November 14, 2007.

118 Based on J. Calano and J. Salzman, "Ten Ways to Fire Up Your Creativity," *Working Woman*, July 1989, p. 94; J. V. Anderson, "Mind Mapping: A Tool for Creative Thinking," *Business Horizons*, January–February 1993, pp. 42–46; M. Loeb, "Ten Commandments for Managing Creative People," *Fortune*, January 16, 1995, pp. 135–136; and M. Henricks, "Good Thinking," *Entrepreneur*, May 1996, pp. 70–73.

Chapter 10

1 Opening vignette based on M. Parker, "Identifying Enablers and Blockers of Cultural Transformation," *Canadian Business Online*, May 17, 2007 (accessed February 4, 2009); E. Lazarus, "Building the Perfect Franchise," *Profit*, February 2006, p. 48ff; M. Parker, "Why Can't Employers See The Paradox?" *Financial Post*, March 19, 2008, p. WK7.

2 "Organization Man: Henry Mintzberg Has Some Common Sense Observations About the Ways We Run Companies," *Financial Post*, November 22/24, 1997, pp. 14–16.

3 K. McArthur, "Air Canada Tells Employees to Crack a Smile More Often," *Globe and Mail*, March 14, 2002, pp. B1, B2.

4 K. McArthur, "Air Canada Tells Employees to Crack a Smile More Often," *Globe and Mail*, March 14, 2002, pp. B1, B2.

5 C. O'Reilly, "Corporations, Culture and Commitment: Motivation and Social Control in Organizations," *California Management Review* 31, no. 4 (1989), pp. 9–25.

6 E. Schein, "Coming to a New Awareness of Organizational Culture," *Sloan Management Review*, Winter 1984, pp. 3–16; E. Schein, *Organizational Culture and Leadership* (San Francisco, CA: Jossey-Bass, 1992); and E. Schein, "What Is Culture?" in *Reframing Organizational Culture*, ed. P. J. Frost, L. F. Moore, M. R. Louis, C. C. Lundberg, and J. Martin (Newbury Park, CA: Sage, 1991), pp. 243–253.

7 T. G. Stroup Jr., "Leadership and Organizational Culture: Actions Speak Louder Than Words," *Military Review* 76, no. 1 (January–February 1996), pp. 44–49; B. Moingeon and B. Ramanantsoa, "Understanding Corporate Identity: The French School of Thought," *European Journal of Marketing* 31, no. 5/6 (1997), pp. 383–395; A. P. D. Van Luxemburg, J. M. Ulijn, and N. Amare, "The Contribution of Electronic Communication Media to the Design Process: Communicative and Cultural Implications," *IEEE Transactions on Professional Communication* 45, no. 4 (December 2002), pp. 250–264; L. D. McLean, "Organizational Culture's Influence on Creativity and Innovation: A Review of the Literature and Implications for Human Resource Development," *Advances in Developing Human Resources* 7, no. 2 (May 2005), pp. 226–246; and V. J. Friedman and A. B. Antal, "Negotiating Reality: A Theory of Action Approach to Intercultural Competence," *Management Learning* 36, no. 1 (2005), pp. 69–86.

8 See www.palliser.com/CompanyInfo.php (accessed August 23, 2009).

9 Seven-item description based on C. A. O'Reilly III, J. Chatman, and D. F. Caldwell, "People and Organizational Culture: A Profile Comparison Approach to Assessing Person-Organization Fit," *Academy of Management Journal*, September 1991, pp. 487–516; and J. A. Chatman and K. A. Jehn, "Assessing the Relationship Between Industry Characteristics and Organizational Culture: How Different Can You Be?" *Academy of Management Journal*, June 1994, pp. 522–553. For a description of other popular measures, see A. Xenikou and A. Furnham, "A Correlational and Factor Analytic Study of Four Questionnaire Measures of Organizational Culture," *Human Relations*, March 1996, pp. 349–371. For a review of cultural dimensions, see N. M. Ashkanasy, C. P. M. Wilderom, and M. F. Peterson, eds., *Handbook of Organizational Culture and Climate* (Thousand Oaks, CA: Sage, 2000), pp. 131–145.

10 See C. A. O'Reilly and J. A. Chatman, "Culture as Social Control: Corporations, Cultures, and Commitment," in *Research in Organizational Behavior*, vol. 18, ed. B. M. Staw and L. L. Cummings (Greenwich, CT: JAI Press, 1996), pp. 157–200.

11 T. E. Deal and A. A. Kennedy, "Culture: A New Look Through Old Lenses," *Journal of Applied Behavioral Science*, November 1983, p. 501.

12 J. Case, "Corporate Culture," *Inc.*, November 1996, pp. 42–53.

13 T. Cole, "How to Stay Hired," *Report on Business Magazine*, March 1995, pp. 46–48.

14 S. L. Grover, "The Truth, the Whole Truth, and Nothing but the Truth: The Causes and Management of Workplace Lying," *Academy of Management Executive* 19, no. 2 (May 2005), pp. 148–157.

15 R. McQueen, "Bad Boys Make Good," *Financial Post*, April 4, 1998, p. 6.

16 The view that there will be consistency among perceptions of organizational culture has been called the "integration" perspective. For a review of this perspective and conflicting approaches, see D. Meyerson and J. Martin, "Cultural Change: An Integration of Three Different Views," *Journal of Management Studies*, November 1987, pp. 623–647; and P. J. Frost, L. F. Moore, M. R. Louis, C. C. Lundberg, and J. Martin, eds., *Reframing Organizational Culture* (Newbury Park, CA: Sage Publications, 1991).

17 See J. M. Jermier, J. W. Slocum Jr., L. W. Fry, and J. Gaines, "Organizational Subcultures in a Soft Bureaucracy: Resistance Behind the Myth and Facade of an Official Culture," *Organization Science*, May 1991, pp. 170–194; S. A. Sackmann, "Culture and Subcultures: An Analysis of Organizational Knowledge," *Administrative Science Quarterly*, March 1992, pp. 140–161; R. F. Zammuto, "Mapping Organizational Cultures and Subcultures: Looking Inside and Across Hospitals" (paper presented at the 1995 National Academy of Management Conference, Vancouver, August 1995); and G. Hofstede, "Identifying Organizational Subcultures: An Empirical Approach," *Journal of Management Studies*, January 1998, pp. 1–12.

18 T. A. Timmerman, "Do Organizations Have Personalities?" (paper presented at the 1996 National Academy of Management Conference, Cincinnati, OH, August 1996).

19 S. Hamm, "No Letup—and No Apologies," *BusinessWeek*, October 26, 1998, pp. 58–64.

20 Based on "Rising on Three Pillars Strategy; 10 Most Admired Corporate Cultures," *Financial Post*, November 26, 2008, p. WK4; and www.bostonpizza.com.

21 E. H. Schein, "The Role of the Founder in Creating Organizational Culture," *Organizational Dynamics*, Summer 1983, pp. 13–28.

22 E. H. Schein, "Leadership and Organizational Culture," in *The Leader of the Future*, ed. F. Hesselbein, M. Goldsmith, and R. Beckhard (San Francisco: Jossey-Bass, 1996), pp. 61–62.

23 "PCL's Biggest Investment: Its People," *National Post*, September 2, 2008, p. FP10.

24 See, for example, J. R. Harrison and G. R. Carroll, "Keeping the Faith: A Model of Cultural Transmission in Formal Organizations," *Administrative Science Quarterly*, December 1991, pp. 552–582.

25 See B. Schneider, "The People Make the Place," *Personnel Psychology*, Autumn 1987, pp. 437–453; J. A. Chatman, "Matching People and Organizations: Selection and Socialization in Public Accounting Firms," *Administrative Science Quarterly*, September 1991, pp. 459–484; D. E. Bowen, G. E. Ledford Jr., and B. R. Nathan, "Hiring for the Organization, Not the Job," *Academy of Management Executive*, November 1991, pp. 35–51; B. Schneider, H. W. Goldstein, and D. B. Smith, "The ASA Framework: An Update," *Personnel Psychology*, Winter 1995, pp. 747–773; and A. L. Kristof, "Person-Organization Fit: An Integrative Review of Its Conceptualizations, Measurement, and Implications," *Personnel Psychology*, Spring 1996, pp. 1–49.

26 S. Fralic, "Even Playland's Interviews Are Fun for Job-Seekers," *Vancouver Sun*, Monday, July 14, 2008, www.canada.com/vancouversun/news/story.html?id=7ba15dd4-cbe8-4a09-a08c-cce86c73a694 (accessed August 23, 2009).

27 S. Fralic, "Even Playland's Interviews Are Fun for Job-Seekers," *Vancouver Sun*, Monday, July 14, 2008, www.canada.com/vancouversun/news/story.html?id=7ba15dd4-cbe8-4a09-a08c-cce86c73a694 (accessed August 23, 2009).

28 D. C. Hambrick and P. A. Mason, "Upper Echelons: The Organization as a Reflection of Its Top Managers," *Academy of Management Review*, April 1984, pp. 193–206; B. P. Niehoff, C. A. Enz, and R. A. Grover, "The Impact of Top-Management Actions on Employee Attitudes and Perceptions," *Group and Organization Studies*, September 1990, pp. 337–352; and H. M. Trice and J. M. Beyer, "Cultural Leadership in Organizations," *Organization Science*, May 1991, pp. 149–169.

29 *OB in the Workplace* based on B. Stone and A. Vance, "Apple's Obsession With Secrecy Grows Stronger," *New York Times*, June 23, 2009, p. B1.

30 See, for instance, J. P. Wanous, *Organizational Entry*, 2nd ed. (New York: Addison-Wesley, 1992); G. T. Chao, A. M. O'Leary-Kelly, S. Wolf, H. J. Klein, and P. D. Gardner, "Organizational Socialization: Its Content and Consequences," *Journal of Applied Psychology*, October 1994, pp. 730–743; B. E. Ashforth, A. M. Saks, and R. T. Lee, "Socialization and Newcomer Adjustment: The Role of Organizational Context," *Human Relations*, July 1998, pp. 897–926; D. A. Major, "Effective Newcomer Socialization into High-Performance Organizational Cultures," in *Handbook of Organizational Culture & Climate*, ed. N. M. Ashkanasy, C. P. M. Wilderom, and M. F. Peterson (Thousand Oaks, CA: Sage, 2000), pp. 355–368; and D. M. Cable and C. K. Parsons, "Socialization Tactics and Person-Organization Fit," *Personnel Psychology*, Spring 2001, pp. 1–23.

31 J. Impoco, "Basic Training, Sanyo Style," *U.S. News & World Report*, July 13, 1992, pp. 46–48.

32 G. Probst and S. Raisch, "Organizational Crisis: The Logic of Failure," *Academy of Management Executive* 19, no. 1 (February 2005), pp. 90–105; D. L. Ferrin and K. T. Dirks, "The Use of Rewards to Increase and Decrease Trust: Mediating Processes and Differential Effects," *Organizational Science* 14, no. 1 (2003), pp. 18–31; J. R. Dunn and M. E. Schweitzer, "Too Good to Be Trusted? Relative Performance, Envy, and Trust," *Academy of Management Best Conference Paper Proceedings*, 2004, CM, pp. B1–B6.

33 See, for instance, D. Miller, "What Happens After Success: The Perils of Excellence," *Journal of Management Studies*, May 1994, pp. 11–38.

34 G. Probst and S. Raisch, "Organizational Crisis: The Logic of Failure," *Academy of Management Executive* 19, no. 1 (February 2005), pp. 90–105; R. Deshpande, J. U. Farley, and F. E. Webster, "Corporate Culture, Customer Orientation, and Innovativeness in Japanese Firms: A Quadrate Analysis," *Journal of Marketing* 57, no. 1 (1993), pp. 23–27; and C. Homburg and C. Pflesser, "A Multiple Layer Model of Market-Oriented Organizational Culture: Measurement Issues and Performance Outcomes," *Journal of Marketing Research* 37, no. 4 (2000), pp. 449–462.

35 See C. Lindsay, "Paradoxes of Organizational Diversity: Living Within the Paradoxes," in *Proceedings of the 50th Academy of Management Conference*, ed. L. R. Jauch and J. L. Wall (San Francisco, 1990), pp. 374–378; and T. Cox Jr., *Cultural Diversity in Organizations: Theory, Research & Practice* (San Francisco: Berrett-Koehler, 1993), pp. 162–170.

36 A. F. Buono and J. L. Bowditch, *The Human Side of Mergers and Acquisitions: Managing Collisions Between People, Cultures, and Organizations* (San Francisco: Jossey-Bass, 1989); S. Cartwright and C. L. Cooper, "The Role of Culture Compatibility in Successful Organizational Marriages," *Academy of Management Executive*, May 1993, pp. 57–70; R. J. Grossman, "Irreconcilable Differences," *HR Magazine*, April 1999, pp. 42–48; J. Veiga, M. Lubatkin, R. Calori, and P. Very, "Measuring Organizational Culture Clashes: A Two-Nation Post-Hoc Analysis of a Cultural Compatibility Index," *Human Relations*, April 2000, pp. 539–557; and E. Krell, "Merging Corporate Cultures," *Training*, May 2001, pp. 68–78.

37 C. Isidore, "Daimler Pays to Dump Chrysler," *CNNMoney.com*, May 14, 2007, http://money.cnn.com/2007/05/14/news/companies/chrysler_sale/index.htm (accessed August 23, 2009); T. Watson, "In the Clutches of a Slowdown: Plant Closures Might Loom in DaimlerChrysler's Future as the Carmaker Tries to Correct Past Management Errors, a Misread of What Consumers Wanted to Drive Off the Lot and a Clash of Cultures From Its Recent Merger," *Financial Post* (*National Post*), December 23, 2000, p. D7; T. Watson, "Zetsche Runs into Perfect Storm: Chrysler's Crisis," *Financial Post* (*National Post*), December 13, 2000, pp. C1, C4; M. Steen, "Chrysler to Improve: Schrempp: Shareholders Are Embittered by Steep Losses and Imprecise Earnings Forecasts: Better Operating Results," *Financial Post* (*National Post*), April 11, 2002, p. FP12; and "DaimlerChrysler Boss to Step Down," *BBC News World Edition*, July 28, 2005.

38 K. W. Smith, "A Brand-New Culture for the Merged Firm," *Mergers and Acquisitions* 35, no. 6 (June 2000), pp. 45–50.

39 H. L. Sirkin, P. Keenan, and A. Jackson, "The Hard Side of Change Management," *Harvard Business Review* 83, no. 10 (October 1, 2005), pp. 108–118.

40 See, for instance, K. H. Hammonds, "Practical Radicals," *Fast Company*, September 2000, pp. 162–174; and P. C. Judge, "Change Agents," *Fast Company*, November 2000, pp. 216–226.

41 K. Lewin, *Field Theory in Social Science* (New York: Harper and Row, 1951).

42 P. G. Audia, E. A. Locke, and K. G. Smith, "The Paradox of Success: An Archival and a Laboratory Study of Strategic Persistence Following Radical Environmental Change," *Academy of Management Journal*, October 2000, pp. 837–853.

43 J. B. Sorensen, "The Strength of Corporate Culture and the Reliability of Firm Performance," *Administrative Science Quarterly*, March 2002, pp. 70–91.

44 J. Amis, T. Slack, and C. R. Hinings, "The Pace, Sequence, and Linearity of Radical Change," *Academy of Management Journal*, February 2004, pp. 15–39; and E. Autio, H. J. Sapienza, and J. G. Almeida, "Effects of Age at Entry, Knowledge Intensity, and Imitability on International Growth," *Academy of Management Journal*, October 2000, pp. 909–924.

45 J. P. Kotter, "Leading Changes: Why Transformation Efforts Fail," *Harvard Business Review*, March–April 1995, pp. 59–67; and J. P. Kotter, *Leading Change* (Boston: Harvard Business School Press, 1996).

46 See, for example, A. B. Shani and W. A. Pasmore, "Organization Inquiry: Towards a New Model of the Action Research Process," in *Contemporary Organization Development: Current Thinking and Applications*, eds. D. D. Warrick (Glenview, IL: Scott, Foresman, 1985), pp. 438–448; and C. Eden and C. Huxham, "Action Research for the Study of Organizations," in *Handbook of Organization Studies*, eds. S. R. Clegg, C. Hardy, and W. R. Nord (London: Sage, 1996).

47 See, for example, G. R. Bushe, "Advances in Appreciative Inquiry as an Organization Development Intervention," *Organizational Development Journal*, Summer 1999, pp. 61–68; D. L. Cooperrider and D. Whitney, *Collaborating for Change: Appreciative Inquiry* (San Francisco: Berrett-Koehler, 2000); R. Fry, F. Barrett, J. Seiling, and D. Whitney, eds., *Appreciative Inquiry & Organizational Transformation: Reports from the Field* (Westport, CT: Quorum, 2002); J. K. Barge and C. Oliver, "Working With Appreciation in Managerial Practice," *Academy of Management Review*, January 2003, pp. 124–142; and D. van der Haar and D. M. Hosking, "Evaluating Appreciative Inquiry: A Relational Constructionist Perspective," *Human Relations*, August 2004, pp. 1017–1036.

48 G. R. Bushe, "Advances in Appreciative Inquiry as an Organization Development Intervention," *Organization Development Journal* 17, no. 2 (Summer 1999), pp. 61–68.

49 P. G. Audia and S. Brion, "Reluctant to Change: Self-Enhancing Responses to Diverging Performance Measures," *Organizational Behavior and Human Decision Processes* 102 (2007), pp. 255–269.

50 J. P. Kotter and L. A. Schlesinger, "Choosing Strategies for Change," *Harvard Business Review*, July–August 2008, pp. 130–139.

51 A. E. Reichers, J. P. Wanous, and J. T. Austin, "Understanding and Managing Cynicism About Organizational Change," *Academy of Management Executive* 11, 1997, pp. 48–59.

52 R. H. Hall, *Organizations: Structures, Processes, and Outcomes*, 4th ed. (Englewood Cliffs, NJ: Prentice Hall, 1987), p. 29.

53 J. Lee, "Canadian Businesses Not Good at Adjusting, Survey Says," *Vancouver Sun*, December 14, 1998, pp. C1, C2.

54 D. Katz and R. L. Kahn, *The Social Psychology of Organizations*, 2nd ed. (New York: John Wiley & Sons, 1978), pp. 714–715.

55 J. P. Kotter and L. A. Schlesinger, "Choosing Strategies for Change," *Harvard Business Review*, March–April 1979, pp. 106–114.

56 J. E. Dutton, S. J. Ashford, R. M. O'Neill, and K. A. Lawrence, "Moves That Matter: Issue Selling and Organizational Change," *Academy of Management Journal*, August 2001, pp. 716–736.

57 P. C. Fiss and E. J. Zajac, "The Symbolic Management of Strategic Change: Sensegiving via Framing and Decoupling," *Academy of Management Journal* 49, no. 6 (2006), pp. 1173–1193.

58 Q. N. Huy, "Emotional Balancing of Organizational Continuity and Radical Change: The Contribution of Middle Managers," *Administrative Science Quarterly*, March 2002, pp. 31–69; D. M. Herold, D. B. Fedor, and S. D. Caldwell, "Beyond Change Management: A Multilevel Investigation of Contextual and Personal Influences on Employees' Commitment to Change," *Journal of Applied Psychology* 92, no. 4 (2007), pp. 942–951; and G. B. Cunningham, "The Relationships Among Commitment to Change, Coping with Change, and Turnover Intentions," *European Journal of Work and Organizational Psychology* 15, no. 1 (2006), pp. 29–45.

59 D. B. Fedor, S. Caldwell, and D. M. Herold, "The Effects of Organizational Changes on Employee Commitment: A Multilevel Investigation," *Personnel Psychology* 59, 2006, pp. 1–29.

60 S. Oreg, "Personality, Context, and Resistance to Organizational Change," *European Journal of Work and Organizational Psychology* 15, no. 1 (2006), pp. 73–101.

61 J. A. LePine, J. A. Colquitt, and A. Erez, "Adaptability to Changing Task Contexts: Effects of General Cognitive Ability, Conscientiousness, and Openness to Experience," *Personnel Psychology*, Fall 2000, pp. 563–593; T. A. Judge, C. J. Thoresen, V. Pucik, and T. M. Welbourne, "Managerial Coping with Organizational Change: A Dispositional Perspective," *Journal of Applied Psychology*, February 1999, pp. 107–122; and S. Oreg, "Resistance to Change: Developing an Individual Differences Measure," *Journal of Applied Psychology*, August 2003, pp. 680–693.

62 Paragraph based on M. Johne, "Wanted: A Few Good Egocentric, Self-Serving Risk-Takers," *Globe and Mail*, May 27, 2002, p. C1.

63 See J. Pfeffer, *Managing With Power: Politics and Influence in Organizations* (Boston: Harvard Business School Press, 1992), pp. 7, 318–320; and D. Knights and D. McCabe, "When 'Life Is but a Dream': Obliterating Politics Through Business Process Reengineering?" *Human Relations*, June 1998, pp. 761–798.

64 See, for instance, W. Ocasio, "Political Dynamics and the Circulation of Power: CEO Succession in U.S. Industrial Corporations, 1960–1990," *Administrative Science Quarterly*, June 1994, pp. 285–312.

65 Adapted from K. H. Chung and L. C. Megginson, *Organizational Behavior*, Copyright © 1981 by K. H. Chung and L. C. Megginson. Reprinted by permission of HarperCollins Publishers, Inc.

66 Based on "Organizational Culture at TerraCycle," *Organizational Behavior Video Library*, 2008. Copyrighted by Prentice-Hall.

67 Ideas in *From Concepts to Skills* were influenced by A. L. Wilkins, "The Culture Audit: A Tool for Understanding Organizations," *Organizational Dynamics*, Autumn 1983, pp. 24–38; H. M. Trice and J. M. Beyer, *The Cultures of Work Organizations* (Englewood Cliffs, NJ: Prentice Hall, 1993), pp. 358–362; H. Lancaster, "To Avoid a Job Failure, Learn the Culture of a Company First," *Wall Street Journal*, July 14, 1998, p. B1; and M. Belliveau, "4 Ways to Read a Company," *Fast Company*, October 1998, p. 158.

Glossary/Subject Index

Key terms and the pages on which they are defined appear in **boldface**.

Name and Organization Index

List of Canadian Companies

Photo Credits

Author photographs: page xxii: Gary Schwartz; page xxiii (top): Courtesy of Stephen P. Robbins.

Chapter 1

Page 3: Photo by Bruce Cole, Sequel Naturals; page 4: AP Photo/Elaine Thompson; page 13: Reprinted by permission of RBC Financial Group; page 20: China Photos/Getty Images.

Chapter 2

Page 33: Dick Hemingway; page 35: Ward Perrin/*Vancouver Sun*; page 40: Nathan Denette/*National Post*; page 46: AP Photo/Manish Swarup; page 48: Reprinted with permission from *The Globe and Mail*; page 50: Jason Kempin/FilmMagic; page 57: Kimberly White/Reuters/Corbis.

Chapter 3

Page 75: Courtesy of Michael Bach/KPMG Canada; page 83: The Canadian Press/Steve White; page 88: Presented by ACE-Canada; page 91: © 2006 Eros Hoagland/Redux Pictures; page 92: STR/AFP/Getty Images; page 104: Moosehead Breweries Ltd.

Chapter 4

Page 113: CP PHOTO/Ryan Remiorz; page 117: AP Photo/Nick Ut; page 121: CP PHOTO/*Hamilton Spectator*–Barry Gray; page 127: Patrick Price/Reuters/Landov; page 132: Courtesy of Purdy's Chocolates; page 133: Joe Raedle/Getty Images.

Chapter 5

Page 157: Bjorn Larsson Rosvall/SCANPIX/Canadian Press Images; page 158: AP Photo/Alexandra Boulat/VII; page 161: Bob Daemmrich/Corbis; page 167: Courtesy of IKEA Canada; page 170: Ruth Fremson/*The New York Times*; page 175: Redlink/Corbis; page 176: Mike Cassese/Reuters/Landov.

Chapter 6

Page 193: Courtesy of Suncor Energy; page 197: Courtesy of Claude Norfolk; page 201: Carlo Allegri/*National Post*; page 204: Noah Berger/*The New York Times*/Redux Pictures; page 208: Adam Pretty/Getty Images; page 209: Courtesy of Donna Cona Inc.; page 210: Peter J. Thompson/*National Post*; page 218: CP PHOTO/Adrian Wyld.

Chapter 7

Page 229: Lucas Oleniuk/GetStock.com; page 232: Courtesy of Naina Lal Kidwai; page 235: © 2006 Christopher LaMarca/Redux Pictures; page 238: Kim Kyung-Hoon/Reuters/Corbis; page 240: Courtesy of Great Little Box Company Ltd.; page 243: King Shipman Production/Getty Images; page 246: Courtesy of Aris Kaplanis/Teranet; page 260: Chris Rout/Alamy.

Chapter 8

Page 267: © 2007 Ben Baker/Redux Pictures; page 270: AP Photo/Scott Cohen; page 279: AP Photo/Paul Sakuma; page 284: STRDEL/AFP/Getty Images; page 290: Courtesy of Bill Young, President, Social Capital Partners; page 291: Reprinted with permission from *The Globe and Mail*.

Chapter 9

Page 303: The Canadian Press/Sean Kilpatrick; page 305: Kim Kulish/Corbis; page 319: Courtesy of Electronic Arts; page 324: Courtesy of Stewart Leibl; page 327: Todd Korol; page 329: AP Photo/Jakub Mosur.

Chapter 10

Page 343: CP PHOTO/*Edmonton Sun*–Brendon Dlouhy; page 346: Steve Bosch/*Vancouver Sun*; page 348: AP Photo/Elaine Thompson; page 352: Spencer Platt/Getty Images; page 363: Courtesy of Advantech.